The Bible
and
Liberation

The Bible & Liberation

An Orbis Series in Biblical Studies

Norman K. Gottwald and Richard A. Horsley, General Editors

The Bible & Liberation Series focuses on the emerging range of political, social, and contextual hermeneutics that are changing the face of biblical interpretation today. It brings to light the social struggles behind the biblical texts. At the same time it explores the ways that a "liberated Bible" may offer resources in the contemporary struggle for a more human world.

Already published:

The Bible
and
Liberation

Political and Social
Hermeneutics

Revised Edition

Edited by
Norman K. Gottwald
and
Richard A. Horsley

The Catholic Foreign Mission Society of America (Maryknoll) recruits and trains people for overseas missionary service. Through Orbis Books, Maryknoll aims to foster the international dialogue that is essential to mission. The books published, however, reflect the opinions of their authors and are not meant to represent the official position of the society.

Copyright © 1993 by Orbis Books
Published by Orbis Books, Maryknoll, NY 10545
Published in Great Britain 1993 by the Society for Promoting Christian Knowledge, Holy Trinity Church, Marylebone Road, London NW1 4DU

Grateful acknowledgment is made to the following for permission to reprint from previously published material:

Augsburg Fortress Publishers: Renita Weems, "Reading Her Way through the Struggle," from *Stony the Road We Trod*, edited by Cain Hope Felder, copyright © 1991 Augsburg Fortress; Phyllis A. Bird, "To Play the Harlot: An Inquiry into an Old Testament Metaphor," from *Gender and Difference in Ancient Israel*, edited by Peggy Day, copyright © 1989 Augsburg Fortress; Excerpts from *Power, Politics, and the Making of the Bible* by Robert and Mary Coote, copyright © 1990 Augsburg Fortress. Reprinted by permission of Augsburg Fortress.

HarperCollins Publishers: "The Imperial Situation of Palestinian Jewish Society" and "The Kingdom of God and the Renewal of Israel" from *Jesus and the Spiral of Violence* by Richard Horsley, copyright © 1987. Reprinted by permission of HarperCollins Publishers.

The Crossroad Publishing Company: "Liberating Narrative and Liberating Understanding: The Christmas Story," from *The Liberation of Christmas* by Richard Horsley, copyright © 1989; Excerpts from *The Scandalous Message of James* by Elsa Tamez, copyright © 1992. Reprinted by permission of The Crossroad Publishing Company.

Beacon Press: Excerpt from *But She Said* by Elisabeth Schüssler Fiorenza, copyright © 1991 by Elisabeth Schüssler Fiorenza. Reprinted by permission of Beacon Press.

Wm. B. Eerdmans Publishing Co.: "Biblical Hermeneutics and Black Struggle in South Africa: The Use of the Bible" and "Materialist Reading of Micah" from *Biblical Hermeneutics and Black Theology* by Itumuleng Mosala, copyright © 1989. Reprinted by permission of Wm. B. Eerdmans Publishing Co.

The Pilgrim Press: "The Deuteronomic Law Code and the Politics of State Centralization" by Naomi Steinberg, and " 'Enemies' and the Politics of Prayer in the Book of Psalms" by Gerald T. Sheppard, from *The Bible and the Politics of Exegesis: Essays in Honor of Norman K. Gottwald*, edited by David Jobling, Peggy L. Day, and Gerald T. Sheppard, copyright © 1992 The Pilgrim Press. Edited and reprinted and used by permission of the publisher.

Judson Press: Excerpt from *Paul's Message of Freedom* by Amos Jones Jr., copyright © 1984. Used by permission of Judson Press.

Semeia: "Discovering the Bible in the Nonbiblical World" by Kwok Pui Lan; "Social Class and Ideology in Isaiah 40-55," by Norman K. Gottwald; "A Chamberlain's Journey and the Challenge of Interpretation for Liberation," by Clarice Martin.

University Press of America: "Bitter Bounty," by Marvin L. Chaney, excerpted from *Reformed Faith and Economics*, Robert L. Stivers, ed., copyright © 1989. Used by permission of University Press of America.

SPCK/ISBN 0-281-04719-7
ORBIS/ISBN 0-88344-849-1

Contents

v

Part II
Sociopolitical Readings of the Hebrew Bible

Abbreviations

AB	Anchor Bible
AJA	*American Journal of Archaeology*
ASOR	American Schools of Oriental Research
ATANT	Abhandlungen zur Theologie des Alten und Neuen Testaments
AThR	*Anglican Theological Review*
BA	*Biblical Archaeologist*
BAR	*Biblical Archaeological Review*
BASOR	*Bulletin of the American Schools of Oriental Research*
BBB	*Bulletin de Bibliographia Biblique*
BDB	F. Brown, S. R. Driver, and C. A. Briggs, *Hebrew and English Lexicon of the Old Testament*
Bib	*Biblica*
BO	*Bibliotheca Orientalis*
BT	*The Bible Translator*
BTB	*Biblical Theology Bulletin*
BZAW	Beihefte zur *ZAW*
CBA	Catholic Biblical Association
CBQ	*Catholic Biblical Quarterly*
EAJT	*East Asian Journal of Theology*
ET	*Expository Times*
EvT	*Evangelische Theologie*
ETL	Ephemerides Theologicae Lovanienses
FOTL	The forms of Old Testament Literature
HALAT	W. Baumgartner et al., *Hebräisches und aramäisches Lexikon zum Alten Testament*
HSM	Harvard Semitic Monographs
HTR	*Harvard Theological Review*
IB	*Interpreter's Bible*
IDB	*Interpreter's Dictionary of the Bible*
IDBSup	Supplementary volume to *Interpreter's Dictionary of the Bible*
IEJ	*Israel Exploration Journal*
Int	*Interpretation*
JAAR	*Journal of the American Academy of Religion*
JAOS	*Journal of the American Oriental Society*
JB	Jerusalem Bible
JBAC	*Jahrbuch für Antike und Christentum*
JBC	*The Jerome Biblical Commentary*, R. E. Brown, et al., eds.

JBL	Journal of Biblical Literature
JEA	Journal of Egyptian Archaeology
JESHO	Journal of Economic and Social History of the Orient
JFSR	Journal of Feminist Studies in Religion
JITC	Journal of the Interdenominational Theological Center
JNES	Journal of Near Eastern Studies
JPFC	S. Safrai and M. Stern (eds.), *The Jewish People in the First Century*
JR	Journal of Religion
JRT	Journal of Religious Thought
JSNT	Journal for the Study of the New Testament
JSOT	Journal for the Study of the Old Testament
JSOTSup	JSOT Supplements
JSS	Journal of Semitic Studies
JThSt	Journal of Theological Studies
JTS	Journal of Theological Studies (New Series)
JTSA	Journal of Theology for Southern Africa
KJV	King James Version
LCL	Loeb Classical Library
LXX	Septuagint
MT	Masoretic Text
NAB	New American Bible
NICNT	New International Commentary on the New Testament
NJV	New Jerusalem Version
NT	Novum Testamentum
NTSup	NT Supplements
NTS	New Testament Studies
OTL	Old Testament Library
PEQ	Palestine Exploration Quarterly
PG	Patrologia graeca
PL	Patrologia latina
Q	Sayings Source of the Synoptic Gospels
RAC	Reallexikon für Antike und Christentum
RB	Revue biblique
RevExp	Review and Expositor
RSV	Revised Standard Version
SBL	Society of Biblical Literature
SBLDS	Society of Biblical Literature Dissertation Series
SBLMS	Society of Biblical Literature Monograph Series
SBLSP	Society of Biblical Literature Seminar Papers
SBT	Studies in Biblical Theology
SNTSMS	Society for New Testament Studies Monograph Series
SNTS	Society for New Testament Studies
ST	Studia theologica
TDNT	G. Kittel and G. Friedrich (eds.), *Theological Dictionary of the New Testament*

TDOT	G. J. Botterweck and H. Ringgren (eds.), *Theological Dictionary of the Old Testament*
THAT	*Theologisches Handwörterbuch zum Alten Testament*
ThStThSt	*Theological Studies*
ThZ	*Theologische Zeitschrift*
TynNTC	Tyndale New Testament Commentary
UF	Ugarit-Forschungen
USQR	*Union Seminary Quarterly Review*
VT	*Vetus Testamentum*
VTSup	*Vetus Testamentum* Supplements
WHJD	B. Mazar (ed.), *The World History of the Jewish People*
WMANT	Wissenschaftliche Monographien zum Alten und Neuen Testament
ZA	*Zeitschrift für Assyriologie*
ZAW	*Zeitschrift für die altitestamentliche Wissenschaft*
ZNW	*Zeitschrift für die neutestamenliche Wissenschaft*
ZwTh	*Zeitschrift für Wissenschaftliche Theologie*

EXTRABIBLICAL JEWISH LITERATURE

ExR	Exodus Rabbah, a rabbinic midrash
1QM	War Scroll, from Qumran Cave 1
1QS	Rule of the Community, from Qumran Cave 1
1QSa	Rule of the Congregation, from Qumran Cave 1
11QTemple	Temple Scroll, from Qumran Cave 11

Introduction

The Bible and Liberation

Deeper Roots and Wider Horizons

In 1975 the *Radical Religion* collective published a special issue of the journal on "Class Origins and Class Readings of the Bible" and in 1976 expanded it into a Reader entitled *The Bible and Liberation: Political and Social Hermeneutics* (edited by Norman K. Gottwald and Antoinette Wire). The immediate demand quickly exhausted all copies. In 1983 Orbis Books published a revised and expanded anthology featuring the emerging sociological and materialist analyses of biblical texts and issues for use in both academic and church study circles.

Meanwhile, particularly in the last ten years, there has been an explosion of articles and books pursuing a variety of liberative readings and analyses of the Bible. Latin American liberation theology has been joined by parallel voices around the world. Feminist readings of problematic biblical texts and criticism of androcentric presuppositions have multiplied, deepened, and sharpened. What appear to those living in the North Atlantic countries as Third-World voices have claimed a hearing for their perspective on the Bible, which they received originally through Western colonialism. African Americans are eloquently articulating a sharp criticism of how the Bible has been used to legitimate racist domination and exploitation as well as the liberative resonance that parts of the Bible had for enslaved and subordinated people. Meanwhile, studies of the generative historical context of the biblical texts themselves have become much more sophisticated and precise, leading to the recognition that some of the nascent sociological interpretation may have been domesticating rather than liberative of the Bible. It is impossible to hold together all of these perspectives and analyses, but it is essential to widen the scope of the discussion and include representatives of these different attempts to explore liberation in, of, and perhaps from the Bible.

AIMS AND RATIONALE OF THE ANTHOLOGY IN A REVISED EDITION

The original Reader had two primary aims for studying the Bible: (1) To elucidate the original historical struggles of our biblical ancestors and the human and religious resources they drew upon, and (2) to tap those biblical struggles and understandings as resources that might inform our current social struggles. The wider debate and discussion of various facets of "the Bible and liberation" in a diverse range of situations of historical social conflict has dramatized the necessity of a more comprehensive awareness of the politics involved in the interpretation and use of the Bible—now a third aim of this anthology.

The original Reader set out to bridge certain frustrating and destructive chasms that had emerged in modern Western study and use of the Bible. It is now clear from the discussion of the last decade or so that those chasms have been addressed and, if not bridged, now appear possibly as illusions created by the abstracting idealist modern Western mentality itself.

1. It is increasingly clear that the chasm *between religion and the rest of life* experienced by many in "structurally differentiated" modern societies does not exist in biblical history and literature. Religion is inseparable from, often embedded with politics and economics in the social struggles portrayed in the Bible. Recognition that the religious dimension is inseparable from the political-economic dimension means that it is far less possible for modern interpreters to reduce the scope and implications of biblical stories, prophecies, and struggles.

2. A related chasm was perceived *between the past as "dead history" and the present as "real life."* But recognition both that the Bible is about political-economic life inseparable from religious perspective and inspiration and that the Bible is full of political-economic-religious conflict and struggle, as well as how the Bible has influenced us, makes it appear dramatically, perhaps even problematically, "relevant."

3. The chasm many felt *between thought and practice* also turns out to be an "illusion" of modern Western idealism and the acquired cultural habit or assumption that the Bible is to be understood primarily as "revelation" or "the word of God." But with the discovery/realization that both the contents of the Bible and the process by which the Bible was written and became revered scripture involved intense political-economic struggles, it becomes evident that thought and practice are no more separated in the Bible than are religion and political-economy. The oracles of the Israelite prophets and Jesus' preaching of the kingdom of God, for example, were about social policy and practice.

4. The chasm *between biblical academics and popular lay Bible study* remains. But as biblical scholars recognize that their own enterprise and points of view are historically determined and parochial (e.g., Eurocentric and androcentric), and further recognize that certain popular readings display an affinity or analogy with certain views or struggles represented in biblical literature, even this chasm begins to seem bridgeable.

As the bridging of these chasms continues, new issues and conflicts emerge to prominence. Thus rather than more narrowly focusing and tightening the anthology, we are attempting to make more accessible selections that will stimulate a wider and more multifaceted, as well as sharply critical, discussion of the Bible and liberation. We hope that, with a broad selection of articles available, readers can engage the issues of political and social hermeneutics at points of immediate interest to them and, in that very process of choice, be lured to think about the interconnecting factors that they might otherwise be inclined to overlook or downgrade in importance. In this way perhaps theorists will be nudged toward practice and activists toward reflection; Hebrew Bible devotees will be drawn toward the New Testament as well (and vice versa); lovers of history will sense the need for social theory; and social theorists will attend to social history. Text-oriented Bible readers will be driven to consider their presuppositions in interpreting texts as they do, just as the fanciers of hermeneutics will have to check their theories against the texts as socially generated documents.

As a result, conversations and collaborations among people dealing with the Bible in various functional roles in our society may be encouraged. We are beginning to recognize that the liberated/liberating Bible — seen only by the scholar, or only by the academic teacher, or only by the pastor, or only by the church teacher, or only by the community organizer, or only by the social analyst — is far from the Bible that will be adequate for liberation. Our very functional specializations constitute both a strength and a limit to interpretation, as well as a way of specifying our bondage within a highly instrumental and people-separating capitalist culture. Not only must we question both the intellectually dismembered Bible and the spiritually unified Bible that scholarship and church now respectively present us, but we must also question our own scattered and stereotyped religious and academic roles that separate us from one another and that incline us to be structurally unable to receive the liberating insights and energies that we desire.

SELECTION AND ORGANIZATION

The principles of selection and the organization of this new edition are somewhat different from those of the first edition. It is essential to include representative voices of Asian, African, and African American, as well as Latin American peoples, and feminist interpretations and analyses. Moreover, a far wider range of critical sociological, sociohistorical, and political-hermeneutical studies and/or feminist studies of New Testament as well as Hebrew Bible texts and issues is available now than ten years ago. Difficult choices were necessary. Retaining less than half of the 1983 edition, we have attempted to select representatives of a wide range of perspectives and positions in political hermeneutics and social analysis. We simply collapsed the sections on social-scientific method, social class as a hermeneutical factor, and political theology in the first edition into a broad general range of readings from a particular social base, political perspective, and/or critical approach. In the sections on Hebrew Bible and New Testament, the sociological approach taken in most of the selections in the first edition is now complemented by political hermeneutics and/or perspectives critical of the androcentric and Eurocentric assumptions of established biblical studies.

Part I. Readings for Liberation

Distinctive readings of the Bible from a number of particular social locations are now challenging the ideological dominance of established scholarly biblical interpretation. Carlos Mesters pungently reports on the process of "grassroots" biblical study among base communities of politically disprivileged Christians in Brazil. Kwok Pui Lan argues that as a counter to the historical imposition of the Bible on Asians by Western Christian missionaries as "the running dogs of imperialism," the Bible can work for liberation only insofar as it is allowed to interact with Asian resources in a process of "dialogical imagination."

Writing from the heritage of slaves who were forbidden to read the Bible and were taught the Bible according to their masters' interests, Renita J. Weems argues that it is possible to learn to discern different voices embedded in different kinds of texts. In some, the voice of oppressed people can still be heard clearly, while in others it is overwritten and obscured by the concern of the dominant interests. Itumeleng J. Mosala illustrates how the Bible contains materials and ideologies that legitimate domination in his discussion of the way Europeans used the story of Israel's "conquest" of the land in their dispossession of Black Africans. Yet precisely because biblical literature itself is the product of struggle, it has liberative potential. By critically discerning the class, gender, and/or racial struggles that went into the formation of particular biblical texts it may be possible to engage them in the service of current struggles for liberation.

Latin American liberation theologians, oriented to the concrete situation of the people, have discerned emphases and concerns in the Bible different from those they learned from European biblical scholarship. Accordingly, they have also explored alternative analyses and explicitly political hermeneutics. Arthur F. McGovern sums up the pivotal dimensions of scripture that inform Latin American liberation theology and rebuts the criticisms of its "unbiblical" character as largely due to deliberate misunderstanding by its critics. George V. Pixley reaches back into classical philosophy to help explain how God can be understood to have acted in history in bringing Israel out of Egypt and, by implication, in an analogous way in contemporary struggles. Juan Luis Segundo uses communication theory about first- and second-level learning to distinguish two separate but related ways of reading the many ideological expressions of faith in the Bible. We read them for "simple learning" about the many ways that faith has been and can be materialized, but we also read them in a process of "learning to learn" in which we have to choose the ideological form of analysis/action most appropriate for our situation.

Both Latin American and European biblical interpreters have been far more open than their North American counterparts to adapt certain kinds of Marxist analysis as aids both in breaking the dominance of idealist hermeneutics and in formulating an approach more sensitive to the political and economic dimensions of biblical history. José Míguez Bonino outlines how Marxist analysis can awaken readers to their own political-economic context as well as to the concrete sociopolitical orientation of biblical stories and prophecies. Kuno Füssel explains "the materialist reading of the Bible" that is now widely followed among lay and university-based Bible study circles in Europe. David Lochhead adopts a method for group Bible study in North America that insists on recognizing our own ideological assumptions as well as those of the biblical text.

While broadening and deepening sociological analysis, North American biblical scholars are increasingly learning from others' struggles with the Bible, which are particularly pertinent to emerging political hermeneutics. Norman K. Gottwald, in an important reflection on the methodological framework he developed in writing the groundbreaking study, *The Tribes of Yahweh*, reviews the tasks and limits of a sociological criticism of ancient Israel indebted to macrosociological and anthropological theory. Suggesting that North Americans can learn from the way in which Central American *campesinos* "read" the "Christmas story," which rationally enlightened scholars had dismissed as historically unreliable "myth," Richard A. Horsley explores how such realistic narrative, read in the concrete context of imperial domination, can help keep alive subversive memory and aid the recovery of unfulfilled historical possibilities.

Feminist criticism is becoming increasingly sophisticated and complex as it explores the multifaceted fabric of patriarchal social and cultural forms. Elisabeth Schüssler Fiorenza applies a multifaceted hermeneutical model for critical feminist biblical interpretation to a key Lucan text in which liberative elements were previously found, challenging apologetic interpretations that prematurely defend the Bible as liberative and squarely facing the ambiguities of the biblical text.

Part II. Sociopolitical Readings of the Hebrew Bible

The sociological criticism and political hermeneutics of biblical texts and historiography pertaining to early Israel pioneered by Norman Gottwald and others have now been extended to many other Hebrew Bible texts and aspects of biblical history. Walter Brueggemann's survey of the results of literary and sociological studies provides a critical summary of the basic framework and lines of analysis that have been pursued. He suggests that the history of Israel involved a struggle between a "Mosaic liberation" trajectory and a "royal consolidation" trajectory. Although incomplete in detail and problematic in structure, this study is suggestive of some of the principle features of a fuller socioreligious history of ancient Israel that is now beginning to emerge from subsequent studies.

Gottwald's groundbreaking sociological analysis of Israelite origins as involving a popular "revolt" has decisively shaped subsequent investigations and discussion. The two reviews of *The Tribes of Yahweh*, by Walter Brueggemann and Franklin J. Woo, summarize the new model of Israel's origins and probe its implications. Gottwald himself reflects on the particular theological implications he discerns in his own and others' more politically critical revisionist construction of the origins of Israel.

Interpretation of Israel's prophets is set on a solid foundation by recent analysis of the historical social conditions they were addressing, along with a new appreciation of the historical political struggles involved in the shaping of the prophetic books as we have them. Marvin L. Chaney sketches a far more precise picture of the political-economy of the Davidic monarchy than before available, drawing on evidence generated by archaeological investigations as well as by textual analyses, and utilizing comparative historical sociological studies. He thus provides readers of the eighth-century prophets Micah and Isaiah in Judah and, to a degree, Amos and Hosea in Northern Israel, a vivid sense of the concrete political-economic exploitation the prophets were protesting. Itumeleng J. Mosala then reads the prophecies of Micah against the determinative historical social conditions Chaney illuminates. Mosala's reading of Micah, however, also involves the recognition that the text as we have it was the product of the reuse, supplementation, and reframing of Micah's original oracles in such a way that indictments of exploitative rulers were transformed into self-legitimation by later generations in the same ruling groups. Mosala further explores how the current struggles for social-economic justice and human dignity in South Africa illuminate and are illuminated by the struggles evident in and through the book of Micah.

As products of a traditional patriarchal society, the prophetic books, like other Hebrew biblical literature, pose severe problems for concerns about gender domination. Phyllis A. Bird sorts carefully and critically through the difficulties of translation and sociological analysis involved in the highly problematic metaphor in Hosea of Israel as a woman of harlotry, and examines the closely-related scholarly polemics focused on "cult prostitutes."

Henri Mottu reformulates and transforms the issue of true versus false prophecy in concrete terms of the respective ideologies arising from particular social locations, focusing on Jeremiah's encounter with the rival prophet Hananiah. Gottwald's analysis of Isaiah 40–55 is a pioneering essay in ideological criticism, exploring the web of social forces at work in the production of a text (in this case emerging from the about-to-be-restored Judahite ruling class) and the political functions of a text, both intended and unintended.

The Torah or Pentateuch, like the prophetic books, was the product of religious-political struggles over the interpretation and application of Israel's history and covenantal traditions. Robert B. Coote and Mary P. Coote sketch the broad outlines of a sequence of writing and rewriting of history by a succession of rulers as a way of establishing or enhancing their legitimacy, from the Davidic monarchy to the rival priestly factions of second-temple Jerusalem. Naomi Steinberg similarly locates stages in the development of Israel's law-codes in the explicit and implicit concerns of ruling groups to control the society, focusing on attempts to shape the loyalty of families and the social position and role of women.

Moving beyond the modern psychologizing and formal cultic interpretation of the Psalms, Gerald T. Sheppard argues that many of the Psalms were a form of public discourse. Spoken in the presence of "enemies," such prayers apparently functioned to provide public exposure of certain social conflicts, protection from further attack, or indictments against exploitation.

Part III. Sociopolitical Readings of the Second Testament

The modern Western assumption has been that New Testament texts—and New Testament studies—are more "individualistic" and "nonpolitical" than the Old Testament/Hebrew Bible. It is increasingly difficult to follow that assumption. In the New Testament as well as in the Hebrew Bible, as in the societies and communities that produced them, politics and economics were inseparable from religion. New Testament texts also presuppose and address certain political-economic structures and conditions such that a purely "religious self-understanding" or "theology" cannot be abstracted from community and historical circumstances.

The ministry of Jesus, the development of the Gospel traditions, and the emergence of rabbinic Judaism can hardly be understood without taking into account the pervasive impact of the imperial situation in ancient Palestine. Richard Horsley sketches how domination by one foreign empire after another, particularly by the Hellenistic and Roman empires, made a powerful impact on the lives of the Palestinian Jewish people, turning the Jewish high-priestly leaders into mediators of imperial domination and causing the disintegration of local village and family life.

Developing in close interrelation with a fuller and more precise sense of the social structure and social conflict in ancient Jewish Palestine are recent attempts to do a more concrete reading of Jesus-traditions and the Gospels. Horsley explores the implications of such a concrete reading of Jesus' proclamation of "the kingdom of God," suggesting that a social dimension was included with the transcendent theological dimension, indeed that Jesus' preaching and practice of "the kingdom" meant a renewal of Israel. Ched Myers, combining a sophisticated literary analysis of the whole Gospel of Mark with a concrete sociopolitical reading, suggests that the Gospel articulates a broad political and economic strategy for resistance against the faltering established system along with the particular practice of a discipleship community.

The role of women in the New Testament has prompted even more inquiry and discussion than the corresponding issue in the Old Testament. Luise Schottroff and Elisabeth Schüssler Fiorenza use critical tools to uncover the coequality of women and men in the circle of Jesus' followers and in the early church that was eclipsed before long as the church accommodated itself to the male-dominated Roman world. Schottroff gives us vivid portraits of Mary of Magdala and Priscilla, while Schüssler Fiorenza calls for a retrieval of earliest Christian legitimation of gender equality in order to unmask and reverse the patriarchal-hierarchic "power-play" that still dominates the Christian church.

Early Christianity turns out to have been more inclusive racially as well as more egalitarian in male-female relations than the traditional church and established academic biblical studies have recognized. Clarice J. Martin challenges the blatantly Eurocentric map (figurative *and* literal) of the New Testament world as well as the standard exegesis of the early chapters of Acts in marshalling abundant evidence from the Greco-Roman world that an Ethiopian was unambiguously understood to be an African from (one of) "the ends of the earth." The conversion of the "Ethiopian eunuch" in Acts 8 thus clearly indicates not only the fulfillment of Jesus' prophecy-commission in Acts 1:8 but that the Christian movement included Africa and Africans as well.

The letters of Paul himself and particularly 1 Corinthians, along with the Pastoral Letters, have been criticized as ambiguous at best and at points simply oppressive, not liberative, with respect to the position of women and slaves. Indeed, some Black theologians have simply rejected Paul because of his apparent stance on slavery and the use made of Pauline letters in the religious legitimation of slavery in U.S. history. Countering both this rejection of Paul and established scholarly exegesis, Amos Jones, Jr., argues, from a critical rereading of 1 Corinthians 7 in the context of the early Christian movement as an alternative political-economic community, that Paul's message and strategy entailed the liberation of slaves.

Finally, one of the most neglected books of the New Testament is the Letter of James. Clearly this is partly, if not largely, because of its sharp criticism of the exploitation of the poor by the wealthy. In a direct challenge to the ways in which traditional exegesis has avoided the uncomfortable implications of James, Elsa Tamez identifies the circumstances of oppression the letter addresses and the social-ethical integrity it calls for in a praxis of persistent hope and resistance to that oppression.

READER AIDS

Certain aids for the reader have been included to enhance this volume as a textbook, reference resource, or collection of supplementary readings.

Each of the articles and excerpts from books is prefaced with an abstract that will help the general reader, academic instructor, or Bible study leader to ascertain quickly which selections are most germane to the purposes at hand.

The volume is supplied with indexes according to authors, biblical citations, and subjects.

INCLUSIVE LANGUAGE

Unfortunately, inclusive and bias-free language is not yet fully accepted among those who write on the subject of the Bible and liberation.

In the original Reader (1976), a concerted effort was made to use nonsexist language. We avoided "man" as a false generic for men and women, and "he/ him" where the context called for a feminine or an indefinite pronoun. In biblical and historical argumentation we tried to be alert for cases where either the original language or later interpreters overlooked or distorted the presence or activity of women because of masculine mindsets or forms of expression. In the first edition and this revised edition, Elisabeth Schüssler Fiorenza's and Luise Schottroff's articles forcefully document many instances of sexist language (sometimes by New Testament writers and more often by biblical translators and commentators). As they demonstrate, far from being mere peccadillos, these "small" instances combine to obscure the creative role of women in Christian origins.

Because this revised edition of *The Bible and Liberation* draws upon materials from many independent sources, the editors have not attempted a thoroughgoing bias-free correction of all the essays. The inconsistencies in practice among the writers serve to remind us that one of the *major* incomplete tasks of liberation is a reworking of normal language (including the language of scholars) to eliminate the unintended perpetuation of gender stereotypes. To carry forward this refashioning of language, it will be necessary to know practical alternatives to inappropriate gender-specific and other biased language. Every writer committed to the coequality of men and women is well advised to make regular use of bias-free stylebooks such as Casey Miller and Kate Swift, *The Handbook of Nonsexist Writing for Writers, Editors and Speakers* (New York: HarperCollins, 2d ed., 1988) and *Language, Gender, and Professional Writing: Theoretical Approaches and Guidelines for Nonsexist Usage* by Francine Wattman Frank and Paula A. Treichler (New York: Modern Language Association, 1989).

Liberation perspectives call us to align theory and practice. If we really mean that women are coequal with men, our practice of language must accord with the intention of our theory.

Norman K. Gottwald
Richard A. Horsley

The Bible
and
Liberation

PART I

READINGS FOR LIBERATION

1

CARLOS MESTERS

The Use of the Bible in Christian Communities of the Common People

The typical grassroots Bible study setting among Brazilian Catholics is a community of people meeting around the Bible who introduce the concrete reality of their own situation into the discussion. Using language studded with the pungent speech of the people themselves, the author notes obstacles they face and how they surmount them: inability to read, slavish literalism, differing conceptions of time, dependence on the learned expert, lack of tact in pastors and teachers, erudite language, and fundamentalist dogmatism.

As the ordinary Christian Bible readers gain in confidence to claim the Bible as their own, dislocations or shifts in interpretation take place from an upper class toward a lower class perspective, from biblical text to real life, from a text enclosed in itself to a text with meaning for us, from an abstract individualistic understanding to a community sense, from neutrality to taking sides in society, and from overly spiritualized concepts to the concrete meanings and demands of faith in a present lived situation.

Reprinted from Sergio Torres and John Eagleson, eds., *The Challenge of Basic Christian Communities*, Papers from the International Ecumenical Congress of Theology, February 20–March 2, 1980, São Paulo, Brazil (Maryknoll, N.Y.: Orbis Books, 1981), 197-210.

PRELIMINARY OBSERVATIONS

Limitations of This Report

The information I am going to pass along to you is limited for several reasons. First of all, I am going to talk to you only about Brazil because I am not that familiar with the rest of Latin America. Second, I am going to talk only about the Catholic church in Brazil because I know relatively little about other Christian churches. I am just now beginning to make an acquaintance with them. Third, my report is limited by the fact that there is this "opening up" process now going on in Brazil. That may well force me to rethink a lot of the things I am going to say about the past twelve years or so in Brazil. Finally, my report is limited by my own eyesight. Even though I wear glasses and have good intentions, I find it hard to grasp certain sides of reality—the political side in particular. That may be due to the fact that when I got my education the social sciences and their findings were not a part of the picture.

The Importance of the Bible in Grassroots Christian Communities

The Bible is very important in the life and growth of grassroots communities. But its importance must be put in the right place. It's something like the motor of an automobile. Generally the motor is under the hood, out of sight. It is not the steering wheel. The history of the use of the Bible in grassroots communities is a bit like the history of car motors. Way back when the first cars came out, the motor was huge. It was quite obvious and made a lot of noise. It also wasted a lot of gasoline and left little room for passengers. Today the motors are getting smaller and smaller. They are more powerful, but they are also quieter and better hidden. There's a lot more leg room and luggage room in the car. Much the same is true about the Bible and its function in the life of Christian communities. The Bible is supposed to start things off, to get them going; but it is not the steering wheel. You have to use it correctly. You can't expect it to do what it is not meant to do.

My Relative Optimism

Perhaps what I am going to say to you may seem a trifle optimistic. If so, it is something like the optimism of a farmer watching the grain surface above ground. A storm may come later and wipe out the whole crop. But there is room for optimism, and it's good to be optimistic.

INTRODUCING THE ISSUE: THREE BASIC SITUATIONS

First Situation

In Brazil there are many groups meeting to focus on the Bible. In this case the motivating occasion for the group is some pious exercise or special event:

a feast day, a novena, a brotherhood week, or what have you. The people meet on the parish level. There is no real community context involved. The word of God is the only thing that brings them together. They want to reflect on God's word and put it into practice.

Second Situation

In Brazil some groups are meeting within a broader context. They are meeting on the level of the community and its life. I once went to give a course to the people in such a community. In the evening the people got together to organize the course and establish basic guidelines. In such groups you generally get questions such as these: "How do you explain the Apocalypse? What does the serpent stand for? What about the fight between David and Goliath?"

The questions, you see, are limited to the Bible as such. No hint of their own concerns, no hint of real-life problems, no hint of reality, no hint of problems dealing with economic, social, and political life. Even though they are meeting as a community, the real-life problems of the people are not brought up.

Third Situation

To introduce the third situation, I am going to tell you a typical story about my experience in this area. I was invited to give a course in Ceará, in northeast Brazil. The group was made up of about ninety farmers from the backlands and the riverbanks. Most of them couldn't read. In the evening we met to get things organized. They asked me about a dozen basic questions, but these are the ones I remember:

1. What about these community activities we are engaged in? Are they just the priest's idea? Are they communism? Or do they come from the word of God?

2. What about our fight for land? (Most of them had no land. But they had plenty of problems and fights on their hands.) What about our labor struggles and our attempts to learn something about politics? What does the word of God have to say about all that?

3. What about the gospel message? Does it have to do just with prayer, or is it something more than that?

4. The other day, in a place where there was a big fight going on between the landlord and his tenants, this priest came, said Mass, and explained the gospel in a way that made the landlord right. Then the local priest of the parish read the same gospel and explained it in a way that made the tenant farmers right. So who really is right?

5. The landlord gives catechism lessons that teach subservience and bondage. In our community we have a catechetics of liberation, and the landlord persecutes us for it. So how do we settle the matter and figure it all out? We want to know whether the Bible is on our side or not!

Here we have three basic situations. In the first situation the group involved comes together solely for the sake of discussing the Bible; the Bible is the only thing that unites them and they stick to it. In the second situation the people focus on the Bible, too, but they come together as a community. In the third situation we have a community of people meeting around the Bible who inject concrete reality and their own situation into the discussion. Their struggle as a people enters the picture. So we can formulate the following basic picture:

Community
the con-text

Hearing the word
of God today

the Bible   *Reality*
text   the pre-text

We find three elements in the common people's interpretation of the Bible: the Bible itself, the community, and reality (i.e., the real-life situation of the people and the surrounding world). With these three elements they seek to hear what the word of God is saying. And for them the word of God is not just the Bible. The word of God is within reality and it can be discovered there with the help of the Bible. When one of the three elements is missing, however, interpretation of the Bible makes no progress and enters into crisis. The Bible loses its function.

When the three elements are present and enter the process of interpretation, then you get the situation that I encountered when I gave a course in Ceará. People asked me to tell them the stories of Abraham, Moses, Jeremiah, and Jesus. That is what I did. But in their group discussions and full meetings, the Bible disappeared. They hardly ever talked about the Bible. Instead they talked about real life and their concrete struggles. So at the nightly review the local priest asked them what they had learned that day. They quickly got to talking about real life. No one said anything about the Bible. Ye gods, I thought to myself, where did I go wrong? This is supposed to be a course on the Bible and all they talk about is real life. Should I feel upset and frustrated, or should I be satisfied? Well, I decided to take it easy and feel satisfied because the Bible had achieved its purpose. Like salt, it had disappeared into the pot and spiced the whole meal.

It's like what happens when you take a sponge and dip it in a little bowl of water. The water is soaked up and disappears inside the sponge. At the end of the nightly review the people were asked what they had learned from the biblical explanations. They squeezed the sponge a bit and let a few drops of water out. I could see that the sponge was filled with water. At the final ceremony for the week, which lasted four hours, they squeezed the sponge completely and everything inside came out. I realized that when the three elements are integrated—Bible, community, real-life situation—then the word of God becomes a reinforcement, a stimulus for hope and courage. Bit by bit it helps people to overcome their fears.

Conclusions

1. When the community takes shape on the basis of the real-life problems of the people, then the discovery of the Bible is an enormous reinforcement.

2. When the community takes shape only around the reading of the Bible, then it faces a crisis as soon as it must move on to social and political issues.

3. When the group closes itself up in the letter of the biblical text and does not bring in the life of the community or the reality of the people's struggles, then it has no future and will eventually die.

4. These three factors or situations characterize the use of the Bible by the common people and reveal the complexity involved. The three situations can be successive stages in a single ongoing process, or they can be antagonistic situations that obstruct and exclude each other. It all depends on how the process is conducted.

5. It doesn't matter much where you start. You can start with the Bible, or with the given community, or with the real-life situation of the people and their problems. The important thing is to do all you can to include all three factors.

SOME OBSTACLES AND HOW THE PEOPLE ARE SURMOUNTING THEM

It is not always easy to integrate all three factors in the interpretation of the Bible. There are many obstacles along the way that the people are trying to surmount in various ways.

Many Don't Know How to Read

Many people don't know how to read, and the Bible is a book! Sometimes no one in the group knows how to read. They are inventing ways to get around this problem. They are using song and story, pictures and little plays. They are thus making up their own version of the "Bible of the poor." Thanks to songs, for example, many people who have never read the Bible know almost every story in it.

Slavish Literalism

Another obstacle is slavery to the letter or fundamentalism. This usually occurs when the Bible is read in dissociation from a real-life community and concrete situation. The circle closes and the letter becomes a source of further oppression rather than of liberation.

The Bible is ambiguous. It can be a force for liberation or a force for oppression. If it is treated like a finished monument that cannot be touched, that must be taken literally as it is, then it will be an oppressive force.

Three things can help to overcome this obstacle. The first is the good sense of the people. In one community composed of blacks and other farmers the people were reading the Old Testament text that forbade the eating of pork.

The people raised the question: "What is God telling us today through this text?" Their conclusion was: "Through this text God today is ordering us to eat the flesh of pork." How did they arrive at such a contrary conclusion? They explained: "God is concerned first and foremost with life and health. In those times eating the flesh of pork was very dangerous to people's health. It was prohibited in God's name because people's lives had to be protected. Today we know how to take care of pork meat, and the only thing we have to feed our children are the piglets in our yards. So in this text God is bidding us to eat the flesh of pork."

A second thing of great importance in breaking through enslavement to the letter is the ongoing action of a local church that takes sides with the poor. The ongoing movement of the church in this direction is helping to ensure that questions focused exclusively on the letter of the biblical text gradually give way to others. Literalist questions are falling from the tree like dry leaves to make room for new buds. The larger complex of a local church that sides with the poor and joins their fight for justice is very important in correctly channelling the people's interpretation of the Bible.

The third thing has to do with various devices of a fairly simple kind. For example, we can show people that many of the things we talk about in words cannot be taken literally. Symbolism is an integral part of human language. In many instances the first step towards liberation comes for people when they realize that they need not always take the biblical text literally. They discover that "the letter kills, the Spirit gives life." This realization unlocks the lid and lets new creativity out.

The Conception of Time

Another problem or obstacle is the people's conception of time. Often folks will ask questions like these: "Did Abraham come before or after Jesus Christ? Did David live before or after Cabral discovered America? Was it Jesus Christ who created the world?" Such questions may seem to indicate a great deal of confusion to us, but I think not. Apart from a certain amount of ignorance about the content of the Bible, I don't think it is a matter of confusion at all. Instead it is an expression of their circular conception of time. In such a conception you don't know exactly what comes at the beginning and what comes at the end. A simple explanation will not suffice to change this view of time, because it is a cultural problem rather than a problem of mere ignorance. In their minds the people simply don't have a peg on which to hang a concept of linear time.

How do we help them to overcome this obstacle? How do we unroll the carpet of time in their consciousness? Perhaps the best way we can help is to help them discover their own ongoing journey in their lives today. We can help them to recover the memory of their own history, of struggles lost and forgotten. We can help them to begin to recount their own history. In Goiás a group of farmworkers was asked: "How did the Bible come about?" An old farmer gave this reply: "I know. It was something like this. Suppose fifty years from now someone asks how our community arose. The people will reply: In the beginning there was nothing here. . . ." Thanks to his own concrete journey in life, the old farmworker perceived that the Bible had arisen from narrative accounts, from stories people told to others about their history. He realized that the Bible was the collective memory that gave a people its identity.

Dependence on Informational Knowledge and the Learned Expert

You often hear people say something like this: "I don't know anything. You or Father should do the talking. You're the ones who know things. We folks don't know anything." In the past we members of the clergy expropriated the Bible and got a monopoly on its interpretation. We took the Bible out of the hands of the common people, locked it with a key, and then threw the key away. But the people have found the key and are beginning again to interpret the Bible. And they are using the only tool they have at hand: their own lives, experiences, and struggles.

Biblical exegetes, using their heads and their studies, can come fairly close to Abraham; but their feet are a long way from Abraham. The common people are very close to Abraham with their feet. They are living the same sort of situation. Their life-process is of the same nature and they can identify with him. When they read his history in the Bible, it becomes a mirror for them. They look in that mirror, see their own faces, and say: "We are Abraham!" In a real sense they are reading their own history, and this becomes a source of much inspiration and encouragement. One time a farmworker said this to me: "Now I get it. We are Abraham, and if he got there then we will too!" From the history of Abraham he and his people are drawing the motives for their courage today.

Now here is where the danger comes in. Some teacher or learned expert may come along. It might be a pastoral minister, a catechist, or an exegete. This expert may arrive with his or her more learned and sophisticated approach and once again expropriate the gains won by the people. Once again they grow silent and dependent in the presence of the teacher or expert. Our method is logical. It involves a reasoning process, a careful line of argument. We say it is scientific. When the people get together to interpret the Bible, they do not proceed by logical reasoning but by the association of ideas. One person says one thing; somebody else says another thing. We tend to think this approach has little value, but actually it is just as scientific as our approach! What approach do psychoanalysts use when they settle their patients into a chair or couch? They use the free association of ideas. And this method is actually better than our "logical" method. Our method is one for teaching information; the other is one for helping people to discover things themselves.

Lack of Tact on the Part of Pastoral Agents

Another obstacle that crops up at times is the lack of tact on the part of pastoral workers among the people. They are in a hurry and have no patience. They ride roughshod over some of the natural resistance that people have to our interpretations of the Bible. One time a nun went to give a course on the Old Testament. Halfway through she had to close down the course because no one was showing up. The people said: "Sister is destroying the Bible!" A certain priest offered an explanation of the Exodus. Many people never came back. "He is putting an end to miracles," they complained.

Meddling with the faith of the people is very serious business. You must have deep respect and a delicate touch. You must try to feel as they would and intuit their possible reaction to what you are going to say. The people should be allowed to grow from the soil of their own faith and their own character. They should not be dragged along by our aggressive questions.

Erudite Language

Another obstacle is erudite language, abstruse words. We talk a difficult idiom, and the language of translations is difficult. Today, thank God, various efforts are being made to translate the Bible into more popular terms. Nothing could be more desirable. People now feel that they are getting the point at least. The first and most basic requirement is that people talk in such a way that their listeners can understand them. It sounds simple enough, but often it is very hard to do.

Another important point is that we must not lose the poetry of the Bible. We must not reduce it to concepts. The Bible is full of poetry, and poetry is more than a matter of words. It is the whole way of seeing and grasping life.

From Confrontation to Practical Ecumenism

Another problem crops up on the grassroots level with "fundamentalist" groups. They head for people's homes with the Bible in their hands and make it clear that they have the only right answer. This leads to a defensive reaction and sectarian apologetics. It is hard to foster any ecumenism around the Bible in such an atmosphere.

In some areas, however, practical biblical ecumenism is growing from other starting points. Roman Catholics and Protestants are meeting each other and working together in labor unions, in fights for land ownership, and in other real-life struggles. Gradually other sectarian issues are taking a back seat to practical ecumenism.

CHARACTERISTICS OF THE PEOPLE'S INTERPRETATION OF THE BIBLE

In a sense we can say that the tabernacle of the church is to be found where the people come together around the word of God. That could be called the church's "holy of holies." Remember that no one was allowed to enter the holy of holies except the high priest, and he was allowed in only once a year! In this holy of holies no one is master—except God and the people. It is there that the Holy Spirit is at work; and where the Spirit is at work, there is freedom. The deepest and ultimate roots of the freedom sought by all are to be found there, in those small community groups where the people meet around the word of God. One song in Ceará has this line: "It is the tabernacle of the people. Don't anyone touch it!" Certain characteristics are surfacing in this tabernacle, and I should like to point them out here.

The things I am going to mention now are not fully developed and widespread. They are more like the first traces of dawn in the night sky. We are dipping our finger into the batter to savor how the cake will taste when it is baked and ready. The following characteristics are just beginning to surface here and there in the ongoing journey of various communities. I think they are very important.

The Scope of the Biblical Message

In the eyes of the common people the word of God, the gospel message, is much broader than just the text itself. The gospel message is a bit of everything: Bible, community, reality. For the common people the word of God is not just in the Bible; it is also in the community and in their real-life situation. The function of the Bible, read in a community context, is to help them to discover where God is calling them in the hubbub of real life. It is as if the word of God were hidden within history, within their struggles. When they discover it, it is big news. It's like a light flicking on in their brains. When one leper in Acre made this discovery, he exclaimed: "I have been raised from the dead!" He used the idea of resurrection to express the discovery he had made.

Theologians say that reality is a *locus theologicus*. The common people say: "God speaks, mixed into things." A tinker defined the church this way: "The church is us exchanging ideas with each other to discover the idea of the Holy Spirit in the people." If it hadn't come from Antonio Pascal, I would have said it came from St. Augustine. But it came from Antonio Pascal. It is us exchanging ideas with each other to discover the idea of the Holy Spirit in the people. Not in the church, in the people!

So you see, when they read the Bible, basically they are not trying to interpret the Bible; they are trying to interpret life with the help of the Bible. They are altering the whole business. They are shifting the axis of interpretation.

The Unity of Creation and Salvation

The common people are recovering the unity or oneness of creation and salvation, which is certainly true in the Bible itself. The Bible doesn't begin with Abraham. It begins with creation. Abraham is not called to form some separated group apart. Abraham is called to recover for all peoples the blessing lost by the sin of Adam. This is the oneness between life and faith, between transforming (political) activity and evangelization, that the people are concretely achieving in their praxis.

The Reappropriation of the Bible

The Bible was taken out of the people's hands. Now they are taking it back. They are expropriating the expropriators: "It is our book! It was written for us!" It had always been "Father's book," it seemed. Now it is the people's book again.

That gives them a new way of seeing, new eyes. They feel at home with the Bible and they begin to link it with their lives. So we get something very interesting. They are mixing life in with the Bible, and the Bible in with life. One helps them to interpret the other. And often the Bible is what starts them developing a more critical awareness of reality. They say, for example: "*We* are Abraham! *We* are in Egypt! *We* are in bondage! *We* are David!" With the biblical data they begin to reflect on their real-life situation. The process gradually prompts them to seek a more objective knowledge of reality and to look for a more suitable tool of analysis elsewhere. But it is often the word of God that starts them moving.

The rediscovery of the Bible as "our book" gives rise to a sense of commitment and a militancy that can overcome the world. Once they discover that God is with them in their struggles, no one can really stop them or deter them. One farmworker from Goiás concluded a letter this way: "When the time comes for me to bear my witness, I will do so without any fear of dying." That is the kind of strength that is surfacing. A sort of resurrection is taking place, as I suggested earlier.

We who have always had the Bible in hand find it difficult to imagine and comprehend the sense of novelty, the gratitude, the joy, and the commitment that goes with their reading of the Bible. But that is why these people generally read the Bible in the context of some liturgical celebration. Their reading is a prayer exercise. Rarely will you find a group that reads the Bible simply for better understanding. Almost always their reading is associated with reflection on God present here and now, and hence with prayer. They live in a spirit of gratefulness for God's gift.

History as a Mirror

Another characteristic which I hinted at already is the fact that the Bible is not just history for the people; it is also a mirror. Once upon a time we used to talk about the Bible as "letter" and "symbol." Today we might do well to talk about it as "history" and "mirror." The common people are using it as a mirror to comprehend their own lives as a people.

We who study a great deal have a lot more trouble trying to grasp the point of images and symbols. If we want to get a handle on symbolic language, we have to go through a whole process of "demythologizing." We have to go through a long process of study to get the point of the symbol. To us images are opaque glasses; we can't see through them at all. To see at all, we have to punch out the glass and smash it. To the common people in Brazil, an image or symbol is a pair of glasses with a little dust or frost on it. They just wipe them a bit and everything is as clear as day.

I don't think we pay enough attention to this educational item. We are awfully "Europeanized" in our training. Take the question of the historicity of a text. I think you have to approach it very differently, or worry about it differently, when you are dealing with ordinary people. Very often pastoral workers are talking about the Bible and they ask questions like these: "Did that really happen? Did Jesus walk on top of the water? Were there only five loaves and two fishes?" They think that this is the most important problem that the people have with the text in front of them. I don't think so. Once, in Goiás, we read the passage in the New Testament (Acts 17:19) where an angel of the Lord came and freed the apostles from jail. The pastoral worker asked his people: "Who was the angel?" One of the women present gave this answer: "Oh, I know. When Bishop Dom Pedro Casaldáliga was attacked in his house and the police surrounded it with machine guns, no one could get in or out and no one knew what was going on exactly. So this little girl sneaked in without being seen, got a little message from Pedro, ran to the airport, and hitched a ride to Goiana where the bishops were meeting. They got the message, set up a big fuss, and Dom Pedro was set free. So that little girl was the angel of the Lord. And it's really the same sort of thing."

The people don't always take things literally. They are far smarter than you would think. Our question simply will have to take more account of the way that ordinary people understand history. They are far more capable of understanding symbols than we assume.

DISLOCATIONS

When there are only five people in a room, then each one can be pretty much at ease. When fifty more people enter the room, then the original five find themselves a bit crowded and some moving around has to take place. Well, the common people have entered the precincts of biblical interpretation and they are causing much shifting and dislocation.

A Shift in Standpoint

First of all, the Bible itself has shifted its place and moved to the side of the poor. One could almost say that it has changed its class status. This is important. The place where the people read the Bible is a different place. We read the Bible something like the wealthy car owner who looks out over the top of his car and sees a nice chrome finish. The common people read the Bible something like the mechanic under the car who looks up and sees a very different view of the same car.

The common people are discovering things in the Bible that other readers don't find. At one session we were reading the following text: "I have heard the cries of my people." A woman who worked in a factory offered this commentary: "The Bible does not say that God has heard the praying of the people. It says that God has heard the cries of his people. I don't mean that people shouldn't pray. I mean that people should imitate God. Very often we work to get people to go to church and pray first; and only then will we pay heed to their cries." You just won't find that sort of interpretation in books.

The Bible has changed its place, and the place where the common people read the Bible is different. It is the place where one can appreciate the real import of Jesus' remark: "I thank thee, Father . . . that thou hast hidden these things from the wise and understanding and revealed them to babes; yea, Father, for such was thy gracious will" (Matt. 11:25-26). If you take sides with the poor, you will discern things in the Bible that an exegete does not see. All of us have a slight blind spot that prevents us from seeing certain things.

From Biblical Text to Real Life

Another shift mentioned earlier has to do with the fact that the word of God has moved in a certain sense from the Bible to real life. It is in the Bible but it is also in real life—especially in real life. So we come to the following conclusion: the Bible is not the one and only history of salvation; it is a kind of "model experience." Every single people has *its own* history of salvation.

Clement of Alexandria said: "God saved the Jews in a Jewish way, the barbarians in a barbarian way." We could go on to say: "God saves Brazilians in a Brazilian way, blacks in a black way, Indians in an Indian way, Nicaraguans in a Nicaraguan way, and so on." Each people has its own unique history. Within that history it must discover the presence of God the Liberator who journeys by its side. The scope of this particular dislocation is most important.

From Meaning in Itself to Meaning for Us

Another dislocation is to be found in the fact that emphasis is not placed on the text's meaning in itself but rather on the meaning the text has for the people reading it. At the start people tend to draw any and every sort of meaning, however well or ill founded, from the text. Only gradually, as they proceed on their course in life, do they begin to develop an interest in the historical import and intrinsic meaning of the text. It is at this point that they can benefit greatly from a study of the material conditions of the people in biblical times: i.e., their religious, political, and socioeconomic situation. But they do so in order to give a better grounding to the text's meaning "for us." In this framework scientific exegesis can reclaim its proper role and function, placing itself in the service of the biblical text's meaning "for us."

From Abstract Understanding to a Community Sense

The common people are doing something else very important. They are reintroducing faith, community, and historical reality into the process of interpretation. When we studied the Bible back in the seminary in the old days, we didn't have to live as a real community or really know much about reality. We didn't even have to have faith. All we needed was enough brains to understand Greek and Hebrew and to follow the professor's line of reasoning.

Now the common people are helping us to realize that without faith, community, and reality we cannot possibly discover the meaning that God has put in that ancient tome for us today. Thus the common people are recovering something very important: the *sensus ecclesiae* ("sense of the church"). The community is the resonance chamber; the text is a violin string. When the people pluck the string (the biblical text), it resonates in the community and out comes the music. And that music sets the people dancing and singing. The community of faith is like a big pot in which Bible and community are cooked just right until they become one tasty dish.

From Neutrality to Taking Sides

The common people are also eliminating the alleged "neutrality" of scholarly exegesis. No such neutrality is possible. Technology is not neutral, and neither is exegesis.

Clearing up Overly Spiritualized Concepts

The common people are giving us a clearer picture of concepts that have been excessively spiritualized. Let me give just one example. Some time ago Pope Paul VI delivered an address in which he warned priests not to become overly preoccupied with material things. He urged them to show greater concern for spiritual things. One farmworker in Goiás had this comment: "Yes, the pope is quite right. Many priests concern themselves only with material things, such as building a church or decorating it. They forget spiritual things, such as food for the people!"

This is what the people are doing with such notions as grace, salvation, sin, and so forth. They are dusting them off and showing us that these notions have to do with solid, concrete realities of life.

Putting the Bible in Its Proper Place

Finally, the common people are putting the Bible in its proper place, the place where God intended it to be. They are putting it in second place. Life takes first place! In so doing, the people are showing us the enormous importance of the Bible and, at the same time, its relative value – relative to life.

PROBLEMS, CHALLENGES, REQUIREMENTS

There are many problems, difficulties, and failings associated with the interpretation of the Bible by the common people. But every good tree has a strong, solid limb that can be pruned when the time comes. The point is that its roots are okay. The common people are reading and interpreting the Bible as a new book that speaks to them here and now. And this basic view of the Bible is the view that the Church Fathers of the past had when they interpreted the Bible.

Here I simply want to enumerate a few further points that need greater attention.

1. There is the danger of subjectivistic interpretation. This can be combated in two ways: by more objective grounding in the literal sense of the Bible and by reading the Bible in community.

2. It is possible to read the Bible solely to find in it a confirmation of one's own ideas. In this case the biblical text loses its critical function. Community-based reading and interpretation help to overcome this tendentious use of the Bible. In addition, people must have a little humility and a little signal-light in their brains that call them up short when they are tempted to absolutize their own ideas.

3. People may lack a critical sense in reading and interpreting the biblical text. They may be tempted to take the ancient text and apply it mechanically to today, without paying any serious attention to the difference in historical context.

4. The above three points underline the proper and necessary function of scientific exegesis. Exegesis is being called upon to concern itself, not with the questions it raises, but with the questions that the common people are raising. In many cases the exegete is like the person who had studied salt and knew all its chemical properties but didn't know how to cook with it. The common people don't know the properties of salt well, but they do know how to season a meal.

5. We need biblical interpretation that will reveal the material living conditions of the people in the Bible. We need a materialistic reading and interpretation of the Bible, but not a narrow and confined reading. It must be broad and full.

6. We urgently need to give impetus to ecumenism on the grassroots level. It is a hard and challenging task, but a beginning has been made here and there.

7. The Bible is a book derived from a rural environment. Today we live in an urban environment. Re-reading the Bible today here in São Paulo, in this urban reality, presents no easy task of interpretation.

8. There is the matter of revolutionary effectiveness and gratitude for the Father's gift. This is another matter that needs further exploration.

9. Criticism can be derived from the word of God to foster transforming action.

2

KWOK PUI LAN

Discovering the Bible
in the Nonbiblical World

To many peoples of the world, the Bible is linked with Western domination. As the North Atlantic powers built their empires in Asia and Africa, missionaries often brought the Bible as the revealed Word of God to people they viewed as culturally inferior "heathens" mired in idolatry and superstition. The scripture was implicated with Christianity as "the running dog of imperialism" to many Chinese, for example. Chinese theologian Kwok Pui Lan argues that the Bible can no longer be understood through the "general politics" of truth by which established Western scholars or clergy have sole authority to determine meaning. If the Bible is to work for liberation instead of domination, biblical themes can be allowed to interact with Asian resources in a process of "dialogical imagination." Folk tales and legends cultivated for centuries among the common people may "have the power to illumine many biblical stories." Particularly fruitful may be the reading of biblical stories through the corporate spirit and concerns (as opposed to Western individualism!) of what Koreans call the minjung, *the mass of people subjected by others, whether a race, an ethnic group, a class, or women. For example, the* social *biography of the Korean* minjung, *repeatedly under domination by powerful surrounding nations, and the* social *biography of the Israelites in the Hebrew Bible can provide mutual illumination. For women as well as for Asian and other* minjung

Reprinted from *Semeia* 47 (1989): 25–42.

generally, the authority and critical principle of receiving the Bible lie not in the "sacred" biblical canon established by Western male Christianity, but in the experience of the community of women or minjung *generally who read with dialogical imagination.*

'To the African, God speaks as if He [*sic*] were an African; to the Chinese, God speaks as if He [*sic*] were a Chinese. To all men and women, the Word goes out over against their particular existing environment and their several cultural settings.' Thus spoke T. C. Chao, a Protestant theologian from China.[1] The central *Problematik* of biblical hermeneutics for Christians living in the 'non-Christian' world is how to hear God speaking in a different voice — one other than Hebrew, Greek, German or English.

Christianity has been brought into interaction with Chinese culture for many centuries, but the Christian population in China never exceeded 1 percent. Since the nineteenth century, the Christian missionary enterprise has often been criticized as being intricately linked to western domination and cultural imperialism. Chinese Christians have been struggling with the question of how to interpret the biblical message to our fellow Chinese, the majority of whom do not share our belief.

In fact, this should not only be a serious concern to the Chinese, but a challenge to all Christians with a global awareness, and to biblical scholars in particular. For two-thirds of our world is made up of non-Christians and most of these people are under the yoke of exploitation by the privileged one-third of our world. The interpretation of the Bible is not just a religious matter within the Christian community, but a matter with significant political implications for other peoples as well. The Bible can be used as an instrument of domination, but it can also be interpreted to work for our liberation.

This paper attempts to discuss some of the crucial issues raised by the interaction of the Bible with the nonbiblical world. My observation will be chiefly based on the Chinese situation, with which I am most familiar, drawing also upon insights from other Asian theologians. I shall first discuss biblical interpretation in the context of the political economy of truth. The second part will focus on biblical interpretation as dialogical imagination based on contemporary reappropriation of the Bible by Asian Christians. Finally, I shall offer my own understanding of the Bible from a Chinese woman's perspective.

BIBLICAL INTERPRETATION AND THE POLITICS OF TRUTH

Biblical interpretation is never simply a religious matter, for the processes of formation, canonization and transmission of the Bible have been imbued with the issues of authority and power. The French philosopher Michel Foucault helps us to see the complex relationship of truth to power by studying the power mechanisms which govern the production and the repression of truth. He calls this the 'political economy' of truth:

Each society has its regime of truth, its 'general politics' of truth: that is, the types of discourse which it accepts and makes function as true; the mechanisms and instances which enable one to distinguish true and false statements, the means by which each is sanctioned; the techniques and procedures accorded value in the acquisition of truth; the status of those who are charged with saying what counts as true.[2]

Foucault's analysis leads me to examine the power dynamics underlying such questions as: What is truth? Who owns it? Who has the authority to interpret it? This is particularly illuminating when we try to investigate how the Bible is used in a cross-cultural setting.

Who owns the truth? In the heyday of the missionary movement of the late nineteenth century, John R. Mott, the chief engineer of what was called the campaign of the 'evangelization of the world in this generation,' cried out:

The need of the non-Christian world is indescribably great. Hundreds of millions are today living in ignorance and darkness, steeped in idolatry, superstition, degradation and corruption. . . . The Scriptures clearly teach that if men are to be saved they must be saved through Christ. He alone can deliver them from the power of sin and its penalty. His death made salvation possible. The Word of God sets forth the conditions of salvation.[3]

Mott and others saw the Bible as the revealed Word of God which had to be made known to all 'heathens' who were living in idolatry and superstition. The Bible was to be the 'signifier' of a basic deficiency in the 'heathen' culture. This is a western construction superimposed on other cultures, to show that western culture is the norm and it is superior. It might be compared to the function of the 'phallus' as a signifier of the fundamental lack of the female superimposed on women by men in the male psychological discourse.[4] It is not mere coincidence that missionary literatures describe Christian mission as 'aggressive work' and western expansion as 'intrusion' and 'penetration.'

The introduction of the Bible into Asia has been marked by difficulty and resistance mainly because Asian countries have their own religious and cultural systems. The issue of communicating 'The Christian message in a Non-Christian World' was the primary concern of the World Missionary Conference in 1938. Hendrik Kraemer, the key figure in the Conference, acknowledged that non-Christian religions are more than a set of speculative ideas, but are 'all-inclusive systems and theories of life, rooted in a religious basis, and therefore at the same time embrace a system of culture and civilization and a definite structure of society and state.'[5] But his biblical realism, influenced much by Karl Barth's theology, maintains that the Christian Gospel is the special revelation of God, which implies a discontinuity with all cultures and judges all religions.

This narrow interpretation of truth has disturbed many Christians coming from other cultural contexts. T. C. Chao, for example, presented a paper on 'Revelation' which stated: 'There has been no time, in other words, when God has not been breaking into our human world; nor is there a place where men have been that He [sic] has not entered and ruled.'[6] Citing the long line of sages, moral teachers of China, such as Confucius, Mencius and Moti, he questioned, 'Who can say that these sages have not been truly inspired by the spirit of our God, the God of our Lord Jesus Christ? Who can judge that the Almighty has not appeared to them in His [sic] Holy, loving essence and that they have not been among the pure of heart of whom Jesus speaks?'[7]

In this battle for truth, many Chinese Christians reject the assumption that the Bible contains all the truth and that the biblical canon is rigidly closed. Po Ch'en Kuang argued in 1927 that many Chinese classics, such as Analects, Mencius, the Book of Songs and Rites, are comparable to the prophets, the Psalms, and the Book of Deuteronomy of the Old Testament.[8] Since the Bible contains the important classics of the Jewish people which preceded Jesus, he could see no reason why the Chinese would not include their own. Others such as Hsieh Fu Ya[9] and Hu Tsan Yün[10] argue that the Chinese Bible should consist of parts of the Hebrew Bible, the Christian Bible, Confucian classics, and even Taoist and Buddhist texts! For a long time, Chinese Christians have been saying that western people do not own the truth simply because they bring the Bible to us, for truth is found in other cultures and religions as well.

Who interprets the truth? Another important issue in the political economy of truth concerns who has the power to interpret it. In the great century of missionary expansion, many missionaries acted as though they alone knew what the Bible meant, believing they were closer to truth. The Gospel message was invariably interpreted as being the personal salvation of the soul from human sinfulness. This interpretation reflects an understanding of human nature and destiny steeped in western dualistic thinking. Other cultures, having a different linguistic system and thought form, may not share similar concerns. As Y. T. Wu, a Chinese theologian, notes, 'Such terms as original sin, atonement, salvation, the Trinity, the Godhead, the incarnation, may have rich meanings for those who understand their origins and implications, but they are just so much superstition and speculation for the average Chinese.'[11]

More importantly, this simplistic version of the Gospel functions to alienate the Christians in the Third World from the struggle against material poverty and other oppressions in their society. But in the name of a 'universal Gospel,' this thin-sliced biblical understanding was pre-packaged and shipped all over the world. The basic problem of the so-called 'universal Gospel' is that it not only claims to provide the answer but defines the question too! The American historian William R. Hutchison rightly observes that American missionary ideologies at the turn of the century shared the belief that 'Christianity as it existed in the West had a "right" not only to conquer the world, but to define reality for the peoples of the world.'[12] If other people can only define truth according to the western perspective, then Christianization really means westernization! Chinese Christians began a conscious effort to re-define what the Gospel meant for them in the 1920s, as a response to the anti-Christian movement which criticized Christianity as 'the running dog of imperialism.' Chinese Christians became collectively aware that they had to be accountable to their fellow Chinese in their biblical interpretations, not just to the tiny Christian minority. They tried to show that biblical concepts such as 'agape' were compatible to 'benevolence' in Chinese classics and that the moral teachings of Jesus were comparable to the teachings of the Confucian tradition. As foreign invasion became imminent, the central concern of all Chinese was national salvation and the gospel message, too, became politicized.[13] Y. T. Wu, for example, reinterpreted Jesus as 'a revolutionary, the upholder of justice and the challenger of the rights of the oppressed'[14] in the mid-1930s, anticipating the kind of liberation theology that developed decades later. These attempts of indigenization clearly show that biblical truth cannot be pre-packaged, but that it must be found in the actual interaction between text and context in the concrete historical situation.

What constitutes truth? The last point I want to consider briefly concerns the norm by which we judge something as truth. Here again, Chinese philosophical tradition is very different from the west in that it is not primarily interested in metaphysical and epistemological questions. On the contrary, it is more concerned with the moral and ethical visions of a good society. The Neo-Confucian tradition in particular has emphasized the integral relationship between knowing and doing. Truth is not merely something to be grasped cognitively, but to be practiced and acted out in the self-cultivation of moral beings.

For most Chinese, the truth claim of the Bible cannot be based on its being the supposed revealed Word of God, for 99 percent of the people do not believe in this faith statement. They can only judge the meaningfulness of the biblical tradition by looking at how it is acted out in the Christian community. Some of the burning questions of Chinese students at the time of foreign encroachment were: 'Can Christianity save China?,' 'Why does not God restrain the stronger nations from oppressing the weaker ones?,' 'Why are the Christian nations of the west so aggressive and cruel?'[15] These probing questions can be compared to what Katie G. Cannon, an Afro-American ethicist, has also asked: 'Where was the Church and the Christian believers when Black women and Black men, Black boys and Black girls were being raped, sexually abused, lynched, assassinated, castrated and physically oppressed? What kind of Christianity allowed white Christians to deny basic human rights and simple dignity to Blacks, these same rights which had been given to others without question?'[16]

The politics of truth is not fought on the epistemological level. People in the Third World are not interested in whether or not the Bible contains some metaphysical or revelational truth. The authority of the Bible can no more hide behind the unchallenged belief that it is the Word of God, nor by an appeal to a church tradition which has been defined by white, male, clerical power. The poor women, and other marginalized people, are asking whether the Bible can be of help in the global struggle for liberation.

BIBLICAL INTERPRETATION AS DIALOGICAL IMAGINATION

To interpret the Bible for a world historically not shaped by the biblical vision, there is need to conjure up a new image for the process of biblical interpretation itself. I have coined the term 'dialogical imagination' based on my observation of what Asian theologians are doing. I will explain what this term means and illustrate it with some examples of the contemporary use of the Bible in Asia.

Dialogue in Chinese means talking with each other. It implies mutuality, active listening, and openness to what the other has to say. Asian Christians are heirs to both the biblical story and to our own story as Asian people, and we are concerned to bring the two into dialogue with one another. Kosuke Koyama, a Japanese theologian, has tried to explain this metaphorically in the title of his latest book, *Mount Fuji and Mount Sinai*. He affirms the need to do theology in the context of a dialogue between Mount Fuji and Mount Sinai, between Asian spirituality and biblical spirituality.[17] Biblical interpretation in Asia, too, must create a two-way traffic between our own tradition and that of the Bible.

There is, however, another level of dialogue we are engaged in because of our multi-religious cultural setting. Our fellow Asians who have other faiths must not be considered our missiological objects, but as dialogical partners in our ongoing search for truth. This can only be done when each one of us takes seriously the Asian reality, the suffering and aspirations of the Asian people, so that we can share our religious insights to build a better society.

Biblical interpretation in Asia must involve a powerful act of imagination. Sharon Parks[18] shows that the process of imagination involves the following stages: a consciousness of conflict (something as not fitting), a pause, the finding of a new image, the repatterning of reality, and interpretation. Asian Christians have recognized the dissonance between the kind of biblical interpretation we inherited and the Asian reality we are facing. We have to find new images for our reality and to make new connections between the Bible and our lives.

The act of imagination involves a dialectical process. On the one hand, we have to imagine how the biblical tradition which was formulated in another time and culture can address our burning questions today. On the other hand, based on our present circumstances, we have to re-imagine what the biblical world was like, thus opening up new horizons hitherto hidden from us. Especially since the Bible was written from an androcentric perspective, we women have to imagine ourselves as if we were the audience of the biblical message at that time. As Susan Brooks Thistlethwaite suggested, we have to critically judge both the text and the experience underlying it.[19]

I have coined the term 'dialogical imagination' to describe the process of creative hermeneutics in Asia. It attempts to capture the complexities, the multi-dimensional linkages, the different levels of meaning in our present task of relating the Bible to Asia. It is dialogical, for it involves a constant conversation between different religious and cultural traditions. It is highly imaginative, for it looks at both the Bible and our Asian reality anew, challenging the established 'order of things.' The German word for imagination is *Einbildungskraft*, which means the power of shaping into one.[20] Dialogical imagination attempts to bridge the gap of time and space, to create new horizons, and to connect the disparate elements of our lives in a meaningful whole.

I shall illustrate the meaning of dialogical imagination by discussing how Asian theologians have combined the insights of biblical themes with Asian resources. We can discern two trends in this process today. The first is the use of Asian myths, legends and stories in biblical reflection. The second is the use of the social biography of the people as a hermeneutical key to understand both our reality and the message of the Bible.

For some years now, C. S. Song, a theologian from Taiwan, has urged his Asian colleagues to stretch their theological minds and to use Asian resources to understand the depths of Asian humanity and God's action in the world. He says: 'Resources in Asia for doing theology are unlimited. What is limited is our theological imagination. Powerful is the voice crying out of the abyss of the Asian heart, but powerless is the power of our theological imaging.'[21] To be able to touch the Hindu heart, the Buddhist heart, the Confucian heart, we have to strengthen the power of theological imaging.

C. S. Song demonstrates what this means in his book, *The Tears of Lady Meng*,[22] which was originally delivered in an Assembly of the Christian Conference of Asia. Song uses a well-known legend from China, the story of Lady Meng, weaving it together with the biblical themes of Jesus' death and resurrection. In one of his recent books, *Tell Us Our Names*, Song shows how fairy tales, folk stories and legends, shared from generation to generation among the common people, have the power to illuminate many biblical stories and other theological motifs. Song reminds us that Jesus was a master storyteller who transformed common stories into parables concerning God's Kingdom and human life.[23]

The use of Asian resources has stimulated many exciting and creative ways of re-reading the scriptures. A scholar from Thailand, Maen Pongudom, uses the creation folktales of the Northern Thai to contrast with the creation story in Genesis, arguing that people of other faiths and traditions share certain essential ideas of creation found in the biblical story.[24] Archie Lee, an Old Testament scholar from Hong Kong, uses the role of the remonstrator in the Chinese tradition to interpret the parable of Nathan in the context of political theology in Hong Kong. His creative re-reading of the stories from two traditions shows that 'story has the unlimited power to capture our imagination and invite the readers to exert their own feeling and intention.'[25]

Asian women theologians are discovering the liberating elements of the Asian traditions as powerful resources to re-image the biblical story. Padma Gallup reinterprets the image of God in Genesis 1:27–8 in terms of the popular Arthanareesvara image in the Hindu tradition which is an expression of male/female deity. She argues that 'if the Godhead created humans in its image, then the Godhead must be a male/female, side-by-side, non-dualistic whole.'[26] I myself have used Asian poems, a lullaby, and a letter of women prisoners to interpret the meaning of suffering and hope.[27] I have also used the story of the boat people in Southeast Asia to reappropriate the theme of the diaspora.[28]

In her observations concerning the growing use of Asian resources in theologizing, Nantawan Boonprasat Lewis, a Thai woman theologian, makes the following perceptive remarks:

The use of one's cultural and religious tradition indicates the respect and pride of one's heritage which is the root of one's being to be authentic enough to draw as a source for theologizing. On the other hand, it demonstrates a determination of hope for possibilities beyond one's faith tradition, possibilities which can overcome barriers of human expression, including language, vision, and imagination.[29]

The dialogical imagination operates not only in using the cultural and religious traditions of Asia, but also in the radical appropriation of our own history. We begin to view the history of our people with utmost seriousness in order to discern the signs of the time and of God's redeeming action in that history. We have tried to define the historical reality in our own terms and we find it filled with theological insights.

In Korean *minjung* theology, Korean history is reinterpreted from the *minjung* perspective. *Minjung* is a Korean word which means the mass of people, or the mass who were subjugated or being ruled. *Minjung* is a very dynamic concept: it can refer to women who are politically dominated by men, or to an ethnic group ruled by another group, or to a race when it is ruled by another powerful race.[30] The history of the *minjung* was often neglected in traditional historical writing. They were treated as either docile or as mere spectators of the rise and fall of kingdoms and dynasties. *Minjung* theology, however, reclaims *minjung* as protagonists in the historical drama, for they are the subject of history.

Korean theologians stress the need for understanding the corporate spirit — the consciousness and the aspirations of the *minjung* — through their social biography. According to Kim Yong Bock: 'The social biography is not merely social or cultural history: it is political in the sense that it is comprehensively related to the reality of power and to the "polis," namely the community. . . . Social biography functions to integrate and interrelate the dimensions and components of the people's social and cultural experiences, especially in terms of the dramatic scenario of the people as the historical protagonists.'[31]

The social biography of the *minjung* has helped Korean Christians to discover the meaning of the Bible in a new way. Cyris H. S. Moon reinterprets the Hebrew Bible story through the social biography of the *minjung* in Korea. He demonstrates how the story of the Korean people, for example, the constant threat of big surrounding nations, and the loss of national identity under Japanese colonialization, can help to amplify our understanding of the Old Testament. On the other hand, he also shows how the social biography of the Hebrew people has illuminated the meaning of the Korean *minjung* story. Through powerful theological imagination, Moon has brought the two social biographies into dialogue with one another.[32]

The hermeneutical framework of the *minjung*'s social biography also helps us to see in a new way the relationship between Jesus and the *minjung*. According to Ahn Byung Mu, the *minjung* are the *ochlos* rather than the *laos*. In Jesus' time, they were the ones who gathered around Jesus — the so-called sinners and outcasts of society. They might not have been the direct followers of Jesus and were differentiated from the disciples. They were the people who were opposed to the rulers in Jerusalem.[33] Concerning the question of how Jesus is related to these *minjung*, theologian Suk Nam Dong says, in a radical voice, '[T]he subject matter of *minjung* theology is not Jesus but *minjung*. Jesus is the means for understanding the *minjung* correctly, rather than the concept of *'minjung'* being the instrument for understanding Jesus.'[34] For him, 'Jesus was truly *a part of the minjung*, not just *for* the *minjung*. Therefore, Jesus was the personification of the *minjung* and their symbol.'[35]

Social biography can also be used to characterize the hopes and aspirations of the women, as Lee Sung Hee has demonstrated.[36] The question of whether Jesus can be taken as a symbol for the women among the *minjung* has yet to be fully clarified. Social biography is a promising hermeneutical tool because it reads history from the underside, and therefore invites us to read the Bible from the underside as well. Korean *minjung* theology represents one imaginative attempt to bring the social biography of *minjung* in Korea into dialogue with the *minjung* of Israel and the *minjung* in the world of Jesus. It shows how dialogical imagination operates in the attempt to reclaim the *minjung* as the center of both our Asian reality and the biblical drama.

LIBERATING THE BIBLE: MANY VOICES AND MANY TRUTHS

After this brief survey of the history of the politics of truth in the Chinese Christian community and a discussion of dialogical imagination as a new image for biblical reflection, I would like to briefly discuss my own understanding of the Bible. I shall focus on three issues: (1) the sacrality of the text, (2) the issue of canon, and (3) the norm of interpretation.

Sacrality of the text. The authority of the Bible derives from the claim that it is the Scripture, a written text of the Word of God. However, it must be recognized that the notion of 'scripture' is culturally conditioned and other religious and cultural traditions, such as Hinduism and Confucianism, may understand it differently. This may partly account for the relative fluidity of these traditions, which can often assimilate other visions and traditions. These traditions also do not have a crusading spirit to convert the whole world.

Why has the Bible, seen as sacred text, shaped western consciousness for so long? Jacques Derrida's deconstruction theory, particularly his criticism of the 'transcendent presence' in the text and the logocentrism of the whole western metaphysical tradition, offers important insights. In an earlier volume of *Semeia*, which focuses on 'Derrida and Biblical Studies,' the editor Robert Detweiler summarizes Derrida's challenge to biblical scholarship:

The main characteristic of sacred texts has been their evocation and recollection of sacred presence—to the extent that the texts themselves, the very figures of writing, are said to be imbued with that divine immanence. But Derrida argues that such a notion of presence in writing is based on the false assumption of a prior and more unmediated presence in the spoken word; this spoken word in the religious context is taken to be none other than the utterance of deity, which utterance is then reduced to holy inscription in and as the text. For Derrida, however, written language is not derivative in this sense; it does not find its legitimacy as a sign of a 'greater' presence, and the sacred text is not rendered sacred as an embodiment of an absolute presence but rather as the interplay of language signs to designate 'sacred.'[37]

The notion of the 'presence' of God speaking through the text drives us to discover what the 'one voice' is, and logocentrism leads us to posit some ultimate truth or absolute meaning which is the foundation of all other meanings. But once we recognize the Bible is one system of language to designate the 'sacred,' we should be able to see that the whole biblical text represents one form of human construction to talk about God. Other systems of language, for example, the hieroglyphic Chinese which is so different from the Indo-European languages, might have a radically different way to present the 'sacred.' Moreover, once we liberate ourselves from viewing the biblical text as sacred, we can then feel free to test and reappropriate it in other contexts. We will see more clearly that the meaning of the text is very closely related to the context and we will expect a multiplicity of interpretations of the Bible. As Jonathan Culler says, 'meaning is context-bound but context is boundless.'[38]

The issue of canon. Canonization is the historical process which designates some texts as sacred and thus authoritative or binding for the religious community. This whole process must be analyzed in the context of religio-political struggles for power. For example, scholars have pointed out that the formation of the canon of the Hebrew Bible was imbued with the power-play between the prophets and priests. The New Testament canon was formed in the struggle for 'orthodoxy' against such heresies as Marcionism and Gnosticism. Recently, feminist scholarship has also shown how the biblical canon has excluded Goddess worship in the ancient Near East and that the New Testament canon was slowly taking shape in the process of the growing patriarchalization of the early church.

The formation of the canon is clearly a matter of power. As Robert Detweiler so aptly puts it: 'A Text becomes sacred when a segment of the community is able to establish it as such in order to gain control and set order over the whole community.'[39] This was true both inside the religious group as well as outside of it. Inside the religious community, women, the marginalized, and the poor (in other words, the *minjung*) did not have the power to decide what would be the truth for them. Later, when Christianity was brought to other cultures, the biblical canon was considered to be closed, excluding all other cultural manifestations.

As a woman from a nonbiblical culture, I have found the notion of canon doubly problematic. As my fellow Chinese theologians have long argued, Chinese Christians cannot simply accept a canon which relegates their great cultural teachings and traditions to the secondary. As a woman, I share much of what Carol Christ has said, 'women's experiences have not shaped the spoken language of cultural myths and sacred stories.'[40] Women need to tell our own stories, which give meaning to our experience. As Christ continues, 'We must seek, discover, and create the symbols, metaphors, and plots of our own experience.'[41]

I have begun to question whether the concept 'canon' is still useful, for what claims to safeguard truth on the one hand can also lead to the repression of truth on the other. A closed canon excludes the many voices of the *minjung* and freezes our imagination. It is not surprising that feminist scholars of religion are involved in the rediscovery of alternate truths or the formulation of new ones. Rosemary R. Ruether's recent book, *Womanguides*, is a selection of readings from both historical sources and modern reformulations that are liberating for women.[42] Elisabeth Schüssler Fiorenza's reconstruction of the early Christian origins borrows insights from non-canonical sources.[43] Carol Christ describes women's spiritual experiences from women's stories and novels.[44] Black women scholars such as Katie G. Cannon[45] and Delores Williams[46] have also emphasized black women's literature as a resource for doing theology and ethics. These stories of the liberation of women as well as other stories from different cultural contexts must be regarded as being as 'sacred' as the biblical stories. There is always the element of holiness in the people's struggle for humanhood, and their stories are authenticated by their own lives and not the divine voice of God.

The norm for interpretation. Since I rejected both the sacrality of the text and the canon as a guarantee of truth, I also do not think that the Bible provides the norm for interpretation in itself. For a long time, such 'mystified' doctrine has taken away the power from women, the poor and the powerless, for it helps to sustain the notion that the 'divine presence' is located somewhere else and not in ourselves. Today, we must claim back the power to look at the Bible with our own eyes and to stress that divine immanence is within us, not in something sealed off and handed down from almost two thousand years ago.

Because I do not believe that the Bible is to be taken as a norm for itself, I also reject that we can find one critical principle in the Bible to provide an Archimedian point for interpretation. Rosemary Ruether has argued that the 'biblical critical principle is that of the prophetic messianic tradition,' which seems to her to 'constitute the distinctive expression of biblical faith.' This is highly problematic for three reasons: (1) The richness of the Bible cannot be boiled down to one critical principle. Ruether often makes comments like 'God speaks through the prophet or prophetess ... the spokesperson of God ...'[47] as if the utterance of God is the guarantee of the one principle. Here again we discern the need for 'absoluteness' and 'oneness' which Derrida questions. The *minjung* need many voices, not one critical principle. (2) The attempt to find something 'distinctive' in the biblical tradition may have dangerous implications that it is again held up against other traditions. (3) Her suggestion that this critical principle of the Bible can be correlated with women's experiences assumes that the prophetic principle can be lifted from the original context and transplanted elsewhere. She fails to see that the method of correlation as proposed by Tillich and Tracy presupposes the Christian answer to all human situations, an assumption which needs to be critically challenged in the light of the Third World situation today.

Conversely, I support Elisabeth Schüssler Fiorenza's suggestion that a feminist interpretation of the Bible must 'sort through particular biblical texts and test out in a process of critical analysis and evaluation how much their content and function perpetuates and legitimates patriarchal structures, not only in their original historical contexts but also in our contemporary situation.'[48] The critical principle lies not in the Bible itself, but in the community of women and men who read the Bible and who, through their dialogical imagination, appropriate it for their own liberation.

The communities of *minjung* differ from each other. There is no one norm for interpretation that can be applied cross-culturally. Different communities raise critical questions to the Bible and find diverse segments of it as addressing their situations. Our dialogical imagination has infinite potential to generate more truths, opening up hidden concerns we have failed to see. While each community of *minjung* must work out their own critical norm for interpretation, it is important that we hold ourselves accountable to each other. Our truth claims must be tested in public discourse, in constant dialogue with other communities. Good news for the Christians might be bad news for the Buddhists or Confucianists.

The Bible offers us insights for our survival. Historically, it has not just been used as a tool for oppression, because the *minjung* themselves have also appropriated it for their liberation. It represents one story of the slaves' struggle for justice in Egypt, the fight for survival of refugees in Babylon, the continual struggles of anxious prophets, sinners, prostitutes and tax collectors. Today, many women's communities and Christian base communities in the Third World are claiming the power of this heritage for their liberation. These groups, which used to be peripheral in the Christian church, are revitalizing the church at the center. It is the commitment of these people which justifies the biblical story to be heard and shared in our dialogue to search for a collective new religious imagination.

In the end, we must liberate ourselves from a hierarchical model of truth which assumes there is one truth above many. This biased belief leads to the coercion of others into sameness, oneness, and homogeneity which excludes multiplicity and plurality. Instead, I suggest a dialogical model for truth where each has a part to share and to contribute to the whole. In the so-called 'non-Christian' world, we tell our sisters and brothers the biblical story that gives us inspiration for hope and liberation. But it must be told as an open invitation: what treasures have you to share?

NOTES

1. T. C. Chao, 'The Articulate Word and the Problem of Communication' (*International Review of Mission*, 36, 1947), p. 482.

2. M. Foucault, *Power/Knowledge: Selected Interviews and Other Writings 1972-1977*, ed. C. Gordon (New York: Pantheon, 1980), p. 131.

3. J. R. Mott, *The Evangelization of the World in This Generation* (New York: Arno, 1972), pp. 17-18 (reprinted from the original 1900 edition).

4. J. Lacan and the école freuidienne, *Feminine Sexuality*, ed. J. Mitchell and J. Rose (New York: W. W. Norton, 1982), pp. 74-85.

5. H. Kraemer, *The Christian Message in a Non-Christian World* (Grand Rapids, Mich.: Kregel, 1956), p. 102.

6. Chao, p. 42.

7. Ibid., p. 43.

8. Po Ch'en Kuang, 'Chung-kuo ti chiu-yüh' (Chinese Old Testament) (*Chen-li yu Sheng-ming* [*Truth and Life*]: 2, 1927), pp. 240-4.

9. Hsieh Fu Ya, 'Kuan-hu chung-hua chi-tu-chiao sheng-ching ti pien-ting wen-ti' (On the issues of editing the Chinese Christian Bible), in *Chung-hua chi-tu chiao shen-hsueh lun-chi* (*Chinese Christian Theology Anthology*) (Hong Kong: Chinese Christians Book Giving Society, 1974), pp. 39-40.

10. Hu Tsan Yün, 'Liang-pu chiu-yüh' (Two Old Testaments) in *Chung-hua chi-tu-chiao shen-hsueh lun-chi*, pp. 67-71.

11. Y. T. Wu, 'The Orient Reconsiders Christianity' (*Christian Century* 54, 1937), p. 836.

12. W. R. Hutchison, 'A Moral Equivalent for Imperialism: Americans and the Promotion of Christian Civilization, 1880-1910,' in *Missionary Ideologies in the Imperialist Era 1880-1920*, ed. T. Christensen and W. R. Hutchison (Arhus: Aros, 1982), p. 174.

13. Ng Lee Ming, 'The Promise and Limitation of Chinese Protestant Theologians, 1920-50' (*Ching Feng* 1978-79), pp. 178-9.

14. Wu, p. 837.

15. Ibid., p. 836.

16. K. G. Cannon, 'A Theological Analysis of Imperialistic Christianity' (unpublished paper), p. 9.

17. K. Koyama, *Mount Fuji and Mount Sinai: A Critique of Idols* (Maryknoll, N.Y.: Orbis Books, 1984; London: SCM Press, 1984), pp. 7, 8.

18. S. Parks, *The Critical Years: The Young Adult Search for a Faith to Live By* (San Francisco: Harper & Row, 1986), p. 117.

19. S. Brooks Thistlethwaite, 'Every Two Minutes: Battered Women and Feminist Interpretation of the Bible,' in *Feminist Interpretation of the Bible*, ed. L. M. Russell (Philadelphia: Westminster Press; Oxford, Basil Blackwell, 1985), p. 98.

20. Parks, p. 113.

21. C. S. Song, *Theology from the Womb of Asia* (Maryknoll, N.Y.: Orbis Books, 1986), p. 16.

22. C. S. Song, *The Tears of Lady Meng* (Geneva: WCC, 1981 and Maryknoll, N.Y.: Orbis Books, 1982).

23. C. S. Song, *Tell Us Our Names: Story Theology from an Asian Perspective* (Maryknoll, N.Y.: Orbis Books, 1984), p. x.

24. M. Pongudom, 'Creation of Man: Theological Reflections Based on Northern Thai Folktales' (*East Asia Journal of Theology*, 32, 1985), pp. 222-7.

25. A. C. C. Lee, 'Doing Theology in the Chinese Context: The David-Bathsheba Story and the Parable of Nathan' (*East Asia Journal of Theology*, 32, 1985), pp. 243-57.

26. P. Gallup, 'Doing Theology—An Asian Feminist Perspective,' in *Commission on Theological Concerns Bulletin* (Christian Conference in Asia, 4, 1983), p. 22.

27. P. Lan Kwok, 'God Weeps with Our Pain' (*East Asia Journal of Theology*, 22, 1984), p. 228-32.

28. P. Lan Kwok, 'A Chinese Perspective,' in *Theology by the People: Reflections*

on Doing Theology in Community, ed. S. Amirtham and J. S. Pobee (Geneva: WCC, 1986), pp. 78-83.

29. N. Boonprasat Lewis, 'Asian Women's Theology: A Historical and Theological Analysis' (*East Asia Journal of Theology*, 42, 1986), p. 21.

30. Y. B. Kim, 'Messiah and Minjung: Discerning Messianic Politics over against Political Messianism,' in *Minjung Theology: People as the Subjects of History*, ed. by the Commission on Theological Concerns of the Christian Conference of Asia (Maryknoll, N.Y.: Orbis Books, 1983; London: Zed Press, 1983), p. 186.

31. Y. Bock Kim, 'Minjung Social Biography and Theology' (*Ching Feng*, 28: 4, 1985), p. 224.

32. See C. H. S. Moon, *A Korean Minjung Theology: An Old Testament Perspective* (Maryknoll, N.Y.: Orbis Books, 1985).

33. A. B. Mu, 'Jesus and the Minjung in the Gospel of Mark,' in *Minjung Theology: People as the Subjects of History*, pp. 138-39.

34. S. N. Dong, 'Historical References for a Theology of Minjung,' in *Minjung Theology: People as the Subjects of History*, p. 160.

35. Ibid., p. 159.

36. S. H. Lee, 'Women's Liberation as the Foundation for Asian Theology' (*East Asia Journal of Theology* 4: 2, 1986), pp. 2-13.

37. R. Detweiler, 'Introduction' (*Semeia*, 23, 1982), p. 1.

38. J. Culler, *On Deconstruction: Theory and Criticism After Structuralism* (Ithaca, N.Y.: Cornell University Press, 1982), p. 128.

39. R. Detweiler, 'What is a Sacred Text?' (*Semeia*, 31, 1985), p. 217.

40. C. P. Christ, 'Spiritual Quest and Women's Experience,' in *Womanspirit Rising: A Feminist Reader in Religion*, ed. C. P. Christ and J. Plaskow (San Francisco: Harper & Row, 1979), p. 230.

41. Ibid., p. 231.

42. R. R. Ruether, *Womanguides: Readings Toward a Feminist Theology* (Boston: Beacon Press, 1985).

43. E. Schüssler Fiorenza, *In Memory of Her: A Feminist Theological Reconstruction of Christian Origins* (New York: Crossroad, 1983; London: SCM Press, 1983).

44. C. P. Christ, *Diving Deep and Surfacing: Women Writers on Spiritual Quest* (Boston: Beacon Press, 1980).

45. K. Geneva Cannon, 'Resources for a Constructive Ethic in the Life and Work of Zora Neale Hurston' (*JFSR*: 1, 1985), pp. 37-51.

46. D. Williams, 'Black Women's Literature and the Task of Feminist Theology,' in *Immaculate and Powerful: The Female in Sacred Image and Social Reality*, ed. C. W. Atkinson, C. H. Buchanan and M. R. Miles (Boston: Beacon Press, 1985), pp. 88-110.

47. R. R. Ruether, 'Feminist Interpretation: A Method of Correlation,' in *Feminist Interpretation of the Bible*, p. 117.

48. E. Schüssler Fiorenza, 'The Will to Choose or to Reject: Continuing Our Critical Work,' in *Feminist Interpretation of the Bible*, p. 131.

3

RENITA J. WEEMS

Reading *Her Way* through the Struggle

African American Women and the Bible

African Americans' first exposure to the Bible was oral/aural, in subjection to slavemasters who forbade teaching slaves to read. The Bible, moreover, was taught to slaves according to the interests of the slavemasters. That the androcentric orientation of the ancient world pervades biblical stories and teachings only compounds the problematic character of the Bible for African American women. Yet "the Bible has been the only book passed down from her ancestors." Although the dominant culture has consistently used the Bible to legitimate the subjection of people, significant passages nevertheless "speak to the deepest aspirations of oppressed people for freedom, dignity, justice, and vindication." Moreover, it is possible to learn to discern different voices embedded in the text and different categories of texts, such that in some passages the voice of the oppressed can still be heard clearly, while in others it is mixed with or obscured by the voice of the dominant interests. This opens up a listening/reading strategy in which one can hear and identify with the voice of the oppressed, wary of texts that express the concerns of dominant forces, and critical of ambiguous passages.

Reprinted from Cain Hope Felder, ed., *Stony the Road We Trod: African American Biblical Interpretation* (Minneapolis: Fortress Press, 1991), 57–77.

An ongoing challenge for scholars committed to a liberation perspective on the Bible is explaining how and why modern readers from marginalized communities continue to regard the Bible as a meaningful resource for shaping modern existence. This is a challenge because in some crucial ways not only do biblical authors at times perceive reality very differently from these groups, but the Bible itself is often used to marginalize them. For example, feminist biblical scholars have made the helpful insights that the androcentric milieu of the ancient world pervades biblical texts, and they have convincingly demonstrated that specific texts are unalterably hostile to the dignity and welfare of women; because of these and other similar findings, these scholars are hard pressed to explain why large numbers of religious women (including feminists) still identify with many of the ideals and characters found in the Bible. Likewise, African American scholars have brought eloquent and impassioned charges against the Bible as an instrument of the dominant culture that was used to subjugate African American people. However, the Bible is still extremely influential in the African American religious life, and these scholars are hard pressed fully to explain why. Scholars must realize that something is at work here that involves more than the reader's lack of sophistication, or a slavish dogmatic devotion to the Bible.

Exploring the true reasons, in this post-Enlightenment, postintegrationist, and supratechnological age, becomes important because the Bible is still able to influence, persuade, and arrest so many modern readers.

In this chapter, I wish to explore the rationale by which African American women (marginalized by gender and ethnicity, and often class) continue to regard the Bible as meaningful. This rationale has much to do with how African American women assess the Bible's portrait of how human beings relate to one another. African American women have, in the past, regarded this portrait as credible; they have judged that it coincides with the way they—as African, American, and women—have experienced relationships with other people. I suggest that black women find this portrait especially meaningful because it reflects a distinctive way of living that African American women have valued and continue to advocate with great energy.

Over the last decade or so, a number of illuminating studies have been produced by feminist literary critics who, building upon the discussions taking place in such areas as linguistics, psychology, sociology, and philosophy, have focused attention on the reading strategies of women. Their aim has been to determine whether women interpret literature differently from men, and if so, to what extent gender itself accounts for that difference.[1] Beyond this, other insightful works have focused more specifically on comparing how women read texts written by men and how they read those written by women.[2] Moreover, scholars writing particularly in the area of African American religious history have frequently commented on the different ways in which Anglo- and African Americans have historically interpreted the Bible. These scholars have speculated that the differences may be due in large part to the contrasts in the social and political status of these groups.[3] It is my hope in this chapter to move such a thesis from the realm of speculation to an insight that is methodologically demonstrated. I will identify a few ways that factors in American society (associated with gender, race, and, in some cases, class) have shaped African American women's relationship with the Bible—a relationship that has some ambivalence. Of course, there are manifold factors inherent to American history that played a role in shaping African American women's consciousness, factors which, in turn, influenced how African American women read literature in general. My scope is necessarily restricted here to a few salient factors that have particular importance for how and why African American women read the Bible.

Reading can be a sublime and complex process. Such sublimity and complexity are magnified all the more when the book is imbued with the kind of power that the Bible has had over Western women's lives. The Bible is in many ways alien and antagonistic to modern women's identity; yet, in other ways, it inspires and compels that identity. An example of the complexity of this situation is this: How African American women read the Bible is a topic that has to do with not only uncovering whose voice they identify with in the Bible—female as opposed to male, the African as opposed to the non-African, the marginalized as opposed to the dominant. It has equally and more precisely to do with examining the *values* of those readers and the corroboration of those values by the text; it has to do with how the text arouses, manipulates, and harnesses African American women's deepest yearnings.

Moreover, African American women have not attempted to negotiate fully the socio-literary universe of the Bible as paradigmatic of a truly liberationist and liberated hermeneutic. Negotiating and interpreting texts are processes that are both empirical and intuitive, rational and transrational, recoverable and unrecoverable. Obviously, many factors, tangible and intangible, cultural and psychological, have shaped African American women's attitudes and reading habits. I will use a select few of these in this study. My discussion is organized in two parts. The first part consists of an examination of the socio-cultural location of African American women against the backdrop of American history. Here, I will show that history has impacted African American women's reading in general, and their reading of the Bible in particular, given the way that the written text has been presented to them as "authoritative." The second part consists of looking at some of the varying types of texts found in the Bible in terms of the voices and values of African American women.[4]

THE AFRICAN AMERICAN FEMALE READER CONFRONTING THE BIBLE

Only within the last one hundred years or so have African Americans in large numbers been able to read. In America, prior to that time, their enslaved ancestors were not simply unable to read, they were *forbidden* to read.[5] This clarification makes all the difference in the world. In fact, so determined was the American slavocracy to censure reading among slaves that, in addition to the laws prohibiting citizens from teaching slaves to read, aggressive, hostile measures were taken to discourage slaves and free Africans from seeking to learn to read. *Forbidding slaves from reading was, undoubtedly, intended to restrict the slaves' contact with the outside world and to insure that the slaves were totally dependent upon their slavemasters to interpret and manage their environment for them.* As a result of this aspect of American history, African Americans to this day continue to view reading as an act clouded with mystery, power, and danger. The truth of this is evident in the ambivalence toward reading one can still detect within segments of the African American community — many still view reading as an activity that is at once commendable and ominous.[6]

Because slaves were not permitted to read for themselves, their exposure to ideas, notions, concepts, knowledge, and information was chiefly through word of mouth. Indeed, the one piece of literature that was intentionally and consistently made "available" to them, namely the Bible, was communicated through public readings or sermons. As to be expected, the transmitters of the Bible in a slave culture rehearsed and interpreted the contents of the Bible as they saw fit.[7] Thus, what the slaves learned of the Bible's content, however distorted, depended upon an aural tradition for its sustenance, transmission, and assimilation. What the slavemasters did not foresee, however, was that the very material they forbade the slaves from touching and studying with their hands and eyes, the slaves learned to claim and study through the powers of listening and memory. That is, since slave communities were illiterate, they were, therefore, without allegiance to any official text, translation, or interpretation; hence once they heard biblical passages read and interpreted to them, they in turn were free to remember and repeat them in accordance with their own interests and tastes. Sermons preached by slave preachers attest amply to the ways in which slaves retold the biblical message in accordance with their own tastes and hermeneutic.[8] Hence, for those raised within an aural culture retelling the Bible became one hermeneutical strategy, and resistance to the Bible, or portions of it, would become another. Howard Thurman's story of his grandmother's listening habits illustrates this last point.

> Two or three times a week I read the Bible aloud to her. I was deeply impressed by the fact that she was most particular about the choice of Scripture. For instance, I might read many of the more devotional Psalms, some of Isaiah, the Gospels again and again; but the Pauline epistles, never — except, at long intervals, the thirteenth chapter of First Corinthians. . . . With a feeling of great temerity I asked her one day why it was that she would not let me read any of the Pauline letters. What she told me I shall never forget. "During the days of slavery," she said, "the master's minister would occasionally hold services for the slaves. Old man McGhee was so mean that he would not let a Negro minister preach to his slaves. Always the white minister used as his text something from Paul. At least three or four times a year he used as a text: 'Slaves, be obedient to them that are your master . . . , as unto Christ.' Then he would go on to show how it was God's will that we were slaves and how, if we were good and happy slaves, God would bless us. I promised my Maker that if I ever learned to read and if freedom ever came, I would not read that part of the Bible."[9]

Thurman's grandmother presumably never learned to read the Bible for herself, and it is clear that she never became attached to every word printed in the Bible. In fact, her aural contact with the Bible left her free to criticize and reject those portions and interpretations of the Bible that she felt insulted her innate sense of dignity as an African, a woman, and a human being, and free to cling to those that she viewed as offering her inspiration as an enslaved woman and that portrayed, in her estimation, a God worth believing in.[10] Her experience of reality became the norm for evaluating the contents of the Bible.

It is a fact that the slaves' earliest exposure to the Bible was aural and was set within the context of a slaveholding society that forbade teaching slaves to read. It is also a fact that the Bible was transmitted to slaves in accordance with the interests of slave owners. Both of these facts *must not be underestimated* when considering how modern African American women read the Bible.[11] The strategies one employs in reading a text will depend in large part upon what one's overall disposition is toward the act of reading itself. That is, reading begins with what the reader has been taught about literature and the very act of reading. Texts are read not only within contexts; a text's meaning is also dependent upon the pretext(s) of its readers. Hence, African American women's earliest exposure to the Bible was characterized by their history as a community of enslaved women of color trying to find meaning and hope for their (communal) existence from a text that was held out as congenial to them as long as they remained slaves, but censorious of them should they seek to become free human beings. Indeed, whether one considers their history from the context of North American women's history or African American history, one discovers that the Bible has been the most consistent and effective book that those in power have used to restrict and censure the behavior of African American women.

Thurman's grandmother's refusal to have the Pauline portions of the Bible read to her highlights two important ways in which the experience of oppression has influenced African American women's disposition toward reading the Bible. First, the experience of oppression brought African American women to understand that outlook plays an important role in how one reads the Bible—it became clear that it is not just a matter of whose reading is "accurate," but whose reading is legitimated and enforced by the dominant culture. Second, the experience of oppression has forced the marginalized reader to retain the right, as much as possible, to resist those things within the culture and the Bible that one finds obnoxious or antagonistic to one's innate sense of identity and to one's basic instincts for survival. The latter, however, has not always been easy.

After all, the Bible (rather, its contents) has not been presented to African American women as one of a number of books available to her to read or not read as she pleases. For African American (Protestant) women, the Bible has been the *only* book passed down from her ancestors, and it has been presented to her as *the* medium for experiencing and knowing the will of the Christian God. The Bible's status within the Christian community as an authoritative text whose content is seen as binding upon one's existence always has been a complicated matter. Its role for marginalized readers—especially those who read the Bible in order to get some idea of who they are in the presence of God or who they are in relation to other people—is even more complicated and problematic.[12] Depending upon the social location of the reader, the history of African Americans exemplifies the ways in which the Bible can and has been used, in the name of its supposed authority, to sanction the subjugation and enslavement of people or to instigate insurrection and buttress liberation efforts of oppressed people. Indeed, the seemingly mercurial dexterity of Bible interpreters has had dire implications for both African Americans and women. Nevertheless, the Bible has some power on its own, and it is certainly true that it has been able to arrest African American female readers and persuade them to make their behavior conform according to certain of its teachings. This is due in part to at least two factors. First, the Bible, or portions of it, is believed to provide existential insight into the dilemmas that grip African American women's existence. Second, it reflects values and advocates a way of life to which African American female readers genuinely aspire. But the fact that it has been used most often in American society to censure rather than empower women and African Americans has forced them to approach the task of reading the Bible with extreme caution.

Within recent years, there has been growing attention to the influence that readers themselves exert in interpreting texts. Meaning is no longer seen, as it has been in formalist circles, as the sole property of the text, and the reader is no longer viewed simply as one who is to perform certain technical operations (literary analysis, lexical studies, etc.) upon the text in order to extricate its carefully guarded, unadulterated message. Rather, meaning in contemporary discussions is viewed as emerging in the interaction between reader and text; that is, the stimulus of the text (language, metaphors, literary form, historical background, etc.) interacts or enters into exchange with the stimulus of the reader (background, education, cultural values, cosmology, biases, etc.).[13] From this perspective, moreover, reading is acknowledged to be a social convention, one that is taught, reinforced, and, when "done properly," rewarded. That is, what is considered the appropriate way to read or interpret literature is dependent upon what the dominant reading conventions are at any given time within a culture. Indeed, it should be added, the dominant reading conventions of any society in many instances coincide with the dominant class's interests in that society. In fact, one's socio-cultural and economic context exerts enormous influence upon not only how one reads, but what one reads, why one reads, and what one reads for. Thus, what one gets out of a text depends in large measure upon what one reads into it.

When we consider more specifically the matter of the Bible's status as an authoritative text, again the histories of both African Americans and women in this country show rather clearly that it is not texts per se that function authoritatively. Rather, it is reading strategies, and more precisely, *particular* readings that turn out, in fact, to be authoritative.[14] After all, the history of Protestantism aptly points out that different readings (and hence interpretations) of the one fixed text, the Bible, have existed simultaneously. However, in any given period in history, by and large, only one reading convention is deemed to be *the* appropriate way to read (e.g., the allegorical method during the Middle Ages and the historical-critical method during the nineteenth century). What is construed as the appropriate way to read and write is a convention that is passed along during a person's educational and cultural development and is reinforced in the way the dominant culture rewards (e.g., through promotion, public readings, publication) certain readings and penalizes others. And, as we will have occasion to consider shortly, the dominant reading conventions and the dominant class interests in many instances reinforce one another. In other words, readers and reading strategies have far more power than isolated ancient texts in themselves.

One distinctive American way of teaching blacks to read has had profound implications upon the way many African Americans view the printed word. This method suggests that in order to read and understand a literary work "properly," one must be prepared to abandon oneself completely to the world of that literary work. Here, the African American woman, when confronted with a work, must agree to renounce her experience of reality, suspend her understanding of life, and waive her right to her own values, so that she may without encumbrances surrender herself to the experiences, world view, values, and assumptions embedded in the work. This, we have been told, is to allow the text to speak for itself; and only under these circumstances, when we permit the text to speak to us on its own terms, without our mediation, do we have the chance, so we have been taught, of apprehending accurately the true meaning of a text. To do otherwise is to impose one's prejudices upon the text. It is a technique for reading that is taught in the schools and reinforced by the dominant culture.

Strongly influenced by eighteenth- and nineteenth-century European historiographic debates, the notion that a text can be properly understood only after one has thoroughly assessed its historical context originally emerged as a challenge to what was, at the time, the doctrinal way of reading. In the case of the Bible, texts were read literally or figuratively to conform to church doctrine without any regard for the way historical settings influenced language and ideas, without regard for the differences that existed among biblical authors, and without regard for the differences between ancient and modern audiences.[15] On the one hand, the value of the historical-critical technique was to reclaim the autonomy of a historical work by attempting to protect the text for as long as possible from the biases of the reader, so that the work might be appreciated within its own context. On the other hand, the negative result, especially as it has become evident in the way this position has been used by those in power, has been to undermine marginalized reading communities by insisting that their questions and experiences are superfluous to Scripture and their interpretations illegitimate, because of their failure to remain objective. But, as the story of Thurman's grandmother demonstrates, the emotional, psychological, and religious health of African American women has been directly related to their refusal to hear the Bible uncritically and their insistence upon applying what one might call an "aural hermeneutic." This hermeneutic enables them to measure what they have been told about God, reality, and themselves against what they have experienced of God and reality and what they think of themselves as it has been mediated to them by the primary community with which they identify. The community of readers with whom they identify as they read tends to influence how they negotiate the contents and contexts of the Bible.

Describing what reading male texts does to women, Judith Fetterley writes, "The cultural reality is not the emasculation of men by women, but the *emasculation* of women by men. As readers and teachers and scholars, women are taught to think as men, to identify with a male point of view, and to accept as normal and legitimate a male system of values, one of whose principles is misogyny."[16] In other words, according to Fetterley, in order to read texts by men, women have to read like men. That is, the African American female reader of the Bible has, like other women, been taught to suspend her female identity long enough to see the world through the eyes and ears of the male narrator. Failing that, she is expected to agree to become the male reader/audience for whom the text was originally written. As a result of their training in school, church, and the home, African American women, like women everywhere who read and find meaning within the Bible despite the clutter of silenced biblical women, have been taught to and indeed have felt it necessary to identify with the male voice in texts.

But the male voice in texts is not the problem per se. For man qua man is not for African American women the presumed nemesis. It is rather a certain kind of man. Obviously, when they encounter biblical texts, Anglo-American women, like African American and other culturally marginalized female readers, are confronted with works in which they share neither the author's gender nor, in some cases, cultural viewpoints. However, as I have already pointed out, texts are not the sole determinants of meaning. Reading strategies and social interests are endorsed and enforced by ruling interpreting communities that can be not only androcentric, but also, as in the case of Anglo-feminist readings, class-centered and ethnically chauvinistic. That is, within the Anglo-Saxon religious hegemony, the female voice has been suppressed because it comes from a woman. The Anglo woman has, nevertheless, benefited from (and hence contributed to) the hegemonic legacy of the dominant culture in her complicity in reading the Bible like a man who insists upon securing and retaining his domination over others and his control over his surroundings. Thus, one characteristic of the African American woman's reading of the Bible is that she has refused to read (and respond) like a certain kind of man.[17] Therefore, the insistence on the part of Anglo (Eurocentric) feminists for recognition within the Western religious and literary tradition might be viewed as an unwitting admission that, as Anglos, they too have played a part in shaping the Eurocentric texture of that religious and social hegemony.

Further, how one reads or interprets the Bible depends in large part on which interpretative community one identifies with at any given time. That is, the average reader belongs, in actuality, to a number of different reading communities, communities that sometimes have different and competing conventions for reading and that can make different and competing demands upon the reader. In fact, the interpretative community with which one identifies will have a lot to say about what "reading strategy" one will adopt. For, in the end, it is one's interpretative community that tends to regulate which reading strategies are authoritative for the reader and what ought to be the reader's predominant interests.[18] For example, Christian African American women belong to at least four communities of readers: American/Western, African American, female, and Christian. Each community has its own ideas about what the reader should be reading for in a text, and each one is governed by its own vested interests. Hence, an African American woman, confronted, say, with the Old Testament story of Ruth, may be forced, depending upon the context in which she is reading, to focus predominantly on Ruth the woman, Ruth the foreigner, Ruth the unelected woman, Ruth the displaced widow, or, perhaps, Ruth the ancestress of the king of Israel, King David, to name a few.

Indeed, a full analysis of the ways in which these interpretative communities individually and collectively influence African American women's reading habits is beyond our present scope. Yet, when one looks at how this experience as *women* has shaped their attitude toward reading, one finds that there have been very few incentives for African American women *as women* to read. Until recently, the production of literature of consequence in this culture has been a male enterprise that has left the African American woman, like other female readers, to read about and reflect upon the meaning of her existence through the viewpoint of a largely androcentric canon. It is a canon that has by and large proved itself to be incapable of transcending gender restraints against women in antiquity and, by implication, modern female readers. That canon has consistently assigned women to the category of "the other." Because of that, the African American female reader, in essence, finds herself permanently reading as an outsider as long as she is unwilling and incapable to deal creatively in partitioning out her double identity as woman and African American. She experiences what it means to be a woman as she experiences it as an African American, and her African Americanness as she experiences it as a woman. Admittedly, there is no evidence to suggest that, in addition to the fact that she was a slave, the African woman was prohibited from reading *because* she was a woman. Still, one must consider that (1) the Bible's world view is pervasively androcentric; (2) the official interpreters of the Bible over the centuries have been almost exclusively male; and (3) the Western canon is predominantly male in origin. These facts help one to see that although the African American woman was not forbidden to read *because* she was a woman, the Bible projects her femaleness as a problem. The Bible purports to address the existential dilemmas of its intended audience, but its less than favorable treatment of women, at times, has created some ambivalence in the ways African American women read the Bible. The fact is that the literary canon of Scripture was not written with African American women as the intended audience.

In short, the Bible has often conveyed to the African American woman its mixed messages within a context that has denied that such a woman has any substantive heritage in the printed word. The message of her environment has been that, as a woman, she has had no one to write for her, and, as an African, she has had no one to write to her.[19] We have seen already in the example of Howard Thurman's grandmother at least one way in which, as African American, a woman responded to the Bible's teaching on slavery. In those contexts, however, where the African American female reader identifies predominantly with the interests of a female interpretative community, she has by and large had the same options for responding to the Bible as Anglo and other female readers. She could elect either to reject totally the Bible on account of its androcentric bias,[20] to elevate portions of the Bible that in her estimation are central for understanding God's liberating activity and allow those passages to become the norm by which all other passages are judged,[21] or to supplant the biblical account of salvation history altogether with extrabiblical accounts that help provide a fuller, more egalitarian reconstruction of biblical history.[22]

To the extent, however, that the African American woman has insisted upon holding in creative tension her African American and female identities simultaneously, her history overwhelmingly shows that—with neither the permission nor paradigms for doing so—*African American women have sought to be sensitive to oppression wherever it exists, whether in society or in narrative plots.*[23] They, like other women marginalized by virtue of sex and culture, have consistently called attention to texts where individuals (both male and female) are slaughtered, subjugated, silenced, or isolated as a result of their identity—and not their deeds.[24] In fact, of all the interpretative communities to which she belongs, the African American female interpretative community (whether in the church, the academy, or the civic club) is the only one that has consistently allowed her to hold in tandem all the components of her identity.[25] It is the only one where, so that she may be included in the universe of readers, she is not required to suppress some one aspect of her identity in order to assert another. Both the feminist and the African American male interpretative communities have seemed unable to tolerate (when not ignoring them altogether) the multiple and simultaneous identities of the African American female reader.

Where the Bible has been able to capture the imagination of African American women, it has been and continues to be able to do so because significant portions speak to the deepest aspirations of oppressed people for freedom, dignity, justice, and vindication.[26] Substantial portions of the Bible describe a world where the oppressed are liberated, the last become first, the humbled are exalted, the despised are preferred, those rejected are welcomed, the long-suffering are rewarded, the dispossessed are repossessed, and the arrogant are prostrated. And these are the passages, for oppressed readers, that stand at the center of the biblical message and, thereby, serve as a vital norm for biblical faith. Therein is a portrait of a God that oppressed readers can believe in. In the process of the Bible's description of an ethic of divine reversal, some of those who will be abased may be African or women, and the overthrow of the proud may seem to come about only through more violence, but these factors pale in the face of the overall promise of liberation. The fact that these factors are suppressed in the reading process says more about the depth of human yearning for freedom than it does about any lack of sophistication on the part of the readers. If, therefore, African American women have acquiesced to the dominant reading convention of identifying with the male voice within a text, and, thereby, have read in most cases with the "eyes of a man," and I believe they have, then their indelible status as marginalized readers has seen to it that they have read the Bible by and large with the eyes of an *oppressed* man! This statement should not be construed as an attempt to justify the way African American women read the Bible; rather it is an effort to suggest rather broadly the very complex ways in which those who are multiply marginalized negotiate their multiple identities when reading. That said, let me summarize the discussion so far.

The concentration up to this point has been on the reader in the reading process. I have attempted to outline some of the social factors that have impinged upon the consciousness and reading habits of the African American woman. By situating the African American female reader within the context of the American religio-literary tradition, with its history of systematically denying African Americans access to the world of reading and with its strictly defined androcentric canon, I have contended that the African American woman reads the Bible having on the one hand to resist what she has been taught about her lack of any right to read, and having on the other hand to comply in some critical ways with what she has been taught about how to read. For African American women, therefore, to read the Bible and to presume that they recognize themselves and their world in the socio-literary world they find there are in many respects subversive claims. They are subversive because they run counter to much that African American women have been taught about themselves as potential consumers of literature.

The nature and extent of that subversion can be seen best in the active role African American women who have identified themselves with the Christian faith have played in the major social and civil rights movements of this country.[27] They and others have attributed their activism, in many cases, to their reading of the Bible. Indeed, one can find many fine studies devoted to examining from any number of perspectives (e.g., literary, historical, sociological, theological, archaeological) the unique contents of the Bible. The results of that work will be presupposed in the following remarks where I will consider the second half of the reading process, namely, the biblical text. In that discussion I will explore whether and to what extent the social values and perspectives encoded in the text reflect the sentiments of the oppressed.

THE BIBLICAL PERSPECTIVES CONFRONTING THE READER

Aspects of biblical interpretation in America have definitely impacted the lives of African Americans and women. This would seem to suggest that the Bible has been an important device for shaping social reality. That is, the Bible is not merely an entity of intellectual or religious achievement. It is rather, as canon, a document that was produced to advocate and shape social behavior according to certain ideals. The ideals that the Bible *in the name of God* advocates represent just a few of what no doubt were a number of positions that were at the time advocated by rival thinkers, religious groups, and authors. The production and utilization of the Bible, therefore, were activities whose aim (intentionally or unintentionally) was to take sides in the struggle of one ideological faction against another. While the conspicuous ethos of the Bible is the viewpoints of those in history whose claims won out, close scrutiny of the Bible will yield in some cases sketchy hints of the counterclaims of rival groups.

In the first half of this chapter, I cited one of the ways that we in the West have been taught to read that has been used against the marginalized to the benefit of the hegemony, namely the notion that readers are to subjugate their experiences to those of the dominant voice in a literary work. I have also noted before that the dominant reading conventions within a society often reinforce the dominant class's interests in that society. In the case of biblical literature, the dominant voices are often those whose interest was to undermine counterclaims, to delegitimize counter-revelations, and to control those people who posed a threat to the class interests of the dominant group. The consequence of the above mentioned reading strategy is that one is not only forced to subjugate oneself to the voice embedded in the text, but by identifying with the dominant voice, the modern marginalized reader is forced to side against the marginalized in the Bible and is made to identify with the ideological efforts of the dominant group. For women, this means identifying with texts written by men, for men; in many instances it means female readers are required to be insensitive to women in texts. For African Americans, this means identifying with texts interpreted by those within the dominant cultural group; for those who belong to the dominant cultural group, it means defending one's claims against rival cultural groups. For African American women, this means identifying with texts written by those in power for those in power against the powerless. *A challenge for marginalized readers in general, and African American women in particular, has been to use whatever means necessary to recover the voice of the oppressed within biblical texts.* Here again, they have had to rely upon their own experience of oppression as their guide.

In an article on the social effects and hermeneutical implications of the Philippians Hymn in Philippians 2:6-11, a hymn that makes its christological statement through the metaphor of slavery, Sheilah Briggs begins her discussion by noting that there are three categories of texts that confront readers committed to a liberationist perspective when they read the Bible. Each one poses a different set of hermeneutical problems, and each one, presumably, requires a different set of hermeneutical operations. In the first category of texts the voice of the oppressed, despite the processes of canonization and redaction, can still be heard. In the second category, the voices and values of the dominant group are clearly reflected. The third category of texts, in which the Philippians Hymn belongs, consists of those texts whose social effects upon their audience were unclear, the language, imagery, and perspective being oblique and incorporating "a range of different performances, hearings, readings."[28]

Briggs, unfortunately, does not cite specific examples of biblical texts that fall under the first and second of her categories. One New Testament text that might qualify for the first category is the Letter to Philemon, which concerns a runaway slave. Admittedly, the text tells us hardly anything about the perceptions and actions of Onesimus, the slave. The brief epistle discloses more about the writer's regard for his friendship with the slavemaster Philemon, and the lengths to which the writer went to protect the reputation of the budding church movement from being seen as a threat to the social and economic fiber of the Roman Empire. Nonetheless, the occasion that gave rise to the letter—from a religious leader to a slaveholding Christian friend—is that a slave who had escaped is now being returned to the latter. From the point of view of the liberationist reader, it is important that however ineradicable slavery might have been in Rome, and however pastoral and tactful the tone of the letter, the runaway slave, Onesimus, ran away in all likelihood because he did not want to remain a slave, even the slave of a Christian. Moreover, that Paul speaks of returning or "sending" Onesimus to Philemon suggests that Onesimus, despite his conversion or perhaps because of his conversion, is not returning to his slavemaster freely. This is an instance where the voice of the oppressed, despite the considerations of the dominant voices, deserves fuller examination.[29]

African Americans have been ambivalent in their treatment of this story. They have recognized themselves in Onesimus's act of self-determination, and they have been sympathetic to Paul's subtle attempt to hint rather broadly that the good-hearted slavemaster free the slave (1:16, 17). However, the manner in which Paul handles the matter of slavery in the Letter to Philemon has served to remind both African American male and female readers of two things. First, the social location of biblical authors, like those of modern interpreters, can influence their theology. Paul makes much of his persecution and imprisonment for the sake of the gospel, and this fueled his commitment to evangelize the empire and inspired his vision of the imminent return of Jesus as the Lord of all the earth. Nevertheless, he claimed his birthright as a "Hebrew among Hebrews" (e.g., male, educated, Benjaminite [see Phil. 3:4f.]) and as a citizen of Rome (Acts 23:22-29), with social and political privileges. These credentials, in view of his teachings on women and slaves, appear to have restricted his vision of the kingdom of God to that of a vindicated community of religiously oppressed men; it appears, then, that he did not envision the kingdom as a totally reconstructed and reconciled humanity. Second, the Bible attests, however obliquely, that there were some—a segment of society and a subclass within the Christian movement, not unlike modern marginalized readers—who understood their humanity and their religiosity differently from that of the dominant voices of the text, however irretrievable in the end the declarations of the former may be.

As for possible examples in the Old Testament, an obvious and widely commented upon case is the story of the Hebrews' escape from Egyptian slavery. For the Hebrew community, the events told in the Book of Exodus stand at the center of Israel's identity and testimony about the character of Israel's God. In fact, the claim has been made that what one finds in the entire saga of Israel's Exodus from Egypt and its earlier attempts in the wilderness recounts the details of a social revolution. It tells of Israel's efforts to constitute itself as a theocratic community that would be the voice of an oppressed people who sought intentionally to stand in radical contradistinction to the elitist, despotic, totalitarian, oppressive values and policies of neighboring societies. In this way, the Pentateuch in general and particular books, such as Exodus and Deuteronomy, reflect the hopes, dreams, ambitions, and manifesto of a band of runaway slaves imagining for themselves a new way of being in the world.[30] This explains, in large part, the significance attached to the Exodus event and story by liberation movements and theologians, African, Asian, Latin American, feminist, and African American alike. A reading of slave narratives will show that for African American slave women and men Christian hope was anchored in the story of a God who heard the outcries of the enslaved and in turn delivered them from the bondage inflicted by their taskmasters.[31] For American slaves who were themselves descended from Africans, that the taskmasters in the Exodus story were Africans was subordinate to the fact that the victorious underdog in the story was a people whose plight as slaves was only too well understood.[32]

Within that same larger complex of material in the Book of Genesis is the story of the Egyptian woman Hagar and her slaveholding mistress, the Hebrew Sarah (see Gen. 16:1-16; 21:1-21). Here the status, ethnicity, gender, and circumstances of a biblical character have been seen as unmistakably analogous to those of the African American reader.[33] It is a story of the social and economic disparity between women, a disparity that is exacerbated by ethnic backgrounds. It is the story of a slaveholding woman's complicity with her husband in the sexual molestation of a female slave woman. It is a story of the hostility and suspicion that erupt between women over the plight and status of their male sons. It is the story of an enslaved Egyptian single mother who is subjected to the rule of a vindictive and brutal mistress and an acquiescent master. It is a story familiar, even haunting, to African American female readers. Indeed, in actuality the story of Sarah and Hagar is a story about neither woman, but is Abraham's story, and the drama between these two women shows the rival and petty efforts of the two to manipulate the deity's promise of an heir for the patriarch Abraham.[34] Nevertheless, African American female readers have taken the sketchy incidental details of the story of Hagar—a sexually and economically exploited slave woman who first runs away and is eventually banished—and have perceived uncanny parallels between the plight and status of Hagar and themselves. While the details of Hagar's story offer for the African American female reader minimal positive strategies for survival, the story, by way of a negative example, reminds such a reader what her history has repeatedly taught her: *That women, although they share in the experience of gender oppression, are not natural allies in the struggles against patriarchy and exploitation.* The Genesis story of Hagar and Sarah is an important story, therefore, because it reinforces and coincides in some crucial ways with African American women's experience of reality.

Finally, one might object, and correctly so, to this selection of episodic biblical instances of resistance against the hierarchical social structures of the times. The voice of the oppressed in the end is not the predominant voice. In fact, theirs is a voice that could be viewed as random aberrant outbursts in a world otherwise rigidly held together by its patriarchal attitudes and androcentric perspective. "One can talk of more or less androcentric texts," argues Briggs, "but only with the recognition that androcentricism pervades the whole of the New Testament."[35] The same holds true within the Old Testament. Whatever hints of the values and struggles of the oppressed in the Bible that one happens upon, they are, in the end, conveyed to the reader through the perspective of the dominant group. While there is admittedly remarkable variety in their perspectives, the voices that came to dominate and be embedded in the Bible are for the most part male, elitist, patriarchal, and legitimated. About that segment of society and subclass within biblical religion who opposed the voices of the dominant groups, we can say only that they were both female and male and evidently powerless.

It has proved the task and responsibility of marginalized readers today, both female and male, to restore the voices of the oppressed in the kingdom of God.[36] In order to do this, they have had to be able as much as possible to read and hear the text for themselves, with their own eyes and with their own ears. And in the final analysis, they have had to be prepared, as I have tried to highlight in this exploration of African American women's reading strategies, to resist those elements of the tradition that have sought, even in the name of revelation, to diminish their humanity. In so doing, African American women have continued to read the Bible in most instances because of its vision and promise of a world where the humanity of everyone will be fully valued. They have accomplished this reading in spite of the voices from within and without that have tried to equivocate on that vision and promise.

NOTES

1. Working in this important area of reader criticism, Jonathan Culler has raised the provocative question, "Suppose the informed reader of a work of literature is a woman. Might this not make a difference . . . ?" (*On Deconstruction: Theory and Criticism after Structuralism* [Ithaca, N.Y.: Cornell University Press, 1982], 43). For fine anthologies of research devoted to pursuing the implications of this kind of question, see Elizabeth A. Flynn and Patrocinio P. Schweickart, eds., *Gender and Reading: Essays on Readers, Texts, and Contexts* (Baltimore: Johns Hopkins University Press, 1986); Judith Spector, ed., *Gender Studies: New Directions in Feminist Criticism* (Bowling Green, Ohio: Bowling Green State University Popular Press, 1986).

2. See, e.g., David Bleich, "Gender Interests in Reading and Language," in Flynn and Schweickart, eds., *Gender and Reading*.

3. There are many excellent works on the role that so-called slave religion played in shaping and/or sustaining African American history. Two notable examples in this area are Albert Raboteau, *Slave Religion: The "Invisible Institution" in the Antebellum South* (New York: Oxford University Press, 1978); and Mechal Sobel, *Trabelin' On: The Slave Journey to an Afro-Baptist Faith* (Westport, Conn.: Greenwood Press, 1979).

4. Throughout this essay, when I speak of African women or African American women, I admit that I am employing language that tends to obscure the enormous differences among African American women in terms of their perspectives, backgrounds, religious traditions, and self-understandings. One might be justified in

claiming that, in fact, I am referring to myself (and a small sample of women with whom I am personally familiar) as the surrogate for all African American women. Although this no doubt reflects one of the numerous shortcomings of scholarly discourse, the more modest intention here is simply to call attention to the special circumstances of a segment of readers who previously have been overlooked in biblical and theological studies and to reclaim their presence in American religious history.

5. According to the historian Leon Litwack, at the time of their emancipation, around 5 percent of the emancipated population could read (*Been in the Storm So Long: The Aftermath of Slavery* [New York: Random House, 1979], 111).

6. It is important to point out that those African Americans like myself who were born during or shortly after World War II are a mere two or three generations removed from slavery. For example, my grandfather and his sisters, all in their eighties and with varying literacy skills, can still recall the stories that their emancipated parents and grandparents told them about the hardships of slavery and the measures that were taken to keep them from being able to read. Although African Americans as free citizens have had the right to learn to read for the last one hundred and twenty-five years or so, it has been only since the landmark Supreme Court decision of *Brown v. Topeka Board of Education* in 1954, which declared that segregated schools were unconstitutional (which was translated more specifically to mean that African American children had the right to a quality education), that many of the accoutrements of culture that cultivate and support reading and learning have been made available, even nominally, to African Americans.

7. Scholars frequently comment upon the importance of the Bible and biblical religion in the African American religious experience. A recent article by an African American female scholar involved in theological scholarship deserves special comment. Katie G. Cannon, a womanist ethicist, has written about the hermeneutical strategies that were employed by the hegemonic culture to legitimate and sacralize slavery (see "Slave Ideology and Biblical Interpretation," *Semeia* 49 [1989]: 9-24). Cannon argues that three ideological notions undergirded the exegetical strategies of the slaveholding apologists: (a) the charge that African Americans were not human; (b) the claim that God had foreordained black people to a life of subjugation and servitude to white people; and (c) the assumption that because the Bible does not expressly prohibit the bartering of human flesh, slavery, therefore, was not a violation of divine law.

8. As an example, see John G. Williams, *De Ole Plantation* (Charleston, S.C.: published by the author, 1895).

9. Howard Thurman, *Jesus and the Disinherited* (Nashville: Abingdon Press, 1949), 30-31.

10. Deborah Gray White argues that the female slave network was an important institution for the survival and resistance of slaves and one which provided the opportunity for African women to maintain autonomous religious rituals and positions within the community (see *Ar'n't I a Woman? Female Slaves in the Plantation South* [New York: W. W. Norton, 1985], 119-41).

11. Their detachment from the Bible as a textual phenomenon explains in part why African Americans have been absent from doctrinal battles that have characterized American Protestantism, and why, until recently, there has been a paucity of written sermons and exegetical works by African Americans. In an aural culture, textual motifs and fragments predominate. Cheryl T. Gilkes has discussed how one

such biblical fragment has imprinted itself upon the African American cultural imagination and has been preserved in a locution, widely repeated in African American religious lore ("Mother to the Motherless, Father to the Fatherless: Power, Gender, and Community in an Afrocentric Biblical Tradition," *Semeia* 47 [1989]: 57-85).

12. For a helpful discussion of the ways in which Protestant biblical tenets have influenced Protestant feminist biblical scholarship, see Mary Ann Tolbert, "Protestant Feminists and the Bible: On the Horns of a Dilemma," *USQR* 43 (1989): 1-17.

13. While it shares many of the assumptions of New Criticism, which focused on the autonomy of the text, the contemporary perspective emphasizes the role that the reader plays in construing meaning within texts. Reader-response criticism, as this perspective is called, is considered to have started with the writings of I. A. Richard in the 1920s and in recent times has come to be associated with names like Wolfgang Iser, Stanley Fish, and Michael Riffatere, who, despite the differences in their emphases, share a common interest in such elements as the reader, reading process, and response. One of the more widely commented upon works in the area is Wolfgang Iser's *The Implied Reader* (Baltimore: The Johns Hopkins University Press, 1974). For helpful collections of essays on the development of this perspective, which will simultaneously point out the broad spectrum of viewpoints associated with it, see Susan R. Suleiman and Inge Crosman, eds., *The Reader in the Text: Essays on Audience and Interpretation* (Princeton: Princeton University Press, 1980); Jane P. Tompkins, ed., *Reader-Response Criticism: From Formalism to Post-Structuralism* (Baltimore: The Johns Hopkins University Press, 1980).

14. In other words, even if one concedes that the Bible is authoritative, one still has not said anything about how the Bible should be interpreted. For example, the Bible can be read figuratively or literally, from a christocentric or theocentric perspective, from a historical-critical or fundamentalist point of view, and still be viewed as an authoritative book.

15. Arguing that the kind of confessional, precritical reading of the Bible advocated by fundamentalism (a movement to which African Americans have become attracted in recent years due to very particular sociopolitical reasons) is potentially self-destructive, Vincent Wimbush maintains that a historical-cultural reading allows African Americans "an increased measure of *hermeneutical control* over the Bible" in a way that allows Afro Christian churches "to articulate self-understanding, maintain integrity as separate communities, and determine their mission in the world" ("Historical/Cultural Criticism as Liberation," *Semeia* 49 [1989]: 47-48). See Wimbush's article for a discussion of the dangers of the fundamentalist interpretative strategies for the survival of the African American community.

16. Judith Fetterley, *The Resisting Reader: A Feminist Approach to American Fiction* (Bloomington, Ind.: Indiana University Press, 1978), xx.

17. Writes one reader-response critic, "A bad book [then] is a book in whose mock reader we discover a person we refuse to become, a mask we refuse to put on, a role we will not play" (Walker Gibson, "Authors, Speakers, Readers, and Mock Readers," in Tompkins, ed., *Reader-Response Criticism*, 5).

18. And within those communities, a reader's identity may be compounded by any number of other factors—class, geography, sexual preference, physical health—all of which may impinge upon what perspective she or he brings to the reading act (see Stanley E. Fish, *Is There a Text in This Class? The Authority of Interpretive*

Communities [Cambridge: Harvard University Press, 1980]).

19. In the introduction to the volume he edited on the significance of race as a meaningful category in the study of literature and criticism, Henry Louis Gates, Jr., writes: "Race has become a trope of ultimate, irreducible differences between cultures, linguistic groups, or adherents to specific belief systems which—more often than not—also have fundamentally opposed economic interests. Race is the ultimate trope of difference because it is so very arbitrary in its application. The biological criteria used to determine 'difference' in sex simply do not hold when applied to 'race.' Yet we carelessly use language in such a way as to *will* this sense of *natural* difference into our formulations. . . . We must, I believe, analyze the ways in which writing relates to race, how attitudes toward racial differences generate and structure literary texts by us *and* about us. We must determine how critical methods can effectively disclose the traces of ethnic differences in literature. But we must also understand how certain forms of difference and the *languages* we employ to define those supposed differences not only reinforce each other but tend to create and maintain each other" ("Race," in Henry Louis Gates, Jr., ed., *"Race," Writing, and Difference* [Chicago: University of Chicago Press, 1985], 5, 15).

20. If one can use the work of African American female theological scholars as an example, one finds that they have not *as yet* endorsed some of the more radical options taken by Anglo-feminist theological critics, like Mary Daly and proponents of goddess worship, who reject the Bible and biblical religion altogether as hopelessly misogynistic and patriarchal. I believe, at this juncture in their history, African American female theological scholars want to stand, for as long as they can, with their constituency within the Christian and biblical traditions.

21. See Jacqueline Grant's discussion of the role and significance of the person and ministry of Jesus for the African American female self-understanding in *White Women's Christ and Black Women's Jesus: Feminist Christology and Womanist Response* (Atlanta: Scholars Press, 1989).

22. There are indeed specific occasions when African American women may elect to respond in either of these manners, e.g., in women's Bible study, in the feminist academy.

23. Most recently, the distinctiveness of our message has been underscored by the poet and novelist Alice Walker. She coined the term *womanist* as indigenous to African American folklore, and she has captured the commitment of African American women to the survival of all peoples. She writes, "A womanist [is] committed to the survival and wholeness of entire people, male *and* female. Not a separatist, except periodically, for health . . . " (*In Search of Our Mothers' Gardens: Womanist Prose* [New York: Harcourt, Brace, and Jovanovich, 1983], xi). Almost one hundred years earlier, in 1892, in a speech to the Congress of Representative Women on the status of black women, the educator, suffragette, and "race woman" Anna Julia Cooper sought to broaden the vision of her predominantly white audience by appealing to the example of her constituency: "Now, I think if I could crystallize the sentiment of my constituency, and deliver it as a message to this congress of women, it would be something like this: Let woman's claim be as broad in the concrete as in the abstract. We take our stand on the solidarity of humanity, the oneness of life and the unnaturalness and injustice of all special favoritism, whether of sex, race, country, or condition" (*A Voice from the South, by a Black Woman of the South* [1892; reprint, Westport, Conn.: Greenwood Press, 1976], 94).

24. For a fine discussion of the synergistic relationship that has existed between

black women's experience and their literary traditions, see Katie G. Cannon, *Black Womanist Ethics* (Atlanta: Scholars Press, 1988).

25. Commenting on the distinguishing feature of black women's literature, Mary Helen Washington writes, "If there is a single distinguishing feature of the literature of Black women—and this accounts for their lack of recognition—it is this: their writing is about Black women, it takes the trouble to record the thoughts, words, feelings, and deeds of Black women, experiences that make the realities of being Black in America look very different from what men have written" *(Invented Lives: Narratives of Black Women, 1860-1960* [New York: Anchor Press, 1987], xxi).

26. For an insightful discussion of the way texts capitalize on the reader's desires, see Frederic Jameson's *The Political Unconscious: Narrative as a Socially Symbolic Act* (Ithaca, N.Y: Cornell University Press, 1981). Jameson writes: "The effectively ideological is also at the same time necessarily utopian" (286).

27. Some of the more popular collections of testimonies from and biographical information on slave women and their nineteenth-century free colored sisters amply attest to the extent to which these women attributed their heroic and persistent acts of resistance to their faith in God. For example, see Bert Lowenberg and Ruth Bogin, eds., *Black Women in Nineteenth-Century American Life* (University Park, Pa.: Pennsylvania State University, 1976); Dorothy Sterling, ed., *We Are Your Sisters: Black Women in the Nineteenth Century* (New York: W. W. Norton & Company, 1984).

28. Sheilah Briggs, "Can an Enslaved God Liberate? Hermeneutical Reflections on Philippians 2:6-11," *Semeia* 47 (1989): 139.

29. See Lloyd A. Lewis, "An African American Appraisal of the Philemon–Paul–Onesimus Triangle," in *Stony the Road We Trod*, Cain Felder, ed., (Minneapolis: Fortress Press, 1991), 232-46.

30. For the most classic formulation of this viewpoint, see Norman Gottwald, *The Tribes of Yahweh: A Sociology of the Religion of Liberated Israel* (Maryknoll, N.Y.: Orbis Books, 1979). However, this viewpoint has been seriously challenged (see Jan Dus, "Moses or Joshua: On the Problem of the Founder of the Israelite Religion," in *The Bible and Liberation* [Berkeley: Community for Religious Research and Education, 1976]). Of course, this viewpoint is an ideologically motivated, highly idealistic assessment of Israel's history. This becomes clear when one considers that this block of material was probably composed in an early form significantly later in Israel's history, say, during the period of King Josiah's reforms in 621 B.C.E., when Israel had become a political bureaucracy seeking its own self-preservation.

31. One such collection of slave experiences is found, for example, in Charles H. Johnson, ed., *God Struck Me Dead: Religious Conversion Experiences and Autobiographies of Ex-slaves* (Philadelphia: Pilgrim Press, 1969).

32. For illuminating discussion of the significance of race in the Bible for African Americans and Africans, see Charles B. Copher, "3000 Years of Biblical Interpretation," *JITC* 13, no. 2 (Spring 1986): 225-46; and Cain H. Felder, *Troubling Biblical Waters: Race, Class, and Family* (Maryknoll, N.Y.: Orbis Books, 1989), 37-48.

33. See my comments on this story from the interpretative context of African American Christian women in the chapter entitled, "A Mistress, a Maid, and No Mercy," in my book, *Just a Sister Away: A Womanist Vision of Women's Relationships in the Bible* (San Diego: LuraMedia Publishers, 1988).

34. See John W. Waters, "Who Was Hagar?," in Felder, ed., *Stony the Road We Trod*, 187-205.

35. Briggs, "Can an Enslaved God Liberate?" 137.

36. This is Briggs's position when she argues far more carefully than I have been able to do here that the past that biblical interpretation seeks to recover cannot be made transparent solely through exegetical operations, but requires an intuitive component that in fact only those in analogous circumstances can bring to bear upon texts. Writing about Philippians 2:6–11, Briggs states, "The subjectivity which might have been the slaves' as they subverted the text . . . is not historiographically recoverable. It is a past that can only be invented, a theological task proper to the narrative creativity of biblical proclamation within the communities of the oppressed today" (ibid., 149).

4

ITUMELENG J. MOSALA

Biblical Hermeneutics and Black Theology in South Africa

The Use of the Bible

Writing in the context of the struggle of South African Blacks against apartheid and exploitation, Mosala contends that it is contradictory/ delusory both to believe that the Bible is all liberative and to claim the Bible as a basis for liberation while still adhering to universalizing interpretations. The basis for this lies in the Bible/biblical literature itself. Scholarship of the last century has shown that biblical literature is the product of struggle. In the course of those struggles, meanings and uses became transformed. For example, in the latter chapters of the book of Isaiah we can see how the Exodus story of liberation of the Hebrews from slavery in Egypt is transformed into an ideology of their own restoration to power and privilege in Jerusalem by the exiled Judean ruling class. Dominant groups today can both exploit other people in various ways and simultaneously claim to be biblically based because the Bible contains materials and ideologies that legitimate just such forms of domination. The story of Israel's settlement in the land, portions of which were clearly written to legitimate the "conquest" of Canaanites by the Davidic monarchy, was thus virtually ready-made for the (European) whites' dispossession of Black South Africans. It is

Reprinted from Itumeleng J. Mosala, *Biblical Hermeneutics and Black Theology in South Africa* (Grand Rapids: Eerdmans, 1989), 13–42.

thus delusory to believe that the Bible is unambiguously all on the side of human rights and oppressed people. "The issue of social class, race, and gender struggles is the single most undetected feature of the biblical literature." The recognition that biblical literature may contain mixtures, even layers of contradictory meanings in the same books, however, opens up whole new possibilities for critical, liberative reading. "The Bible is rent apart by the antagonistic struggles of the warring classes of Israelite society in much the same way that our world is torn asunder by society's class, cultural, racial, and gender divisions." Thus, by critically discerning the class, gender, and/or racial struggles that went into the formation of particular biblical literature, we may be able to engage them anew in the service of current struggles for liberation.

In this chapter I presuppose the important contribution of black theology to the black struggle for liberation and therefore will make no attempt to catalog the virtues of this theology. But it is appropriate to mention that among its key contributions is its insistence on the necessary *ideological* roots of all theology. Black theologians have not always identified this in an explicit way. They have, however, exposed the cultural assumptions of white theology and shown its link with white society and white values. In this way black theology has exploded the myth of rational objectivity in theology, which presumes to preclude cultural and ideological conditioning.

But black theology does not take its own criticism of white theology seriously enough. This is particularly true with regard to the use of the Bible. The first part of this chapter, therefore, extrapolates features of black theology that represent an ideological captivity to the hermeneutical principles of a theology of oppression. I will argue that it is precisely this slavery to the hermeneutics of white theology that is responsible for the inability of black theology to become a viable theoretical weapon of struggle in the hands of the exploited masses themselves. In this respect it is appropriate to consider the words of Marx:

The weapon of criticism cannot, of course, replace criticism of the weapon, material force must be overthrown by material force; but theory also becomes a material force as soon as it has gripped the masses. Theory is capable of gripping the masses as soon as it demonstrates *ad hominem*, and it demonstrates *ad hominem*, as soon as it becomes radical. To be radical is to grasp the root of the matter. But for man the root is man himself.[1]

It is incontestable that, although black theology has made a vital contribution to the black struggle,[2] it has not yet, as a weapon of theory, become the property of the struggling black masses. To this extent it is a theory that has not yet become a *material force*, because it has not gripped the masses. It has served its purpose well as a weapon of criticism against white theology and white society. That activity, however, does not replace criticism of the weapon itself. Part of the reason black theology has not become the property of the toiling masses may lie in the class positions and class commitments of its proponents.[3]

BLACK THEOLOGY'S EXEGETICAL STARTING POINT

All major black theological studies in South Africa draw in some way on the work of James Cone. Cone cannot be faulted for omissions in South African black theology; it is nonetheless necessary to trace the trajectory of the biblical hermeneutics of black theology back to its first and most outstanding exponent in order to see how it has been uncritically reproduced in South Africa. Black theology's exegetical starting point expresses itself in the notion that the Bible is the revealed Word of God. The black theologian's task is to reveal God's Word to those who are oppressed and humiliated in this world.[4] For Cone, the Word of God, therefore, represents one structuring pole of the biblical hermeneutics of black theology, while the black experience constitutes the other. He summarizes black theology's hermeneutical position in this way:

The Bible is the witness to God's self-disclosure in Jesus Christ. Thus the black experience requires that Scripture be a source of Black Theology. For it was Scripture that enabled slaves to affirm a view of God that differed radically from that of the slave masters. The slave masters' intention was to present a "Jesus" who would make the slave obedient and docile. Jesus was supposed to make black people better slaves, that is, faithful servants of white masters. But many blacks rejected that view of Jesus, not only because it contradicted their African heritage, but because it contradicted the witness of Scripture.[5]

Thus the black experience of oppression and exploitation provides the epistemological lens through which to perceive the God of the Bible as the God of liberation. This process, however, does not alter Cone's perception of the nature and function of the Bible as the Word of God. Rather, Scripture in its status as the Word of God "establishes limits to white people's use of Jesus Christ as a confirmation of black oppression."[6]

Paradoxically, black theology's notion of the Bible as the Word of God carries the implication that there is such a thing as a nonideological appropriation of Scripture. Black theologians condemn white people's view of God and Jesus Christ as *apolitical*, that is, above ideologies, on the one hand; but they maintain a view of Scripture as the absolute, nonideological Word of God that can be made ideological only by being applied to the situation of oppression, on the other hand. Even the most theoretically astute of current black theologians, Cornel West, takes this position. He argues:

An interpretation of the black historical experience and the readings of the biblical texts that emerge out of this experience constitute the raw ingredients for the second step of black theological reflection. By trying to understand the plight of black people in the light of the Bible, black theologians claim to preserve the biblical truth that God sides with the oppressed and acts on their behalf.[7]

To be fair to West, one must add that he goes a step further than do Cone and other black theologians by not resting the case at interpreting the black experience in the light of the Bible; he also interprets the Bible in the light of the black experience. Nevertheless, West, like Cone, insists that it is a biblical truth that God sides with the oppressed in their struggle for liberation. This is true as far as it goes; but, as any hermeneutics deriving from the crucible of class struggle will attest, the biblical truth that God sides with the oppressed is only one of the biblical truths. The other truth is that the struggle between Yahweh and Baal is not simply an ideological warfare taking place in the minds and hearts of believers but a struggle between the God of Israelite landless peasants and subdued slaves and the God of Israelite royal, noble, landlord, and priestly classes. In other words, the Bible is rent apart by the antagonistic struggles of the warring classes of Israelite society in much the same way that our world is torn asunder by society's class, cultural, racial, and gender divisions.

What, then, do we mean by the Bible as the "Word of God"? The ideological import of such a theological question is immense, because presumably the Word of God cannot (by definition) be the object of criticism. Furthermore, the Word of God cannot be critiqued in the light of black experience or any other experience. The only appropriate response is obedience. At best, the black experience can be seen in the light of the Word of God but not vice versa. Does the definition of the Bible as the Word of God, therefore, mean that even the "law and order" God of David and Solomon cannot be the object of criticism in the light of the black experience? Does it mean that the black struggle cannot be hermeneutically connected with the struggles of the oppressed and exploited Israelites against the economic and political domination of the Israelite monarchical state, which was undergirded by the ideology of the Davidic-Zionist covenant (2 Sam. 7)? Does it mean that no hermeneutical affinity can be established between working-class blacks and landless peasants, exploited workers, and destitute underclasses that made up the followers of Jesus? One cannot select one part of the "Word of God" and neglect others.

It is clear that South African black theologians are not free from enslavement to the wider neoorthodox theological problematic that regards the notion of the Word of God as a hermeneutical starting point. Sigqibo Dwane displays this exegetical bondage when he writes:

Liberation theology as an aspect of Christian theology cannot play to the gallery of secular expectations. It seeks to understand and to articulate what in the light of this revelation in the past, God is doing now for the redemption of his people. Liberation theology is theocentric and soundly biblical insofar as it points out that God does not luxuriate in his eternal bliss, but reaches out to man and to the world. To say that liberation theology is not a Gospel of liberation is to state the obvious. The Gospel, it is true, is good news for all men. And no theology, Western or African, has the right to equate itself with the Gospel. The entire theological enterprise is concerned with the interpretation of the one Gospel for all sorts and conditions.[8]

The attempt to claim the *whole* of the Bible in support of black theology is misdirected because it ignores the results of biblical scholarship over the last century and has its roots in ruling-class ideology. By ruling-class ideology I mean the desire and attempts by the dominant classes of society to establish hegemonic control over other classes through a rationalizing universalization of what are in effect sectional class interests. James Joll makes this point succinctly:

The hegemony of a political class meant for Gramsci that that class had succeeded in persuading the other classes of society to accept its own moral, political and cultural values. If the ruling class is successful then this will involve the minimum use of force, as was the case with the successful liberal regimes of the nineteenth century.[9]

The insistence on the Bible as the Word of God must be seen for what it is: an ideological maneuver whereby ruling class interests evident in the Bible are converted into a faith that transcends social, political, racial, sexual, and economic divisions. In this way the Bible becomes an ahistorical, interclassist document. Sergio Rostagno exposes the ideological roots of this line of thinking when he argues:

Historically speaking the church has always been a church of the bourgeoisie, even when it claimed to transcend class barriers or labored under the illusion that it pervaded all classes in the same way. Indeed it has been a truly bourgeois church, if the notion of interclassism is taken as part of bourgeois ideology. ... The church has been the church of the class which has identified itself with the history of the West, in which Christianity may have been considered to have been a major force. Only those members of the working class who accepted this view of history attended church. But most of the working people never accepted this view and only gave the church the kind of formal allegiance subjects give to the claims of their rulers. They could not really belong to the church of another class.[10]

Just as the church has always been the church of the bourgeoisie, theology and biblical exegesis have always represented bourgeois theological and exegetical interests. And it is a tragedy that rebel theologies like black theology and liberation theology should uncritically adopt the biblical hermeneutics of bourgeois theological interests. According to Rostagno, bourgeois exegesis shows the sterility of its ahistoricism in that

It claims to consider humanity in certain typical existential situations which provide analogies for all historical situations resulting from the human condition. It deals, therefore, with *humanity*, rather than with *workers* as they try to wrest from the dominant class its hold on the means of production and its hold over the vital spheres of human life. In this sense, it could be said that exegesis was an interclass affair. . . . This was an indication that biblical exegesis had been effectively estranged from the labor movement.[11]

The belief in the Bible as the Word of God has had similar effects. It is pro-humanity but anti-black-working-class and anti-black-women. It has, to all intents and purposes, been bourgeois exegesis applied to the working-class situation. The theoretical tragedy of such a state of affairs is that claims in that direction have been made with confidence and pride. Allan Boesak, for instance, states unashamedly:

> In its focus on the poor and the oppressed, the theology of liberation is not a new theology; it is simply the proclamation of the age-old gospel but now liberated from the deadly hold of the mighty and the powerful and made relevant to the situation of the oppressed and the poor.[12]

An approach to the study or appropriation of the Bible that begins with the theological notion of the Bible as the Word of God, therefore, presupposes a hermeneutical epistemology for which truth is not historical, cultural, or economic. For such an epistemology the Word of God is pre-established. The political, cultural, economic, or historical relevance of this Word of God comes out of its capacity to be applied to the various facets of human life, and in this case of black human life. Its relevance does not issue out of its very character as a historical, cultural, political, or economic product. Because Boesak sees the Word of God as above history, culture, economics, or politics, he resorts to a mere contextualization approach in biblical hermeneutics, which he rightly perceives as nothing new but simply the proclamation of the age-old gospel.

The problem with the contextualization approach is that it conceals the hermeneutically important fact that the texts of the Bible, despite being overladen by harmonizing perspectives, are problematical — if only because they are products of complex and problematical histories and societies. By this I mean that as products, records, and sites of social, historical, cultural, gender, racial, and ideological struggles, they radically and indelibly bear the marks of their origins and history. The ideological aura of the Bible as the Word of God conceals this reality. A black biblical hermeneutics of liberation must battle to recover precisely that history and those origins of struggle in the text and engage them anew in the service of ongoing human struggles.

The point, therefore, is not that Boesak and other black theologians are mistaken in finding a liberating message in the Bible. Rather, I contend that the category of the Word of God does not help to bring out the real nature of the biblical liberation because it presumes that liberation exists everywhere and unproblematically in the Bible. I argue here that this category is oblivious, even within biblical communities themselves, to the history of ruling-class control and co-optation of the discourses and stories of liberation of the ancient Israelite people. The appropriation by the exile community in Babylon of the exodus story to express their yearning for freedom to return to Zion and rebuild the Davidic dynasty, for example, conceals—with devastating ideological effects—the class and political differences between the first exodus and this second exodus. This kind of reuse of the exodus story goes against the invectives of the prophets and their view of Jerusalem and Zion: "Listen to me, you rulers of Israel, you that hate justice and turn right into wrong. You are building God's city, Jerusalem, on a foundation of murder and injustice" (Mic. 3:9-10, Good News Bible). The ethos of the original exodus theology is incompatible with the ideology and culture implied in the struggle for the reconstruction of Zion and Jerusalem.

Black theology needs a *new* exegetical starting point if it is to become a material force capable of gripping the black working-class and peasant masses. Such an exegetical point of departure must itself be grounded in a materialist epistemology that is characterized, among other things, by its location of truth not in a world beyond history but indeed within the crucible of historical struggles.[13] The social, cultural, political and economic world of the black working class and peasantry constitutes the only valid hermeneutical starting point for a black theology of liberation.

THE PROBLEM OF UNIVERSALITY AND PARTICULARITY IN BLACK THEOLOGY

The abstract exegetical point of departure of black theology leads inevitably to problems concerning the validity of the particularistic character of this theology. If the Word of God transcends boundaries of culture, class, race, sex, and so forth, how can there be a theology that is concerned primarily with the issues of a particular race? Conversely, if black people are correct when they claim that in their struggle for liberation Jesus is on their side, how can the same Jesus remain the supreme *universal* disclosure of the Word of God?

This simultaneous concern for a cultureless and culturebound, classless and class-based, raceless and race-oriented Jesus manifested itself fairly early in the development of black theology. Simon Gqubule says:

Black Theology is not an attempt to localize Christ in the black situation, but to make him so universal that the Red Indian, the Pigmy, the Maori, the Russian, the Hungarian, the Venda and the American, may each say: "This man Jesus is bone of my bone; he speaks in my own accent of things that are true to me!" Viewed in this way Christianity can never be a white man's religion although it was brought to us by a white missionary. It is natural that any white artist would portray Jesus as a white man.[14]

Elliot Khoza Mgojo endorses this line of thinking when he sees black theology as contextual. By this he seems to understand that it is the application of universal theological principles to a particular situation. Consequently, he traces the development of universal theology from the Age of Apology through to the period starting in 1720, which he characterizes as the era of evolving theological responses to a technological society. He concludes:

> In looking at the history of doctrine we can see in every period, theology developed in response to challenges from the larger society. This being the case there is nothing strange in a particular segment of the Christian community reflecting on the nature of God in relation to its experience of suffering and oppression. Hence today there is Black Theology.[15]

Thus Mgojo's understanding of the origins and function of black theology is rooted in a belief in the fundamental universality of the gospel. This understanding stems from a hermeneutical commitment to the Bible as the "Word of God." As a result, he sees the emergence of black theology as a logical historical development of Christian theology, not a rebellion against Christian theology. There is thus no theoretical break with traditional Western theology. Indeed, black theology is simply *contextual* theology, that is, white theology in black clothes. It is little wonder that he applies the following strictures against James Cone:

> Cone's understanding of the theological task in his early work is in conflict with our definition of theology, in fact it is in direct opposition. His focus is on the analysis of the black man's condition, ours is on God as revealed in Jesus Christ and his relationship to the world and man. Cone's approach here could be classified as christian sociology rather than christian theology.[16]

This apologetic attitude on the part of black theologians is related to their enslavement to traditional biblical hermeneutics, which we discussed above.[17] There are also forms of colonization that are connected to this hermeneutical bondage. In South African black theology the debate between African theologians, whose emphasis is more heavily cultural, and black theologians, whose focus—like that of the Afro-American theologians—is predominantly socio-political, exemplifies this crisis of cultural identity. Simon Gqubule, for instance, in addressing one of the points of conflict between Christianity and African religion, locates himself unproblematically in a framework that reflects at once a cultural desertion and a biblical hermeneutical position based in the dominant Western culture. He argues:

> There is a widespread belief about the role of the ancestors. One view is that they are an object of worship. Another view is that they are intermediaries who, because they know our lot on earth, are better able to mediate to God on our behalf. However, for the Christian only the Triune God can be the object of worship; moreover, the Christian Scriptures say: "There is *one God*, and also *one mediator* between God and men, Christ Jesus" (1 Tim. 2:5). [*italics mine*][18]

The most explicit and often-quoted criticism of African theology and religion, which feeds on this cultural self-deprecation, is the one made by Manas Buthelezi. Buthelezi correctly directs his strictures against tendencies to reify the African past, especially African culture. However, the terms of his strictures display an uneasiness about culture that characterizes the conflict between the universal and the particular in black theology. He writes:

> There is a danger that the "African past" may be romanticized and conceived in isolation from the realities of the present. Yet this "past" seen as a world view is nothing more than a historical abstraction of "what once was." Rightly or wrongly, one cannot help but sense something panicky about the mood which has set the tenor and tempo of the current concerns about "indigenous theology."[19]

Notwithstanding this rigorously antiabstractionist stance, Buthelezi proceeds to suggest equally abstractionist solutions to the problem of indigenous theology in South Africa:

> The shift from the "ideological" to the "human" expressions of ecclesiastical kinship solidarity will serve as a freeing factor for indigenous theology. Considerations of *esprit de corps* will no longer be a haunting spector for theological freedom in Africa, since there will be another way of expressing this kinship solidarity.[20]

The abstract universalizing category of the "human" as opposed to the concrete particularizing concept of the "African" helps Buthelezi maintain ties with what is "universal"—and for him nonideological—while simultaneously intending his theology to address the indigenous—and therefore ideological—situation. One might even argue that for Buthelezi the "human" or "anthropological" is finally given in the Word of God, which, he asserts, addresses him within the reality of his blackness.[21] That is why, in his view, black theology is no more than a methodological technique of theologizing.[22]

Bereft of a theoretical perspective that can locate both the Bible and the black experience within appropriate historical contexts, Buthelezi and other black theologians are unable to explode the myth of the inherent universality of the Word of God. In so doing they are surpassed by the largely illiterate black working class and poor peasantry who have defied the canon of Scripture, with its ruling-class ideological basis, and have appropriated the Bible in their own way by using the black working-class cultural tools emerging out of their struggle for survival.[23] To be able to reopen the canon of Scripture in the interests of black liberation, black theologians will need to take the materialist-hermeneutical significance of the black experience much more seriously.

Black theology's inability to connect adequately with the culture of resistance of the oppressed and exploited black people needs to be considered in the light of the class bases and commitments of the black theologians. Thus, while they

oppose the racial exclusiveness of social privileges and how these are legitimated by the existing white theology, they are uncritical of their own structural
lines to the societal institutions that produce these privileges. The contradictory
insertion of black theologians into the social structure of the South African
capitalist society and its cultural institutions, including the churches, accounts
for the contradictory character of their theological practice. On the one hand,
black theology represents a revolutionary rhetoric against social discrimination
and oppression. On the other hand, it is the mechanism through which black
theologians try to deal with an identity crisis occasioned by their exclusion from
the privileges of white culture despite their secret admiration of and class qualification for it. This conflict between a critique of oppression and a hunger to
occupy and control the institutions of power that produce this oppression has
affected black theologians' choice of biblical hermeneutical tools.

Thus the problem of an absence of a black biblical hermeneutics of liberation
has its roots in the inherent crisis of the petite bourgeoisie of all shades, but
especially those of the colonized countries. Amilcar Cabral diagnoses the inherent malaise of this class when he says:

> As I said, regarding culture there are usually no important modifications
> at the summit of the indigenous social pyramid or pyramids (groups with
> a hierarchical structure). Each stratum or class retains its identity, inte-
> grated within the larger group, but distinct from the identities of other
> social categories. By contrast in urban centers and in urban zones of the
> interior where the colonial power's cultural influence is felt, the problem
> of identity is more complex. Whereas those at the base of the social
> pyramid—that is, the majority of working people from different ethnic
> groups and those at the top (the foreign ruling class) keep their identities,
> *those in the middle range of this pyramid (the native lower middle class) —
> culturally rootless, alienated or more or less assimilated—flounder* in a social
> and cultural conflict in quest of their identity. [*italics mine*][24]

Cornel West has raised the same question of the cultural crisis of the petit-
bourgeois class in relation to Latin American liberation theology. The problem
there expresses itself in terms of the conspicuous absence of blacks and Indians—or the issues related to them—in liberation theology. He suggests that
when Marxists are preoccupied with an analysis that denigrates the liberating
aspects of the culture of oppressed people, they share the ethos not of the
degraded and oppressed minorities but of the dominant European culture.[25]

Thus universal abstract starting points derived presumably from the biblical
message will simply not work for a biblical hermeneutics of liberation. Black
theology will have to rediscover the black working-class and poor peasant culture in order to find for itself a materialist-hermeneutical starting point. The
particularity of the black struggle in its different forms and faces must provide
the epistemological lens with which the Bible can be read. Only this position
seems to represent a theoretical break with dominant biblical hermeneutics;
anything else is a tinkering with what in fact must be destroyed.

OPPRESSION AND OPPRESSORS, EXPLOITATION AND EXPLOITERS IN THE TEXT OF THE BIBLE

The need for a biblical hermeneutics of liberation rooted in the cultural and political struggles of the black oppressed and exploited people is underscored when we realize that black theology's propensity to appeal to the same ideology as do its oppressors in fact represents the extent of its slavery. For while the deceptions of the theology of oppression concerning its basis especially in the Yahwistic and Jesus movements must be exposed with all the might that can be mustered, it is equally crucial—if not more so—to recognize the presence of the oppressor and oppression in the text itself. It is fatal to mistake oppression for liberation and an oppressor for a liberator. Boesak exemplifies how some black theologians are hermeneutically ill equipped to make this identification:

> Can the whites succeed? How can they succeed if the gospel itself rejects everything that white society attempts to maintain and defend? How can the whites succeed if the gospel of liberation that Jesus Christ effects condemns white "Christianity"? Against what paganism does white society struggle if its "Christian civilization" can be maintained only by trampling justice underfoot? This "Christian civilization" is established on self-centredness, selfishness, murder, and the theft of the land. . . . To defend what I have been describing, you must be alienated from the gospel.[26]

Indeed, one wishes it were really true that, to defend what Boesak describes, one must be alienated from the gospel. That is in fact what most innocent Christians assume is the case. The real reason the dominant groups in society are able to claim to be grounded in the best traditions of Christianity and at the same time to be part of structures and societal processes that alienate and impoverish others is that that accommodation happened in the formation of the biblical texts themselves. Thus to overlook that internal biblical contradiction is to be in danger of uncritically—albeit often inadvertently—transmitting such struggle-ridden texts as part of the unproblematical Word of God. There is a trajectory of struggle that runs through all biblical texts, and a recognition of this fact means that it is no longer accurate to speak of the gospel or the Word of God unproblematically and in absolute terms. Both the Word of God and the gospel are such hotly contested terrains of struggle that one cannot speak in an absolutizing way of being alienated from the gospel. What one can do is take sides in a struggle that is not confirmed by the whole of the Bible, or even of the Gospels, but is rather encoded in the text as a struggle representing different positions and groups in the society behind the text. That provokes different appropriations of those texts, depending on one's class, gender, culture, race, or ideological position and attitude.

Underlying Boesak's assertion is the assumption that there exists a "gospel" that all social classes, genders, and races can recognize equally as representing the essential message of Jesus of Nazareth. This perspective derives from the assumption that the entire biblical text is, in an unproblematical way, God's message to and intention for the world. Once black theology colludes with the text in obscuring its oppressors and oppression and in presenting the text as divine discourse emanating from among the poor and oppressed, then the way is open for it to defend and claim, as part of the underclass, the program of the dominant classes.

The impotence of black theology as a weapon of struggle comes from this useless sparring with the ghost of the oppressor, whom black theology has already embraced in the oppressor's most dangerous form, the ideological form of the text. There is a real sense in which it does not bother the oppressors that black theologians attack their "Christian civilization" for being established "on self-centredness, selfishness, murder, and the theft of the land." It does not matter, as long as before or after this attack, blacks or oppressed peoples can embrace and own the same processes and their agents in the text as part of the "Word of God" or as integral to that "gospel."

The issue of social class, race, and gender *struggles* is the single most undetected feature of the biblical literature. It is overlooked even by those theologies that originate from contexts of fierce struggles and come into being specifically as weapons of struggle. Among these theologies is black theology. The problem is illustrated by the manner in which black theologians speak and write of the "biblical message" rather than the "biblical messages" (plural); the "biblical God" rather than "biblical Gods"; the "biblical right" rather than "biblical rights." As a consequence, for example, Boesak, attacking the brutalities perpetrated by white people on black people, argues that despite their manipulation of God (by which he means their false claims to the favor of God) and their economic and military power, white people cannot escape God's judgment. A biblical hermeneutician of liberation cannot but ask, Which God— Baal, or El, or Yahweh? the white God or the black God? the male God or the female God? No theology of struggle can any longer afford not to recognize the biblical texts' witness to the fact that there are many Gods.

Motivated by what is undoubtedly a politically righteous conviction, Boesak asserts further:

> The right to live in God's world as a human being is not the sole right of whites that eventually, through the kindness of whites, can be extended to "deserving" (obsequious?) Blacks as a "special privilege." *Human dignity for all is a fundamental biblical right.* Nevertheless, many whites seem to think that Blacks live by the grace of whites. [*italics mine*][27]

As a matter of historical, political, and ideological fact, blacks in South Africa *do* live by "the grace of whites." Boesak is correct in arguing that there is no *ontological* reason why this should be so; nevertheless, the Bible is not an ontological product in which the human dignity of all is ontologically inscribed.

The reason the Bible cannot be read as a bill of rights pertains to the very nature of the Bible itself. A century of historical-critical scholarship has demonstrated beyond any doubt that the Bible is made up of a multiplicity of varying and often contradictory traditions that are a function of both a long history over which they were produced and a variety of situations that produced them. Recent sociological and materialist exegeses of biblical texts have added to this understanding the role of contradictory and conflicting social and political interests, even within the same time frame or society, in the production of the Bible. Thus, while many texts of the Bible clearly represent human rights values, there are surely many others that emanate from the biblical counterparts of our contemporary oppressors and violators of such human rights. The biblical story of the settlement of Israelite tribes in Canaan, for example, is totally oblivious of any understanding of human rights until it is rescued by the kind of sociological reassessment of the rise of ancient Israel such as Norman K. Gottwald undertakes in his *The Tribes of Yahweh*.

In South Africa the use of the story of settlement to justify the colonial dispossession of blacks by whites and the maintenance of an ideology of white people's superiority over black people is well known. Protestations to the effect that white people are misusing the Bible have neither empowered black people to deliver themselves from this white slavery nor successfully explained to anybody, except the beneficiaries of apartheid, why such a tradition of conquest exists in the Bible in the first place. My contention is that the only adequate and honest explanation is that not all of the Bible is on the side of human rights or of oppressed and exploited people. Recognition of this is of vital importance for those who would use the Bible in the service of the struggle for the liberation of oppressed and exploited people.

Existentialist uses of the Bible in the struggle for liberation cannot be allowed to substitute for a theoretically well-grounded biblical hermeneutics of liberation. The reason for this is that, while texts that are against oppressed people may be co-opted by the interlocutors of the liberation struggle, the fact that these texts have their ideological roots in oppressive practices means that the texts are capable of undergirding the interests of the oppressors even when used by the oppressed. In other words, oppressive texts cannot be totally tamed or subverted into liberating texts.

For this reason a biblical hermeneutician of liberation must respond, "Yes, but . . . " to Boesak when he writes:

> God acts openly, not secretly. God does this as a challenge to the powers that be and to the powerful ones who think that they can manipulate God's justice, or that they can escape God's judgement. God acts openly so that the world may know that Israel's God lives—lives for the people of Israel; that Yahweh is the liberator of the oppressed and the warrior who fights for justice on behalf of the downtrodden. God is not ashamed to be called "the God of the oppressed." "You have seen what I did to the Egyptians, and that I have brought you to me" (Exod. 19:4, 5). Of course! You have *seen!*[28]

Boesak's argument must be embraced to the extent that it expresses, albeit inadvertently, something of what Gottwald describes when he argues that Yah-

weh is unlike other gods because Israel is unlike other social systems; Yahweh
forbids other gods because Israel forbids other social systems; Yahweh is so
different from other gods because Yahweh is the God of such a different social
organization. In Israel Yahweh acted for and through the people instead of for
and through kings and dynasties and centralized political entities. "Moreover,
Yahweh acts for and through a whole people acting on their own behalf."
Yahweh brings a people into being because Yahweh is a God of a people who
bring themselves into being. Yahweh is at once the cause and the effect of a
particular historical choice. Israel in the premonarchic period created a just
and egalitarian society because it trusted in Yahweh, and Israel trusted in
Yahweh because it had created a just and egalitarian society.[29]

To the extent, however, that Boesak's existential appropriation of the Bible
is founded on questionable historical and theoretical grounds, one must agree
with Hugo Assmann, contrary to Boesak, that there is a

> need to reject a "fundamentalism of the Left" composed of short-circuits:
> attempts to transplant biblical paradigms and situations into our world
> without understanding their historical circumstances. It is equally false to
> state that the whole biblical framework, with its infinite variety of para-
> digms and situations, is an adequate basis for establishing a satisfactory
> complex dialectics of hermeneutical principles.[30]

In a recent study, Gottwald has driven home Assmann's point with an even
more poignant clarity. He says of liberation theologians, including black theologians:

> While invoking biblical symbols of liberation, liberation theologians sel-
> dom push those biblical symbols all the way back to their socio-historic
> foundations, so that we can grasp concretely the inner-biblical strands of
> oppression and liberation in all their stark multiplicity and contradictory
> interactions. ... A thinness of social structural analysis and a thinness of
> biblical analysis combine to give many expressions of liberation theology
> the look of devotional or polemical tracts. ... The picking and choosing
> of biblical resources may not carry sufficient structural analysis of biblical
> societies to make a proper comparison with the present possible. Like-
> wise, those most oriented to biblical grounding for liberation theology
> may lack knowledge or interest in the history of social forms and ideas
> from biblical times to the present, so that unstructural understanding of
> the Bible may simply reinforce and confirm unstructural understanding
> of the present.[31]

My fundamental objection to the biblical hermeneutics of black theology is
that not only does it suffer from an "unstructural understanding of the Bible,"
but—both as a consequence and as a reason—it also suffers from an unstructural understanding of the black experience and struggle. In point of fact, black
theologians fail in what Terry Eagleton has called the threefold task of a rev-

olutionary cultural worker. According to Eagleton, a revolutionary cultural worker must (1) participate in the production of works and events, thereby intending those effects commensurate with the victory of socialism; (2) function as a critic, exposing the rhetorical structures of works and combating whatever deceptions are intended through them; (3) interpret works and events "against the grain." Presumably, in making this last point Eagleton seeks to remind us that the appropriation of works and events is always a contradictory process that embodies in some form a "struggle."[32]

I will argue that this struggle is a key category in developing a biblical hermeneutics of liberation. The struggle is, depending on the class forces involved, either to harmonize the contradictions inherent in the works and events or to highlight them with a view toward allowing social class choices in their appropriation. In brief, then, Eagleton summarizes the tasks of a cultural worker as "projective, polemical, and appropriative."

The interrelatedness of the tasks of a revolutionary cultural worker can scarcely be overemphasized. There is no doubt that black theology is "projective" and "appropriative," albeit vaguely and loosely, in its use of the Bible. It is certainly *not* polemical — in the sense of being critical — in its biblical hermeneutics. Rather, it lifts and appropriates themes from the Exodus, the prophetic, and the Jesus traditions into the service of a liberation project. It uncritically enlists the rhetorical structures that inhere in and circumscribe those themes — and which have an inbuilt proclivity to produce politically undesirable effects — on the side of the struggle for the liberation of the oppressed. And it fails to detect oppression and oppressors, exploitation and exploiters in the text of the Bible. Nothing, of course, could be more subversive to the struggle for liberation than enlisting the oppressors and exploiters as comrades in arms.

The most glaring example of this fighting of the class enemy with his own weapons is Boesak's appropriation of the text of Genesis 4:1-16, the story of Cain's killing of Abel. Boesak's reading of this story is in complete ideological collusion with the text and its rhetorical intentions: to legitimate the process of land expropriation by the ruling classes of David's monarchy from the village peasants in the hill country of Palestine during the tenth century B.C.E. Boesak maintains that Cain shirked his responsibility for his brother: "Cain rejects this human responsibility in the most abominable manner: he murders his brother."[33] According to Boesak, God's punishment was justified: Cain had to be ruptured from the land. But what is more, he had to be made a wanderer, a vagabond, in the world. Boesak then draws this hermeneutical conclusion:

What does that mean for us? I think the story meant to tell us that oppressors shall have no place on God's earth. Oppressors have no home. Oppressors do not belong to, are not at home in, God's objectives for this world. They have gone out of bounds. They have removed themselves from the world. Cain did not only break his relationship to the land, but also his relationship to God.[34]

"Kgakgamatso! Mohlolo! Isimanga! What a miracle!" Africans would say. The story of the oppressed has been stolen by the oppressors and is being used as an ideological weapon against the oppressed in subsequent histories. The point is that there is no historical basis in this period of Israel's history to support the argument that the oppressors were made homeless, wanderers, and vagabonds. Neither is there any historical evidence in previous or subsequent epochs to support the assertion that oppressors can be made homeless, even by their murder of the oppressed.

The category of social struggle as a biblical hermeneutical tool necessitates a historical-critical starting point for an exegesis of Genesis 4. The questions that emanate from this approach are, among others: What historical point is reflected by the discursive practice this text represents? what are the social, cultural, class, gender, and racial issues at work in this text? what is the ideological-spiritual agenda of the text, that is, how does the text itself seek to be understood?

It is generally accepted within biblical scholarship that Genesis 4 is part of the J-document of the Pentateuch. Most scholars also concur that the J-document is to be located historically in the Davidic-Solomonic era of the Israelite monarchy. The royal scribes of Solomon, in particular, are credited with having undertaken to write the history of the united monarchy using the traditions of the various groups. This production of the history of Israel by the royal scribes is acknowledged to be dominated in its discursive practice by the concerns of the Davidic-Solomonic state. These concerns involve such matters as the change of socioeconomic structures, for example, from the premonarchical egalitarian tribal system to the tributary-exploitive monarchical system. They also involve the need for an ideological explanation of the creation in Israel of large estates (*latifundia*), and the simultaneous large-scale dispossession of peasant producers of Israel from their *naḥalahs* (2 Kgs. 21), or inherited plots of land. Included in these concerns are matters such as the development of the social division of labor on which was predicated deep class distinctions. New social struggles developed around this division of labor in the monarchy, into which the prophetic movement was to insert itself in very specific ways, most of them not necessarily revolutionary.

Genesis 4 represents one such production of the royal scribes of Solomon and David's monarchy. The question of the division of labor is excellently inscribed in this text through the struggle between the pastoral sector and the agricultural sector of the economy. The agenda of this story seems to be the legitimation of the process of dispossession of freeholding peasants by the new class of estate holders under the protection of the monarchical state. Clearly, Cain the tiller of the soil must be seen to represent the freeholding peasantry who became locked in a life-and-death struggle with the emergent royal and latifundiary classes, represented in this story by Abel. Obviously, the text favors Abel and enlists divine pleasure on his side. The reason Abel is depicted as a pastoralist must have something to do with the division of labor mentioned above and the way in which it fed the regional specialization so important to the ruling classes. Marvin Chaney, commenting on these dynamics from the point of view of the text of 2 Chronicles 26:10, says:

Here we learn that under royal tutelage, herding was increased in the steppe by means of guard towers and cisterns, plowing—the cultivation of cereal crops, the predominant of which was wheat—was intensified in the plain and piedmont region, and viticulture and orcharding were pressed in the uplands. In each case, the economic exploitation of a given region was specialized to the one or two products by whose production that region could contribute maximally to the export trade and/or to the conspicuous consumption of the local elite.[35]

Expropriating the lands of the peasant producers for purposes of increasing and intensifying ruling-class herding, plowing, viticulture, and orcharding was a practice that is very well attested in Israelite traditions, not least in Genesis 4. The problem, of course, is that these traditions must be understood as ideological productions—spiritual ideological productions certainly, but ideological productions nonetheless. Thus their signification of the historical and social processes of Israel is necessarily in some way reflective of, even though not exhausted by, the class and political interests of the conditions of their production.

In the case of Genesis 4 roles are changed around. The story chooses to depict the victorious and successful groups of the tenth and ninth century B.C.E., the Israelite monarchy, as the victims and vice versa, thus lending ideological legitimacy to the process of latifundialization and peasant land dispossession that took place.

On the issue of whether an offering was acceptable or unacceptable to the Lord, a critical biblical hermeneutics of liberation would have immediately thought of the question of the Israelite monarchy's ruling classes' practice of exacting a tribute from the village peasants. This perspective would have raised the question of the class struggle in monarchical Israel and how its reality is signified in a discursive ideological textual practice such as Genesis 4 represents.

There is also evidence that village peasants often resisted encroachments on their *naḥalahs*. While no indications of their victories exist in the texts of the Bible, except in the New Testament (Matt. 21:33ff.), it is reasonable to believe that the murder of Abel may stand for one such victory. But, of course, the text comes to us from the hands of the ruling class, and thus one can hardly expect a celebration of Abel's representative demise. The class and ideological commitments of Genesis 4 are unequivocal. This factor, however, is not immediately obvious to the reader. It requires a reading that issues out of a firm grounding in the struggle for liberation, as well as a basis in critical theoretical perspectives that can expose the deep structures of a text.

Desmond Tutu is even more deeply steeped in traditional biblical hermeneutics than is Allan Boesak. Like Boesak, he also fails to identify the oppressor in the text. At a memorial service for Steve Biko, the leader and founding member of the Black Consciousness Movement in South Africa, Tutu likened the sacrifice that Biko had made of his life to that of Jesus of Nazareth. While Jesus the liberator of the oppressed in certain parts of the New Testament is indeed comparable to Biko in hermeneutical ways that can spell liberation for present-day black South Africans, not all Jesuses of the New Testament have such effects. The point is that the ideological appropriations of Jesus by the various New Testament authors are different and do not all always adequately represent the ideological concerns of Jesus' own earthly program. There are, therefore, different approximations of Jesus' ministry by the different discourses of the New Testament. The argument here is that Luke's signification of Jesus' program, in particular, is problematical in terms of the liberation struggle of black people in South Africa.

The tradition that Tutu appropriates in the service of this struggle is especially problematical. Having made the Jesus connection, he proceeds to collude with the oppressors in the Bible by describing Jesus—as do other black and liberation theologians—in terms of Isaiah 61:1-7. He ignores the class basis of the text, as it now stands, in the royal ruling-class ideology (the Hebrew term *mašiah* is thoroughly royal). This is true notwithstanding the liberating aspects of the text. For although the text appeals to a tradition of liberation that probably goes back many centuries, it is now framed by the interests of a formerly Zion-based elite, a ruling-class people now displaced from Jerusalem. This group is in Babylonian exile, where an ideology of return—not liberation—is being hammered out on the basis of the old liberation traditions of Israel and the political and ideological interests of a formerly Zion-based ruling class: "To appoint unto them that mourn in Zion—to give unto them beauty instead of ashes, the oil of joy for mourning, the garment of praise for the spirit of heaviness; that they may be glorified. And they shall build the old wastes, they shall raise up the former desolations, and they shall repair the waste cities, the desolation of many generations."[36]

Surely it is the liberation—if one may speak of it as that—of the exiled elites that this text has in mind. It is their restoration to the luxuries and privileges of Zion that the text predicts. If this text had had in mind the oppressed and exploited peasants and underclasses of monarchical Israel, their vision of the future would have been different. It would certainly not have been symbolized by the possession of luxury items such as oil, a garment of praise, buildings, and cities. Rather, it would have been the repossession of land, the tools, the control of their labor for productive use, and their security (Mic. 4:3b-4; 1 Sam. 8:22).

Of course, the real difficulty in criticizing Tutu's biblical hermeneutics here is one's assumption that he shares an ideological uneasiness about ruling-class values. This assumption is based on his speaking of liberation as the goal of his theology. It is, however, sometimes difficult to maintain that assumption in the face of assertions such as the following:

> My dear Brothers, you are being prepared for one of the most wonderful moments in your life—when you will be ordained priests. This means that you will have a special share in *the one royal priesthood* of our Lord and Savior Jesus Christ, the true High Priest of our faith who ever lives to make intercession for us. . . . [*italics mine*][37]

The basic question here is: which side of the class struggle in the social history of the biblical communities do we hermeneutically connect with when, like

Tutu, we describe our vision in terms of a share in the *royal* priesthood of our Lord (i.e., our ideological landed nobility)?

In all fairness to Tutu, Boesak, and black theologians in general, I am not questioning their personal intentions here. The problem is basically one of contradiction. It has to do with the difficult area of the interface between personal existential commitments and structural-ideological locations as well as frameworks of political activity. It is not enough to be existentially committed to the struggles of the oppressed and exploited people. One must also effect a theoretical break with the assumptions and perspectives of the dominant discourse of a stratified society. Thus, unless the nature of this contradiction at the heart of the theologies of Boesak and Tutu is identified and dealt with adequately, the effect of black theology will be no more than what Cornel West describes regarding the black American scene in the 1960s:

> The working poor and underclass watched as the "new" black middle class visibly grappled with its identity, social position and radical political rhetoric. For the most part, the black underclass continued to hustle, rebel when appropriate, get high and listen to romantic proletarian love songs produced by Detroit's Motown; they remained perplexed at their idolization by the "new" black middle class which they sometimes envied. The black working poor persisted in its weekly church attendance, struggled to make ends meet and waited to see what the beneficial results would be after all the bourgeois "hoopla" was over. In short, the black nationalist moment, despite its powerful and progressive critique of American cultural imperialism, was principally the activity of black petit bourgeois self-justification upon reaching an anxiety-ridden middle-class status in racist American society.[38]

Gottwald offers a way out of the dilemma of black and other liberation theologians: that is, gleaning liberation themes and perspectives from biblical texts. Specifically regarding feminist biblical hermeneutics, he says:

> Instead of straining after possible "feminine" elements in the overwhelming masculine deity of Israel, women and men who care about the future of feminism in our religious communities should be examining the techno-environmental and socio-political conditions of ancient Israel to see what parameters actually existed for a feminist movement and to assess the extent to which Israelite women benefitted or lost from the transition between elitist hierarchical Canaan and a generally much more egalitarian intertribal Israel. A careful calculus of these gains and losses will ultimately be of far more significance to the contemporary religious feminist movement than attempts to make ancient Israelite religion look more feminist than it actually was. . . . For feminists who wish to keep in continuity with their religious heritage, I believe it is sufficient to assert that contemporary feminism in church and synagogue is a logical and necessary extension of the social egalitarian principle of early Israel, which

itself did not exhibit any appreciable independent feminist consciousness or praxis.[39]

Clearly, however, black theologians are correct in detecting glimpses of liberation and of a determinate social movement galvanized by a powerful religious ideology in the biblical text. The existence of this phenomenon is not in question; rather, the problem here is one of developing an adequate hermeneutical framework that can rescue those liberating themes from the biblical text. One cannot successfully perform this task by denying the oppressive structures that frame what liberating themes the texts encode. The need for such a framework can be seen from the use of even a semiological approach to texts. Describing how this approach underscores the urgency of *materialist* readings, Michel Clévenot says:

> But the reading that is interested only in the meaning is idealist, believing in the innocence and transparency of the text. The exchange is governed here by the general equivalent—just as on the economic level, fascinated by the signifier "gold," workers are unable to see the real process of production; and just as on the political level, fascinated and intimidated by power and its signifiers such as king and Caesar, the subjects find the established order natural. So on the ideological level, fascinated by a "god" or the "truth" and by the false evidence of the signified (the meaning of the text), people read with the eyes of faith and "good sense."[40]

It is this manner of reading the biblical text as an innocent and transparent container of a message or messages that has caused black and liberation theologians not to be aware of—or, more correctly, to appropriate as otherwise— the presence and significance of oppression and oppressors, exploitation and exploiters in the *signified practices* that the biblical texts really are. In reading a biblical text, one can decode its message using any number of reference codes. One can read the text accepting the code in which its message has been inscribed, thus colluding with it. Stuart Hall calls this the "dominant" or "hegemonic" code of a text. According to him, there are at least three other codes within which the messages of a text or discourse can be decoded: (1) The professional code attempts to communicate messages that are already signified in a hegemonic manner. While this code has a relative autonomy, it nonetheless operates within the hegemony of the dominant code. As Hall aptly puts the matter,

> Indeed, it serves to reproduce the dominant definitions precisely by bracketing the hegemonic quality, and operating with professional codings. . . . It may even be said that the professional codes serve to reproduce hegemonic definitions specifically by not overtly biasing their operations in their direction: ideological reproduction therefore takes place here inadvertently, unconsciously, "behind men's backs." Of course, conflicts, contradictions, and even "misunderstandings" regularly take place between

the dominant and the professional significations and their signifying agencies.[41]

(2) The negotiated code combines within itself adaptive and oppositional elements. It takes dominant codes as a starting point, while it allows itself "a more negotiated application to 'local conditions.' "[42] Hall succinctly captures its essence when he says that negotiated codes

... operate through what we might call particular or situated logics: and these logics arise from their differential and unequal relation to power.[43]

(3) The oppositional code is another means by which a message may be decoded. This particular framework, while understanding perfectly the preferred code inherent in a text or discourse, may choose to read such a text or discourse in a contrary and often alternative framework. "This is the case of the viewer who listens to a debate on the need to limit wages, but who 'reads' every mention of the 'national interest' as 'class interest.' "[44]

NOTES

1. Karl Marx and Friedrich Engels, *On Religion* (New York: Schocken Books, 1964), 50.

2. See Ishmael Noko, "The Concept of God in Black Theology" (Ph.D. diss., McGill University, 1977); Lulamile Ephraim Ntshebe, "A Voice of Protest" (M.A. thesis, Rhodes University); Stanley Mogoba, "The Faith of Urban Blacks" (M.A. thesis, Bristol, 1978); Takatso A. Mofokeng, "The Crucified among the Crossbearers" (Ph. D. diss., Kampen, 1983); and numerous articles in the various issues of the *Journal of Theology for Southern Africa*.

3. I have argued this in "Black and African Theologies" (paper read at the University of Cape Town, 1982). See also the "Final Statement of the Black Theology Seminar," *Institute for Contextual Theology News* 1 (No. 2, Sept. 1983): 9ff. Sam Noplutshungu, writing on the political interpretation of the so-called black middle class, corroborates this contention. He writes: "As things stand, it is not surprising that attempts to define a modern cultural sensibility for Blacks in the late 1960s and early 1970s were so derivative in idiom and style—deep and authentic through the anguish which they expressed. 'Middle class' Blacks remained, even so, firmly attached to the common culture and even in the area of religion where much was written about the need for a black theology, radical dissent was still expressed by separatist churches that were predominantly non-middle-class in following." *Changing South Africa* (Cape Town: David Philip, 1983), 125.

4. Cf. James Cone, *God of the Oppressed* (New York: Seabury Press, 1975), 8.

5. Ibid., 31.

6. Ibid.

7. Cornel West, *Prophesy Deliverance* (Philadelphia: Westminster Press, 1982), 109.

8. "Christology and Liberation," *JTSA* 35 (1981): 30.

9. James Joll, *Gramsci* (Danbury, Conn.: Franklin Watts/Fontana Paperbacks, 1977), 99.

10. Sergio Rostagno, "The Bible: Is an Interclass Reading Legitimate?" in *The Bible and Liberation*, ed. N. K. Gottwald (Maryknoll, N.Y.: Orbis Books, 1983), 62.

11. Ibid.

12. Allan Boesak, *Farewell to Innocence* (Maryknoll, N.Y.: Orbis Books, 1976), 10.

13. Marx and Engels, *On Religion*, 42.

14. Simon Gqubule, "What is Black Theology?" *JTSA* 8 (1974):17.

15. Elliot K. M. Mgojo, "Prolegomenon to the Study of Black Theology," *JTSA* 21 (1977): 26f.

16. Ibid.

17. See also Ephraim K. Mosothoane, "The Use of Scripture in Black Theology," in *Scripture and the Use of Scripture* (Pretoria: Unisa, 1979), 32.

18. Gqubule, "What Is Black Theology?," 17.

19. Manas Buthelezi, "Toward Indigenous Theology in South Africa," in *The Emergent Gospel* (Maryknoll, N.Y.: Orbis Books, 1978), 62.

20. Ibid., 73.

21. Ibid., 74.

22. Ibid.

23. For a helpful study of this process, see Matthew Schoeffeleer's "African Christology" (unpublished paper, Free University, Amsterdam, 1981), *passim*.

24. Amilcar Cabral, "The Role of Culture in the Liberation Struggle," *Latin American Research Unit Studies* 1 (Toronto, No. 3, 1977), 93.

25. "The North American Blacks," in *The Challenge of Basic Christian Communities* (Maryknoll, N.Y.: Orbis Books, 1981), 256.

26. Allan Boesak, *Black and Reformed* (Maryknoll, N.Y.: Orbis Books, 1989), 5.

27. Ibid., 6.

28. Ibid., 8.

29. Norman K. Gottwald, *Tribes of Yahweh: A Sociology of the Religion of Liberated Israel, 1250-1050 B.C.E.* (Maryknoll, N.Y.: Orbis Books, 1980), 692f.

30. Hugo Assmann, *Theology for a Nomad Church* (Maryknoll, N.Y.: Orbis Books, 1976), 104.

31. Gottwald, "Socio-Historical Precision in the Biblical Grounding of Liberation Theologies" (an address to the Catholic Biblical Association of America at its annual meeting, San Francisco, August 1985), 5f.

32. Terry Eagleton, *Walter Benjamin, or Towards a Revolutionary Criticism* (London: Verso, 1981), 113.

33. Boesak, *Black and Reformed*, 138.

34. Ibid., 151.

35. Martin L. Chaney, "Latifundialization and Prophetic Diction in Eighth Century Israel and Judah" (Society of Biblical Literature, Sociology of the Monarchy Seminar, Anaheim, CA, 1985), 5.

36. See Desmond Tutu, *Hope and Suffering* (Grand Rapids: Eerdmans, 1984), 7.

37. Ibid., 17.

38. West, "The Paradox of the Afro-American Rebellion," in *The 60s Without Apology*, ed. S. Sayres et al. (Minneapolis: University of Minnesota Press, 1984), 53.

39. Gottwald, *Tribes of Yahweh*, 797 n. 628.

40. Michel Clévenot, *Materialist Approaches to the Bible* (Maryknoll, N.Y.: Orbis Books, 1985), 67f.

41. Stuart Hall, *Encoding and Decoding in the Television Discourse* (Birmingham: Centre for Contemporary Cultural Studies, 1973), 22.

42. Ibid., 23.

43. Ibid.

44. Ibid.

5

ARTHUR F. McGOVERN

The Bible in Latin American Liberation Theology

Four related biblical themes recur in liberation theology as the foundational expressions of an integral process of salvation involving all realms of life: God as liberator, notably in the Exodus; God's command to "do justice"; Jesus as proclaimer and doer of the kingdom of God; and the political dimension of Jesus' conflicts with authorities.

Liberation theology is frequently charged with reducing faith to politics, one-sidedly stressing politics and human activity in the Bible, and using theology to justify pre-established political positions. These charges are shown to derive largely from misunderstandings of critics who display their own reactionary position or from revolutionary groups who employ the rhetoric of liberation theology in a simplistic way. The central claims of liberation theology, which understand liberation as a broad process inclusive of but not exhausted by politics, are consistent both with the Bible and with the role of critical faith in the present oppressive situation in Latin America.

The critique of development policies and the critique of ideological elements in church doctrine supportive only of reformism led liberation theologians to a new awareness. Authentic liberation, Gutiérrez claimed, could come to Latin America only through a liberation from domination exercised by the great cap-

Reprinted from Arthur F. McGovern, *Marxism: An American Christian Perspective* (Maryknoll, N.Y.: Orbis Books, 1980), 188–97.

italist countries and their domestic allies who control the national power structure. Such a liberation would require creating an entirely new kind of society. It would mean being open to socialism; it would mean learning from Marxism about structural causes and from Paulo Freire about conscientization.[1] It would also require the active participation of the oppressed. "It is the poor who must be protagonists of their own liberation."[2]

This new awareness led to the discovery of new dimensions in scripture about God's liberating power, and to new convictions about the role of the church. Liberation, Assmann noted, means more than just freedom or improvement. It implies a judgment on, a condemnation of, the present state of affairs. It is a word of confrontation and conflict. It expresses a new historical awareness among Latin American peoples, and awareness that they are not just insufficiently developed but dominated and oppressed peoples.[3] But with this new consciousness of oppression came also a new way of experiencing God and understanding Christian faith.

What in the Bible and Christian faith speaks to hopes of liberation from conditions of oppression and bondage?[4] Four related biblical themes recur most often in liberation theology as a response to this question: God as liberator, with the Exodus as a special prototype; God's command to "do justice," reflected in the denunciations of the prophets; Jesus, liberation, and the kingdom of God; Jesus and the confrontations in his life which gave a "political dimension" to his actions. These four themes will serve as a basis for discussing new biblical dimensions in liberation theology.

GOD AS LIBERATOR: EXODUS

Through the influence of Greek philosophy on Christianity, God came to be thought of as eternal, unchangeable, and outside of human history. Theology consequently said little about God's role in history apart from the one moment of the Incarnation. Recent biblical scholarship, however, has placed great stress on God's part in history, noting that God revealed himself only gradually over a period of time and by entering into human history. Thus the expression "the God of Abraham, Isaac, and Jacob" communicates this sense of God gradually revealing more of himself to successive generations in the course of Israel's history. He reveals himself by acting in history to bring salvation.

God initiates human history by his gift of creation. He saves humanity from destruction by floods when he appears to Noah; he promises to make Abraham the father of a new nation; through Joseph he acts to spare the descendants of Abraham from starvation; through Moses he liberates the Israelites from slavery in Egypt and leads them to the promised land. Thus, as Gutiérrez observes, "biblical faith is, above all, faith in a God who reveals himself through historical events, a God who saves in history."[5] The salvation which God brings, moreover, is not just the salvation of the soul in a life hereafter. As these historical events manifested, God acted to affect the lives of persons on earth, to free them from hunger and misery, to liberate them from Egyptian oppression, to bring them to a promised land.

The Exodus, especially, provides liberation theology with a striking paradigm of God's liberating power. The Exodus out of Egypt molded the consciousness of the people of Israel and revealed God's power to them.[6] It showed that God's actions take place *in* history and *as* history, and it showed the political character of this history, for it embraced the total life of the people.[7] The Exodus liberated the Israelites physically from the bondage of Egypt.[8] The Exodus speaks to the present situation of Latin America for it reveals that God works in history and not outside it, and God works to liberate the oppressed in the fullest political sense of the word.[9]

GOD'S DEMAND: "DOING JUSTICE"

God identifies with the poor and oppressed. To be a Christian one must share in this love. Love of God and love of neighbor, especially love of the poor, cannot be separated.[10] The central mystery of our faith is that God shared our humanity, so that every person must be seen as the living temple of God. The parable of the last judgment in Matthew 25 summarizes the very essence of the gospel message. Christ is to be found in the hungry, the thirsty, the naked. "Whatever you did for the least of my brethren you did unto me."

God's identification with the poor, however, is not just a question of charity but of justice. The prophets make this point clear: to know the Lord is to do justice. Míguez Bonino cites Jeremiah 22:16, in which Josiah is praised for doing justice: "He judged the cause of the poor and the needy; then it was well. Is not this to know me? says the Lord." Hosea 4:1-2 makes the same point by equating lack of knowledge of God with failure to do justice.[11]

José Miranda's *Marx and the Bible* provides a detailed study of this identification of knowledge of God and doing justice. Miranda argues first of all that Western translations of the Bible, since the sixth century A.D., robbed biblical texts of their force. What the Hebrew text intended to connote as "justice" the translations rendered as "almsgiving." Thus deeds we have come to consider works of charity or supererogation were in the original Bible texts called works of justice.[12]

Miranda's central theme is that one cannot claim to know Yahweh except by doing justice. To know Yahweh is to achieve justice for the poor. Miranda insists, moreover, that the Bible does not just mean that justice is one sign or manifestation of knowledge of God. It is *the* way. Citing another biblical scholar, H. J. Kraus, he concludes: "Amos, Hosea, Isaiah, and Micah know only one decisive theme: justice and right."[13] In the view of the Bible, Yahweh is the God who breaks into human history to liberate the oppressed. "I Yahweh, have called you to serve the cause of justice . . . to free captives from prison and those who live in darkness from the dungeon" (Isa. 42:5-7). Or again in Exodus 6:3, God says, "Say this to the sons of Israel, 'I am Yahweh *and therefore* I will free you of the burdens which the Egyptians lay on you. I will release you from slavery to them.' "[14] Liberation flows from his very nature.

Miranda believes not only that injustice is denounced by Yahweh but that his justice is "fiercely punitive against the oppressors," that it is for their injustice that Yahweh defeats nations for Israel.[15] But it is likewise Israel's own injustices that are the direct cause of its rejection by Yahweh. Thus we read in Micah 3:9–12: "Now listen to this, you leaders of Jacob, rulers of Israel, you who loathe justice and pervert all that is right; . . . because of this since the fault is yours, Zion will be ploughed like a field."[16]

In short, justice is decisive for God. One cannot claim to know, love, or worship God except through doing justice.

JESUS AND LIBERATION: THE KINGDOM OF GOD

Jesus proclaimed the coming kingdom of God. He preached primarily not about himself or even about God but about the kingdom. Jon Sobrino writes: "The most certain historical datum about Jesus' life is that the concept which dominated his preaching, the reality which gave meaningfulness to all his activity, was 'the kingdom of God.' "[17]

To understand the import of the term "kingdom of God," says Sobrino, we must understand what it meant to the people of Israel. They had suffered the destruction of the northern and southern kingdoms, the Babylonian captivity, and had failed to achieve national self-determination after these. But the prophets held out to them the promise of liberation, of a Messiah who would fulfill their hopes. This salvation was viewed as something radically new. Thus Yahweh announced: "Lo, I am about to create new heavens and a new earth; the things of the past shall not be remembered or come to mind. Instead there shall always be rejoicing and happiness in what I create" (Isa. 65:17). Jesus shared that prophetic vision and understood his task of proclaiming the kingdom in that context.[18]

The kingdom comes as a grace, it is due to God's initiative. But it is a salvation and liberation expressed in deeds. Jesus equates "proclaiming God" with "realizing God's reign in practice." His deeds, his healings, his driving out of demons, his raising to life, are signs of the coming kingdom. They also show that kingdom means transformation of a *bad* situation, of an oppressive situation. The kingdom must overcome sin, not merely personal sin but sin in its social and collective dimensions, in groups that oppress and the structures they represent.[19]

It is not enough, however, to know what the kingdom of God meant in Jesus' time. It must be grasped in the light of present experience. Today in Latin America, Leonardo Boff asserts, the kingdom expresses a people's utopian longing for liberation from everything that alienates them: pain, hunger, injustice, death.[20] But it also conveys the absolute lordship of God who will carry out this liberation. Jesus proclaims that the kingdom will no longer be utopian but the real fulfillment of happiness for all people. This kingdom of God is not only spiritual but also a total revolution of the structures of the old world; it is *this* world transformed and made new. The cross symbolizes the suffering that unjust structures can impose on the world. The resurrection is an experience of liberation not only for Jesus but in every instance where elements of oppression are overcome and new life breaks through. If the church is to be the bearer of the kingdom, then demands of liberation are not only political demands but demands of the faith.[21] On this last point Gutiérrez writes: "To place oneself in the perspective of the kingdom means to participate in the struggle for the liberation of those oppressed by others. That is what many Christians who have committed themselves to the Latin American revolutionary process have begun to experience."[22]

JESUS AND CONFLICT: THE POLITICAL DIMENSION

Many Christians, Gutiérrez observes, take for granted that Jesus was not interested in political life, that his mission was purely religious. To look for the characteristics of a contemporary political militant, he continues, would be to misrepresent his life and witness. He rejected the narrow nationalism of the Zealots and their belief that they could realize the kingdom through their own efforts alone. He opposed all political-religious messianism which did not respect the depth of the religious realm and the autonomy of political action. He attacked instead the very foundation of injustice and exploitation, the disintegration of community. In doing so his actions took on a very definite political significance. He confronted the major power groups of his society. He called Herod a "fox"; he denounced the hypocrisy and legalism of the Pharisees; his teachings threatened the privileged position of the Sadducees; and he died at the hands of political authorities.[23]

Several other liberation theologians argue for the political dimension of Jesus' life by focusing on his confrontations and conflicts with authorities. Ignacio Ellacuría contends that Jesus lived in a highly politicized atmosphere in which all he did necessarily carried political implications.[24] His criticisms interfered with the whole sociopolitical power structure. In criticizing the Scribes and Pharisees he was attacking their monopoly over the faith and consequently he undermined the power base of the priestly class. He also threatened the power balance between the Jewish nation and the Romans. His condemnation of wealth carried the same political implications. Míguez Bonino adds that the universality of Jesus' love cannot be interpreted as a compromise with or acceptance of evil, and that he was *rightly* accused of taking the side of the oppressed against the constituted religious and political authorities.[25]

Sobrino emphasizes the targets of Jesus' denunciations. If Jesus does not speak in contemporary terms of unjust structures or institutions, his denunciations are almost always *collective*. They are aimed at the Pharisees because they pay no attention to justice, at the legal experts because they impose intolerable burdens on the people, at the rich because they refuse to share their wealth with the poor, and at the rulers of the world because they govern despotically. The anathemas are also directed against abuse of power, be it religious, intellectual, economic, or political.[26]

In a powerful chapter on the death of Jesus, Sobrino argues that the crucifixion can be explained only as the historical consequence of Jesus' life and preaching of the kingdom. Jesus proclaimed a God of liberation, a God concerned about human life and dignity, a God whose love is so deeply affected by all that is negative that *he suffers* from the death of his Son and from human suffering. But this God whom Jesus proclaimed conflicted with the God of religion, the God of external rituals and temple worship, the God in whose name privileged classes subdue others. Jesus was charged with blasphemy for proclaiming such a God, but he suffered the punishment imposed on political agitators (crucifixion) rather than the punishment dealt out to religious blasphemers (stoning) because his denunciations challenged every claim to power which does not embody God's love and truth.[27]

Jesus seems clearly to have renounced the use of violence in his own defense or as a means of confronting injustice. He drove moneychangers out of the temple. He did not, however, use or condone violence against persons. But given the violence of oppressive conditions in Latin America would not revolutionary violence be justifiable? Liberation theologians do not deal with this issue as often as one might expect. Gutiérrez, in *A Theology of Liberation*, speaks often of oppressive institutional violence in Latin America and of the necessity of class struggle to oppose it. But he does not discuss to any extent a recourse to revolutionary violence. Some liberation theologians have affirmed nonviolence as an essential Christian stance on liberation. Leonardo Boff affirms that the power of God, to which Jesus bore witness, is love. "Such love rules out all violence and oppression, even for the sake of having love itself prevail." The apparent efficacy of violence does not manage to break the spiralling process of violence.[28] Segundo Galilea argues that liberation from violence, both from institutional violence and from subversive violence, is one of the most important tasks confronting Christianity. He holds that liberation theology and Christianity "tell us that violence cannot be overcome with purely human means or with other forms of violence."[29]

Juan Luis Segundo, on the other hand, believes that Jesus' message of nonviolence is not a matter of faith but an ideological stance taken in a particular historical context. The Israelites felt that God commanded them to exterminate their enemies; Jesus insisted on love and nonresistance to evil; each ideology had its own historical function to carry out. What theology must do is decide what ideology is needed in the light of the present situation of sociopolitical oppression in Latin America. Since it would be unrealistic to look centuries back to biblical situations for an answer, the best approach would be to ask: "What would the Christ of the Gospels say if he were confronting our problems today?"[30]

SOME COMMENTS ABOUT BIBLICAL PERSPECTIVES

Critics of liberation theology charge that it oversimplifies the biblical message of the faith and tends to reduce it to politics with a definite ideological thrust.[31] Their criticisms might be grouped and considered under three charges: that liberation theology reduces faith to politics, that it interprets political dimensions of the gospel one-sidedly, overemphasizing human efforts, and that it uses scripture to justify its own political positions.

Liberation theology is criticized for reducing faith to politics. Liberation theologians *do stress* the political dimensions and political implications of scripture because they see Latin America's most urgent problems as bound up with politics. But stress cannot be equated with denial of all other aspects. A theologian who writes on prayer is not accused of ignoring marriage. More qualifying statements within liberation theology might have averted some of the criticism. Segundo, for example, makes a claim for liberation theology which could be used as an objection to the response that it only stresses the political. He writes: "Liberation is meant to designate and cover theology as a whole" and it is "the only authentic and privileged standpoint for arriving at a full and complete understanding of God's revelation in Jesus Christ."[32] The fact that he moves on to discuss the political problem of socialism versus capitalism as a test of theology might add to the impression that liberation theology deals only with politics. But Segundo does not say that *politics* is the privileged standpoint or covers theology as a whole; he says that *liberation* is. Liberation has a much fuller meaning than political action. Certainly other liberation theologians in the same volume of *Frontiers of Theology in Latin America* quite clearly take liberation in a broad sense and say explicitly that politics is only one dimension of the faith.[33]

The second objection raised against liberation theology is that when it treats the political dimension of the Bible it gives a one-sided and oversimplified interpretation, and it overstresses human activity in achieving liberation. Some liberation theologians have presented one-sided interpretations of biblical passages. Miranda's *Marx and the Bible* falls into this. His major thesis that justice is the prevailing theme of scripture has been supported by other scripture scholars.[34] His book, moreover, contains a powerfully moving call to justice. But Miranda also makes strong, sweeping statements that do present only one dimension of the biblical message. He claims, for example, that the justice proclaimed by Isaiah is "fiercely punitive against oppressors," without mentioning numerous passages that extol God's great mercy.[35] He claims that not even the anarchist Bakunin made assertions more subversive of the law than St. Paul, overlooking Paul's admonitions that slaves obey their masters and wives their husbands.[36] Phillip Berryman, in an otherwise very positive presentation of liberation theology, comments on the extreme form of Miranda's arguments.[37] And as the title of the book would suggest, Miranda often does impose a Marxist framework on the Bible.

Biblical passages have many dimensions and hence lend themselves to different interpretations. The sources most often cited by liberation theologians could be used to show that liberation does *not* come through struggle and oppression. If the Exodus account serves as a paradigm of liberation, it is not an example of overthrowing oppressors. The Jews fled Egypt; they did not overcome their oppressors and establish a new social order in Egypt. Yahweh told them that it was not because of their efforts, but because of him, that they were liberated. They struggled and fought wars to gain possession of the promised land, but not against oppressors over land they could claim was due to them in justice. Yahweh told them: "It is not for any goodness of yours that Yahweh gives you this rich land to possess, for you are a headstrong people"

(Deut. 9:6). Similarly, when the prophets denounced injustice they did not call for collective political action but for conversion of the powerful and wealthy. They insisted moreover that only God could provide true justice (Isa. 1:24ff.; Exod. 3:7-9). Neither did Jesus organize the masses to overthrow unjust structures.

These examples, however, do not negate the central claims made by liberation theology that God acts in history to bring human, physical liberation and that he defends the poor and denounces injustice. The examples only serve to illustrate Segundo's argument about the distinction between faith and ideology. These central claims of liberation theology pertain to faith; how they were acted upon in biblical times was conditioned by cultural ideologies. If exact imitation of what the prophets did or what Jesus did is made a matter of faith, then few of the institutional ministries of the church could be justified. Jesus never started a school or built a parish church; nor did he instruct his apostles to do so. The essential thing is to discover and act upon the spirit and intention that underly God's revelations and Jesus' actions. Dorothee Soelle articulates this well:

> Social awareness of transformation cannot and need not be justified biblically. . . . It is not a matter of compiling in a biblicistic sense materials pertaining to the political activity of Jesus and using them to establish whether or not he was a revolutionary. The main thing is not to describe his concrete behavior and to imitate it, but rather to discern the intention or tendency of that behavior and to realize anew his goals in our world.[38]

Leonardo Boff's essay on "Christ's Liberation via Oppression" complements what has already been said about the meaning, spirit, and tendency of Jesus' words and behavior. Jesus preached good news to the poor and was born and lived among them; he denounced injustice; he put human good above legalism when he healed on the Sabbath; he died for values he refused to compromise. Yet at the same time he forgave and he maintained a deep love for every person and respect for each person's liberty.[39] To combine the strength to oppose and overcome injustice with a love that is forgiving is, I believe, to live with the spirit of Jesus. Combining these, moreover, could be the distinctive contribution of Christianity to human liberation.

The third criticism raised against liberation theology is that it uses theology to justify political positions already taken. A criticism often heard about liberation theology is that it identifies God's will and Marxist socialism: it identifies the poor with the proletariat, prophetic denunciation with Marxist critiques of capitalism, God's liberation with socialist revolution, and the kingdom of God with a new socialist society. But if liberation theology made no effort to correlate the poor of the Bible with the poor in Latin America, and injustice denounced in the Bible with contemporary injustices, it would lose all meaning. The very purpose of liberation theology is to relate the word of God and historical praxis.[40] The issue is whether liberation theology determines in advance what it will find in praxis by adopting only Marxist categories. If the summaries we have given on biblical perspectives accurately reflect liberation theology as a whole, the identification of biblical and Marxist categories is *not* characteristic. Opponents of liberation theology, Galilea observes, often fail to distinguish between liberation theology as such and political documents published by revolutionary Christian groups. Some forms of liberation theology, he acknowledges, do tend to be "ideologized" and to rely on Marxist categories, but this current is limited and not representative of liberation theology as a whole.[41] To his remarks could be added those of other liberation theologians who criticize the "absolutizing" of any one ideological position.[42]

Quite often it is the opponents of liberation theology who read into theological statements a Marxist-Leninist identification. Bishop Alfonso López Trujillo's *Liberation or Revolution?* exemplifies this tendency. The book cover, not inappropriately in light of its tone, presents the title in dripping paint to suggest bloodshed. Where liberation theologians speak of the political dimension of Jesus' mission, López Trujillo treats them as militant proponents of violent revolution. "Is Christ a Zealot who seeks radical change by means of violence. ... Does He impatiently seek the 'Kingdom,' and does He want to speed his mission by means of violence?"[43] In short, where facile identifications of liberation and Marxism are made, they are most often the product of opponents, or of militant political groups using liberation theology, not from within liberation theology itself.

A way of reading liberation theology more sympathetically, while at the same time testing the basic faithfulness of liberation theology to scripture, would be to list points that they hold and ask: "which of these should be *denied*?" Could any of the following be judged contrary to faith or scripture?

> God reveals himself in history.
> God desires the full human freedom of his people, at every level of their life.
> God reveals a very special concern for the poor and is angered by injustice done against them.
> Jesus sought to bring God's liberating power and justice to all.
> Jesus identified in a very special way with the marginal people of society, the outcasts, the poor.
> Jesus denounced those who placed burdens upon the poor and who placed legalism (law and order) over human need.
> Jesus sought to "break the power of evil and sin" in the world.
> Jesus' actions were seen as a threat to those in positions of power.

A similar set of statements could be drawn up to reflect the role of faith in the present as expressed in liberation theology. Which of these should be denied?

> The issue of poverty and oppression is the gravest problem facing the great masses of people in Latin America.
> Without denying the value of other ministries, primary importance should be attached to the work of helping the poor.

The poor of Latin America are the landless peasants, the marginal people in the barrios of the city, the underpaid, underemployed, or unemployed workers.

In Latin America capitalism has failed to serve the common good, and developmental policies have not succeeded in bettering the situation.

These failures suggest the need for a more profound analysis of causes, using the best tools available from the social sciences.

The church should be willing to evaluate its own social teachings to see if they are adequate to the present situation.

Some church teachings may reflect cultural attitudes or "ideologies."

To work directly with the poor is certainly consistent with the spirit of Jesus and the mission of the church. It might prove more effective for social change than educational work with upper and middle classes, a work which seems to have had very limited success in changing conditions in Latin America.

Working with the poor and striving with them for liberation can lead to a very enriching and new understanding of the faith.

In its concern for the poor and for ending injustice the church should be willing to take stands, even if this involves conflict with some of its own members, for example regarding land reform.

It may be argued that this list of statements, and other efforts made to strike a balance, are out of harmony with liberation theology which concerns itself with praxis and the process of liberation, not with theological propositions. But an important political issue is involved, namely, whether liberation theology wants to build support for its positions within the institutional church.

NOTES

1. Gustavo Gutiérrez, *A Theology of Liberation: History, Politics and Salvation*, trans. and ed. Caridad Inda and John Eagleson (Maryknoll, N.Y.: Orbis Books, 1973), pp. 88-92.

2. Ibid., p. 113.

3. Hugo Assmann, *Theology for a Nomad Church*, trans. Paul Burns (Maryknoll, N.Y.: Orbis Books, 1976), pp. 49-51.

4. See Jon Sobrino, S.J., *Christianity at the Crossroads*, trans. John Drury (Maryknoll, N.Y.: Orbis Books, 1978), p. 35. See also Leonardo Boff, "Christ's Liberation via Oppression," in *Frontiers of Theology in Latin America*, ed. Rosino Gibellini, trans. John Drury (Maryknoll, N.Y.: Orbis Books, 1979), pp. 100-131.

5. Gutiérrez, *A Theology of Liberation*, p. 154.

6. See Assmann, *Theology for a Nomad Church*, p. 66, and Rubem Alves, *A Theology of Human Hope* (Washington, D.C.: Corpus Books, 1969), p. 89.

7. See José Míguez Bonino, *Revolutionary Theology Comes of Age* (London: SPCK, 1975); and U.S. edition, *Doing Theology in a Revolutionary Situation* (Philadelphia: Fortress, 1975), pp. 134–35.

8. Alfredo Fierro, *The Militant Gospel: A Critical Introduction to Political Theologies*, trans. John Drury (Maryknoll, N.Y.: Orbis Books, 1977), pp. 140–45.

9. Assmann, *Theology for a Nomad Church*, p. 35.

10. See Sobrino, *Christology at the Crossroads*, pp. 169-73, 204-5.

11. José Míguez Bonino, *Christians and Marxists: The Mutual Challenge to Revolution* (Grand Rapids, Mich.: Eerdmans, 1976), pp. 31-33.

12 . José Miranda, *Marx and the Bible: A Critique of the Philosophy of Oppression*, trans. John Eagleson (Maryknoll, N.Y.: Orbis Books, 1974), pp. 14–15.

13. Ibid., p. 46.

14. Ibid., pp. 78–79.

15. Ibid., pp. 83 and 121.

16. Ibid., p. 165. In Scripture see also Amos 4:1–3 and Hosea 10:13.

17. Sobrino, *Christology at the Crossroads*, p. 41.

18. Ibid., pp. 42–44.

19. Ibid., pp. 50–55.

20. Leonardo Boff, "Salvation in Jesus Christ and the Process of Liberation," in *The Mystical and Political Dimension of the Christian Faith*, Concilium 96, ed. Claude Geffré and Gustavo Gutiérrez (New York: Herder/Seabury, 1974), pp. 81–88.

21. Ibid., p. 88. Opponents of liberation theology have accused it of identifying the kingdom as something human activity alone can achieve. Boff clearly does not, p. 89.

22. Gutiérrez, *A Theology of Liberation*, p. 203. Also, on the distinction noted above between the kingdom and human efforts, pp. 227, 231.

23. Ibid., pp. 225–32.

24. Ignacio Ellacuría, *Freedom Made Flesh*, trans. John Drury (Maryknoll, N.Y.: Orbis Books, 1976), pp. 31–45.

25. Míguez Bonino, *Revolutionary Theology Comes of Age*, pp. 121–24.

26. Sobrino, *Christology at the Crossroads*, p. 53.

27. Ibid., pp. 204–9. On God's suffering, see pp. 224–26.

28. Leonardo Boff, "Christ's Liberation via Oppression," in *Frontiers of Theology in Latin America*, p. 120.

29. Segundo Galilea, in ibid., "Liberation Theology and New Tasks Facing Christians," p. 175.

30. Juan Luis Segundo, *The Liberation of Theology*, trans. John Drury (Maryknoll, N. Y.: Orbis Books, 1976), pp. 116–17. See also Míguez Bonino, *Christians and Marxists*, p. 124, who comments only briefly on the question of violence by saying that if socialist revolution involves violence a Christian should be concerned with keeping it at a minimum.

31. See the criticism of the International Theological Commission "Human Development and Christian Salvation," in *Origins* 7 (November 3, 1977). As an advisory group to the pope, the Commission's criticism of "some forms" of liberation theology constituted the most formal critique. The criticisms focused chiefly on biblical interpretations which were found oversimplified. The Commission itself was criticized for not including a liberation theologian in its deliberations. Clark H. Pinnock, "Liberation Theology: The Gains, the Gaps," in *Christianity Today* 20 (January 16, 1976), is critical of liberation theology.

32. Juan Luis Segundo, "Capitalism versus Socialism: Crux Theologica," in *Frontiers of Theology*, p. 241.

33. Gutiérrez, "Liberation Praxis and Christian Faith," in *Frontiers*, insists that Christian liberation is not restricted to political liberation, but stresses its universal

transcendence (p. 128). Also in *Frontiers*, Boff, pp. 107–8; Raul Vidales, "Methodological Issues in Liberation Theology," pp. 35–36, and Galilea, "Liberation and New Tasks," pp. 169–70.

34. See, for example, John R. Donahue, S.J., "Biblical Perspectives on Justice," in *The Faith That Does Justice*, ed. John C. Haughey, S.J. (New York: Paulist Press, 1977), p. 68.

35. Miranda, *Marx and the Bible*, p. 83.

36. Ibid., p. 187.

37. Phillip Berryman, "Latin American Liberation Theology," in *Theology in the Americas*, ed. Sergio Torres and John Eagleson (Maryknoll, N.Y.: Orbis Books, 1976), pp. 71–73.

38. Dorothee Soelle, *Political Theology*, trans. John Shelley (Philadelphia: Fortress, 1974), p. 64.

39. Boff, in *Frontiers*, pp. 100–31.

40. See Vidales, in *Frontiers*, p. 41.

41. Galilea, in ibid., pp. 169–70.

42. In *Frontiers*, see Gutiérrez, pp. 22–23; Vidales, p. 47; José Comblin, "What Sort of Service Might Theology Render?," p. 76; Enrique D. Dussel, "Historical and Philosophical Presuppositions for Latin American Theology," p. 212; Juan Carlos Scannone, "Theology, Popular Culture, and Discernment," pp. 218, 221.

43. Alfonso López Trujillo, *Liberation or Revolution?* (Huntington, Ind.: *Our Sunday Visitor*, 1977), pp. 16–17.

6

GEORGE V. PIXLEY

In What Sense Did Yahweh Bring Israel Out of Egypt?

Israel's exodus from bondage in Egypt is the central event of biblical history for liberation theology. But to conceive of God as active in particular historical events is difficult for Christians whose way of thinking has been heavily influenced by an Aristotelian concept of God as pure, impassive Being utterly transcending the imperfect and corruptible world of change. Pixley takes up the challenge of biblical narratives to reconceptualize God as an actual participant in contingent events that involve free human agency.

In Exodus 20:2 the God of Israel says "I am Yahweh your God who brought you out of the land of Egypt, out of the house of slavery." In part 2 of my commentary (Exod. 2:23–13:16) the spelling out of this statement in narrative form—reworked by generations of Israelites—has been examined. We have seen that, if there is a single central affirmation in the faith of Israel, this is that affirmation. To the question Who is God? the Bible replies: Yahweh, who brought us out of slavery in Egypt. Martin Noth, the most lucid of the researchers of the origins of Israelite traditions, maintains that Exodus is the original nucleus of the Pentateuch (*History*, 47–51). Without the exodus event there would be no people of Israel and no Pentateuch.

Reprinted from George V. Pixley, *On Exodus: A Liberation Perspective* (Maryknoll, N.Y.: Orbis Books, 1987), 76–80.

But this profession of faith, constituting the kernel of the faith of Israel, poses two serious theoretical questions. The first is historical, the second philosophical.

The historical question arises from the fact that Israel was a tribal alliance formed only by the unification of various groups that were rebelling against the kings of Canaan. The Levites (or whoever were the group that followed Moses) were incorporated into this alliance only once they reached Canaan. Of course, this group that had been delivered from Egypt was of the very greatest importance in giving the tribes a sense of their historical destiny. But strictly speaking one cannot say that "Israel" was the group that Yahweh brought out of Egypt. What occurred, historically, is that the Levitical group liberated from slavery in Egypt came to be ideologically dominant in Israel, and now all the tribes could declare that they themselves had been present in the exodus—that ancient paradigm of the new liberation struggles being waged by these tribes.

The philosophical question is, in what sense is it correct to speak of God as the agent of a historical event such as the liberation of the Hebrew slaves? In the account of the plagues, God is represented as the principal agent, assaulting the pharaoh and the Egyptians in order to force them to permit the departure of the Israelites.

Let us begin by excluding two extreme interpretations of the action of God in history. First, there is the notion that God is external to the world, which constitutes a more or less closed chain of causality in which God can nevertheless intervene. We find something like this in Exodus 14:13–14:

Have no fear! Stand firm, and you will see what Yahweh will do to save you today. . . . Yahweh will do the fighting for you: you have only to keep still.

In this first view, when God acts the ordinary chain of human events comes to a halt. The more the divine action, the less the human action. God is an exceptional cause, who takes the place of normal causes.

This interpretation enjoys the advantage of permitting a more or less direct reading of any biblical passage that speaks of God's intervention in history. But it suffers from the disadvantage of disqualifying any criteria for recognizing the divine activity other than that taking place in the absence of known causes. And it has the further, practical disadvantage of encouraging political passivity. Human organization would imply a lack of faith in divine activity. Surely we should be able to develop an interpretation of divine initiative that will not detract from the value of active human involvement.

At the other extreme is the position that Israel only *believed* that God intervened in its favor. In this interpretation, Exodus would be only the expression of the naive faith of a primitive people, and any actual divine involvement would be excluded from the objective world a priori. To be sure, Israel believed that Yahweh delivered the people from the land of Egypt. But if we deny the possibility of a genuine, objective divine participation, we postulate a humanity that will make history "by itself." No longer will our collective actions have any transcendent orientation. The poor are at the mercy of the mighty, and religion may serve to control the credulous masses, but not to instruct the elite. I resist this view of history. Indeed, I believe that the history of philosophy can be of help to us in avoiding both the extremes here presented.

Philosophical reflection in the West on the relationship between God and history begins with the Greek philosophers' critique of the official religion of their time. The received and officially countenanced religion of Athens and other Greek cities of the fifth and fourth centuries B.C. was a cult of heroic gods and goddesses, and fostered respect of the virtues of war. Socrates, Plato, and Aristotle developed a systematic critique of this religion, in the name of the more intellectual and civilized virtues. It seemed unworthy that gods would suffer the bodily passions of hunger, sexual desire, and jealousy. The philosophers held the divine to be necessarily incorporeal, and hence not subject to these passions. The human correlate of the divine was the soul, the spiritual part of human nature. The highest function of the soul was knowledge. The mind, unlike the senses, which are of the body and bound to concrete perceptions, is ignorant of concrete, tangible things, knowing only eternal, unchangeable "forms," as for example a mathematical formula. The perfection of the human soul, then, would consist in the everlasting contemplation of these unchangeable forms. But human souls, bound as they are to the body with its needs, can contemplate these perfect forms only from time to time. A divine being, not subject to these passions, would contemplate the forms without interruption.

The best expression of a spiritual theology in early Greek philosophy is probably that of Aristotle in the tenth book of his *Physics*. Here the philosopher posits the existence of God. Change is totally foreign to God: God is perfect. Were God to undergo change, God would have to become either better or worse, Aristotle held, and both alternatives were unacceptable: either the alternative would postulate a less than perfect state for this divine being—either the condition before the hypothetical change, or the condition after. God cannot change, then, even in the content of divine knowledge—and so, neither can God know change, i.e., know a changing thing.

But if God cannot know change, then how can God relate to our world, where change is universal? To solve this difficulty, Aristotle's theology postulates a God who moves the world only as the object of its desire. God moves the world by attraction alone, not by impulse. God is the "unmoved mover." Imperfect, changeable beings are moved by their desire for God. In the celestial sphere of the stars (Greek astronomy had heavenly spheres for the sun, the moon, and the planets, too), with their perfectly regular movements, we have the closest approximation of a movable being to the immovable God: this sphere moves in a perfect circle, which daily repeats itself with perfect regularity. As we descend from the sphere of the stars, however, sphere by sphere we begin to discern a progressive distancing from perfection.

With the Jewish philosopher Philo, a new and important step was taken. Philo lived in Alexandria in the first century A.D., and was equally familiar with the Bible and with Greek philosophy. For Philo, God's perfection is the ability to create from nothing. God gives existence to the totally nonexistent. God guides human beings by sending prophets to orientate them. But God continues to be outside, or above, the world. Although God knows historical events (Aristotle's God did not), God is not affected by them. God influences history through the word of the prophets. Harry A. Wolfson, in a whole series of works, has demonstrated the enormous influence that this view of the relationship between God and the world exerted on Jewish and Christian thought. (The series begins with *Philo: Foundations of Religious Philosophy in Judaism, Christianity and Islam.*)

With the nineteenth-century discovery of evolution, philosophers' attitudes toward change underwent a modification. Historical change basically comports progress. Now creation was no longer seen as something that had happened once and for all. The world is being shaped over the course of millions of years by a slow but sure process of the emergence of the new and the better. For Henri Bergson, the great miracle is newness. Claude Tresmontant interprets the Bible within this theoretical framework. God is God because of the creation of what is new. God is eternally the creator. (See, for example, Tresmontant's *A Study of Hebrew Thought.*)

This history of critical reflection on God and the world provides us with the elements we need in order to answer our initial question about God's activity in the exodus. I shall synthesize these elements here in the form in which they have been developed by Alfred North Whitehead. (Whitehead's most important work in this area is *Process and Reality.*) According to Whitehead, it is essential that we assimilate the transformation that we have undergone in our evaluation of change. The real, the valid, is not the unchangeable, but precisely the emergence of what is new. The changeless forms held by the Greeks to be the most perfect reality are mere potentialities which become real only when they take flesh. Without events, there is nothing. The ultimate reality is the emergence of newness, and if God exists, God will have to be intervening in this creative process.

We need not enter too deeply into these considerations in order to answer our question about God's activity in the exodus. I shall simply give examples of this new attitude toward change, applying it to the two areas of (1) time and (2) God's passivity.

1. If the emergence of newness is real, then the future is a series of mere potentialities—possibilities that have in no way become real as yet. In Philo's tradition, God's eternity meant that God knew everything simultaneously, whereas from the perspective of creatures time unfolded in a series of instants, unfolded little by little. For God, according to Philo, the future is as real as the present and the past. The problem with this doctrine, which does ascribe a certain importance to change (in contrast with the interpretation of the Greek philosophers), is that at least for God, there is no newness. And if there is no newness for God, then is newness only apparent? In Whitehead's philosophy, God indeed knows the future perfectly, but knows it as future, which means that God knows all the potentialities that the present contains. Which of these potentialities are actually to be realized depends on the actions of a multiplicity

of agents. Only their collective actions will make this determination. This is the nature of creativity.

2. Anselm of Canterbury taught that God is that being than which no greater can be conceived. This is the logic of perfection, and the grammar of all language about God. But in speaking of passivity—of the capacity to be affected by others—correct conclusions have not always been drawn. Aristotle thought that a perfect being could not be affected by anything other than itself. But if a sensation of things, an awareness of things, is not a defect, then, quite the contrary, God's perfection will consist in "sensing," being aware of, everything. God, then, is "universally passible." Only in this way can God offer to each event as it arises an ideal of newness that will be relevant to its particular past.

Thus it is not beyond the realm of possibility that Exodus is correct when it asserts that God heard the cry of the Hebrews. For a biblical vision of reality, it is essential to assert that God hears everything—but with discernment, to be sure. It is also necessary to assert that God acts—universally. That is, there is no event of the past by which God is not affected, and no event in the present in which God is not an agent. There is no event in which God does not intervene—not as exclusive cause, but as a force that inclines created causes (and hence their effects) toward the realization of the most harmonious and comprehensive ideals possible for a particular event, given the circumstances of that event.

God, then, is the universal "instigator" of the new and better, within the spectrum of the real potentialities of each new event. In order to be this "instigator" in an appropriate way in a world of emerging newness, God must be perfectly aware of everything that is realized in this world.

In sum, God does nothing—if by "do" we mean God is the exclusive agent of anything. On the other hand, God does everything—if by "do" we meant that God is present in every event, prompting it to the realization of its fullest and best potential. God is the co-creator of everything new that emerges in this historical world.

Having made this rapid survey of the philosophical problems involved, we are now in a position to state the sense in which it is correct to say that Yahweh indeed delivered Israel from Egypt. As in every event in which a new reality arises, here too it was God who was the inspirer of the better, of the best. To a people condemned to servitude, exploitation, in Egypt, Yahweh sent Moses to sow the seed of the "good news" of a liberation that would lead to a land where milk and honey flowed.

To establish and maintain the real possibility of this totally original ideal was by no means an easy task. When Moses first arrived in Egypt and told the elders of his and God's plans for liberation, the elders joined him in these plans. But when, after the first interview with the king, the Israelites' work load was increased, the elders protested to Moses: "You have made us hated by Pharaoh and his court; you have put a sword into their hand to kill us" (Exod. 5:21)— and the vision of the possible ideal grew dim. The account solves this particular problem by having Yahweh and Moses work miracles before the pharaoh, with the people reduced to the role of spectators. It is difficult to say what this direct intervention of God could have been. God does not take action of major significance in irrational creatures — frogs, flies, and the like — because these creatures have too little margin for newness. If God effectuates the newness that consists in the actualization of the maximum potential of the real, then what God effectuates in a frog will be real, but severely limited. With Martin Buber, we may rather see in the plagues the activity of the prophet of God who interprets natural portents as God's judgment on a king who refuses to release slaves to celebrate a religious festival. It may be that the massacre of the exodus night was a terrorist action — inspired by God.

A frequent theme of the stories of the Israelites in their wanderings in the wasteland is their loss of faith in the pursuit of liberation and their wish to return to Egypt. "Were there no graves in Egypt that you must lead us out to die in the wilderness? ... Better to work for the Egyptians than die in the wilderness!" (Exod. 14:11-12). More than once it is said that the people cursed Moses, and wanted to return to Egypt. The text reminds us of the need for continual activity on God's part to move a people toward a better destiny than that of servitude.

It is within this reflective framework that we may understand in what sense "Yahweh brought Israel out of the land of Egypt, out of the house of slavery."

7

JUAN LUIS SEGUNDO

Faith and Ideologies in Biblical Revelation

Faith is basic commitment to liberation, but the options for concretely realizing liberation in history must be learned through specific modes of political analysis and action, namely, by means of ideologies. The debate over whether the New Testament continues or corrects the Old Testament, or gives it a "fuller sense," is best resolved by stressing the continuity of revelation and the coexistence of faith and ideologies in all levels of the Bible.

There is an inescapable "empty space between the conception of God that we receive from our faith and the problems that come to us from an ever-changing history." We must bridge the gap by a system of means and ends. Our reading of the Bible on two simultaneous levels may be explained from the communication theory concepts of proto-learning, *which is simple learning, and* deutero-learning, *which is learning to learn. When, for example, we read how faith came to expression at one time in an ideology of fighting one's way out of bondage and at another time in nonviolent resistance to bondage, we are engaged in simple learning. When we reflect on these expressions, together with other strategies of fighting oppression, in order to determine what we should do about oppression in our situation, we are learning to learn.*

Faith and ideologies, simple learning and learning to learn, are different but vitally linked aspects of our relation to the biblical revelation. The Fourth Gospel and Paul pointedly express the Christian reality of a fundamental process of learning to learn that works within

Reprinted from *The Liberation of Theology* (Maryknoll, N.Y.: Orbis Books, 1976), 108-122.

and beyond the limitations of simple learning about biblical laws and about the historical Jesus.

What, then, does the faith say to me in the concrete? What is its truth *content*? If I remain logically consistent in deducing conclusions from the above principles, then my only response can be: *nothing.* Let me repeat that in another way. If someone were to ask me what I have derived from my faith-inspired encounter as a clear-cut, absolute truth that can validly give orientation to my concrete life, then my honest response should be: nothing.

However, we are carrying the balance of faith to an irrational extreme in talking about *one* encounter with the objective font of absolute truth. If it is in fact a matter of only *one* encounter, then there is no solution to the problem. The absolute truth would remain totally obscured behind the ideology exhibited in that one historical encounter. It is quite clear that in history we can only have historical encounters, that is, encounters bound up with relative contexts.

This *reductio ad absurdum* prompts us to rediscover the decisive importance of the (historical) *density* of the Bible. Over a period of twenty centuries different faith-inspired encounters took place between human beings and the objective font of absolute truth. All of these encounters were historical; hence each one of them was relative, bound up with a specific and changing context. What came to be known or recognized in each of these encounters was an ideology, but that is not what was learned. Through the process people *learned how to learn* with the help of ideologies. This deutero-learning has its own proper content, and when I say that Jesus had two natures, one human and one divine, I am saying something about the *content* of this learning process. But these contentual items cannot be translated into one or another specific ideology because they belong to a secondary stage or level of learning. They are essentially methodological symbols. On the one hand they have no direct ideological translation; on the other hand they have no other function but to be translated into ideologies.

From these remarks it should at least be clear that one pretension of the ecclesiastical hierarchy makes no sense at all in theology. They often attempt, quite openly, to maintain a distinction if not an outright separation between faith and ideologies in order to safeguard the former. But while faith certainly is not an ideology, it has sense and meaning only insofar as it serves as the foundation stone for ideologies.

Regarding the attempt to separate faith from ideologies, I should like to cite the following remarks in an article by Thomas W. Ogletree:

Man must answer for what he does. Being able to answer cannot be equated with success in "measuring up" to some pre-established standard. The openness of the historical process continually erodes the authority of such standards, unless they are given a highly abstract form, e.g., "loyalty to being," or "doing what love (agape) requires." Since the abstractness of such formulations makes their applicability to concrete situations problematic, it is clear that there is no precise measuring instrument by which human behavior can be tested. ... There is no way to remove the moral risk from human action, partly because no one can ever adequately grasp the nature of his situation or the possible consequences of his action, but also because the appropriate tack in a given context may be to innovate, to give rise to the new possibility which cannot be comprehended in terms of previous values and understandings.[1]

This passage is not alluding specifically to a Christian reading of the gospel message or to the difference between faith and ideologies. But it is perfectly applicable to those areas. Even though endowed with absolute value, the Christian faith totally lacks any precise instrument for measuring the historical life of Christians by pre-established standards. And since the human sciences also lack any such value standards, Christians cannot evade the necessity of inserting something to fill the void between their faith and their options in history. In short, they cannot avoid the risk of ideologies.

The problem is of course that we are used to picturing our faith as a plane of eternal certitudes which are destined to be professed on the one hand and translated into actions on the other. Rubem Alves comments on this fact in a reference to the thought of Ebeling:

There are elements in the consciousness of the community of faith, however, which suggest that it is not only possible but indeed necessary to understand faith in exactly the opposite sense, as a radically historical mode of being, as "the acceptance of truly historical existence." If this is the case, its language consequently must express the spirit of *freedom for history, of taste for the future, of openness for the provisional and relative.*[2]

It is worth noting, by the way, that certain passages in the documents of Vatican II, particularly in *Gaudium et spes*, can only make sense if they are interpreted in this light. It is one more proof of the powerful ecumenism implicit in the methodology of liberation theology. The first passage deals with the orientation of faith, not toward other-worldly certitudes, but toward historical problems and their solutions: "Faith throws a new light on everything, manifests God's design for man's total vocation, and thus *directs the mind to solutions which are fully human*" (*Gaudium et spes*, no. 11). Are we to assume from this that the faith *possesses* such solutions? Vatican II unexpectedly rejects such an assumption, the standard assumption of classical theology: "In fidelity to conscience, Christians are joined with the rest of men *in the search for truth, and the genuine solution* to the numerous problems which arise in the life of individuals and from social relationships" (ibid., no. 16).

The latter passage by itself, and even more so when combined with the first passage cited, forces us to a different conception of revealed truth. It is not a *final* truth, however absolute it may be. Instead it is a fundamental element in the search for *the truth*. In other words, it helps to support and verify what was said about faith as a process of learning to learn, as a deutero-learning. However lofty it may be, it is ever in the service of historical solutions to human problems—even though the latter solutions will always be provisional and incomplete. Faith, then, is a liberative process. It is converted into freedom for history, which means freedom *for ideologies.*

Our remarks so far suggest that we would do well to take a final look at certain biblical elements which must be considered if we wish to verify the path that has led us to those conclusions. We are particularly interested in one central point: the relationship between the revelation of Jesus and his own particular moment in history. We are interested in elucidating the relationship between faith and ideologies as it is to be found in this central event of Christianity. We want to consider the life and teaching of Jesus in his own moment of history within the overall historical process.

1. Insofar as content is concerned, liberation theology is known to have a preference and a partiality for the Old Testament in general, and for the Exodus event in particular. The reason for this is clear enough. The Old Testament, and the Exodus event in particular, show us two central elements completely fused into one: i.e., God the liberator and the political process of liberation which leads the Israelites from bondage in Egypt to the promised land. In no other portion of scripture does God the liberator reveal himself in such close connection with the political plane of human existence. Moreover, it is a well-known fact that from the time of the Babylonian exile on, the *sapiential* literature became more individualistic, inner-directed, and apolitical. And at first glance the New Testament would seem to deprecate or even reject any connection between liberation and politics, even though it might talk about the former.

Jesus himself seems to focus his message on liberation at the level of interpersonal relationships, forgetting almost completely, if not actually ruling out, liberation vis-à-vis political oppression.[3] The same would seem to apply to Paul[4] and almost all the other writings in the New Testament.

Here liberation theology is faced with a pastoral problem of the first magnitude. If concern and commitment constitute the elements fundamental to any encounter with the gospel message, then the results can be and often are disastrous. Why? Because the Gospels seem to center Jesus' main interests on another plane entirely, on an apolitical plane. The young Christian is often advised in advance that he must "translate" the language of Jesus into political dimensions. Aside from the fact that such "translation" is not an easy process, the youth's first encounter with the gospel message often proves to be disheartening anyway. That is not one of the least reasons why liberation theology prefers the Old Testament and, in particular, the Exodus account.

In recent years, to be sure, various exegetes in Latin America and Europe[5] have tried to read between the lines of the Gospels and find a close connection between the activity of Jesus and the Zealots of Israel. I personally think that their interpretations are a bit forced, quite aside from the fact that they do not resolve the problem we have just posed in pastoral terms.

Even though it does not solve the latter problem, I think it is more sensible to realize that we are guilty of an anachronism when we assume that the decisive and critical political plane—precisely in political terms—was the opposition between Judea and the Roman Empire. It is quite possible that some contemporary groups such as the Zealots thought it was. But it seems to me that the political reality that really structured the Israel of Jesus' time and determined people's role and relationships in society was not the Roman Empire but the Jewish theocracy grounded on, and controlled by, the religious authorities who had charge of the Mosaic Law. We have already noted how Jesus destroyed the foundation of that oppressive power structure by teaching the people to reject its theological foundations. His teaching was such a political threat that the authorities of Israel made use of Rome's authorities to eliminate this dangerous *political* adversary. That is precisely what Jesus was.

Whether my last hypothesis is correct or not, indeed even assuming that for a variety of sound reasons[6] Jesus had decided not to take an interest in any political sort of liberation, it is important to realize that we must still explain either attitude in terms of an *ideology*. We must explore the problem in terms of the necessity of combining means and ends vis-à-vis a concrete situation. And it cannot be approached in other terms that are not equally concrete.

More interesting in terms of our purpose here is the fact that two theological explanations are usually offered for liberation theology's preference for certain passages of divine revelation—or, if you prefer, for certain *ideologies* expressed in its content. The first, and more naive, explanation maintains that the Exodus event is the key to the interpretation of scripture as a whole, including the Gospels and the rest of the New Testament.[7] I consider this position naive because it is very easy for a scientific biblical theology to tear apart any such pretension. To begin with, the Book of Exodus is an historical reconstruction. It is very important, of course, but it can hardly compete with the vivid reflections of living people who are facing the prospect and then the reality of the event—to take just one example.[8] Moreover, Exodus is certainly not the central axis of the sapiential literature. The latter relates to an era of foreign domination in which the historical vocation of Israel was either lost from view or projected into eschatological terms. Still less can it be the central axis of the New Testament unless we go in for a terrible process of mutilating the latter. We could maintain that liberation was the only theme of the New Testament, I suppose, but only if we were willing to go in for a great deal of abstraction.

That brings us to the second argument against this naive attempt to suppress the rich variety of biblical experiences and to replace them with an abstract summary. In any such attempt we lose the pedagogical intent of the whole scriptural process. We also cannot explain the why and wherefore of all that concrete content, if a few summary words could have done the job equally well.

The second theological explanation for the preferences of liberation theology is more complicated. At first glance it seems more immune to attack from critical scholarship. The argument in this case is that the pedagogical principle of the Bible as a whole not only justifies but demands partiality. God reveals himself to human beings who are preoccupied with their own concrete situation. We can only understand and appreciate the word of God if we take that fact into account. Only in connection with the problems that are embodied in the questions of the community can we comprehend who exactly this responding God is. If we fail to understand the situation and problems of the community, we cannot possibly come to know that God. At first glance there may seem to be contradictions in God's revelation and his responses, but they are clarified when we uncover the different historical situations and the different questions addressed to him from within those situations.

This more complex explanation does justice to the pedagogical principle of divine revelation. To cite a different example, let us consider the educational process of any child. If we want to understand that process but do not have direct access to the words or methodology of the educator—as is the case with the pedagogy of scripture—then we must try to infer all that from what the child says about many different things, in different situations, over a long period of time. The first thing we must keep in mind is that the child does not tell us exactly what the educator is thinking. The educator is attentive to the child, and even the latter's mistakes can help in the pedagogical process. But that does presume that the educator is aware at every moment of the child's own situation, for that is and remains the starting point of education. The fact that at a given point in time the child may insist upon the real existence of Red Riding Hood does not indicate anything in the nature of a pedagogical error. Faced with a real-life situation at that point, the educator felt it made no sense to argue with the child over that point, but that it did make sense to try and draw certain lessons from the story, and so forth.

We can assume that in the scriptures the people of Israel have accumulated and set forth for us an educative process directed by God. But God does not show up on the tape. All that we get are the *results* that flowed from the reflections and responses of the Israelites to that divine instruction.

2. That brings us to a second problem. What is the exact relationship between, for example, the revelation of Jesus in the New Testament and the revelation of God in the Old Testament? Though it may seem hard to believe, the fact is that this basic and important question has scarcely been given a clear answer over the past twenty centuries of Christian living. And that fact has conditioned the whole of theology.

The usual responses tend to move in two opposite directions. One response stresses the fact that Jesus represents one more link in a chain of revelation, the revelation itself being one basically and all of it being true. Jesus himself lends support to this view when he says: "Do not suppose that I have come to abolish the Law and the prophets; I did not come to abolish but to complete. I tell you this: so long as heaven and earth endure, not a letter, not a stroke, will disappear from the Law until all that must happen has happened" (Matt. 5:17-18). As we all know, "the Law and the prophets" was a common shorthand way of referring to all of Sacred Scripture in Jesus' day; it did not refer solely to the legal or prophetical books. Jesus, therefore, is referring to the whole of what we call the Old Testament; and he seems to be saying that he himself and his message represent an additional element that is directly and positively a continuation of past revelation.

The implication seems to be that the scriptures are not a body of law in the modern sense of the term. Instead they embody a divine plan of long-term duration. Jesus did not come to alter this plan, but to bring it to its fulfillment and completion. And if we consider that plan as an educational one, then we are forced to conclude that Jesus is making himself a part of that plan rather than upsetting it. Thus when he goes on to say, on several occasions, "But I tell you . . . ," he is simply trying to purify the moral law of the Old Testament of its grosser material features.

But other features of the Gospel accounts point us in the opposite direction. They show us a break in continuity, a qualitative leap in Jesus' revelation beyond the older divine teaching—even though the exact nature of this leap may be hard to spell out. At the very least it looks more like outright correction than mere continuation.

At the end of the Sermon on the Mount, for example, Matthew informs us: "When Jesus had finished this discourse the people were astounded at his teaching; unlike their own teachers he taught *with a note of authority*" (Matt. 7:28-29). Now this special air of authority by contrast with the teaching of the scribes could be viewed as a revival of prophetic authority in Israel after a long period of prophetic silence. There is no doubt that Jesus presented himself as prophet and was taken as such from the very beginning. But in this connection we must note that it would never have occurred to the prophets to challenge the very content of the Mosaic Law. That is precisely what Jesus did, Matthew's previous remark notwithstanding. Mark certainly saw Jesus in that new light, for he notes that Jesus declared all foods clean when in fact there was a huge corpus of Mosaic Law and related commentaries on the matter of pure foods (Mark 7:19).

Then there are Jesus' authoritative statements on gratuitous love (Luke 6:27-36), which Paul sums up in his letter to the Romans:

> Let your aims be such as all men count honorable. If possible, so far as it lies with you, live at peace with all men. My dear friends, do not seek revenge, but leave a place for divine retribution; for there is a text which reads, "Justice is mine, says the Lord, I will repay." But there is another text: "If your enemy is hungry, feed him; if he is thirsty, give him a drink; by doing this you will heap live coals on his head." Do not let evil conquer you, but use good to defeat evil (Rom. 12:17-21).

Now if we take Jesus' authoritative statements in this vein as authentic moral precepts, then he certainly did *correct* passages which the Old Testament attribute to God himself and which command such things as the slaying of neighboring peoples who might constitute a threat to the freedom and religion of Israel (e.g., Deut. 7:14 ff.).

Some time ago another view was popular, particularly in Catholic circles, which stood somewhere between the *continuation* view and the *correction* view. It was the notion of the *sensus plenior*, the "fuller sense," of scripture. Jesus' revelation allegedly pointed up the true sense of older revelation, a sense that had not been appreciated even by those who wrote down God's revelation. With this revelation, in other words, Jesus provided people with new light for understanding the real import of persons, doctrines, and events in the Old Testament: e.g., Moses and the law, Adam and sin.

Now in some way or other we will always be compelled to recognize a fuller sense in God's later revelation. But the notion of the *sensus plenior* presents two very serious difficulties to any attempts to explain and resolve the contradictions cited above. The first difficulty is that unless one chooses to appeal to miracles as part of the scientific hermeneutic process, then one must assume that the whole notion of *sensus plenior* extends to all the different stages of the Old Testament as well. But, to take one example, can one really maintain that the authentic import of the Exodus event is more clearly spelled out in the more spiritualistic and subjective interpretation of the sapiential books? Are we to assume that in analogous circumstances the Israelites should henceforth act in a very different manner than they did the first time around? Clearly that is a basic and important question for any liberation theology.

Let us consider another example from the New Testament. Paul can certainly be considered a proponent of the *sensus plenior*. Looking at Moses and his law in the light of Christ, Paul believes he can pinpoint the true significance of that early legislation. The Mosaic Law was not a restrictive condition imposed by God on the unconditional promise made to Abraham. Rather, it was a preparation for Christ insofar as it revealed the reality and enslaving power of sin. This logically leads Paul to assert that with Christ human beings cease to be subject to the Law. It no longer makes any sense to ask whether some course of action is *licit* or not, when one is faced with some moral doubt. The new meaning brought by Christ serves to correct old, outmoded attitudes and approaches. But that brings us back to the critical question: if we do find thoroughgoing correction in divine revelation, can we really say that there is a oneness of faith from past to present? Can we Christians really say that we have faith in the Old Testament, in the Exodus revelation for example? Is it worth going back to the Mosaic Law when its real meaning is spelled out in the New Testament, to the point where the Law itself is abolished? And in such a case what is the point of preferring the Exodus account to the New Testament in our liberation theology?

3. The first response of liberation theology to the problem posed above involves going back to the notion that there is real continuity in the whole of divine revelation and distinguishing two elements in it. One element is permanent and unique: *faith*. The other is changing and bound up with different historical circumstances: *ideologies*.

If God's revelation never comes to us in pure form, if it is always fleshed out in historical ideologies, then we cannot appeal to the historical Jesus in order to throw out the solutions of the Old Testament. If circumstantial conditions and exigencies are decisive, then Jesus' remarks about turning the other cheek in no way correct the command of Deuteronomy to physically exterminate certain foreign peoples.

Our theory, in other words, assumes that there is an empty space between the conception of God that we receive from our faith and the problems that come to us from an ever-changing history. So we must build a bridge between our conception of God and the real-life problems of history. This bridge, this provisional but necessary system of means and ends, is what we are calling *ideology* here. Obviously each and every ideology presented in scripture is a human element even though in the intensely unified psychological processes of human beings it may seem to be a direct and straightforward translation of the proper conception of the God who has been revealed.

Consider the Israelites who arrived in the promised land. For them the extermination of their enemies was concretely the most clear-cut way of conceiving who God was and what he was commanding in the face of specific historical circumstances. Thus the extermination of enemies was the ideology that faith adopted, with or without critical thought, at that moment in history. And to be logical here, we must say the same thing with regard to the gospel message. When Jesus talked about freely proffered love and nonresistance to evil, he was facing the same problem of filling the void between his conception of God (or perhaps that of the first Christian community) and the problems existing in his age. In short, we are dealing here with another ideology, not with the content of faith itself.

This view of the matter gives liberation theology greater freedom to move, in principle, through the scriptures and to work with the faith. Moreover, it is actually the scientific approach used by exegesis in dealing with the content of both the Old and the New Testaments. For exegesis regards that content as a succession of religious ideologies, each one being bound up with its historical context and being comprehensible only in terms of that context. As a scholarly science, biblical exegesis is much less concerned about the oneness or unity of the whole complex. It does not decide, for example, whether a specific orientation or line of thinking is incompatible with the rest or not, is heretical or not. Of course it assumes some sort of unity between the Exodus and Jesus, since it is dealing with a process going on in the same cultural world, a world that differs from other cultural worlds of the same era. But it refuses to make a theological value judgment as to whether one of those ideologies is superior to another or not. Each ideology has its historical function to carry out.

Needless to say, liberation theology cannot accept or adopt that impartiality. Its concern is not to describe what happened in the past but to make a decision vis-à-vis new problems that either were not dealt with in scripture or were dealt with in a very different context.

In this situation theology has two ways open to it in trying to relate the faith to new historical situations—e.g., to the situation of sociopolitical oppression that prevails in Latin America. One way is to seek out the biblical situations most akin to those of the present day and to accept the ideology that scripture presents in those situations as the correct response of faith. If, for example, the relationship between the Exodus situation and our own today seems closer than the situation of the Hebrews in the time of Christ and ours today, then the Exodus rather than the Gospels should serve as our source of inspiration in trying to find a present-day ideology that will dovetail with the faith.

The other possible approach is to invent an ideology that we might regard as the one which would be constructed by a gospel message contemporary with us. What would the Christ of the Gospels say if he were confronting our problems today? If the faith is one amid the diversity of history, then there must be some ideology that can build a bridge between that faith and our present-day situation even as there were such ideologies in the past.

These would seem to be the only two approaches open to us. The problem is that the first approach becomes more unrealistic and anti-scientific as time goes on. There seems to be less and less sense in trying to look for similar situations in cultural milieus dating back thirty-five centuries, particularly since the pace of history seems to be accelerating every day. The second approach does call for creativity here and now. But if we must try to imagine what the gospel message would be if it were formulated today, it is becoming more and more obvious to Christians that *secular* inventiveness and creativity are more appropriate and fruitful.

4. These difficulties prompt us to take a further step and to ask a further question: Can the content of faith offer us the precision we so far lack? Here we run into a serious problem. For while ideologies are defined by their content, we run into problems when we try to do the same thing with our faith. What is the faith in *objective* terms, in terms of information rather than merely subjective attitudes? Is there anything left in scripture once we have discarded the ideological element?

It is too easy to say that what remains is precisely the conception of God that runs through the centuries and that the various ideologies attempt to relate to specific historical circumstances. It is too easy because that conception of God is never found separated from the ideologies that attempt to interpret God by applying his demands to a specific historical situation. Both processes are inextricably linked. You cannot get rid of one without emptying the other of content.

In other words the idea of a liberating God cannot be separated from historical situations and actions, such as the slaying of the firstborn, because no liberating God is revealed outside of such historical situations. As James Cone noted, there are no universal truths in the process of liberation; the only truth is liberation itself.[9] Though some people may feel disappointed, there is no "universal God" in the ordinary sense of the word "universal."[10]

Now this view frees us from the necessity of *reducing* the whole Bible to one singular conception of reality for the sake of maintaining the oneness of our faith. But it does not offer us much help in trying to use our faith as the orientation we need to solve our problems in history. But is it possible that we are confusing the issue for ourselves? When we talk about some objective content of faith and try to dissociate it from the content of various ideologies as if the two were disputing the same ground, may we not be confusing *two simultaneous but different levels of learning?* To borrow the terminology that communication theory uses with reference to such fields as cybernetics, biology, and psychology, may we not be confusing a *proto-learning* with a *deutero-learning*, a first-level learning with a second-level learning?[11] The former is *simple learning*, the latter is *learning to learn*.

Consider Pavlov's experiments, for example. His dogs learned that the sound of a bell signified food, and their salivary glands began to secrete as soon as the bell sounded. Here we clearly have a process of *simple learning.* The dogs learned to react to a specific stimulus, and that is all. They could be taught in the same way to react to a second stimulus. Now the characteristic feature of learning at that stage is that information is *added* or *subtracted.* Information about two stimuli tells the dogs nothing about a possible third stimulus, and a mistake represents a subtraction. Thus if a dog were given food one hundred times after a bell was rung and not given food one hundred times after a bell was rung, the sum of information at the end of the experiment would be exactly zero.

On the human level, however, we repeatedly experience a second-level learning, a process of *learning to learn.* The main characteristic of this process is that new information *multiplies* or *divides* the balance of previous information. Let us take mathematics as a case in point. After a certain period of learning, a child is able to solve a certain set of problems. But suddenly we notice that he or she is solving a problem that is not a mere copy of, or addition to, the previous problems. We have reason to assume that in the process of learning mathematics the child did more than merely learn isolated answers to isolated problems. The child acquired a bibliography, as it were, which it could then consult in order to solve a new problem. The information possessed by the student is not a simple sum of the problems already learned and the bibliography previously acquired. It is the product of a multiplication of those two factors. The student, in other words, possesses objective information that enables him to solve new problems which he has not studied before. An inadequate or jumbled bibliography, on the other hand, does not represent a mere subtraction of information already learned; it represents a division of that information because it wipes out much of what had been previously learned. But when they are part of the overall process and do not disorient the child, even errors are helpful. They do not represent subtraction or addition of information; they represent a multiplication of information.

The important point here is that simple learning and learning to learn do not dispute control of the informational content. The bibliography, for example, is not a mathematical formula. The mathematical formulas that the child may retain or construct are dependent on the bibliography, but they are not in competition with it.

Perhaps this allusion to a bibliography may not be the most satisfactory way to explain or comprehend the relationship between faith and ideologies, since a bibliography always remains external to mathematical knowledge and understanding itself. A student who is truly creative in mathematics might afford us a suitable example. Once introduced to the learning process, such a student not only acquires specific formulas but also the possibility of creating them when faced with new problems. The relationship between simple learning and learning to learn becomes more intimate, and it becomes more difficult to distinguish between the content of the two levels. But even in this case what we said of the bibliography above remains true: on one level information is added or subtracted, on the other it is multiplied and divided.

We can say without fear of error that the ideologies present in scripture belong to the first level. They are responses learned vis-à-vis specific historical situations. Faith, by contrast, is the total process to which man submits, a process of learning in and through ideologies how to create the ideologies needed to handle new and unforeseen situations in history. The scriptures can and should be examined and studied from both points of view since both processes are in the sacred writings and do not compete with each other over content. This means that fighting one's way out of bondage in Egypt is one experience and turning the other cheek is another experience. Someone who has gone through both experiences and has reflected on them has learned how to learn; he has multiplied his faith-based information, not subtracted it to zero.

These remarks will help us to better understand two basic problems of liberation theology, even if they will not enable us to fully resolve them. The *first* problem has to do with the continuation of revelation. It seems clear in the thinking of John the Evangelist that divine revelation is destined to continue after the physical disappearance of Jesus. Classical theology, however, talks about revelation as a "deposit" closed at the death of the last apostle, the last eyewitness to the teaching of Jesus.

In the Fourth Gospel Jesus has this to say as he is about to bid farewell to his disciples: "There is still much that I could say to you, but the burden would be too great for you *now*. However, when he comes who is the Spirit of truth, he will guide you into all the truth; for he will not speak on his own authority. . . . He will glorify me, for everything that he makes known to you he will draw from what is mine" (John 16:12-14).

Jesus clearly affirms that many things remain to be said and that they will be said, although in a different manner. The *Spirit* of truth will take many things which Jesus himself had not spoken and will make them comprehensible as obviously belonging to the same divine revelation. Jesus' language is very clear. It points not towards a better understanding of what has already been spoken but towards the learning of new things.

Can we, in that case, substitute the word "ideologies" for "things"? We have already seen that the concrete responses of the Israelite community or the Christian community at any given moment necessarily constitute ideologies. Well, we have exactly the same situation here. There are things that Jesus *cannot say* because they do not dovetail with the historical situation in which his disciples are living. They could not bear them *now*. When they are spoken by the Spirit, however, they will automatically be converted into ideologies associated with a specific historical situation that renders them comprehensible and useful.

What will be the relationship between these new ideologies and *faith*, the latter being understood as a divine revelation that entails recognition of its revealer? The logical answer is that the former revealer, Christ, is replaced by the Holy Spirit. But the Spirit is not a visible, identifiable revealer, which would seem to indicate that one can really have faith only in past revelation. The only coherent hypothesis is to have recourse once again to the notion of a *deutero-*

learning process, a process of learning to learn. This process is by its very definition the opposite of any sort of deposit, for it involves an unending process of acquiring new pieces of information that multiply the previous store of information. That being the case, the only visible guidepost is the presence or absence of the teacher outside of the pupil. At a certain point, however, the external teacher disappears from the scene; yet the internal process of learning goes on continually, based on external experience.

This seems to be the obvious import of Jesus' promise. The Spirit of truth is not an external teacher as Jesus himself was. Or we might say instead that no external teacher after Christ will add any information to the educational process. The process will go on internally, as the pupil confronts reality with new ideologies. Jesus is saying that one stage of the process is ended, but he is also promising that the process can continue through its own proper means. And those means are nothing else but a succession of ideologies vis-à-vis the concrete problems of history. In short, after Christ history itself is entrusted with the task of carrying on the process. The Spirit of Christ, that is, the dynamic, intrinsic result of the revelatory education process, ensures a process that will lead to the full and complete truth.

The *second* problem is intimately bound up with the first, and it is the same problem with which we have been dealing from the very start of this essay. From what we have said so far it seems clear that it makes no Christian sense at all to try to separate ideologies from faith in order to safeguard and preserve the latter. Without ideologies faith is as dead as a doornail, and for the same reason that James offers in his epistle: it is totally impracticable (James 2:17).

From this standpoint it is very instructive to give a brief summary of Paul's interpretation of the Christian's moral obligations in the light of Christ's revelation. Remember that Paul's interpretation antedates the redaction of the four Gospels in their present form. His view can be summarized as follows:

(a) Only concrete love gives meaning and value to any kind of law existing in the universe (Rom. 13:8-10).

(b) Any and every type of law represents a decisive element for Christian conduct insofar as it points up more or less constant relationships between things and persons. But such laws are not decisive as moral laws (Rom. 14:14). They are decisive as constants in the service of the love-based plans and projects of human beings (1 Cor. 6:12 ff.; 10:23 ff.), since they furnish these projects with criteria for judging what is or is not *expedient* in carrying them out (1 Cor. 10:23-29; Rom. 14:7-9).

(c) Since this desacralizes the law as a static inventory of questions concerning the intrinsic morality of a given line of conduct, the conduct of the Christian must undergo a basic change. *Faith* rather than the law must serve as the springboard for launching into a new adventure. One's destiny will depend on this venture, but it possesses no a priori criteria established in advance. The Christian must accept the riskiness of projects that ever remain provisional and will often go astray (Gal. 5:6 and passim; Rom. 14:1 ff.).

(d) Therefore this faith does not consist in intellectual adherence to a certain body of revealed content as the definitive solution to theoretical or practical problems. Nor does it consist in having confidence in one's own salvation, thanks to the merits of Christ. Instead it entails the freedom to accept an educational process that comes to maturity and abandons its teacher to launch out into the provisional and relative depths of history (Gal. 4:1 ff.; Rom. 8:19-23; 1 Cor. 3:11–15).

Faith, then, is not a universal, atemporal, pithy body of content summing up divine revelation once the latter has been divested of ideologies. On the contrary, it is maturity by way of ideologies, the possibility of fully and conscientiously carrying out the ideological task on which the real-life liberation of human beings depends.

NOTES

1. Thomas W. Ogletree, "From Anxiety to Responsibility: The Shifting Focus of Theological Reflection," in *Chicago Theological Seminary Register*, March 1968. Reprinted in *New Theology* 6 (New York: Macmillan, 1969), p. 61.

2. Rubem A. Alves, *A Theology of Human Hope* (Washington, D.C.: Corpus Books, 1969), p. 71.

3. If we agree with Gutiérrez that the realm of politics is the most prevalent and pervasive factor in present-day human life, it is anachronistic to ask what Jesus' attitude might have been toward this *present-day* situation of ours. The discovery of the pervasive influence of politics is our contemporary discovery, not his. Hence Jesus' stance vis-à-vis the Roman Empire or the Zealots, as a political stance, is also relatively beside the point. The fact is that the concrete systematic oppression that Jesus confronted in his day did not appear to him as "political" in our sense of the term; it showed up to him as "religious" oppression. More than officials of the Roman Empire, it was the religious authority of the scribes and Sadducees and Pharisees that determined the sociopolitical structure of Israel. In real life this authority was political, and Jesus really did tear it apart. This is evident from the fact that the concern to get rid of Jesus physically—because he threatened the status quo—was primarily displayed by the supposedly "religious" authorities rather than by the representatives of the Roman Empire.

4. See the passages where Paul exhorts slaves to obey their masters (e.g., Eph. 6:5; Col. 3:22; Titus 2:9; and Philemon), or the passages where he tends to minimize but not reject the fact of slavery in the novel light of Christ (e.g., Col. 3:11; 1 Cor. 7:21-22; 12:13; Gal. 3:28).

5. See Gustavo Gutiérrez, *A Theology of Liberation* (Maryknoll, N.Y.: Orbis Books, 1973), Chapter 11.

6. One reason of utmost importance should be noted. Any liberation process— e.g., political liberation—would have concrete historical limitations of its very nature. That fact would have seriously diminished the universality of Christ's message about total liberation, applicable to all human beings and all phases of human existence. To be sure, it is impossible to *talk* about liberation without implementing some concrete forms of liberation if one wants to be credible to others. Jesus submitted to this basic law. But the obligation of summoning human beings to a universal liberation while bearing real witness to some concrete liberation is what explains the curious dialectic in Jesus' life. He first points up the concrete liberations he is effecting, only to try to draw people's attention away from them later in order

to emphasize a broader and more profound message. That, in my opinion, is the proper explanation of the so-called "messianic secret" in Mark. The explanation of liberal exegesis is incorrect.

7. The most profound and scholarly effort in this direction is, in my opinion, that of Severino Croatto, *Exodus: A Hermeneutics of Freedom* (Maryknoll, N.Y.: Orbis Books, 1981).

8. See, for example, Gerhard von Rad, *Old Testament Theology* (New York: Harper & Row, 1965), vol. 2, Part II.

9. James H. Cone, *A Black Theology of Liberation* (Philadelphia: Lippincott, 1970), p. 33.

10. Ibid., p. 156.

11. On this process of *deutero-learning* on different scientific levels, see Gregory Bateson, *Steps to an Ecology of Mind* (New York: Ballantine Books, 1974), especially Parts II, V, and VI.

8

JOSÉ MÍGUEZ BONINO

Marxist Critical Tools

Are They Helpful in Breaking the Stranglehold of Idealist Hermeneutics?

Modern idealist biblical interpretation replaced the concrete events and conflicts narrated and addressed in the Bible with words addressed to the individual believer's subjectivity. The (re-)discovery of Marxist critical "materialist" analysis among Bible-study groups, particularly among workers and students in Europe and in popular church circles in Latin America, opened up a way to recover the concrete sociopolitical orientation of biblical stories, prophecies, and theology. Marxist analysis helps interpreters discern the socio-historical context of biblical texts. But it also helps awaken interpreters to their own political-economic context, to the fact that they "always already" read the biblical text in a concrete historical situation, both "out of" a praxis and "into" a praxis in their own concrete historical situation. Moreover, Marx's insight that religion is a protest against as well as an expression of distress points to the dynamism of much of the Bible, which not only gives powerful expression to human misery, but "announces, narrates, and demands historical events which overcome that misery," as well.

Reprinted from *Holy Bible: The Politics of Bible Study* (London: SCM, 1974).

The question of the title, given to me by the editor, is both puzzling and tempting. Marxism presents itself, whether as scientific analysis or as revolutionary theory and ideology, as a blunt negation (or overcoming) of religion in general and of the Christian religion in particular. The acceptance of a Marxist vision should logically result, therefore, not in the interpretation of the Biblical message but in its dissolution. On the other hand, Marx and his followers have offered an interpretation of the Christian religion and even of the Biblical (particularly but not exclusively the New Testament) writings. Is there anything in this interpretation which could help a Christian today to a better grasp of his own faith? Or, coming more specifically to our question: is there in the way in which Marx and some of his followers come to the interpretation of Christian origins and development anything that a Christian interpreter can learn when he faces the Scriptures? My subtitle tries to summarize my answer to this question. It is offered here very tentatively, as comments and questions to be discussed and pursued rather than as an elaborate analysis. And it is offered out of the concrete context of Christians who are engaged in the struggle for the liberation of man and society, and who are engaged in that struggle together with many Marxists in a common — though not undifferentiated — socialist commitment. It seems to me that, translated to the area of Biblical study, the Marxist insights are a powerful instrument to free interpretation from its idealist captivity. This is what I shall try to illustrate.

TRACKING DOWN "IDEOLOGY": THE CRITICISM OF INTERPRETATION

It is well known that Marxism places religion in the area of ideologies — the intellectual constructions whose real significance is in the economic and social relations which they reflect (or hide). Among the criticisms that Marx directs against Christianity within this framework is the accusation that it provides religious sanction to the oppressive capitalist bourgeois system (in fact, that 'Christian principles' have justified all forms of exploitation and oppression). The concrete form to which he points is the Christian buttressing of the Prussian absolutist state.

Whatever qualifications one might have to make concerning this interpretation, I submit that 'ideological suspicion' is a fundamental critical tool for interpretation. I think the first application has to do with the 'history of interpretation' because, as a matter of fact, our study of the Bible is always placed within a stream of interpretations. We modify, correct, qualify, even reverse, 'meanings' which have already been given, traditioned, almost incorporated into the texts. It is, therefore, crucial to ask about the ideological presuppositions and functions which such interpretations may have had.

Marx said, for instance, that Protestant ethics had reflected the capitalist bourgeois ideology by substituting 'having' for 'being': man had to forgo all aesthetic, material, and social enhancement of the self in order to work and save — 'the more you save . . . the greater will become your treasure which neither moss nor rust will corrupt — your capital'. We know that — although in a different way—Max Weber's sociological studies have borne out the operation (if not the reasoning) of this interpretation. But if this is so, should not we ask how has this affected Biblical interpretation? How has, in fact, Biblical interpretation dealt with the texts which relate being and having?

1. The first thing that comes to mind are Jesus' sayings about 'riches' and 'the rich'. Even a cursory look to Biblical commentaries in the Protestant tradition shows the almost uniform ideological train of thought: riches (in themselves) are good—therefore Jesus could not have condemned them as such, nor rich people as such—consequently the text must mean something else—this something else must be found in the 'subjective' sphere (intention, attitudes, motivations). Once this framework of interpretation is in operation, all texts gather around it in one coherent whole. Exegesis follows suit: Luke's version of the Beatitude of the poor for instance, is interpreted through Matthew's 'in spirit'; this is in time disconnected from the prophetic-Psalmic relation of 'poor' and 'oppressed' or the whole is 'spiritualized' as devotion (humility before God). The ideological function of such interpretation is evident (however different the intention of the interpreter may have been); you can rest assured in your capitalist accumulation of wealth (or your attempt to reach it); religion (reverence for God) legitimizes and blesses your effort! The persistence of such ideological stereotypes is forcefully attested in the interpretation of such an honest and responsible exegete as J. Jeremias. He—perhaps correctly—argues that in the parable of the rich man and Lazarus, 'Jesus does not want to comment on a social problem'. But when verse 25 (Luke 16:19-31) poses the question of the reversal of the condition of the poor, Jeremias argues from the 'ideological supposition' and asks: 'Where had Jesus ever suggested that wealth in itself merits hell and that poverty in itself is rewarded by paradise?' To which, clearly, there are at least two answers that an interpretation free from the bourgeois presupposition could not have failed to see. One: that Jesus never speaks of wealth *in itself* or poverty *in itself* but of rich and poor as they are, historically. The 'in itself' abstraction is clearly a piece of liberal ideology. Second: a whole number of texts, or rather practically all texts dealing with the subject (with the exception of Matthew 13:12 and parallels if interpreted in this connection), point in the clear direction of this reversal, whatever explanation we may want to give them. Moreover, its relation to one trend of the prophetic tradition—to which Jesus is evidently related in several other aspects of his teaching—makes it all the more clear. We reach the real ground of Jeremias' interpretation in the strange affirmation that 'Jesus does not intend to take a position on the question of rich and poor'.

2. A host of other examples could easily be given. The problem is not one of particular texts but of the total framework into which interpretation is cast. Once the 'mythical' cosmic dimension in which traditional interpretation had projected the Biblical story began to slip away at the advent of the modern world, the peculiar atmosphere of liberal bourgeois 'spirituality', individualistic and subjective, became normative for interpretation. Thus, historical and political events like the death of Jesus, the Parousia, or mission, were decoded out of their cosmic representation into an individualistic and inward 'existential'

moment, experience or appropriation. A reinterpretation of the texts requires the explosion of the ideological straitjacket in which they have been imprisoned.

THE SOCIOECONOMIC MATRIX: THE CRITICISM OF THE SOURCES

Deeper than the discovery of the ideological functions of religion is Marx's understanding of it as the projection of man's 'misery', of his suffering from and protest against an unjust and oppressive world. In this line, Engels, Kautsky and others have understood the emergence of Christianity as the 'slave's' protest against oppression, finding a (substitutionary) satisfaction in the hope of an apocalyptic (and later otherworldly) vindication. Lately Ernst Bloch has called attention to the dynamism of that hope. A dynamism that can only find historic realization when the religious 'heritage' is wrenched from its transcendent-mythical and incorporated into a historic-scientific (Marxist) projection.

We need not concern ourselves with the details of this interpretation. They suffer from serious historical oversimplifications and inaccuracies. Moreover, we must reject—even on Marxist grounds—all simplistic and mechanistic explanations of religion as a mere 'reflex' of economic conditions. The religious reality is a complex phenomenon which has its own laws and internal coherence. It would be ridiculous—though a wooden orthodox Marxism sometimes has tried it—to explain the Biblical texts as a direct consequence of economic and social situations. But it is quite another thing to ask for the socioeconomic matrix in which these texts were born. This is more than the already established determination of the *Sitz im Leben* in order to illumine a text. It is the question of whether and in what form a religious outlook which finds expression in texts expresses the socioeconomic relations and circumstances of a given society.

1. The 'social' prophets offer a good illustration. Socially engaged and progressive Christians rightly appeal to them. Their scathing denunciation of exploitation and oppression, their condemnation of a religion which covers up injustice with ritual, their call to repentance and their announcement of judgment are all relevant to our present situation. But one may wonder whether the prophets can be so directly 'enrolled' for socioeconomic revolution. As conservative exegetes are always ready to point out, most prophets are actually opposed to progress and change; they rather dream of a former (perhaps never existent) society in which every family freely cultivated its field, cared for its cattle and enjoyed a self-sufficient situation. In fact, sometimes they even go back to a pre-agricultural, nomadic ideal. The real crisis which prompts their message is the 'progress' to a more differentiated society in which class differences become accentuated and the structural class-relationships (landowner and laborer, producer and tradesman, the intermediation of business, and the corresponding political differentiations) take the place of face-to-face and intra-familial ones. Their prophecy is indeed 'the sigh of the oppressed creature' alienated in this change and 'the protest' of that creature. But it is cast in the form of a utopian projection of a previous real or imagined harmony.

What is the importance of this distinction? It is this: that unless we identify the utopian character of the prophetic projection, we run the risk (to which most 'progressive' interpretation succumb) of merely *moralizing* the prophetic message into a well-meaning admonition to those in power to repent and put an end to injustice. The real question posed by the prophetic message so understood is not how to translate into modern terms the prophetic demands. This can only result in a new set of idealistic principles. The question is: how can we, in the present historical conditions, give adequate expression to the prophetic protest against the disruption of human life created by the conditions of our capitalist society and how can we in the present historical conditions give adequate expression to the prophetic hope of a reintegration of human life and society in justice and solidarity?

2. Again, there is no need to provide many illustrations of the point we are trying to make. In one sense, what we are saying is that Biblical texts—like all texts—can be (and at one level must be) seen (as Marxism indicates) as an expression of the human misery and hope generated by the socioeconomic conditions and finding expression in mythical or utopian projections. The 'eschatological reversal' of rich and poor to which we alluded previously, the thaumaturgic (healing) expectations and performances, the forms of communal solidarity which we find both in the Old and the New Testament, cannot be exempted from this level of analysis.

3. The previous affirmation will immediately prompt a question: is not God's reality and power evacuated in this interpretation? Because it seems clear that it is precisely in this 'mythical' or 'utopic' space where the Bible locates God's presence: God raises the Assyrian to punish Israel, he appoints Cyrus to bring his people back, he strikes down with sickness the wicked king. Jesus miraculously heals the sick, feeds the hungry, raises the dead—i.e. brings the sign of the coming Kingdom. A divinely ordained catastrophic event ushers in the new age. It seems to me that this question points to a deeper level of Biblical interpretation in several ways.

Firstly, it is this question which helps us to see one peculiarity of the Biblical witness: its own tendency to historicize the space of God's intervention; thus, God judges and liberates 'in, with and under' historical, worldly events. Jesus relativizes his own role as *thaumaturg* by relating it to faith on the one hand and subordinating it to his message of the Kingdom on the other. Paul historicizes the eschatological expectation by demanding in the Christian community the reality of the eschatological reversal (no more woman and man, Jew or Greek, slave or master). Using the terms of the Marxist analysis: the Bible is not satisfied with expressing human misery, nor with otherworldly or subjective realms—it announces, narrates and demands historical events which, at least in principle and initially, *overcome in reality* this misery. Biblical interpretation looks for the presence of these pointers not by denying the socioeconomic matrix but by bringing it to light.

PRAXIS AND INTERPRETATION: WHAT IS THE "TRUTH" OF THE BIBLE?

Are we really entitled to take the step indicated in the last paragraph? Is this not a dissolution of God's message into human activism, an unwarranted secularization of the Gospel? The answer to this question hinges on the understanding of the character of God's Word. If it is understood as a *statement* of what God is or does, then the mythical or utopian frameworks (or the subjectivistic inversion of reality of liberal hermeneutics) has the last word. But if the Biblical message is a *call, an announcement-proclamation (kerygma)* which is given in order to put in motion certain actions and to produce certain situations, then God is not the *content* of the message but the *wherefrom* and the *whereto*, the originator and the impulse of this course of action and these conditions. Then, *hearing* the message can mean no other than becoming involved in this action and this creation of conditions and situations. By defining an event as 'God's action', the Bible is not withdrawing it from history — even if the ideological framework used is mythical — but pointing to the divinely wrought and revealed background and power of the human action demanded. This is even so in the New Testament references to Christ's resurrection: mission, the new life, community, active love, are the human historical content of which Christ's resurrection is the ground and power.

1. In this perspective we are forced to transform our understanding of interpretation itself. Even in the Bible-study renewal which has been so significant for the SCM and the ecumenical movement, we have been used to the 'idealist' method of trying to establish the meaning of the text in the first place, and then to relate it to our historical conditions and to listen to what the text will say to us. There are two misunderstandings in this procedure. The first is that it does not take seriously enough the fact that the text itself is an 'action', the record of an involvement in God's call. We are not faced with a naked divine word but with a human obedience or disobedience in which God's Word is made present to us. We enter into these courses of action.

But — and this is even more important — we always read the texts 'out of' a praxis and 'into' a praxis. As Christian citizens, workers, intellectuals, husbands or wives, we already have an 'enacted interpretation' of the text which will be confirmed, deepened, challenged or rejected in the confrontation — but which will set the terms of that confrontation. The relation between theory and praxis — to which Marxist thinking has called our attention — is by no means simple. It does not deny that any course of action already incorporates (conscious or unconscious) theoretical presuppositions. It underlines the importance of theoretical thinking which examines the practical course of action in terms of its relevance to the direction of the process and criticizes the theoretical presuppositions in terms of the development of the process. There is, in this respect, a constant relation between theory and praxis. We cannot and need not at this point enter further into this discussion. But we need to stress the importance of this basic understanding for Biblical interpretation.

2. Let me take an illustration from a very controversial person and situation in my continent: the Colombian priest Camilo Torres. When he reads in the Gospel: 'If you are offering your gift at the altar and then remember that your brother has something against you, leave your gift before the altar and go; first be reconciled to your brother, and then come and offer your gift' (Matt. 5:23-24). He asks himself — using all the tools of knowledge available to him: who is

my brother who has something against me? Not merely in an individual and subjective sense but as a priest who belongs to a particular historical structure of religious and political power, as an intellectual who belongs to a group who has played a role in history, as a member of a (economically powerful and dominating) class. The answer is clear: the poor, the worker, the peasant, he 'has something against me'. Furthermore, what he has against me is objectively real — my action in the solidarity of the institution, the group, the class to which I belong is an oppressive action. Therefore, if I interpret the text as merely affecting my subjective interpersonal relation to those whom I know personally (within the circle of my relations) I am rejecting and denying the real estrangement. My interpretation in such a case is an ideological occultation, bound to the interests of my class. I can only read the text authentically from within the recognition of the class conflict in which my relation to the largest number of my brothers places me. The command to 'reconcile myself with my brother' can only be understood, therefore, as objectively demanding me to remove the objective alienation between my brother and myself.

We can perhaps question the course of action taken by Camilo Torres as he moves into political action and finally into the guerrilla. But this discussion misses (or eludes) the point; Camilo reads the text in and out of the explicit recognition of his total involvement as an historical man and re-acts his praxis out of the total impact of the text on his involvement. He refuses to take refuge in a 'normative' course of behavior which would be found in the text without exposing himself to it, without bringing to it his total present reality. Otherwise he might have been satisfied to fulfill the 'normative requirement' within the self-understood limits of his unexposed and therefore unchallenged sociological condition (i.e. resolve the personal quarrel he may have had with a fellow-priest or a colleague-professor). And he refuses to let the command hover over the concrete historical circumstances in which his actions take place. Otherwise he might have been satisfied with an action of charity — which leaves the objective conflict untouched. Only by incorporating his action within a total 'praxis' in which the cause of 'offense' might be objectively removed could the reading of Jesus' word be actually 'heard'. Naturally, the relation between interpretation and praxis understood in this way requires the use of all the analytical tools at our disposal — both in the understanding of our present praxis, of the text, and of the conditions for a new praxis. This is precisely the 'theoretical' work. And this is the only justification for doing theology . . . when it fulfills its task!

3. This is, in fact, the kind of theology that we meet in the Biblical 'reading of the Bible'. Modern scholarship has shown us, for instance, how the story of creation, or the exodus, is 'read' in the course of the tradition of Israel. When Deutero-Isaiah, for instance, tells the 'exodus' in chapter 35, he reads it as the exile who mourns in captivity far from the Promised Land and who waits for the return. The road in the desert, the springs of water, the power that comes to the weary, is *the new road* to the return from exile. He does not 'deduce' from the Exodus story a 'moral' for his time: he is invited to enter the exodus *now*, the first exodus as God's action is the *wherefrom* and the *power* of this call. This is what happens when people in the Third World receive today this same story. As a Latin-American theologian puts it:

If our reading of the Biblical kerygma has any purpose, the 'memory' of the Exodus becomes for us—oppressed people of the Third World—a pro-vocative Word, an announcement of liberation. . . . It is our call to prolong the exodus, because it was not an exclusive Hebrew event but God's liberating purpose for all peoples. In an hermeneutic line it is perfectly legitimate to understand ourselves *out* of the Biblical exodus and, above all, to understand it *out of* our situation as peoples living in political, social, economic or cultural 'slavery'.[1]

God's Word: The Limitations of the Tools

An interpretation which would limit itself to a Marxist analysis could not, certainly, make sense of what we have been saying, particularly in the last section. There is no 'wherefrom' and no 'power' in such interpretation, except in people's own action. Anything else is a human projection, the reification of relationships which man has not yet understood or wants to mystify. The Bible can—at best—record this dynamism of human action. Marxism gives it its real name. At this point no doubt there is a basic divergence. What for a Christian is the ultimate ground and power of his praxis is for an orthodox Marxist an ultimate alienation. This divergence cannot be solved in discussion or through argument. The faithfulness of his commitment is the only verification—not certainly proof—that a Christian can offer for the reality of the source and the power which sustains it. But a few brief theological points may be in order for a Christian who intends to take seriously the critical tools that Marxism has developed.

1. The overcoming of an idealist interpretation, far from being a surrender to a materialistic conception of reality, seems to me—to use a Marxist analogy—placing the Biblical perspective 'back on its head'. Idealist interpretation, in fact, particularly in its modern subjectivist form, inverted the direction of the Biblical message by projecting the historical events of God's action into consciousness as subjective events. This is precisely the reverse of the Incarnation: while God's Word becomes history, idealist interpretation replaces history by words. God in the flesh is the rejection of the idealist resolution of objective conflict and liberation into subjective transactions.

2. God's Word—the power of the Risen Lord—is a dynamic reality. It cannot be tied down to the merely logical continuity of dogmatic formulae but it impinges creatively on historical circumstances. Jesus Christ is the same yesterday, today and forever not in the static identity of a thing or a formulation, but in the dynamic unity of his redemptive purpose working itself out within the conditions and possibilities of a human history which itself is in movement. As a normative witness of that purpose, the Biblical record has a 'reserve of meaning' which becomes concrete as men read it in obedience, within the conditions of their own history. To claim normativity for the sociological limitations of understanding and action of the eighth-century prophets or the first-century Apostles is to stultify the Word of God. This is certainly not to surrender to arbitrary interpretation. There is a direction and a congruity in God's

purpose — and the tools of historical and literary criticism cannot be underestimated in helping to clarify this direction and congruity. But to look for a direct unmediated transposition is to deny the reality of the Holy Spirit.

3. 'Discernment of the spirits' is not, therefore, a purely analytical process. Analytical processes (which are indispensable both in relation to the reading of the text and our relation to them) are assumed into and have their place within a synthetic act of commitment. Not the mere 'hearer' but only the 'doer' can understand God's Word.

NOTE

1. J. Severino Croatto, *Exodus: A Hermeneutics of Freedom* (Maryknoll, N.Y.: Orbis Books, 1981), 14-15.

9

KUNO FÜSSEL

The Materialist Reading of the Bible

Report on an Alternative Approach to Biblical Texts

Three influential studies on the materialist reading of the Bible have been written since 1974 by Fernando Belo, Michel Clévenot, and Georges Casalis. They have as their aim to clarify how the biblical texts relate to their socio-historic settings as ideological productions. A combination of Marxist historical material analysis and of literary structuralism is employed to illuminate the literature as a product of the social formation which has its own unique character as a written system of symbolic codes.

The author briefly develops a materialist theory of literature and sets forth the steps typically involved in doing a materialist reading of a biblical text, including the distinctive mixture of sequential codes and cultural codes that are embodied in the structure of the writing. This type of biblical study is finding a widespread audience principally among lay groups in France, Spain, and Italy, and among university-based groups in Germany, Austria, Switzerland, and the Netherlands. Leftist Christians, dedicated to changing their own socio-historic circumstances, are aided by a materialist reading to grasp the connection

Reprinted from Willy Schottroff and Wolfgang Stegemann, eds., *The God of the Lowly: Socio-historical Interpretations* (Maryknoll, N.Y.: Orbis Books, 1984), 13-25.

between the biblical symbols they are nurtured on and the social practice of the biblical symbolizers.

CLASSICS OF THE MATERIALIST READING OF THE BIBLE

The year 1974 saw the appearance of Fernando Belo's *Lecture matérialiste de l'évangile de Marc.*[1] With this book, Belo, a Portuguese who was at that time living in French exile as a foreign worker and a laicized priest, set in motion a search for alternative readings of the Bible that has continued down to the present. His approach is not only fascinating but is marked by a certain inexorability; both qualities result from his ability to bring almost the entire arsenal of Parisian theoretical production in the linguistic and social sciences to bear on a single basic question: What is the connection between political and radical Christian practice? Or, to spell this question out in greater detail: How do economic, political, and ideological class struggles influence the production and reception of biblical texts? What material presuppositions, interests, and needs lead to which concepts, ideas, and theories? What are the laws regulating not only the exchange of goods but also the circulation of signs in those systems of a social formation that mediate meaning?

In the first part of his book Belo admittedly requires the reader to climb a whole mountain of methodological problems; the effort needed has certainly deterred many a reader from continuing with the book or has forced them to approach it in a different way. But as early as the second part of the book the reader's perseverance receives its first reward when Belo comes to the conclusion that the Old Testament is shaped by two main opposed lines of thought. These are the expression not only of distinctive religious and theological traditions but, at a deeper level, of contrary socioeconomic interests and power relationships. A system based on gift (a system that is Yahwist and concerned with equality and self-rule in the framework of tribal society) stands over against a system based on purity vs. pollution (this system is priestly, centralizing, and bureaucratic with its focus in the exercise of sacral and royal power).

The struggle between these two approaches continues into the New Testament. At their point of intersection stands the cross of Jesus. Belo shows why this was inevitable, by means of a clear analysis of the function of the temple in Israelite religion. The proceedings against Jesus are really concerned with the role of the temple as the economic, political, and ideological focus of power. Jesus dies because he wishes to tear down this temple and build a new one distinct from the old temple and outside the holy city. This purpose distinguishes him from the Zealots, who die for and in the temple.

In Belo's view, the entire development of theology that follows on the death of Jesus (it begins in the Bible, although least of all in Mark, whose Gospel Belo analyzes and comments on, sequence by sequence) must be described as an attempt to blunt and adapt the radical messianic practice of Jesus. Perhaps

Belo is here throwing out the infant (theology) with its idealist bath, but no one can dispute his claim that to follow Jesus without accepting his messianic practice is simply to play games with labels.

In 1976 Michel Clévenot published his *Approches matérialistes de la Bible.*[2] His study picks up the main points of Belo's book but puts the latter into a form better suited to group reading. Clévenot not only provides a simple methodological introduction to the interrelations of historical materialism, linguistics, and Scripture study, but also makes stimulating comments in explaining the Bible as a collection of literary texts and in interpreting the Gospel of Mark as the story of the subversive practice of Jesus. As for the main task, which is to ascertain and map the traces of the practice of Jesus at the level of the various societal instances, Clévenot seeks to accomplish this by reconstructing the class relationships current around A.D. 70 and by deciphering the codes used in Mark's literary production.

In 1977 Georges Casalis published his book *Les idées justes ne tombent pas du ciel* [Correct Ideas Don't Fall from the Skies],[3] which describes numerous and varied approaches to a materialist hermeneutic that is valid not only for a materialist reading of the Bible but also for a theologico-political reading of Christian revolutionary practice in general. This brilliantly written account of the journey of a militant French professor of theology from a politically sensitive Barthian theology to a clear option for the oppressed classes may be regarded as a first contribution to a European theology of liberation. Casalis energetically continues the struggle, begun by Belo, against bourgeois logo-centrism in theology (that is, the exorcism of rational thinking as a supposedly impartial grasp of objective thought-forms).

He shows that human alienation is not to be overcome by an ever-new submission to ever-new scientific considerations but only by liberation from what divides us from God, our neighbor, and ourself. In Casalis's view, theological thinking is primarily a trailblazing engagement in revolutionary practice; it is a risking of one's existence, and this usually means initially that one becomes an outcast in one's own church. Such an approach to theology means the end of theology as conceptual representation; it is a farewell to spectator theologians. Another characteristic of this new kind of theologizing is a new manner of reading, which does not get entangled in abstract problems of understanding but uses book lore in order to experiment on behalf of life and thus to change one's own practice. The world's structure of meaning, its intelligibility, "does not fall from the skies" as a gift, but must be created.

WHO ENGAGES IN AN ALTERNATIVE READING OF THE BIBLE, AND WHY DO THEY DO IT?

No one who is familiar with the professional scene will deny that, if the publication of technical studies be taken as a criterion, exegesis and the auxiliary biblical sciences have made great progress in the last thirty years. A decisive factor in this progress has been the acceptance of the historical critical method by all scholars in these disciplines, almost without exception. It seems, however, that the undeniable multiplicity of exegetical results has not satisfied an equally great number of diverse interests and needs. In fact, there is reason for thinking that scholarly exegetical interest and the hermeneutic which guides it (rather than the formal method as such) have been directed unilaterally to the acquisition of authoritarian knowledge in the service of an elitist claim to dominance on the part of a few "reading experts" in the church. Exegesis has thus become, in large measure, a legitimating science, and authentic exegesis has turned into ideology.

When Belo, Casalis, Clévenot, and many others denounce this tendency as idealist, they are at least able to point out how surprisingly little of real history appears in the immediate work done on the biblical text by outstanding representatives of the historical critical method, such as Rudolf Bultmann. At the very time (1941) when Nazi Germany was attacking the Soviet Union and Jews were being murdered in the concentration camps, Bultmann, who was certainly not a fascist, published his book *Neues Testament und Mythologie* in which he accepts the modern spirit as the criterion for interpreting the Bible. Yet Bultmann does not allow the pitiless consequences of this spirit and of the technological mind to which it has given birth, as seen in war and the Holocaust, to exercise any influence on his exegetical principles.[4] It is clear that even in Bultmann "history" still means simply such residues of the past as can be established and that criticism is limited to the analysis of world views, forms, redactions, and traditions. Nothing is seen of history as the presently operative product of the class struggle, or of a revolutionary "critique of the status quo" as a valid interpretive horizon for contemporary reading and for the discernment of spirits that is needed today.

In view of this observation, which is representative of many that might be made, we can understand the severity with which Belo criticizes this elimination of social contradictions and conflicts from the existential hermeneutic of the demythologization program:

> Bourgeois exegetes, working on the basis of anthropocentric logo-centrism, have sought with varying success to undo the closure of the MYTH codes that play in the New Testament texts. The name of Bultmann especially is connected with this attempt at demythologization. For a symptom of the fact that the attempt is being made on the basis of bourgeois logo-centrism I need point out only the appeal to "the modern consciousness," to scientific reason, and to advancing modernity that seems always to be the ultimate argument in texts aiming at demythologization. This effort at demythologization fails to understand the Scriptures and the narrative of power (the messianic narrative). This bourgeois form of the theological discourse ends up in *interiority* (even if it be called spiritual experience or a spiritual attitude).[5]

Ecclesiastical authorities and the dominant exegetes have reacted strongly to the charge of idealism. Catholic exegetes especially insist that in matters of scriptural exegesis they will allow no alien gods besides them, and therefore any approach to the Bible that differs from theirs or represents a critical reaction to theirs is labeled as unbridled or unscientific or as a temporary fad (assuming that they do not join the bishops and reach for a stronger weapon, disqualifying other approaches as un-ecclesial or even un-Christian).

It is evident, therefore, that attempts at a non-idealist approach to the Bible do not originate in the academic world of university theology, but rather in the commitment of the leftist Christians who opt for the oppressed in the class struggles of our time and join them in the fight for liberation.

Revolutionary practice thus becomes the starting point for a comprehensive hermeneutic that not only makes possible a new interpretation of political and ideological reality in society but also becomes the basis for a new understanding of faith.

If a church of the oppressed is to be built and if the folly of the cross is to be taken seriously in politics, then there is need not only of bidding farewell to bourgeois religion and the church of the established classes, but also of forming a new identity. A materialist reading owes its existence to this need, springing from an altered practice, for a Christian-socialist identity and for an appropriation of the tradition of faith and its sources that will make this identity secure.

Like every conversion, this new beginning has its problems. There is a need to avoid two dangers: that of an individualistic, spontaneous biblicism, and that of a completely functional approach to the Bible which looks upon it solely as a source of motivation for political action. A conscious and sustained materialist reading is therefore compelled, first of all, to be clear about its own limitations, the methods required, and the state of utilizable preliminary work. It is here that Belo and, following him, Clévenot and Casalis have made a valuable pioneering contribution.

Numerous groups throughout the world (at present there are about a hundred) have therefore adopted the program suggested by these men and have made it the basis for their common study of the Bible. In addition, the groups have moved beyond the now prototypical Gospel of Mark and have applied the method to other texts of Scripture: in the Old Testament to the Books of Samuel and Kings, to Genesis and Jeremiah; in the New Testament, to I Thessalonians and I Corinthians, to the Gospel of John and the Acts of the Apostles. The Acts of the Apostles especially has attracted increasing interest, and this for two reasons. First, it provides a document in which the entire range of problems created by the entry of the church into the place left by Jesus ("Jesus went and the church came") may be studied. Second, it makes possible a closer examination of living conditions among the early Christians and especially of their common possession and sharing of goods.

In the Romance-language (and especially in the French- and Spanish-speaking) countries a materialist reading is practiced chiefly by groups made up of members from left-oriented church associations (in which an ecumenical composition is taken for granted), the trade unions, and the Christians for Socialism movement. The important thing seems to be not the reading as such but rather the liberation and enlightenment it brings within the family, at work, and in the Party. In terms of trade or profession, the members of the groups are quite varied: technicians, workers, elementary school teachers, nurses, housewives, students, retirees. There are few academic people or professional theologians.

The composition of the groups is quite different, however, in the German-speaking countries (West Germany, East Germany, Austria, Switzerland). Here the universities and the student associations provide the milieu for the groups devoted to the materialist reading of the Bible; in terms of methodology these groups frequently take their lead from the school of the Dutchman F. Breukelmann (thus, for example, T. Veerkamp and J. van Zwieten). Pastors, teachers, theology students, and church workers largely determine the manner in which these groups go about their work. The situation is similar in the Netherlands, although here the phenomenon of the base-level communities and the general ecclesial climate of tolerance also provide a favorable atmosphere. In both of these language areas, however, it can be said that Christians for Socialism plays an important role in coordinating and giving guidance. This is true also of Belgium, England, Norway, Canada, Peru, Colombia, and Mauritius.

The work of these groups derives the essentials of its structure from the leftist Catholic periodical *Lettre* which is published in Paris[6] and has M. Clévenot as one of its editors. Since the appearance of Belo's book, *Lettre* has promoted the common cause in trailbreaking articles and has provided a forum for supraregional and international discussion. The Supplement to No. 237 (1978) may be regarded as a first comprehensive survey of the subject of alternative readings. It contains reports of new groups, new exegetical findings, and new tools of analysis.

With this Supplement as a basis and preparation, a first international meeting took place in Paris on November 11-12, 1978. There were more than 100 participants from sixteen countries; among these were "of course" Belo, Clévenot, and Casalis, but it was the laity, and not the professional textual analysts who gave the event its stamp. The pentecostal power of Christian-socialist internationalism supplied the normative codes: the primacy of experience, the equal standing of all readers, unity in political commitment, the impulse to ongoing personal work.

The Bible is, of course, not the only book these groups use in their often discouraging struggle against the establishment in church and society. Perhaps it is not even the most important of the tools they use.

Christians who sum up in the term "socialism" their ideas and suggestions for the improvement of the present social order realize that they cannot derive their views directly from the Bible. On the other hand, it would be at the very least imprudent to take it for granted that militant Christians can in their political involvement dispense with the rich treasures of the Bible and the stimuli it affords. On the contrary, it is to be presupposed that the texts of the Bible have something in common with the hope that keeps us going in the political struggle, the hope, I mean, of a society without oppression and alienation. Consequently, the Bible is an indispensable aid to survival on the long journey through the wilderness of capitalism. Many of the groups mentioned know from experience that a reading of the Bible done in common not only brings new knowledge and helps eliminate old misapprehensions of the Bible as being a collection of pious statements for use on feastdays, but also affords an authentic joy. Texts of the Bible and the reading of them have contributed to the loosing of the tongues of many in the groups. As a result, conflicts in the groups have found their voice and a solution, whereas previously they had been unadmitted and had unconsciously hindered practical action.

From this it can be seen that a materialist reading of the Bible has three goals. 1. It aims at showing that the Bible does not simply contain scattered expressions of the lives of the oppressed but has the poor for its real subject. 2. It aims therefore at rescuing the Bible from those who have wrongfully appropriated it and put it in chains. 3. It aims at reading the Bible in such a way that in its light our political practice will receive a new clarification, while at the same time this practice and its clarification will help us find in the writings of the Old and New Testaments hitherto undiscovered paradigms of a subversive practice.

WHAT DOES THE TERM "MATERIALIST" MEAN IN THIS CONTEXT?

The primary point of reference for a materialist reading is "revolutionizing practice"[7] as a concrete epistemological principle. In other words, the transformative practice determines in each instance the range of concepts and theories that is developed, and serves as criterion of truth for statements made with the help of these. This applies to a hermeneutic for interpretation of the Bible.

The materialism in question here is therefore practical and not metaphysical. It begins with the concept of production which, according to Marx, is determinative for the human species. "The act by which they [living human individuals] distinguish themselves from animals is not the fact that they think but the fact that they begin to produce their means of subsistence."[8] Under the heading of productive activities Marx includes art and therefore literature as particular forms. "Religion, family, state, law, morality, science, art, etc., are only particular modes of production, and fall under its general law."[9] At the same time, however, there are serious differences between the various productive activities just mentioned, between art and science, for example: "The whole as it appears in the mind as a conceptual totality [scientific investigation of social reality in its entirety] is a product of the thinking mind, which appropriates the world in the only way possible to it, a way that is distinct from the artistic, religious, or practical appropriation of the same world."[10] But in order to appraise correctly the place of writing, reading, and literature (the Bible belongs here), recourse must be had to a materialist theory of literature.[11]

By way of a rough and condensed formula, then, the following can be said with regard to a materialist theory of literature: Applying Marx's maxim to the literary production of texts we may assert that literature is to be understood as a product of social practice and derives its character from the relations at work in each case.

Literary production is a *form of ideological production.* Like every other ideological production literary production is determined by the relation between basis and superstructure and by the class struggle. The production of texts is the privileged field of the conflict between the rival ideologies at work on a social formation. The basic structure of literary texts emerges from considera- tion of this primary contradiction. In itself, therefore, literature is always incom- plete, incoherent, and open to new readings. What is called "the unity of a work of art" is simply a metaphor for the effort to resolve social conflicts in a symbolic way and achieve a fictive reconciliation by creating a secondary semi- otic system (= literary language).

A materialist theory of·literature identifies types of texts and genres of texts as variations within a general social determination of literary form, and analyzes the religious, political, juridical, etc., themes of a text in light of its function. This emphasis on the objective character of literature as a reflection of real life means the rejection of a conception that regards literature as resulting from the genial or even fully mysterious creative action of individuals.

Once literature is understood as a particular form of ideological *practice*, it follows that it is not to be classified as an achievement of consciousness and removed from reality, but that it is a material, that is, a practico-transformative, factor of social reality. Literary texts are not simply mental products of material life but rather themselves in their turn play a part in shaping this life. To produce and utilize literature is always at the same time to intervene and take sides in the struggle between the rival ideologies at work in a social formation, and it is therefore to make an active contribution to the shaping and differ- entiating of its contradictions.

A materialist reading (this applies not only to the Bible) must therefore strive to do justice, in dealing with a text, to the viewpoints of productivity and materiality. But productivity and materiality must themselves be seen from two points of view, lest we fall into the error of an esthetics of production, on the one hand, or an esthetics of reception, on the other.[12] Productivity and reception must be considered in relation to the labor of the authors, who make the text out of the given material of their own language, but also in relation to the readers (interpreters), who make the text their own by their reading of it, implant it in their own speech, and so incorporate it into themselves. As far as reading is concerned, this process means that the constitutive elements must be interrelated: (a) the given language; (b) the author who uses it, and the original addressees of the text; and (c) the present-day reader—while paying attention to the conditions in which the text was produced and those in which it now discloses itself, as these conditions are determined by the social situation of the author and that of the reader.

Clévenot therefore sets down the following minimal requirements for a mate- rialist reading: It must lead the reader to the point at which (a) at least the basic syntactical structure of the text and the structure of its statements or actions is clear; (b) the manner in which the author says something to others with the means which his language provides likewise emerges; (c) the author- reader relation and the influence of each on the other are clarified; and (d) enough information about the social situation of author and reader is brought to bear on the analysis of the text.[13]

WHAT METHOD IS TO BE PREFERRED IN READING?

The categories and methods a person needs and the degree of differentiation he claims for them will depend (a) on the field of practical needs and requirements in which he is taking his stand, and (b) on the degree of theory-development which he regards as obligatory and considers to be fruitful and helpful to him in his options. Since the reading groups are made up of militants and not of university professionals, much less theoreticians of science, the first of these two criteria will be decisive for the choice of linguistic methods.

For such an initial understanding,[14] which has not surveyed, and does not intend to survey, the entire discussion that goes on among modern theoreticians of texts, texts are to be regarded, in a quite general way, as linguistic entities which were produced under certain social conditions. Materially speaking, texts are collections of signifiers (signs that convey meaning) which are connected with one another by precise relations. The totality of these relations reveals the structure of the text. For a structural analysis of a text[15] one particular relation is especially important: the opposition between two elements (good/evil, stay/go, Jerusalem/Samaria, etc.). The oppositions that occur in a text reveal the purpose of the text. This is also one of the most important formal bridges to historical materialism with its methodological emphasis on contradictions.

The ascertainment of the conditions of production and reception requires not only reliable information on the pertinent social formation and its general instances: economy, politics, and ideology (consultation of the pertinent technical literature is indispensable here), but also a clarification of the type of text. What is meant by "type of text"?

Most people (this is something drilled into them in school) read texts (a newspaper, a book, a letter) either because they want to know what the author (a friend, a teacher, a politician, etc.) intended to say to them or others, or because they want to find out what happened, what it was really like then or now, who was involved, who did what.

Given these two basic interests, it seems plausible to divide the texts we meet in reading the Bible into two main groups: discourses or speeches, on the one hand (e.g., the letters of Paul), and stories or accounts, on the other (e.g., the Gospel of Mark).

A discourse is a text that establishes a relation between an I and a You and then fashions this relation (developing it, intensifying it, weakening it). At the level of linguistic features discourses are recognizable by the present tense of the verbs, the role of pronouns and adverbs, and the structure of the statements.

A story or narrative, on the other hand, eliminates references to the author's role in the process of expression. Events seem to narrate themselves, so that we do not know clearly who is speaking to whom. Consequently, the third person and the past tense are linguistic signposts of narrative. The change produced by the text is the change that takes place between the actants or agents who make their appearance in the text.

The distinction between discourse and narrative is usually made at the beginning of joint work on the text.

According to Roland Barthes (whom many study groups follow on this point in their reading), the mode of production peculiar to a text, and the structure that emerges from the text, are to be determined by deciphering the sequential codes used, whereas the insertion of the text into a particular situation can be known by the indicial or cultural codes.[16]

Sequential codes may be subdivided into three types: the actantial code, the analytic code, and the strategic code.[17] The working of these codes can be further specified depending on whether they are used in a discourse or in a narrative:

1. The actantial code enables us to see who the actors or actants are and what they do (Jesus, the Pharisees, the disciples, and so on).

2. The analytic codes show us how the actants read and analyze the events (the Pharisees and Jesus pass divergent judgments on cures worked on the sabbath).

3. The strategic code permits us to evaluate the behavior of the actants in terms of the attitudes they adopt toward each other (e.g., the summoning of a sick person into the midst of the synagogue).

Once the overall plan of the text is known, the indicial or cultural codes tell us how the individual components of it are related (e.g., place names), in order that we may thus come to grasp the meaning of the whole. The most important thing here is the serial connections among the individual terms (e.g., whether they all have to do with health, sickness, healing, and so on, or whether they deal with landed property, money, selling, contracts, and so on).

The most important cultural codes are the following:

1. The geographical code: it tells us the regions whence the information comes or where the action takes place.

2. The topographical code: it indicates locales, at least in a narrative: a house, the street, the sea, the temple.

3. The chronological code: it specifies the temporal sequence.

4. The mythological code: it establishes connections with the store of myths that were current throughout the entire East.

5. The symbolic code: it makes reference to the system of values and norms found in the Bible.

6. The social code: it indicates relations to the economic and political instances of society and to practical life generally.

Most groups begin their work by first investigating the way in which one particular code works and then adding code after code until the entire fabric has been reconstituted.

WHY HAS THE MATERIALIST READING UNDERTAKEN TO LINK HISTORICAL MATERIALISM AND STRUCTURALISM?

A materialistic reading of literary texts may be described, from the viewpoint of methodology, as an effort to draw profit, for an intensive reading, from the sociohistorical analysis of the production and reception of texts, on the one hand, and from the determination of their specific literary form, on the other.

In the process, the social background for the analysis is derived from historical materialism as a theory of the formation and history of societies. This is followed by a consideration of the text on the basis of linguistic structuralism. Is this combination of approaches accidental or necessary?

At least on historical grounds the claim that the conjunction is accidental can be dismissed. Ever since the beginning, in the twenties, of Russian formalism,[18] which continues to exert an influence on French structuralism by way of R. Jacobson and T. Todorov, there has been a complementarity (often ignored) between the problems dealt with in the Marxist/materialist theory of literature and those in the formalist/structuralist theory:

1. The Marxists insist on the need of showing how literary texts depend even in their multiplicity of meanings on the sociohistorical context.

2. The formalists are interested primarily in the way in which a literary text manages to establish between sign and reality a relationship that is free from any utilitarian compulsion to represent reality. It is in this freedom that the autonomy of the work of art consists.

3. In concrete work on texts each party gladly avoids the approach taken by the other or, by way of diversion, criticizes the other for neglecting its own (the criticizing party's) side of the investigation. There are only a few theories of literature that try to deal with both aspects at the same time and in a balanced way; some of the exceptions are W. Benjamin and T. W. Adorno, along with E. Balibar and P. Macherey.[19] Belo is very close to the last-named, even though he takes Julia Kristeva as his explicit point of departure.[20]

The attempt to link historical materialism and structuralism in a dialectical way when working on a text is in keeping with an older aspiration, although one that is difficult to satisfy. In this context a dialectical approach implies the need of remaining aware that both the esthetic and the sociofunctional aspects of a text are socially determined but are not on that account reducible to one another by any means. Theory of ideology and structural analysis of texts can therefore usefully complement one another when the goal is to explain how a literary work such as the Bible not only permits different and even contrary types of reading (one which confirms the dominant understanding of reality; another which shatters it), but is itself already the product of rival types of reading and represents their fictive reconciliation.

It is still possible, however, to argue about whether the alliance of methods and the practice of reading that are exhibited in this book are meaningful and helpful and carry us forward. It may be asked whether an equally fruitful or perhaps even more productive combination of the historical critical method and the analysis of societal formation may not be possible. In my opinion, the likelihood of a positive answer to these questions has for the first time increased, now that L. Schottroff and W. Stegemann have published their book[21] which so brilliantly combines readableness, thorough information, and knowledge of the present state of scholarship with the concern for a concrete sociocritical reading.

NOTES

1. Fernando Belo, *Lecture matérialiste de l'évangile de Marc. Récit — Pratique — Idéologie* (Paris: Du Cerf, 1974; 2nd ed., 1975); Eng. *A Materialist Reading of the*

Gospel of Mark, trans. M. J. O'Connell (Maryknoll, N.Y.: Orbis Books, 1981). I also refer the reader here to the exegetical journal, *Texte und Kontexte*, which is published by the Alektor-Verlag (Stuttgart) and contains contributions from the area of alternative interpretations of the Bible.

2. Michel Clévenot, *Approches matérialistes de la Bible* (Paris, 1976); Eng. *Materialist Approaches to the Bible*, trans. William J. Nottingham (Maryknoll, N.Y.: Orbis Books, 1985). In an appendix to the German translation of Clévenot's book, *So kennen wir die Bibel nicht* (Munich, 1978), I have gone more fully into the theoretical background; I refer the reader to it for a more detailed discussion of the subject.

3. Georges Casalis, *Les idées justes ne tombent pas du ciel* (Paris, 1977), Eng. *Correct Ideas Don't Fall from the Skies: Elements for an "Inductive Theology,"* trans. Jeanne Marie Lyons (Maryknoll, N.Y.: Orbis Books, 1985).

4. Cf. also Casalis's critique in Chapter 4 of his book.

5. Belo, *A Materialist Reading of Mark*, p. 286.

6. *La Lettre* is published by *Temps Présent* (68, rue de Babylone, Paris 7).

7. Marx's third thesis on Feuerbach, in L. S. Feuer, ed., *Karl Marx and Friedrich Engels: Basic Writings on Politics and Philosophy* (Garden City, N.Y.: Doubleday & Co., 1959), p . 244.

8. Karl Marx and Friedrich Engels, *The German Ideology*, Part I, in ibid., p. 409.

9. Karl Marx, *The Economic and Philosophical Manuscripts of 1844*, ed. Dirk J. Struik, trans. Martin Milligan (New York: International Publications, 1964), p. 136.

10. Karl Marx, *Einleitung zur Kritik der politischen Ökonomie*, in *Marx-Engels Werke* 13: 632-33.

11. I have indicated elsewhere the sources on which Belo and Clévenot depend; cf. my essay, "Anknüpfungspunkte und methodisches Instrumentarium einer materialistischen Bibellektüre," in M. Clévenot, *So kennen wir die Bibel nicht*, pp. 145-70.

12. Cf. P. V. Zima, *Kritik der Literatursoziologie* (Frankfurt, 1978), pp. 72-112.

13. Cf. M. Clévenot, "Lectures matérialistes de la Bible," in *Introduction à la lecture matérialiste de la Bible* (Geneva, 1978).

14. There is here an understandable difference in level between the reflections and researches of Belo and that which individual groups can absorb of these.

15. There is a survey of the various methods in M. Titzmann, *Strukturale Textanalyse* (Munich, 1977).

16. Cf. especially Roland Barthes, *S/Z*, trans. Richard Miller (New York: Hill and Wang, 1976).

17. Cf. Füssel, art. cit. (n. 11, above), pp. 150-52.

18. Cf. J. Striedter, ed., *Texte der russischen Formalisten* 1 (Munich, 1968); V. Erlich, *Russischer Formalismus* (Munich, 1964); M. Bakhtin, *Marxismus und die Philosophie der Sprache. Grundprobleme der soziologischen Methode in der Wissenschaft von der Sprache* (Leningrad, 1929; Frankfurt, 1976).

19. Cf. E. Balibar and P. Macherey, "Thesen zum materialistischen Verfahren," *Alternative*, no. 98 (1974), 193-221.

20. Cf. Füssel, "Anknüpfungspunkte," pp. 152-54; see note 11 above.

21. Cf. L. Schottroff and W. Stegemann, *Jesus von Nazareth — Hoffnung der Armen* (Stuttgart: Kohlhammer, 1978), Eng., *Jesus and the Hope of the Poor* (Maryknoll, N.Y.: Orbis Books, 1986).

10

DAVID LOCHHEAD

The Liberation of the Bible

People read the Bible from different points of view and see different meanings in its texts. Since the eighteenth century, we have come to realize that such a "partial" or "prejudicial" stance is a necessary aspect of our knowing anything. "Ideology" refers to the social, economic, cultural, and political dimensions of one's point of view. The Bible itself is not ideologically neutral, nor do all its parts form a harmonious ideological unity. The Bible does not prescribe an ideology for our time in any simple or direct way.

By insisting on full and honest analysis of the ideological assumptions of the Bible and of our own ideological assumptions, it is possible to increase our awareness of what we hold to be true (theory) and of what we do (praxis). By gaining more consciousness through the interaction of theory and praxis, we also make it possible to change our ideology. In Bible study, this process can both free the Bible *from our naive prejudgments about it and free us to alter our judgments about ourselves and our society.*

The discipline of producing a "biblical" sermon each week, together with the necessity which circumstances forced on me to come to terms with the

Reprinted from David Lochhead, *The Liberation of the Bible* (Student Christian Movement of Canada, 1977, and the World Student Christian Federation of North America, 1979), 4–7, 18, 27–28, 40–52.

charismatic movement, led me to reflect on my own praxis in relation to the Bible. The whole train of thought was triggered by a very simple remark by a charismatic friend. In the middle of a conversation he remarked that the Bible could be considered to be infallible *as long as it was interpreted in context.*

This is a rather commonplace remark, but for the first time it struck me how significant this qualification *in context* really is. This insight became an important tool for analyzing my own approach to the Bible as a preacher. I pursued the logic of this remark to the point at which the interpretation of the Bible became, for me, the crucial contemporary theological issue.

In brief, the problem was this: In the late '50s and early '60s there was a great interest in existentialism. We approached theological questions through existential questions—personal identity, dialogue, estrangement as sin, God as ultimate concern—and all that. Of course, the existential questions were never solved. The later '60s took care of that! Under the impact of the '60s, the existential questions gave way to political questions.

The title and shape of this work have been chosen for a variety of reasons. In the pastorate, I am particularly aware of the pressure of the religiopolitical right wing. I want to challenge as forcefully as I can the assumption that the Bible is a reactionary book.

The other major reason for the title and shape of the work comes from my persuasion that the only rigorous program which relates faith to the total context of life is that of "liberation" theology. Yet at this point I feel a certain embarrassment. This is not a work in liberation theology. At best, it is prolegomena to an indigenous Canadian liberation theology.

The reason for my embarrassment is simply this: I am white and male and North American. On every count I am numbered with the oppressor! At the same time, I am very aware of my own powerlessness. I believe that the basic insight of liberation theology is quite correct. God does identify himself with the oppressed. The struggle for liberation in the third world, in the women's movement, among racial minorities, in native groups—that is where the theological action is! Yet that is not where I am!

Where I am—and where the people are with whom I must deal day by day—is terribly ambiguous in a theological sense. I and my parishioners are people of good will. We are people who are concerned about, and are willing to sacrifice for, the oppressed of the world. We, too, are oppressed. We are powerless. We lack either the will or the determination even to influence the future of our immediate environment. We doubt that we could change things, even if we had the will and the determination. So we watch, immobilized, while our orchards are appropriated for the recreational use of people from the city. No option but immobility seems reasonable in our circumstances.

Yet coexisting with the consciousness of our powerlessness is the fact that we know we are being paid very well. The farmer who sells his orchards for recreational use can look forward to a reasonably comfortable and independent retirement. We all benefit from the fact that North America pays low prices for raw materials and receives high prices for manufactured goods. I benefit because I am unilingual in English rather than in French. I benefit from my sex and my color. I am oppressor and oppressed—and I don't seem to have much choice about either.

I do not believe that I am alone in this sense of ambiguity. It is precisely in the recognition of the ambiguity of our situation that any white, male, North American theology of liberation must begin. We do not need a theology for the oppressor. We have that in abundance. What we need is a theology for the oppressed who are simultaneously the oppressor. That is much more difficult. Prior to that, we need to understand ourselves better. We need an adequate analysis of the ambiguity of our situation. This task, as fundamental as it is, is not attempted in this book. It still awaits us.

For some, the theoretical openness that this work leaves to ideological pluralism will be offensive. I leave this option open for a number of reasons. First, I do not believe that the Bible is of one ideological piece. Only a falsification of history could, for example, represent the royal theology of the Old Testament as expressing identical ideological interests to the prophetic theologies—at least, during the period of the monarchy. Secondly, I believe that we North Americans have a lot of listening to do both to Scripture and to the world before our options can become sufficiently clear. Thirdly, I am convinced that the truth of a statement like "God identifies himself with the oppressed" is not at issue. What is at issue is the *praxis* which is associated with this kind of affirmation.

By *praxis*, I mean the way that theory and practice fit together. I say certain things; I hold to certain opinions; I do certain things. How are these interrelated? How does what I think fit together with what I do? That interrelatedness, that "fitting together," is my *praxis*. That is how the word is used here. Other uses may be quite legitimate, but those other meanings are not intended in this work.

I use the words "prejudice," "perspective," "viewpoint," and "ideology" more or less synonymously. Furthermore, the terms "prejudice" and "ideology" are never meant in a disparaging sense. I argue that, in understanding reality, our understanding always reflects our perspective on reality. For every view of reality, there is always a "point of view." The term "prejudice" is used when it is important to emphasize that we come to reality with certain expectations of what we are going to find. Any perspective "prejudges" reality in certain ways. The term "ideology" is used to emphasize the social, cultural, economic, and political dimensions of one's "point of view."

The treatment of ideology in the first chapter may seem hopelessly idealistic. It could be read as if I believed that ideologies were caused by people deciding to have one ideal rather than another. No such thesis is intended. I am quite aware of those theories which would see ideologies as reflections of social relationships. I have no argument, in general, with such a thesis. My point in chapter one is simply to identify certain ideals as typifying (not causing) ideological commitments in order to see, in a simple model, what happens when the Bible is read from an ideological point of view.

In case any theologians should happen to pick up this work, I should add that I am aware of the many questions I have begged or over-simplified. I am not writing for theologians. In case any biblical scholar should be listening, I plead *nolo contendere*. I am not a biblical scholar. But neither are those who are my intended readers. We all have a desperate need to hear. This book is not about what to hear, but *how* to hear. It is a book for communities of people who are not content to leave the *doing* of theology to the experts.

THE MIRROR OF THE MIND

One of the dominant myths of modern Western culture is that the mind is something like a mirror of reality. The mind knows the world. What the mind "knows" is like an image of reality—a representation. Ideally the mind itself neither adds to nor subtracts from the facts which it encounters in the world. Like a good mirror which represents what is placed before it without distortion, the mind should reproduce in the form of knowledge only what exists in the world independently of mind.

But just imagine if things were the opposite. Imagine that, in the encounter of the mind and the world, it was the *world* which resembled the mirror. Instead of having knowledge which represented an objective world, what we would "know"—what we would perceive in the world—would simply be a reflection of ourselves.

The contrast between these simple analogies—the mind as mirror vs. the world as mirror—illustrates a basic tension in our recent intellectual history. In the seventeenth and eighteenth centuries the idea of knowledge as an objective representation of reality was certainly dominant. Yet many of the major thinkers of the nineteenth and twentieth centuries have raised the possibility of an alternative: Perhaps what we know, however it may represent a world which exists quite independently of our minds, may also reflect something that our minds contribute as well. Perhaps, at least partly, what we see when we look at the world is our own reflection.

The question of how much we see our own reflection in what we "know" puts the problem of an ideological captivity of the Bible in a radically new perspective. Ideological readings of the Bible are not *simply* attempts to manipulate the texts to our own purposes. If it should be a condition of knowing that we must see the world from the perspective of our own prejudices, we have to read the Bible that way too. We need to consider the implications of the possibility that prejudice is a necessary condition of having any knowledge at all. . . .

It has not been the purpose of this chapter to endorse any particular view which has been briefly sketched here. It has been the intention, however, to endorse the major conclusion which has emerged: *The world is "known" only from the unique perspective of the knower. What is understood reflects not only the reality which is understood but the perspective from which it is understood.*

At the same time we must be clear that we are not endorsing a kind of reductionism which might be suggested by some of the views we have discussed. Among Marxists, for example, it is sometimes suggested that economic factors are the only significant variables in understanding. Similarly, McLuhan often seems to hold that everything can be explained by media studies. We don't wish to move in this direction. What we want to stress is that every "knower" has a unique perspective on the "known." We each belong to some particular social class in a particular socioeconomic system. Each of us has a unique set of parents and a unique upbringing. We speak a particular language with a particular grammatical structure. We are part of a particular culture in which particular media of communication are used. Each of these factors plays a role in defining the perspective from which we experience and understand our world. Each of these factors is reflected in what we see in the world.

It will be clear that if everything that we understand reflects our own unique perspective, this will also be true of how we understand the Bible. There is no reason to complain about this or deplore it. Without a perspective—without prejudices—we could not begin to understand anything. The important thing is to be aware that this is so. It is just not possible to talk about what the Bible says as if our exposition of the biblical view of things were quite independent of our own perspective on reality. To ignore this is to make the Bible captive to our prejudices. Our task is to read the Bible in such a way that it is liberated from our blindness to the relativity of our own point of view.

To put this point another way, we have to learn to read the Bible so that it is able to liberate us from the bonds of our own perspective. To a remarkable degree, our point of view is not something of our own making. We are not asked when we want to be born, what nationality and social class we will have, what language we will speak, what ideological framework will accompany our instruction in Sunday School, and so on. The temptation is to force the Bible to fit the perspective we have inherited. Yet a Bible which must "fit" a perspective is not one that is going to tell us anything new. It becomes an ideological weapon in our defense of our own version of the status quo.

In this study we will henceforth assume the relativity of knowledge. In making this assumption it is important to make a few qualifications. In particular it should be clear that while any given expression of truth is relative to the perspective of the beholder, it is quite another thing to hold that truth itself is relative. The latter position is a metaphysical theory which we shall not discuss. Relativism can be used as an excuse for the abdication of any intellectual and moral seriousness. It can justify exploitation and irrationalism. This is not the conclusion we wish to draw here. Rather we wish to ask, given the fact that any understanding of the Bible reflects the relativity of the perspective from which it is read, how we can proceed in our search for valid theological insight which is relevant to the reality in which we live? . . .

THE POLITICS OF UNDERSTANDING

We have seen that our goal of the liberation of the Bible is closely related to our ability to see the text in its own contexts. To be more precise, a liberated and liberating reading of the Bible must, at the level of *explicatio*, fulfill two conditions. First, the method must be available to groups of ordinary people who wish to listen to the Bible as a part of their reflection on the reality in which they live and on their own relationship to that reality. Second, the group must be free and able to distinguish the perspective of the group from the perspective of the text.

Yet at this point the method as we have outlined it is in danger of falling into a contradiction in practice. The problem is this: The method requires that the participants be aware of the context of the text. This awareness involves a relatively sophisticated knowledge of biblical scholarship. "Where," groups ask, "can we find the information we need to establish the contexts of the passages we study? How do we discover the passages which are relevant to the reality we are addressing?"

The temptation is to call in an expert. The expert locates the relevant texts. The expert supplies the background material.

Here the contradiction is introduced. The expert has a point of view too! The expert has ideological commitments. The very selection of the passage has to be studied; the way that the background material is structured cannot help but reflect the perspective of the expert. From the beginning the expert dominates the course of the study. There may be no intention to manipulate on the part of the expert. The contradiction is built into the expert's role.

The contradiction poses the dilemma which plagues many attempts at Bible study. The choice seems simple. One can do away with the expert in a burst of anti-intellectual populist enthusiasm. We know the result. The group is then dominated by the more aggressive representatives of the unofficial ideology of the group: the most pious or the most militant. What is worse, in dispensing with the expert the group dispenses with the kind of information that the expert can provide. Such an approach must, therefore, take history less than seriously. Turning one's back on the historical reality of the world of the Bible means that the text is treated, in practice if not in theory, as a fairy tale, a once-upon-a-time kind of story. (Note that the socioeconomic environment of Goldilocks is not very relevant to the story *Goldilocks and the Three Bears*. The date of Goldilocks' visit to the home of the bears is also irrelevant.) In theological terms, this denial of the relevance of history to the study of the Bible may be seen as a practical denial of the reality of the word of God.

The first approach, then, has the virtue of recognizing and rejecting the dominance of the expert. It fails to be liberating because, transforming history into fantasy, it is vulnerable to various kinds of ideological manipulation. The alternative approach, of course, is to affirm the dominance of the expert. Thus the relevance of the special knowledge and skills which are possessed by the expert is affirmed. The price is that the group is submitted to the prejudices and the personal agenda of the expert. Such an approach cannot be called liberating.

Is there a way out? Let us look at the problem again. We have assumed that all understanding involves prejudice. If so, it follows that no attempt to understand a text can be free of the perspective of the interpreter. If an ideologically free reading of the Bible is what we mean by liberation, we might as well forget it. There can be no such thing. Then what is the problem? If our understanding of the text is going to be "contaminated" by ideology anyway, why not "sin the more that grace may abound"?

What we need to clarify is that the problem of the liberation of the Bible is not ideology itself. The problem is the *dominance* of our ideology over the text. The struggle of *explicatio* is a struggle against the ways in which we allow our ideologies to *control* our reading of the text. Thus, in the use of experts, we are in danger of surrendering our reading of the text to the control of the expert's point of view. If we dispense with the expert, we apparently surrender control of our reading to prejudices we share, largely unconsciously, with our peers.

The aim of *explicatio* must be to approach the world of the text as consciously and as critically as we can of our own prejudices. The truth or falsity of our prejudices is not at issue here. What is at issue is that our prejudices should not dominate the text. On the contrary, we should be in a position to allow the text to expose and illumine the prejudices we bring to it. Our experience in entering the world of the text should be a form of consciousness raising.

But how? The information we need to enter the world of the text has to come from somewhere. We need the expertise of the specialist. Yet our very need seems to place us under the domination of the expert. We still have the dilemma. It is a dilemma which has plagued the churches since the rise of modern historical and critical Bible scholarship. In churches where this dependence on the expert has been rejected, the Bible is a living and powerful force in the lives of the people. In churches which have accepted the historical-critical method, and thereby the dominance of the expert in biblical studies, the people are alienated from a book which, they assume, is too difficult and too remote to understand.

It would be possible to examine this apparent alienation of people from the Bible in "liberal" churches from a number of perspectives. The dynamics are complex and take varied and subtle forms. At base, however, the study of the Bible has tended to become a problem of marketing biblical knowledge. The scholar produces knowledge about the Bible. The preacher is the distributor of the scholar's product. The layperson is the consumer. Given this underlying structure to our attitude to the Bible, it is not surprising that so many attempts to deal with the problem of biblical illiteracy have the appearance of a search for a new and better package for the product. No wonder people are alienated!

Without wishing to labor the analogy, it should be clear that if we wish to speak of the liberation of the Bible, the kind of marketing of biblical knowledge which moves from producer through distributor to consumer needs to be challenged. But how?

Let us recall what is involved in *explicatio*. There are two basic questions here. The first involves getting as complete a picture as we can of the world of the text. Here, it must be granted, some source of information is necessary. We can't all carry around the knowledge of archaeology, history, and textual studies that we require for any text we might wish to study. Yet we must recognize that what we need is not information about what the Bible *means*, but about the *context* within which the text has its basic meaning. There is a difference and, at this point, a very important one.

The "meaning" of a text must be understood in context. However, the meaning of a text is not identical to the context. One could know all there is to know about the context of a text and still miss the point. One can know relatively little about the context of a text and still make a pretty good guess about its basic intention. Ultimately, the intuition of what a text means in context is not a matter of expertise. It is a matter of creative insight.

What we look to the specialist for is not an exposition of a given text. Rather we need the background information which will help us to listen to the text in its own context. This distinction does not entirely remove the threat of the domination of a reading by the expert's viewpoint. If this distinction is ignored, however, the domination is virtually inevitable.

We might state this conclusion in another way by saying that the role of the specialist in biblical reflection is that of a resource rather than of an "expert." The problem of the group which is engaged in biblical reflection is that of finding resources. How do you go about it?

It means work. Unless a group includes a number of members with a relatively sophisticated knowledge of the history and culture of the ancient Middle East, it will be necessary to research the background of the text before the group deals with it. The questions which should be answered are these:

1. When was the text written?
2. Who was the author of the text?
3. What important historical events and developments were taking place at the time of the text?
4. What forms of social organization are reflected in the text?
5. To whom is the text addressed?

The answers to these questions will be found most easily in general introductions to the Bible and in commentaries. Groups should be careful to do their research with more than one resource. Every resource has its own set of prejudices. Watch for them!

Understanding is always political in this sense: What we "know," what we understand, always takes place in a social context. The social context is constituted by a complex system of social relationships. Among other things, these relationships are power relationships. They are relationships between the dominating and the dominated. This fact of the sociology of understanding is put very simply in Marx's remark that the dominant ideas of any society are the ideas of the dominant classes of that society. Put more generally, we can say that understanding never occurs in a political vacuum. Dominance and submission in the realm of ideas is still dominance and submission.

There can be no escape from this kind of politics of understanding. In terms of our analysis of the method of biblical reflection, relations of dominance and submission arise at every stage. *Who selects the text? Why is this text chosen? What interests are reflected in the resources which the group is using? In whose interest is it to read a text the way we do? Why do we analyze our contemporary reality the way we do? Why do we apply the text in one way rather than another?* In relation to all our questions we need to ask, *whose interest is being served?*

If we find this notion disturbing, it is very likely our liberal conditioning at work. In the understanding of the feudal church (an understanding which survived in the Roman Catholic church at least until Vatican II and which still appears to be alive and well in the Curia) there was no question about the right of the hierarchy to dominate the church's theory and practice of faith. In many right-wing groups there is similarly no question about the right of the leader who is "blessed by God" to dominate the thinking of the group. On the left, radicals understand quite well—particularly in the relation of class interest to ideology—the connections between understanding and power.

The problem is not to eliminate relationships of power from the study of the Bible. That would be an illusory task. Neither is the problem to legitimate those relationships that would be oppressive. The problem is to be aware of the politics of biblical reflection. Only when we are aware of the power relationships which we bring into the process of reflection can we begin to think and act freely in relation to them.

The power relationships which are relevant to biblical reflection exist on two levels. First, there are the external power relationships; the relationships which order society as a whole. Since we live our lives in the context of these relationships we necessarily bring to the task of biblical reflection a type of thinking which is molded by the world we live in. We then have to ask, in relation to any specific text, the question of class interest. Who stands to benefit if we read the text one way rather than another? Second, we have to deal with the internal relationships within the study group. Who is dominating the discussion? How is he doing it? Why? On both levels, a liberated reading of the Bible must be accompanied by a healthy exercise of suspicion.

DOING THEOLOGY

When we speak of the "liberation" of the Bible we mean two things. First of all, we mean the liberation of the Bible in quite a public sense. We observed that in the media there has been a tendency for the Bible to be presented as a reactionary document. The question we face, then, is how we can effectively challenge this view of what the Bible is. At the same time, most of us who have been raised in the so-called mainline denominations face another kind of captivity. The Bible as we have been exposed to it in Sunday School and in sermons is a very liberal document. So here the challenge of the liberation of the Bible is a challenge to something that is very much part of ourselves. How can we get the kind of critical distance from our own assumptions so that this kind of ideological captivity can be questioned?

This brings us to the second meaning of the term *liberation*. In liberating the Bible from its various captivities we find that we have to engage in a process of personal liberation as well. The mechanisms which allow the Bible to be placed in ideological captivity are built into the very nature of understanding. We have found that self-criticism and consciousness-raising are absolutely necessary in any attempt to engage in a liberated reading of the Bible.

To help ourselves along the way we have formulated a "method" for Bible reflection consisting of four steps in two movements. The first movement takes us into the world of the text. It consists of (1) determining the context of the text, and (2) reading the text in the light of its context. We have called this movement *explicatio*. The second movement, which we have called *applicatio*, brings the text into relation with our contemporary reality. *Applicatio* consists of two steps: (1) reflection on the similarities and differences between the world of the text and our world and (2) a decision on how the text might be relevant to our reality in the light of this reflection.

Now it must be confessed that the method is really not a method at all. It is simply a formalization of what happens of necessity in any theological reflection on the Bible. To read a biblical text, one must presuppose a context for it. If we do not know the context of a text, we must imagine one. We may very well imagine wrong. It is not possible to understand a text in abstraction from any context at all. Similarly to decide that a text applies to our world in a specific way is to assume that our world is sufficiently like the world of the text to make our application appropriate.

What the method does is simply to analyze the act of theological reflection and to identify the steps we perform. What is important is that we recognize what we are doing and to acknowledge the need to perform each step in a responsible way.

This formulation of the steps involved will be helpful to those who are new to biblical reflection. To this extent, it is appropriate to see the formalization as a method. As a method, however, it is meant to be put aside once its purpose has been achieved. Ultimately biblical reflection cannot be separated neatly into *explicatio* and *applicatio*. To enter the world of the text, in *explicatio*, is already to gain new perspective on one's own world. *Explicatio* involves *applicatio*.

There are two major weaknesses in the formalization when it is considered as a method. The first weakness is that no method can program creative insight into the reading of the Bible. Yet without creativity it is difficult to see how any reading could be described as liberated and liberating.

In *explicatio*, we have already indicated the need for creative insight. It is one thing, for example, to know everything that there is to know about the world of Paul. It is quite another thing to see that world through Paul's eyes. The latter step is an act of creative imagination. Here method is no substitute for creativity.

The role of creativity in *applicatio* is just as decisive. Here creativity takes the form of seeing new possibilities in the text, the risk of departing from old and well-worn applications.

The first weakness of the formalization, considered as method, is that it does not create imaginative insight. The second weakness lies in apparently isolating *applicatio* as a discrete step in the method. It seems that once you have done everything else, it is time to make up a moral to the story. When actually performed that way, the applications come out sounding pompous and cliché-ridden. To consider the relevance of a text as a distinct step in the process of biblical reflection is to expect too little and too much. It is to expect too much of a formal process to hope to capture in words the impact of the text on our world. It is to expect too little of *applicatio* to confine it to a formal step in biblical reflection.

Applicatio is theological praxis. It is "doing theology." The term *praxis* designates the interrelationship of thought and action. *Applicatio* is the bridge between reflection and action.

What we have to notice is that biblical reflection is not something which is autonomous. It is possible, of course, to attempt a kind of autonomous Bible study. One could discuss the application as a kind of ideal, leaving it quite open and optional whether the discussion would actually affect the lives of the participants. Indeed, this is often done. We have to insist that this kind of reading of the text is not liberated because it is not liberative. By stopping the application at the level of ideas, the Bible is held in a kind of captivity which, if not ideological, is at least idealistic. It is only when *applicatio* is construed as *praxis* that we can speak in any genuine sense of the liberation of the Bible.

What this implies is that a liberated and liberating reflection on the Bible is possible only on the basis of a theological commitment. Biblical reflection involves a commitment to listen to Scripture and to act on the word we hear.

To this point we have avoided traditional theological language as much as possible. It is time we drew some connections between what we have been saying and some of the theologians which we are used to hearing. By calling Scripture "the word of God," the church has expressed the confidence that in a faithful hearing of Scripture the will of God can, in fact, be encountered by human beings. The qualification "faithful" is important. It implies that not every hearing of the word of Scripture is a hearing of the word of God. The church has further made the qualification that only the Holy Spirit is the legitimate interpreter of Scripture—a warning that no automatic and mechanical application of Scripture is possible. *No method will ensure a liberated and liberative reading of the Bible.*

It is not the purpose of this study to elaborate on the traditional theological formulations. Yet the term "faith" needs particular attention. This word has had an unfortunate history in that it has been perennially interpreted as something which is contrasted with human *activity*. Thus, if we think of human life in terms of thought, emotions, and activity, faith tends to be understood as a kind of thinking or a kind of feeling. In doctrinaire churches, faith has tended to be understood as a kind of belief, as a matter of one's religious opinions. In revivalistic churches and sects, on the other hand, faith has come to be associated with the emotions, a matter of the heart. In neither case is faith interpreted directly as a matter of activity.

This assigning of faith to what we may call human passivity (as opposed to activity) is not something new. When the Pauline doctrine of salvation by faith alone gained some standing in the early church, it was opposed by the Epistle of James, for just this reason. The author of James assumes that faith is something other than activity. "Show me your faith apart from your works, and I by my works will show you my faith. You believe that God is one; you do well. Even the demons believe—and shudder" (James 2:18-19). Clearly faith is here equated with belief.

It is worth setting against James something that Paul says. In the epistle to the Romans, Paul had been concerned to spell out his objections to a doctrine of salvation by works of the law. Yet after stating and restating his conviction that salvation can only be by faith, Paul remarks: "If you confess with your lips that Jesus is Lord and believe in your heart that God raised him from the dead, you shall be saved" (Rom. 10:9). It might be easy to miss the significance of this remark. We must remember that in Paul's context the confession "Jesus is Lord" was not a kind of automatic doctrinal cliché. To confess with one's lips that Jesus is Lord was, to those in Paul's time, a political act of no little consequence. What Paul suggests, here and elsewhere, is that "faith" somehow includes activity with thought and feeling.

Instead of seeing faith as a matter of belief or of feeling, we are well advised to see faith as *praxis*. Faith, in relation to Scripture, is the commitment to listen to Scripture and to act on the word we hear. Faith is presupposed in any genuine *applicatio*.

The association of the words "faith" and "belief" is very strong in our culture and, of course, they are connected. They are not, however, identical. Let us characterize "belief" as belief of doctrines. (In philosophy of religion, a distinction is often made between "belief that" and "belief in." The latter is close to what we mean by "faith." We are considering belief as "belief that.") Belief expresses itself as the assent to certain propositions about God and man. "I believe that there is a God." "I believe that Jesus is the Son of God." "I believe that Jesus died to save humankind." "I believe that there is life after death." And so on.

It is important to understand the nature of doctrine which is the substance of belief. The classical creeds—particularly the Apostles' Creed and the Nicene Creed—can be seen as models of doctrinal statements. What are the creeds? And where do they come from?

Recall the basic principle with which we insisted the Bible be interpreted. Texts must be understood in context. The context of the creeds is the life of the early church. The creeds arose out of the *praxis* of the early church. As Christians moved between the poles of listening to the testimony of the Apostles and facing the challenges of the reality in which they lived, certain statements became important as expressing the difference between an authentic *praxis* and a false one. Behind each creedal statement lay practical issues which the church felt were matters of life and death for the community.

What happens, however, when these statements are formalized into creeds and passed on from generation to generation is that the creeds become statements without a context. It is assumed that in the creeds we have statements which can say essentially the same thing in any and every context.

In fact, the creeds have done rather well in presenting a distillation of belief to which Christians in various eras have been able to give their assent. The assumption that belief can be constant in changing circumstances is naive and fallacious, however. Only propositions of mathematics have this kind of constancy. Statements of substance are always embedded in history.

We need to make a distinction here between theology and doctrine. This distinction may have to be drawn at the price of making a bit of a caricature of the word "doctrine." If so, I apologize. The distinction is important even though some may wish to dispute the words with which the distinction is made.

Theology is the community's reflection on its *praxis*. Theology is the representation in terms of ideas which arises from the community's hearing of Scripture and its acting on the word it hears. Theology is, therefore, part and parcel of the ongoing life of the community.

Doctrine is what happens when theology is presented in abstraction from the concrete life of the community in which it arises. Doctrine is saying that Jesus is "very man and very God" without reference to the very concrete temptations which the church of the fifth century faced to say that Jesus was *not quite* "very man" and *not quite* "very God," and without reference to the implications that such temptations held for the life of the Christian community.

This distinction is necessary to talk about the "theological commitment" which we have claimed to be necessary for a liberated and liberative reading of the Bible. The point which has to be made is that what we call a "theological commitment" is not necessarily a "doctrinal commitment."

Faith is not equivalent to belief. Theology is not equivalent to doctrine. A doctrinal commitment would be a commitment which placed a priori limitations on what could be heard from Scripture. It would determine in advance what Scripture would have to tell us. This kind of limitation is just a variant on what we have called the "ideological captivity" of the Bible.

What we mean by theological commitment can be put most simply in biblical terms: "He who has ears to hear, let him hear." There is no need to set doctrinal pre-conditions here. Obviously a person to whom all "God-talk" is simply nonsense will not have much desire to listen. The theological commitment is simply commitment to a *praxis* of hearing and acting. In the process of doing theology, the problems of doctrine will present themselves in their own place and in their own way. It would be improper, indeed self-defeating, to determine them in advance.

Theological commitment is commitment to *praxis*. We need to be warned. Biblical reflection is not something one does as a hobby, in one's spare time. Biblical reflection is not something which can be done as a kind of philosophical discussion, a kind of playing with ideas because ideas are interesting. Biblical reflection cannot be separated from the response we make to the reflection in the face of the concrete questions and concerns which life throws at us. In biblical reflection we are responsible to each other, not only for our ideas but for our *praxis* as a whole. One cannot liberate the Bible privately. That is an individualistic illusion characteristic of our liberal heritage. The liberation of the Bible can happen only when people come together in faith and hope and love to seek a unity of belief and action which is the essence of theological *praxis*.

The forms which this coming together may take can vary quite widely. It may happen in issue-oriented groups who wish to get a theological perspective of the questions with which they are already involved. It may happen in groups who gather simply to study the Bible and find what they are hearing directs them to grapple with specific personal, social, and political issues. It may even happen in the ongoing life of a local congregation in its recurring movement from world to word and back again. Yet it is only when this coming together happens that the Bible demonstrates its freedom to speak to the world in which people live.

Let us close where we started: the problem of ideology. We have seen that there is no simple correspondence between the ideological options of the contemporary world and those of the world of the Bible. Further, we have seen that although the Bible is not ideologically neutral, neither is it an ideological unity. The Bible does not prescribe an ideology for our time in any simple and direct way.

Yet we live in a world where crucial ideological issues are at stake. How are we to live in a world and to mold the future of a world in crisis — a world divided between rich and poor, oppressor and oppressed, powerful and powerless? And what does theological *praxis* have to do with it? How do we choose our options with theological responsibility?

These questions can be answered only in the *doing of theology*. An ideological choice which could be specified a priori would simply bind the Bible once again to ideological bondage. It is only in the commitment to hear and to do that the Bible can demonstrate its relevance to the world we inhabit.

11

NORMAN K. GOTTWALD

Sociological Method in the Study of Ancient Israel

Sociological method in Old Testament studies supplements and enriches historical method by providing a complementary grid of understanding for viewing biblical communities as social entities in process. The biblical communities arose, developed, and declined according to regularities known from a wide range of studies in comparative anthropology and social history.

The fruitfulness of sociological method for understanding the origins of Israel as a social revolutionary movement primarily of peasants; for delineating Israel in relation to Canaanites, 'apiru, pastoral nomads, and Philistines; and for assessing the social organization presupposed in the patriarchal narratives is illustrated. The necessity of carefully applied sociological theory and method in order to avoid arbitrary and unsupportable comparisons between Israel and other peoples is underscored by these examples.

The article explains the methodological framework that informs the author's The Tribes of Yahweh: A Sociology of the Religion of Liberated Israel, 1250-1050 B.C.E. *(Maryknoll, N.Y.: Orbis Books, 1979).*

Reprinted from *Encounter with the Text: Form and History in the Hebrew Bible*, ed. M. J. Buss (Philadelphia: Fortress Press, and Missoula: Scholars Press, 1979), 69-81.

Historical method and sociological method are different but compatible methods for reconstructing ancient Israelite life and thought. Historical study of ancient Israel aims at grasping the sequential articulation of Israel's experience and the rich variety of its cultural products, outstandingly its literature and religion. Sociological study of ancient Israel aims at grasping the typical patterns of human relations in their structure and function, both at a given moment or stage (synchronics) and in their trajectories of change over specified time spans (diachronics). The hypothetically "typical" in collective human behavior is sought by comparative study of societies and expressed theoretically in "laws," "regularities," or "tendencies" that attempt to abstract translocal and transtemporal structural or processual realities within the great mass of spatiotemporal particularities. In such terms, the tribal phase of Israel's social history is greatly illuminated by a theoretical design of social organization (as developed by Sahlins and Fried, among others).[1]

Historical method embraces all the methods of inquiry drawn from the humanities (e.g., literary criticism, form criticism, tradition history, rhetorical criticism, redaction criticism, history, history of religion, biblical theology). Sociological method includes all the methods of inquiry proper to the social sciences (e.g., anthropology, sociology, political science, economics). Sociological method in data collection and theory building enables us to analyze, synthesize, abstract, and interpret Israelite life and thought along different axes and with different tools and constructs from those familiar to us from historical method. Sociological inquiry recognizes people as social actors and symbolizers who "perform" according to interconnecting regularities and within boundaries or limits (social systems).

If we wish to reconstruct ancient Israel as a lived totality, historical method and sociological method are requisite complementary disciplines. Historical method has long recognized the need for collaboration with archaeology, which as a discipline does not fit immediately or comfortably into the molds of the humanities. It is increasingly clear that the need of historical method for sociological inquiry into ancient Israel is just as urgent as its need for archaeology.

The social system of ancient Israel signifies the whole complex of communal interactions embracing functions, roles, institutions, customs, norms, symbols, and the processes and networks distinctive to the subsystems of social organization (economic production, political order, military defense, judicatory procedure, religious organization, etc.). This social system must be grasped in its activity both in the communal production of goods, services, and ideas and in the communal control of their distribution and use.

We must resist the tendency to objectify Israel's social system into a static and monolithic hypostasis. It developed unevenly, underwent change, and incorporated tension and conflict. It was a framework for human interaction in which stability struggled against change and change eroded away stability. To call this complex of human interaction a social system is meaningful in that it was something more than an aggregation of discrete interhuman relations. There were regularities in the ways that Israelites organized their actions and thoughts, cooperated and contended with one another and with outside groups. These regularities form an analyzable system in the additional sense that they placed Israelite behavior and valuing under impulses and pressures toward normativeness or standardization. The social system tended to validate particular uses and distributions of natural and human resources and to delimit the exercises and distributions of personal and public power. The social system supplied the constraints of physical coercion and symbolic persuasion. By carefully noting the regularities and normative tendencies, it is possible to identify deviations and idiosyncrasies, both those that appear to have been "social waste" and those that augured "social innovation."

The materials for sociological study of ancient Israel are the biblical text and all available extrabiblical evidence, written and material. In addition, the contents, structures, and developmental trajectories of other social systems — whether in Israel's immediate milieu or far beyond in time and space — are potentially relevant for comparative study. What is vital is that those contents, structures, and trajectories be examined in their total contexts and that they be compared with Israel in its total context. Alleged comparison of isolated social data torn out of systemic context is not comparison at all, but superficial juxtaposition lacking criteria for evaluation.

Sociological method works as a totality with its own analytic tools and theoretical perspectives quite as much as does historical method. Since historical method has already "staked out" the field of biblical study, sociological method tends to arrive on the scene as a "tacked on" adjunct to the customary privileged methods. As long as it performs in the role of supplying addenda or trying to do "rescue work" on texts and historical problems that are momentarily resistant to historical methods, sociological method in biblical study will appear tangential and quixotic, as a problematic interloper.[2]

In any given text the sociological data may be no more than traces or shattered torsos. What are we to make, for example, of the kinship and marriage patterns attested in the patriarchal accounts? When sociological method is called in to assist on this problem, it must try to contextualize the fragments within their larger complexes. So far, what is loosely called "sociological" inquiry in this instance is a ransacking of ancient Near Eastern societies for parallel social phenomena. As in the appeal to Nuzi parallels to patriarchal kinship and marriage practices, insufficient attention is paid to the nature of the compared texts and to the social systems presupposed by the texts.

We are becoming freshly aware of the scandalous imprecision of such "sociological" dabbling in the patriarchal traditions. The historical and social loci of the patriarchal traditions are simply not specifiable with any degree of confidence, and, in fact, there is every reason to believe that the historical and social horizons of the separate units and cycles of tradition are highly diverse.[3] In this stalemated situation, sociological inquiry can be most helpful when it extends the examination of how biblical texts with similar social data function in relation to texts or traditions of a similar nature among other peoples, whether literate or preliterate. Working on its own ground, sociological method will try to build up a body of knowledge about types or families of texts and traditions containing social data of certain kinds. How do these tradition types reflect or refract

social reality in various types of social systems? How, for example, do genealogies function in oral and written traditions, as separate pieces and as elements
within larger compositions, in tribal and in statist societies, etc.?[4]

In other words, a sociology of ancient Israel can be a proper complement to
literary and historical inquiry only as it pursues its own proper object of reconstructing the Israelite social system as a totality, without prejudging which of
its results are likely to be germane to understanding specific texts or historical
problems and without diverting too much energy at the start to narrowly or
obscurely framed "social puzzles" in idiosyncratic literary and historical contexts.

In order to approximate comprehensive reconstruction of the Israelite social
system, sociological method depends upon literary and historical criticism to
undertake their tasks in a similarly comprehensive and systemic way. It also
relies upon archaeology to break loose from the domination of historically
framed orientations and to become an instrument for recovering the total material life of ancient Israelites irrespective of immediate applications to texts or
to historical and sociological problems.

We may illustrate the way the integral projects of sociological method inter-
sect with historical methods by noting the impact of the introduction of a new
model for understanding the origins of Israel within its Canaanite matrix. The
proposal that earliest Israel was not an invading or infiltrating people but a
social revolutionary peasant movement within Canaan is at least a quasi-soci-
ological model.[5] This heuristic model gives a new way of looking at all the old
texts, biblical and extrabiblical, and the material remains.[6] Its effect has been
to shift attention away from the precise historical circumstances of Israel's
occupation of Canaan and toward the social processes by which Israel came to
dominance. The effort to reconstruct a history of the occupation has long been
deadended by the sparse historical data. A sociological model in this case provides a way of reviewing the fragmentary historical data and in the end may
help us to understand why the historical data are as obscure as they are. Finally,
the specifically historical project of identifying the agents and spatiotemporal
course of the emergent dominion of Israel in Canaan may be freshly facilitated
by the working out of a different conception of the process at work in that
achievement.

The effect of the peasant-revolt model of the origins of Israel has been to
replace uncritical cultural assumptions about Israel's alleged pastoral nomadism
with sharper sociological inquiry into the internal composition of early Israel,
demographically and socioeconomically.[7] What exactly was this formation of
people called Israel which took control in Canaan and whose social system took
form as it gained the upper hand in the land? From what social spaces in Syro-
Palestine did these people derive? What brought them together, enabled them
to collaborate and to succeed? What were the goals these people shared and
what social instrumentalities and material conditions contributed to their
accomplishment? How does this social system of earliest Israel relate to those
that preceded it and those against which it was counter-posed? In other words,
a proper model of the Israelite emergence in Canaan is not attainable apart

from a proper model of the social system of the people who gained dominion in the land.[8] And of course neither the historical course of Israel's coming to power nor its emergent social system can be grasped without an understanding of the cultic-ideological process of tradition formation.

Up to the present, biblical studies have grappled with a model of the settlement and with a model of the cultic production of traditions, but there has been no adequate mediation between these two forms of inquiry within a larger analytic model of the social system involved in the twin process of taking power in the land and of building its own traditions. Martin Noth and George Mendenhall have made suggestive, incomplete, and at times mistaken attempts at an encompassing societal model. By drawing together the seminal contributions of Noth and Mendenhall, while weeding out their errors and false starts, we have the beginnings of a comprehensive social model for early Israel—or, more precisely, we have an inventory of the questions to be pursued and a general sense of the appropriate range of model options.[9]

A theoretical model of the origins and operations of early Israelite society will entail two axes of investigation: (1) the analysis of Israel's internal composition and structure at its several organizational levels and in its sectoral subsystems; (2) the characterization of Israel's social system as an operational and developing totality in comparison and contrast with other social systems. Both types of inquiry have synchronic and diachronic dimensions, and both types of inquiry will proceed dialectically in movement back and forth between concrete data about specific social systems and more abstract heuristic models, such as a theoretical design of "tribalism."[10]

As for the first task, evidence of the internal composition and eclectic structure of early Israel is largely biblical, but there are significant checkpoints in the Ugaritic, Alalakh, and Amarna texts, as well as rich resources concerning the material culture which have yet to be sufficiently mined. These immediate social data must be reflected upon against the backdrop of the large body of information and theory we now possess as a consequence of anthropological field studies, work in pre-history, and theorizing about social organization.

To what levels, ranges, and functions of social organization do the designations *ševeṭ, mišpaḥa,* and *beth-'av* refer? To date it has seemed sufficient to give them the native meanings of "tribe," "clan," and "household" or "extended family," without further ado. If early Israel is conceivable as a form of "retribalization," what were the bonding organizational elements for holding together the segmented "tribes" of diverse origin? Noth provided the summary answer of "a sacral league," but his analogy between the Greek amphictyony and the intertribal league of Israel holds good at such an abstract level that it is of doubtful value in illuminating the crucial features of Israel's retribalization process. If Israel was a revolutionary movement within Canaanite society, how did matters develop from the uncoordinated restiveness of peasants and '*apiru* in Amarna days into the coalition of Israelite tribes? So far only Alt has offered a bare sketch of diachronic possibilities.[11] Merely appealing to Mosaic traditions and Yahwistic faith as "explanations" for this coalescing process does not clarify and reconstruct the arduous struggle by which Israel put itself together in Canaan.

As for the second task, what was the over-all character of Israel's social system in comparison with other preceding and contemporary social systems? Such a comparison depends upon prior analysis of the social systems compared, and this analysis must follow an inventory of social desiderata so that we do not simply accept at face value either the form or the preponderance of specific social data as they happen to appear to us in texts. The comparison of social systems must constantly contextualize social systems and subsystems within the systems as a whole and in terms of the direction of their movement (e.g., expansion, differentiation, decline, transition to new systems, etc.).

Whether two different social complexes can be meaningfully compared is of course a matter of much discussion.[12] In biblical studies there has been an abundance of hasty and superficial cross-cultural comparisons. With each new discovery in the ancient Near East—such as the Amarna, Mari, Ugaritic, or Ebla texts—there has been a rush of claims for direct correlations between them and the biblical text, or for wholesale borrowings of systems or institutions or offices by Israel. On more careful analysis these "parallels" either vanish or are greatly scaled down and nuanced. Such defaults establish the urgency of developing more reliable ways of comparing and contrasting social data and systems. If we wish, for example, to compare early Israelite society with its Canaanite counterpart and matrix, we face serious gaps in our knowledge of aspects of both entities, but these difficulties need to be brought out more systematically so that we will be clearer about the explanatory strength or weakness of our theory and thereby more aware of the kinds of research needed to test and improve theory.

It is evident that comparison of early Israel with other contemporary social systems entails diachronic and synchronic approaches. The social systems under comparison were not static, isolated entities; they developed internally and stood in varying relations to one another over spans of time and in different regions. A great deal of nuancing in treating these societal interfaces is required, often dismally lacking, for example, in the way "Canaan" and "Israel" are counter-posed by biblical scholars, like characters in a morality play. According to all known analogies of revolutionary movements, we should expect that by no means all of the people of Canaan will have been "polarized" by the nascent Israelite movement. It should be expected that as the Canaanite and rising Israelite social systems collided and conflicted, there will have been many people—probably a majority at first—who were conflicted in their own feelings and stances toward the two options. We should expect to find those who strove for neutrality, by choice or necessity, some who were half-hearted converts and those who switched sides, others who were secret supporters and yet others who were opportunist in their allegiances.[13] A reexamination of Israel's early traditions in terms of these dynamics of social revolutionary movements will reveal unexpected results toward a clearer conception of how Israel arose. The result is likely to be that the initially simplistic-appearing peasant revolt model will turn out to be even more complex and nuanced than the previous conquest and immigration models of Israel's origins.

In pursuing the comparative approach to Israelite society a major issue is how we are to decide which social systems should be compared with Israel's. Here we encounter the vexed problem of determining the boundaries of social systems in relation to the boundaries of the various historic state, tribal, and cultural formations which appear under various, vaguely depicted proper names and gentilics in the biblical and extrabiblical texts. No doubt we should identify the Canaanite city-state system as the dominant and definitive social system within earliest Israel's horizon.[14] But do the *'apiru* of the Amarna period form another such system? Here the time trajectory enters into consideration. The *'apiru* appear as a sub-set within Amarna "feudalism" or Asiatic mode of production,[15] but insofar as the *'apiru* are seen as forerunners and one of the contributors to early Israel, they may indeed merit attention as another social system in embryo or as one trajectory along which the Canaanite social system declined and the Israelite social system rose. And it would be a grave methodological error to assume that early Israel arose along only one such trajectory. More often than not, the relation of the *apiru* to early Israel has been examined as though it was the only or the primary pertinent relationship and that, if the *apiru* data could not account for all or most of the features of early Israel, then they were irrelevant.

Pastoral nomadism as the supposed socioeconomic condition of early Israel might be viewed as another social system, but we now see how doubtful it is that we can locate an autonomous pastoral nomadic system in the immediate environment of Canaan contemporary with early Israel. The trans-human, village-based pastoral nomadism of Israel's environment was a minor sub-set of village tribalism subordinated socioeconomically and politically to sedentary Canaan. This pastoral nomadism was at most a minor contributor to early Israel. Nonetheless, it is necessary that this pastoral nomadic sub-specialization of village tribalism be carefully analyzed in order to reassess properly its vastly overstated role in Israelite origins.[16]

Other possible social systems in Israel's milieu come to mind. Do the Philistines constitute a new social system or are they merely heirs of the Canaanite system with new organizational twists, mostly of a political and military nature?[17] And what are we to make of the Ammonites, Moabites, and Edomites, whose origins were roughly contemporary with Israel and yet who did not become a part of Israel? Did these people feel the tug of Israel's social mutation, did some of them actually engage in social revolution, and if so, why did they accept kingship earlier than did Israel itself?[18]

Against this methodological sketch, we can see why the patriarchal traditions are particularly resistant to sociological analysis. From all appearances, those traditions belong to any number of peoples moving along various trajectories toward their convergence in early Israel. The patriarchal groups are proto-Israelites. Just as Noth recognized that the patriarchal traditions can only be approached backwards, working out of the congealing traditions of united Israel in Canaan, so the sociological analysis of the patriarchal communities must be approached backwards from the coalescing peoples of the intertribal community in Israelite Canaan. No sociological wonders will be workable on the patriarchal traditions until much more is known of their literary form and function, of their temporal horizons, and of their rootage in one or another of the social trajectories along which sectors of the Syro-Palestinian peoples converged toward their unity in Israel.[19]

An instance of the great difficulties in precise sociological analysis of the groups represented in the patriarchal traditions of Genesis 25-35 is the practice of using the connubium reported in Genesis 34 between Shechemites and Israelites as evidence for clan exogamy, a habit that goes back at least to the nineteenth-century anthropologist E. B. Tylor.

Genesis 34 tells us only that the two parties began to reach agreement on an alliance that was to include the exchange of wives. It does *not* tell us that a presupposition for the proposed wife-exchange was that Israelites or Shechemites could not marry among themselves and thus were obliged to get wives from outside. It does *not* tell us that the wives to be exchanged between the group constituted all or most of the marriage arrangements to be made by Israelites and Shechemites, thereby sharply reducing or excluding intragroup marriages or intermarriage with other groups. In other words, since we do not know the actual scope demographically or the internal social structure of the two contracting entities in Genesis 34, we have to try out various hypotheses to see how clan-exogamous they look on close examination. The results are not reassuring.

If, for example, "Israel" in Genesis 34 was actually only a relatively small social group (still proto-Israelite), the connubium formula might be read—especially noting the phrase "we will become one people" (v. 16)—as alluding to an early endeavor to meld together two groups of people into one tribal formation as complementary moieties. We might in that case be witnessing an initial act by which a member of later Israel (Manasseh or a section of Manasseh?) was formed from two originally separate groups that become segments practicing exogamy and thus exchanging wives within the newly shaped tribe. Granted that the formation was not carried through according to Genesis 34, it could at least be construed that connubium covenant was a means by which some peoples did come together as tribal entities within Israel, the tribes being built up by exogamous clans.

If, on the other hand, we imagine (as the final state of the text certainly does), that many Israelite tribes are present and that this is an "external" arrangement between autonomous entities, a matter of intertribal "foreign policy," we could say that Israel developed, or sought to develop, peaceful relations with some surrounding peoples by connubium covenant. But would a tribal organization (Israel) and a city organization (Shechem) be likely to enter into such an exogamous connubium? Would a large assemblage of tribes be able to get enough wives from one city for an exclusive connubium if exogamy forbade marriage of Israelites to fellow Israelites? The anthropological evidence is that whole tribes are not exogamous; it is clans within a tribe that are exogamous and that take wives from and give wives to other exogamous clans, the tribe as a whole remaining endogamous (although marriages may be allowed or prescribed outside the tribe in certain cases). The more large-scale the Israelite partner in the proposed connubium is conceived to have been, the more likely it becomes that the group already would have worked out marriage patterns, exogamous or otherwise (that cannot be known from the text), among its member units, and thus the more peripheral the connubium with Shechem would become as a wife-exchange mechanism and the more it would look like an alliance sealed with limited intermarriage bearing no correlation whatsoever with exogamy rules. Maybe the difficulties can be eased by conceiving the proposed connubium as an arrangement involving only a single clan or group of clans (of Manasseh?) located in the vicinity of Shechem. In that way a possible symmetrical, exogamously based exchange of wives could be made plausible, but that hypothesis still fails to deal with the issue of whether a city would be interested in, or capable of, wholesale exogamy.

The farther our analysis and speculation about alternatives runs, the more evident it becomes that even if Genesis 34 goes back to early times, the obstacles to perceiving its exact sociohistoric context, the parties involved, and the mechanisms posited, are insuperably opposed to any reasonable confidence that this tradition shows the existence of exogamous clans in early Israel. A careful examination of other early biblical traditions thought to attest to clan exogamy yields similarly doubtful or flatly negative results.[20]

A main sociological task in the study of early Israel is the development of an adequate socioeconomic and cultural material inventory. This will require further historicoterritorial and topological studies (of the sort begun by Alt and carried on by Rowton). Archaeology will have to attend not only to fortified cities but to the agricultural village/neighborhood complexes that included settlements, roads, fields, springs, irrigation, terrace systems, etc. Renewed attention will have to be given to population size, density, and distribution. The role of technological factors taken in combination will have to be explored more thoroughly: the introduction of iron, waterproof cisterns, improved terracing, and irrigation works. The archaeology of biblical Israel, previously overwhelmingly oriented to direct synchronizations with biblical literature and history (e.g., who were the kings of Genesis 14:1?), will increasingly offer a wider spectrum of data for the social and cultural reconstruction of the early Israelite movement. More and more we can hope for the collaboration of all methodologies in clarifying the material and socioreligious processes by which the Israelites came into dominance in the hill country of Canaan.[21]

The sociological inquiry which I have here illustrated in the instance of Israel's origins will equally apply to the major social transition to the monarchy and the resulting tensions and conflicts between state, empire, and tribe, as well as to the later period of the disintegration of the Israelite states and the survival and reconstruction of social forms into the postexilic age. It is obvious that in this task it will be necessary to call upon a host of specialists so far only sporadically enlisted in the task of reconstructing ancient Israel, e.g., agronomists, botanists, hydrologists, geologists, demographers, etc. The reconstructed cultural-material complexes will bear important indicators for social, military, and religious organization, especially when contextually compared with agrarian complexes and urban center/rural periphery complexes of similar sorts that can be studied at first hand by contemporary ethnologists.

In sum, it is essential that we devise a constructive model of the Israelite social system in its own right, firmly rooted in its material conditions, a model which delineates the major subsystems and segmented organization, as well as a model that grasps the integrating mechanisms and the solidifying ideology of the social whole.[22] This model will necessarily be viewed genetically in order to show how Israel arose, achieved its first cohesive form, and then passed over into other forms in the course of time through a combination of internal and external pressures. Synchronics and diachronics, internal dynamics and external interfaces and interpenetrations will be drawn together under the principle or law of internal relations whereby an alteration in any element of the whole will be seen to bring about alterations in the entire system.

A model of the Israelite social system will incorporate the highly centralized and richly articulated religion of Yahweh. But it must do so sociologically by understanding the religion as a social phenomenon (institutionally and symbolically) and therefore related to all the other social phenomena within the system by the law of internal relations. This socioreligious inquiry must proceed without simplistic recourse to the tautological, philosophically idealist claim that because religion was central to the social system, it can be posited as the unmoved mover of the Israelite mutation.[23]

The sociological contribution to biblical hermeneutics is that the Israelite traditions must not only be interpreted within their original matrices, but must be interpreted from out of the social matrix of the interpreter. In the end it will be learned that an adequate biblical hermeneutics will require the investigation of the evolution of social forms and systems from biblical times until the present![24] Any interpreter who claims continuity with the biblical texts must also assume the continuity of the history of social forms as an indispensable precondition of the hermeneutical task.

NOTES

1. Marshall Sahlins, *Tribesmen* (Englewood Cliffs, N.J.: Prentice-Hall, 1968); Morton H. Fried, *The Evolution of Political Society: An Evolutionary View* (New York: Random House, 1968).

2. Frank S. Frick and Norman K. Gottwald, "The Social World of Ancient Israel," *SBLSP* 1 (1975), pp. 165-78.

3. The precariousness of attaching patriarchal tradition to Bronze Age historical and social settings is independently demonstrated by Thomas L. Thompson, *The Historicity of the Patriarchal Narratives: The Quest for the Historical Abraham* (Berlin: de Gruyter, 1974) and John Van Seters, *Abraham in History and Tradition* (New Haven: Yale University Press, 1975).

4. Renger, working with Amorite texts in which he finds exogamous clan organizations, posits patriarchal exogamy for the biblical patriarchs, but can only succeed by capriciously regarding the biblical genealogies sometimes as actual descent lineages and sometimes as fictitious or eponymous constructs (J. Renger, *"mārat ilim:* Exogamie bei den semitischen Nomaden des 2 Jahrtausends," *Archiv für Orientforschung* 14 [1973]: 103-7). Much more sophisticated in using comparative methods and thus advancing our comprehension of biblical genealogies are Abraham Mala-

mat, "Tribal Societies: Biblical Genealogies and African Lineage Systems," *Archives Européennes de Sociologie* 14 (1973): 126-36, and Robert R. Wilson, *Genealogy and History in the Biblical World*, Yale Near Eastern Researches, 7 (New Haven: Yale University Press, 1977). See also Norman K. Gottwald, *The Tribes of Yahweh: A Sociology of the Religion of Liberated Israel, 1250-1050* B.C.E. (Maryknoll, N.Y.: Orbis Books, 1979), pp. 308-10, 334-37.

5. See George E. Mendenhall, "The Hebrew Conquest of Palestine," *BA* 25 (1962): 66-87, and *The Tenth Generation: The Origins of the Biblical Tradition* (Baltimore: Johns Hopkins University Press, 1973). The same broad conclusion that early Israel was "the *first* ideologically based socio-political revolution in the history of the world" was reached independently by Jan Dus, "Moses or Joshua? On the Problem of the Founder of the Israelite Religion," *Radical Religion* 2, nos. 2 and 3 (1975): 26-41. See also the discussions in the May 1978 issue of *JSOT*: by Alan J. Hauser, "Israel's Conquest of Palestine: A Peasants' Rebellion?," pp. 2-19; Thomas L. Thompson, "Historical Notes on 'Israel's Conquest of Palestine: A Peasants' Rebellion?,'" pp. 20-27; and Norman K. Gottwald, "The Hypothesis of the Revolutionary Origins of Ancient Israel: A Response to Hauser and Thompson," pp. 37-52.

6. A striking example of heuristic value of a sociological model for textual criticism and historical reconstruction is Marvin L. Chaney, "ḤDL-II and the 'Song of Deborah': Textual, Philological, and Sociological Studies in Judges 5, with Special Reference to the Occurrences of ḤDL in Biblical Hebrew" (Ph.D. diss., Harvard University, 1976).

7. Norman K. Gottwald, "Were the Early Israelites Pastoral Nomads?" in *Rhetorical Criticism: Essays in Honor of James Muilenburg*, ed. J. J. Jackson and M. Kessler (Pittsburgh: Pickwick, 1974), pp. 223-55; idem, "Nomadism," IDB*Sup* (1976), pp. 629-31; idem, *The Tribes of Yahweh*, pp. 464-92.

8. Gottwald, *Tribes of Yahweh*, pp. 493-587.

9. My critiques of Noth's and Mendenhall's models for early Israel will be found in *Tribes of Yahweh*, pp. 220-33, 345-57, 376-86, 599-602. See Note 5 above for Mendenhall, and Martin Noth, *A History of the Pentateuchal Traditions* [1948] (Englewood Cliffs, N.J.: Prentice-Hall, 1972).

10. For an elaboration of this programmatic statement, see *Tribes of Yahweh*, pp. 228-33, and for provisional conclusions on the content, see pp. 237-587.

11. Albrecht Alt, "The Settlement of the Israelites in Palestine [1925]," *Essays in Old Testament History and Religion* (Oxford: Blackwell, 1966), pp. 175-204.

12. Walter R. Goldschmidt, *Comparative Functionalism: An Essay in Anthropological Theory* (Berkeley: University of California Press, 1966).

13. For an analysis of Israel's Canaanite converts, allies, and neutrals, see *Tribes of Yahweh*, pp. 555-583.

14. W. Helck, *Die Beziehungen Aegyptens zu Vorderasien im 3. und 2. Jahrtausend v. Chr.* (Wiesbaden: Harrassowitz, 1962); M. A. K. Mohammad, "The Administration of Syro-Palestine during the New Kingdom," *Annales du Service des Antiquités de l'Egypte* (Cairo) 56 (1959): 105-37; Giorgio Buccellati, *Cities and Nations of Ancient Syria*, Studi Semitici, 26 (Rome: Università di Roma, 1967).

15. Norman K. Gottwald, "Early Israel and 'The Asiatic Mode of Production' in Canaan," *SBLSP* (1976), pp. 145-54.

16. On classificatory typology of pastoral nomadism, see Douglas L. Johnson, *The Nature of Nomadism* (Chicago: University of Chicago Press, 1969), and for

ancient Near East pastoral nomadism, see M. B. Rowton, "Autonomy and Nomad-ism in Western Asia," *Orientalia* 42 (1973): 247-58, and "Urban Autonomy in a Nomadic Environment," *JNES* 32 (1973): 201-15.

17. Cf. Albrecht Alt, "Aegyptische Tempel in Palaestina und die Landnahme der Philister [1944]," in *Kleine Schriften*, I (Munich: Beck, 1953), pp. 216-30; Hanna E. Kassis, "Gath and the Structure of the 'Philistine' Society," *JBL* 84 (1965): 259-71.

18. Cf. S. H. Horn, "Ammon, Ammonites," *IDBSup* (1976): 20; J.R. Bartlett, "The Rise and Fall of the Kingdom of Edom," *PEQ* (1972): 26-37, and "The Moabites and the Edomites," in *Peoples of Old Testament Times*, ed. D. J. Wiseman (Oxford: Clarendon, 1973), pp. 229-58.

19. Gottwald, *Tribes of Yahweh*, pp. 32-44, 105-10.

20. Ibid., pp. 301-15.

21. Ibid., pp. 642-63.

22. Ibid., pp. 191-663.

23. Ibid., pp. 591-691.

24. Ibid., pp. 692-709.

12

RICHARD A. HORSLEY

Liberating Narrative and Liberating Understanding

The Christmas Story

Attempting to bridge historical criticism's "distancing" of modern interpreter from ancient text, the "hermeneutics of consent" sought to listen to the text's "truth claim" while recognizing rather than avoiding the interpreter's prejudgments. But, besides retaining an individualistic and exclusively "religious" orientation, this approach fails to recognize the depth of the historical determination of its own interests and prejudgments. Historical criticism serves to recognize the reality of concrete historical differences and keeps alive the "irritation" of the original text, its challenge to our own assumptions, worldview, and politics. As interpretations of significant events, critically read biblical stories such as those of Jesus' birth can help keep alive subversive memory and aid the recovery of unfulfilled historical possibilities that have been closed off by the dominant contemporary "reality principle." Indeed, North Americans have much to learn from the way in which Central American campesinos *"read" biblical history through "the Christmas story," which rationally enlightened scholars had dismissed as historically unreliable "myth." Modern-day Third-World peasants discern in these legends of Jesus' birth analogies that are provocative,*

Reprinted from Richard A. Horsley, *The Liberation of Christmas* (New York: Crossroad, 1989), 144–61.

if also threatening, to the modern-day Caesars and Romans busy enjoying their "bread and circus" in the imperial metropolis.

A great deal of energy in biblical studies has been devoted to mitigating or avoiding the distancing effects of historical-critical analysis of biblical literature and history. Critical biblical scholarship, having become institutionalized in theological schools for the training of the clergy, had so distanced the Bible from the personal and ecclesial concerns of theologians, clergy, and laity that "what it meant" seemed virtually irrelevant for contemporary faith. Following upon legitimate objections to historical criticism's pretensions of "value-free" investigation and "objective" analysis in its concern to free biblical texts from traditional dogmatic biases of established Christianity, various ways were found to restore the Bible's relevance and revelatory power. Through all the emphasis on historical-critical study, its own practitioners had never come to grips with its implications for either the Bible or their own situation. Indeed, they, along with other theologians, had never really relinquished the older traditional understanding of the Bible as the "word of God." The whole discussion of what the Bible "meant" versus what it "means" is a manifestation of this schizophrenic dilemma of modern theologian-scholars torn between two ostensibly conflicting understandings of the Bible—as historical document or as the word of God.[1]

Attempts to salvage the biblical text as the word of God for people today from the distancing effects of historical criticism either avoid or mitigate the historical reference of the biblical texts. Of great recent popularity is the reading of biblical texts simply as literature. Thus their intrinsic beauty or structure or their rhetorical power can be appreciated by the reader. On the analogy of modern drama, for example, an elaborate scheme of acts and scenes is discovered in the brief, twenty-three-verse narrative of Matthew 2.[2] Given the modern individualistic orientation, particularly in North America, it is not surprising that psychological interpretations are popular. Parts of the text or the whole are applied to the self; for example, in the birth of the Christ-child the self is being born (or the self is giving birth, or the child is being born in the heart).[3] Such psychological interpretations are, in effect, the modern equivalents of traditional allegorical interpretation, except that the system of spiritual understanding into which the text is being transposed is derived not from Plato but from Jung or Freud. How the fundamental motifs of the infancy narratives as a whole are transformed into a psychological pattern of meaning can be seen, of course, in Rank's Freudian treatment of "the myth of the birth of the hero."[4]

The way most people have any contact at all with the Bible, of course, is in the context of a church service. There, when it is not simply utilized as a source for prooftexting and illustration, it is reduced to paragraph-or story-length "lessons" selected according to either the preacher's current agenda or an established liturgical lectionary. A historical understanding of the text may well inform the preacher's preparation of a sermon on such a text, but the people's reading is structured and oriented by the contemporary ecclesial (or personal piety) context. In such a case, of course, the infancy narratives are read in the context of the Advent season, which is part of an annual cycle of celebrations as well as part of the contemporary cultural Christmas atmosphere. With all of these approaches available and operative, the infancy narratives as "the word of God" would appear to have plenty of channels to the minds and hearts of the faithful with virtually no interference from the distancing effects of historical criticism.

HERMENEUTICS OF CONSENT

Others have attempted to find a way to let the text, the word of God, speak to the contemporary faithful, while still utilizing historical criticism. Anxious that historical criticism simply distances biblical text and history from the present, the "hermeneutics of consent" seeks an interpretation that listens as well as critically dissects, that allows the text to make a truth claim on the interpreter.[5] Bridging the gulf between historical criticism and word of God, or between past and present, is particularly important for theologians in the Lutheran tradition, for whom the very identity of the church depends upon its connection with Holy Scripture. For those anxious about this gulf, the historical criticism that once emancipated us from the constraints of tradition now appears even "absolutist." Consensual hermeneutics wants to utilize but to mitigate the effects of historical criticism by a new openness or consent to the textual spiritual tradition, which makes a claim on the interpreter.

This approach offers some concepts and concerns that might prove important for biblical interpretation if they could be implemented. First, in contrast with the Enlightenment and the "scientific" historical criticism that emerged from it, this hermeneutics attempts to take its prejudices or prejudgments (preunderstanding) into account rather than to escape or suppress them. The interpreter who seeks understanding of a text is unavoidably embedded in a particular situation, of which there is little possibility of any objective knowledge. In fact, the very presupposition of historical knowledge is that the interpreter is involved in a tradition, part of which is constituted by the effects that the text has had on her or his situation and preunderstanding. The power of those effects, moreover, does not depend on their being recognized.[6] Because "the self-awareness of the individual is only a flickering in the closed circuits of historical life," of course, one's prejudgments are far more determinative of understanding than one's judgments. "Thus the hermeneutically trained mind . . . will make conscious the prejudices governing our own understanding so that the text, another's meaning, can be isolated and valued on its own."[7]

Second, the concept of horizon has been used since Nietzsche with reference to how one's thoughts or views are determined by the situation. It includes potentially the whole range of vision, everything that could be seen from a particular vantage point. The implications are that one is not necessarily limited to seeing what is nearest but can see broad ranges of things with a certain perspective, even that one's horizon could be shifted and expanded. Historical understanding requires placing ourselves within the horizon out of which the tradition or text we are seeking to understand speaks. Simply to place ourselves in the situation or horizon of the text, however, would be like a one-way conversation in which we listen attentively to another person in order to understand another's views but without agreeing or letting it make a claim on us. If, on the other hand, we were to consent to the text's having something valuable or true for us, then we would have to engage in a genuine two-way conversation, allowing our own viewpoint or horizon to be further questioned and challenged. Genuine understanding would involve a "fusion of the horizons." Thus in seeking understanding of a text, we would not only place ourselves in another situation, within another horizon, but we would also resist a facile assimilation of the text or past to our own unexamined situation or horizon. Encounter with the texts from the tradition that has affected us is important to the testing of our prejudgments and the informing of our self-understanding.

There are a number of problems with this consensual hermeneutics, however, when it comes to the infancy narratives and other biblical materials. Some of the problems are simply inherent in the approach. Consensual hermeneutics appears still to assume that a religious dimension of life is separable from other dimensions, such as the political and economic. The Bible is understood, accordingly, as "the word of God," which evokes "faith" in the believer. Consensual hermeneutics does not appear to be any more open to nonreligious dimensions of life, past or present, than historical criticism is to transcendence (divine causation). Historical criticism, however, has made clear that most if not all biblical narratives and prophecies are concerned with life as a whole, and not simply a religious realm. As noted above, "he who was born king of the Jews" is not presented in Matthew 1–2 or Luke 1–2 as merely a spiritual savior. Consensual hermeneutics assumes an individualistic stance and focus. The infancy narratives, by contrast, manifest a sociopolitical stance and focus. Interconnected with the previous two points, consensual hermeneutics is concerned with self-understanding. The latter, moreover, is conceived in abstract, intellectual and spiritual terms of humankind in general. The infancy narratives, like the exodus narratives, however, are concerned with the concrete liberation of a whole people. Thus, insofar as this approach in effect confines itself to the claim of texts from its own religious tradition, it limits that claim to the impact that spiritual ideas from the past might have on its own self-understanding. The horizons involved are, in effect, the past and present spiritual and intellectual ones from the same religious tradition.

On the other hand, if this approach is seriously committed to pursuing historical criticism in a way that the concerns, foci, and horizons of past texts are allowed to challenge our own preunderstanding, then consent to and dialogue with biblical texts such as the infancy narratives should eventually have the effect of calling our limiting assumptions into question. Dialogic hermeneutics appears almost naive in its expectation that this openness will happen, virtually by sheer willpower, for there are severely limiting factors that it has apparently not taken into account. The placing of oneself in another horizon and the questioning of one's own prejudices supposedly take place within a continuous religious or intellectual tradition, but no critical principle is supplied for the conversation other than the continuing circular dialogue between interpreter and text. We can predict how the conversation would work, for example, between North American interpreters and the infancy narratives. The history of effects of the biblical tradition is such that North Americans identify strongly with the biblical people of Israel and see themselves as those to whom the Christ-child was sent and to whom the "peace on earth" was proclaimed. No critical principle is provided that suggests that such an identification with the people of God in the tradition is invalid. Consensual hermeneutics relies on the willingness of Europeans and Americans (particularly those who are hermeneutically trained) to test their own prejudices. But biblical texts suggest that people in positions of relative power and privilege (kings, princes, priests, scribes, Pharisees) tend not to test their own prejudices and horizons but to use their power to impose them on others.

Perhaps consent to and confrontation with biblical texts are needed, but a far greater sense of suspicion is clearly in order with regard both to our own situation and prejudice (most of which we are unaware of) and to the ways in which the tradition has affected our situation and prejudices, the power of which goes unrecognized. We want to be near to the scriptural text once more, and an objectifying historical criticism is blamed for the alienation that has occurred. But perhaps, as the result of historical processes, we have in fact become distant from the biblical past in various respects (socially, politically, religiously), and historical criticism discerns the distance already there, however much it also tends to objectify. Thus historical criticism would appear to have a highly important role in two respects. Not only would critical historical reconstruction of the biblical texts and their circumstances discern the difference and distance of the biblical past from the situation and prejudices of the present. Historical criticism must also be applied to the ways in which the biblical text or past has affected our situation and preunderstanding. Such critical distancing may provide one of the primary bases for suspicion and criticism of our own position.[8]

The distancing of historical criticism helps make possible the distancing necessary for difficult self-criticism. Schüssler Fiorenza delineates important ways in which historical criticism of the Bible can function in the interpretation and use of Scripture:

1. It asserts the meaning of the original witness over later dogmatic and social usurpations, for different purposes.
2. It makes the assimilation of the text to our own experience of parochial pietism and church interests more difficult.
3. It keeps alive the "irritation" of the original text by challenging our own assumptions, world views, and practice.
4. It limits the number of interpretations that can be given to a text. The "spiritual" meanings of a biblical text are limited by its historical meanings.[9]

Although consensual hermeneutics has critical intentions, its inherent problems are such that the very historical criticism whose effects it is attempting to mitigate must be pursued even more rigorously in order to accomplish its stated agenda of listening to the claims of biblical texts.

UNDERSTANDING THE BIBLE HISTORICALLY

The above discussion, however, assumes that the Bible is being understood as text, or more important, that what we are attempting to understand is text or "word." One of the results of historical criticism and of some recent hermeneutical discussions is that this is not the only way to view the Bible, particularly biblical narratives and prophetic material. The Bible was the product of communities of people.[10] The biblical text as we have it was preceded by oral and written traditions that were also produced and cultivated by historical communities, such as early Israel, disciples of the prophets, or followers of Jesus. The tradition and the texts they produced are expressions and reflections of their own experiences or events that were highly significant for them. The Book of Exodus provides accounts that express the significance of the people's deliverance from bondage in Egypt. The biblical text is a "word" about the event. It is the exodus event that Israel proclaims as its liberation, while the biblical "word" or account is a medium of communication about that liberating event (and becomes highly revered or "sacred Scripture" just for that reason). Similarly the infancy narratives are accounts of the significance of a liberating event. Because of our own recent objectifying and positivist historical orientation, we may be skittish or embarrassed with regard to the texts' imperviousness to discovery of "what really happened," but the infancy narratives originated and were cultivated and written as accounts of the significance of Jesus' birth. It is the latter event, not the "word" or text in itself, which is important—as is indicated by the subsequent formulation of the doctrine of the incarnation as one way to help protect it.

What may be only implicit in narratives such as the Exodus or the infancy stories is stated explicitly by Paul. Over against some of the Corinthians who were apparently reading the biblical text as a word of spiritual wisdom with salvific qualities, Paul insists that the Bible is about past historical events. What had significance was not the word or the text itself but the events, which "were written down for our instruction" (or warning; see 1 Cor. 10:1-11). In fact, in his understanding of the Torah as an account of significant historical events, Paul has the audacity to insist that the function of the text or word was relative to its particular historical period in the overall sequence of events. That is, the Law as text or word served as the means of salvation from the time of its institution through Moses, but it had not so functioned in the prior events that it itself recounted and it was now historically superseded in its function by the events of Jesus' crucifixion and resurrection (Gal. 3). Thus, whether explicit in Paul or implicit in narratives such as the Exodus or the infancy narratives, much of the biblical text presents itself as an account about events of significance. The events, moreover, are not confined to a religious dimension but are events of politicoeconomic as well as (and inseparable from their) spiritual significance.

In a now-famous essay, the great literary critic Erich Auerbach delineated how leaders of the ancient church developed, and medieval biblical interpretation elaborated, the *figural* reading of the Bible as past history pertinent to subsequent history. A key step was the retention of the Jewish Scriptures as the Old Testament and the decision not to interpret it only abstractly and allegorically. Christianity thus maintained "its conception of a providential history, its intrinsic concreteness, and with these no doubt some of its immense persuasive power."[11] Not only are biblical narratives read as referring to concrete life and events, but they are also understood as pertaining to and elucidating later—including present—life and events, and not simply some spiritual dimension. This figural approach

> implies the interpretation of one worldly event through another; the first signifies the second, the second fulfills the first. Both remain historical events; yet both, looked at in this way, have something provisional and incomplete about them; they point to one another and both point to something in the future, something still to come which will be the actual, real, and definitive event. This is true not only of Old Testament prefiguration, which points forward to the incarnation and the proclamation of the gospel, but also of these latter events, for they too are not the ultimate fulfillment, but themselves a promise of . . . the true kingdom of God.[12]

As recently as the American Revolution and formulation of the United States Constitution, many North Americans still understood the Bible as accounts of historical events, including politicoeconomic as well as religious affairs; and they understood that biblical life and events pointed forward and could illuminate subsequent history. In a sermon entitled "The Republic of the Israelites an Example to the American States," preached before the General Court (state legislature) of New Hampshire in June 1788, for example, Samuel Langdon declared that, "as to everything in their constitution of government . . . the Israelites may be considered as a pattern to the world in all ages; and from them we may learn what will exalt our character, and what will depress and bring us to ruin."[13] For understandable reasons, established biblical interpretation retreated into a primarily religious reading of the Bible understood as a religious text. In recent times, however, black, women's, and third-world communities and liberation movements are showing the way toward rediscovery and critical appropriation of the Bible as history.

When the Bible is read as an account of experiences or events significant to the people of Israel or followers of Jesus, the focus is not on the text itself, removed from historical life to a separate sacred status, but on the people and their struggles. The Bible recounts the founding events of God's deliverance of the people, other paradigmatic events of liberation, and numerous experiences of conflict, failure, judgment, or renewal. When the account leaves off, however, the history of the people continues, being informed, inspired, and warned by biblical events and prophecies. For contemporary communities and movements that identify with or look seriously to biblical history, the reading and historical criticism of the Bible thus takes on some constructive roles or functions, while expanding the scope of its distancing and critical functions delineated in the preceding section. Several of these can be illustrated from the infancy narratives.

Any reconstruction of history is done for a group of people or for a certain position or purpose, whether it is consciously acknowledged or not.[14] But this fact accords well with the stance of biblical accounts such as the infancy narratives, in which God is, in no uncertain terms, effecting liberation for the subjected Israelite people, saving them from their enemies. Thus the infancy stories readily open toward a reconstruction of the historical relations involved in the birth of the Christ-child for purposes of liberation and movements among the oppressed. Liberative reconstructions, moreover, appear to be solidly supported by a reading of these narratives in the historical context of ancient Roman Palestine.[15] Biblical history, of course, can be reconstructed for purposes of domination as well as liberation. Herod consulted the biblical scholars of his day concerning messianic prophecies to determine where he should concentrate his military action to suppress any nascent resistance to his control. In today's more subtle reconstruction, the massacre of the innocents (or any indication of political conflict) is suppressed in order to produce a politically innocuous Christmas story for the holidays.

Bible reading and historical reconstruction are important for the cultivation of memory. Selective memory can be used in the service of domination. But unrestrained historical memory is usually threatening to oppressive or repressive order.[16] Memory of the infancy narratives would be "dangerous" in two respects especially. These stories and songs articulate the eager hopes and longings of ordinary people for deliverance from their domination by indigenous and alien rulers—indeed, their excitement over the birth of the one who is to lead their redemption. Elizabeth, Mary, Simeon, and Anna, as well as the shepherds (and the heavenly armies), were all ecstatic that here, finally, was "the consolation/redemption of the people." The stories also present a memory of suffering and struggle. The rulers were threatened and struck out violently; Joseph, Mary, and the child had to flee the country and, even when they returned, had to avoid recognition by the threatened and threatening rulers; and innocent children were slaughtered, and their mothers mourned. Memory of the longings and the sufferings of predecessors or forebears is subversive; it sustains the longings, mitigates the suffering, and nourishes the resolve to resist among those who remember.

In the interrelation between memory and the reconstruction of history, biblical criticism can help determine what shall be remembered and how or in what connection it is remembered. Is the mention of Caesar and the census simply a literary device in Luke 2, as suggested in christologically oriented interpretations? Our awareness of the imperial situation of first-century Palestine indicates that the Roman demand of tribute evoked intense resistance among the Jewish peasants and teachers and was important in biblical memory (Acts 5:37). Is the memory of the liberative deeds of Jael or Judith to be evoked in the recitation of Elizabeth's greeting of Mary, "Blessed are you among women," or is it too threatening? The pre-Matthean traditions and pre-Lucan canticles, along with Matthew and Luke, make possible and encourage that Caesar's demand of tribute, Herod's cruel and violent repression, and Jael's and Judith's as well as Mary's acts of deliverance be remembered in connection with the birth of Jesus. Closely related to the issue of what is to be remembered, there may be more to the biblical history that can be remembered than initially meets the eye from reading the text. Historical criticism can discern, for example, that women were more important in the leadership of early Christianity than is portrayed in the androcentric New Testament texts. In the infancy narratives in particular, women play a more significant role than in other New Testament narratives, and the dialogue or songs by women in the stories allude to the tradition of women's prominence in historical deliverance as charismatic figures and prophets.

A particularly important function of both memory and historical criticism is the recovery of unfulfilled historical possibilities.[17] One of the dominant themes of biblical history is promise and fulfillment. The community of priests and scribes who wove revered traditions together and gave final form to the Torah included, in a prominent position, God's promise to Abraham and Sarah that their descendants would have land and would be a great people and that all peoples would receive blessings through them. But, writing in circumstances of exile, they end the historical narrative and covenantal exhortation prior even to Israel's entry into the land. History went on after the historical narrative of the Torah stopped, and the promises were partially fulfilled. Paul, in his excitement over the final fulfillment of the promises, proclaimed that the traditional social divisions between Jew and Greek, slave and free, and male and female were no longer valid (Gal. 3:28). But in his social practice he implemented only the first, and acquiesced in the perpetuation of the other inequalities and their attendant oppressions. Although the biblical account of people's struggles left off, the history of faithful communities continued. Finally in the nineteenth and twentieth centuries there was a serious return to the unfulfilled historical possibilities of liberation for slaves and women.

The narratives of the birth of Jesus occupy in the New Testament (or the new biblical history) the place that corresponds to the promises to the ancestors in the Hebrew Bible (and Israel's history). The savior and messiah is born, the good news of liberation is proclaimed, and the people rejoice as well as begin the difficult struggles involved. The infancy narratives set the theme and thrust of the gospel history as a whole: Israel is finally being redeemed, and then (at the end of Matthew and at the beginning of Acts) deliverance is opened to all peoples. After recounting Jesus' proclamation of the kingdom, his martyrdom and vindication, and the extension of the mission to the other peoples, the biblical story leaves off before the anticipated final fulfillment in the *parousia*. (Of course, by the end of Acts the gospel has at least finally reached the imperial capital.) But the history of peoples' yearning and struggle continues. The memory of Christmas in the infancy narratives, however, keeps alive the hopes for and the commitment to the unfulfilled historical possibilities that the birth of the child inaugurated. There is nothing in the infancy narratives themselves or in the rest of Matthew or Luke to suggest that the possibilities of "deliverance from our enemies" is deferred as only eschatological, that is, possible only at the end of historical conditions. That view is a carryover from the older tendency to read the biblical text literalistically. In fact, the eschatological reading only serves to discourage the yearning and struggle toward realization of the unfulfilled historical possibilities as illegitimate (according to the authoritative scholarly reading of the "word of God") and to dissipate the subversive memory that Christmas would keep alive.

Like history that is reconstructed for some purpose or community, memory is not necessarily oriented toward the past. Considering the prominence of promise and fulfillment and the memory of unfulfilled historical possibilities that are juxtaposed with concrete, formative experiences of deliverance in the Bible, biblical memory and biblical history are if anything oriented toward the future (or as Paul says, biblical history was written down "for us"). Thus yet another function of biblical history and memory is "to provide paradigms in which the life of a later time, i.e., the future from the viewpoint of the texts themselves, may be illuminated."[18] Not only prophecies but many narrative passages, which ostensibly refer to the past, become paradigmatic for present experiences.[19] Stories of Abraham and Sarah were told or written not to provide information about the past but to offer patterns of hope and trust, or the lack thereof, in the fulfillment of God's promises. Such stories still function paradigmatically in the present. The same illumination of present historical experience by the biblical past happened for black slaves in North America and is happening today for Central Americans on the basis of biblical memories of the exodus and the birth of Jesus, respectively.

Historical criticism has an important role in relation to this future orientation and pertinence of biblical history, but its function is more enabling than definitive.

> The future direction of scripture can be rightly realized and exploited only in conjunction with its past references, for it is the past references that, though historically imprecise, provide the historically given definitions of its terms. And here again we have a reason why the Bible has to be understood with a fully historical understanding, aligned with disciplines lying outside the biblical and theological fields: only that can guard us from systematic misunderstanding of the range of possible meanings of biblical terms in their reference of present and future.[20]

The role of historical criticism and reconstruction here, however, is only that of assistance to communities or movements. The illumination of present experience and events from the biblical past is a matter of discernment, although without historical criticism there would be less to discern.[21]

In a number of respects these functions of memory and criticism of biblical history, such as the attention to unfulfilled historical possibilities and the discernment of how biblical paradigms illumine present affairs, represent a rediscovery of the figural interpretation prominent prior to the Reformation and rise of rationalism. Yet, they differ in important respects as well. That is, they are no longer tied to the Platonic cultural heritage of late antiquity, with the historical *figurae* as a tentative form of something eternal and timeless as well as concrete in themselves. And with less standardized patterns fixed in the minds of contemporary historical actors, they allow current events their own full concrete integrity and flow without conforming them to biblical prototypes.

A LIBERATING CHRISTMAS STORY

The infancy narratives are about liberation. The birth of the Christ-child means that God has inaugurated the long-awaited deliverance of the people of Israel from their enemies. More precisely, God has begun to free the people from domination and exploitation by the imperial ruler and from their own rulers, particularly the tyrannical king. The people's liberation evokes brutal repression and involves suffering, but the dominant tone is one of relief and excitement as the people respond readily to God's initiative.

Memory of the stories of Jesus' birth have been among the most cultivated of all biblical narratives, partly because of the widespread celebration of Christmas. Correspondingly, however, with regard to the history of its influence on cultural tradition, there has been all the more opportunity for that memory to have become selective and for the stories to have become used with other than liberative effects. Nevertheless, these biblical narratives are among the most laden with unfulfilled historical possibilities because they tell of and rejoice in liberation initiated but remaining potential rather than actualized. Like the stories of the promises to Abraham and Sarah and those of the temporary heavenly enthronement of Jesus, they are strongly oriented toward future historical realization.

Those in the present likely to find themselves particularly addressed by these stories are people of similar life circumstances. People dominated and exploited by local or foreign rulers are the ones likely to discern that these biblical stories illuminate their own situation and experiences. The *campesinos* of Solentiname, Nicaragua, under the rule of Somoza provide a vivid illustration.[22] By contrast, North American society generally has moved away from its earlier identification with and celebration of the birth of the Christ-child, or strikingly domesticated adaptable parts of the Christmas story, into a festival of gift-giving consumption legitimated and motivated primarily by the symbol of Santa Claus. Vast numbers of North Americans, living in a culture no longer familiar with the Bible as people's history, have little sense of how the stories behind "Christmas" could be about the deliverance of an oppressed people. Thus it may be useful to explore the liberative function of the infancy narratives as memory or history for basic Christian communities, focusing particularly on the process of "conscientization" (consciousness raising) that takes place in many of these small Latin American communities of the poor.[23] In the process some interesting points of difference will emerge between the attitudes and approaches of established European and North American biblical studies and those of the basic Christian communities.

For many if not most peoples in oppressive situations, the world appears as

fated. Given their own utter powerlessness, combined with the traditional religious and other cultural forms utilized by their rulers to legitimate their own
rule and control their subjects, it is not surprising that the people's stance
toward reality is often fatalistic. It is not difficult to appreciate how the infancy
narratives, like much other biblical material, provide a direct challenge or alternative to such fatalism. A benign god not only is in full control of the situation
but is acting to liberate the people. The old myths and mystification are exposed
by the birth narratives, and alternative explanations are suggested. The emperor
or other ruler is not divine; tribute and taxes are not the legitimate claim of
rulers and conquerors. And true peace is not tranquility and prosperity for the
privileged on the basis of the people's subjection. Moreover, the infancy narratives portray the people's difficult circumstances of life, which they would
otherwise have accepted as simply "the way things are," as caused by human
agents to whom God's action is sharply opposed. It is a powerful but mortal
Caesar who decrees taxation, not God. Those who dominate and exploit the
people are viewed as enemies whom God is about to overthrow. Rulers can be
seen to exercise such violence against the people because they sense the ille-
gitimacy and insecurity of their own domination.

In contrast to oppressed peoples' internalized sense of subjection to and
dependency on their masters, the infancy narratives present a striking case of
God's dealing directly with the ordinary people. The divine will and action,
moreover, is for their own liberation, not their further oppression. If ordinary
people are valued by God, then perhaps they can value themselves. The ordinary people in the infancy narratives, moreover, display no deference to their
rulers and have no apparent anxieties or hesitation about their own imminent
liberation. The people in the birth narratives thus become paradigms or prototypes for later readers or hearers: seeing that God helped earlier people, who
ventured to assert their freedom, they come to believe that God will help them
as well and are able to take action in shaping their own lives.

As has been noted by reflective participants in the discussions of communities of the poor, and as can be readily observed in Cardenal's transcripts from
Solentiname, the people readily relate or even mix biblical stories, events, or
figures with their own lives and circumstances, and vice versa. *They* are Mary
or the Christ-child or the shepherds. Herod's killing of the children is Somoza's
National Guard turned loose on fellow Nicaraguans. Or *they* are in bondage in
Egypt. Biblical stories are history for the people but are also reflections or
portrayals of their own lives and situations. Hearing and discussing the biblical
stories is a way of beginning to understand their own situation and of reflecting
what might be done about it. They are not focused on trying to interpret the
Bible as an activity in itself (and separate from other activities). In effect, they
are interpreting their own lives and circumstances with the help of or by means
of the biblical stories. The word of God is not in the Bible but somehow emerges
from the community's discussion of their life situation in relation to biblical
figures and events. In contrast with the traditional European and North American Protestant emphasis that the reading and exposition of Scripture evokes
faith, but in a separate religious dimension, the basic communities' reading and

discussion of biblical stories do not differentiate life and faith, do not separate politicoeconomic concerns from religious activities.[24]

It might legitimately be charged that such communities are giving the Bible only a relative position or even second place. But that position is in integral relation with life as a whole, whereas when North Atlantic Christians, particularly Protestants who emphasize the *sola scriptura* principle, give the Bible first place, it is only within a separate sphere of faith or religion. Finally we should note the basic communities' strengthening conviction that God is with them in their struggles, and not simply active in past struggles. Directly or indirectly, this conviction leads to taking action in regard to their own lives on matters such as education, labor organization, access to land, or health care, as well as the Eucharist and prayer. But such actions should not be surprising, since biblical stories have provided some suggestive prototypes of organization for taking control of one's life and having land as well as a positive self-image and a spirit of group solidarity.

How might North Americans learn to read the liberating story of Christ's birth and begin to discern how it might illumine our situation? Because we have become so distant historically (i.e., socially, economically, politically, and religiously) from the birth narratives, historical criticism may indeed have an important role in preparation for discernment. One of the ways that has been developed to deal with the historical distance is the principle of "dynamic analogy." In interpreting biblical statements such as prophecies or the teachings of Jesus (i.e., the Bible as word), for example, one would apply the message to "those dynamically equivalent to those challenged in the text."[25] If this principle of dynamic analogy can be expanded in scope and complexity to deal with the Bible not only as word but as history as well, then it might well provide a device by which some discernment could be induced.

As noted above, in early generations analogies (often elaborate) were made between biblical history and United States history. More recently, with the scope of history narrowed to that of religious institutions, analogies have frequently been drawn between facets of the biblical people of God and their modern equivalents. Not only do theologians often see themselves in Paul's image, but (more self-critically) they even acknowledge that the established clergy correspond to the Pharisees in ancient "Judaism." Were we to draw a dynamic analogy between United States society and ancient Jewish society as a whole as portrayed in the infancy narratives, then the wealthy and powerful generally would correspond to Herod and the high priests, and educated professionals generally would correspond to the scribes, and so forth.

However, to press such an analogy between a tiny ancient society and one of the great modern world powers strains historical credibility. The analogy discerned by the peasants in Solentiname is far more credible. What corresponds to Jewish society under Roman rule in New Testament times is a third-world country such as their own Nicaragua, while the United States, with a number of small countries under its domination, corresponds to Rome. Such an analogical interpretation simply extends a prophetic principle used in biblical history itself both in Amos and by John the Baptist. A people that confidently understood its continuity with those specially favored by God in the past as a guarantee of continued divine blessing (whether because of the promise to Abraham or because of the redemption from Egyptian bondage) is disabused of its presumptuous illusion: God can raise up children to Abraham out of stones; and perhaps God is concerned as much about the Philistines and Syria as about Israel (Luke 3:7–9; Amos 9:7–8). The extension here, in broad analogy to the infancy narratives, is from the recognition that the United States can no longer pretend to be "God's New Israel" to the realization that it has apparently become the new Rome.

Once we recognize the imperial position of the U.S. in the dynamic historical analogy, it may be possible to discern important facets of the present-day "Caesar's" rule through a fresh reading of the infancy narratives, informed additionally from our historical-critical reconstruction of their broader context. Thus we can discern that the equivalent of Caesar's decree that all the world should be laid under tribute is North American economic exploitation of smaller countries. And just as Caesar sent in the legions to enforce Rome's extraction of tribute, so U.S. military power is used to protect investments, profits, and trade. One of the purposes of Rome's economic exploitation of subject peoples was to provide the "bread and circus" necessary to keep the Roman mobs under control. Moreover, just as Rome dominated through client-rulers such as Herod, so the U.S. maintains its interests and influence through governments, often military, that it designates and supports. Pressing the analogy to greater complexity, we can see our own equivalent to the ancient Roman religious ideology of "peace" established by the imperial "savior." "Democracy" and "development" or "progress" are the blessings of the "free world" established and dominated by U.S. military power.

The foregoing aspects of a dynamic analogy were all drawn from ancient Roman history, as represented in the infancy narratives (Caesar, tribute, peace, Herod) and applied to contemporary United States practices. The analogy could be drawn or discerned in the other direction as well. Thus, for example, the hundreds of thousands of Central American refugees in the United States might have an analogue in the flight of the Christ-child and parents to Egypt, especially considering the similar causes of their flight (repression by client-regimes threatened by nascent liberation movements).

Having determined the corresponding cast of characters and some of their practices by means of the expanded dynamic analogy with the infancy narratives, we can probe the thrust of the stories as well, particularly the implications for "Caesar" and other "Romans." In the stories and songs about the birth of Jesus, God, in acting for the people, is acting against Caesar and Herod. The emphasis, particularly in Luke 1–2, is that the birth of Jesus means salvation of the people from their enemies. But it is abundantly clear, both from the fundamental relationships portrayed in the narratives and from the Magnificat in particular, that raising up the lowly and feeding the hungry also entail pulling down the mighty from their thrones and sending the rich away empty. The unmistakable implication in the birth stories that God is rejecting the rulers, moreover, is part of a consistent pattern of God's historical action. In liberating the Israelites from bondage in Egypt, for example, God took action against Pharaoh and his armies (Exod. 15); in reasserting the independence of the covenant people in their land, God fought against Canaanite kings (e.g., Judg. 5); in delivering Israel from the harsh rule of Ahab and Jezebel, God inspired a revolt through the prophets Elijah and Elisha (1 Kings 19 and 2 Kings 9); to preserve the traditional covenant with the people, God inspired resistance and revolt against the imperial rule of Antiochus Epiphanes (e.g., Dan. 11; 1 and 2 Maccabees). Thus if the infancy narratives are to be read analogically, the present-day Caesars and their client-rulers are implicated. If, analogous to God's action recounted in the infancy narratives, and in pursuit of the unfulfilled historical possibilities that opened in the birth of Jesus, God is still today acting for the liberation of poor and subjected people, it would seem clear that such action entails opposition to their domination and exploitation by North American political and economic practices.

The infancy narratives and the Gospels that they introduce, however, are neither deterministic nor vindictive. The Magnificat and the Beatitudes are not announcements of "eschatological reversal," whereby the downtrodden will finally lord it over their oppressors in some end time. And there are no lurid descriptions of how cruel and arrogant rulers are to suffer horrendous torments. Although under the influence of powerful social and cultural forces, the wealthy and powerful are not thought to be inevitably and hopelessly condemned. Later in the gospel story, Jesus does not simply turn away the "rich young ruler" (Luke 18:18–25). What the Gospels, like the prophets, appear to be calling for is a change of practice, and not simply an expansion or adjustment of one's "horizon." In this connection the actions of certain groups—some of them church or church-related organizations—rather than hermeneutical discussions, are providing indicators of how the citizens of today's "Rome" might respond to the implications of the infancy narratives.

Some churches or church groups have taken advantage of the supposed "separation of church and state" to offer a biblically based sanctuary to refugees. A number of independent organizations help channel donations for medical aid and other forms of relief from the effects of U.S.-sponsored destruction of life, limb, and livelihood. The complex politicoeconomic system centered in the United States, however, calls for a more systematic approach, including use of contemporary social criticism along with historical criticism, by biblically informed citizens of the modern analogue to Rome. Although the economic system has become highly intricate, for example, with union and professional retirement funds being invested in multinational corporations that exercise extraordinary power in "underdeveloped" countries, there is still a degree of structural differentiation among political and economic institutions, and some degree of pluralism, hence of personal and group independence of any particular institution. Hence it is possible for North American individuals and groups to quit (at least partially) living from the "bread and circus" provided, for a profit, by the huge agribusinesses that are exploiting dependent laborers in Central America. North Americans, who still enjoy political rights, can demand that their own government cease enforcing the "tribute" taken by U.S.-based corporations and cease placing and supporting in power client-regimes that expropriate and brutalize their subjects. Some groups, with substantial church participation, have already pledged resistance by civil disobedience to any further direct military intervention in Central America by the United States government. Although perhaps to a diminishing degree, the present-day "Caesar" is still dependent on the consent of the citizenry, which was not the case in ancient Rome.

In the heyday of rational criticism, biblical expressions of future hope were dismissed as utterly unrealistic, as fanciful myths. Besides being viewed as "mythical" (hence to be rejected as accounts of anything that might really have occurred), the stories surrounding Jesus' birth were dismissed as fantasies with regard to their hopes of salvation. Like Jesus' promise of the kingdom of God (read, of course, in Matthew's wording of "the kingdom of heaven"), the Christmas story's proclamation of peace on earth and salvation of people from their enemies appeared to rational modern men and women as expressions of pious fantasies that merely provided spiritual compensation for unenlightened people's suffering. Memory that the birth of Jesus included the promise of peace on earth and excited responses to God's nascent deliverance by ordinary people such as Mary, Elizabeth, Simeon, Anna, and the shepherds was cultivated in the traditional celebration of Christmas. But that event too was understood as a special, mythical, magical time.

The increasing abandonment or subordination of the biblical Christmas story in contemporary North American celebration of "the holidays" invites us to read the former over against the latter. The current celebration of "Christmas" now appears to take place in a fantasyland, a magical, fairy-tale world—which no one takes too seriously, of course. Whereas Enlightenment reason was driven to criticize the stories of Christ's birth and other biblical "myths" as parts of the traditional forms of authoritarian domination, few today are bothered by the new forms of myth and magic. The latter are forms of domination no less than were the biblical revelation and the Christian theological doctrines attacked by Enlightenment rationalists. If they were not effective in inducing massive retail spending from Thanksgiving to Christmas, then manufacturers and retailers would hardly utilize them so extensively in costly advertising in the communications media. Perhaps the fact that these new forms of myth and magic help keep the economy humming tends to mitigate any discomfort over the manipulation and domination involved.

The infancy narratives of Jesus, on the other hand, once freed both from the domesticating cultural context of "the holidays" and from rationalist dismissal as "myth," can be read again as stories of people's liberation from exploitation and domination. The people who may respond most immediately are probably those whose situation is similar to that portrayed in the stories. But for the modern-day citizens of "Rome," uncomfortable about their intricate involvement in the web of the new forms of domination, they also offer a challenge and inspiration to regain control of their own lives in response to God's liberating initiative in the birth of Jesus.

NOTES

1. See, e.g., K. Stendahl, "Biblical Theology, Contemporary," *IDB*, vol. 1:418-32.

2. E.g., Raymond Brown, *Birth of the Messiah* (Garden City, N.Y.: Doubleday, 1977), 178-79.

3. For a sophisticated and dialogic use of a psychoanalytic approach, see W. Wink, *The Bible in Human Transformation* (Philadelphia: Fortress, 1973), 49-63.

4. See R. A. Horsley, *The Liberation of Christmas* (New York: Crossroad, 1989), Appendix: "Legend of the Birth of the Hero: A Critical Appraisal," 162-72.

5. This hermeneutical position, which builds heavily on the thought of H.-G. Gadamer, particularly *Truth and Method* (New York: Seabury, 1975), is sketched briefly in P. Stuhlmacher, *Historical Criticism and Theological Interpretation of Scripture: Toward a Hermeneutics of Consent* (Philadelphia: Fortress, 1977), 61-91.

6. Gadamer, *Truth and Method,* 268.

7. Ibid., 245, 266.

8. So also L. E. Keck, "Will the Historical-Critical Method Survive? Some Observations," in *Orientation by Disorientation: Studies . . . in Honor of W. A. Beardslee* (ed. R. A. Spencer; Pittsburgh: Pickwick, 1980), 124.

9. E. Schüssler Fiorenza, *Bread Not Stone: The Challenge of Feminist Biblical Interpretation* (Boston: Beacon, 1984), 130-31.

10. J. Barr, "The Bible as a Document of Believing Communities," in *The Bible as a Document of the University* (ed. H. D. Betz; Chico, Calif.: Scholars, 1981), 25-28; J. S. Croatto, *Biblical Hermeneutics* (Maryknoll, N.Y.: Orbis Books, 1987), 36-50.

11. E. Auerbach, "Figura," in *Scenes from the Drama of European Literature* (Minneapolis: University of Minnesota, 1984; original English trans., 1959), 52.

12. Ibid., 58.

13. Pamphlet published in 1788 at Exeter, N. H., by Lamson and Ranlet; more accessible in C. Cherry, ed., *God's New Israel* (Englewood Cliffs, N.J.: Prentice-Hall, 1971), 93-105.

14. H. White, "Historicism, History, and the Figurative Imagination," *History and Theory* 14 (1975), 54.

15. See Horsley, *The Liberation of Christmas,* chaps. 2-6.

16. Recent reflections on the functions of memory appear in J. B. Metz, *Faith in History and Society* (New York: Seabury, 1980), 184-204; and S. D. Welch, *Communities of Solidarity and Resistance* (Maryknoll, N.Y.: Orbis Books, 1985), 35-44.

17. Schüssler Fiorenza, *Bread Not Stone,* 105, 147.

18. Barr, "Bible as a Document," 39-40.

19. "Implicit in the movement from memory to tradition to text to scripture to canon is the fulfilled expectation that the material from the past illumines the ever moving present, that the past is repeatedly paradigmatic" (Keck, "Will the Historical-Critical Method Survive?," 124).

20. Barr, "Bible as a Document," 40.

21. Keck, "Will the Historical-Critical Method Survive?," 124.

22. Ernesto Cardenal, *The Gospel in Solentiname* (Maryknoll, N.Y.: Orbis Books), 4 volumes. See also Horsley, *The Liberation of Christmas,* chap. 7.

23. For the classic exposition of the widely effective "conscientization" process,

see Paulo Freire, *Pedagogy of the Oppressed* (New York: Herder & Herder, 1971). The following paragraphs presuppose conversations such as those recorded by E. Cardenal in *Gospel in Solentiname.*

24. See further C. Mesters, "The Use of the Bible in Christian Communities of the Common People," in chap. 1 in this book, 3-16.

25. J. A. Sanders, "Hermeneutics," *IDBSup.*, 406.

13

ELISABETH SCHÜSSLER FIORENZA

The Practice of Biblical Interpretation

Luke 10:38−42

Apologetic interpretations concerned to defend the Bible may move prematurely to claim liberative elements in texts whose broader agenda legitimate forms of domination. The Gospel of Luke, for example, was often thought to portray women positively as well as frequently. More comprehensive and probing analysis of the biblical text in the context of the increasing subordination of women in the development of early Christianity discerns something very different in Luke. Elisabeth Schüssler Fiorenza here applies her multifaceted hermeneutical model for critical feminist biblical interpretation to a key Lucan text in which liberative elements were previously found. A hermeneutics of suspicion *detects the androcentric assumptions and patriarchal interests of both biblical texts and modern interpreters, including the dualistic antagonism between Mary and Martha which does not lie in the text itself. A* hermeneutics of remembrance *realizes that the story in Luke 10:38−42 is directed not to a situation in the ministry of Jesus but to a later situation in which Luke and others are attempting to delimit and subordinate the ministry of women from its earlier unrestrained fullness. A* hermeneutics of proclamation *insists that this text is recognized as the word of Luke (not of God), and should be used in critical*

Reprinted from Elisabeth Schüssler Fiorenza, *But She Said: Feminist Practices of Biblical Interpretation* (Boston: Beacon Press, 1992), 51-76.

explorations of the ways in which women and men have internalized the patriarchal tendencies of this and other biblical texts. Finally, a hermeneutics of actualization *seeks to articulate alternative, liberating interpretations.*

The feminist literary critic Nancy K. Miller[1] has argued that postmodern literary theory has replaced the notion of text as a "veil," behind which is to be found a more or less hidden truth or reality, with the notion of the text as texture, tissue, lace, or weaving. This language of textiles privileges the spider's web over the spider, the threads of lace over the lace-maker, the trophology of the loom over the weaver. Such a recasting of the text as texture not only spells the "death of the author," but it also forecloses the discussion of the writing, reading, and interpreting subject insofar as it assumes that "lost in this tissue — this texture — the subject unmakes himself [*sic*] like a spider dissolving in the constructive secretions of [her] web."[2] Miller suggests that a feminist poetics must replace the neologism of the text as "hyphology" with the notion of "arachnology," that is, with the study of the woman weaver of texts. Such a study is a "critical positioning which reads *against* the weave of indifferentiation to discover the embodiment in writing of a gendered subjectivity; to recover within representation the emblems of its constructions."[3]

Since such a critical positioning is not a fixed standpoint but a shifting and moving position, I suggest that we add to the image of spider and text that of the dance. Insofar as the feminist biblical critic repeats strategic moves of interpretation, she is best imaged as a dancer who engages in a circle-dance that spells not only movement but also embodiment.[4] The biblical figures of Miriam, Judith, and Sophia come to mind as leaders in the ongoing, never closing, shifting movement of a feminist biblical interpretation for liberation.

In *Bread Not Stone* I have proposed *four reading strategies* which I seek to further theorize here. The crucial moments in a critical feminist hermeneutical process are: ideological suspicion, historical reconstruction, theoethical assessment, and creative imagination. However, these strategies of interpretation are not undertaken in a linear fashion. Rather, they must be understood as critical movements that are repeated again and again in the "dance" of biblical interpretation.

These four rhetorical movements can only be sustained when contextualized in a feminist critical process of *conscientization,* or learning to recognize sociopolitical, economic, cultural, and religious contradictions.[5] This process of conscientization strives to create critical consciousness and has as its goal both a praxis of solidarity and a commitment to feminist struggles that seek to transform patriarchal relations of subordination and oppression.[6] Such a process of conscientization is engendered by experiences of cognitive dissonance. These "breakthrough" and "disclosure" experiences bring into question the "common-sense" character of patriarchal reality. Such "breakthrough" experiences and the systemic critique of oppressive patriarchal reality are made possible through emancipatory movements. The critical feminist paradigm of reading as a "transformative dance of interpretation" must thus begin with the critical moments of *consciousness raising* and *systemic analysis*.[7] For these two moments are the ingredients of a *hermeneutics of suspicion.*

Although these four interpretive strategies can be distinguished theoretically, they interact with each other in the process of interpretation. A hermeneutics of suspicion, for instance, must be applied not only to biblical texts and interpretations, but also to an imaginative feminist retelling. The *hermeneutics of imagination,* on the other hand, is a crucial ingredient in historical reconstruction and critical evaluation. Moreover, before engaging historical, literary, and theological reading strategies and methods within a critical feminist paradigm of reading, a feminist practice of interpretation must interrupt the perspectives and relations between text, reader, and context which have been construed by dominant doctrinal, literary, or historical reading formations.

A hermeneutics of suspicion is misunderstood if it is labeled "paranoid" and construed as assuming a "conspiracy" of biblical writers and contemporary interpreters.[8] Rather, such an interpretive method turns its searchlight first on the reader's own reading practices and assumptions. It seeks to detect and analyze not only the androcentric presuppositions and patriarchal interests of the text's contemporary interpretations and historical reception but also those of biblical texts themselves. Rather than presuppose the feminist character and liberating truth of biblical texts, a hermeneutics of suspicion rests on the insight that *all* biblical texts are articulated in grammatically masculine language — a language which is embedded in a patriarchal culture, religion, and society, and which is canonized, interpreted, and proclaimed by a long line of men. Without doubt the Bible is a *male-centered* book!

A *hermeneutics of remembrance,* therefore, can not take grammatically masculine, allegedly generic language and texts "about women" at face value. Instead, it must read them as intimations that much of what remains is submerged in androcentric historical consciousness. If the reading strategies of a hermeneutics of suspicion can be likened to the practices of a detective or a sleuth, those of a hermeneutics of remembrance resemble the activity of a quilt-maker who stitches all surviving historical patches together into a new overall design. To that end, a hermeneutics of remembrance must develop designs or models for historical reconstruction which can dislodge the eradicating frame of the androcentric biblical text. In positive terms, such reconstructive models must allow one to reintegrate women and other marginalized people into history as agents and at the same time to write biblical history as the history of women and men. A hermeneutics of historical remembrance reconstructs early Christian history not as reified artifact, but as memory and heritage for the *ekklesia* of women.

While a hermeneutics of remembrance seeks to recover all possible remnants of textual and material information in order to rearrange them in a different and more plausible historical picture, a *hermeneutics of proclamation* insists that texts which reinscribe patriarchal relations of domination and exploitation must not be affirmed and appropriated. In theological terms, they should not be proclaimed as the word of G-d but must be exposed as the words of men. Otherwise, Christian discourses about G-d continue ultimately to legitimize patriarchal oppression. If the first two hermeneutical strategies can be likened to the practices of a detective and of a quiltmaker, this third strategy resembles the activity of a health inspector who tests all food and medicine for possible harmful ingredients.

Like a health inspector, a hermeneutics of proclamation for the sake of life and well-being, ethically evaluates and theologically assesses all canonical texts to determine how much they engender patriarchal oppression and/or empower us in the struggle for liberation. Such an ethics of interpretation transforms our understanding of Scripture as "the foundation stone of truth" to that of "nourishing bread and food." Like a public health investigator, it not only attempts to test which foods are poisoned and which are not, but it also seeks to judge to whom and under what circumstances such "food" can be given. For instance, one might agree that a biblical injunction such as "love your neighbor" does not promote oppressive relations. Yet when it is quoted by a minister who is counseling a battered woman to remain in a destructive marriage, such an injunction serves patriarchal purposes.

Finally, a *hermeneutics of liberative vision and imagination* seeks to actualize and dramatize biblical texts differently. The social function of imagination and fantasy "is to introduce possibilities ... [for] we can work toward actualizing only that which we have first imagined."[9] Creative re-imagination employs all our creative powers to celebrate and make present the suffering, struggles, and victories of our biblical foresisters and foremothers. It utilizes all kinds of artistic media to elaborate and enhance the textual remnants of liberating visions. It retells biblical stories from a different perspective and amplifies the emancipatory voices suppressed in biblical texts. It elaborates on the role of marginal figures and makes their silences speak. Lynn Gottlieb captures the goals of such a creative re-imagination:

> ... some of us remain at the beginning, the word still to be formed, waiting patiently to be revealed, to rise out of the white spaces between the letters in the Torah and be received. I am speaking of the tradition of our mothers, our sister-wives, the secret women of the past. How would they have spoken of their own religious experiences, if they had been given a space to record their stories? ... In order for Jewish women truly to be present in Jewish history and everyday life we must find the female voices of the past and receive them into our present.[10]

Whereas in the first chapter I have situated a critical feminist process of interpretation for liberation within a rhetorical paradigm of reading, in this chapter I seek to engage such a feminist model of interpretation in the reading of a Lukan text. Luke 10:38–42, the story about Martha, Mary, and Jesus, is only found in Luke's Gospel, where it is part of the so-called Lukan travel narrative. It reads in the RSV translation as follows:

> Now as they went on their way, he entered a village; and a woman named Martha received him into her house. And she had a sister called Mary

who sat at the Lord's (*tou kyriou*) feet and listened (*ēkousen*) to his teaching (*ton logon autou*). But Martha was distracted with much serving (*diakonian*); and she went to him and said: "Lord (*kyrie*) do you not care that my sister has left me to serve (*diakonein*) alone? Tell her then to help me. But the Lord (*ho kyrios*) answered her: "Martha, Martha, you are anxious (*merimnas*) and troubled about many things; one thing is needful. Mary has chosen the good portion, which shall not be taken away from her.

The great emotional attraction which this story has for many biblical readers is eloquently expressed in the following introductory statement to an essay on this text:

And there is something else about this story. It simply will not let us go. I mean at the personal level. It is many years now since the Martha and Mary story first took hold of my attention. Since then I have spent many hours of study on it and many more pondering and reflecting on what it might mean. Each time when I put it down or let it go, it clings to me and refuses to let me go. I know that I have not yet gotten to the heart of its mystery. . . . We may be able to say some things which point toward the story's greatness, and we may enable others and ourselves to see various aspects of the story which we had not noticed before. But to define and possess it? Can we possess the greatness of the flowers of the field? Greatness is recognized, not defined.[11]

How does a feminist critical interpretation approach this text, which is so highly valued by biblical scholars and theologians? Feminist biblical interpretation begins with experience. Many women greatly identify with Martha's plight. Traditionally women have been told that their feminine vocation is to take care of men and their children. They do all the work in the house and in the kitchen, clean and shop, give dinner parties for the advancement of their husbands, and at the same time are supposed to be relaxed, entertaining, and well-groomed. In the church they wash the altar linen, run the bingo games, and hold bake sales. They do all of this, often without ever receiving a "thank you." They secretly identify with Martha who openly complains, and they resent Jesus who seems ungrateful and unfair in taking Mary's side. Yet because Jesus is not supposed to be faulted, women repress their resentment of Jesus' action. Instead they vent their resentment against other women who, like Mary, have abandoned traditional feminine roles. The right-wing backlash in society and church feeds on this resentment of women who feel that their work and contributions are not valued but that it would be unfeminine to express their resentment.

Other women feel guilty because they are not able to fulfill Martha's role of perfect housekeeper and entertaining hostess. Pondering this story one student writes of her mother:

I watched my own mother neglect the housekeeping in order to talk to someone or listen or read and I joined my father in feeling embarrassed about the untidy house. I was ashamed about the mess and always surprised when my friends wanted to come home with me. Some have later explained that my mother made them feel welcome and important and they liked that housekeeping wasn't the first priority ... Yet within her own family and within herself this was a conflicted issue. I am sure my mother shared this conflict with Martha.

Such an exploration of women's experience with the Martha and Mary story calls for a hermeneutics of suspicion even though this passage is usually hailed as one of the most positive biblical texts about women.

I. A HERMENEUTICS OF SUSPICION

A *hermeneutics of suspicion* seeks to explore the liberating or oppressive values and visions inscribed in the text by identifying the androcentric patriarchal character and dynamics of the text and its interpretations. Since biblical texts are written in androcentric language within patriarchal cultures, a hermeneutics of suspicion does not start with the assumption that the Martha and Mary story is a feminist liberating text just because its central characters are women. Rather it seeks to investigate *how and why* the text constructs the story of these two women as it does.[12]

The meaning of this passage is most difficult to establish because of the textual critical problems in verses 41 and 42.[13] Jesus' pronouncement is the climax of the story and therefore key to the meaning of the story. The six textual variations indicate that the story was controverted very early on. The variations represent, basically, two different readings. The longer reading, on the one hand, assumes a meal setting: "Martha you are anxious and troubled about many things; few things are needful or one," could mean, as one commentator puts it, that a couple of olives, or even one, will suffice at present. Mary has the main course already. The shorter reading, on the other hand, which is preferred by most contemporary interpreters, reads: "Martha you are anxious and troubled about many things, one thing is needful." The "one thing" probably refers to the activities of the two protagonists. The climactic word of Jesus then asserts that Mary has chosen the one thing, the good part.

Since the text does not directly refer to a meal or explicitly to "serving at table" but uses the more general expressions *diakonian, diakonein* the longer reading's assumption that a meal is being served cannot be justified. Moreover, the climactic word of Jesus does not mention *diakonia* or *diakonein* but reproaches Martha because she is anxious and troubled about many things. The Greek expression for being anxious—*merimnan*—reminds one of Luke 12:22, 26, where the disciples are told not to worry about eating, drinking, and clothing, and not to be anxious about their lives. Instead they should seek God's *basileia*.

No consensus can be found among interpreters as to the story's basic meaning. A critical review of divergent interpretations can distinguish two basic approaches, which highlight in different ways the text's dualistic character.[14]

An *abstractionist* interpretation reduces the two sisters to theological principles and types. It is supported by the form-critical classification of the text as a biographical apophthegm, that is, an ideal scene or construct for the climactic saying of Jesus in which the many worries of Martha are contrasted with the one thing needful chosen by Mary. Such abstractionist interpretations, for example, have understood Martha and Mary as ciphers for the theological principles of justification by works and justification by faith, alms-giving and prayer, Judaism and Christianity, synagogue and church, people who are preoccupied with worldly cares and those who listen to God's word and seek spiritual things.

According to traditional interpretations of the story, Martha and Mary symbolize either the labors of this world and the bliss of the world to come (Augustine) or the active and the contemplative life in this world, or life according to the flesh and according to the Spirit (Origen). The contemporary version of this traditional interpretation emphasizes the importance of love of God over and against the social activism that stresses the importance of love of neighbor. Such interpretations not only dehistoricize the narrative, but they also make women historically invisible. They obscure the androcentric dynamics of the text which uses *women* to make its point.

Those interpretations which acknowledge that Martha and Mary are two female characters, that is, that actual women are the protagonists of the story, work with a "good woman/bad woman" polarization. The traditional Catholic interpretation gives women the choice of two lifestyles in the church: active (Martha) and contemplative (Mary). There are those women who serve God and those women who serve men. Active women do the housework, rear the children or take care of the sick, and concern themselves with mundane business. Contemplative women do not allow worldly things to interfere with their quiet study, prayer, contemplation, and service to the Lord. Women are either laywomen or nunwomen, secular or religious, serving their husbands or serving the Lord, their heavenly bridegroom.

Protestant interpreters have a more difficult time with this story since the Reformation replaced the role of nuns with that of the "pastor's wife," and the ascetic lifestyle with the cult of domesticity. Therefore they insist that women must fulfill their duties as housekeepers. Nevertheless, they must not overdo it. In other words, they should be accomplished hostesses of dinner parties and church suppers, but they should take some time out to "listen, to pray and to learn." Martha is told that only "a few things" are needed. She must still be the hostess, yet she has to keep it simple so that she can also fulfill her religious obligations. To quote a widely read work, *Women in the Ministry of Jesus,* Jesus' "remarks, however, are neither an attempt to devalue Martha's efforts at hospitality, nor an attempt to attack a woman's traditional role; rather Jesus defends Mary's right to learn from Him [*sic*] and says this is the crucial thing for those who wish to serve Him [*sic*]. Jesus makes clear that for women as well as men one's primary task is to be a disciple; only in that context can one be a proper hostess."[15]

Apologetic feminist interpretations in turn continue this dualistic interpretation. They focus on Mary's rejection of the traditional housewife role and stress her option for theology. They celebrate her vindication by Jesus without carefully analyzing the androcentric implications of Luke's story. Mary is compared to a student or disciple of a rabbi since she is seated at Jesus' feet. Just as Paul was the Pharisaic student of Gamaliel (Acts 22:3), so Mary is a disciple of Jesus, dedicated to listening to his word. Mary's role is characterized as very unusual in view of the place of women in Jewish culture whose work was to serve but not to study with a rabbi. Unlike any Jewish rabbi, it is then asserted, Jesus accepts women as disciples studying the Torah, while he rejects the role of housewife as women's proper role.

However, this interpretation highlights Christian women's role as disciples at the expense of Jewish women and their tradition. It assumes that Jewish women were relegated to the kitchen and excluded from the study of the Torah. Apologetic feminist interpretations have not invented such an anti-Jewish explanation; rather, they have uncritically taken it over from malestream exegesis. They do so in order to show that Christianity, far from being anti-women, has actually liberated women. Nevertheless, a feminist critical hermeneutics of liberation must reject such an anti-Jewish interpretation, because it seeks to eliminate the oppression and marginality of Christian women by historically perpetuating that of Jewish women. It overlooks that both Mary and Martha are Jewish women.

Another way to "save the story" from its critics emerges in the interpretive attempt to psychologize and eroticize its protagonists. One psychological reading, for instance, stresses that Mary showed sympathetic understanding toward the anguish of Jesus, who was on his way to Jerusalem where he was to face death, whereas Martha could not meet his needs. Jesus expected such a sympathetic understanding, though it was almost unheard of that a woman would be sought out as a confidante or that a man would discuss matters of life and death with a woman.[16] Other psychological readings understand the competition between Martha and Mary as either sibling rivalry or sexual jealousy. Martha, the older of the two sisters, expects Mary, the younger, to take over her share of work. Since John 11:5 states that Jesus "loved Mary and her sister," it is asked what sort of love this was: "Could there indeed have been sexual jealousy between the sisters for the attention of Jesus? Or was it platonic, a friendly relationship? As lively, physical human beings we cannot discount the possibility that there was more than friendly interaction between the three, a factor which could have entered into the resentment Martha expresses."[17]

Such psychologizing readings of the story overlook the insight of historical-critical exegesis that biblical texts are not interested in the psychological attitudes and emotions of their protagonists. They also perpetuate the patriarchal cultural stereotype of women as rivals, as merely the emotional support or love object of a man, or as both. Finally, such an interpretation also relies on the negative contrast of Jewish society.

In short, a hermeneutics of suspicion indicates that in one way or another most interpretations of Luke 10:38–42 underline the dualistic antagonism either between the two women or between the timeless principles or lifestyles which they symbolize. One must therefore ask whether such an androcentric dualism is a projection of traditional and contemporary interpretations, or whether it is generated by the text itself.

The same two women are also mentioned in John 11:1–44 and 12:1–11.[18] In distinction to the Fourth Gospel, the writer of Luke-Acts mentions neither the name of the town, Bethany, nor the brother of the two sisters, Lazarus. We can no longer know with certainty whether this silence is due to redactional considerations, or whether Luke did not have the same information about the two sisters as the Fourth Evangelist had. Nevertheless, a comparison between the gospels of John and of Luke indicates that the dualistic opposition characterizing Luke's text is absent from that of the Fourth Gospel.

A form-critical analysis shows that Luke's story itself constructs this opposition between Martha and Mary. Bultmann therefore classifies this story form critically as a biographical apophthegm, rather than as a controversy dialogue that was composed as an ideal scene to illustrate the final word of Jesus.[19] Apophthegms or pronouncement stories generally utilize antagonistic characterization to make a point and to espouse behavioral norms. The narration tends to stylize and typify certain persons or situations so that readers can identify with them and imitate their behavior. What seems to be clear is that the Lukan account is not concerned with the two women as individuals; rather, it is interested in them as representatives of two competing types or roles of discipleship: *diakonia-service* and *listening to the word.*

A linguistic-structural analysis further underlines the text's dualistic-oppositional structure.[20] In such an analysis, Mary functions as the positive figure to which the figure of Martha serves as a negative foil. The text itself inscribes the oppositions: rest/movement; lowliness/upright posture; listen/speak. Martha's intervention as a speaking subject reinforces this contrasting opposition:

Mary	*Martha*
student	householder
listening	speaking
rest	movement
receptiveness	argument
openness	purposefulness
passivity	agency
better choice	rejection

In addition, a narrative analysis that charts the interventions of the characters can highlight the dualistic dynamics of the text. The three characters of the story are Martha, her sister Mary, and the *Kyrios,* the Lord. The relationship of Martha and the Lord in the beginning of the story is that of "equals": Martha welcomes Jesus into her house. Mary's relationship to the Lord is that of a "subordinate": she seats herself at his feet. Martha is absorbed in the preoccupations of *diakonia;* Mary gives her whole attention to the "word of the Lord." This opposition already hints at a conflict in which Martha becomes the protagonist. Martha's speech has two parts, one referring to the present and one pointing to the future, insofar as she aims to change the situation. Whereas the first part consists of a question which contains two accusations, the second is an imperative sentence which contains two demands. Martha's strong reference to her own person and needs contrasts with Mary's silence and passivity as she is focused on the *Kyrios* (v. 39bc). Both parts of Martha's speech are directed explicitly to the *Kyrios* and only indirectly to Mary.

Martha does not speak to Mary directly but she appeals to Jesus[21] as a little girl might run to her father to tell on a sibling who misbehaved. She complains to the Lord about her sister[22] and asks him to use his authority to tell Mary to share in the work. In doing so she relinquishes the more egalitarian relationship between hostess and guest in favor of the dependency relationship between child and parent. The Lord rejects Martha's appeal and sides with Mary. He approves of Mary's choice to listen to him but discredits Martha's choice of *diakonia,* which is not the "one thing necessary."

In the beginning, the emotional dynamics of the scene lead us to expect an intervention of the *Kyrios* in favor of Martha. Readers understand her impatience with Mary's self-absorption and sympathize with her. Yet, Martha's active intervention shifts the reader's sympathy against her. Whereas in the beginning the story opposes Martha's welcoming of Jesus and attention to service to Mary's position at his feet and attention to his word, the end of the narrative stresses Martha's exaggerated service, anxiety, and worry in contrast with Mary's choice of the better part which will not be taken away from her. Martha's desire to change the situation is rejected as too much worrying and busybodiness. In the course of the narrative, Martha, the independent and outspoken woman, is rebuffed in favor of the dependent Mary, who chooses the posture of a subordinate student.

In short, the story places the *Kyrios* in the center of the action. Insofar as he is characterized in masculine terms, the story is clearly kyriocentric, i.e., master-centered. Moreover, Mary, who receives positive approval, is the *silent* woman, whereas Martha, who argues in her own interest, is *silenced.*[23] Those who praise Mary's extraordinary role as a disciple generally overlook the fact that Mary's discipleship only includes listening but not proclamation. Finally, the text is not descriptive of an actual situation. Rather the narrative is *prescriptive,* pitting sister against sister in order to make a point. But what is the point that Luke wanted to make in his own social-ecclesial situation?

II. A HERMENEUTICS OF REMEMBRANCE

A *hermeneutics of remembrance*[24] seeks to move against the grain of the androcentric text to the life and struggles of women in the early churches. It seeks to reconstruct early Christian history as the history of men and women, as memory and heritage for women-church. Rather than taking the androcentric text or historical model of Luke-Acts at face value, a hermeneutics of remembrance seeks to uncover both the values inscribed in the text and the patriarchal or emancipatory interests of its historical contextualization. When discussing the role of women in early Christianity, exegetes usually affirm that women have a prominent place in the Lukan double-work. However, they generally situate Luke's stories about women in the life of the historical Jesus rather than in the situation of the early Christian communities to whom Luke writes. Such an interpretive move allows them to psychologize and historicize the characters in the text and to stress, for example, Mary's personal relationship to Jesus.

That Luke 10:38–42 was generated by and addressed to a situation in the life of the early church—rather than an episode in the life of Jesus—is linguistically signaled by the title *Kyrios*. The text appeals not to the authority of the historical Jesus but to that of the resurrected Lord. Thus it is important to explore the story's inscribed historical situation and rhetorical function in order to identify the theological-pastoral interests of the author. Exegetes have pointed out that the inscribed historical situation is that of the early Christian missionary movement which gathered in house-churches.[25] Therefore, the householder Martha welcomes the Lord into her house. One reading of the story contextualizes it in terms of Gerd Theissen's claim that the Jesus movement consisted of itinerant (male) missionaries and local households who supported the apostolic mission with material means.[26]

The text supports such an interpretation insofar as the *diakonein* of Martha refers back to that of the women in Jesus' and the apostles' company (Luke 8:1–3). As such a local householder, Martha makes too much fuss about hosting Christian itinerant preachers. Just as the twelve apostles (Luke 9:1–6) and the seventy (Luke 10:1–24) are admonished to stay as officially authorized delegates at the same house, to eat and drink whatever is put before them (10:7–8, cf. 9:4), and not to worry about their sustenance (12:22–26), so Martha's worries about hosting such traveling missionaries are rejected in favor of listening to their words. Such a construction of the historical subtext not only presupposes Theissen's historical reconstructive model of the Jesus movement, but in so doing it relegates women householders to providing hospitality for male preachers. Ultimately, such an interpretive model colludes with and reinscribes Luke's editorial interests, which relegate the *diakonein* of the women disciples to wealthy women's patronage and support for the apostolic male leaders.

Luke 8:1–3 is best understood as a Lukan editorial summary account (see 4:14f; 6:17; 9:51) which changes the Markan tradition by distinguishing clearly between the circle of the twelve and that of their female supporters. By adding Joanna, the wife of Herod's steward, he underlines that they are wealthy women who support Jesus and his male followers. They are not characterized as disciples, *akolouthein*, as in Mark, but they are motivated by gratitude because Jesus heals them.[27] That Luke intends to downplay women's equal discipleship comes to the fore not only in his attempt to subordinate women to the circle of the male disciples, but also in his characterization of them as wealthy benefactors. Studies of the social world of Luke have pointed out that he uses the Greco-Roman patron-client relationship as a model for his construction of the social world of Jesus, but that he insists on its modification.[28] Such patron-client relationships are characterized by inequality in status and power, as well as by exchange and reciprocity. "A patron has social and economic resources; in return a client can give expression of solidarity and loyalty. Generosity from the patron can be translated into honor and power."[29]

The Greco-Roman patron-client exchange system was a significant opportunity for marginalized wealthy but low-status people, such as freeborn women or freed persons, to achieve status and power. Are we then to understand that in exchange for their economic service the women who supported Jesus and the male apostles were to gain honor, status, and power equal to that of the male apostles? In fact, this is not the case, because the Lukan Jesus insists again and again that the expected behavior is the opposite of that produced by the patron-client relationship. The text insists that wealthy persons and leaders cannot expect to receive repayment in the form of honor and influence. Their only reward is from G-d, who is the only patron.

By undercutting the reciprocity of the patron-client system, the Lukan narrative produces the power-inequality between rich and poor men, male leaders and their subordinates. In doing so, it forecloses a significant social avenue to status and influence in the church for wealthy freeborn women and freedpersons. Thus the Lukan rhetoric of 8:1-3 undercuts women's equal discipleship on several levels: The women followers of Jesus are portrayed not only as serving Jesus and the male apostles with their possessions but also as owing gratitude to Jesus for having been healed. At the same time the text introduces "class" differences between women by turning the women disciples into elite married women and wealthy patrons. Ultimately, a historical reading that contextualizes the Martha and Mary story in terms of Luke's historical model as it has been theorized by G. Theissen is not able to break the hold of the androcentric texts but reinscribes it. Consequently, one must ask whether another reading is plausible.

It is important to note that the text itself does not directly place Martha in the kitchen preparing and serving a meal. In fact, the text merely states that she is preoccupied with too much "serving." *Diakonia* and *diakonein* had already become technical terms for ecclesial leadership in Luke's time. Traveling missionaries and house-churches were central to the early Christian mission, which depended on special mobility and hospitality. According to the Pauline literature, women as well as men were traveling missionaries and leaders of house-churches. The house-church provided space both for the preaching of the word and for eucharistic meal celebrations. Scholars project patriarchal bias onto the early Christian missionary movement, however, when they conclude that the *diakonia* of women consisted either in serving traveling male missionaries and doing housework for communal gatherings or that it was restricted to the house.

In early Christian usage, *diakonia* refers to eucharistic table service in the house-church. It was not, however, restricted to such service, since it also included the proclamation of the word. That this was the case comes to the fore in Acts 6-8 despite Luke's redactional interests to the contrary. Although the "seven" Hellenists are said to have been appointed to devote themselves to the *diakonia* of the tables so that the twelve could dedicate themselves to the preaching of the word, they nevertheless become the initiators of the Christian missionary movement and are depicted as powerful preachers and founders of communities. They are characterized similarly to the rival missionaries, preachers, and apostles of Paul in Corinth.

The structural affinity of Acts 6:1-6 and Luke 10:38-42 has long been recognized.[30] Just as Martha complains that Mary leaves (*katalipein*) the *diakonein* to her in order to listen to the word (*ton logon*) of the *kyrios,* so the twelve apostles maintain that they cannot leave (*katalipein*) the word (*ton logon*) of G-d in order to serve (*diakonein*) at tables. Luke's text not only distinguishes the *diakonia* of the word from that at table and restricts both to different groups, but, in so doing, Acts 6:1-6 subordinates one to the other. Lukan redactional interests seem remarkably similar to those of the Pastoral Epistles, which also distinguish between ministers who labor "in preaching and teaching" (1 Tim. 5:17) and those who "serve" (1 Tim. 3:8ff).

Luke 10:38-42 stresses that the *diakonein* of Martha is not the "one thing needful" and hence must be subordinated to "listening to the word." However, it must not be overlooked that the "good portion" chosen by Mary is not the *diakonia* of the word: it is not the preaching but rather the listening to the word. The characterization of Mary as a listening disciple corresponds to the narrative's interests in playing down the leadership role of women.

It has often been pointed out that it is a major Lukan literary strategy to parallel a story about a woman with one about a man and vice versa.[31] One of the earliest feminist articles has therefore argued that this male-female dualism reflects the "important constituency of women and men who shaped the missionary and catechetical movement."[32] Such an observation is correct in that it describes the audience of Luke's "catechetical" instruction as consisting of women and men. Yet the Lukan text represses the knowledge that women and men have *shaped* the missionary movement, insofar as the gospel does not parallel a single story about a leading male disciple, such as Peter, with that of a leading female disciple, such as Martha. By paralleling stories about male and female characters who are the objects of healing and instruction, the Lukan work genderizes membership in Jesus' community of disciples while simultaneously subordinating the women disciples to the male leaders.

This portrayal of women as *members* but not leaders of the Jesus movement corresponds to Luke's picture in Acts of the role of women. Acts tells us that women as well as men listen to the Christian message and become disciples.[33] However, the public speeches in Acts use the address "men, brothers" (*andres, adelphoi*) eleven times.[34] More importantly, Acts does not tell us a single story of a woman preaching the word, leading a congregation, or presiding over a house-church.

While the Pastoral Epistles explicitly prohibit women to teach men, the Lukan work fails to tell us stories about women preachers, missionaries, prophets, and founders of house-churches. Thus while the Pastorals silence our speech, Acts deforms our historical consciousness. In addition, Luke plays down the ministry of those women leaders of the early church whom he has to mention because they were known to his audience. Martha and Mary are a case in point.

Such a critical feminist interpretation of the Lukan text has met with strong disagreement.[35] These objections assert that the above interpretation does not sufficiently take into account the story's contextualization in the so-called travel-narrative and the overall tendencies of the Lukan redaction that are widely held to be positive with regard to women.[36] Such objections insist that the story characterizes Mary as a disciple of Jesus contrary to contemporary religious-cultural expectations. My point, however, is not that Mary is not to be understood as a follower or disciple of Jesus, but rather that she is not seen as a "minister of the word."

Even a cursory review of the placement of the story in the Lukan macrotext can substantiate my argument. Jesus is on his way to Jerusalem (9:51) and the reader knows he will die there. Chapter 10 begins with the official commissioning of the seventy-two disciples. They are told to expect food and shelter and to eat and drink what is set before them when they are received into a house (10:7). The vignette of the Martha and Mary story explicitly directs readers back to the sending out of the seventy-two disciples in that it refers to the journey and to the reception of Jesus in Martha's house. In doing so it clearly distinguishes between the disciples, who, like Jesus, are sent to proclaim the good news, and those in the community, who receive the disciples and listen to their preaching. The Lukan contextualization of the story thus marks Mary's discipleship as being like that of the members of the Christian community.

In addition, the placement of the Martha and Mary story in the immediate context of instructions for Christian practice is telling. The story is sandwiched between the example story of the Good Samaritan (10:25-37) and Jesus' teaching on how to pray (11:1-4).[37] While the story of the Good Samaritan addresses the question, "Who is my neighbor?," the section 11:1-4 answers the disciples' request for Jesus to teach them how to pray. The Martha and Mary story in turn climaxes in the assertion that Mary has chosen "the good portion."

Finally, the Lukan travel narrative in which the Martha and Mary story is situated has three journey sections. These are marked in 9:51, 13:22, and 17:11. The first narrative complex (9:52 to 10:42) in the first journey section (9:52 to 13:21) of the macrotext ends with the Mary/Martha story.[38] Whether the example story of the Good Samaritan and the pronouncement story of Martha and Mary are interrelated is debated. Yet both can be read as answering the question of the lawyer, "What am I to do to inherit eternal life?" Both are thus explications of the great commandment. They teach members of the Christian community what true discipleship is all about. They express the same message in narrative form as the blessing of Jesus in Luke 11:28, which praises those "who listen to the word of God and observe or do it (see 8:21)."[39] In short, the contextualization of the Martha/Mary story within Luke's macrotext of the travel narrative supports my argument that, although Luke's rhetorical strategy acknowledges women as members of the Christian movement,[40] it downplays their apostolic leadership.

That Martha and Mary were well-known apostolic figures in the early churches can be seen from the Fourth Gospel. Martha, Mary, and Lazarus are characterized as Jesus' friends whom he loved (11:5). They are his true disciples and he is their teacher. After expressing her faith in Jesus' word, Martha goes and calls Mary (11:20), just as Andrew and Philip called Peter and Nathanael. According to the Fourth Evangelist, Jesus' public ministry climaxes in the revelation that he is the resurrection and the life (11:1-54). While in the original miracle source the resurrection of Lazarus was the heart of the story, in the gospel the climax is the christological confession and dialogue of Martha and Jesus.

As a "beloved disciple," Martha becomes the spokeswoman for the messianic faith of the community. Her confession parallels that of Peter (6:66-71), but hers is a christological confession in the fuller Johannine sense: Jesus is the revealer who has come down from heaven. Indeed, Martha's confession has the full sense of the Petrine confession at Caesarea Philippi in the Synoptics, especially in Matthew 16:15-19. Thus Martha represents the full apostolic faith of the Johannine community, just as Peter does for the Matthean community.

While Martha of Bethany is responsible for articulating the community's christological faith, Mary of Bethany exemplifies the right praxis of discipleship. She is explicitly characterized as the "beloved disciple" whom the teacher has specifically called. She has many followers among her people who came to believe in Jesus (11:45). Though in the narrative of John 11 Mary plays a subordinate role to Martha, in 12:1-8 she is the center of the action. That Martha "served at table" could be an allusion to Luke 10:40, but in John 11 and 12 she is characterized as fulfilling both the ministry of the word and of the table.

Moreover, in John the two sisters are not seen in competition with each other or played out against each other as they are in Luke. Mary is not portrayed as Martha's opposite but as Judas' counterpart. The centrality of Judas both in the anointing and in the footwashing scene emphasizes the evangelistic intention to portray the true female disciple, Mary of Bethany, as the alternative to the unfaithful male disciple, Judas, who was one of the twelve. This opposition lends itself to an anti-Jewish reading if it is overlooked that Mary is portrayed as a leading Jewish woman. Whereas according to Mark 14:4, "some," and according to Matthew 26:8, "the disciples," protest the waste of precious oil, in John it is Judas who objects.[41] The male objection to Mary's ministry is discredited and rejected by Jesus' harsh rebuke: "Let her alone." Mary not only prepares Jesus for his hour of "glory," she also anticipates Jesus' command for each to wash the feet of the other as a sign of the agape praxis of true discipleship.

To sum up: A hermeneutics of remembrance can show that both Luke and the Fourth Gospel repress but nevertheless inscribe the struggle of early Christian women against the patriarchal restrictions of their leadership and ministry at the turn of the first century.[42] The Fourth Gospel indicates how women might have told stories which portrayed women as leaders in the Jesus movement to legitimate their own ministry and authority. By contrast, the rhetorical construction of Luke 10:38-40 pits the apostolic women of the Jesus movement against each other and appeals to a revelatory word of the resurrected Lord in order to restrict women's ministry and authority. The rhetorical interests of the Lukan text are to silence women leaders of house-churches who, like Martha, might have protested, and to simultaneously extol Mary's "silent" and subordinate behavior. Such a reconstruction of women's struggles in the early church also indicates why women have always identified more with Martha than with Mary. That is, it confirms women's "suspicion" that in the Lukan account Martha received a "raw deal." Yet it is not the *Kyrios* but the writer of Luke 10:38-40 who promotes such patriarchal restrictions.

III. A HERMENEUTICS OF EVALUATION AND PROCLAMATION

The preceding critical feminist theological exploration of this Lukan text has important implications for contemporary feminist readings, for preaching, counseling, and individual Bible study. Such a hermeneutics has two significant interfaces: first, a critical assessment of the text, and, second, a critical assessment of the reading situation or context.[43]

First, instead of reinscribing the dualistic, oppositional, and kyriocentric dynamics of the biblical texts, a hermeneutics of proclamation must critically assess the values and visions the text promulgates in order to help women to name their alienation from and oppression within biblical religions. My critical exploration of the literary dynamics of Luke 10:38-42 has shown that the androcentric tendencies of traditional and contemporary interpretations are not completely read into the text; rather, they are generated by it. If this is the case, a feminist interpretation that defends the story as positive for women cannot but perpetuate the androcentric dualism and patriarchal prejudice inherent in the original story. This text is patriarchal because it reinforces the societal and ecclesiastical polarization of women. Its proclamation denigrates women's work while insisting at the same time that housework and hospitality are women's proper roles. It blames women for too much business and simultaneously advocates women's "double role" as "super women." Women ought to be not only good disciples but also good hostesses, not only good ministers but also good housewives, not only well-paid professionals but also glamorous lovers. A hermeneutics of proclamation therefore must insist that theologians not clothe such a patriarchal text with divine authority and proclaim it as the word of God. Instead it must be proclaimed as the word of Luke! We must evaluate all aspects of such a text to assess whether, how much, and in what kind of situations it continues to sustain patriarchal internalization in the name of G-d or Christ.

To say that we cannot simply proclaim Luke 10:38-42 as the liberating and salvific word of G-d does not, however, mean that we should not critically use this text in preaching and teaching. Since women and men have internalized its androcentric and patriarchal tendencies as the "word of G-d," Bible studies and sermons must critically explore its oppressive functions and implications. Not only the hermeneutics of suspicion, but also a hermeneutics of remembrance enables us to do so, since the androcentric character and patriarchal interest of Luke 10:38–42 can be elaborated with the help of historical reconstruction. A comparison with the Fourth Gospel's depiction of Martha and Mary, for example, helps one to understand that Luke's story functioned as prescriptive rhetoric in women's struggle against the gradual patriarchalization of the church at the turn of the first century. Such a comparison can also help readers to break the dualistic construction of the Lukan text and to celebrate the two female characters as historical and independent apostolic figures in their own right. In short, it allows us to reclaim the speech as well as the theological agency of these two women.

Second, a hermeneutics of proclamation must not only evaluate the androcentric dynamics inscribed in the structures of the text, it must also assess the sociopolitical contextualizations that determine how the Lukan text is read and heard today. Since such contextualizations are complex, I will outline four possibilities in order to emphasize the need for a critical evaluation for proclamation.

1. Ever since antiquity, Western culture has especially praised elite women's silence as proper feminine behavior. Mary, sitting at or lovingly washing the feet of Jesus and silently listening to his word, becomes the example par excellence for the proper feminine behavior of elite educated women in such a cultural context. Yet, when contextualized in the life of lower and working-class women, Mary's audacity in taking time out from work to sit idle and to relax in good company can have a liberating effect. As Janice Radway has pointed out, while the content of romance novels insists on the desirability and benefits of heterosexual feminine behavior, the act of *reading* itself for many women readers is oppositional. It allows women readers of romance fiction to take time out from work and family obligations and to "refuse momentarily their self-abnegating role." Such an act of reading is a "declaration of independence" and a way to say to others, "This is my time, my space. Now leave me alone." A homily stressing Mary's right to study and to read can therefore be liberating in a community where women's activity is restricted to caring and working for others in the family, on the job, or in the church. However, the example of Mary should not be used just to encourage the practice of biblical or religious reading; such a practice can also stifle the desire to struggle for satisfaction in real life insofar as women's emotional needs are successfully met in fantasy.[44]

2. The dualistic character of Luke's story is not discarded if the figure of Martha is held up to women as an exemplary figure fulfilling women's role of service. By taking the author's picture of Martha and the other women supporters of the Jesus movement at face value and interpreting such a picture in terms of sacrificing service, apologetic or literary feminist readings neither question nor subvert the androcentric tendencies of Luke's redaction. Therefore, they cannot but reinforce cultural stereotypes of femininity internalized by women and men. Such interpretations reinscribe cultural-religious gender, class, and race stereotypes when they stress, for instance, that the women "have given all for Jesus," or when they assert that the women "whom Luke so fondly speaks of" need not be remembered as "simply idle wealthy women."

A feminist interpretation which understands the Lukan texts about women in a historicizing way and which uncritically follows the patriarchalizing tendencies of the Lukan rhetoric cannot but recuperate these tendencies in its own reading. The women disciples are then seen as female workers who sacrificed everything to follow the "man" Jesus. Like women today, these women disciples are pictured as carrying a double burden.

They too traveled with Jesus, along with the male disciples, but they were not only teaching; they also did the cooking and the mending. They were not just donating their funds, but also their time. Just as faithful, sacrificing church women have always done! Ben Witherington III puts it succinctly: "Being Jesus' disciples did not lead these women to abandon their traditional roles in regard to preparing food, serving, etc. . . . The transformation of these women involved not only assuming new discipleship roles, but also resuming their traditional roles for a new purpose."[45]

3. Whereas feminist theology has challenged the restriction of women's roles to housework and service, it has not sufficiently questioned the notion of ministry as service. In spite of the feminist critique of the cultural and religious socialization of women and other subordinated peoples to self-sacrificing love and selfless service for others, the notion of ministry as service is still a powerful symbol for Christian feminists. They have argued that Christian theology cannot avoid the expression, despite its oppressive overtones, since *diakonia* is central to the understanding of the mission and ministry of Christ, as well as to that of the church.[46] Such a feminist retrieval of servanthood-ecclesiology basically divides along two strategies of interpretation: The first elaborates the early Christian distinction between *diakonein* and *douleuein* to stress that freely chosen service means liberation. *Diakonia*-service is to be differentiated from servility. Servanthood without choice is not *diakonia* but slavery (*douleia*). However, "servanthood through choice" is said to be an act of the total self. The powerlessness of servanthood can be redemptive only when it results from "free and conscious choice." Such "freely chosen" servanthood is not to be understood as self-denial, self-elimination, self-ignorance, or self-immolation. Rather it is said to be the "capacity to look beyond our selves to see the needs of others." It is the "empathy" that wants to help and the skill that knows how to help.

Jesus models such "freely chosen" service, according to this interpretation, because he made the choices of self-giving and self-sacrifice rather than allowing society to dictate his behavior. Thus *diakonia* is realized in the life of Jesus, who came "not to be served but to serve and to give his life as ransom for many" (Mark 10:45). If "servanthood is being in love with the world as God is in love with it," then servanthood in the final analysis means liberation. "We find ourselves liberated into servanthood."[47] However, this feminist proposal for the theological recuperation of servanthood does not take into account that people who are powerless in a patriarchal culture and church; those singled out and socialized into subservience and a life of servanthood are not able to "choose servanthood freely."

By revalorizing service and servanthood theologically, this interpretive strategy extends the theological "double-speak" about service to the theological concept of liberation. For those who are destined by patriarchal culture and sociopolitical structures to become "servants" to those who have power over them, the theological or ecclesiological retrieval of "service/servant/slave/waiter" cannot have a liberating function as long as patriarchal structures continue to divide people into those who serve and those who are served. Rather than elaborate the theological symbols of service/servitude/self-sacrifice, a critical feminist theology of liberation must seek biblical concepts such as *dynamis/ exousia/soteria,* i.e., power/authority/well-being, that can critically challenge the cultural-religious production of a servant mentality.

4. Another feminist theological strategy for retrieving the theology of service for ministry concentrates on redefining ministry. By combining the theology of "freely chosen" service with an understanding of ministry not as "power over" but as "power for," it seeks to recover the early Christian understanding of ministry as serving G-d and building up the community. It also takes Jesus Christ and his incarnation as "suffering servant" as the model of Christian ministry:

> Such dismantling of clericalism is implied in the Gospel concept of ministry as *diakonia* or service. Diakonia is kenotic or self-emptying of power as domination. Ministry transforms power from power over others to empowerment of others. The abdication of power as domination has nothing to do with servility. . . . Rather ministry means exercising power in a new way as a means of liberation of one another.[48]

Although this reconceptualization of ministry seeks to retrieve the New Testament model of *diakonia* — service for a feminist ecclesial self-understanding in and through a redefinition of power — it nevertheless valorizes the patriarchal concept and institution of service/servanthood theologically. The theological language of ministry as service, i.e., as "power for" rather than "power over" the church and the world, obfuscates the fact that the patriarchal church continues to exercise its ministry as "power over" its people as long as it is structured into a hierarchy of power-dualisms: ordained/nonordained, clergy/laity, religious/secular, church/world. Continuing to use the theological notion of service as a central feminist category for ministry, this approach reduplicates the cultural pattern of self-sacrificing service for women and other subordinate peoples, while at the same time it continues to serve as a moralistic appeal to those who have positions of power and control in church leadership. Dependence, obedience, second-class citizenship, and powerlessness remain intrinsic to the notion of "service/servanthood" as long as society and church structurally reproduce a "servant" class of people. Therefore, when seeking to define women's ministry, a feminist ecclesiology of liberation must reject the categories of service and servanthood as disempowering to women.

Luke and later theologians did not understand the radical paradox of the discipleship of equals when they called those in positions of wealth and power to "charitable service," which did not question but actually confirmed their patriarchal status and privileges. In the interest of "good citizenship," the post-Pauline writers advocate adapting the Christian community as "the household of God" to its patriarchal societal structures. The restriction of women's ministry and the separation of the *diakonia* of the word and that of the table, of proclamation and service, go hand in hand. Religious authority and power is no longer used for the service and well-being of people; it is no longer understood as enabling power but as controlling power, as patriarchal superordination and subordination.

Since this patriarchal adaptation of some segments of the early church has defined mainline Christian self-understanding and community and has institutionalized structures of "domination and authority," a feminist theology of ministry must deconstruct such a patriarchal Christian self-understanding and structure, refusing to perpetuate it by valorizing the notion of service and servanthood. The ministry of women is no longer to be construed as "service" or as "waiting on someone." Instead, ministry should be understood as "equality from below," as a democratic practice of solidarity with all those who struggle for survival, self-love, and justice. Since the *ekklesia* of women as the discipleship of equals has been overshadowed by the reality of the patriarchal church, we need to re-envision women's ministry as such a practice of solidarity and justice.

IV. A HERMENEUTICS OF IMAGINATION

Finally, a *hermeneutics of creative imagination and ritualization* seeks to articulate alternative liberating interpretations that do not build on the androcentric dualisms and patriarchal functions of the text. It allows women to enter the biblical text with the help of historical imagination, narrative amplifications, artistic recreations, and liturgical celebrations.[49] Such imaginative embellishments and retellings of the text, however, must also always be submitted to a hermeneutics of suspicion. For instance, a cursory survey of feminist retellings of the Martha and Mary story shows that many such feminist re-creations remain caught up in the cultural feminine role expectations when they place Martha "in the kitchen" preparing a meal for Jesus.[50]

The following is an attempt at an imaginative feminist reinterpretation, made by a participant in one of my workshops:

That Mary is invited to sit at Jesus' feet is only to coopt Mary, but not necessarily to set her free. Freedom would have come if Jesus and Mary would have shared the work so that everyone could have "the good portion." Jesus does invite Martha to put down her burdens and partake. He does lift up and validate Mary's choice to change roles. However, the pause still lingers on "one thing is needful." If the one thing that will help Martha with her anxieties and troubles is a shift in her view of herself and her role, the repercussions will be told around the world. She will no longer speak through a male authority figure, she will no longer put up with a group who expect to be waited on, she will take the good portion as she wants it and demand it as it is forthcoming. She will find a relationship to God Herself that fits for her which may well include both preaching and serving at table. She will reclaim her friendship with Jesus. She will raise hell.[51]

While this revisioning of the Mary and Martha story is articulated in terms of women's contemporary experience, the following account attempts a feminist retelling of the Mary and Martha story that allows us to discard the message that divides, subordinates, and alienates one sister from another. It allows us to understand the struggles of women in Luke's time and our own against patriarchal subordination, silencing, and oppression as one and the same struggle for liberation and wholeness. Out of the distorted web of history it lifts women of power and action and calls us to solidarity with them. One might want to quibble with its historicizing narrative, but I suggest that the following account is useful for illustrating a *hermeneutics of creative imagination:*

I am Martha the founder of the church in Bethany and the sister of Mary, the evangelist. All kinds of men are writing down the stories about Jesus but they don't get it right. Some use even our very own name to argue against women's leadership in the movement. Our great-great grand-daughters need to know our true stories if the discipleship of equals is to continue.

They had been travelling for a long time when they finally came to our village. I invited them to join my sister Mary and me. Jesus and the disciples with him sat down and began talking. Mary sat at the teacher's feet and I joined her in asking him about his latest journeys. He told us the story of the Syrophoenician who came to him asking that her daughter who was possessed be healed. Preoccupied with all the ministry to be done in Galilee Jesus refused: "I have come to serve only the lost and outcast of my own people."

But to his great surprise—Jesus continued—the woman persisted and started to argue with him: God's gracious goodness is so abundant that the crumbs falling from Israel's table are sufficient for nourishing those who do not belong to God's special people. Her argument and faith was like a flash of revelation in which Jesus realized that the good news of liberation and God's power of wholeness was for all people, Gentile and Jew, male and female, slave and free, poor and rich. And her daughter was healed.

By the time the teacher finished this story, evening had approached and it was time for sharing the meal. I asked Jesus if he would stay to eat with us. He said yes, and added: "Martha don't go to a lot of trouble. Whatever you were going to have will be fine. Let me help you." We started toward the kitchen when one of the males hollered: "The women can go but you, Jesus, stay here. After all we have important things to talk about and they don't really understand theology."

But an Essene who had become one of the disciples travelling with Jesus said: "Isn't God's word for all people? Before I joined your movement I had always studied the Torah with other women. Are we women disciples to be excluded? After all, didn't your story about the woman from Syrophoenicia show that your message isn't just for some but for all, women and men, Gentile and Jew, slave and free, rich and poor?" And Jesus replied: "Susanna thank you for speaking out. You are much blessed by Holy Wisdom, for you are right." And he asked me to preside at the breaking of the bread and invited Susanna to say the blessing and to teach the Torah lesson for the day. There was grumbling among the men, but we women were excited by the new possibilities God had opened up to us.

My sister Mary helped me to write this down. May God Herself speak to us now and forever.[52]

In this chapter I have sought to exemplify the "dance of interpretation" as a critical rhetorical process. Such a critical practice of interpretation for liberation is not restricted to biblical texts but can be applied successfully to other religious or cultural classics. I am told that it has been used for instance in graduate education, in parish discussions, in college classes, in interreligious dialogue, or in work with illiterate Andean women.

The *ekklesia* of women, I have argued in *Bread Not Stone,* constitutes the practical center and normative space for the hermeneutical circle-dance of a critical feminist rereading of the Bible for liberation. Since such a critical process of biblical interpretation seeks not just to understand biblical texts but also to change biblical religions and cultures in the interest of all women and other marginalized people, it requires a theological reconception of the Bible. Such a reconception construes the Bible as a formative root-model rather than as a foundational archetype. In this understanding the canon is neither the foundational constitution nor a set of norms defining Christian community and identity. Rather, as the formative prototype of biblical faith and community, the Scriptures offer paradigms of struggles and visions that are open to their own transformations through the power of the Spirit in ever new sociohistorical locations.

This model of the Bible as formative prototype conceives of biblical interpretation as a site of struggle and conscientization. It raises several sets of questions which not only require a reconceptualization of historical and theological hermeneutics in rhetorical terms, but also challenge biblical scholarship in general and feminist interpretation in particular to become more sophisticated by attending to its sociopolitical locations and religious contextualization, as well as its rhetorical interests and functions in the struggle for a more just church and world.

NOTES

1. Nancy K. Miller, "Arachnalogies: The Woman, the Text, and the Critic," in *The Poetics of Gender,* ed. Nancy K. Miller (New York: Columbia University Press, 1986), 271ff.

2. Roland Barthes, *The Pleasure of the Text* (New York: Hill and Wang, 1975), 64.

3. Miller, "Arachnalogies," 272.

4. Such a critical feminist model of text and interpretation has affinities with the understanding of midrash developed by Gerald L. Bruns, "The Hermeneutics of Midrash," in *The Book and the Text: The Bible and Literary Theology,* ed. Regina Schwartz (Oxford: Basil Blackwell, 1990), 189-213.

5. See Paolo Freire, *Pedagogy of the Oppressed* (New York: Seabury Press, 1973).

6. Cf. Beverly Wildung Harrison, *Making the Connections: Essays in Feminist Social Ethics* (Boston: Beacon Press, 1985), 235-263.

7. See Christine Schaumberger, "Subversive Bekehrung," in *Schuld und Macht: Studien zu einer feministischen Befreiungstheologie*, ed. C. Schaumberger and L. Schottroff (Munchen: Kaiser Verlag, 1988), 153-182, 202-216, for a discussion of the difficulties in moving women's groups from the sharing of experience to a critical political analysis.

8. For such a deliberate misreading, see George W. Stroup, "Between Echo and Narcissus: The Role of the Bible in Feminist Theology," *Interpretation* 42 (1) (1988): 25.

9. Jean Wyatt, *Reconstructing Desire: The Role of the Unconscious in Women's Reading and Writing* (Chapel Hill: University of North Carolina Press, 1990), 215f; see also Linda K. Christian-Smith, *Becoming a Woman Through Romance* (New York: Routledge, 1990): "Popular fiction, a literary fantasy in which one can dream about an identity and pleasures often beyond what is socially possible or acceptable ... encourages reflection on problems from everyday life and on various alternatives in the imagination" (9).

10. Lynn Gottlieb, "The Secret Jew: An Oral Tradition of Women," in *On Being a Jewish Feminist: A Reader*, ed. Susannah Heschel (New York: Schocken Books, 1983), 273.

11. Eugene LaVerdier, "The One Thing Required," *Emmanuel* (September 1983): 398-399.

12. For literature and discussion of this text, see Joseph Fitzmyer, *The Gospel According to Luke X-XXIV* (Garden City: Doubleday, 1985), 891-895; for more popular commentaries, see Frederick W. Danker, *Jesus and the New Age: A Commentary on St. Luke's Gospel*, rev. ed. (Philadelphia: Fortress Press, 1988), 224-226; David L. Tiede, *Augsburg Commentary Series* (Minneapolis: Augsburg Publishing House, 1988), 210f.

13. It is usually shocking but potentially liberating to students who have internalized in one form or another a doctrine of the Bible as verbal inspiration to come to realize that scholars not only interpret but also establish the original text of the Bible. For a critical discussion of these textual variants, see Juttah Brutscheck, *Die Maria-Martha-Erzählung: Eine redaktionsgeschichtliche Untersuchung zu* Lk 10,38-42. BBB 64 (Frankfurt-Bonn: Verlag Peter Hanstein, 1986), 4-29; M. Zerwick, "Optima Pars (Le 10,28-42)," *Verbum Domini* 27 (1929): 294-298; M. Augsten, "Lukanische Miszelle," *New Testament Studies* 14 (1967/68): 581-583; A. Baker, "One Thing Necessary," *Catholic Biblical Quarterly* 27 (1965): 127-135; Gordon D. Fee, "One Thing Needful? Luke 10:42," in *New Testament Criticism*, ed. E.J. Epp and G. D. Fee (Cambridge: Cambridge University Press, 1981), 61-76.

14. See Daniel A. Scanyi, "Optima Pars. Die Auslegungsgeschichte von Lk 10, 38-42 bei den Kirchenvatern der ersten vier Jahrhunderte," *Studia Monastica* 2 (1960): 5-78; A. Kemmer, "Maria und Martha: Zur Deutungsgeschichte von Lk 10,38ff im alten Mönchtum," *Erbe und Auftrag* 40 (1964): 355-367; J. B. Lotz, "Martha und Maria," *Geist und Leben* 32 (1959): 161-165.

15. Ben Witherington III, *Women in the Ministry of Jesus*, SNTSMS 51 (Cambridge: Cambridge University Press, 1984), 101.

16. See W. H. Wuellner and R. C. Leslie, *The Surprising Gospel: Intriguing Psychological Insights from the New Testament* (Nashville: Abingdon Press, 1984), 110; see also Wuellner's response to my interpretation of the text in E. Schüssler Fiorenza, "Theological Criteria and Historical Reconstruction."

17. R. Conrad Wahlberg, *Jesus According to a Woman* (New York: Paulist Press, 1976), 79.

18. However, please note that I do not analyze John 11 and 12 here in terms of a hermeneutics of suspicion but only in terms of a hermeneutics of reconstruction. If I were to focus here on the Fourth Gospel, such a hermeneutics of suspicion and critical evaluation would be absolutely necessary for a critical feminist interpretation for liberation.

19. Rudolph Bultmann, *History of the Synoptic Tradition* (New York: Harper & Row, 1968), 33.

20. See Jutta Brutscheck, *Maria-Martha-Erzählung*, 30-49.

21. To explain away this dynamic of the story with reference to notions of the Eastern world is to miss the point. "The immediate reaction of most of us in the Western world is to ask why Martha didn't go directly to Mary. Why was it necessary to go to Jesus at all? But the ways of the Eastern world follow precisely the route that Martha took. Instead of open and direct confrontation, the Eastern world characteristically works through a third person to avoid any loss of face on anyone's part. Martha's approach to Jesus was thoroughly consistent with the culture in which she lived" (Wuellner and Leslie, *The Surprising Gospel*, III). It is obvious, however, that Luke did not plot the story in such a way because he wanted Martha to save face. The opposite seems to be the case. The narrative discredits Martha.

22. Mary Rose D'Angelo, "Women Partners in the New Testament," *Journal of Feminist Studies in Religion* 6/1 (1990): 65-86, suggests that *adelphe*, sister, should be read as a missionary title and Martha and Mary understood as a missionary pair. Such a contextualization in the practices of the early Christian missionary movement as I have developed them in *In Memory of Her*, 160-184, is likely and supports my interpretation here. However, her further conclusion that both are a paradigm for lesbian couples who shared "their lives in the Christian mission in relationships that were parallel to those of husband and wife missioners" cannot be substantiated since we do not know whether female-male teams, such as Prisca and Aquila, were married couples.

23. Unfortunately the article of Adele Reinhartz, "From Narrative to History: The Resurrection of Mary and Martha," in Amy-Jill Levine, ed., *"Women Like This,"* 161-184 was not yet available when I revised this chapter. However, her argument against my interpretation overlooks that the rhetoric of kyriocentric texts functions differently with respect to women and men.

24. For elaboration and documentation of such a hermeneutics, see my *In Memory of Her: A Feminist Theological Reconstruction of Christian Origins* (New York: Crossroad, 1983).

25. For the patriarchal shaping of the household and the householder motifs in Luke-Acts that "mollifies the revolutionary eschatological language of the Q-tradition" and in Acts "portrays conversion of households from the top down," see L. Michael White, "Scaling the Strongman's 'Court,' " *Forum* 3(3) (1987): 18.

26. Gerd Theissen, *Sociology of Early Palestinian Christianity* (Philadelphia: Fortress Press, 1978) and the critical review by W. Stegemann, "Vagabond Radicalism in Early Christianity? A Historical and Theological Discussion of a Thesis Proposed by Gerd Theissen," in *The God of the Lowly: Socio-Historical Interpretations of the Bible*, ed. W. Schottroff and W. Stegemann (Maryknoll, N.Y.: Orbis Books, 1984), 148-168.

27. For further discussion and literature, see my *In Memory of Her*, 139f. For a

more positive evaluation of Luke's remark in 8:1-3, see Witherington, *Women in the Ministry of Jesus*, 117. Yet by construing Luke's historical context as rabbinic Judaism, he succumbs to an anti-Jewish reading.

28. See F. W. Danker, *Benefactor, Epigraphic Study of a Graeco-Roman and New Testament Semantic Field* (St. Louis: Clayton Press, 1982); David Lull, "The Servant Benefactor as a Model of Greatness (Lk 22:24-30)," *Novum Testamentum* 28 (1986): 289-305.

29. H. Moxnes, *The Economy of the Kingdom: Social Conflict and Economic Relations in Luke's Gospel* (Philadelphia: Fortress Press, 1988), 133f.

30. See especially E. Laland, "Die Martha-Maria-Perikope Lukas 10, 38-42," *Studia Theological* 13 (1959): 70-85.

31. Such parallel stories are: Zechariah and Mary (1:8-56); Simeon and Anna (2:25-38); the healings of the demoniac and of Simon's mother-in-law (4:31-39); centurion's slave and the son of the widow of Nain (7:1-17); the good Samaritan and the sisters at Bethany (10:29-42); the Sabbath healing of the woman bent double and of the man with dropsy (13:10-17; 14:1-6); the parables of mustard seed and leaven (13:18-21) and of the lost sheep and lost coin (15:4-10); the stories of the widow and tax-collector (18:1-14); of Simon the Cyrene and the women of Jerusalem (23:26-31); the healings of Aeneas and Dorcas (Acts 9:32-42); the vision of the Macedonian and the conversion of the Lydian (Acts 16:9-15); the conversions of Dionysus and Damaris (Acts 17:34).

32. Constance F. Parvey, "The Theology and Leadership of Women in the New Testament," in *Religion and Sexism*, ed. Rosemary Radford Ruether (New York: Simon & Schuster, 1974), 139.

33. Acts 8:3; 9:1f; 17:11f; 22:5f.

34. Acts 1:16; 2:29,37; 13:15,26,38; 15:7,13; 23:1,6; 28:17.

35. Compare, e.g., Hermann-Josef Venetz, "Die Suche nach dem 'einen Notwendigen,'" *Orientierung* 54 (1990): 185-189; see also W. S. Anderson and the minutes of the overall discussion found in H. Waetjen, ed., *Protocol of the Fifty-Third Colloquy*, 10 April 1986, 17-20, 41-63.

36. See now also Steven Davies, "Women in the Third Gospel and the New Testament Apocrypha," in Amy-Jill Levine, ed., *"Women Like This,"* 185-198. In this article Davies has abandoned his positive reading of the Lukan double-work and therefore no longer believes that it was authored by a woman.

37. Robert W. Wall, "Martha and Mary (Luke 10:38-42) in the Context of a Christian Deuteronomy," *Journal for the Study of the New Testament* 35 (1989): 19-35, connects all three pericopes in terms of the deuteronomic Shema.

38. I am following here the analysis of Jutta Brutscheck, *Maria-Martha-Erzählung*, 50-64.

39. See the analysis of the dualisms structuring this passage and its Lukan context by Kerry M. Craig and M. A. Kristjansson, "Women Reading as Men/Women Reading as Women: A Structural Analysis for the Historical Project," in *Poststructural Criticism and the Bible: Text/History/Discourse,* ed. Gary Phillips, *Semeia* 51 (1990): 119-136. However, their structural analysis reinscribes cultural gender dualism insofar as they assume without question that one reads either *as a man or as a woman.*

40. At stake for theologians in such an interpretation that privileges the listening Mary is their own "masculine" authority to speak which requires a "feminine" audience to listen. See for a similar discussion but with a somewhat different empha-

sis, Walter Magab, "Maria und Martha—Kirche und Haus: Thesen zu einer institutionellen Konkurrenz," *Linguistica Biblica* 27(28) (1973): 2-5.

41. The contrasting opposition between Mary and Judas corresponds to the anti-Jewish tendencies in the Fourth Gospel. Whereas the "sectarian" tendencies of the Fourth Gospel allow for women's leadership, the apologetic interests of Luke's gospel vis-à-vis the Roman patriarchal order leads to the downplaying of women's leadership roles. A clue to this editorial tendency is found in Acts 16:21, where Paul is accused of advocating "customs which it is not lawful for Romans to practice."

42. For a similar interpretation see Frances Beydon, "A temps nouveau, nouvelles questions: Luc 10, 38-42," *Foi & Vie: Cahier Biblique* 28 88/5 (1989): 25-32. However, she does not refer to my work.

43. Since such an exploration generally does not belong to the task of professional exegesis, it is also not very well developed in feminist biblical studies. See, however, Susan Brooks Thistlethwaite, "Every Two Minutes: Battered Women and Feminist Interpretation," in *Feminist Interpretation of the Bible*, ed. Letty M. Russell (Philadelphia: Westminster Press, 1985), 96-110; Renita J. Weems, *Just a Sister Away: A Womanist Vision of Women's Relationships in the Bible* (San Diego: Lura Media, 1988); and the feminist collections of sermons by Annie Lally Milhaven, ed., *Sermons Seldom Heard* (New York: Crossroad, 1991).

44. Janice Radway, *Reading the Romance: Women, Patriarchy and Popular Literature* (Chapel Hill: University of North Carolina Press, 1984), 209-222.

45. Ben Witherington III, *Women in the Ministry of Jesus* SNTSMS 51 (Cambridge: Cambridge University Press, 1984), 118.

46. Letty M. Russell, "Women and Ministry," in A. L. Hageman, *Sexist Religion and Women in the Church* (New York: Association Press, 1974), 55ff.

47. All quotes are taken from R. Richardson Smith, "Liberating the Servant," *The Christian Century* 98 (1981): 13-14; see also R. Propst, "Servanthood Redefined: Coping Mechanism for Women Within Protestant Christianity," *Journal of Pastoral Counseling* 17 (1982): 14-18.

48. Rosemary Radford Ruether, *Sexism and God-Talk: Toward a Feminist Theology* (Boston: Beacon Press, 1983), 207; see also the various contributions of Letty M. Russell.

49. Examples of such a hermeneutics of imagination are, e.g., Martha Ann Kirk, CCVI *Celebrations of Biblical Women's Stories: Tears, Milk and Honey* (Kansas: Sheed & Ward, 1987), and Miriam Therese Winter, *WomanWord: A Feminist Lectionary and Psalter: Women of the New Testament* (New York: Crossroad, 1990).

50. See for instance, Heidemarie Langer and Herta Leistner, "Mary and Martha," in *Women's Prayer Services*, ed. Iben Gjerding and Katherine Kinnamon (Mystic: Twenty-Third Publications, 1987), 71-73, and the interpretation of the Ecumenical Women's Group Aarhus, "Mary and Martha," ibid., 55.

51. Quoted from a paper by Jean Young, written after a workshop in the Feminist Spirituality Program of Immaculate Heart College in Los Angeles, August 1984.

52. Revised and quoted from a paper by Gena Marie Stinnett, who participated in the same workshop.

PART II

SOCIOPOLITICAL READINGS
OF THE HEBREW BIBLE

14

WALTER BRUEGGEMANN

Trajectories in Old Testament Literature and the Sociology of Ancient Israel

By drawing lines of connection between the work of G. E. Mendenhall and N. K. Gottwald on premonarchic Israel, F. M. Cross on the priest-hoods during the monarchy, and P. D. Hanson on exilic and postexilic apocalyptic, Brueggemann "maps" two major lines of tradition-for-mation in the Old Testament which show close linkages between the-ology and social organization. These are traceable as competing "trajectories" that run through all the major Old Testament periods.

The "Mosaic liberation" trajectory emerges in an early Israelite peas-ant revolt, in the Mushite priesthood of Shiloh and Nob, in the prophetic critiques, in the Deuteronomists before they later harden into dogmatists, and in postexilic visionaries from the displaced Levitical priesthood and other "have nots." The "royal consolidation" trajectory surfaces in the Davidic-Solomonic state coup, in the Aaronid priesthood of Hebron and Jerusalem, in the institutions of monarchy, in the Priestly writer, and in the postexilic Zadokite priesthood and other empowered "haves."

Various points of tension and conflict between the trajectories and their intermixture in particular Old Testament documents are explored. In the Old Testament, "the shape and character of human community are in question along with the God question," with very large implica-tions for biblical interpreters and scholars in all religious disciplines, since "there is no disinterestedness in the text or in the interpreter."

Reprinted from *Journal of Biblical Literature* 98 (1979): 161-85.

It has long been recognized that there are two circles of tradition in Israel's literature concerning covenant, one derived from Moses and the other Davidic in its formulation.[1] The biblical tradition itself wishes to suggest that the two are continuous, so that the Davidic is a natural derivation from that of Moses and fully faithful to it. Undoubtedly, the circles around David urged this perception of the matter. Recent critical scholarship, however, has now made it reasonable to assume that these two articulations of covenant are not only distinct but also came from very different centers of power and very different processes of tradition building.[2]

Tension, and in some ways, conflict between the traditions can be sensed even when one is not attempting to be precise about the points of origin or settings for the two circles of tradition. Recent traditio-historical analyses confirm such a judgment.[3] Two additional observations need to be made in order to provide a better understanding of these circles of tradition. First, we may speak of trajectories running through the tradition. To my knowledge, the categories of Robinson and Koester[4] have not been applied to Old Testament studies. They urge that pieces of literature and tradition should not be studied in isolation nor in terms of mechanical dependence and relationship through a literary process, but that special attention should be paid to the continuities which flow between various pieces of literature. As a result of social value, use, and transmission, continuities both in terms of cultural context and in terms of theological perspective[5] become decisive for interpretation. Applied to the two covenantal traditions in the Old Testament, "trajectories" suggest that we might be able to trace continuities in the literature shaped and energized by the Mosaic and Davidic covenants. Specifically, as will be evident in what follows, the Mosaic tradition tends to be a movement of protest which is situated among the disinherited and which articulates its theological vision in terms of a God who decisively intrudes, even against seemingly impenetrable institutions and orderings. On the other hand, the Davidic tradition tends to be a movement of consolidation which is situated among the established and secure and which articulates its theological vision in terms of a God who faithfully abides and sustains on behalf of the present ordering.[6] As is clear from the work of Robinson and Koester, attention to trajectories is at best imprecise and does not permit a rigid schematization. It does, however, provide a way to see a coherent and persistent *Tendenz* in each stream.

Second, the presence and meaning of two alternative covenant traditions are richly illuminated by the recent attention to sociological factors. While we still do not have a comprehensive overview of this data, the recent work of George Mendenhall, Norman Gottwald, and Paul Hanson provides some beginnings. Such work makes clear that the literature that stands within the various trajectories is never sociologically disinterested nor singularly concerned with matters theological. Each text and each trajectory reflect important socioeconomic and political concerns.

The following discussion will consider the two covenant traditions in terms of literary trajectories and sociological considerations which may be related to them. Thus far, scholarly presentations have been concerned only with smaller historical periods and not with a comprehensive pattern for the whole. This paper suggests the provisional discernment of a comprehensive pattern which may significantly alter our understanding of the theological import of the texts and the literary-historical questions relating to them.

I

It will be useful to consider recent scholarly literature in terms of various periods of Israel's history which have been subjected to study. Our presentation will reflect a certain periodization of Israel's history; however, that periodization is used simply as a way of reporting various scholarly studies. None of the scholars mentioned has urged a pattern of periodization, so that it may be regarded simply as organization of convenience. For the present discussion, the stress is on the continuity of the trajectory rather than the periodization.

As early as 1962, Mendenhall proposed a fresh way of understanding the conquest and the premonarchial period of Israel (1250–1000 B.C.).[7] In contrast to the dominant views of conquest, either by invasion or infiltration, Mendenhall urged that Israel was formed by an intentional "bond between persons in an intolerable situation."[8] Oppressed people with an alternative vision of social order were able to "reject the religious, economic, and political obligations to the existing network of political organizations."[9] The "habiru" mounted a revolution against tyrannical Canaanite city-kings, rejecting the given social order. Bound to a nonhuman overlord by covenant and the solidarity of the newly formed community, they set about fashioning a deliberate alternative social ordering which became Israel. Thus Mendenhall has interpreted the "conquest" in the categories of oppressed people revolting for liberation versus tyrannical city-kings. In what follows, it will be suggested that these categories provide entry into the two dominant trajectories of Israelite literature.

Related to this hypothesis, several observations emerge from sociological considerations. First, the dominant view of early Israel as nomadic has been sharply placed in question. The sociological data, summarized by Mendenhall,[10] Gottwald, and Frick,[11] require a fresh sociological realism about Israel as an alternative to the city-state. What is different is not mobility or lack of a place but a social ordering which is characterized by political decentralization and social egalitarianism in contrast to urban centralization and social stratification with the power in the hands of an elite. In his preliminary paper, Gottwald contrasts the city and the countryside as available alternative models,[12] whereas Mendenhall presents Israel's egalitarian movement as a more radical step. Thus, Israel is not to be understood as a group of geographical outsiders but as sociopolitical outsiders who were only geographically present but not permitted to share in the shaping of their own destiny. Their marginality is not geographical in character, but rather social, economic, and political. Thus, instead of nomad, the suggested sociological identity is that of peasant, a term which means the politically-economically marginal element of society from whose produce the elite draw their life. Peasant is characterized as one whose labor yields produce enjoyed by others.[13]

Second, Mendenhall has urged a rethinking of the notion of "tribe" in characterizations of early Israel.[14] Tribe, he urges, is not to be understood as a natural ethnic grouping but as an intentional community deliberately committed to a different ideology and a different social organization.[15] Such a notion suggests that the central social unit in early Israel is not to be confused either with conventional notions of nomadism nor with anthropological ideas of kinship groups.

These groups are historical and not natural. In Israel they did not originate because of necessity or nature, but through historical decision-making. The tribe in Israel is to be contrasted with the state, a distinction that has received various presentations in the history of sociology. It is especially to be noted that the historical decision-making from whence comes such a tribe is an intentional action which is the first step away from historical marginality.

Third, such an understanding of the social unit provides a way by which greater stress may be placed on covenant as an ideology and form of social organization. The hypothesis of covenant (anticipated by Buber[16] and articulated especially by Baltzer[17] and Mendenhall[18]) of course provides a major conceptual category for understanding Israel. But that conceptualization has in scholarly discussion stayed largely in the sphere of theological interpretation. Indeed, Baltzer's excellent study is confined to literary and form-critical concerns. Only recently has the notion of covenant been handled sociologically to suggest that it provided ground for a "systematic, ethically and religiously based, conscious rejection of many cultural traits of the late Bronze Age urban and imperial cultures."[19] The covenant, then, is more politically radical and historically pertinent to early Israel than has often been recognized, for it permitted a political *novum* in history and a radical break with urban culture. Mendenhall has in schematic fashion contrasted the regnant social organization and the alternative made possible by covenant.[20]

While Mendenhall in 1955[21] did turn scholarship in a new direction, his major sociological intent has been neglected. Mendenhall's crucial presentation had two parts. The first dealt with the "treaty-form" and ancient Near Eastern parallels discovered in Hittite and Assyrian texts. The second was concerned with the innovative social vision and social organization derived from a covenant-treaty. Scholarship has largely embraced the former and has busily identified elements of the treaty form in many places, although some identifications are exceedingly doubtful.[22]

Until very recently, Mendenhall's major concern for social vision and social organization has not been recognized or pursued by scholars. It has been Mendenhall's own more recent work which has indicated that covenanted Israel embodied not only a theological novelty but also a social experiment as well.[23] The theological factor has required a quite new discernment of God as a faithful covenanter who engaged in the history of Israel and who was impacted by Israel's history, her acts and praises, but nonetheless a faithful covenanter who has independent purpose and authority not derived from his covenanted partner. Conversely, the theological self-understanding of Israel permitted a new people which had no other identity—linguistic, racial, ethnic, or territorial—

except exclusive allegiance to its God. That much has been widely observed.[24]

What has not been sufficiently appreciated are the social implications of this theological novelty. Covenantal commitment to this God, unknown by name and without credential in the empire, carried with it a rejection of loyalty to the gods of the empire and a rejection of the ways of ordering that society.[25] Thus, the theological vision, either as impetus or as justification,[26] made possible a radical discontinuity in the social organization of Israel. Israel was no longer bound to the religion of the empire, which had now been effectively delegitimated, and Israel could no longer and need no longer rely upon the self-securing technology of the empire.

This way of interpreting the data presumes a close link between theological vision and sociological organization. A totalitarian, hierarchical social order has its counterpart and justification in the static religion of the empire in which the gods have no independent existence but are only an integral part of the social system.[27] Most obviously, the pharaoh, manager of the social process, is at the same time embodiment of the gods. There is an identity of social process and theological vision, an arrangement which assured changelessness and which denied any standing ground for theological criticism of social reality.[28]

When the "new" God of freedom and justice is accepted as covenant partner, the totalitarian, hierarchical social order is no longer necessary or viable. Thus the Israelite order from Moses until the time of David, 1250–1000 B.C., represents a sociological experiment to determine if a society is possible when not sanctioned and protected by the imperial gods. It is admittedly a precarious social experiment based on a precarious theological vision. That experimentation stands in sharp discontinuity with its political context as well as its theological milieu and is justified only by the bold theological novelty of Yahwism, a novelty focused on justice and freedom.[29]

So far as I am aware, Mendenhall at no point appeals to a Marxist criticism of society. Gottwald, however, does allow for it.[30] The discernment of the new situation is in keeping with the insight of Marx that the ultimate criticism is the criticism of heaven which then radically criticizes all earthly historical institutions.[31]

This insight, only recently reasserted by Mendenhall in a discussion of the covenant hypothesis, presents a quite shifted paradigm for biblical study, one that will need carefully to be studied, tested, and considered. In both the "peasant revolt" theory of "conquest" and the "covenant law" theme, Mendenhall has understood Israel in sharp discontinuity with its context. It may be argued that this is simply a "class conflict" reading of the text, or perhaps the emergence of an alternative consciousness.[32] In any case, it provides a way to hold together (a) a sense of religious radicalness which either is unexplained or appeals to "revelation" and (b) the awareness of urgency about social reality evident in the text. For the moment, setting aside literary critical judgments, such a view permits us to understand the militancy of Deuteronomy[33] as it urges an alternative understanding of reality and the high-risk venture Israel's faith is shown to be in the Book of Judges. Much more is now seen to be at stake in the pressure of syncretism, for it is not just a choosing among gods or a matter of loyalty to this especially jealous one, but the shape and character of human community are in question along with the God question. Human society, as ordered by Moses, is covenantal because the covenant God both sanctions and expects it. And Israel must resist every religion and every politics which would dismantle the covenant.

These discussions of peasants, tribe, and covenant prepare the way for Gott-wald's major study of early Israel as a community of radical liberation. His book has not yet appeared, but we have hints[34] about his argument that conventional historical interpretations do not appropriate the sociopolitical radicalness of a movement which is profoundly religious in its commitment to the God of the exodus and dangerously political in its rejection of the status quo with its oppressive consciousness and practice.

We do not have (nor are we likely to have) a parallel consideration of the religion of the tyrannical city-kings of Canaan. Obviously, that lies outside the scope of Israel's normative faith and is treated by the Old Testament texts only in reaction and with contempt and hostility. The social organization of the period, however, provides a clue to the religious ideology that undoubtedly legitimated it. We may presume that this religion concerned a god of order who surely served to legitimate the way things already were. While one cannot be very precise, clearly the structure of liberation faith vis-à-vis a religion of legit-imated order is already evident. That trajectory of a religion of God's freedom and a politics of justice will be important for the subsequent periods.

II

The second period we shall consider is that of united monarchy. Obviously something decisive happened to Israel in this period. The tensions revealed in 1 Samuel reflect a battle for Israel as to whether it will be "like the other nations (1 Sam. 8:5, 20) or whether it shall be *'am 'qadōš*, a people holy to the Lord. While that issue has long been perceived, it is now possible to conclude that this was not only a battle over gods and theological identity but also a battle concerning social values and social organization. The innovations and inventiveness of David and Solomon (expressed, e.g., in temple, bureaucracy, harem, standing army, taxation system, utilization of wisdom) embody an imi-tation of urban imperial consciousness of Israel's more impressive neighbors and a radical rejection of the liberation consciousness of the Mosaic tradition. While the texts shaped under the aegis [note the word] of the monarchy in their present form stress continuity with and purpose fidelity to the tradition of Moses, the discontinuities can scarcely be overstated.

Mendenhall has described this as the "paganization of Israel."[35] It is clear from his work that the social innovation of Moses and its corresponding theo-logical novelty of a God aligned with the marginal ones were abandoned in monarchic Israel. Social innovation and theological novelty sustained the com-munity for 250 years, but only as a marginal, minority community preoccupied with survival. That now is given up when the community has the resources and breathing space not only to survive but also to dominate its context, as Solomon was able to do.[36] The radical experiment of Moses is given up and there is in Israel an embrace of the very imperial notions rejected from Egypt.[37] This imperial consciousness combines a religion of a static, guaranteed God together with a politics of injustice and social domination, precisely antithetical to the religion of the freedom of God and the politics of justice introduced by Moses and kept alive in the community of premonarchic Israel.

The change can be observed in a variety of ways. First, the organizational and institutional changes are well known: from traditional to bureaucratic leadership, from tribal ordering to governmental districts, from "holy war" ideology to hired mercenaries, and the introduction of a harem as an appropriate royal accouterment. Thus the presuppositions of public life were drastically altered, indicating an abandonment of the vision which powered the "peasant revolt."

Second, the discernment of God's relation to the community is reshaped. That change may be presented in terms of tent and house. The old tradition of "tent" asserts a claim of mobility and freedom for God. The "house" tradition is surely royal in its orientation and stresses the abiding presence of Yahweh to Israel. Thus the tension of the freedom of God and the accessibility of God to Israel is now tilted in a new direction.[38] The older Mosaic tradition stressed the freedom of God and the notion of presence was precarious. Now the notion of presence is primary and God's freedom is severely constricted, for the royal regime must depend on a patron and legitimator who is unreservedly committed to the shrine and its social arrangement.

Third, in the context of social transformation and theological revision, Frank M. Cross has offered a persuasive construction of the history of priesthood in Israel.[39] Clearly, the priestly narratives must be read with attention to the conflicts and political interests that seem always to have been at stake. It is clear that David was able to achieve a remarkable balance in having two priests, Abiathar and Zadok, and it is equally clear that Solomon brashly dissolved the balance with the enhancement of Zadok and the elimination of Abiathar (1 Kings 2:26–27).

By carefully piecing together the fragmentary evidence, Cross concludes that David held together the priestly rivalry to serve his dominant interest of political unification. According to Cross, one priestly interest, represented by Abiathar, is the Mushite house with old links to Shiloh and Nob; the other is the house of Aaron, represented by Zadok, with roots in Hebron and, ultimately, in Jerusalem.[40] Further, after the period of the united monarchy, Jeroboam I, in setting up his two shrines, balanced a Mushite shrine in Dan with the Aaronid Shrine of Bethel.[41] Thus, the narrative, as Alt has recognized, shows David holding together the imperial and covenantal constituencies. In terms of social vision and organization, it is plausible that David managed the process so that he did not finally force the issue which was so clearly and ruthlessly forced by Solomon.

The Davidic-Solomonic tradition with its roots in Abrahamic memory provides an important alternative theological trajectory.[42] We may identify two theological elements which are surely linked to this movement and which are important to the subsequent faith and literature of the Bible. First, it is generally agreed that the emergence of creation faith in Israel has its setting in Jerusalem and its context in the royal consciousness.[43] The shift of social vision is accompanied with a shifted theological method which embraces more of the imperial myths of the ancient Near East and breaks with the scandalous historical particularity of the Moses tradition. The result is a universal and comprehensive worldview which is more inclined toward social stability than toward social transformation and liberation. Thus, creation theology, like every theological effort, is politically interested and serves to legitimate the regime, which in turn sponsors and vouches for this theological perspective.

Second, clearly from this tradition comes messianism, the notion of God's promise being borne in history by an identifiable historical institution. Thus, the Davidic house now becomes not only historically important but theologically decisive for the future of Israel and all promises and futures are now under the dominance of this institution. It will be clear that in both ways, creation and messianism, the royal perspective is in tension with the Mosaic tradition. In the Mosaic tradition, narratives of concrete liberation are much preferred to comprehensive myths of world order. In the Mosaic world, precarious covenant premised on loyalty is in deep tension with the unconditional affirmation of an historical institution. In these major ways, the Davidic-Solomonic period witnesses the emergence of an alternative both in theology and politics which is in radical tension with Mosaic tradition and congenial to the non-Mosaic and pre-Mosaic royal traditions.[44]

For purposes of tracing literary-theological trajectories, it is important to recognize that the Mushite priesthood was heir to the liberation faith rooted in Moses and preserved among the northern tribes, likely at the shrines of the confederation. Conversely, the Zadokite rootage, from what can be reconstructed, belongs to a royal consciousness based in an urban context. The priestly conflict is not just an in-house power struggle of priestly interests, but it is again a battle for the life of Israel between a liberation faith and a religion of legitimated order. The issue of the earlier period (to use the construct of Mendenhall) between "peasants" and "city-kings" appears to apply here.

On the basis of such a reading of the evidence, the Hebron/Shiloh, Aaronid/ Mushite, Aaron/Moses pattern and the vindication of the former in each case shows that the consciousness of the united monarchy was finally shaped decisively by a tradition rooted in very old pre-Israelite royal traditions. Specifically, it provided a shrine which legitimated order at the expense of justice, which presented the king as the principle of order and not as a child of the torah, and which placed stress on dynastic continuity at the expense of critical transcendence in history.

The tradition of the Canaanite city-kings to whom Mendenhall has applied the term "tyrannical" found its continuation in the royal theology focused on creation and messiah. The Mosaic tradition found its muted continuation in the priestly house of Abiathar, in occasional prophetic criticism, in the symbolic but revolutionary rejection of the Davidic house (2 Sam. 20:1; 1 Kings 12:16), in protests against the institution of monarchy (1 Sam. 8:12), and its "sacred space" (1 Kings 8:27).

III

The two trajectories can be discerned in development throughout the period of the divided monarchies, 922-587 B.C. For this period there has not been the enormous scholarly activity of a sociological character as for the other periods. The tensions revealed here are also better understood when placed in the frame of the earliest confrontation of peasants/city-kings.

The political institutions of the northern and southern kingdoms are likely vehicles for these two traditions of religion and social vision. Thus the split of 1 Kings 12 represents a departure of the community of historical liberation from the ordering regime of David. It is important that the split did not happen over a theological dispute, nor was it simply a gradual growing apart, but it was triggered by a concrete issue of political oppression and social liberation. There is no doubt that the royal consciousness was committed to the maintenance of order at the cost of justice. This is not, of course, to claim that the northern kingdom did not practice similar oppression as under Ahab, but the northern kingdom appears to have been peculiarly open to and vulnerable to the transforming impact of the Moses tradition.

This entire phase of Israel's history is easily understood as a confrontation of kings and prophets, thus continuing the claims of the Davidic-Solomonic commitment to order and continuity and the Mosaic affirmation of freedom even at the cost of discontinuity. We may mention four occasions of the traditions in conflict, in which these trajectories are at work.

1. The confrontation of Elijah/Ahab (Jezebel) in 1 Kings 21 is nearly a pure paradigm of the issue. Elijah stands in the old tradition of "inheritance" (*naḥalah*) whereas the royal figures are committed to the right of royal confiscation which overrides older inheritance rights (*yaraš*).[45] The prophet appeals to the unfettered work of Yahweh which calls kings to accountability and dismantles kingdoms (vv. 17-19), whereas the king utilizes mechanizations of the torah for the sake of royal interest. Elijah believes that covenant curses follow violations of torah, even against the royal person, whereas Ahab believes the torah is only a tool of royal policy.

2. The confrontation between Amos and Amaziah (Amos 7:10-17) is of the same character. Amos speaks against any who violate torah[46] or who try to stop the free word of Yahweh, even if it touches the king. By contrast, Amaziah does not doubt the authority of torah but believes the royal reality has immunity. Thus the king's world has created a situation in which there is no transcendence outside royal management to which appeal can be made. It follows that there is no free God who can evoke or sanction radical social change, precisely the situation Pharaoh wished for in the Egypt of the thirteenth century.

3. The confrontation of Isaiah and Ahaz (Isa. 7:1-9:7) is somewhat different because Isaiah is not so unambiguously placed in the Mosaic trajectory,[47] though of course he does affirm a transcendence beyond royal perception in his use of the key words "glory" (*kabôd*) and "holy" (*qadôš*). Thus it is not quite so clear that his position in the face of the king is so unambiguously critical. Nonetheless,

he calls the king to radical faith (7:8) and urges the king to a wholly new perception of reality which calls the king out from his self-securing posture.

The resolution of the unit on the Syro-Ephraimite War (Isa. 9:2-7) demonstrates the delicate balance worked by the prophet. On the one hand, the future is indeed Davidic, with appeal to the royal promissory tradition rooted in 2 Sam. 7. The promise indicates enormous confidence in the royal tradition and royal institution, for it makes reference to Yahweh's unreserved commitment to this institution. Thus, the expectation of the prophet (if it is in fact his poetry) is very different from the radicalness of Amos. Amos, in extraordinary boldness (now placed after the Amaziah encounter), had finally said "end" (*qēṣ*).[48] There had never been a pronouncement more radical than this. In a different way, Isaiah in his appeal to the Davidic promise concludes "no end" (*'în qēṣ*) (v.6).[49] (If, as some argue, Amos is committed to the Davidic reality, then his word is against the north and not in conflict with Isaiah; but that seems unlikely, even if Amos' words refer to the north.)

4. A final example we cite of the tension of traditions in this period is in the poem of Jer. 22:13-19, in which Jeremiah contrasts two kings, Jehoiakim and Josiah. Jehoiakim, so quickly dismissed by the Deuteronomist (2 Kings 24:1-7), is presented as an embodiment of royal self-serving, dominated by injustice and unrighteousness. The son practiced oppression and violence, the father cared for the poor and needy, i.e., he understood covenantal knowing. The poetry of Jeremiah (passing over the death of Josiah) presents him as "well," i.e., faithful in covenant, and Jehoiakim as destined to an ignoble death (which did not happen). The poem is not a report on what happened but a projection of what may be anticipated from the tradition.

Special note should be taken of Josiah, who occupied a crucial place in this period near its end and who also holds an enigmatic position between the traditions. On the one hand, he is clearly a Davidic figure. His credentials are unquestioned and his conduct of office shows he did not flinch from that role. But it is equally clear that unlike almost every other Davidide, he subordinated his Davidic role to the claims of torah. In terms of traditions which concern us, the Davidic claims are subordinated to Mosaic claims.[50]

The contrast of Jehoiakim (*lô'-ṣedeq, lô'-mišpaṭ*) and Josiah (*mišpaṭ, ṣedeq*) articulates well the trajectories of the older period. Jehoiakim is obviously a practitioner of the same oppression as the city-kings and no doubt had a theology of order to legitimate it. Josiah, from a religion of torah, engages in political practice quite in keeping with the liberation movement of Moses.

It is possible that the trajectories in this period can be discerned in the variant expressions of the normative tradition designated J and E. There is little doubt that J is an attempt at unitive and comprehensive theologizing. Concerned both to secure the place of the Davidic house in normative theology and to make cosmic claims in terms of linking Jerusalem's centrality and creation theology.[51] Conversely, the E tradition, to the extent it is a distinct and identifiable piece, is a separatist statement concerned for the purity of the community and aware of the threat of syncretism.[52] Clearly, purity is no concern of J and unitive issues are remote to E. Thus the old trajectory of marginal people with a primary concern for freedom and established people with a large concern for stability are reflected in the shape of the J and E traditions. The main issue, in terms of community identity (south and north) communal function and office (king and prophet) and tradition (J and E), stayed alive until the loss of Jerusalem.[53]

IV

The next period we may identify is that of the exile, for which the conventional dates are 587-537 B.C. Even if those dates are somewhat problematic, this period presents an identifiable crisis and a responding literature which permits disciplined consideration.

It is clear that with the crisis of 587, the faith trajectories we have presented are thrown into disarray. Particularly is this the case with the Mosaic prophetic covenantal trajectory which seems now to have failed. From the perspective of the normative literature of the Old Testament, the pre-exilic period is dominated by the Mosaic trajectory, with the royal alternative subordinated (though undoubtedly flourishing in practice). With the exile, we may in broad outline speak of an inversion of the traditions so that the Mosaic theme is in crisis and is apparently less germane, while the promissory royal tradition now becomes the dominant theological mode for Israel.

In recent scholarly discussion the following are relevant to our theme:

1. The deuteronomic corpus, either shaped or revised in the exile, represents an insistence upon the Mosaic way of discerning reality and its insistence on radical obedience.[54] It is a call for radical obedience to torah, an embrace of Yahweh's will for justice with appropriate sanctions (positive and negative) for obedience. Thus, it continues the urgent call for purity (2 Kings 17:7-41) with its militant, uncompromising social vision.

Following Von Rad, it has been argued that Davidic themes of assurance are also present in the corpus.[55] These may perhaps be found in the conclusion of 2 Kings 25:27-30, or in the three texts now generally regarded as later additions (Deut. 4:29-31; 30:1-10; 1 Kings 8:46-53).[56] It is possible that these somewhat tone down the uncompromising rigor of the literature, but it is equally clear that they do not measurably affect the main theme of the piece, namely, Yahweh's will for a community of obedience and justice.

There can be no doubt that this primal liberation word of Moses has now hardened into an ideology. It serves as a critique of comfortable, cult accommodating religion, whether toward Babylonian imperialism or Canaanite city-kings. Thus the call for repentance and disengagement from culture religion persists.

2. In sharp contention with that trajectory, two pieces of literature growing out of the promissory tradition are rooted in another view of reality. First Albrektson has argued that Lamentations is a response to the harshness of Deuteronomy.[57] In the poetry of Lamentations, appeal is made to the claims of Jerusalem. Thus, Lamentations casts itself much more willingly upon the graciousness and freedom of Yahweh, the abiding faithfulness of Yahweh which

is unconditional and unreserved. That modest affirmation (3:22-24) cannot be derived from the abrasion and urgency of the Mosaic tradition but appeals to an alternative theological model more likely rooted in the confidence of the Jerusalem traditions and institutions. Thus both the assurance of 3:22-24 and the confidence of 3:31-33 appear to be echoes of the promise of *hesed* in 2 Sam. 7:11-16. The allusions to the royal psalms which Albrektson has noted strengthen the likelihood of such an appeal.

In a similar though more frontal way, the poem of Job may be understood as a protest against the crisp certitude of Deuteronomy. If indeed Deuteronomy can in moralistic simplicity reduce everything to discernible moral causes, Job counters with an awareness that life will not be so easily explained, that mystery moves in ambiguity and lack of clarity, and that God in his freedom has other concerns than exact response to human behavior.[58] Thus the God of Job is not inordinately preoccupied with "the human condition." There is no doubt that Job protests the moral singularity of his friends who speak out of a perspective not unlike that of Deuteronomy. The speech of Yahweh completely rejects those categories.

The rootage of the alternative perspective of the poet is not so easy to identify. We may note two attempts pertinent to our investigation. Samuel Terrien has located the poem of Job in the new year festival in the Babylonian exile as a para-cultic drama of one for whom history no longer holds any promise.[59] The innocent sufferer "has lost all, and for all practical purposes of historical realism, he has died, but will live again by faith."[60] Terrien sees that an appeal to the creation myths (older than Israel's historical memories) makes possible "a poetic discussion of the theology of grace." Indeed the poet presents himself as "theologian of pure grace, over against the fallacies of proto-pelagianism."[61] Thus the basic themes of the religion of the city-state, a royal person and a creation myth, surface here as resources for Israel when the historicizing morality of Deuteronomy has failed. Such a difference of trajectory is apparent, even if linkage of the poem of Job to an historical crisis cannot be sustained.

From a quite different perspective, Cross has reached conclusions similar to those of Terrien.[62] "Yahweh the Lord of history has failed to act. El or Baal, the transcendent creator, spoke."[63] In Job, opines Cross, the ancient myths regained their meaning. Cross draws the radical conclusion that Job brought the ancient religion of Israel to an end and evoked the resurgence of the oldest pre-Israelite myths, precisely those myths to which the creation faith of Israel made appeal.

We should not neglect the sociological implication of the embrace of older myth at the expense of historical self-awareness in a time of crisis. Needful though that choice was in exile, such a decision is inherently socially conservative. There is not within the return to myth the nerve or energy to take the actions which would transform historical circumstance. Indeed, it was the rejection of those very myths which permitted the Israelite *novum* in history and religion.[64] Conversely, such a "theology of grace" contains within it the acceptance of things as they are, and there is here no call to repentance in terms of historical engagement. Thus, from one perspective Job reacts against the passionate stridency of Deuteronomy which knows too much and asks too much. On the other hand, it reduces historical nerve and asks an embrace of help-lessness in the face of the terror of history and the hiddenness of God. Thus Miles, in a socially conservative position albeit faithful to Job, sees that "there was truth in what had been excluded, and in the book of Job that truth returns."[65] The poet is challenged to retain the old knowledge against the new; and the old knowledge is that God is not always victorious and "Job's comforting is a play about the return of the truth that God and natural reality are inex-tricably one."[66]

The trajectories are clear in the apparent tension between Job and Deuter-onomy. Job does indeed represent the "old truth" that oppressive life must be accepted as ordained, surely a comfort in exile, while Deuteronomy bears the "new truth."[67] Exile brings these truths to sharp conflict, the one offering assur-ance of grace, the other the urgency of repentance. Exile may be read, then, either as a destiny to be embraced or as an historical situation to be trans-formed.

3. Second Isaiah, it is commonly agreed, is the poetic matrix in which the crisis of the trajectories receives a new articulation.[68] In an earlier essay,[69] Bern-hard Anderson showed the extent to which Deutero-Isaiah utilized the exodus traditions to announce that his own time was a time like that of Moses, in which Israel as a newness in history had been willed by God. Thus, Second Isaiah is a statement about historical redemption, making ready use of the Mosaic tra-dition.

More recently and with more precise focus on covenant, Anderson has con-cluded that it is the Abrahamic/Davidic covenant which dominates Second Isa-iah.[70] Moreover, "the Mosaic covenant is appropriately absent from Second Isaiah's prophecy, for obedience to commandments is not regarded as a pre-requisite for blessing and welfare."[71] "The ground for hope, therefore, is not a change on the side of man but, so to speak, on the side of God."[72]

Second Isaiah is the primary locus in Scripture where the trajectories do come together in a remarkably synthetic way. Both the history-transcending God of Job and the militant historicality of Deuteronomy come to positive expression. But on balance, Anderson has rightly discerned that the promises of God are the ultimate word of the poet. Thus Second Isaiah shows how it was necessary in the exile to make a major reorientation in traditions and move the normative faith of Israel from the one trajectory to the other.

In Second Isaiah, as in Job, creation themes reshape Israel's memory and hope according to the Jerusalem trajectory. It is the royal theme of Abraham/ Noah/David which gives the poetry of Second Isaiah its energizing power.[73]

Anderson's stress makes it unmistakable that in exile the Abrahamic tradi-tion has gained a new centrality which tilts the religion of Israel essentially toward promise. In that context, we should note the bold proposal of Van Seters that the Abraham materials were formulated in this period to meet the situation of dislocation.[74] That perhaps claims too much. We can observe that the the-ological inventiveness of the period shows a tendency to return to the royal-creation-promise tradition with its social conservatism, the very tradition which the "new truth" of Moses challenged.

4. Finally for this period, we should note the way in which Wolff[75] has juxtaposed the traditions of D and P in the exile. He begins with the two-sided covenant formula: "I will be your God and you shall be my people," and argues that P and D, reflecting their two trajectories, each stress one part of the formula. P gives emphasis to "I will be your God," and D stresses "You shall be my people." That is a fair summary of the issue in the exile. Obviously, both statements bear a truth and both are essential in exile. The alternative stress indicates not only a different theological reading of the promise and of the resources but also a very different sociological analysis of what is required and what is possible.

V

The final period we shall consider, the postexilic period, may be briefly mentioned by reference to the work of Paul Hanson.[76] Hanson has presented a major proposal, admittedly too schematic, for organizing the postexilic literature of the canon. He proposes that the beginning point for understanding this literature is the dialectic Deutero-Isaiah articulated between vision and reality.

In the period after Deutero-Isaiah, various groups in Israel each embraced a part of the dialectic and made that part its standing ground for faith and literature. Thus, Second Isaiah provides poetic and theological rationale for both the "pragmatists" and the "visionaries." For Hanson, the pragmatists are identified as the group in power, centering around the accommodating priesthood in Jerusalem. The visionaries are those groups now shut out of power and driven to hope in a new act of God which would invert historical reality and bring them to power. This latter group, pressed by its "worldweariness" to apocalyptic, may be identified with the circles of the Levites who were previously influential and now had become increasingly marginal.

Hanson's work utilizes the sociological paradigm of Karl Mannheim with its definition of ideology as a self-serving justification for the status quo and utopia as the passionate hoping for an alternative future. In presenting such a paradigm, Hanson limits his attention to rootage in Second Isaiah and does not go behind this literature for his purposes. But for our purposes, it is important to observe that Second Isaiah is not the first articulator nor the inventor of this dialectic. It lies deep and old in the tradition of Israel. Thus the "visionaries" and "pragmatists" of the postexilic period continue, in a way appropriate to their time and place, the same stances already discerned in the hopeful liberation movement of Moses and the accommodating, embracing creation-royal faith of the Davidic circles. The visionaries continue the hope and passion of the liberation tradition which believes that the present order is sharply called into question by God's promises. The pragmatists continue the confident affirmation of the present as the proper ordering willed by God, perhaps to be gradually changed but on the whole to be preserved. It is the substantive connections between the work of Gottwald and Mendenhall in the early period, Cross in the history of the priesthood, and especially Hanson in the later period, which permit us to speak of trajectories.

VI

We may then suggest a schematic way in which the trajectories can be understood. A trajectory, of course, is not a straitjacket into which every piece of data must be made to fit, but it lets us see the tendencies which continue to occur and to observe the influences which flow from one period to another. Over the five periods we have considered, generally following the periodization used by recent scholars in delimiting their work, the continuities may be outlined in the form of a chart.

Up to this point, scholars have focused on the tension in various periods. Mendenhall and Gottwald have concentrated on the early period, Cross on the monarchial period, and Hanson on postexilic developments. The point argued here is that continuities may be traced through the various periods in each of the strands, thus permitting us to term them "trajectories."[77]

Moreover, we may suggest, again in quite schematic fashion, common elements which appear continuously in each of the trajectories. Among them are:

A. *The Royal Trajectory*
  (1) prefers to speak in myths of unity
  (2) speaks a language of fertility (creation) and continuity (royal institutions)
  (3) preferred mode of perception is that of universal comprehensiveness
  (4) appears to be fostered by and valued among urban "haves"
  (5) tends to be socially conserving with a primary valuing of stability
  (6) focuses on the glory and holiness of God's person and institutions geared to that holiness

B. *The Liberation Trajectory*
  (1) prefers to tell concrete stories of liberation
  (2) speaks a language of war and discontinuity
  (3) preferred mode of perception is that of historical specificity
  (4) appears to be fostered by and valued among peasant "have nots"
  (5) tends to be socially revolutionary with a primary valuing of transformation
  (6) focuses on the justice and righteousness of God's will

To the extent that the schematic presentation below is correct, it means that these tendencies will be found at every period in the appropriate trajectory. A history of traditions approach must include a sociological analysis so that we are aware of the social function of each of the traditions, the authority assigned to it, the claims made for it and the power and social vision deriving from it.[78]

VII

It is perhaps premature to speak of the emergence of a new paradigm for scholarship, but there are hints in that direction.[79] It is clear that the older

	I. Mosaic Period (emergence of liberation)	II. The United Monarchy ("paganization")	III. Divided Monarchy (the clash of traditions)	IV. Exile (traditions in crisis)	V. Postexilic Period
A.	imperial power and city-kings	Zadok: the Aaronite priesthood, royal theology and creation faith	royal history	P: "I will be your God"	Zadokite priesthood: pragmatists urban "haves" scribes comfortable syncretists Ezekiel 44
			in tension	2nd Isa.	
			1 Kings 21: Ahab/Elijah Amos 7:10–17: Amaziah/Amos	"Look to the Rock from which you were hewn" (51:1)	
			Isa. 7:1–9:7: Ahaz/Isaiah	"Behold, I am doing a new thing" (43:18)	
			Jer. 22:13-19: Jehoiakim/Josiah		
B.	revolt of peasants	Abiathar: the Mushite priesthood	prophetic alternatives	D: "You will be my people"	Levitical priesthood: visionaries peasant "have nots" apocalypticists waiting purists Isaiah 60–62

syntheses are now generally perceived as inadequate. This applies not only to the evolutionary scheme of Wellhausen but in a less incisive way also to the credo-tradition hypothesis of Von Rad.[80] Evidences of the emerging consensus around this provisional paradigm are as varied as Westermann's proposal of a contrast of blessing and salvation[81] and the suggestive title of Cross's statement, *Canaanite Myth and Hebrew Epic*. Westermann, in a programmatic way, has shown that blessing and salvation represent quite different theological worlds. He has not gone on to draw sociological conclusions nor to suggest that Old Testament interpretation may be largely organized this way. Cross has finely shown the dialectic of epic, which seeks to be concretely historical, and myth, which moves in the direction of syncretism. Cross means both to move beyond the historical emphasis of the American and German schools and the mythic inclination of the Scandinavians to show that the perspectives of the two are mutually corrective.

1. It can be argued that such a reading of Israel's faith and history is possible only by an appeal to a particular theory of history. And there is no doubt that a Marxist class reading of the Bible is not unrelated to this paradigm. Concerning the early period, Gottwald acknowledges this influence and makes a deliberate use of such a frame of reference.[82] Concerning the later period, Hanson is decisively guided by the conceptualization of Mannheim.[83] Having acknowledged the influence (explicit or not) of this theory of society, several comments are in order:

(a) There has been some critical objection to the use of such a model for interpretation. Alan J. Hauser[84] has objected to the decisive role played by a Marxist model. More judiciously, Brian Kovacs[85] observed that by the use of Mannheim's model, Hanson has been led to and permitted certain conclusions which would have been very different given a different sociological model. Undoubtedly, much more testing remains to be done, and a clear consensus in this direction is far from established.

(b) It will, of course, be tempting to dismiss the entire approach by a rejection of Marxist presuppositions.[86] In response to such a criticism, Robert McAfee Brown has rightly said that the real issue is not if Marxist categories may be used but if the presentation and discernment is correct in terms of the data and if the categories serve responsible interpretation.[87] When that question is answered, the issue of Marxist presuppositions becomes largely irrelevant.

(c) Most importantly, it will need to be recognized again that there is no "presuppositionless" exegesis. It is not a matter of using Marxist categories or continuing "objective" interpretation. The paradigm suggested here requires that the critical guild become aware of its own categories and, indeed, of its own "embourgeoisement."[88] For example, Hauser seems quite unaware of his own presuppositions and seems to imagine that his own critical approach is socially disinterested. In this view, John McKenzie seems also to misunderstand and deliver a polemic against Marxist categories without discerning what the argument is about. There is no doubt that every paradigm, that of Wellhausen, Von Rad, or any other, including this one, contains presuppositions which govern interpretation. Thus, the present sociological discussion presses hermeneutical considerations even upon our more "objective" work in literature and history.[89]

2. The trajectories suggested here may illuminate the various alternatives in current theological discussion. Most broadly, the alternatives may be grouped in terms of process hermeneutics and liberation hermeneutics.[90] In terms of our previous discussion, process theologies may be generally placed in the trajectory of royal theology which is concerned with large comprehensive issues, which regards the concreteness of historical memory as a matter of little interest, and which is concerned with the continuities of the process. Current scholarly investigation within this trajectory: (a) is likely seeking meaningful interface with

current cultural forms; (b) is most likely to be lodged in university contexts and their epistemological commitments and not primarily interested in the forming of the synagogue/church as an alternative and distinct community of faith; and (c) is likely to have an inherent bias toward social conservatism. Of course, persons engaged in this scholarship may indeed be found elsewhere, but the reference group is likely to be the same. It is equally clear that persons in this scholarly tradition may themselves be concerned for an ethical radicalness, but it is not likely to be rooted in this epistemological tradition.

We may cite one recent example, the judgment of Miles about the "old truth" that "God and the harshness of nature, though they may not be One, are not separable."[91] Such an affirmation clearly inclines to seeing God simply as part of the process and runs the ready danger of giving sanction to the way things are because they cannot in any case be changed. Of course, Miles does not even hint at such an extrapolation. The slide from nature which is not separable from God and cannot be changed to history understood the same way, however, is not a difficult one. Such an understanding of the trajectory does not, of course, imply a criticism of the persons who work in the trajectory for they themselves may be passionate in other directions. The *Tendenz* itself inclines toward uninterrupted development. Moreover, that *Tendenz* has a remarkable capacity to coopt and contain the specific angularities of the other tradition, as, for example, Solomon containing the ark in the temple.

3. Conversely, the various liberation theologies in their epistemological abrasiveness likely may be located on the trajectory rooted in Moses. They are inclined to focus on the concreteness of historical memory and regard more sweeping unitive statements as less important and compelling. Current scholarly work in this trajectory: (a) is likely not so directly concerned with contact with cultural forms and values but is addressed to a particular faith community living in uneasy tension with the dominant cultural forms and values; (b) is most likely to be lodged in a confessing community or a school of it. It is inclined to be concerned primarily with the faithful effectiveness of the confessing community and to believe that the dominant rationality will permit no ready point of contact without coopting. And, if the scholar is lodged in a university context, it is still likely the case that the main referent is a confessing group; (c) is likely to have an intrinsic bias toward social, ethical radicalness. This does not mean, of course, that in every case the person involved is socially radical, for he/she may in fact be conservative. But the practice of this scholarship will predictably lead to the surfacing of such issues, even without the person intentionally doing so.

The pursuit of this paradigm of trajectories from early Israel until current scholarship, informed as it is by sociological considerations, is important in two ways, both affirming that there is no disinterestedness in the text or in the interpreter. Such a paradigm will permit texts to be understood more effectively in terms of their placement in Israel's faith and life and in the traditioning process. Such a paradigm will regularly force more attention to the interest and hermeneutical presuppositions of the interpreter and his/her community of reference. The pursuit of these trajectories may be a major service biblical study can offer to colleagues in other disciplines, for it may provide ground from which to do serious criticism. This discernment might lead one to expect a very different kind of scholarship, each faithful to a stream of tradition, depending on the context of the interpreter.

NOTES

1. On the extensive literature, see L. Rost, "Sinaibund und Davidsbund," TLZ 72 (1947): 129-34; and "Erwägungen zu Hosea 4:14f," *Festschrift Alfred Bertholet,* ed. W. Baumgartner, O. Eissfeldt, K. Elliger, and L. Rost (Tübingen: Mohr, 1950), pp. 459-60; M. Sekine, "Davidsbund und Sinaibund bei Jeremia," VT 9 (1959): 45-57; A. H. J. Gunneweg, "Sinaibund und Davidsbund," VT 10 (1960): 335-41; Murray Newman, *The People of the Covenant* (New York: Abingdon, 1962); David N. Freedman, "Divine Commitment and Human Obligation," *Int* 18 (1964): 419-31; Delbert Hillers, *Covenant: The History of a Biblical Idea* (Baltimore: Johns Hopkins University Press, 1969); Tomoo Ishida, *The Royal Dynasties in Ancient Israel,* BZAW 142 (Berlin: de Gruyter, 1977), pp. 99-117; Ronald Clements, *Abraham and David,* SBT 2/5 (London: SCM Press, 1967); and the general comments of Dennis McCarthy, *Old Testament Covenant* (Richmond: John Knox Press, 1972), especially Chapters 2 and 5.

2. Murray Newman, *People of the Covenant,* had already argued that the Abraham-David tradition is derived from the south and the Mosaic tradition from the north. The difference, of course, is more cultural and sociological than geographical. Bernhard W. Anderson, *Creation versus Chaos* (New York: Association Press, 1967) has shown the creative power of the Jerusalem establishment as expressed in the various creation and royal traditions.

3. Cf. the summary of Douglas Knight, *The Traditions of Israel,* SBLDS 9 (Missoula: Scholars Press, 1973).

4. James M. Robinson and Helmut Koester, *Trajectories through Early Christianity* (Philadelphia: Fortress Press, 1971).

5. On the issue of continuity and discontinuity, see especially the discussions of Peter Ackroyd, *Continuity: A Contribution to the Study of the Old Testament Religious Traditions* (Oxford: Blackwell, 1962) and "Continuity and Discontinuity: Rehabilitation and Authentication," *Tradition and Theology in the Old Testament,* ed. Douglas Knight (Philadelphia: Fortress Press, 1977), pp. 215-34.

6. See the summary of Claus Westermann, "Creation and History in the Old Testament," *The Gospel and Human Destiny,* ed. V. Vajta (Minneapolis: Augsburg, 1971), pp. 11-38. Westermann has observed how the different traditions yield very different presentations of God. He has not pursued the sociological dimension of the argument, but it is clear that the theological *Tendenz* of a trajectory serves specific interests.

7. George Mendenhall, "The Hebrew Conquest of Palestine," BA 25 (1962): 66-87. His alternative hypothesis has been given a positive treatment by John Bright, *A History of Israel,* 2nd ed. (Philadelphia: Westminster, 1972), p. 133, n. 69, and John L. McKenzie, *The World of the Judges* (New York: Prentice-Hall, 1966), pp. 95-98.

8. Mendenhall. "The Hebrew Conquest," p. 87.

9. Ibid., p. 75.

10. George Mendenhall, "The Conflict between Value Systems and Social Con-

rol," *Unity and Diversity,* ed. Hans Goedicke and J. J. M. Roberts (Baltimore: Johns Hopkins University Press, 1975), pp. 169-80; "The Monarchy, " *Int* 29 (1975): 155-70; "Samuel's Broken Rib: Deuteronomy 32," *No Famine in the Land,* ed. James W. Flanagan and Anita Weisbrod Robinson (Missoula: Scholars Press, 1975), pp. 63-74, and his synthesis in *The Tenth Generation* (Baltimore: Johns Hopkins University Press, 1973), especially Chapters 1, 7, and 8. These studies are derivative from his early work on covenant in 1955. Only now is he exploring the sociological aspects of that study.

11. Norman K. Gottwald, "Biblical Theology or Biblical Sociology?" *Radical Religion* 2 (1975): 46-57; "Domain Assumptions and Societal Models in the Study of Pre-Monarchic Israel," *VTSup* 28 (1974): 89-100, and "Were the Early Israelites Pastoral Nomads?" *Rhetorical Criticism,* ed. Jared J. Jackson and Martin Kessler (Pittsburgh: Pickwick, 1974), pp. 223-255; Norman K. Gottwald and Frank S. Frick, "The Social World of Ancient Israel," SBLSP (1975): 165-78.

12. For our argument and its implications, it is important to note that both Gottwald and Mendenhall are engaged in the construction of alternative models. Obviously, increased data can still be adapted to the regnant models, but the importance of their work is precisely in the proposal of a new comprehensive model for interpretation.

13. Eric Wolf, *Peasants* (Englewood Cliffs, N.J.: Prentice-Hall, 1966), has provided a basic study of this social factor. Cf. John H. Halligan, "The Role of the Peasant in the Amarna Period," SBLSP (1976): 155-70. Concerning what is perhaps a contemporary parallel to this crisis in Israel, Hugo Blanco *(Land or Death* [New York: Pathfinder, 1972¹], p. 110) asserts, "We must always keep in mind that the one problem of the peasant around which all others revolves is the problem of land.

14. *Tenth Generation,* Chapter 7, and more recently, "Social Organization in Early Israel," *Magnalia Dei: The Mighty Acts of God,* ed. Frank Cross, Werner Lemke, and P. D. Miller, Jr. (Garden City, N.Y.: Doubleday, 1976), pp. 132-51.

15. Mendenhall, *Tenth Generation,* pp. 19-31.

16. Martin Buber, *The Kingship of God,* 3rd ed. (New York: Harper & Row, 1966), especially Chapter 7. It is remarkable that Buber had seen this long before the work of Mendenhall and Baltzer.

17. Klaus Baltzer, *The Covenant Formulary* (Philadelphia: Fortress Press, 1971; first published in 1964).

18. George Mendenhall, *Law and Covenant in Israel and the Ancient Near East* (Pittsburgh: Biblical Colloquium, 1955).

19. Mendenhall, *Tenth Generation,* p. 12.

20. Mendenhall, "The Conflict between Value Systems and Social Control." In tabulating the contrasts between social theories based on "covenant" and "law," it is likely that he uses "law" in the same sense as does Paul in his radical critique of the theological function of the law.

21. Mendenhall, *Law and Covenant.*

22. See the summary of Dennis McCarthy, *Old Testament Covenant.*

23. The earlier scholarly consideration of Mendenhall's work focused on the radical theological break with the religion of the day. Only more recently has the social counterpart of that radical theology been more widely considered. The links between the theological and sociological are evident in *Tenth Generation.* See also Gottwald, "Biblical Theology or Biblical Sociology?" and especially M. Douglas Meeks, "God's Suffering Power and Liberation," *JRT* 11 (1977): 44-54.

24. A model articulation of that insight is offered by G. Ernest Wright, *The Old Testament against Its Environment*, SBT 2 (London: SCM Press, 1950).

25. Gottwald, "Biblical Theology or Biblical Sociology?" is especially attentive to the social use and function of religion, an insight surely Marxist in its awareness. His summary of the break in sociology asserted by Yahwism is this: "In brief the chief articles of Yahwistic faith may be socio-economically 'de-mythologized' as follows: 'Yahweh' is the historically centralized primordial power to establish and sustain social equality in the face of oppression from without and simultaneously provincialism and non-egalitarian tendencies from within the society. . . . Yahweh is unlike the other gods of the ancient Near East as Israel's egalitarian inter-tribal order is unlike the other ancient Near Eastern social systems. . . . The social-organization principle in Israel finds its counterpart in a symbolic ideological exclusionary principle in the image of the deity" (p. 52).

26. Acknowledgment must of course be made of Feuerbach's criticism that every religious statement is indeed a projection of social reality. Gottwald (ibid., p. 48) appears to move in this direction. "It seems that it is primarily from the historico-social struggle of a sovereign inter-tribal community that the major analogies for conceiving Yahweh are drawn." Mendenhall more readily appeals to the category of revelation and exercises a kind of theological positivism. Thus there is a difference between them on this point. Mendenhall *(Tenth Generation*, p. 16) alludes to the problem. "Do the people create a religion, or does the religion create a people? Historically, when we are dealing with the formative period of Moses and Judges, there can be no doubt that the latter is correct, for the historical, linguistic, and archaeological evidence is too powerful to deny. Religion furnished the foundation for a unity far beyond anything that had existed before, and the covenant appears to have been the only conceivable instrument through which the unity was brought about and expressed." In any case, their critical approaches disclose in fresh ways the fact that not only the dominant theology but the dominant scholarly methodology is not disinterested.

27. My colleague, M. Douglas Meeks ("God's Suffering Power and Liberation") has discerned how a notion of God who is passionless serves well a psychology and a sociology which are passionless. This observation appears to be especially important to liberation movements as they address the theological and sociological paradigms of dominance. Cf. Jane Marie Luecke, "The Dominance Syndrome," *Christian Century* 94 (1977): 405-7, for a summary of the matter.

28. Mendenhall has seen that to the extent that God is continuous with the social, economic system, outsiders have no court of transcendent appeal against the dominant ordering. That linkage of sociology and theology is especially evident in Egyptian religion which on the one hand is committed to order and on the other hand regards Pharaoh as an embodiment of that ordering divinity. On both sociological and theological grounds, revolution is unthinkable. See Henri Frankfort, *Kingship and the Gods* (Chicago: University of Chicago Press, 1948). The subtitle is telling: "A study of Ancient Near Eastern Religion as the Integration of Society and Nature." Such integration brings with it social conservatism.

29. The Mosaic tradition is premised on the affirmation of a God who has freedom from the regime. On the freedom of God in this tradition, see Walther Zimmerli, "Prophetic Proclamation and Reinterpretation," *Tradition and Theology in the Old Testament*, pp. 69-100. Zimmerli sees the tradition as being concerned with the fact that "Yahweh in his freedom can utter his word anew."

30. In addition to the various articles in *The Bible and Liberation* (Berkeley: Radical Religion, 1976) which make primary use of Marxist critical tools, see especially Gottwald, "Early Israel and 'the Asiatic Mode of Production,' " SBLSP (1976): 145-54.

31. Marx's programmatic statement in his "Critique of Hegel's Philosophy of Right," is: "Thus the criticism of heaven is transformed into the criticism of earth, the criticism of religion into the criticism of law, and the criticism of theology into the criticism of politics." Cf. *The Marx-Engels Reader,* ed. R. C. Tucker (New York: W. W. Norton, 1972), p. 13. My criticism of Gottwald, from whom I have learned so much, is that he has not given sufficient attention to a critique of heaven.

32. In Israel, poetry may be understood as the rhetoric of the alternative community which refuses to abide by the prose of the empire. On the act of poetry as an assertion of liberation, see David N. Freedman, "Pottery, Poetry and Prophecy: An Essay on Biblical Poetry, " *JBL* 96 (1977): 5-26, and less directly, "Divine Names and Titles in Early Hebrew Poetry," *Magnalia Dei: The Mighty Acts of God,* pp. 55-107. In the latter essay, the discernment of "militant," "revival," and "syncretism" in poetry (pp. 56-57) is worth noting because these aspects suggest the social use of the poems. On rhetoric as a tool for an alternative community, see Rubem Alves, *Tomorrow's Child* (New York: Harper & Row, 1972).

33. See Norbert Lohfink, "Culture Shock and Theology," *BTB* 7 (1977): 12-21, on culture crisis and the constructive function of Deuteronomy. For an alternative understanding of the social function of Deuteronomy, see Joseph Gutmann, *The Image and the Word* (Missoula: Scholars Press, 1977), pp. 5-25. Gutmann appeals especially to the hypothesis of W. E. Claburn, "The Fiscal Basis of Josiah's Reform," *JBL* 92 (1973): 11–22.

34. The book promised from Orbis Books is entitled, *The Tribes of Yahweh: A Sociology of the Religion of Liberated Israel, 1250-1050* B.C.E. [published 1979].

35. Mendenhall, *Tenth Generation,* pp. 16, 182, 195-96; "The Monarchy," pp. 157-66; "Samuel's Broken Rib," p. 67.

36. It is evident that the critical perversion came not with David but with Solomon. See Frank M. Cross, *Canaanite Myth and Hebrew Epic: Essays in the History of the Religion of Israel* (Cambridge: Harvard University Press, 1973), pp. 237-41, and W. Brueggemann, *In Man We Trust* (Richmond, Va.: John Knox Press, 1972), pp. 64-77.

37. On the Solomonic fascination with Egypt, see T. N. D. Mettinger, *Solomonic State Officials* (Lund: Gleerup, 1971) and G. Ernest Wright, *Biblical Archaeology* (Philadelphia: Westminster, 1957), pp. 120-63.

38. On this tension, see W. Brueggemann, "Presence of God, Cultic," *IDBSup,* pp. 680-83.

39. Cross, *Canaanite Myth and Hebrew Epic,* pp. 195-215.

40. Cross's location of Zadok clearly is an advance beyond the position of H. H. Rowley (see Cross, p. 209). Nonetheless, Rowley ("Zadok and Nehustan," *JBL* 58 [1939]: 113-41; "Melchizedeq und Zadok [Gen. 14 and Ps. 110]," *Festschrift Alfred Bertholet* [Tübingen: Mohr, 1950], pp. 461-72) had already seen that Zadok represents a cultic tradition essentially alien to the Mosaic tradition.

41. Cross, *Canaanite Myth and Hebrew Epic,* p. 211.

42. Here we are concerned with the traditioning process and not with consideration of historically objective issues. But note must be taken of the radical position of John Van Seters, *Abraham in History and Tradition* (New Haven: Yale University

Press, 1975) and T. L. Thompson, *The Historicity of the Patriarchal Narratives,* BZAW 133 (Berlin: deGruyter, 1974).

43. See Anderson, *Creation versus Chaos.*

44. On Ezekiel's resolution of the role of the Messiah in the Mosaic tradition, see Jon D . Levenson, *Theology of the Program of Restoration of Ezekiel 40-48,* HSM 10 (Missoula: Scholars Press, 1976), Chapter 2. On the reassertion of the older pre-Mosaic traditions, see Cross, *Canaanite Myth and Hebrew Epic,* pp. 343-46.

45. Questions of literary history and unity in the narrative are difficult. See O. H. Steck, *Überlieferung und Zeitgeschichte im der Elia-Erzahlungen,* WMANT 26 (Neukirchen-Vluyn: Neukirchener, 1968), pp. 40-53, and G. Fohrer, *Elia,* ATANT 53 (Zurich: Zwingli, 1968), pp. 24-29.

46. On Amos and the torah, see R. Bach, "Gottesrecht und weltliches Recht in der Verkündigung des Propheten Amos," *Festschrift Gunther Dehn* (Neukirchen-Vluyn: Neukirchener, 1957), pp. 23-24.

47. That the Isaiah traditions will not fit any neat scheme is evidenced by the decision of Von Rad *(Old Testament Theology* [London: Oliver and Boyd, 1965], Vol. 2, pp. 147-75) to place him in the Jerusalem tradition. For a more refined judgment see O. H. Steck, "Theological Streams of Tradition," *Tradition and Theology in the Old Testament,* pp. 193-94.

48. Ronald Clements *(Prophecy and Covenant,* SBT 43 [London: SCM Press, 1965], pp. 39-43) has observed that the drastic announcement of an end represents a new radical announcement in Israel.

49. It may of course be too subtle to relate the "end" of Amos to the "no end" of Isaiah, for Isaiah clearly refers to Davidic Israel, while Amos presumably refers to the northern kingdom. See also Frank Crüsemann, "Kritik an Amos in Deuteronomistischen Geschichtswerk," *Probleme Biblischer Theologie,* ed. H. W. Wolff (Munich: Kaiser, 1971), pp. 57-63.

50. It is clear that the Davidic promises do not function in the poetry of Jeremiah. Indeed it is precisely his opponents who continue to rely on them. And in Deuteronomy, surely closely related to Jeremiah, the balance between Mosaic and Davidic factors is in dispute, but there is little doubt that the Mosaic tradition is decisive. The situation is quite different in Ezekiel, as Levenson has shown.

51. See W. Brueggemann, "David and His Theologian, *CBQ* 30 (1968): 156-81; "From Dust to Kingship," *ZAW* 84 (1972): 1-18; and Walter Wifall, "Gen. 6:1-4, A Royal Davidic Myth?" *BT* (1975): 294-301; "The Breath of His Nostrils," *CBQ* 36 (1974): 237-40.

52. See H. W. Wolff, "The Elohistic Fragments in the Pentateuch," *The Vitality of Old Testament Traditions,* ed. W. Brueggemann and H. W. Wolff (Atlanta: John Knox Press, 1975), pp. 67-82, and Alan Jenks, *The Elohist and North Israelite Traditions,* SBLMS 22 (Missoula: Scholars Press, 1977).

53. See J. A. Soggin, "Ancient Israelite Poetry and Ancient 'Codes' of Law, and the Sources of 'J' and 'E' of the Pentateuch," *VTSup* 28 (1974): 193-95.

54. The most recent discussion is that of Werner E. Lemke, "The Way of Obedience: 1 Kings 13 and the Structure of the Deuteronomistic History," *Magnalia Dei: The Mighty Acts of God,* pp. 301-26, unambiguously placing Deuteronomy in the tradition of Moses and the prophetic demand for obedience. Lemke further develops the direction of Wolff's important essay.

55. Von Rad, *Old Testament Theology* (New York: Harper & Row, 1962), Vol.

1, pp. 334-47. See my derivative discussion, "The Kerygma of the Deuteronomistic Historian," *Int* 22 (1968): 387-402.

56. See H. W. Wolff, "The Kerygma of the Deuteronomistic Historical Work," *The Vitality of Old Testament Traditions*, pp. 91-97.

57. B. Albrektson, *Studies in the Text and Theology of the Book of Lamentations* (Lund: Gleerup, 1963), pp. 214-39.

58. The fact that both Job and Deuteronomy have important connections with Jeremiah makes it quite plausible that Job is grappling with the issues forced by the Deuteronomist. Cf. James A. Sanders, "Hermeneutics in True and False Prophecy," *Canon and Authority*, ed. George Coats and Burke Long (Philadelphia: Fortress Press, 1977), p. 28: ". . . Job was surely written in part to record a resounding No to such inversions of the Deuteronomic ethic of election." There is, to be sure, a counter opinion among scholars that it is not possible to link the poem of Job to any specific historical situation. See especially J. J. M. Roberts, "Job and the Israelite Religious Tradition," *ZAW* 89 (1977): 107-14. Even if that be granted, the religious tendency of the poem is surely in a direction other than that of Deuteronomy.

59. Samuel Terrien, "The Yahweh Speeches and Job's Responses," *RevExp* 68 (1971): 497-509.

60. Ibid., p. 508.

61. Ibid., p. 498.

62. Cross, *Canaanite Myth and Hebrew Epic*, pp. 343-46.

63. Ibid., p. 344.

64. The break and the discontinuity caused by the emergence of Israel have been stressed by Mendenhall. Cf. *Tenth Generation*, pp. 1-19, and "Migration Theories vs. Culture Change as an Explanation for Early Israel," *SBLSP* (1976): 135-43. The problem with a history of religions approach to these issues is that it is ideologically and methodologically committed to continuity as the primary agenda.

65. John A. Miles, Jr., "Gagging on Job, or the Comedy of Religious Exhaustion," *Semeia* 7 (1977): 110.

66. Ibid., pp. 110-13.

67. The "new truth" of the Mosaic revolution contrasts with the "old truth" of which Miles writes. When the old imperial gods are embraced, social stability is assured. Freedman ("Divine Names and Titles") identifies Judges 5 among the poems of "Militant Mosaic Yahwism." It is the coming of the new God, unknown in the empire, which causes a new social possibility.

68. Deutero-Isaiah has the capacity to utilize all the various traditions. See Von Rad, *Old Testament Theology*, Vol. 2, pp. 238–43.

69. Bernhard W. Anderson, "Exodus Typology in Second Isaiah," *Israel's Prophetic Heritage*, ed. Bernhard W. Anderson and Walter Harrelson (New York: Harper & Row, 1962), pp. 177-95.

70. Anderson, "Exodus and Covenant in Second Isaiah and Prophetic Tradition," *Magnalia Dei: The Mighty Acts of God*, pp. 339-60.

71. Ibid., p. 356.

72. Ibid., p. 355.

73. It is the faithfulness of God to which appeal must be made in exile. In the categories of Freedman, now Israel must speak of "divine commitment" and not of "human obligation." On the abiding *hesed* of Yahweh to his people, see Otto Eissfeldt, "The Promises of Grace to David in Isaiah 55:1-5," *Israel's Prophetic*

Heritage, pp. 177-95. While the point of connection is unclear, the oracle of 55:3 is not unrelated to the anticipation of Lam. 3:22-24.

74. See Note 42. Aside from the specific critical judgments he makes, Van Seters has made a strong case that a situation of exile and a theology of promise are precisely appropriate to each other.

75. Hans Walter Wolff, *The Old Testament: A Guide to Its Writings* (Philadelphia: Fortress Press, 1973), pp. 32-44.

76. Paul Hanson, *The Dawn of Apocalyptic* (Philadelphia: Fortress Press, 1975).

77. Steck, "Theological Streams of Tradition," has pursued a parallel investigation utilizing the word "stream." However, Steck's presentation tends to identify so many diverse streams that the concept is diffused. Here I suggest that several of Steck's streams might be considered together as belonging to the same general context.

78. An important resource for further investigation is the book edited by Douglas Knight, *Tradition and Theology in the Old Testament.* Knight's own essay, "Revelation through Tradition," suggests the decisive way in which the traditioning community is engaged in the process of trajectory development.

79. It is of course presumptuous to speak of an emerging paradigm. The definitional statement of Thomas Kuhn, *The Structure of Scientific Revolutions* (Chicago: University of Chicago Press, 1970), has created a new awareness of the ways in which scholarship changes and/or advances. Gottwald ("Biblical Theology or Biblical Sociology?" pp. 52, 55) both critiques the paradigm of "biblical theology," by which he means a quite identifiable approach, and hints at the alternative informed by sociology. From quite another scholarly perspective, John Dominic Crossan, *Raid on the Articulate* (New York: Harper & Row, 1976), p. iv, suggests that he is raising the question of "a shift of the master paradigms of our research." He quotes Kuhn in referring to "a reconstruction that changes some of the field's most elementary theoretical generalizations as well as many of its paradigm methods and applications." Such reasoning is not far removed from the issue raised by Gottwald in "Domain Assumptions and Societal Models in the Study of Pre-Monarchic Israel." While both Crossan and Gottwald may speak of a shift of paradigms, the substance of their urging is in quite divergent directions.

80. It is likely that Gottwald's critique of the paradigm of "biblical theology" refers especially to the method and synthesis achieved by Von Rad. Brevard Childs, *Biblical Theology in Crisis* (Philadelphia: Westminster, 1970), has presented a formidable critique of that synthesis.

81. Claus Westermann has developed this dialectic in various writings, but his major presentation is in the Sprunt lectures soon to be published, in which he contrasts the saving and blessing of God. Most telling is his assertion that the God who blesses cannot fail or suffer. Such a conclusion has enormous sociological implications.

82. Most evident in his utilization of the "Asiatic Mode of Production."

83. Hanson, *Dawn of Apocalyptic*, pp. 213-20.

84. Alan J. Hauser, "Israel's Conquest of Palestine: A Peasants' Rebellion?" *JSOT* 7 (1978): 2-19.

85. Brian Kovacs, "Contributions of Sociology to the Study of the Development of Apocalyptic," paper read at the 1976 meeting of the Society of Biblical Literature.

86. See, for example, the review by John L. McKenzie of the book by José

Miranda, *Marx and the Bible: A Critique of the Philosophy of Oppression* [Maryknoll, N.Y.: Orbis Books, 1974] *JBL* 94 (1975): 280-81.

87. Robert McAfee Brown, "A Preface and a Conclusion," *Theology in the Americas,* ed. Sergio Torres and John Eagleson (Maryknoll, N.Y.: Orbis Books, 1976), p. xvii: "But the important question is, 'Is the analysis true? Does it make sense of what it is describing? Do we understand the world better when we look at it in this way?' "

88. The term is from Helmut Gollwitzer, "Kingdom of God and Socialism in the Theology of Karl Barth," *Karl Barth and Radical Politics,* ed. George Hunsinger (Philadelphia: Westminster, 1976), p. 105.

89. For a persuasive critique of ideological objectivism, see Alvin Gouldner, *The Coming Crisis of Western Sociology* (New York: Basic Books, 1970).

90. On an attempt to engage the two perspectives, see Burton Cooper, "How Does God Act in America? An Invitation to a Dialogue between Process and Liberation Theologies," *USQR* 32 (1976): 25-35. See also Robert T. Osborn, "The Rise and Fall of the Bible in Recent American Theology," *Duke Divinity School Review* 41 (1976): 57-72.

91. Miles, "Gagging on Job," p. 110.

15

WALTER BRUEGGEMANN AND FRANKLIN J. WOO

Theological Issues in *The Tribes of Yahweh* by N. K. Gottwald

Two Critical Reviews

While recognizing the substantive importance of the book's hypothesis of Israel's origin in a revolutionary peasant movement, these reviewers of The Tribes of Yahweh *call attention to the challenge of its radical methodological proposal for biblical hermeneutics and for theology.*

W. Brueggemann observes in Tribes *"the tilt toward a radical theology" in which religion not only integrates and legitimizes but also evokes, criticizes, initiates, and energizes. He connects Gottwald's program of biblical analysis with J. Habermas's formulation of a critical rationality that uncovers the social presuppositions and implications of every exercise of instrumental rationality and of hermeneutical rationality.*

F. Woo calls Tribes *"unabashedly incarnational," which means that traditional concepts of revelation and incarnation, redemption, and resurrection will have to be rethought with a new historical earthiness. At the same time, the religion of ancient Israel gains pertinence to the situation of Third World peoples such as the Chinese, where a great socioreligious peasant revolt (the Taiping Revolution, 1851-1864) evidenced close parallels to Israel's peasant revolt.*

Reprinted from book reviews by Walter Brueggemann in *Journal of the American Academy of Religion* 48 (1980): 44–51, and by Franklin Woo in *China Notes* 18 (1980): 142-43.

Norman K. Gottwald, *The Tribes of Yahweh: A Sociology of the Religion of Liberated Israel, 1250-1050* B.C.E. (Maryknoll, N.Y.: Orbis Books, 1979), xxv plus 916 pp.

1. WALTER BRUEGGEMANN IN *JOURNAL OF THE AMERICAN ACADEMY OF RELIGION*

Gottwald has wrought a peculiarly impressive intellectual achievement. There are few among us who could so capably move among the disciplines of critical sociology and Near Eastern history as he does. Along with that, Gottwald's book is an act of great personal courage, for he has staked out a provocatively imaginative position that will be disputed and controversial for a long time, one bound to be misunderstood in some quarters, for known or unrecognized reasons.

I

It is not too much to say that Gottwald's is a one-idea book. And that one idea is a radical methodological proposal: a most important and neglected interface for Old Testament studies is with *critical sociology,* as distinct from more conventional interfaces with the humanities, explicitly history and literature. More specifically the methodological proposal is that religion must be treated as a function of a coherent socioeconomic structure, a function which both reflects that structure and peculiarly impacts that structure. Positively this means that the "religion of Yahwism" cannot be understood at all apart from the sociopolitical community which articulated, transmitted, and practiced the religion of Yahwism. Negatively the argument permits a criticism of Old Testament scholarship as uncritically idealistic. By "idealism" Gottwald means either that the religion of Yahweh is treated as a thing unto itself with no necessary or integral relation to its social counterparts, or that the religious factor is the decisive and initiative-taking one in forming a social community. Either way, religion is treated as the distinctive element in isolation. And this, Gottwald argues, will not do, for it naively ignores the whole development of critical sociology from Marx, Durkheim, and Weber.

Nowhere does Gottwald explicitly appeal to Marx's programmatic statement, as might be expected from his earlier articles in *Radical Religion.* Nevertheless, Marx's statement may be taken as a premise of the book: "Thus the criticism of heaven is transformed into the criticism of earth, the criticism of religion into the criticism of law, and the criticism of theology into the criticism of politics."[1] Though lacking that particular statement, Gottwald is explicit in his general appeal to a Marxist sociology. To ignore any longer the gains of critical theory in terms of the function of religion is intellectually naive and academically irresponsible. This matter is especially urgent because it appears that alternative directions in Old Testament scholarship (specifically the "new literary criticism") run the risk of bracketing out all the sociologically critical questions. And the result is an uncritical, unwitting embrace of conventional systemic values of American academia.

Gottwald's mehodological proposal brings him close to two programmatic books which greatly illuminate his intent. First, it is instructive that one of Gottwald's early citations (p. 13, n. 6) is to Gouldner's *The Coming Crisis of Western Sociology.* Gouldner has argued that Western sociology, by which he means noncritical positivistic sociology, has been largely a "kept" sociology, confined to technical reason. It has adopted a methodology which screens out the hard questions and operates as a tool for conformity to the way things are. By analogy Gottwald suggests that the "idealism" of historical criticism is also not neutral but *serves interests* about which it is not always aware. I suspect that the impact of Gottwald's book is first of all to call attention to a methodological crisis that is deeper than even Childs or Wink has hinted. Gottwald offers a new set of questions which must be asked. And that inevitably implies a shifted task for scholarship.

Second, at several points Gottwald uses the word "paradigm." Gottwald's book is a prime example of the offer of a new paradigm as Thomas Kuhn describes the function of paradigm in *The Structure of Scientific Revolutions.*[2] That is, Gottwald's book should not be taken simply as another critical analysis, but as a reorganization of the data around quite new categories. What is offered is a bold critical proposal that must be lived with and not simply voted up or down on the basis of data. As Kuhn has seen, a new paradigm, if it is radically new, does not receive or expect ready acceptance, but becomes a field for conflict and battle.

In this book we have a programmatic hypothesis which holds the potential of being an important historical moment in the discipline. Unless I greatly misjudge, the book holds promise of being a point of reference parallel in significance, potential, and authority to Wellhausen's *Prolegomena* and Albright's *From the Stone Age to Christianity.* As is well known, Wellhausen established a new scholarly base for criticism, both literary and historical, with his massive and ingenious synthesis. He broke with a *naive precritical historicism.* In turn, Albright broke with the *evolutionism* of Wellhausen. In a parallel move, Gottwald proposes a break with *idealism* toward a religious functionalism that reflects a dialectic which is profoundly materialistic, and a materialism which is profoundly dialectical.[3]

II

Now of course Gottwald's book is not simply a methodological proposal. The dominant *methodological* proposal of the book is matched by a sustained *substantive* argument: Early Israel, of which religious Yahwism is an important element, is a revolutionary social movement, radically egalitarian in contrast to the hierarchical systems of domination out of which it emerged and against which it worked. Gottwald studies in detail the historical and literary issues and pays attention to the institutional, political life of Israel. He shows that for 200 years (from Joshua to the monarchy, 1250-1050) Israel is a serious, concrete social experiment that was a *novum* in the political world of the Near East. This *novum* utilized, and cannot be understood apart from, both the subversive political actions taken and the triggering of religious Yahwism. The political actions and religious triggering together permitted an alternative social system out of which biblical Yahwism has come.

Among the elements of Gottwald's argument, we can note several of the more important:

1. Tribalism, as distinct from nomadism, is an important feature of the hypothesis. Gottwald does an acute investigation of the nomenclature. First, "tribe" is a sociological unit and not a kinship unit. Second, denying any evolutionism he argues that tribalism comes *after* and in reaction against statism. So he inverts the evolutionary scheme, now dominant, to speak of "retribalization."

2. Gottwald stays close to the German hypothesis of tribal confederation, but takes careful account of the criticism made against Noth's amphictyony. But he does end up with a transtribal organization not unlike that proposed by Noth. His use of Noth's work is a good example of how paradigms shift with both continuities and discontinuities from previous scholarship.

3. Gottwald also posits something much like von Rad's credo or cult hypothesis. That is, after analysis of the "historical" conflict in Joshua and Judges, he understands the main Pentateuchal themes as constructs of the cultic ideological community, i.e., as the theological creativity of the community in providing ideological undergirding for a subversive, egalitarian social system. Gottwald's procedure is to deal with Joshua-Judges as historical foundation (though of course he does not uncritically handle the literature as "history") with Pentateuch materials as part of the "superstructure." Thus we are permitted both the "criticism of heaven" (in the Pentateuch) and the "criticism of earth" (in Joshua and Judges). In his assessment of the Pentateuch, Gottwald moves away from historical questions, very much in the direction of von Rad's more or less liturgical approach. He is, of course, not unaware of or inattentive to the criticisms of von Rad's hypothesis. In his own argument, Gottwald regards the Pentateuch as an ideological construction of an alternative social reality. He does not deny the existence of earlier elements, historical and ideological, but the creative formation is by and in the service of the egalitarian community.

III

Before coming to the main issue, three comments are pertinent to Gottwald's use of and feedback upon Old Testament scholarship:

1. Gottwald has found a way (even if he is not interested in it) of giving substance and credibility to the now discredited "mighty deeds of God" construct. As is well known, Childs saw the problem: "Mighty deeds of God" is a way of speaking that seems to float in the air without historical basis. The approach of Wright and von Rad had not solved the problem of "actual" history and "sacred" history. The recital of sacred history appeared to have no rootage in historicality. Gottwald has found a way for those who will speak in terms of "mighty acts." But now it must be faced that the recital is an ideological articulation of a radical social movement. Obviously the implications for doing Old

Testament theology are acute. Gottwald comes down sharply on Old Testament scholarship which has been idealistic about these matters, as though Israel's was a religion without close linkage to sociopolitical matters. As examples, he applies his strictures to John Bright, Georg B. Fohrer, and, perhaps surprisingly, George Mendenhall.

2. Gottwald proposes two very subtle and, I am not sure, very convincing constructs. I cite these to note that they are advances beyond the synthesis of Noth and to say they are (in this judgment) precarious. The first of these is the twelve-tribe configuration, which Gottwald sees as a backward projection from monarchical administrative districts which both utilized and impeded genuine tribal patterns (p. 363). I doubt if this is persuasive, though it should be noted that no other hypothesis at this point carries more weight.

3. The other oversubtle construct is the hypothesis of an Elohist Israel that is a seedbed for Yahwism. That is, it is already a potentially revolutionary grouping which still lacks the triggering of religious Yahwism (chapter 43). Of course, the problem of Israel's religious antecedents is notorious. I regard this as not much better or worse than other hypotheses.

Neither his proposal about the twelve-tribe system nor his hypothesis on a pre-Yahwistic Elohistic Israel is crucial to his main argument. Not much that is enduring, in this judgment, will hang or fall on these proposals. Both matters will need to be kept under review. In the long run these will not be found any more compelling than some of Noth's work which is now doubtfully regarded.

IV

The crucial issue in the book is the relation between sociology and religion, or, to put it alternatively, the extent to which Yahweh is a "function" of an egalitarian movement and the extent to which Yahweh is a free agent to be understood in religious categories. It may be that finally theologians must learn what they can from such bold sociology, but then must part company and be theologians. But they must learn *much* and make that move away only at the *very last moment*. But from a sociological perspective, and probably from the point of view of Gottwald, any such move toward the independent reality of God is a move toward the very idealism he is trying to combat. Then the substantive question is whether such a theological move can be anything other than mere ideology, an ideology which costs more than it gains.

The question before us is evident if we contrast Mendenhall and Gottwald on this point. Mendenhall is consistent in urging that the initiative runs from religion to social reality: "It is very difficult, if not impossible, for modern Western man to conceive of a new cultural synthesis stemming from a new religious ideology, just as it is virtually impossible to convince the usual secular university professor that religion has occasionally in the past functioned to create new and larger communities, rather than merely to create and perpetuate socio-cultural divisiveness."[4] And that line is pursued in his *Tenth Generation* in his advocacy of Israel's religion and in his strictures against "politics."[5]

By contrast, Gottwald (already in his 1974 Congress paper) had gone far in arguing that the move is in the opposite direction, from social reality to religion. His third domain-assumptive proposal is: "It is assumed that the initially or ultimately prominent or distinctive features of a society or culture must be viewed in the total matrix of generative elements and not overweighed in advance as the all-powerful sources of inspiration or as the selective survival factors in the societal development. Thus, a critical generative role may well have been played by cultural elements which have been lost to view and must be recovered by careful research. In particular, ideational factors must be looked at not as disembodied prime movers but as the ideas of human beings in determinate technological and social settings in which the total mix of culture will tend to exhibit lawful or patterned configurations."[6] And that, of course, is the present argument as well. But Gottwald is acutely sensitive on this point. He will not have Yahwism be *simply* a projection. And so he says: "If it turns out that not only is mono-Yahwism dependably related to sociopolitical egalitarianism, but that likewise sociopolitical egalitarianism is dependably related to mono-Yahwism, we shall be able to speak of two social-systemic entities as interdependently or reciprocally related as functions one of the other" (p. 618).

Especially in Chapter 50, Gottwald not only acknowledges his awareness of the issue, but is extremely sensitive in handling it. He concedes that functionalism has limits in dealing with the question of priority, because it is a tool geared to analyze *interrelations,* but not *priorities.* So Gottwald seeks to move beyond functionalism to a "historical cultural materialism." After some consideration of Durkheim and Weber, he finds Marx (pp. 631ff.) to provide the most coherent strategy for research. Because he insists that religion is best understood on materialist grounds, he concludes (p. 646) that Israelite social relations have priority over Yahwist religion. But at the same time Yahwistic religion has a crucial role to play, not simply as a legitimator, but as a "facilitator" of the egalitarian movement (p. 642). My judgment is Gottwald has gone as far as he can go to face the problem squarely and to give religion its just due. But he will not and must not move beyond his sociological presuppositions or he would vitiate his entire hypothesis. He is, in his own words, "unsurrendered to the end."

Clearly hermeneutical categories from Marx are shown to be not just tools of subversion but responsible ways of discerning the text. Gottwald has made the point in showing that Marxist criticism is not just one more tool with all the others which can be used without changing the others. Rather he shows how these categories place all our methods under criticism in terms of ideological service unwittingly given. While the book is about ancient Israel, it unavoidably raises issues about sociology of our own scholarship. The book pushes toward "canon within canon," a question in which Gottwald has no explicit interest. The problem is this: If this model of religion is understandable only in relation to this egalitarian social system, is it usable as a normative or absolute paradigm? I.e., is it "movable" to other contexts to be used as a critical principle *against* other social systems? Or in other social systems must there only be the matching or appropriate religious symbolization? Perhaps that is when theologians must part company with sociologists. Liberation theologians have gone far in taking this model of religion to use it not only as a *legitimator* and *energizer* of egalitarian movements, but as a *critique* against domination systems. Perhaps in a functionalist approach, that is a "function of dissonance." But in such a use, what is labelled "function" takes on the color of "norm" or of "truth." But then theologians have as their work an articulation of what is normative, work very different from that of a sociologist. Gottwald, of course, fully recognizes this issue. Theologians may wish to have the religion of Yahwism without linkage to that particular intertribal movement. But Gottwald trenchantly observes that is what happened in monarchic Israel, so that "the Yahwistic ideology and traditions were increasingly seen as a self-contained body of beliefs and practices separate from any particular kind of social order" (p. 597). And the social result is a reactionary sociopolitical practice making *reactionary use* of *radical theological rhetoric*. That is a characterization of ancient monarchic Israel, but there are ample contemporary parallels.

V

How can this work be received and assessed by a guild for which these are new questions? It may be useful to locate the book more precisely, epistemologically, in the field. Gottwald's book makes more coherent sense for the field if set in the grid of rationality of Jürgen Habermas.[7] Habermas argues that there are three levels or dimensions of rationality. First, technical knowledge (Habermas calls it "strategic" or "instrumental") is analytical knowledge which seeks only to establish technical control of the data. I suggest it applies especially to historical studies which seek for origins. There is increasing indication in Old Testament studies that scholars grow impatient with those questions. Witness the harsh current judgments on conventional archaeological scholarship.

The second level of rationality for Habermas is hermeneutics. Hermeneutics (by which is meant attention to symbolism and meaning in the interest of "understanding") is commonly regarded as an advance beyond and liberation from historical-critical issues which pursue explanation. In Old Testament studies this second level is especially evident in the new literary criticism and in structuralism, which means to bracket out many of the old critical questions for the sake of meanings. For Habermas, as Pierce was a proponent of technical, instrumental reason, so Dilthey is an example of such a hermeneutical enterprise.

But it is clear in Old Testament studies that "the new literary criticism" tends to work with "history-less" texts and on the whole is uncritical of itself as a method. That is, it is not reflective that such close attention to structure is tilted in a conservative direction with no impetus for newness. Everything falls before an avoidance of the "genetic fallacy." This hermeneutic interest is a reentry to "old truths," by which is meant in general old mythic structures not embarrassed by the scandal of Israel's liberation movement. I suggest Gottwald's program is a practice of Habermas's third form of rationality, a critical perspective that moves behind the hermeneutical to "unmask" its social presuppositions and implications (Habermas cites Freud as a practitioner of this kind of rationality). Gottwald, like Habermas's program, sees that religious symbols reflect, legitimate, energize, and criticize social systems. Thus Gottwald proposes an important task without which our hermeneutical fascination may be accepted too easily without attention to social implications. What Gottwald has done appears not to be an option which some scholars may take up, but an essential ingredient in scholarship, which means to be rigorously critical. Thus we may locate Gottwald by correlation with Habermas's scheme:

> instrumental reason (Pierce).....historical criticism
> hermeneutical (Dilthey).........structuralism and new literary criticism
> critical (Freud)...................Gottwald's sociological investigation

I suggest that this indicates that Gottwald's program is essential to our common work.

VI

Gottwald's final pages suggest a passion that tilts his work in sociology toward a radical theology. These points are worth noting:

1. On pages 684ff., in his consideration of Yahweh's masculinity, the author refers to God as "he" with quotation marks. Clearly Gottwald intends a contemporary critique of such usage.

2. Gottwald comments on the inherent conservatism of Durkheim's sociology of religion (p. 697). But he makes a point that there is another kind of sociology of religion, reflective of Marx, which does not simply personify the spirit of the community. He quotes Buber that this alternative sociology of religion "represents the power which transcends it, happens to it, which changes it, even historicizes it; a power which in a formative hour drives it on to do the unaccustomed and untraditional, in a feud-overcoming gathering together of all clans as a single tribe." On such a material cultural base, there is a sociology of religion which offers the dynamic toward new possibility. Gottwald appeals to categories quite alien to most sociologists of religion who are dominated by Durkheim.

3. Gottwald uses the telling phrase, the "impossible possibility" (p. 701): *"The power of the religious symbolism in early Israel was precisely its integration within and penetration of a total struggle situation,* so that it articulated a willfulness informed by the situation, illuminating a route for those divided Canaanite underclasses to follow as, step by step, they realized 'the impossible possibility' of free communal life in hierarchic Canaan."

In using the phrase "impossible possibility" in this way, Gottwald has in the end done both things which are important. On the one hand, he has used language which links his perception to the most subversive theology of our time. Indeed, Gottwald is fully aware of the theological implications of his sociological analysis for the contemporary scene. But on the other hand and at the same time, Gottwald is clear that the "impossible possibility" is not a contextless theological slogan. It has substance only when used in relation to intentional social struggle. Such religious symbolism has legitimacy only as a form of *praxis* (p. 702). Gottwald has moved well beyond an *integrationist functionalism* to an *historical cultural materialism* that is fully dialectical. Thus the fully dependable function of religious Yahwism is not simply a descriptive counterpart to social reality, but a powerful set of symbols which evoke, initiate, and energize, as well as legitimate. In this way it appears that Gottwald has impressively narrowed the gap between sociology and theology.

It is the impression of this reviewer that Gottwald has not resolved the issues of social criticism and the reality of God. But he has indeed reshaped the context and the issues for our discussion. The book abounds in careful critical detail, comprehensive documentation, and a complete index of authors, personal and geographical names, Scripture passages, and topics. In every way it will be a long-standing teaching instrument. Gottwald's passion for contemporary issues is matched by his peculiar boldness in scholarly questions. And that rare combination is crucial "in the long struggle of human liberation" (p. 709) which finally concerns him. Gottwald has made unmistakably clear that liberated and liberating theology must give careful and sustained attention to methodology, so that it does not at the outset concede the main point in question, or in turn become itself a noncritical ideology. He has shown us how to proceed in that.

Clearly the issue of method is not a formal question of preferring or not preferring Marxist critical categories. It is a substantive question about the nature of early Yahwism as a symbol system, an ideological vision, and a social system. Method cannot be determined on formal grounds, but only in terms of the material before us. And that is not likely to look the same again after Gottwald.

2. FRANKLIN J. WOO IN *CHINA NOTES*

Norman Gottwald's *The Tribes of Yahweh* is a book about the struggle of disenfranchised peasants in Old Testament times for an egalitarian society. For a huge volume of 916 pages, it covers only a thin slice of some 200 years of the history of premonarchic Israel. To see how this history relates to an interest in China and religion is the attempt of this introductory review.

Gottwald is unabashedly incarnational. He sees the religion of people as having to do with their real life. There is always that intimate interaction between life and religion, as banal as this may sound. Gottwald, who is himself trained in humanistic historical methods, chooses to use sociological methods with consistent rigor in unfolding the sociopolitical realities in Canaanite society. He follows his methodology all the way, not giving in to traditional faith assumptions which might lead to a facile relegating of religion to that which comes from out of the blue. For him religion is a social product, and he wants to know the social forces that go into the process of shaping religion. (Instead of the term "religion" Gottwald prefers "ideology" in order to set "a methodological distance between sociological inquiry into Israel's religion and the more familiar historical and theological approaches to Israel's religion, p. 65.)

Gottwald's rigorous application of sociological methodology and his own fidelity to its structural integrity have resulted in what Walter Brueggemann regards as a third turning point in modern Old Testament scholarship. This methodological breakthrough is seen by Brueggemann as comparable to that of Julius Wellhausen's analysis of the Pentateuch and William F. Albright's synthesis of archaeology and biblical history.

The author sees himself as differing from other Old Testament scholars in that he is attempting to complement what they overlook or treat only as "social factors" which are subsumed under what they regard to be universal religious norms. For example, unlike John Bright who has influenced generations of biblical teachers and preachers, Gottwald hesitates to see the uniqueness of Israel in its unique religion while in other areas Israel is seen as similar in every way to other Semitic societies. For Gottwald the tribes of Yahweh were disparate peoples with overlapping concerns. The one basic commonality which they shared was their fighting for a place for themselves within Canaanite society of which they were the underclasses and to which they were marginal.

Gottwald's hypothesis is that there was a coalescing ("retribalization") of marginal peoples within the city-states of Canaan. The underclasses of Canaanite society were held down in their subservient status by the power and authority of the rulers, undergirded by Baal ideology. This hypothesis poses a challenge to prevailing hypotheses which are so familiar to generations of Christians: that the Israelites were pastoral nomads, and that they invaded and conquered Canaan, the land of milk and honey. Building on the work of George E. Mendenhall, especially his peasant revolt thesis, Gottwald nevertheless holds with tenacity to his sociological methodology while staying clear of any one-sided religious idealism. Starting with the known history of Israel, as did Martin Noth, the author finds in Noth a false analogy of the tribes of Israel to the religious league (amphictyony) of ancient Greece. Instead, Gottwald sees a coalition of different marginal peoples who were fighting for a place for themselves under the Canaanite sun. Monotheistic Yahwehism was their religion. It was, however, shaped by the different traditions which they themselves brought to the coalition, and it was commensurate with the egalitarian goals for which they fought.

This is an exciting book. As mentioned, it is an apparent breakthrough in modern Old Testament studies. Furthermore, for people in China concerns, Gottwald's major work offers a possibility of drawing significant parallels from other cultures where similar disenfranchised peoples have also struggled for a place within their own societies. One immediately thinks of the Taiping Revolution (1851-64) which involved millions of land-starved peasants in an expanding population in the Ching period in China. Under a cruel land tenantry system ruled by ruthless feudal elites who were undergirded by a Confucian ideology, the poor peasantry was driven to despair, desperation, and revolt. The already impossible situation was exacerbated by the import of foreign opium and the outflow of Chinese silver. In their quest for an egalitarian society the Taiping's religion was commensurate with the "Heavenly Kingdom of Great Peace" for which they struggled for fourteen years and in which over 20 million lives are estimated to have been lost. Against the Confucian social order their egalitarianism was based on a simple ideology of the fatherhood of God and the brotherhood of man (Taiping egalitarianism included women) provided by Christianity with a Confucian social milieu. Gottwald says that it is easy for scholars including himself to cite all kinds of parallels between Israel and other peoples, but "far fewer have been able to assimilate and assess the comparative phenomena within an adequate theoretical framework" (p. 22). Much remains, therefore, to be done in assessing the role of religion in the Taiping Revolution and how religion was itself shaped by the sociopolitical realities of that historical situation. Here Gottwald's work is most suggestive, as well as providing a rigorous program of mining the Old Testament, part of the written foundation of Christianity, for the material bases of life and religion.

Moreover what Gottwald's rigorous scholarship in sociological criticism of the Old Testament does in effect is to challenge people who are comfortable (as in Plato's Cave) with their understanding of their world, universe, and cosmos. The author begins with people and their historical realities. He does not begin with religion and then look for the people to fit into that religion. He is more interested in the canonizing process of scriptures and its politics than in the finished Canon itself, seen as being authoritative for all times and all places. For people who really want to know, even though such knowledge may be disturbing, Gottwald's pursuit is exciting. For established religion, however, his investigation can be viewed as iconoclastic, threatening, and therefore dangerous. Such time-honored religious concepts as revelation and incarnation, not to mention redemption and resurrection, will have to be seen in new historical light.

Gottwald's work may find much resistance and opposition in the Western world. On the other hand it may find much resonance in China, where from 1949 to 1966 over 3,000 research papers and 100 general books have been published, 50 kinds of source material collected, and 70-80 conferences and symposia on the national level held—all on the Taiping Revolution (see Tan Chung, "Peasant Rebellions in China" in *China Report,* Delhi, Jan.-Feb. 1980). In China, where biblical religion of the Old and New Testaments has never enjoyed an adherence of more than one percent of the total population in any given time of China's 1,300 years of contact with Christianity in its several forms, the problem of rigorous re-examination and self-criticism of faith assumptions may not be as acute as in Western culture.

In China, which has just finished another phase of peasant revolt, where eight people out of every ten in Chinese society are still required to produce food for a quarter of humanity, life is very hard indeed. But life is, as it always has been, also very precious and very much loved. In hardships, suffering, and struggle people form relationships which have dimensions of the sacred. In revolutions they have sought justice, liberation, and human fulfillment for themselves. Even without reference to an incarnator, life is and has been incarnate. Without an ordainer, life is ordained so that the poor do rise up. Without any creation myth, creation is here and now. Life is down-to-earth, and revelation comes, if at all, from the very ground of suffering, struggle, and hope.

What is religion in this setting? A possible answer is that it is *survival.* It is the human struggle for life itself—its meaning, purposes, and destiny even among tremendous and impossible odds. Religion so defined is seen as an integral part of life which is God-given. It is not a *plus* to be appended to life. Though Norman Gottwald did not say these things in his book, his honest investigation of a very important period of the history of premonarchic Israel stimulates new ideas. This is the excitement of the heuristic nature of rigorous scholarship which is always open-ended. Such excitement awaits readers who are not discouraged or intimidated by this 3.4 pound paperback.

NOTES

1. Karl Marx, "Critique of Hegel's Philosophy of Right." Cf. David McLellan *The Thought of Karl Marx* (London: Macmillan, 1971), p. 22.

2. Thomas S. Kuhn, *The Structure of Scientific Revolutions* (Chicago: University of Chicago Press, 1974).

3. That dialectic is quite self-conscious: "In short, the basic tenet for future research and theory is clear and commanding: only as the full *materiality* of ancient Israel is more securely grasped will we be able to make proper sense of its *spirituality*" (*Tribes of Yahweh*, p. xxv).

4. George Mendenhall, "Between Theology and Archaeology," *JSOT* 7 (1978): 31.

5. See esp. his *The Tenth Generation* (Baltimore: Johns Hopkins University Press, 1973), chapters 7 and 8. The point may be traced in his book by the polemical and enigmatic footnotes concerning Harvey Cox, pp. 3, 65, and 202.

6. Norman K. Gottwald, "Domain Assumptions and Societal Models in the Study of Pre-Monarchic Israel," *VTSup* 28 (1974): 93. The contrasting domain assumption which Gottwald rejects is this: "It is assumed that the most idiosyncratic, prominent or distinctive element of the new socio-political phase, especially as viewed in retrospect, must have been the nuclear factor which initiated other sorts of changes and constellated them into a new social system or culture. Since the religio-symbolic and cultic dimensions of Israelite society appear to be the most idiosyncratic elements, particularly as viewed from the perspective of later Judaism and Christianity, Yahwism is to be regarded as the isolate source and agent of change in the emergence of Israel" (ibid., p. 91). The issue with Mendenhall could hardly be more sharply put, though of course Mendenhall has no monopoly on the matter. I submit that this question is the crucial one Gottwald asks of Old Testament scholarship.

7. Jürgen Habermas, *Knowledge and Human Interests* (Boston: Beacon Press, 1968); see also Thomas McCarthy, *The Critical Theology of Jürgen Habermas* (Cambridge: MIT Press, 1979), Ch. 2.

16

NORMAN K. GOTTWALD

The Theological Task after
The Tribes of Yahweh

Socially and theologically, early Israel was embedded in its ancient Near Eastern world, but its distinctive mix of social organization and faith stood out as a critical variation of the general environment. The sociological method of Tribes *contributes to a present theology that understands the "God-talk" of the Bible as symbolic representations of a totalizing and directive sort that are not to be confused with sense perceptions or cognitive concepts.*

Theological representations are developed through critical reflection on active faith in the social sites where believers struggle with the realities of daily life. Such representations provide an "onlook" or orientation toward social theories, analyses, and strategies. Theological representations cannot be dissolved by sociological criticism of the Bible or of present society, but must nonetheless continually reshape themselves in the light of fresh understandings of the social sites where they appear.

The theological task, once sensitized to sociological criticism, is to review and rework Jewish-Christian history as an interplay between faith, theological representation, and social practice. The recovery of an organic theological curriculum of study entails the disciplined exercise of a theory-practice "loop" that links biblical tradition to the present through the mediation of Jewish-Christian history in all its religious, theological, and social aspects.

An address delivered at Yale Divinity School on October 28, 1981.

The title could be heard to strike a pretentious note, as though I were proposing that my sociological study of early Israel now made possible an entirely new theology. The intention rather is to indicate how I believe the theological task is affected or shaped by a thoroughgoing application of sociological criticism to biblical texts. Some readers of *Tribes* have thought either that I announced the end of theology or that, whatever my intentions, no theology would be possible on the basis of such deconstructed reading of the Bible.

By deliberation *Tribes* did not undertake a new theological construction in method or content. Instead, I stated that "I do not present a new theology so much as the *preconditions* for a new theological method which would employ the biblical records as ideological products and instruments of the social formation of Israel" (emphasis added).[1] How then does one begin to spell out the theological implications of the hypothesis of the social revolutionary origins of Israel and of the method and theory by which that hypothesis is reached?

THEOLOGY IN ANCIENT ISRAEL

An important premise of my argument in *Tribes* is to locate ancient Israel in its social matrix and to identify the social structural and developmental conflictual features which have hitherto been described largely as "religious" or, more broadly, as "historical" or "cultural." In doing so I pose a total social formation which includes religion and culture, and which clearly has its own history (although many of the details are inaccessible), but which encompasses the whole constitution and experience of Israelites as determinate human beings who engaged in concrete activities to bring their society into being and to preserve and develop it. A village-based retribalizing movement broke away from city-state control, and in the course of that historical project to enable economic and political emancipation through self-defense and mutual aid, the movement created its own culture.[2] Central to that culture was the religion of Yahweh with a sharply etched symbol system and a centralizing cult practice. This religion was a key factor in achieving unity and perseverance in the historical project of economic and political emancipation.[3]

The socioreligious system of early Israel may be analyzed from as many angles as there were elements that composed it and as there are means for tracing the interactions among the combining and interacting elements. We may, for example, focus on the crops and agricultural technology that formed the base for the solidifying of the movement in the hill country, and go on to clarify the economic impact on residential patterns, forms of governance, and religious cults and symbols.[4] We can also focus on the peculiar "retribalized" social structure of the Israelite movement and its adaptive relationship to the economic, military, and cultural priorities of the movement.[5] Or we can just as legitimately begin with religious symbol and cult and trace how the specific material environment and the forms of social organization came to expression in the religion.[6] What we can no longer do in good conscience is to isolate the religious factors from the total social setting as though, once the historical and social "accidents" are noted as "background," we are free to move on to the self-contained religious essentials.[7] For theology, this is of utmost consequence, not only because of the socially embedded nature of the subject matter in biblical texts, but because of our position as socially situated and conditioned believers and theologians.

In the last section of *Tribes* I try to develop a profile or cross-section of the theological structure of earliest Israel both in its congruence with ancient Near Eastern theology and in its distinctiveness.[8]

It is my judgment that ancient Near Eastern and early Israelite religion participated in or shared a common structure in certain key respects:

1. The high god (either sharing power as one god among others, or as the highest for a given purpose or moment, or as the exclusive deity) is individuated, given personal attributes, and elevated as the comprehensive generative or engendering power behind all that is, or all that has momentary relevance.

2. The high god is active in the world of nature, history, social order, and often in a moral order as well.

3. The high god is conceived by natural and human analogies, which come to expression in titles, iconic symbols, and expressions of the feelings and expectations of worshipers. These analogies include natural elements, atmospheric and meteorological phenomena, topographical features, animals and plants, and familial and sociopolitical roles.

4. The high god is manifested or experienced as powerful, just, and merciful, and likewise effectual in enacting or assuring power, justice, and mercy in human affairs past, present, and future.

5. The high god is in bond with a people, organized in a particular sociopolitical, territorial, and cultural formation, and this relationship tends to be reciprocal—even contractual—in the sense that god and people know what to expect of one another. The god frequently imposes sanctions on the people.

6. The high god is interpreted by human representatives who occupy recognized social roles in accord with the kinds of social organization typical among the worshipers. The relation between god and people is interpreted according to "punishments" and "rewards" which are code-concepts for concrete gains and losses in the natural, historical, and social domains. In times of social conflict and political turmoil, the interpreters of the same god may disagree in their readings of the will or message of the god.

Amid this common theological structure of the ancient Near East, Israel at its inception introduced new developments that marked it as exceptional:

1. The sole high god usurps the entire sacred domain, calling for the exclusive recognition of one deity in the life of the people. The hyperindividuation of Yahweh can be traced in the rhetorical modes of expression concerning divine qualities and doings, in the domains of life where the god is involved and in the behavior prescribed or prohibited by the deity.

2. The sole high god is alone active in the world. Where ancient Near Eastern polytheism tended to diversify, fragment, and disperse human experience, Yahweh's singularity tends toward a more integrated and coherent assertion of the totality of meaning in human experience. Where certain realms, such as death or sexuality, are not immediately penetrable by this sole god, they are none-

theless denied to any other divine powers. Symbolic reflection on *the* activity of *the* one God is encouraged, although it falls short of some alleged single divine plan until apocalyptic times.

3. The sole high god is conceived by egalitarian sociopolitical analogies, by which I mean that the representations of Yahweh are chiefly those of a warrior-leader who brings the distinctive intertribal community into existence and defends it. Of course one cannot properly speak of equality between Yahweh and people, since Yahweh is the superior leader and also creator who benevolently rules human community. The terms chosen to characterize deity, however, show Yahweh to be establishing equality among people by creating Israel. The concretization of El as Yahweh (Yahweh is probably an epithet of El that means "the one who creates the armed hosts of heaven and of Israel")[9] defines the special sphere of divine societal reconstruction as an intertribal network of peoples. By contrast, analogies from nature and narrowly cultic analogies diminish.

4. The sole high god is coherently manifested or experienced as powerful, just, and merciful. The content of the revelation is formally very similar to the content of ancient Near Eastern religious revelation in general, but the faithfulness, reliability, and consistency of the deity in dealing with the people are greatly stressed—to the point that Israel gives much thought to how power, justice, and mercy are interconnected, believing them to be established in one divine ground and thus not at variance with one another. There is an emphatic expectation that all parts of human experience in community will mesh and interact intelligibly and supportively.

5. The sole high god is in bond with an egalitarian people, an intertribal formation. This people is Yahweh's special manifestation, which to misconstrue would be to misconstrue Yahweh. This people is not a land, region, or city; not a descent group formed by actual kinship; not an occupational group or privileged caste; not the protector of single needy persons separated from the whole community. Women share in this equality as members of equal households, and women figure prominently in early Israelite traditions. Yet it seems a chiefly male-led society and the dominant analogies for Yahweh are male, although in many respects it seems as appropriate to refer to Yahweh as "she" as to call Yahweh "he."[10]

6. The sole high god is interpreted by egalitarian functionaries. Consistent with a people of equality is the interpretation of Yahweh by various leaders whose roles are circumscribed and contained within the whole tribal system such that monopolies on priestly or lay leadership are checked. No central government is operative and social stratification is intentionally de-structured. The priestly establishment is sharply contained.

This theological structure of premonarchic Israel can be "demythologized" according to its socioeconomic and communal-cultural referents, in contrast to the usual program of demythologizing into states of existential or mystical consciousness.

"Yahweh" is the historically concretized, primordial power to establish and sustain social equality in the face of counter-oppression from without and against provincial and nonegalitarian tendencies from within the society. "The Chosen People" is the distinctive self-consciousness of a society of equals created in the intertribal order and demarcated from a primarily centralized and stratified surrounding world. "Covenant" is the bonding of decentralized social groups in a larger society of equals committed to cooperation without authoritarian leadership and a way of symbolizing the locus of sovereignty in such a society of equals. "Eschatology," or hope for the future, is the sustained commitment of fellow tribesmen to a society of equals with the confidence and determination that this way of life can prevail against great environmental odds.[11]

Several of the most baffling aspects of Israel's religion are illuminated in terms of their critical social functions. Yahweh's exclusivity and abnormal jealousy correspond to the singularity and excessive passion of the Israelite social revolutionary movement. Yahweh's purposive neglect of the underworld and rejection of sexual commodity fetishism deny elite rulers the power to manipulate people's fear of death and hunger for sex as tools of oppression. The limited socioeconomic demands of the priesthood prevent a theocratic political monopoly over the people. The "popular" historiography of early Israel shows that the people, and not a few privileged heroes, make history. The salvation paradigms of early Israel (exodus, wilderness wandering, seizure of power in Canaan) are ways of showing that the decisive feature of historical events is social struggle.

THEOLOGY TODAY

On the basis of my reading of the theological structure of early Israel in correlation with the people's material-social organizational-cultural structure, I offered in *Tribes* the following brief sketch of what theology is *not* and what it *is*:

> In our attempt to position the socioreligious nexus of mono-Yahwism [the sole high god belief] and egalitarian Israelite society within the context of a larger contemporary understanding of religion, it is necessary to take our cue from the methodological insight that religion is the function of social relations rooted in cultural-material conditions of life. This entails a rejection of forms of theology that separate religion from theology and that abstract religious beliefs from the socially situated locus of the religious believers. The uniqueness of the Israelite religious perception lay in its discovery through social struggle that the concrete conditions of human existence are modifiable rather than immutable conditions. . . .
>
> There is but one way in which those ancient religious symbols can be employed today in anything like their full range and power, and that is in a situation of social struggle where people are attempting a breakthrough toward a freer and fuller life based on equality and communal self-possession. Even then it is a risky business to "summon up" powerful

symbolism out of a distant past unless the symbol users are very self-conscious of their choices and applications, and fully aware of how their social struggle is both like and unlike the social struggle of the architects of the symbols.[12]

In the light of the sociotheological understanding expressed in *Tribes*, I wish to expand briefly on three aspects of the theological task today: the nature and limits of theological representations, the social setting or site of theologizing, and the revitalization of the theological curriculum or encyclopedia.

THEOLOGICAL REPRESENTATIONS

Theological representations or symbols, such as the representations of God as an actor in or a shaper of human affairs, are a special kind of thinking which arises at the immediate level of faith but leads on to critical reflection, both because nontheological experience and knowledge press for an accounting from theology and because faith seeks clarity about itself.[13] Theological representations are general ideas that do not give sense data or cognition such as directly represent the world or directly guide our action within the world; they cannot be operationalized. Theological representations are formed out of tradition and are strongly internalized psychosocially, but they do not replace practical knowledge of all kinds. They are not simply a knowledge alongside other bodies of knowledge but a way of looking at environment and human agency and at the meanings and values associated with various kinds of knowledge. Theological representations are thus totalizing and directive without being exhaustive or prescriptive. They orient and dispose us toward certain kinds of relational perceptions and values and they move us in practical directions, although they are by no means the sole source of totalizing and directive meanings and values.

There are many aspects to the proper comprehension of theological representations. There is the striking inner-biblical tendency to construct, deconstruct, and reconstruct representations of God and of the divine will for people. We also encounter the imperative of analogical or metaphorical limits to our theological representations. Every analogy drawn upon to assert a likeness to God is at the same time qualified by its unlikeness in that God is negatively qualified as one who escapes every analogy. We need especially to recognize how our understanding of theological representations follows on Kant's distinction of ideas such as soul, world, and God as belonging to a different grounding category than sense perceptions and theoretical or operational concepts. Moreover, we need to go on to show how ideas evolve cumulatively and relationally in history (our debt to Hegel), how they ground and function conflictually in a material social base (disclosed by Marx), and how they reverberate intrapsychically (discerned by Freud). The evident universals of the Kantian ideas are seen to be malleable within the strictures created by a developing psychic and social history.

Theological representations belong in a family with art and literature and with ideology conceived as a kind of prevailing "onlook" toward reality, a set of apparent a prioris or preunderstandings which have to be continually raised to consciousness and critically reflected upon. Thus, the theological representations call for incessant movement from first order statements of faith to second order coordination of these statements in themselves and in relation to other orders of experience and thought. Theological representations give an "onlook" toward praxis, as unreflected forms of behavior are self-corrected through intentional commitment and activity in daily life, gathering the behavior that appears to relate to the theological representations into some kind of coherence and relating it to other behaviors which may have their coherencies from other sources. While these theological representations do not operationalize into specific behavior they give an "onlook" toward concepts whose theories can be operationalized.

THE SOCIAL SITES OF THEOLOGICAL REPRESENTATION

Theological representations are the thoughts of people in a particular context. Faith and critical reflection on faith are activities in a given social site. The pertinent site, from which we start and to which we return, is our own social location whose specificity must be felt and analyzed as a determinate one with its own history, special pressures and possibilities, and its own movement toward a future which we consciously or unconsciously help to shape. Past theological representations, rising out of ancient Israel and mediated and enriched through Jewish-Christian history, are totalizing and directive toward our present social sites. Theological representations, far from being "free-floating" universals that give us solutions to problems in every time and place, are rather "engaged" images or models that orient us either to thinking or unthinking life in the here and now. This is because the social world, in which theological representations are formed and communicated, is a humanly constructed world structured by power relations and by power-determined distributions of goods, privileges, ideas, and meanings. The theological representations of biblical Israel are highly political in their scrutiny of social power and the ends for which it is used.

Every way of articulating and prioritizing the theological representations is conditioned by a material base in which people actually produce and reproduce their lives according to certain limits, some of which may be immutable but many of which are changeable. These theological representations express particular social interests which in one way or another are negotiated or imposed. The theological representations can serve to cover over these power realities by denying them or can assist in bringing them to light to justify them or to contest for their change. In the process the theological representations dispose us toward one or another set of theories and operations for dealing with power realities.

Theological representations, like art, literature, and ideology, sensitize and motivate us to deal with power relations in certain ways, but they are not themselves the precise tools for treating power relations, which must rather be theories and methods more exactly tailored to institutional and operational application. We may, for example, entertain a "functional" theory that explains inequality as a rough approximation to people's actual merits, or as the precondition of a social system working at all. Or, we may espouse a "conflict" theory that understands inequality as a forceful or duplicitous imposition of one set of interests on another set of interests without regard to merit.[14] We may accompany functional or conflict social theory with psychological theory that explains how people either necessarily crave mastery and subordination or have been culturally induced to internalize their powerlessness so that they more deeply fear the risk of change than they desire its potential benefits.[15] In our own social sites in capitalist United States, although functional theory is very strong, the impact of the theoretical and methodological currents flowing from Marx and Freud is deepening and widening, precisely because they offer us a leverage on problems that long seemed to be insoluble mysteries, and before which theological representations alone are helpless and even dangerously obfuscating.

Now it is evident that the wielders of theological representations can try to mark off areas of social and psychic life as tabooed ground and thereby resist new theories and methods for a priori reasons. Or they may so rush to embrace new theories and methods that they naively equate theological representations with those theories and methods (for example, the much-too-facile strategy of making Christianity and Marxism mean exactly the same thing), failing to observe the proper ground and limits of theological representations. Or theological representations can be recognized to have no special power to dispose over theory and method but rather a critical negative function of summoning and voicing the interests, meanings, and values that any theory or method will serve or disserve. Both the autonomy and conjuncture of theological representations and of theories and methods must be observed.

In *The Tribes of Yahweh*, I have carried through a radical socioeconomic and religiocultural deconstruction of early Israel without leaving any remainder to save traditional theology by means of the ever-convenient "god who fills the gaps." I have done so by turning theory and method upon the genesis of theological representations in ancient Israel. What I have not done, and could not possibly do by such a project, is to undo the theological representations, both because they are given there in the history and because they inhere in a living tradition today. Just as sense data, theory, and method do not replace art, literature, and ideology, so theological representations coexist with theory and method in the world of praxis. The viability of theological representations rooted in faith and opened to critical reflection is, however, tested by being called upon to give an account of how theological representations relate to their material base and social sites over the whole course of Israelite-Jewish-Christian history.

No mere pasting together of "history of theological ideas" with "history of religious institutions" can possibly accomplish this deconstruction of the history of theological representations in the context of Jewish-Christian praxis within the wider social world from biblical times to the present. The project of *Tribes*, restricted to premonarchic intertribal Israel, needs to be carried forward through all the phases of biblical history, as George V. Pixley has initially sketched in his recent *God's Kingdom* and as Fernando Belo has attempted for one Gospel in *A Materialist Reading of the Gospel of Mark*.[16] At the same time, the material and social base of theologizing throughout the whole of post-biblical Jewish and Christian history must be relentlessly pursued. Simultaneously, the theory and method by which we analyze and reconstruct the social sites of theologizing must be constantly evaluated, corrected, and enriched. It is clear that both Marxist and Freudian traditions are undergoing great ferment in themselves and in interaction with one another. The fertility of the theories and their applications is shown precisely in their capacity to reflect upon themselves and to improve their analytic and operational powers.[17] In this way, around the rubric of the interface between theological representations and social sites, all the disciplines of the theological encyclopedia can be gathered.

THE THEOLOGICAL CURRICULUM/ENCYCLOPEDIA

In a recent article, Edward Farley tackles the forbidding topic of fundamental reform in theological education as a theological task.[18] The theological task is understood by him not as the elevation of traditionally defined dogmatic theology over all the other branches of the curriculum. Rather, the theological task is to grasp the unity of knowledge and understanding requisite to the church and its ministry. I believe that Farley's desiderata for theological reform of the curriculum are met by the following formulation: it is the theological task of the church to grasp the theological representations in their social sites and praxis settings throughout Israelite-Jewish-Christian history and to focus all that critically reworked content on a self-critical praxis of the church and its leadership here and now.

The Reformation, Farley notes, offered a kind of theological vision that grounded the branches of the theological encyclopedia in a unitary study of divinity in which there was a clear movement out of the biblical revelation and the confessions of the church through history and into the ministry of the church in word and sacrament. Modernity has undermined that unitary study of divinity. Science as the theoretical feeder of technological applications has penetrated the theological structure, sapped the primacy of biblical revelation and confessional authority, and reshaped the dismembered branches of the curriculum into professional specializations with their own independent self-justifications, now busily trying to recover the vision by separate enterprises of "bridging the gaps."

Farley believes that the bridgings, redivisions, and rearrangements of curriculum won't work without a new grasp of the theological task. No doubt he is right. But where does one grasp the nettle? A theological curriculum of theory-praxis as the axis of every discipline absolutely requires a substantial base in the church and a faculty fully committed to it. At the moment the main power in the churches and seminaries does not lie in the hands of those who want to revision theologizing, church mission, and the process of leadership education. In short, our current social site favors utter amnesia and mindlessness toward critical thought and action. Nonetheless, the failures of the churches are so colossal, the urgencies of social crisis so insistent, and the resources of a critical social theology so available that new opportunities for deep-going rethinking and reacting of Christian faith may be forced by our very desperation.

To bring theological representations into unabashed and total interface with material base and social site calls for the most unrelenting restructuring of consciousness. Theology really ceases to be higher knowledge, as it also ceases to be the arcane elaboration of a privileged faith that stands apart from worldly experience and meaning. A renewed theological encyclopedia of this sort could only come from Christians with a radical regard for their tradition and with radical trust and courage to commit themselves to the conflictual and open-ended task of restructuring themselves and their world.[19] Just such radical regard, trust, and courage impelled the first Israelites, and it is in part for this reason that they entice and disturb us, making it worth our while to study them so intensively and comprehensively that they might be rescued from the platitudes and dogmas that have nearly cut them off from us.[20]

NOTES

1. Norman K. Gottwald, *The Tribes of Yahweh: A Sociology of the Religion of Liberated Israel, 1250-1050 B.C.E.* (Maryknoll, N.Y.: Orbis Books, 1979), p. 668.

2. Ibid., pp. 210-33, 323-37, 464-85, 489-97, 584-87, 592-602, 611-18, 894-900, 903-13.

3. Ibid., pp. 63-71, 493-97, 592-607, 618-21, 642-49, 692-703, 901-03.

4. Ibid., pp. 650-63.

5. Ibid., pp. 293-341, 611-18.

6. Ibid., pp. 618-21, 660-63.

7. Ibid., pp. 592-607, presents critiques of the pronounced tendency of biblical interpreters to abstract Israel's religion from its society, as exemplified in the work of John Bright, George E. Mendenhall, and Georg Fohrer.

8. Ibid., pp. 670-91.

9. Frank M. Cross, *Canaanite Myth and Hebrew Epic* (Cambridge: Harvard University Press, 1973), pp. 65-71.

10. Gottwald, *Tribes,* pp. 685, 796-97, 913.

11. Ibid., p. 692.

12. Ibid., p. 701.

13. My discussion of theological representations is greatly indebted to Alfredo Fierro, *The Militant Gospel: A Critical Introduction to Political Theologies* (Maryknoll, N.Y.: Orbis Books, 1975), pp. 182-256, 305-62.

14. Michael H. Best and William E. Connolly, *The Politicized Economy* (Lexington, Mass.: D. C. Heath, 1976), offers trenchant analyses of the functional and conflictual explanations of economic inequality.

15. Michael Schneider, *Neurosis and Civilization: A Marxist/Freudian Synthesis* (New York: Seabury, 1975).

16. George V. Pixley, *God's Kingdom: A Guide for Biblical Study* (Maryknoll, N.Y.: Orbis Books, 1981); Fernando Belo, *A Materialist Reading of the Gospel of Mark* (Maryknoll, N.Y.: Orbis Books, 1981).

17. See, among others, Bruce Brown, *Marx, Freud, and the Critique of Everyday Life: Toward a Permanent Cultural Revolution* (New York: Monthly Review Press, 1973); Stanley Aronowitz, *The Crisis in Historical Materialism: Class, Politics and Culture in Marxist Theory* (New York: Praeger, 1981); Alan Gilbert, *Marx's Politics: Communists and Citizens* (New Brunswick, N.J.: Rutgers University Press, 1981).

18. Edward Farley, "The Reform of Theological Education as a Theological Task," *Theological Education* 18 (Spring 1981): 93-117.

19. See, for example, Frederick Herzog, *Justice Church: The New Function of the Church in North American Christianity* (Maryknoll, N.Y.: Orbis Books, 1980).

20. Gottwald, *Tribes,* pp. 700-709, 901-903.

17

MARVIN L. CHANEY

Bitter Bounty

The Dynamics of Political Economy Critiqued by the Eighth-Century Prophets

The projection of religious individualism onto the oracles of the Israelite prophets reduced them to advocates of "ethical monotheism." The projection of capitalist economic assumptions onto the situations addressed by the prophets has obscured their indictment of the institutionalized injustices of the particular political economy of ancient Near Eastern monarchies. Only recently has it become possible, through comparative sociological studies, to organize and interpret archaeological data and textual references into a more adequate reconstruction of the distinctive ancient Near Eastern "tributary" political economy imposed on Israel by the Solomonic monarchy. Thus it is now possible also to discern more precisely the particular dynamics by which the formerly free peasant producers were systematically impoverished by the Israelite monarchies and their agents. Chaney's essay provides important background not only for the discussion of Micah by Itumeleng Mosala and of Hosea by Phyllis Bird, but for the analyses of Jeremiah, Second Isaiah, the Pentateuch, Deuteronomic law, and the Psalms, in the ensuing essays.

Reprinted from Robert L. Stivers, ed., *Reformed Faith and Economics* (Lanham, Md.: University Press of America, 1989), 15–30.

The appropriation of passages from the eighth-century prophets, Amos, Hosea, Isaiah, and Micah by the modern community of faith has often lacked clarity and effect, however, because of a lack of hermeneutical precision. A penchant for abstraction can sometimes be the culprit. The injunction of Amos 5:24 to "let justice roll down like waters," for example, is frequently quoted in tones which presuppose that everyone agrees about what economic justice is, but that certain people must be persuaded to be for it rather than against it. Such are not the terms of reality. People of faith in the vast majority favor economic justice as an abstraction, even as they can almost never agree about what it is or how to achieve it.

If abstraction is the Scylla of an adequate hermeneutic of prophetic economics, particularism is the Charybdis. Under the impress of the extreme individualism of American culture, many modern readers of the prophetic books assume that these texts excoriate a few venal individuals who deviated from norms otherwise observed in what was a healthy and just economic system.

Little could be farther from the realities of ancient Israel and Judah. As a careful reading of the oracles concerning economic dynamics makes clear, the prophets critique certain changes in the political economy as an integrated whole. While these changes benefited the powerful and privileged few who initiated them *as a generic class,* the prophets insist that they did so at the expense of even meager subsistence for the impoverished majority, who are also understood *as a generic class.*

Dozens of oracles in the eighth-century prophets declare the judgment of Yahweh's court against the former because of their oppression of the latter. Although these texts allude to various aspects of the economic dynamics involved, they nowhere describe them in full. All parties to the ancient conflict were familiar with the operations of their economy—even though they valued them quite differently—and thus did not require that they be rehearsed. Modern readers of the prophets share no such preunderstanding, a fact which occasions this preliminary attempt to reconstruct those systemic dynamics for those not participant in them.

Detailed exegesis of the pertinent prophetic texts would require a book far exceeding the bounds of this paper. Attention here will be focused instead on integrating data from disparate sources outside the prophetic books. Against the background thus sketched, it is hoped, many of the more obvious oracles will become self-explanatory.

In an earlier paper, I characterized Israel's economy in the eighth century B.C.E. as follows:

For historical reasons . . . most freeholding peasants in Israel and Judah were located in the highlands. As many small, subsistence plots in this hill country were foreclosed upon and joined together to form large estates, a change in the method of tillage also took place. Upland fields previously intercropped to provide a mixed subsistence for peasant families were combined into large and "efficient" vineyards and olive orchards producing a single crop for market. The increased production of wine and oil resulting from the formation of these plantations or latifundia played at least two roles in the new scheme of things. On the one hand, wine and oil were central to the increasingly consumptive lifestyle of the local elite, epitomized in a sodality called the *marzeaḥ*. On the other, since wine and oil were more valuable than most agricultural commodities per unit of weight or volume, they made ideal exports to exchange for the luxury and strategic imports coveted by members of the ruling classes.

But the *"efficiency"* of these cash crops came at a brutal cost to the *sufficiency* of the livelihood which they afforded the peasants who actually produced them. The old system of freehold had provided this peasant majority secure access to a modest but adequate and integrated living. The new system saw them labor in the same fields, but only according to the cyclical demands of viticulture and orcharding and at wages for day-labor depressed by a sustained buyer's market. During lulls in the agri-cultural calendar, they were as unemployed as landless. Jobless or not, they were forced into the marketplace of which they had little or no experience to buy wheat and barley, the staples of their diet. They had previously produced these cereals sufficiently for themselves in their hill-side plots, but now the same grains were grown "efficiently" on the large estates of the alluvial plains and piedmont region and shipped to market. In the marketplace, the meager and irregular wages of fieldhands bought even less sustenance than they should have because the vulnerable peas-ants were cheated with adulterated grain and dishonest weights and meas-ures. Finally, the processes of foreclosure and expropriation which initiated these dynamics were accelerated by a wholesale suborning of the courts. Instead of stopping foreclosures based upon illegal forms of interest, these corrupted courts sanctioned the proceedings.[1]

The political and military power and territorial expansion of Israel and Judah in the eighth century B.C.E. — particularly during the long and mostly concurrent reigns of Jeroboam II and Uzziah — are beyond doubt. "By the mid-eighth cen-tury the dimensions of Israel and Judah together lacked but little of being as great as those of the empire of Solomon."[2] The particulars are well documented elsewhere,[3] and need not detain us here.

Not since the "United Monarchy" of David and Solomon had Israel and Judah been so secure from immediate, external, military threat. This relative security, coupled with the lengthy tenure in office of both the allied kings, granted a greater than usual opportunity for royal administrations to rearrange their domestic furniture, including that of their economies. The accession of Tig-lath-pileser III to the Assyrian throne in 745 B.C.E. may serve conveniently to symbolize the closing of that window of opportunity. That Jeroboam II and Uzziah had incentive, as well as opportunity, to effect change in the economies of their nations is suggested by the evidence for their active participation in international trade.

As David C. Hopkins recognizes, "the expansion of borders not only meant an increase in sources of income and produce for import/export trade, but also could lead, given propitious geopolitical conditions, to an expansion of transit trade."[4] Morris Silver offers a concise, if maximalist, summary of the evidence for such propitious conditions in eighth-century Israel and Judah.[5] Contra Silver, however, M. Elat is surely correct when he writes of this transit trade that "while it produced profits for the royal court and raised the standard of living of those close to it, it had only a limited influence on the local economy or on the occupational distribution of the country's inhabitants."[6]

It was the import/export trade which heavily impacted the peasant majorities in Israel and Judah and tempted their rulers to become involved in changing the priorities, methods, and distribution of agricultural production. After a penetrating synopsis of the relevant data, Hopkins reaches the widely shared conclusion that "this literary, epigraphic, and artifactual evidence converges on oil, wine, and wheat as the commodities of choice in the monarchic economic network."[7]

These commodities were exported mainly to and through the kingdom of Tyre,[8] a maritime society whose seaborne transportation was cheaper than the overland modes utilized of necessity by the transit trade in Israel and Judah.[9] This differential in transportation costs goes far to explain why a large proportion of Phoenicians could earn their living from transit trade, while most Israelites and Judahites could not. In return for their export of oil, wheat, and wine, Israel and Judah received luxury goods and military material. That such was the nature of the trade between Israel and Tyre can now be documented archaeologically as well as from written records, it would appear.[10]

The interface between this configuration of international trade and the pattern of social stratification in Israel and Judah is significant. Foodstuffs produced by the peasant majority were exported. Luxury goods and arms utilized by the elite minority were imported. While agricultural intensification probably raised the absolute amount of edible commodities produced, there were very finite limits to that increase, and exports competed directly with peasant sustenance. For all its erudition, Silver's "supply-side" analysis of the situation never comes to grips with these simple facts.[11]

Faced with a finite supply of exportable goods but possessed of an almost infinite appetite for imported luxuries, the elites in Israel and Judah had a powerful incentive to increase production of the three major export crops. One method used to gain this increase was a regional specialization of agriculture. 2 Chronicles 26:10, translated according to the known facts of Hebrew syntax and economic geography, records that Uzziah undertook just this process.[12]

He built guard towers in the Steppe and hewed out many cisterns, for he had large herds; and in the Shephelah and in the Plain (he had) plowmen; and vineyard and orchard workers in the Hills and in the Carmel. ...

Here we learn that under royal tutelage, herding was increased in the steppe by means of guard towers and cisterns, plowing—the cultivation of cereal crops, the predominant of which was wheat—was intensified in the plain and piedmont region, and viticulture and orcharding were pressed in the uplands. In each case, the economic exploitation of a given region was specialized to the one or two products by whose production that region could contribute maximally to the export trade and/or to the conspicuous consumption of the local elite. Rainey has analyzed in some detail the exact nature and location of these districts in Judah.[13]

In light of the clarification of the stratigraphy at Lachish and taking this verse as a key, Rainey has been able to demonstrate that the much-discussed *lmlk* seal impressions from Judah witness a system of royal vineyards towards the end of the eighth century B.C.E.[14] Farther north, the Samaria ostraca — despite all the controversies surrounding their exact dating and interpretation — " . . . evidence the flow of oil and wine probably to officials of the royal court . . . "[15] sometime during the eighth century B.C.E. Perhaps the easiest reading of these documents is occasioned by the assumption that the existence of both private and royal vineyards and olive orchards is reflected therein.[16] An ostracon from Tell Qasileh probably witnesses the export of oil in about this period.[17] And epigraphic finds continue. Excavations in the City of David in 1978 produced a large stone plaque fragment from the latter part of the eighth century which may well refer to royal stores, either of grain or of treasure articles.[18]

Anepigraphic archaeology, too, provides further evidence, particularly on the processing of olive oil. While rock-cut olive and grape processing installations are probably almost as old as agriculture itself in Palestine, recent surveys suggest a proliferation of and innovations in such installations in the eighth century B.C.E.[19] Of special interest is the evidence for use of the beam press to extract more oil from the olives. The earliest such press found is apparently from the ninth century B.C.E.,[20] but the device appears to have come into widespread use in the eighth century.[21] As already indicated, the export trade was thirsty for every drop of olive oil it could get. Such intensification of the extraction process, in turn, probably led to different grades of oil. The finest resulted from crushing the olives and using water to extract the oil without presses. Subsequent processing of the pulp and the use of presses often introduced impurities into the oil and reduced its quality.[22] One may reasonably assume that certain of the demands of the export trade tended toward quantity — hence, the beam presses. The tastes of both local and foreign elites, on the other hand, preferred quality, an interpretation which appears to be borne out by the appearance of a term for the finer "washed oil" some dozen times in the Samaria ostraca.[23]

If the processing installations for oil and wine give little hint of who initiated their proliferation, 2 Chron. 26:10, when corroborated by the inscriptional evidence for royal vineyards and olive orchards, strongly suggests elements of a "command economy."[24] Hopkins writes appositely, "the centralizing structure of the monarchy and its characteristic institutions bring about an attenuation of the decisionmaking functions of the primary productive units, perhaps a complete usurpation, in the creation of what has been called a 'command economy'."[25] Such "command economies" are characteristic of advanced agrarian societies as a generic class.[26] Both the comparative data upon which these scholars base their general theories and the specific data adduced for ancient Judah and Israel should give pause to anyone inclined to follow Silver in his position of largely private, free market economies in eighth-century Israel and Judah.[27]

Many of the dynamics already discussed combined to consolidate more and more of the arable land into fewer and fewer hands.[28] Once again, Hopkins has stated the matter with precision: "Besides demands to pay for its costs and the possibility of the loss of labor to the royal projects, the monarchical program of agricultural intensification cut into village-based agricultural systems most directly by its pursuit of land."[29]

The land consolidation reflected in the eighth-century prophets had historical roots. Prior to the founding of the Davidic state, Israel's secure holdings were concentrated in the hill country. "Landholdings in the hills were small in comparison with those in the plains,"[30] a pattern similar to that found in southern Syria.[31] In premonarchic Israel, these small, hill country holdings typically supported a mixed, subsistence agriculture.[32]

This configuration changed with David.

... David not only defeated the Philistines, restricting them to their pentapolis and laying solid Israelite claim to the alluvial plains of Canaan for the first time, but succeeded in subjugating his neighbors on all sides. In that process of empire building, he incurred debts. His military retainers, many loyal to his person since his days as a social bandit, expected to be rewarded when he came into his glory. He had conquered an empire, and its administration necessitated the creation and importation of bureaucrats. In an agrarian context, these categories of obligation were payable in grants of land, that is, in patrimonial and prebendal estates.

But what did David have to grant? Certainly not most of the hill country, which supported his core constituency as peasant freehold. (The forces which led to the formation of the monarchy had produced some larger estates in the hill country [cf., e.g., 1 Sam. 22:6-8], but these were as modest in number and importance as the military professionals whom they supported [Halpern 1981: 86-87 *et passim*; Ben-Barak 1981: 73-91]). But the richer plains had never been a secure part of premonarchic Israel, and were David's to grant by right of conquest. Accustomed to the typical agrarian combination of patrimonial and prebendal domain, the estates of the lowlands simply received new overlords, in this case, newly created Israelite aristocrats and bureaucrats.[33]

If this analysis is correct, the ruling elites of Israel had enjoyed primary control of the "breadbasket" areas of the plains long before the agricultural intensification of the eighth century B.C.E. For them to have implemented on their large, lowland estates measures designed to maximize the production of wheat would have been a relatively simple matter. But what of the hill country? If much of it remained in small plots, tilled by their holders according to the priorities of the village community, such a system would have constituted a major impediment to the goals of the city-based elite.

As already indicated, urban elites in Israel and Judah sought the maximally

efficient production of wheat, oil, and wine for export and for their own consumption. Hill country peasants, left to their own devices in a village, would
have sought to guarantee the sufficiency of their livelihood by spreading the
risks inherent in it as much as possible. "The crucial objective of village-based
agriculture dictates the spreading of risk. The concentration of risk in a costly
investment runs directly counter to this security-conscious objective."[34]

While direct evidence is sparse, a combination of indirect evidence and
broad-based comparisons allows the following sketch of risk spreading in Israelite upland agriculture to be offered with considerable confidence. Fields
which produced cereals were not so used every year. To maintain fertility, they
were periodically fallowed and probably also sown to legumes in at least some
rotations. (Obed Borowski has collected the evidence from the Hebrew Bible
and from archaeological remains for the cultivation of leguminous crops in
ancient Israel.)[35] As well as returning nitrogen to the soil, these pulses would
have been a significant source of protein in the diet. Fallow fields would have
supplemented uncultivable grazing land in providing pasture for the herding of
sheep, goats, and cattle—in varying numbers and proportions. For subsistence
farmers, such herding provided "a hedge against the risk of purely agricultural
pursuits."[36] Animals so raised constituted a "disaster bank on the hoof," which
stored surpluses from good years to be drawn on in lean years. Their manure
helped to fertilize the fallow fields where they grazed, though not so efficiently
as if it had been composted. Herding also made use of labor in the village—
the very young and the very old—which would not otherwise have been productive. Tree and vine crops would have rounded out the repertoire of village
agriculture in the hills. Their labor demands were complementary to those of
cereals, and their processed fruit could be stored stably for extended periods,
making them valuable contributors to the goal of spreading risk.

The demand or encouragement by the urban elite that only oil, wheat, and
wine be produced and in ever increasing quantities

> . . . ran counter to the village's objective of spreading risk and optimizing
> labor through a diversity of subsistence means. Assuming a limitation on
> labor and land, a relative increase of production of these commodities
> meant a relative decrease in the production of others. The absolute
> increase in production if the agricultural village were to contribute a share
> of its produce to the state and also maintain its level of subsistence neces-
> sitated, at least along one likely pathway, an expansion of the percentage
> of village land given over to cultivation of the preferred commodities at
> the expense of grazing lands. Sheep and goats which were integral to the
> risk- and labor-spreading agriculture of the village were not integral to
> the taxation apparatus, and were pushed out of the village system.[37]

When linked with the evidence in 2 Chron. 26:10 for royal herding in the
steppe, such considerations weigh heavily against Silver's statement that " . . .
it is not unreasonable to assume that land consolidation facilitated a transition
from grain to stock farming to take advantage of the emergence of an affluent,

meat-consuming Israelite public."[38] For reasons which are becoming increasingly apparent, we can hardly assume that the Israelite public at large was affluent. Lands in Judah which could support at least seasonal grazing, but were too arid to be cultivable, were scarcely sufficient to supply meat on a regular basis to the general public. All land which was cultivable was increasingly being pressed into producing one of the three preferred export crops.

Animals headed for the tables of a few privileged urbanites were pastured in the steppe during the wet season and then stall-fed in preparation for slaughter. Such stall-feeding would also have facilitated the collection and composting of manure, which in turn would have been in demand for fertility maintenance in the more intensively cropped fields. Lucian Turkowski, at least, reports just such a use of manure in the Judean hills when agriculture was intensified there in the last century:

> From the nineteenth century new systems of increased agriculture spread to the Judaean hills. This demanded that no part of the land should be left unproductive. The part formerly left fallow was now fertilized with manure. . . .[39]

With the fallow went a significant part of village grazing land and its ability to sustain a "disaster bank on the hoof." In its place came hand weeding of cereal fields to provide fodder for stall-fed animals.[40] When this fodder proved insufficient to fatten the delicacies of the rich, precious cereals may well have been used. As Marvin Harris concedes, "it is true that the cost-benefits of intensification are not the same for peasants or workers as for members of the ruling class."[41]

As part of this eighth-century intensification of agriculture in the hill country of Israel and Judah, multi-purpose land which had helped to spread risk was gradually converted into terraces growing vineyards and olive trees.[42] While elite demands on their production tended to be steady or to increase, that production itself was subject to the vicissitudes of the environment and, in the case of the olive, to a pattern of alternating yields.[43] Gone was the "inefficient" diversification which had spread the risk of such fluctuations in the past. Hopkins characterizes the changes and their implications as follows:

> A system-wide increase in crop specialization brings an increase in short-term production and efficiency, but also lowers resistance to catastrophe. The former relative self-sufficiency of the agricultural village gives way increasingly to a dependence upon the centralizing forces and the exchange network that they administer. Constant coordination and direction must emanate from this center, lest the whole structure collapse.
> . . . The period [the eighth century] triggered a sharp jump of the needle that monitors movements on the continuum between autonomous village-based agriculture and an economy dominated by the central state.[44]

Although quantitative data are difficult to secure, there is probably a high correlation generally in agrarian societies between such dynamics, on the one hand, and political stability, territorial expansion, growing import/export trade, and royal construction, on the other.[45]

These latter same factors are also correlated with an increase in what is sometimes called "rent capitalism."[46] In such a system, not only are ownership of the land and labor separated,[47] but each of the factors of agricultural production is segmented from the others and subjected to separate rent.[48] While rural residence of the wealthy favors a multi-stranded patron-client relationship with poor cultivators, a single-stranded relationship of economic exploitation is most often the result when the elite are urban-based.[49]

> This estrangement is favoured by the landlord's urban residence ("absentee landlordism") as well as by the situation of the upper classes which provides both for social prestige and political influence independent of any clientele support.[50]

Inducements for rich landlords to live in the city include import trade in luxury items. "As soon as the market is able to provide luxury goods and gives rise to a corresponding urban life-style ... [,] then exploitation may be a consequence."[51] Under such circumstances, the contrast between the splendor of the cities and the misery of the countryside is stark and "can hardly be exaggerated."[52] Recent studies indicate that this configuration characterized Neo-Assyrian society:

> ... Even under Essarhaddon more revenue was produced from internal provinces than was collected through conquest. Regardless of the wealth of the empire, the economic conditions of the peasant in the countryside never improved, but if anything became worse as the empire expanded. The question was not one of the supply of goods and services but of the demand of a central administration which claimed the right to acquire and redistribute them.[53]

While Israel and Judah were not empires in the sense that Assyria was, every other indication points to similar dynamics there in the eighth century B.C.E.

Such a system pressed the typical peasant cultivator hard even in good years, because there was incentive for the elite to extract every possible surplus, leaving only the barest subsistence necessary to continue production. In less than optimal years cultivators stripped of the insurance of diversification were forced to take out survival-loans. The social systems supported by diversified, subsistence agriculture had most probably included mutual obligations of interest-free survival loans within certain village and/or kinship groupings.[54] But the intensified system saw the only funds available increasingly in the hands of wealthy moneylenders bent on becoming wealthier. "Taking a loan almost automatically leads to long-term or even permanent dependence because of the high interest rates. ... "[55] In many cases, a cycle of encumbered harvests was created, each pledged to repay debts incurred in the prior procurement of the factors of its production. Usurious interest rates — coupled with the nadir of the annual cycle of agricultural commodity values at harvest time, when the debt contracts came due—insured the need for further, even larger loans. Foreclosure on collateral at the discretion of the lender often become a sword of Damocles hanging over the indebted peasantry.

For historical reasons detailed above, the lowlands of Israel and Judah had, for the most part, probably been organized into large estates long before the eighth century B.C.E. Many cultivators there would have been landless tenants, most vulnerable to the dynamics of "rent capitalism." With intensified demand for wheat in the eighth century, these tenants would have been pressed even harder, leading to an increase in all forms of debt incurred for survival reasons, and producing growing numbers of debt-slaves.

The situation in the hill country had been different. Royal vineyards and olive orchards no doubt existed there from the emergence of the monarchy, but in much of the upland a tradition of small freeholders working their own land in mixed subsistence had struck deep root. But as seen above, each of the particulars of that system was under pressure to change in the eighth century. Urban elites could structure state taxation to induce, perhaps even force, increased production of oil and wine, with all the attendant losses in the spreading of risk. Bad years began to bring the necessity of loans from the rent capitalists of the cities, with upland plots offered as collateral.

Although the evidence is spotty and difficult and the secondary literature far too voluminous and controverted to be reviewed here, it seems likely that not all hill country plots were equally alienable. Those planted to vines and orchards were probably most often held in perpetuity by a given family, since such intensive cultivation of perennials takes many years to come to full fruition, and few cultivators will make such improvements on land which is periodically redistributed.[56] Evidence from later periods in Palestine,[57] as well as various comparisons and allusions,[58] combines to suggest that fields used to grow cereals were often held in common by the village as a whole and periodically reapportioned by lot to individual families.

It appears probable that the vineyards and olive orchards may have been the first lands to slip into the hands of the urban elites. They already controlled most of the best grain fields in the lowlands, and would at first have been primarily interested in oil and wine from the hills. Since vineyards and orchards "belonged" to individual families, they would have been less complicated to offer as collateral, even if they could not be sold outright. (1 Kings 21 remains easiest to interpret, I believe, on the assumption that Israelite customary law forbade outright sale or trade of such property.) If the grain lands of the village were taxed in common, as evidence from later periods suggests,[59] heavy state taxes in kind would both have yielded wheat for the export trade and supplied villagers a powerful incentive to terrace former grainfields and convert them to vines and trees. As Hopkins writes,

> the alienation of land, usually the most productive, decreases the farming household's ability to control a variety of ecological niches and pushes the family, which must somehow provide for its subsistence, onto poorer and poorer lands at greater distances from its village.[60]

Unable to grow all their own grain, and in many cases forced off their lands altogether and relegated to agricultural wage labor, former freeholders went, of necessity, to grain traders to procure the staples of their diet.

The mortgaging of and foreclosure upon family lands, members, and property involved court action. While there was a long tradition of consensus justice in the village courts, state officials had long since enjoyed considerable success in limiting and subordinating local judicial functions in the name of the king.[61] Given the priorities of royal policy in the eighth century B.C.E., there can be little astonishment that such courts did not and could not effectively block land consolidation and its concomitants. The bitterness of those whose dispossession was sanctioned by these courts should occasion even less surprise.

Such a sketch of the dynamics of political economy in eighth-century Israel and Judah can be rendered even more probable by close exegesis of the prophetic texts which both reflect and reflect upon these dynamics. That detailed study must await another occasion, as must any attempt to explicate the extended parallels between the world of these prophets and much of the so-called third world today. My only hope is that a slightly firmer foundation has been laid for both enterprises for they are equally intrinsic to any full dialogue between faith and economics in today's world.

NOTES

1. Marvin L. Chaney, "Systemic Study of the Israelite Monarchy," *Semeia* 37 (1986), 72-73. On the sodality called the Marzeah in paragraph one of this quotation, see: Robert B. Coote, *Amos Among the Prophets: Composition and Theology* (Philadelphia: Fortress Press, 1981), pp. 36-39.

2. John Bright, *A History of Israel* 3rd ed. (Philadelphia: The Westminster Press, 1981), p. 258.

3. Ibid., 255-59; S. Yeivin, "The Divided Kingdom: Rehoboam-Ahaz/Jeroboam-Pekah," in *The Age of the Monarchies: Political History*, ed. by A. Malamat, Vol. IV:1 of *The World History of the Jewish People*, ed. by B. Mazar (Jerusalem: Massada Press, 1979), pp. 161-72; and Yohanan Aharoni, *The Archaeology of the Land of Israel*, ed. by Miriam Aharoni, trans. by Anson F. Rainey (Philadelphia: The Westminster Press, 1982), pp. 251-54.

4. David C. Hopkins, "The Dynamics of Agriculture in Monarchical Israel," in *SBLSP*, ed. Kent Harold Richard (Chico, CA: Scholars Press, 1983), p. 195.

5. Morris Silver, *Prophets and Markets: The Political Economy of Ancient Israel* (Boston: Kluwer-Nijhoff, 1983), pp. 49-52.

6. M. Elat, "Trade and Commerce," in *The Age of the Monarchies: Culture and Society*, ed. by A. Malamat, Vol. IV:2 of *The World History of the Jewish People*, ed. by B. Mazar (Jerusalem: Massada Press, 1979), p. 186; cf. Gerhard Lenski and Jean Lenski, *Human Societies: An Introduction to Macrosociology* (5th ed.; New York: McGraw-Hill, 1987), pp. 183-85; and Hopkins, "Dynamics," p. 195.

7. Hopkins, "Dynamics," p. 196; cf. Silver, *Prophets and Markets*, p. 24; and Bernhard Lang, *Monotheism and the Prophetic Minority: An Essay in Biblical History and Sociology*. The Social World of Biblical Antiquity Series, Vol. 1 (Sheffield: The Almond Press, 1983), p. 124.

8. Elat, "Trade and Commerce," pp. 225-28.

9. Lenski and Lenski, *Human Societies*, pp. 216-19.

10. Shulamit Geva, "Archaeological Evidence for the Trade Between Israel and Tyre," *BASOR*, 248 (1982), 69-72.

11. Silver, *Prophets and Markets*, passim.

12. Anson F. Rainey, "Wine from the Royal Vineyards," *BASOR*, 245 (1982), 57-62; Chaney, "Systemic Study," pp. 73-74; cf. Hopkins, "Dynamics," p. 200.

13. Rainey, "Wine," pp. 58-59.

14. Ibid., pp. 57-61.

15. Hopkins, "Dynamics," p. 199.

16. Devadasan N. Premnath, "The Process of Latifundialization Mirrored in the Oracles Pertaining to Eighth Century B.C.E. in the Books of Amos, Hosea, Isaiah and Micah" (unpublished Ph.D. dissertation, The Graduate Theological Union, 1984), pp. 60-62.

17. Silver, *Prophets and Markets*, p. 17; N. Avigad, "Hebrew Epigraphic Sources," in *The Age of the Monarchies: Political History*, ed. by A. Malamat, Vol. IV:1 of *The World History of the Jewish People*, ed. by B. Mazar (Jerusalem: Massada Press, 1979), pp. 33-34; and Benjamin Maisler (Mazar), "The Excavations at Tell Qasileh: Preliminary Report," *IEJ* 1 (1950), pp. 208-210.

18. Silver, *Prophets and Markets*, pp. 36-37; and Yigal Shiloh, "City of David: Excavation 1978," *BA*, XLII (Summer, 1979), p. 170.

19. David Eitam, "Olive Presses of the Israelite Period," *Tel Aviv*, 4 (1979), pp. 146-54.

20. Lawrence E. Stager and S. R. Wolff, "Production and Commerce in Temple Courtyards: An Olive Press in the Sacred Precinct at Tel Dan," *BASOR*, 243 (1981), pp. 95-102; and Lawrence E. Stager, "The Finest Olive Oil in Samaria," *JSS*, 28 (1983), pp. 241-45.

21. Eitam, "Olive Presses."

22. Stager, "Finest Olive Oil."

23. Ibid.

24. Chaney, "Systemic Study," p. 74; Hopkins, "Dynamics," p. 193 and n. 71, p. 200; Premnath, "Latifundialization," p. 56.

25. Hopkins, "Dynamics," p. 193.

26. Lenski and Lenski, *Human Societies*, pp. 183-85; and Robert L. Heilbroner, *The Making of Economic Society* (5th ed.; Englewood Cliffs, N.J.: Prentice-Hall, 1975), pp. 7-46.

27. Silver, *Prophets and Markets,* passim.

28. Ibid., pp. 73-77; 259-63.

29. Hopkins, "Dynamics," p. 200; cf. Chaney, "Systemic Study," pp. 72-73; and J. Andrew Dearman, "Prophecy, Property and Politics," in *SBLSP*, (1984), pp. 389-91.

30. Lawrence E. Stager, "The Archaeology of the Family in Ancient Israel," *BASOR*, 240 (1985), 24.

31. Leon Marfoe, "The Integrative Transformation: Patterns of Sociopolitical Organization in Southern Syria," *BASOR*, 234 (1979), 21-23.

32. Marvin L. Chaney, "Ancient Palestinian Peasant Movements and the Formation of Premonarchic Israel," in *Palestine in Transition: The Emergence of Ancient Israel*, ed. by David Noel Freeman and David Frank Graf, The Social World of Biblical Antiquity Series, Vol. II (Sheffield: The Almond Press, 1983), pp. 50, 64-65.

33. Chaney, "Systemic Study," pp. 67-68; cf. Albrecht Alt, "Der Anteil des Königtums an der sozialen Entwicklung in der Reichen Israel und Juda," in *Kleine Schriften zur Geschichte des Volkes Israel*, ed. by Martin Noth, III (Munich: C. H. Beck, 1959), pp. 348-72. On the larger estates in the hill country supporting military professionals, see: Baruch Halpern, "The Uneasy Compromise: Israel Between League and Monarchy," in *Traditions in Transformation: Turning Points in Biblical Faith*, Baruch Halpern and Jon D. Levenson, eds. (Winona Lake, Ind.: Eisenbrauns, 1981), pp. 86-87 et passim; and Zafrira Ben-Barak, "Meribaal and the System of Land Grants in Ancient Israel," *Biblica*, 62 (1981), pp. 73-91.

34. Hopkins, "Dynamics," p. 201.

35. Obed Borowski, *Agriculture in Iron Age Israel* (Winona Lake, Ind.: Eisenbrauns, 1987), pp. 93-97.

36. Hopkins, "Dynamics," p. 191.

37. *Ibid*, p. 197.

38. Silver, *Prophets and Markets*, pp. 97-98.

39. Lucian Turkowski, "Peasant Agriculture in the Judean Hills," *PEQ*, 101 (1969), p. 24.

40. Ibid., p. 101.

41. Marvin Harris, *Cultural Materialism: The Struggle for a Science of Culture* (New York: Random House, 1980), p. 103.

42. Hopkins, "Dynamics," p. 200; and Gershon Edelstein and Mordechai Kislev, "Mevasseret Yerushalayim: The Ancient Settlement and Its Agricultural Terraces," *BAR*, 44 (1981), pp. 53-56.

43. Hopkins, "Dynamics," p. 197.

44. Ibid., p. 201.

45. Ibid.

46. Lang, *Monotheism and the Prophetic Minority*, p. 167, n. 218.

47. Ibid., p. 118.

48. Eric R. Wolf, *Peasants*, Foundations of Modern Anthropology Series (Englewood Cliffs, N.J.: Prentice-Hall, 1966), pp. 55-56; and Robert B. Coote, *Amos among the Prophets: Composition and Theology* (Philadelphia: Fortress Press, 1981), pp. 29-32.

49. Lang, *Monotheism and the Prophetic Minority*, pp. 118-19.

50. Ibid., p. 119.

51. Ibid.

52. Ibid., p. 120.

53. Dearman, "Prophecy, Property and Politics," pp. 393-94; cf. J.N. Postgate, "Some Remarks on Conditions in the Assyrian Countryside," *JESHO*, 17 (1974), pp. 225-43; and G. van Driel, "Land and People in Assyria," *BO*, 27 (1970), pp. 168-75.

54. Lang, *Monotheism and the Prophetic Minority*, p. 120; and Richard Critchfield, *Villages* (New York: Anchor Press/Doubleday, 1983), p. 345.

55. Lang, *Monotheism and the Prophetic Minority*, p. 117.

56. Chaney, "Ancient Palestinian Peasant Movements," pp. 50, 64-65.

57. Turkowski, "Peasant Agriculture," pp. 23-32.

58. Chaney, "Ancient Palestinian Peasant Movements," pp. 50, 64-65.

59. Turkowski, "Peasant Agriculture," p. 23.

60. Hopkins, "Dynamics," p. 201.

61. Dearman, "Prophecy, Property and Politics," pp. 391-92; and Keith W. Whitelam, *The Just King: Monarchic Judicial Authority in Ancient Israel*, *JSOTSup*, Vol. XII (Sheffield: JSOT Press, 1979), passim.

18

ITUMELENG J. MOSALA

A Materialist Reading of Micah

For some time biblical scholars have pointed out that older traditions have been reused to address new situations. But they have rarely inquired about the politics involved: who was reframing the older traditions for what social-ideological purpose? Now that we have a clearer sense of the dramatic transformation in "political economy" involved in the historic transition from early Israel to the monarchy (see also the preceding essay by Chaney), we have an appropriate background against which to hear the oracles of the Israelite prophets. But it is also necessary, in the appropriate historical (political-economic) context, to develop a dialectical literary and political-ideological analysis of the different literary layers and reframings which produced a given prophetic book in its final form. Only then is it possible to understand the different layers of oracles as addressed to their particular historical situations, and to appreciate the political struggle involved over what prophetic oracles were/are to mean. Following the groundbreaking work of Robert B. Coote on the book of Amos, Mosala here presents the implications of this complex and sophisticated analysis for the book of Micah. Working in the highly charged context of the struggle for human dignity and justice in contemporary South Africa, however, Mosala also demonstrates how the sharp prophetic indictments of ruling class exploitation in the earliest layer of Micah-A can be appropriated by a critical deconstruction of the original historical

Reprinted from Itumeleng J. Mosala, *Biblical Hermeneutics and Black Theology in South Africa* (Grand Rapids: Eerdmans, 1989), 101–103, 105–106, 114–21, 123–53.

*struggle in which those indictments were co-opted into the generalized
exhortations of Micah-B and then the imperialist theology of domination
in Micah-C.*

Biblical scholars have always been aware of the tendency in biblical literature
for older traditions to be reused to address the needs of new situations. The
whole question of the reappearance of themes and motifs in different contexts
at different times exemplifies this process. This practice has, in fact, been seen
as a natural order of things in the internal hermeneutics of the Bible. As Ferdinand Deist has put it, "It is the primary function of tradition to explain the
new in terms of the old and in that way to authorize the new."[1] Von Rad has
gone further and drawn attention to the fact that, in the biblical literature, not
only do we have a reapplication of old themes and motifs, but we are confronted
with what are in fact historical data alongside a "spiritualizing interpretation
of these data."[2] According to him, there is a unifying principle that keeps the
various traditions together:

> In the process the old disassociated traditions have been given a reference
> and interpretation which in most cases was foreign to their original mean-
> ing. . . . Only the reader is not aware of the tremendous process of uni-
> fication lying behind the picture given in the source documents.[3]

Until recently, however, the historical-ideological significance of the "unified
diversity" of biblical literature seems to have eluded biblical scholars. By this I
mean that, although scholars have noticed the disparate character of the material and the manner in which it has been precariously held together by what
they have called "theological interpretative themes," they have nevertheless
failed to see the ideological unity that prevails in most of the Bible. In recent
times new directions have emerged. Norman K. Gottwald's monumental work
The Tribes of Yahweh breaks new ground in a radical way. Among other things,
Gottwald argues convincingly for the cultic-ideological origins of the texts of
the Bible.[4] A number of other scholars follow, *mutatis mutandis*, a procedure
similar to Gottwald's.[5]

We should note, however, that the ideological unity of a text, notwithstanding its literary and other disparities, is not discernible as a matter of *natural*
course to every reader. On the contrary, specific kinds of ideological questions
put to the text as a result of particular kinds of ideological commitments and
practices are necessary to detect the text's own practices. My use of a historical-
materialist method to reconstruct the social system and practices behind the
text of Micah in this chapter is a result of a theoretical commitment that issues
out of a concurrent commitment to the black struggle for liberation from capitalism, racism, sexism, and imperialism in South Africa.

THE MATERIAL CONDITIONS OF THE BOOK OF MICAH

Given a proper theoretical framework, we can discern quite readily that the Israelite monarchical system was based on a tributary mode of production. Gottwald has recently reconstructed the specific mode of production of pre-monarchical Israel. He points among other things to the way in which an egalitarian communal society, arranged in large extended families that were relatively self-contained socioeconomic units and political equals, took advantage of the recent introduction of iron implements for clearing and tilling the land and of slake lime plaster for waterproofing cisterns in order to keep reserve water during the annual dry season.[6]

In premonarchical Israel the basic economic unit was the *beth-'av*, or father's house. The labor of the family was differentiated on the basis of age and sex to accomplish the process of producing the basic means of subsistence. Grain and fruits were grown, and limited animal husbandry was practiced if the *beth-'av* owned some sheep and goats and a few cattle. "The staple crops were barley and wheat, wine and olive oil, which were produced alone or in combination depending on the variable climate and soil from region to region."[7] Cooperation between the *beth-'avoth*, which made up the *mišpaḥa* (extended families networks: II Sam. 6:6; I Sam. 23:1; Ruth 3:2; I Kgs. 22:10), helped to disperse risk and to increase productivity, particularly in view of "the great diversity of the agricultural environment created especially by a variegated landscape overlaid by variations in rainfall, soil and vegetation."[8]

Historically agrarian states depend on surpluses extracted from the agricultural base than on profits from trade.

> Maintaining secure borders and participating in export/import and transit trade were decisive determinants of the extent of the burden imposed by the monarchy upon the village-based agricultural systems. The literary and archaeological record evidences plentitudinous royal-sponsored construction relating to these areas of its concern. The fiscal apparatus which supported these and other activities of the monarchy, with its facilities and personnel expenses, must have required an even greater imposition of taxes. On top of taxes of agricultural produce, Chaney is right to emphasize the pernicious effect of royal enterprise on the availability of tools and labor both of which it siphoned away from possible involvement in the agricultural sector.[9]

The imposition of taxes on agriculturalists, especially under Solomon, marked the dominance of a new mode of production: the tributary mode of production. Gottwald superbly summarizes the fundamental character of this mode:

> We can identify the quantum leap in pressure on free agrarians by noting the officers that Solomon added to those of David's administration:

(1) a chief administrator over the twelve regional areas for the provisioning of an enlarged court establishment with accelerated tastes ...

(2) a large network of officers supervising forced labor operations ...

(3) a head steward who managed the royal household, probably including royal holdings and estates not granted to retainers ....

These added officers indicate a more thorough administration of the court proper, and especially a smoother, more regular, and far more abundant flow of resources *from the Israelite cultivators* to the court and royal bureaucracy, both at Jerusalem and wherever officials were installed throughout the land. In this way Solomon "rationalized," not "modernized," the agricultural base of the economy, for his basic strategy was not to improve the means of production but to improve the flow of as much agricultural surplus as possible into the control of his regime. [Gottwald's italics][10]

The class structure of this formation was characterized by a social division of labor resulting in antagonistic social relations of production, exchange, and distribution. Gottwald identifies especially three forms of surplus extraction:

(a) taxes and tithes imposed by the indigenous Israelite monarchy and priesthood;

(b) tributes imposed on the Israelite ruling classes by foreign oppressors ... both during the period of dependent monarchy and provincial administration;

(c) rents extracted by the growing numbers of latifundiaries, who further stood in diverse and complex relations with the various Israelite dynasties, foreign states, trading partners, etc.[11]

Numerous biblical texts intimate these various forms of surplus extraction directly or indirectly. Gottwald also provides a nuanced class analysis of the Israelite monarchical social formation. The following is a picture of the social classes and fractions of classes as he sees it:

(a) ruling class groups: the Israelite royal houses, during the monarchic period, together with priestly sectors, dependent on taxes and corvées from the peasant communities; the metropolitan ruling classes of the various empires which dominated Israel, dependent on tributes levied on the population and collected by the indigenous ruling classes or imperial administrators; and latifundiaries, dependent on rents from more or less private estates;

(b) middle layers: craftsmen, functionaries, and lower clergy dependent on benefices which do not provide income sufficient to maintain an aristocratic style of life, and independent craftsmen and merchants;

(c) exploited classes: two principal kinds of peasantry: peasants protected by redistributional land tenure and other community guarantees; tenant farmers on the estates of latifundiaries and marginated rural people who have no regular access to the land.[12]

These forms of surplus extraction, together with the social classes and class factions of Israelite society, appear in the biblical text in a signified form that needs to be decoded by an appropriate exegetical and hermeneutical method. They necessarily appear in this form in the Bible because the biblical text was not written as a sociological manual whose purpose would have been to provide straightforward and explicit sociological information.[13]

The book of Micah, therefore, arises out of the tributary mode of production represented by the Israelite monarchy, and the structural elements of this mode are inscribed in a signified form in its text. David inaugurated this social formation, Solomon pushed it to its logical conclusion, and the rest of the Israelites and Judean rulers took it to its grave. We find in Micah, as in other prophetic texts, some of the evidence pointing to the material conditions out of which these biblical texts came. The route to this point has been a long one, but a reconstruction of the material conditions of the text is a necessary first step before we can develop an analysis of the ideological conditions.

CLASS ORIGINS AND INTERESTS OF THE TEXT: GENERAL REMARKS

While the text of Micah offers sufficient indications concerning the nature of the material conditions, the configuration of class forces, and the effects of class rule, it is nevertheless itself cast within an ideological framework that at the same time creates contradictions within the book and distorts the usefulness of its text for struggling classes today. The ideological character of the text has much to do with this.

Ideology is not a lie. It is rather a harmonization of contradictions in such a way that the class interests of one group are universalized and made acceptable to other classes. Also, ideology is not a selection process or filter through which only certain facts pass. On the contrary, it is a process by which the presence of certain facts is constituted by their absence. Therefore, making scientific sense of the ideological condition of a text means knowing that text in a way in which it is incapable of knowing itself. Eagleton makes this point when he says:

> The task of criticism, then, is not to situate itself within the same space as the text, allowing it to speak or completing what it necessarily leaves unsaid. On the contrary, its function is to install itself in the very incompleteness of the work in order to *theorise* it—to explain the ideological necessity of those "not-saids" which constitute the very principle of its identity. Its object is the *unconsciousness* of the work—that of which it is not, and cannot be, aware. [Eagleton's italics][14]

The text of Micah is eloquent about certain issues by being silent about them. Biblical scholars have long been aware of the literary disjunction between Micah 1-3 and Micah 4-7. Broadly speaking, they have designated the first three chapters as genuinely Micah passages and have considered the following three chapters later additions. The issue that has not been faced squarely is: What kind of additions are they?

Viewed ideologically, these chapters fit well into the royal Zion ideology that started during the time of David, and culminated in the ideological activity of the priestly class during the Babylonian exile. Bourgeois biblical scholarship has long been aware of this development but has been unwilling or unable to perceive the political significance of such an ideological setup. Walter Brueggemann was among the first biblical scholars to grasp the political and ideological character of the Bible. He has isolated two different covenant traditions representing two different social, political, and ideological tendencies in the Bible: the Mosaic covenant tradition, which is revolutionary, and the Davidic covenant tradition, which is status-quo-oriented. According to him, the "Davidic tradition . . . is situated among the established and secure."[15] Brueggemann summarizes the tension in the biblical traditions in this way:

> The David-Solomonic tradition with its roots in Abrahamic memory provides an important alternative theological trajectory. We may identify two theological elements which are surely linked to this movement and which are important to the subsequent faith and literature of the Bible. First, it is generally agreed that the emergence of creation faith in Israel has its setting in Jerusalem and its context in the royal consciousness. The shift of social vision is accompanied with a shifted theological method which embraces more of the imperial myths of the ancient Near East and breaks with the scandalous historical particularity of the Moses tradition. The result is a universal and comprehensive world-view which is more inclined toward social stability than toward social transformation and liberation.[16]

The central themes of this monarchical ideology are stability, grace, restoration, creation, universal peace, compassion, and salvation; they contrast radically with the ideology of pre-monarchical Israel, which would have themes such as justice, solidarity, struggle, and vigilance.

The book of Micah, therefore, is eloquent in its silence on the ideological struggle waged by the oppressed and exploited class of monarchical Israel. Apart from making available an otherwise unsuppressible body of information about the material situation of oppression, it simply luxuriates in an elaborate ideological statement of self-comfort by dwelling on issues like the Lord's universal reign of peace (4:1ff.); the promise of return from exile (4:6ff.); God's promise of a ruler from Bethlehem (5:2ff.); the Lord's salvation (7:8ff.), and so forth. These are the dominant ideological themes of the book.

It is little wonder that dominant, traditional theology has found the Bible in general politically and ideologically comfortable, notwithstanding the unsuppressible evidence of a morally distorted material situation. Micah itself, as is true of most of the Bible, offers no certain starting point for a theology of liberation. There is simply too much de-ideologization to be made before it can be hermeneutically usable in the struggle for liberation. In short, viewed as a whole and ideologically, it is a ruling-class document. However, enough contradictions within Micah enable eyes hermeneutically trained in the struggle for liberation today to observe the kindred struggles of the oppressed and exploited of the biblical communities in the very absence of those struggles in the text.

I will undertake a hermeneutical appropriation of the biblical texts of Micah further by exploiting more specifically the contradictions inherent in the text. The presupposition of such an activity will be the black struggle in South Africa — historically and in its contemporary form.

THE CASE OF MICAH

"How is the troubled passage between text and reader to be smoothed, so that literary consumption may be facilitated?" Terry Eagleton's words aptly express the nature of the hermeneutical exercise. They refer to the space between the reader and the text as an arena for a hermeneutical engagement. I would argue, however, that the cultural, historical, and ideological baggage from both the text's side and the reader's side provides the hermeneutical weapons for battling through that "troubled passage." They also provide the hermeneutical lens for reading one's way through it. I contend in this study, therefore, that the social-ideological location and commitment of the reader must be accorded *methodological* priority. And for this reason I see the category of "the black struggle," from precolonial times to the present, as representing an important hermeneutical factor.

I have tried to draw out the cultural and ideological presuppositions inherent in the texts to bounce them off those of the history, culture, and class of the reader. This specific activity takes place in that space between the text and the reader. The best way to smooth the "troubled passage" between text and reader is to unleash the forces of struggle that each brings in the encounter with the other. Thus one can relive the struggle of the communities behind the texts as well as that of the communities this side of the texts as a new *practice*.

However, it is important to realize that the struggles of the biblical communities do not appear in the Bible as mirror reflections of the real. Rather, they have been produced as new textual practices: they come to us as *signified practices*. This understanding is crucial to our circumventing the empiricism that has bogged down the historical-critical method for many years. The biblical texts, therefore, do not represent an unproblematical record of historical events and struggles. On the contrary, they represent particular *productions* of historical and social events and relations. In this chapter we will examine the nature of the productions that the text of Micah represents.

No biblical scholar illustrates and provides the clues for understanding this process of *signification* of reality in the prophetic texts better than does Robert Coote. In his monumental book entitled *Amos Among the Prophets: Composition and Theology*, Coote undertakes an illuminating analysis of the nature of the text of Amos and the process of its production. According to him, however, "it is important to remember that Amos is just an example. To understand the process by which the book of Amos came into being is to learn an approach that will be useful with *all* prophetic literature."[17]

More importantly, Coote has given intelligibility to what has thus far been an elusive trait of scriptural texts: their class and ideological nature. This quality of the biblical texts has tended to hide behind what appeared to be purely logical, historical, and literary inconsistencies and contradictions. The recent use of sociological and ideological analyses of the Bible has re-posed the question of the nature of the biblical literature and opened up new possibilities of understanding and appropriation.

Coote correctly warns, however, against the danger of creating the notion of an original prophet surrounded by secondary additions. This is the danger of an empiricist-historicist approach, which leads to the inference that the original words are truer than those of subsequent editions or recompositions. Such an approach would be inadequate because it would imply a hermeneutics of "selection" by which certain parts of the Bible would be chosen as appropriate and others simply dismissed.

Coote has raised the fundamental question of the class nature and commitments of the various editions or recompositions of the prophetic texts—especially by his division of Amos into Amos A, B, and C. He falls short, however, of providing an adequate hermeneutical *appropriation* of these texts in class and ideological terms. Such an appropriation would seek to avoid a selectivity that amounts to an ideological avoidance tactic, and it would be an appropriate and adequate biblical hermeneutics of liberation because it would raise the question of "struggle" as a fundamental hermeneutical factor in the text, as indeed in the communities behind the text and those appropriating the text presently.

Thus Coote's isolation of the different editions or recompositions of the text put in a framework of biblical hermeneutics of liberation has as its purpose not the selection of one edition and the dismissal of others. On the contrary, the aim is to resurrect and identify the forces of struggle inherent and dominant in each edition. This process then leads to an engagement with these texts that would be framed by the class interests and commitments of the readers. Put simply, it acknowledges the value of all the editions of the texts. But it must be argued forcefully that such value is variable: it could be positive or negative. It is fundamentally framed by the nature of the social and ideological struggles in the text as well as of similar struggles in the life of the readers.

Explaining his method of identifying the various editions of the text, Coote says:

> Suppose author A composed some separate short works (oracles, for example), which we can call 2, 4, and 6. Later editor B, to some extent making use of prophetic tradition (perhaps even some of other A material), composed a similar group—let's call them 3, 5, and 7—to express the concerns of his own person and time. Appropriating A's 2, 4, and 6, B preserved them (possibly modifying them slightly) by joining them to his own words, and composed a new work, 2b−3−4b−5−6b−7, in which 2b stands for A's 2 as preserved or modified by B, 3 for B's 3, and so forth. Then came editor C, who rewrote this work with the addition of an opening and closing, which we'll call 1 and 8. . . . This new work gives a third slant to the words of A and another to the words of B. It

can be schematized as $1-2bc-3c-4bc-5c-6bc-7c-8$, in which 1
stands for C's 1, 2bc for B's 2b as preserved or modified by C, 3c for B's
3 as preserved or modified by C, and so forth.[18]

The following, therefore, is a structural reclassification of the text of Micah
on the basis of the criteria suggested by Coote and on historical-materialist
exegetical considerations being proposed in this study:[19]

Micah A	Micah A B	Micah B	Micah C
1:10-16	1:8-9	1:5b-7	1:1-5a
2:1-5, 8-9		2:6-7, 10-11	2:12-13
3:8-12		3:1-7	
	4:3-4		4:1-2, 5-13
5:9-14		5:1, 4-6	5:2-3, 7-8
6:9-15		6:1-8, 16	
		7:1-7	7:8-20

THE BLACK STRUGGLE AND THE SIGNIFIED
PRACTICE OF MICAH C-TEXTS

Micah C-Texts [Bible translations are the author's, except where otherwise
indicated.]

Micah 1:1-5(a)

1. The word of Yahweh which came to Micah the Moreshite in the days
   of Jotham, Ahaz, and Hezekiah, kings of Judah, which he saw concerning
   Samaria and Jerusalem.
2. Hear, O peoples, every one;
   listen, O earth, and all who are in it;
   that Lord Yahweh may be a witness against you,
   the Lord from his holy temple (palace).
3. For, behold! Yahweh comes forth from his place;
   he descends and treads upon the high places.
4. The mountains melt under him,
   the valleys burst open
   like wax before fire,
   like water pouring down a slope.
5. All this because of the crime of Jacob,
   because of the sins of the house of Israel.

Micah 2:12-13

12. I will surely assemble, O Jacob, all of you;
    I will surely gather the remnant of Israel.
    I will unite him like a flock in the fold,

like a herd in the midst of a pasture;
and that will cause a disturbance.
13. The breaker will ascend,
they will break out before them,
they will cross the gate and go out of it.
Their king will cross before them,
Yahweh in front of them, at their head.

Micah 4:1-2

1. And it shall come to pass in the latter days,
the mountain on which the house of Yahweh stands
will be established at the top of the mountains,
be exalted above the hills.
Peoples will stream to it,
2. and many nations will come.
They will say,
"Come, let us go up to Yahweh's mountain,
to the house of the God of Jacob,
that he may instruct us about his ways,
and we shall walk in his paths."
For from Zion instruction goes out,
the word of Yahweh from Jerusalem.

Micah 4:5-13

5. For all the peoples walk,
each in the name of its God;
but we will walk in the name of Yahweh our God
forever and ever.
6. "On that day,"
oracle of Yahweh declares,
"I will assemble the lame;
I will gather the banished,
those whom I have caused evil to fall on.
7. I will make the lame into a remnant,
and those who are scattered afar (beyond) into a mighty nation."
Yahweh will reign over them in Mount Zion
from now on and forever.
8. But you, Migdal-'eder,
Ophel of Zion's daughter,
to you shall come
the former realm,
the kingdom to Jerusalem's daughter.
9. Now, why do you cry alarm?
Is there no king with you?

Or has your counselor perished
that you should writhe and twist like a woman in labor?

10. Writhe and twist, daughter of Zion,
like a woman in labor,
for now you shall go forth from the city
and dwell in open country.
You shall go to Babylon,
there to be delivered.
There Yahweh shall redeem you
from the grip of your enemies.

11. And now many nations assemble against you.
They say: "Let her be desecrated,
let our eyes gaze on Zion."

12. But they do not know
what Yahweh is contemplating,
nor do they discern his plan.
For he will gather them like sheaves to the threshing floor.

13. Rise up and trample/thresh, daughter of Zion,
for I will make your horn into iron;
for I will make your hoofs into bronze,
and you shall crush many peoples.
You shall devote their booty to Yahweh,
their wealth to the Lord of all the earth.

Micah 5:3-4, 8-9

3. Therefore they shall be handed over until the time
when she who is in labor has given birth
and the rest of his brothers return
to the children of Israel.

4. He shall stand and pasture in the safety of Yahweh,
in the exaltation of the name of Yahweh his God.
They shall dwell (safely), for now he will be great
to the ends of the earth.

8. The remnant of Jacob shall be in the midst of many peoples
like a lion among the beasts of the forest,
like a young lion among flocks of sheep,
which claws when it passes,
when it tears there is no rescue.

9. May your hand be lifted against your enemies,
and may all your enemies be cut off.

Micah 7:8-20

8. Rejoice not over me, my enemy!
Though I have fallen, I shall arise.

Though I sit in darkness,
Yahweh will be my light.

9. Yahweh's anger I bear
because I have sinned against him,
until he pleads my case
and gets me acquitted.
He will bring me out to the light;
I shall see his righteousness.

10. My enemy shall see,
and shame shall cover her who says to me,
"Where is Yahweh your God?"
My eyes shall see her;
now she will be trampled like mud in the street.

11. A day of building your walls!
That day the boundaries will be extended.

12. The day when they shall come to you
from Assyria and Egypt and from Egypt to the river,
from sea to sea and mountain to mountain.

13. The earth will become desolate
because of its inhabitants as a result of their deeds.

14. Shepherd your people with your staff,
the flock of your inheritance,
who dwells alone in the forest,
in the midst of the fertile slopes.
Let them graze in Bashan and Gilead
as in ancient days.

15. As in the days when you went forth from the land of Egypt,
let us see wonders.

16. May the nations see
and refrain from all their power.
Let them lay their hand on their mouths,
their ears be deaf.

17. Let them lick dust like a snake,
like things that crawl on the earth.
Let them come trembling from their strongholds
to Yahweh our God;
let them dread and fear you.

18. Who is God like you,
taking away guilt
and passing over crime
for the remnant of his inheritance?
He does not persist forever in his anger,
for he delights in mercy.

19. He will again have compassion on us,
will subdue our iniquities;
he will cast into the depths of the sea
all our sins.

20. He will show faithfulness to Jacob,
    mercy to Abraham,
    as he has sworn to our fathers
    from days of old.

These texts, scattered throughout and interspersed with others in the book of Micah, have been isolated and grouped together here so that they may be read together. I hold that in this way they give a coherent flavor of their concerns and rhetorical structures. We will follow a similar approach with respect to the other editions of the text of Micah: Micah B, A, and A/B.

A black biblical hermeneutics of liberation should interrogate the Micah C-texts in more or less the following way: What is the nature of the challenge of these texts? Whose class, gender, and race interests does this challenge exist to serve? Who is making the challenge? Where and when? What are the ideological and literary mechanisms whereby the challenge is formulated? And more fundamentally, what effects, then and now, are these texts having on the social classes, genders, and races on whose behalf they were *not* produced?

The C-stage texts provide the dominant ideology of the Micah prophetic discourse. The perspective of these texts frames the various other layers of meaning of the discourse in such a way as to relegate these layers of meaning to a secondary position. In fact, the ideology of Micah-C represents a new production of the discursive practice of Micah. The C-editor of Micah is surely of the same class and ideology as the C-editor of Amos, for here, as in Amos,

> Having already said, through the inclusion of the A and B stages, if you do wrong you will die and I urge you to do right, the C-editor looks to the future, asking who will hear the message? Who *will* obey God's stipulations?
>
> For the C-editor and his readers, the world of meaningful action lies in the future, not the past or the present. With a view to the future, God judges attitude, not action. God is looking for what people today might call "readiness for justice."[20]

Thus Micah 1:2-5a describes the impending action of Yahweh by which he will create a new community. This textual unit can only have the effect of engendering an attitude whose presence or absence will be the basis of God's judgment. The text represents an important part of the core of the ideology of Micah-C material: the shift on the part of God's demands from action to attitude, from concrete relations to abstract principles.

The God of the C-stage material is the God of restoration (2:12-13). Thus this God reconstructs the citadel of power of the former ruling classes of Judah and transforms it into an international meeting place (4:1-2). The theology of the C-stage material feeds on the Zion ideology of the Davidic empire.[21] It is fundamentally imperialist in character (7:11-12).

In this edition of the Micah text Babylon is the new Egypt. The former oppressors of peasants and casual laborers and underclasses in Judah are now seeing themselves as the oppressed in relation to their captors. More importantly, they rewrite the traditions of struggle of ancient Israel to apply to their situation. Thus, instead of the rich and the powerful, it is the nations and the pagans who become targets of Yahweh's judgment. In this tradition the enemy changes:

> My enemy shall see,
> and shame shall cover her
> who says to me,
> "Where is Yahweh your God?"
> My eyes shall see her;
> now she will be trampled like mud in the street. (7:10)

By the time the text of Micah reaches this edition, this production, this signification of reality, vague and generalized descriptions have replaced concrete and specific references to evil. Consequently, this articulation of the enemy in the sight of God does not resonate with the contemporary oppressed and exploited people's knowledge of evil in their situations.

The black working-class people of South Africa do not recognize this enemy. It is not an enemy that their badges of slavery—the passbooks—epitomize; it is not an enemy that torture and death in their detention cells remind them of; it is not the enemy of ignorance, meaninglessness, and abject poverty in their country's various squatter camps, which they have to deal with daily. This enemy is too abstract and too religiously defined. The enemy in this text, as well as the God who is at war with it, are not trappable.

The hermeneutical code with which black working-class Christians operate—which issues out of the struggle for survival in the black ghettos—refuses to appropriate the text of Micah in the code in which it is cast. Micah-C represents the dominant code in which the whole prophetic practice of Micah is cast. It fits the description of dominant definitions provided by Stuart Hall:

> The dominant definitions ... are hegemonic precisely because they represent definitions of situations and events which are "in dominance," and which are *global*. Dominant definitions connect events, implicitly or explicitly, to grand totallizations, to the great syntagmatic views of the world: they take "large views" of issues; they relate events to "the national interest" or to the level of geopolitics, even if they make these connections in truncated, inverted or mystified ways. The definition of a "hegemonic" viewpoint is (a) that it defines within its terms the mental horizon, the universe of possible meanings of a whole society or culture; and (b) that it carries with it the stamp of legitimacy—it appears coterminous with what is "natural," "inevitable," "taken for granted," about the social order.[22]

The process of "grand totallization" and "syntagmatic viewing" of the world is nowhere more evident than in the theology of restoration that pervades the C-stage ideological practice:

And it shall come to pass in the latter days,
the mountain on which the house of Yahweh stands
will be established at the top of the mountains,
be exalted above the hills.
Peoples will stream to it,
and many nations will come. (4:1)

This imperialist theology is more suited to the interests of a formerly powerful class whose pride has been hurt by exile than to a previously oppressed
class whose real interests lie in the building of democratic structures to guarantee its protection and liberation. C-stage theology cannot provide inspiration
to oppressed peoples because it is inherently a theology of domination and
control. The practice of the oppressed cannot draw its hermeneutical weapons
of struggle from this theology. On the contrary, the practice of the oppressed
must engage in struggle with it for a recovery of the suppressed traditions of
liberation in the Bible.

THE BLACK STRUGGLE AND THE SIGNIFIED
PRACTICE OF MICAH B-TEXTS

Micah 1:5(b)-9

5(b). Whose is the transgression of Jacob?
   Is it not Samaria's?
   And whose is the sin [following LXX] of Judah?
   Is it not Jerusalem's?
6. "I will mete out punishment to Samaria.
   I will make her into a vineyard field for planting;
   I will pour her stones into the valley,
   and I will roll away her foundations.
7. All her idols will be crushed;
   all her takings [wages] from prostitution will be burned by fire;
   all her idols I will put to desolation.
   For she collected them as fee for prostitution.
   So to the fee of a prostitute they shall revert."

Micah 2:6-7, 10-11

6. "Stop dripping [prophesying].
   They *drip*. Let them [the prophets] not *drip* about these things.
   Disgrace shall not overtake us."
7. "Is the house of Jacob accursed?
   Is Yahweh impatient?
   Or are these things his deeds?
   Do his acts not benefit
   the one who walks uprightly?"

10. "Arise and go,
    for this is no place of rest.
    Because of uncleanness you shall be destroyed
    by ruinous destruction.
11. If a man came in the spirit [inspired/intoxicated]
    and lied deceptions—'I drip for you in
    wine and beer [intoxicating drink]!'—*he* would
    be the 'dripper' [prophet] for *this* people."

Micah 3:1-7
[Translation follows James Luther Mays, *Micah*, pp. 76f.]

1. And I said,
   "Hear, you chiefs of Jacob
   and magistrates of the house of Israel.
   Is it not your duty to know justice,
2(a). O haters of good and lovers of evil?
3. They eat the flesh of my people,
   and strip their skin off them,
   and break their bones.
   They chop [them] up as if for the pot,
   like meat to put in the cauldron.
2(b). Their skin will be torn off them,
   their flesh off their bones."
4. Then they will cry out to Yahweh,
   but he will not answer them.
   He will hide his face from them in that time,
   since they've turned their deeds to evil.
5. This is what Yahweh said against the prophets:
   "Who mislead my people
   when they have something to chew on,
   they proclaim 'Peace.'
   Let a man fail to put something in their mouth,
   and they sanctify war against him.
6. Therefore it will be night for you without vision,
   darkness for you without divination.
   The sun shall set for the prophets,
   the day go dark for them.
7. The seers shall be confounded,
   and the diviners in consternation.
   All of them will cover their beard
   because there is no answer from God."

Micah 5:2, 5-7

2. "But you, Bethlehem of Ephratha,
   small among the clans of Judah,

from you shall come forth for me
one to be ruler in Israel.
His origins are from old times,
from ancient days."

5. This shall be peace from Assyria,
because he came into our land
and marched against our fortified palaces.
We will raise against him seven shepherds
and eight human chieftains.

6. They shall shepherd the land of Assyria with the sword,
the land of Nimrod with a drawn sword.
He will deliver us from the Assyrians
when he comes into our land,
and when he walks within our borders.

7. The remnant of Jacob shall be in the midst of many peoples
like dew from Yahweh,
like raindrops upon grass,
which does not wait for a man
nor await the sons of humankind.

Micah 6:1-8
[For textual emendation, see Mays, p. 128.]

1. Hear what Yahweh is saying:
"Arise! Make a case with the mountains;
let the hills hear your voice.

2. Hear, O mountains, Yahweh's case,
and listen, O foundations of the earth.
For Yahweh has a case with his people,
with Israel he argues.

3. My people, what have I done to you?
How have I wearied you? Testify against me!

4. For I brought you out from the land of Egypt;
from the house of slavery I ransomed you.
I sent Moses before you,
Aaron and Miriam [5] with him.
Remember what Balak, king of Moab, advised
and how Balaam, son of Beor, answered him.
... from Shittim to Gilgal
in order to know the righteousness of Yahweh."

6. With what shall I meet Yahweh,
humble myself before God above?
Shall I meet him with burnt offerings,
with year-old calves?

7. Would Yahweh be pleased with thousands of rams,
with innumerable streams of oil?

Shall I give my first-born for my crime,
the fruit of my body for the sin of my soul?
8. He has told you, man, what is good.
What Yahweh requires from you is
nothing but to do justice, to love mercy,
and humbly to walk with your God.

Micah 6:16

16. "You have followed the practices of Omri,
every deed of Ahab's house;
you have walked in their counsels.
So I will turn you into a cause of horror,
and your residents into an object of derision.
You shall bear the scorn of the peoples."

Micah 7:1-5

1. How I sorrow!
For I am like the gatherer of summer fruit,
like the gleaners of the vintage,
when there are no grapes to eat,
none of the early figs I crave.
2. The faithful have vanished from the earth;
not one human being is upright.
All lie in wait to shed blood;
each hunts his brother with a net.
3. Their hands are good at doing evil:
the official demands a favorable decision,
and the judge decides to get the reward;
the great speak only of what they want.
4. They twist their good like a brier bush,
their uprightness like a thorn hedge.
The day of their punishment has come;
now their confusion is at hand.
5. Don't rely on a neighbor;
don't trust a friend.
Even with her who lies in your bosom,
be guarded in what you say.

This group of texts is cast in what Stuart Hall calls the "negotiated code":
they represent a mixture of adaptive and oppositional elements. In line with
the social-class practices of its proponents, the negotiated code is shot through
with contradictions. As Hall puts it,

Negotiated codes operate through what we might call particular or situated logics: and these logics arise from the differential position of those

who occupy this position in the spectrum, and from their differential and
unequal relation to power.[23]

This assessment of the B-stage prophetic material is supported by Coote's similar study of Amos. According to Coote, the B-stage material—or material cast
in a "negotiated code," as Hall would put it—exhibits certain distinctive features:

1) It addresses a general audience. In the case of Micah, this means all the
people associated with Jacob or Judah, or Samaria or Jerusalem (1:5b-9). The
closest *specific* description of the B-stage addressees in Micah is in 3:1; but this
concrete description is quickly neutralized by a more general and vague description in a parallel line in 3:2a. The tendency to speak in general terms on the
part of this code is congruent with its blending of adaptive and oppositional
elements within the same discourse. In fact, this is a structural trait, with ideological roots in the middle classes of all social formations. It is the contradictory tendency inherent in a historically marginal but spiritually central class
position. Eagleton describes the historical and ideological dilemma of this group
within a capitalist social formation when he asserts:

> Committed by its nuclear social and economic conditions to a framework
> of overarching authority, to "standards" and "leadership," the petty bour-
> geoisie rejects at once the democratic "anarchy" it discerns below it and
> the ineffectualness of the actual authority posed above it. ... Though
> *empirically* decentred, largely excluded from the ruling academic caste, it
> nevertheless laid claim to be, spiritually, the "real" elite. [Eagleton's ital-
> ics][24]

Thus the nonspecific description of the addressees is a function of the historical
and class contradictions attendant on the proponents of the B-stage material.
Because of their differential relationship to power, especially in the historical
context of Josiah's reform and of the Babylonian siege of Jerusalem, the B-
stage ideologists broadened the indictment against the Jerusalemite and Judean
ruling classes "to include a comprehensive notion of cultic and political idolatry—the practice of pagan religion and trust in military security."[25] It is from
this that the material derives its feature of generality concerning its addressees.

2) On the basis of Micah 3:2, 4-7 and 6:8, it seems reasonable to argue, with
Coote, that the basic message of B-stage prophetic oracles is: "Perform justice
or else."[26] This means that the bearers of tradition of this stage offer the ruling
classes of Judah a chance to survive. But even if the survival option were not
available, the fate of these classes seems bearable, and they are not beyond
redemption: their vision will be darkened, and they will be confounded. There
will be no answer from Yahweh (3:4-7).

3) The B-stage material is characterized by a propensity for abstract rather
than concrete description. Coote says:

> B-stage phrases tend to be *wordy* rather than terse, *vague* rather than
> specific, *abstract* rather than concrete, and *stereotyped* rather than fresh.

... In the B stage one does not "sell the needy into debt slavery for a pair of sandals"; instead one "does wrong." There is ultimately no specific authoritative rationale for the pro-Jerusalemite stance; so the B editor calls it, in effect, "good." [Coote's italics][27]

4) Ambiguity is another feature of the B-stage prophetic oracles. This quality is certainly present in 1:5b-7 and 2:6-7, 10-11; but in 3:1 and 6:6-8 it comes through more clearly. Here the text avoids clarity of statement by posing rhetorical questions on issues that are unambiguously asserted in the A-editions of the prophetic material. The effect is to give the appearance of addressing similar issues as the A-edition, while the concern is weakened by the language structure in which it is cast.

5) The prophetic *rib,* the suit or litigation, with its implication of open-endedness, defines another set of B-stage oracles. "Other forms found in the B-stage include chastisement, exhortation, call to worship, the narrative describing the commissioning of the prophet, the speech in the divine council, prophetic visions, and theophanies."[28] Certainly Micah 6:1-4 represents a perfect example of this feature of the B-stage material. The confidence of the B-stage editors in the justice of the legal system's open-endedness is betrayed in this text. The politics and the sociology of the law courts as well as those of the cultic systems are not an issue for the B-editors.

6) The B-stage text offers an open future. In the case of Micah, it is represented unambiguously by 5:1, 4, 5b-6. The method of "exhortation" is used to communicate this future.

According to Coote, the B-stage material is largely the product of a scribe or scribes who are at the service of a ruling elite;[29] and the features of the oracles of this stage are a function of the class and ideology of this scribal group. I have already pointed out that the discursive productions of this group reflect, unavoidably, its different and unequal relationship to power. The vagueness of the B-stage material, its generality in terms of its addressees, its abstractions and ambiguity, and the open-endedness of the future it offers, represent the extent and nature of the ideology of the class that put it together.

The B-stage oracles derive their identity from a certain kind of incompleteness: they are eloquent by their silence on the struggles of poor and exploited peasants in the Israelite monarchy. Although these oracles condemn evil and injustice and exhort people to good and justice, they do not name the actual actions of oppressors, except vaguely, and the resistance of the oppressed is present only by its absence. The task of a biblical hermeneutics of liberation is to theorize the ideological necessity of this incompleteness, this absence. Black theology as a discursive practice that is rooted in the progressive dimensions of black history and culture should provide the basis for a critical appropriation of these texts.

The first point to make is that this part of the prophetic text of Micah, as seen from the perspective of the hermeneutics of liberation, has a negative identification with the concerns of the poor and the oppressed. It helps to point to the behavior and ideology of a social class that needs careful watching in the

liberation struggle. The B-stage prophetic texts, by virtue of their class character, appeal more to their counterparts in modern society, the petite bourgeoisie, than to the working-class people—the really poor and exploited
members of contemporary societies. Modern middle-class people, who are similarly differentially and unequally related to power structures, display a similar
vagueness, abstractness, generality, and ambiguity as the proponents of the B-
stage texts in relation to oppression and justice. Cabral has this in mind when
he says in regard to this class:

> We must, however, take into consideration the fact that, faced with the
> prospect of political independence, the ambition and opportunism from
> which the liberation movement generally suffers may draw into the strug-
> gle individuals who have not been reconverted. The latter, on the basis
> of their level of education, their scientific or technical knowledge, and
> without losing any class cultural prejudices, may attain the highest posi-
> tions in the liberation movement. On the cultural as well as the political
> level vigilance is therefore vital. For in the specific and highly complex
> circumstances of the process of the phenomenon of the liberation move-
> ments, all that glitters is not necessarily gold: political leaders—even the
> most famous—may be culturally alienated.[30]

A similar dynamic seems to have taken place in the B-stage texts. There
seems to have occurred a cultural alienation of a concrete, direct, specific, and
clear message. The original message of Micah against the ruling classes of Judah
has been reified, in the B-stage, which Henri Mottu describes as, among other
things, a process of recurrence and a process of stealing. Concerning the conflict
between Hananiah and Jeremiah, he writes:

> To the degree that reification as a general phenomenon is "grounded in
> historically recurrent circumstances of human existence in society," one
> can say that Hananiah operates upon the belief that God's fidelity is
> simply a recurrent fact. "Recurrence" is a procedure of demonstration
> that consists in extending to all terms of a series what is valid only for
> the first two terms. This is exactly what he does: he extends the events of
> 701 under Sennacherib to the events of 594/3 under Nebuchadnezzar
> without seeing those events in terms of the historical activity of Babylon
> and Judah.[31]

The nature and orientation of the B-stage prophetic oracles indicate that Hananiah symbolized a whole tradition with firm ideological and social class roots.
Concerning reification as "stealing," Mottu says:

> Reification occurs when certain people "steal" the praxis of others, which
> is the case when Hananiah "steals" [Isa. 9:4] from Isaiah and simply
> transfers a word said in a given situation into a quite different one. This
> process of "stealing" is a far-reaching one and covers many different

situations, as illustrated by the German peasants who saw their praxis being "stolen" from their hands by the princes of Luther. . . . So the text of Isaiah 9 becomes a "thing," even a commodity, at the disposal of anyone at any time. Jer. 23:30 speaks pointedly against this "reification" of the words of God.[32]

Thus, while black theology shares the sentiments expressed in the message about justice in the B-stage texts, it cannot identify with the abstract context in which this message now appears. In these texts both oppression and justice have been "thingified," appearing now as vaguely good and evil. The original message of Micah, which was directed at the ruling classes of Judah during the eighth century B.C.E., has now been stolen from its concrete situation, where it concerned the condition of the poor and exploited, and is being applied to the Judean ruling class in their relationship with their foreign oppressors. The more basic contradiction between exploited peasants and exploiting latifundiaries in Judah has now been replaced by the secondary contradiction between Babylon and Judah or other nations and Israel.

THE BLACK STRUGGLE AND THE SIGNIFIED PRACTICE OF MICAH A-TEXTS

Micah 1:10-15(a)

10. Declare it not in Gath;
    weep, only weep.
    In the streets of Beth-aphrah
    roll in the dust.
11. The Shophar they sound for you,
    rulers of Shaphir.
    From her city she comes not out,
    nobilities/rulers of Zaanan.
    I will make a lamentation, Beth-ezel,
    I will take from you your standing place.
12. Who can hope for good,
    nobilities/rulers of Maroth?
    For evil has come down from Yahweh,
    to the gate of Jerusalem.
13. You harness the chariot to the team,
    nobilities/rulers of Lachish.
    That was the chief sin for the daughter of Zion,
    that in you were found the crimes of Israel.
14. To you they give parting gifts,
    Moresheth-Gath.
    Nobilities/rulers of Achzib have become a failing brook
    to the kings of Israel.
15(a). Shall still the heir come to you,
    nobilities/rulers of Mareshah?

Micah 2:1-5, 8-9

1. Woe to those who contemplate wickedness,
   who do evil upon their couches/beds.
   At morning's light they carry it out
   because they wield power.
2. They covet fields and expropriate them,
   houses and carry them away.
   They oppress a man and his household,
   a producer and his fundamental means of production.
3. Therefore, thus says Yahweh,
   "Behold, I devise evil against these homesteads,
   an evil from which they cannot withdraw their necks,
   and in relation to which they cannot walk upright,
   for it shall be an evil time.
4. In that day a taunt-song shall be raised over you;
   a lament shall be sung, saying:
   'We are utterly ruined.
   The property of my people is exchanged/moved to and fro.
   There is none to remove it, to return our field through
     redistribution.' "
5. Therefore there will be no one to divide property by lot
   in the assembly of Yahweh.
8. But you! against my people
   you arise as enemy. [Following Mays, p. 67]
   From them [in front of them] their garment,
   [their cloak] you strip off [taking away security].
   Causing those who return from war
   to bring over security.
9. The women of my people you drive out,
   from the houses they delight in.
   From their children you take their
   honor forever.

Micah 3:8-12

8. But indeed, I am filled with the spirit of the Lord,
   with justice and power,
   to declare to Jacob his crime,
   to Israel his sin.
9. Hear this, chiefs of the house of Jacob,
   and magistrates of the house of Israel—
   the ones who pervert justice
   and twist the straight thing,
10. building Zion with bloodshed/murder,
    Jerusalem with violence.

11. Her chiefs judge for a bribe,
    her priests give instruction for a price,
    her prophets divine for money.
    And they still trust in Yahweh, saying,
    "Is not Yahweh near us?
    Evil will not come upon us!"
12. Therefore because of you,
    Zion shall become a plowed field,
    Jerusalem will be a ruin,
    and the mount of the house a wooded height.

Micah 5:10-15

10. "It shall be in that day," says the Lord,
    "I will cut off your horses from your midst.
11. I will cut off the cities of your land,
    and I will tear down all your fortresses.
12. I will cut off sorceries from your hand,
    and you will have no soothsayers.
13. I will cut off your idols
    and your sacred pillars from your midst.
    You shall not fetishize again
    the works of your own hands.
14. I will root out the Asherim from your midst
    and will exterminate your cities.
15. I will take vengeance in anger and in wrath
    upon the [nations] that have not heard."

Micah 6:9-15

9. The voice of Yahweh calls to the city
   (and he who hears your name is well-advised),
   "Hear, O tribe and those who assemble in the city.
10. Shall I forget the house of wickedness,
    where treasures of wickedness are stored,
    and the despicable use of an ephah that is too small?
11. Shall I approve anyone with false scales,
    with cheating weights in his pouch?
12. The rich ones are full of violence;
    the rulers speak with deception,
    all their speech is treachery.
13. So I have begun to smite you,
    to lay you waste because of your sins.
14(a). You shall eat and not be satisfied.
14(b). Semen into your womb you will take
    and not bring forth;

and the ones you bring forth
I will give to the sword.
15. You shall sow and not reap.
You shall tread olives and not anoint yourself with oil,
grapes, and not drink wine."

This group of texts is specific about the class of people it addresses. In 1:10-16 the addressees of the A-stage material are described as the "rulers/nobilities/landlords/authorities" of the various cities listed in the lament. The translation of *yoshev* as "ruler/authority" in contexts such as the one in this text has been cogently argued by Gottwald, who builds on the arguments of Albrecht Alt as well as Frank M. Cross and David Noel Freedman. Concluding his study of the use of *yoshev* as referring to political and/or socioeconomic rule, Gottwald writes:

> When referring to the leaders of a region which we otherwise know to have been divided into several political sovereignties, such as Canaan with its independent city-states, the plural views all the heads of state in those several political units as a collectivity sharing similar values, attitudes, policies, or strategies. Therefore, while I incline to view most of the enemy leaders called *yoshev/yoshevim* in the premonarchic sources as kings or princes, I do not agree with Cross and Freedman in restricting the meaning of the term to "reigning princes." The functional import of the general designation is something like this: *yoshev/yoshevim* are leaders in the imperial-feudal statist system of social organization, with primary reference to enemy kings but embracing other functionaries in the statist system. As Israel developed statist sociopolitical organization of its own, the term was increasingly applied to Israelite functionaries in the state apparatus and, on occasion, referred to persons of power in the upper socioeconomic strata irrespective of their political office.[33]

Understood in this way, the lament in 1:10-16 addresses rulers of towns or cities who may or may not have held political power in a specific office. They do, however, wield power (economic or social), and this text laments the behavior and practices that are commensurate with their position as the cause of the disaster that has beset Judah. Mays argues that the historical context for this lament of Micah is the destruction and suffering that descended on Judah following Sennacherib's military campaign along the eastern Mediterranean coast in 701 B.C.E. Mays writes further that

> Sennacherib moved against Judah from the west, overwhelmed Lachish and other "strong cities," according to his count forty-six in all. The defense system of fortified cities in the Shephelah was certainly a focus of his attack. He also claimed countless villages. Two hundred thousand of the population were said to have been deported. Hezekiah was driven inside Jerusalem, held there as though in prison, and finally was spared only by submission and the payment of an impoverishing tribute.[34]

In this lament, however, Micah does not simply bewail the destruction the Assyrians inflicted but, more importantly, the pain the population of Judah has been caused as a result of the practices of the powerful classes of Judah's cities. They were the ones who were exacting tribute from the peasants and squandering it in luxurious lifestyles. It is they for whom the *shophar* has been sounded (1:11), much as it is sounded for the propertied classes and the slave masters on the day of atonement (repossession, restitution, restoration) in the jubilee year (Lev. 25:8ff.).

The A-stage oracles are unambiguous about the crimes of the ruling classes. They are economic exploiters who accumulate wealth by treacherous means: "They covet fields and expropriate them, houses and take them; they oppress a man and his household; a producer and his fundamental means of production" (2:2, 8-9). This class also consists of judicial authorities (communal leaders and magistrates) and religious functionaries (priests and prophets) who participate in the injustices of the ruling classes by perverting the judicial system in the one case and commodifying religious services while invoking the egalitarian religious ideology of Yahwism in the other (3:8-11).

The message of the A-stage oracles is equally direct: Yahweh devises evil for this class. The ruling classes' positions of power, together with their pride, will be destroyed (2:3-5). Similarly, all the symbols of oppression and exploitation will fall prey to the wrath of Yahweh: "Zion shall become a plowed field, Jerusalem will be a ruin" (3:12). The oracles in 5:9-14 and 6:9-15 represent a vivid and dramatic depiction of the forms and instruments of oppression and exploitation against which Micah-A speaks.

Thus the class or group of people on whose behalf the Micah-A oracles are speaking is not sympathetic with the economic, political, and ideological interests of the class under attack. It prophesies the destruction of this class and its political and ideological structures. It represents the God who sees fundamental disruption of the status quo as the only solution to the violence and corruption of the ruling classes. But radical as the oracles of Micah-A are, they lack a dimension that would qualify them as revolutionary. The absence of this dimension is discernible only from the perspective of a hermeneutics of liberation that is rooted in the struggles of oppressed and exploited people today.

While identifying fully with the judgment meted out against the ruling classes by the A-stage oracles, the black working-class people of South Africa would experience an absence of the voice of the laboring and underclasses of Micah's Judah in these texts. This is so because the Micah text as a whole is a curious mixture of A-stage condemnation of injustice with C-stage eschatology. There is a glaring absence of an oppressed people's eschatology, which constitutes the incompleteness of the Micah text as a signifying practice. That is, from the perspective of the poor, the text lacks a vision of the future. It does not even summon the poor people to action. Thus there is a serious ideological lacuna in the text that can only be filled from our side of history. By this I mean that contemporary struggles for liberation, having encountered a void in terms of the actual struggles of the poor and exploited in the text, must offer their struggles — hermeneutically speaking — to complete the text. In this way the

Micah discourse can be liberated to enable contemporary victims of injustice to do what Eagleton has called staging one's "own signifying practices to enrich, modify or transform the effects which others' practices produce."[35]

It is at this point of our thinking about creating alternative discourses and practices that it is appropriate to turn to a minority set of texts in the wider discourse of Micah—the A/B texts.

THE BLACK STRUGGLE AND THE SIGNIFIED PRACTICE OF MICAH-A/B TEXTS

Micah 1:8-9

8. Against this I will mourn and wail;
   I will go stripped and naked.
   I will make a lamentation like jackals,
   a grieving like the young of an ostrich.
9. Because I am sick from her wound;
   for it has come up to Judah, it has reached the gate of my people, right up to Jerusalem.

Micah 4:3-4

3. He will judge between many peoples [see Is. 2:2],
   and decide against the strong nations up to a distant one.
   They will beat their swords into plowshares,
   their spears into pruning knives.
   Nation will not raise sword against nation,
   nor will they learn war again.
4. Each man shall sit under his vine,
   under his fig tree;
   and no one will be terrified,
   for the mouth of Yahweh of hosts has spoken.

This group of texts occupies a position on the border between A-stage and B-stage material. In fact, one might say that this group represents the kind of A-stage texts that have been none too successfully edited by the B-stage signifying practitioner.

The first of these is Micah 1:8-9: this unit of material describes the mourning of the prophet for the state of Judah because of the wrath that Yahweh allows to befall the area. Mays says: "The historical event interpreted by this theological language is Sennacherib's attack on Judah and conquest of many of its cities, leaving King Hezekiah shut in Jerusalem. The situation suggested by the verse [9] is the time when the conquest of the Shephelah and hill country is complete, and only Jerusalem remains."[36] Notwithstanding some vagueness, indirectness, and a certain air of abstractness in this text, there is a concreteness that only the experience of solidarity can signify. It is a concreteness and a directness only tears can express. Walter Brueggemann makes the point succinctly:

> Tears are a way of solidarity in pain when no other form of solidarity remains. And when one addresses numbness clearly, anger, abrasiveness, and indignation as forms of address will drive the hurt deeper, add to the numbness, and force people to behaviors not rooted in experience.[37]

Even more important, "grieving" under certain circumstances may constitute a *revolutionary practice*. The funerals of black victims of police and army violence in South Africa are a case in point. The revolutionary effects of the "grieving" of black masses for their daughters and sons who have fallen in the struggle have forced the powers that be to impose legislative, political, and military restrictions on the freedom of blacks to lament for their dead. For as Brueggemann correctly states,

> Such weeping is a radical criticism, a fearful dismantling, because it means the end of all machismo; weeping is something kings rarely do without losing their thrones. Yet the loss of thrones is precisely what is called for in radical criticism.[38]

The second group of Micah-A/B texts is 4:3-4. There can be no doubt that verse 3a is a B text. It addresses "peoples" and "nations" in general. This verse has replaced what was originally A material, which addressed itself to specific classes within the tributary social formation of monarchical Judah. This B material, however, provides a new hermeneutical framework for what must be the most revolutionary part of the entire biblical discourse (3b-4). The latter redirects attention to the sphere of production of material life. Verse 3b points to an aspect of the productive activity that is destructive not only because the technology it produces is for war but because it is a luxury that consumes human and natural resources that might have been usefully invested in activities supporting the life of the entire community. For the first time, a vision of an alternative society is projected as a result of this realigning and redirecting of production processes: "Each man shall sit under his vine, / under his fig tree, / and no one will be terrified, / for the mouth of Yahweh of hosts has spoken" (vs. 4).

Thus while the oppressed and exploited peasants, artisans, day laborers, and underclasses of Micah's Judah are entirely absent in the signifying practice that the wider text of Micah represents, something of their project and voice has almost accidentally survived in the form of an A/B-stage text. The survival of contradictory texts like these in a discourse that is culminated by contrary perspectives exemplifies the working of ideology. As I have argued elsewhere,

> Ideology is not a lie. It is rather a harmonization of contradictions in such a way that the class interests of one group are universalized and made acceptable to other classes. Also, ideology is not a selection process or filter through which certain facts are constituted by their absence.[39]

There are, therefore, aspects of the texts that provide hermeneutical links with the struggles and projects of the oppressed peoples of biblical communities. These aspects of biblical discourses serve also as a critique of present-day cultural and political discourses of the oppressed. The absences in the text of material concerning the experiences of the oppressed in ancient society also reopen the canon of Scripture in some sense, to the extent that they stimulate the production of new liberating religious discourses that enrich, modify, or transform existing practices. Thus black culture and history as hermeneutical factors in a black theology in South Africa ask questions of the biblical text that seek to establish ties with struggles for liberation in the biblical communities. Similarly, the liberating aspects of the biblical discourses interrogate black culture and history in the light of the values and goals of struggling classes in biblical communities. A theological hermeneutics that brings out this dialectic in the appropriation of biblical texts operates with a clear recognition of the fact that usually in ideological discourses "only the successful . . . are remembered. The blind alleys, the lost causes, and the losers themselves are forgotten."[40] Differently put, this hermeneutics is informed by a perspective recognizing that

> The ideas of the ruling class are in every epoch the ruling ideas, i.e. the class which is the ruling *material* force of society is at the same time its ruling *intellectual* force. The class which has the means of material production at its disposal has control at the same time over the areas of mental production, so that thereby, generally speaking, the ideas of those who lack the means of mental production are subject to it. [Marx's and Engels' italics][41]

The task of a biblical hermeneutics of liberation is to go behind the dominant discourses to the discourses of oppressed communities in order to link up with kindred struggles. In South Africa a common mythological expression of the role of biblical discourses in the dispossession of blacks runs like this: "When the white man came to our country, he had a Bible and we had the land. The white man said to the black man, 'Let us pray.' After the prayer, the white man had the land and the black man had the Bible." The task now facing a black theology of liberation is to enable black people to use the Bible to get the land back and to get the land back without losing the Bible. In order for this to happen, black theology must employ the progressive aspects of black history and culture to liberate the Bible so that the Bible may liberate black people. That is the hermeneutical dialectic.

In order for that to happen, though, a theoretically sound and an ideologically clear approach to the text of the Bible is a prerequisite. The above study of the book of Micah is an example of how this might be done. The point of this textual study has been to confront the class and ideological conditions of production and existence of the text with the class and ideological position and commitment of the reader. In the specific circumstances of the racist and sexist oppression and capitalist exploitation of black people in South Africa, Micah-

A and A/B texts provide a positive hermeneutical connection with the struggles of black workers; but the B and C texts of Micah serve the struggles of oppressed peoples negatively. These latter texts represent the forms of domination and the interests of dominant social classes that are similar to those of contemporary oppressors and exploiters. We can, through an appropriation of these texts, albeit a negative one, once again bring the category of "struggle" to the fore.

NOTES

1. Ferdinand Deist, "Idealistic *Theologiegeschichte*, ideology critique and the dating of oracles of salvation," *Ou Testamentiese Werkgemeenskap van Suid Afrika* 22, 23, (1980): 65.

2. Gerhard von Rad, *Old Testament Theology* (London: SCM Press, 1975), 118.

3. Ibid., 118.

4. Norman K. Gottwald, *Tribes of Yahweh* (Maryknoll, N.Y.: Orbis Books, 1979) 63ff.

5. Michel Clévenot, *Materialist Approaches to the Bible* (Maryknoll, N.Y.: Orbis Books, 1985); Fernando Belo, *A Materialist Reading of the Gospel of Mark* (Maryknoll, N.Y.: Orbis Books, 1981); Walter Brueggemann, *The Prophetic Imagination* (Philadelphia: Fortress Press, 1978); George Pixley, *God's Kingdom* (Maryknoll, N.Y.: Orbis Books, 1981); see also the journals *Opstand* (Christene v/h Socialisme, Amsterdam, The Netherlands) and *Radical Religion* (Community for Religious Research and Education, Berkeley, Calif.).

6. Gottwald, "Domain Assumptions and Societal Models in the Study of Premonarchic Israel," *VTSup* 28 (1974): 95.

7. Gottwald, *Tribes of Yahweh,* 292; Leon Marfoe, "The Integrative Transformation: Patterns of Sociopolitical Organization in Southern Syria," *BASOR* 234 (1979): 5.

8. David C. Hopkins, "The Dynamics of Agriculture in Monarchical Israel," *SBLSP* (1983): 187-88.

9. Ibid., 195.

10. Gottwald, "Social History of the United Monarchy. . ." (paper presented to the SBL Seminar on "Sociology of the Monarchy," Annual Meeting, Dec. 20, 1983), 6.

11. Norman K. Gottwald, "Contemporary Studies of Social Class and Social Stratification and a Hypothesis about Social Class in Monarchic Israel" (Seminar on the Sociology of the Monarchy, ASOR-SBL, Anaheim, Calif. 1985), 18. [The analyses here and in note 12 are dependent on Anthony Mansueto, "From Historical Criticism to Historical Materialism," unpublished paper submitted to a seminar in The Graduate Theological Union, Berkeley, CA., 1983].

12. Ibid.

13. Stuart Hall makes this point exquisitely in relation to television discourse: "The raw historical event cannot in that form be transmitted by, say, a television newscast. It can only be signified within the aural-visual forms of the television language. In the moment when the historical event passes under the sign of language, it is subject to all the complex formal 'rules,' by which language signifies. To put it paradoxically, the event must become a 'story' before it can become a *communicative event*." In Hall, *Encoding and Decoding in the Television Discourse* (Bir-

mingham: Center for Contemporary Cultural Studies, 1973), 2ff.

14. Terry Eagleton, *Criticism and Ideology* (London: Verso, 1980), 89f.

15. Brueggemann, "Trajectories in Old Testament Literature and the Sociology of Ancient Israel," in *The Bible and Liberation* (Maryknoll, N.Y.: Orbis Books, 1983), 308. See Chap. 14 of this volume.

16. Ibid., 314.

17. Robert B. Coote, *Amos Among the Prophets: Composition and Theology* (Philadelphia: Fortress Press, 1981), 2. I will not attempt in this study to rehearse the traditional studies on Micah. Many of these have been debated and adequately assessed by scholars like James Luther Mays in his commentary on Micah quoted below. Suffice it to simply make reference to some of the most useful: Siegfried J. Schwartes, "Critical Notes on Micah 1:10-16," *VT* 14 (1964): 454-461; E. Cannawurf, "The Authenticity of Micah IV:1-4," *VT* 13 (1963): 26-33; B. Stade, "Bemerkungen über das Buch Micha," BZAW (1881): 161ff.; A. S. van der Woude, "Micah in Dispute with the Pseudo-Prophets," *VT* 19 (1969): 245-60; and an even more useful study, Knud Jeppesen's article "New Aspects of Micah Research," *JSOT* 8 (1978): 3-32; D. R. Hillers, *Micah: A Commentary* (Philadelphia: Fortress Press, 1984).

18. Coote, *Amos Among the Prophets,* 5.

19. Ibid.

20. Ibid., 120.

21. J.J.M. Roberts, "The Davidic Origin of the Zion Tradition," *JBL* 92 (1973): 340ff.

22. Hall, *Encoding and Decoding,* 23.

23. Ibid.

24. Eagleton, *Criticism and Ideology,* 14.

25. James Luther Mays, *Micah: A Commentary* (Philadelphia: Westminster Press, 1976), 25.

26. Coote, *Amos Among the Prophets,* 62.

27. Ibid., 63.

28. Ibid., 64.

29. Ibid., 74.

30. Amilcar Cabral, *Unity and Struggle* (London: Heinemann), 45.

31. Henri Mottu, "Jeremiah vs. Hananiah: Ideology and Truth in Old Testament Prophecy," *The Bible and Liberation,* ed. N. K. Gottwald (Maryknoll, N.Y.: Orbis Books, 1983), 242. See Chap. 20 of this volume.

32. Ibid.

33. Gottwald, *Tribes of Yahweh,* 532.

34. Mays, *Micah,* 53.

35. Terry Eagleton, *Literary Theory* (Minneapolis: University of Minnesota Press, 1983), 212.

36. Mays, *Micah,* 41.

37. Walter Brueggemann, *The Prophetic Imagination* (Philadelphia: Fortress Press, 1978), 59.

38. Ibid., 61.

39. I. J. Mosala and B. Tlhagale, eds., *The Unquestionable Right to be Free* (Maryknoll, N.Y.: Orbis Books, 1988), 194.

40. Edward P. Thompson, *The Making of the English Working Class* (Middlesex: Penguin Books, 1963), 13.

41. Karl Marx and Friedrich Engels, *The German Ideology* (London: Lawrence and Wishart, 1970), 64.

19

PHYLLIS A. BIRD

"To Play the Harlot"

An Inquiry into an Old Testament Metaphor

*One of the biblical metaphors and texts found to be most dangerous
and debilitating for women has been the portrayal of Israel as a woman/
wife of harlotry vis-à-vis God as a faithful husband in Hosea 1–3. Such
biblical images, ingrained in Western culture, have served to perpetuate
the blaming of women. In the dominant, androcentric tradition of biblical interpretation, moreover, the behavior of Israel as the faithless
woman promiscuously consorting with the Canaanite fertility god Baal
was compared and confused with what was termed "sacred prostitution." In a close linguistic study, complemented by critical sociological analysis, Phyllis Bird carefully sorts out the meaning of the key
Hebrew terms and their metaphorical usage by Hosea in the context of
Israelite and ancient Near Eastern culture. Hosea's sexual metaphor is
indeed that of the common prostitute and promiscuous wife. But, she
argues, rather than single out women for condemnation, Hosea uses the
metaphor to condemn the socioreligious practices of Israelite men. That
is, by playing on the patriarchal stereotype of a fallen woman, the
prophet confronts his own patriarchal society: "You male Israelites are
that 'fallen woman.'"*

Reprinted from *Gender and Difference in Ancient Israel*, ed. P. Day (Minneapolis: Fortress,
1989), 75–94.

This chapter explores a number of problems related to the translation and interpretation of the Hebrew root *znh*, with particular attention to its metaphorical or figurative use.[1] It is prompted by problems in translation and definition, difficulties in determining the boundary between literal and figurative uses, and interest in the use of a metaphor drawn, apparently, from female behavior to characterize the behavior of collective Israel.

The translation "play the harlot" is RSV's conventional rendering of the Hebrew verb *zana*, in both literal and figurative uses, replacing the familiar but archaic "go awhoring" or "commit whoredom" of KJV. Unlike the whoring language that may describe either male or female activity (to have unlawful sexual intercourse *as* or *with* a whore),[2] the "denominative" rendering of RSV defines the behavior by reference to a female model. Both translations, however, share an orientation toward the professional prostitute. Is this a peculiarity of English idiom or does it represent the Hebrew understanding? A primary question for investigation must be the relationship of verbal uses to the noun *zona* ("prostitute").

Another question concerns the meaning of the verb when used with a masculine subject.[3] Most of the examples represent clearly metaphorical uses, describing pursuit of other gods (Judg. 2:17; 8:33; Deut. 31:11) or participation in illicit cultic activity (Lev. 20:5; 17:7; Judg. 8:27). In Num. 25:1, however, the usual cultic and metaphorical interpretations are strained, and the translation of RSV appears ludicrous: "While Israel dwelt at Shittim the people (*ha'am*) began to play the harlot (*wayyahel . . . liznot*) with the daughters of Moab." Is the usage here figurative or literal, or does it represent some other type of extended use?[4]

A further question is raised by the common identification of prostitution and "sacred or cultic prostitution." The assumption of such an institution as a pervasive and constitutive feature of Canaanite religions is fundamental to most interpretations of the root *znh* and discussion of "fertility cult religion."[5] Although the institution is construed in different ways, the term by which it is designated is never called into question. Yet the concept expressed by combining words for "sacred" (or "cultic") and "prostitution" is not found in the Hebrew Bible or in any ancient Semitic language.

From biblical Hebrew and Akkadian sources we know only of "prostitutes" (Heb. *zona*; Akk. *harimtu*) and "sacred/consecrated women" (Heb. *qedeša*; Akk. *qadištu*) along with other classes of female cult functionaries (*en/entu, naditu, ugbabtu, ištaritu, kulmašitu*).[6] While prostitutes *may* have functioned at times in the cultic sphere (in which case the circumstances require careful attention) and while hierodules[7] *may* have had functions or duties involving sexual activity (here too the circumstances require careful attention), the terms used in the indigenous languages to describe these two classes never connect the sacred sphere with prostitution or prostitution with the cult.[8] It is only through association that the interpretation arises, and it is only in the Hebrew Bible that the association is made in a deliberate manner. It would appear then that the identification is the result of a specifically biblical and, I shall argue, polemical interpretation.[9]

In the limited scope of this essay it is impossible to give attention to all of the interlocking issues that affect interpretation of this root and its unique metaphorical employment in the Hebrew Bible. I shall begin with a summary treatment of the primary meaning(s) of the root and then move to a detailed examination of selected texts in the book of Hosea, which appear to represent the earliest metaphorical usage.

znh/zona

The basic meaning of the root as expressed in the verb *zana* is "to engage in sexual relations outside of or apart from marriage,"[10] activity that is normally understood as illicit; hence the primary definition of BDB: "commit fornication."[11] In relation to *n'p* "commit adultery," with which it is often associated and may at times coincide, *znh* is the more general or inclusive term. Cognate usage (Aramaic, Ethiopic, and Arabic) exhibits a similar broad meaning, especially evident in Arabic *zana* "to commit adultery, fornicate, whore" (cf. *zinan* and *zina*, "adultery, fornication"; *zanin* "fornicator, adulterer"; *zaniya* "whore, harlot, adulteress").[12]

As a general term for extramarital sexual intercourse, *znh* is limited in its primary usage to female subjects, since it is only for women that marriage is the primary determinant of legal status and obligation. While male sexual activity is judged by the status of the female partner and is prohibited, or penalized, only when it violates the recognized marital rights of another male, female sexual activity is judged according to the woman's marital status. In Israel's moral code, a woman's sexuality was understood to belong to her husband alone, for whom it must be reserved in anticipation of marriage as well as in the marriage bond. Violation of a husband's sexual rights, the most serious of sexual offenses, is signified by the term *n'p* "adultery"; all other instances of sexual intercourse apart from marriage are designated by the term *znh*.[13] These include premarital sex by a daughter, understood as an offense against her father or family (Heb. "father's house"), whose honor requires her chastity (Deut. 22:13-21; Lev. 21:9; cf. Gen. 34:31); or sex by a levirate-obligated widow (Gen. 38:6-11, 24-26), understood as an offense against her father-in-law or her deceased husband's family.[14]

It also includes the activity of the professional prostitute, who has no husband nor sexual obligation to any other male. Herein lies a critical distinction. Whereas the promiscuity of a daughter or levirate-obligated widow offends the male to whom each is subject and is penalized accordingly, the harlot's activity violates no man's rights or honor, and consequently is free from the sanctions imposed on the casual fornicator. Strictly speaking, her activity is not illicit — and neither is her role.[15]

The distinction between the two classes of activity (fornication and prostitution) described by the common root *znh* is strikingly illustrated by the account of Judah's reaction to Tamar in two episodes of the narrative in Genesis 38. In the first, he embraces a woman whom he identifies as a *zona* (v. 15, RSV: "he thought her to be a harlot"); in the second he condemns to death a woman whose activity is identified by the verb *zana* (v. 24, RSV: "your daughter-in-law has played the harlot [*zaneta*]"). The irony of the situation, on which the story turns, is that the two women are one, and so too is their action. But it is construed differently according to the perceived circumstances, more particularly, according to the sociolegal status of the woman involved. In the first instance, *znh* describes the woman's profession ("he thought her to be a harlot") and consequently her status—as an ostracized but tolerated purveyor of sexual favors for men. In the second, *znh* describes the activity of a woman whose sociolegal status ("your daughter-in-law" *kallateka*) makes such activity a crime.

Hebrew linguistic usage links the fornicator and the prostitute, but it also distinguishes them, by syntactic and contextual means. A proper understanding of the root *znh* and its usage in the Hebrew Bible requires careful and discriminating attention to linguistic, literary, and sociological factors that determine meaning.

The Hebrew term for "prostitute," *zona*, is the *qal* feminine participle of the verb *zana* used as a noun of profession either alone ([*haz*]*zona* "[the] prostitute") or in apposition to ('*išša* "woman" ('*išša zona* "a prostitute woman")[16] Thus in Hebrew conception the prostitute is "essentially" a professional or habitual fornicator, a promiscuous or unchaste woman, whose role and profession are defined by her sexual activity with men to whom she is not married. The noun represents a special case of the activity denoted by the *qal* verb. Despite this apparent relationship of dependence, however, virtually all discussions of the root reverse the order of influence, pointing to prostitution as the determining content of the verbal usage and thereby perpetuating the fixation on the professional model exhibited in the common English translations "play the harlot" and "go awhoring."[17] Is such a shift justified, and under what conditions?

The semantic relationship between the verbal and nominal uses of the root is, in fact, complex, affected in part at least by the figurative usage that dominates in the Hebrew Bible and invites interchange. Once the participle has become the identifying term for the prostitute, this specialized usage may exercise a secondary or "reverse" influence on the verb. The verb may be understood to describe the exercise of the profession (Amos 7:17), or it may acquire connotations and associations that were originally peculiar to the noun. Nevertheless, the basic meaning of the verb as describing fornication or illicit extramarital relations should be the starting point for interpreting any given use.

Another factor contributing to the problems of determining the meaning of the root is inadequate sociological analysis of the phenomenon of prostitution. The figure designated by the Hebrew participle *zona* represents a recognized institution, known throughout the ancient Near East and most urban cultures, whose relatively constant features can be described and analyzed quite apart from the terminology used for it in any given language or culture.[18] Thus while Hebrew linguistic usage gives important clues to Israel's understanding of prostitution, it does not suffice to describe the nature of the institution or how it functioned. It is the historically functioning institution, however, with all of its associations, that supplies the content of the term *zona*, not the etymology.

What is needed is a sociologically adequate account of the institution as it functioned in ancient Israel. This is especially urgent in view of the widespread assumption of an analogous or allied institution in the sacred sphere likewise identified by the term "prostitution."

In lieu of that needed account a few words of analysis must suffice. Prostitution shares with fornication, as defined in Israel, a fundamentally female profile,[19] despite the fact that both activities require active male participation and may involve male initiation (cf. Gen. 38:15-16). This asymmetry of conception and description is a characteristic feature of patriarchal societies, reflecting a general pattern of asymmetry in gender-related roles, values, and obligations (a phenomenon recognized in a more limited way by the notion of the "double standard"). The anomaly of the prostitute as a tolerated specialist in an activity prohibited to every other woman is a particular feature of patriarchal society, representing an accommodation to the conflicting desires of men for exclusive control of their wives' sexuality (and hence offspring[20]) and, at the same time, for sexual access to other women. The greater the inaccessibility of women in the society as a result of restrictions on the wife and unmarried nubile woman, the greater the need for an institutionally legitimized "other woman." The prostitute is that "other woman," tolerated but stigmatized, desired but ostracized. As I have attempted to show elsewhere, attitudes toward prostitution are characterized by ambivalence in every society, and the biblical evidence does not support the notion of a sharp distinction between Israelite and Canaanite society with respect to the prostitute's legal or social status.[21]

In my analysis, neither the verb *zana* nor the noun *zona* in their primary uses refers to cultic activity or have cultic connotations. Where then does the cultic interpretation arise, and under what conditions? Does it represent Israelite understanding or is it an interpreter's imposition? I shall limit attention to three linked texts in the book of Hosea, which represent, I believe, the primary literary and religio-historical context for the development of the figurative usage. The discussion must remain partial and tentative, since the key texts contain multiple interlocking problems of interpretation, some unresolved and others incapable of summary treatment. I have chosen, nevertheless, to begin with these texts, because I believe they are critical and because they illustrate a number of different interpretive problems.

THE BIRTH OF A METAPHOR: *ZNH* IN THE BOOK OF HOSEA

The opening words of the book present a sign-action that introduces the governing metaphor of chapters 1-3 and the theme of the collected oracles, articulated by use of the root *znh* (1:2).[22] Hosea is commanded to get a "woman/wife of promiscuity" (*'ešet zenunim*) and "offspring/children of promiscuity" (*yalde zenunim*), "because the land is utterly promiscuous (turning) away from Yahweh" (*ki-zanoh tizneh ha'areṣ me'aḥare yhwh*). The prophet is to represent by his marriage and family life Yahweh's relationship to Israel as a relationship subverted by Israel's promiscuous behavior. The use of *znh* in the interpretive *ki* ("for, because") clause is clearly figurative, with the land (grammatically feminine) replacing the usual female subject. Although the underlying metaphor is that of marriage, the use of *znh* rather than *n'p* serves to emphasize promiscuity rather than infidelity, "wantonness" rather than violation of marriage contract or covenant. The connotations of repeated, habitual, or characteristic behavior are reinforced by the emphatic verbal augment (*zanoh*) and by repetition of the noun *zenunim* ("promiscuity, fornication") to characterize both the wife and the children.

The woman is not described as a *zona*, although most commentators speak inaccurately of Hosea's marriage to a harlot.[23] Rather, as an *'ešet zenunim* she is characterized as a woman of loose sexual morals, whose promiscuous nature is exhibited in her "fornications" (*zenunim*). The use of the abstract plural noun points to habitual behavior and inclination rather than profession (cf. *ruḥ zenunim* "spirit of promiscuity" 4:12; 5:4). It is also open to extended or figurative meanings. In fact, the pairing of "woman of promiscuity" with "children of promiscuity" would appear to point in that direction, since, as we have seen, fornication normally describes a woman's activity. What sense can it make applied to the children?

Although *zenunim* can be understood to refer to the woman in both expressions and thus to characterize the children as the product of her promiscuous activity ("children [born] of promiscuity"), the mimicking construction of the paired terms and the linkage without an intervening verb suggest that the author intended to claim for the children the same nature as their mother. The message of the sign-action, enunciated in the following *ki* clause and elaborated in chapter 2, is that the land "fornicates" — and so do its inhabitants (children). The identification and interchange between mother and children, land and people are clear in chapter 2, where the mother's pursuit of her lovers is equated with cultic activities of the general population — and especially males. Thus mother and children should not be sharply differentiated.

What then does *zenunim* mean when applied to the children? I suggest that term be read in its incongruous "literal" (but abstract) sense. The function of the sign-act is to shock, and intimate, and confound — and more particularly to point forward to the explanation that follows. As in other prophetic sign-actions, the sign depends on the interpretive word for its meaning and is chosen and/or formulated in the light of the intended message. The message in this case is that the land is unfaithful to Yahweh — like a promiscuous wife and promiscuous children. The characterization of the wife by *zenunim* makes sense as literal description (even if it raises questions of plausibility), but the duplicate characterization of the children must be heard as strange and enigmatic, raising a question about the meaning of both uses. That, I think, is exactly what it was meant to do, opening the way to the explanation that follows. But the explanation is as enigmatic as the action it interprets. What does it mean to say that the land "fornicates"?

The meaning of the charge is revealed only in chapter 2, to which it points and on which it depends.[24] The implication, however, is clear: the land (people) has relations with other lovers in place of (*me'aḥare*, lit. "from after/behind") Yahweh. The logical supposition is that the "affairs" are with other gods, although 1:2 does not identify the object(s) of Israel's affections. It points, rather, to the aggrieved husband, with a construction that is unique to Hosea. The sequence *zana* + *min/me* "(away) from" occurs only in Hosea, and Ps. 73:27, and appears to be dictated by the marriage metaphor to which Hosea has adapted his usage. Normally *zana* does not carry the notion of infidelity, which is supplied by the context and made explicit here by Hosea's inventive construction. In each of the three occurrences of the sequence in Hosea (1:2; 4:12; 9:1) the *min* is compounded with another preposition that serves to connect the statement to a following expression. In the case of *me'aḥare* the expression that explains the usage is found in 2:5 (cf. 13),[25] where the charge of fornication (*zaneta 'immam* "their mother *znh*-ed") is interpreted by the quotation, "For she said, 'I will go *after ('aḥare)* my lovers.' " The preposition "after" belongs to the idiom *halak 'aḥare* "walk after," "follow." Hosea has appropriated it to describe, in a privative construction (*zana min*), the relationship to the one abandoned.

The charge of fornication that opens the book is elaborated in an extended allegory in 2:2-13 (Heb. 4-15), which develops the figure of the promiscuous bride and points to the activity underlying the metaphor. The opening accusation employs the mother-children metaphor and *zana/zenunim* language of 1:2, and likewise identifies mother and land (2:3; cf. v. 12). In 5b the summary charge of promiscuity (5a) is substantiated with a quotation from the accused:

> For she said, "I will go after my lovers,
> who give me my bread and my water,
>   my wool and my flax, my oil and my drink."

The picture presented in these words is that of a woman who seeks lovers for their gifts, called specifically "hire" (*'etna*)[26] in v. 12. Here the metaphor points to the figure of the professional prostitute, who is distinguished from the casual fornicator by her mercenary motive and multiple partners (pl. "lovers"). But she is also depicted as a wife (vv. 2, 7, 13) and mother (vv. 2, 4, 5) who has "behaved shamefully" (*hobiša* // *zaneta* "committed fornication," v. 5a), and it is her status as wife that is reflected in the punishment envisioned in vv. 3 and 10.[27] It appears that the author has drawn upon the full range of images and attitudes associated with the root *znh* to create his portrait of wayward Israel. It also suggests that the distinction between fornication and prostitution was essentially a legal one and that popular opinion regarded the behavior as essentially the same.

But what is represented by the metaphor, and to what extent are the terms of the figure dictated by the activity it describes? It is clear from the nature of the gifts mentioned in v. 5 that they are, directly or indirectly, the products of the land (cf. vv. 8, 9, 12) that depend on the life-sustaining gift of rain. Israel thinks they come from her lovers, whom she pursues (vv. 5, 7), adorning herself to win their favor (v. 13); but they are in fact the gifts of her husband Yahweh (v. 8), who will take them away, exposing her nakedness (vv. 9, 10, 12; cf. v. 3). The allegory is transparent: Israel has turned to the Canaanite rain god Baal (pejoratively represented as plural lovers) when her covenant lord, Yahweh, is the true God of fertility; the means of her lovemaking is the cult (vv. 8, 11, 13). The allegory is consistent, and daring in its appropriation of the basic fertility myth of the earth mother wed to the rain god.

The fundamental issue, in Hosea's view, is still the same as in the days of Elijah, viz., Who is the true god of fertility, Baal or Yahweh? — but now there is no contest. The battle of rival deities for national homage and state support has been won. What Hosea attacks is a Yahweh cult perverted by practices derived from the old (Baal) religion of the land, so that, in effect, it is really Baal that is worshiped ("courted") in these practices, not Yahweh.[28] The plural reference to the object of Israel's promiscuous devotion ("lovers," vv. 5, 7, 10, 12, 13; "the baals," v. 13; cf. v. 17) is, I suggest, an intentional device for "belittling" Baal, denying him a proper name and the status of a true rival. It also serves to identify the deity with the local cult places, and reinforces the impression of feverish cultic/sexual activity suggested by reference to multiple feasts (vv. 11, 13).

Despite the innuendo of chapter 2, the suggestion of cultic sex remains just that. The sexual language belongs exclusively to the allegory, while the cultic activity to which it points is represented in terms elsewhere descriptive of normative Yahweh worship: pilgrim feast (*ḥag*), new moon, and sabbath — every appointed feast (*kol mo'ed*) (v. 11).[29] It is only in chapter 4 that sexual language is employed in a non-metaphorical way in conjunction with cultic language — and the key term is *znh*.

Hosea 4:11-14 is a judgment oracle framed by short proverbial sentences (vv. 11 and 14b).[30] The indictment begins in v. 12 with a condemnation of oracular practices, followed by an explanatory *ki* clause employing the root *znh*, which functions as a leitmotif in the pericope, uniquely combining literal and metaphorical uses:

> My people[31] inquires of his (= its) "tree"
> and his "rod" gives him answer,
> For a *spirit of fornication* (*ruḥ zenunim*)
> has led (them) astray,
> and *they have fornicated* (*wayyiznu*)
> from under (*mittaḥat*) their God.

The charge of seeking oracular guidance by illicit means is couched in language that suggests both idolatry/apostasy ("tree" and "rod" as cult objects associated with other gods or illicit cult)[32] and sexual activity ("tree" and "rod" as phallic symbols). The sexual innuendo of the opening bicolon is reinforced by the use of *znh* in the following sentence. The language is strongly reminiscent of 1:2 in its combined use of *zana* and *zenunim* and in the syntax of the verb (with *min* + a preposition of position, here *taḥat* "under"). As in 1:2, the language functions metaphorically to characterize the nation as promiscuous in its inclination (*ruḥ zenunim*) and activity (*wayyiznu*). Here, however, the appeal to a female interpretive model cannot be explained by the grammatical gender of the subject. There is no personification of the land as mother; instead the people themselves (*'ammi*) are the subject, represented throughout the pericope by male-defined activity as well as masculine gender. NJV reflects this shift to a masculine subject by employing male-oriented or gender-neutral terminology ("a lecherous impulse," "they have strayed"). Yet the model for the usage continues to be the promiscuous bride, as reference to the wronged partner implies—employing a preposition (*tahat* "under") that is even more sexually suggestive.[33]

The indictment of cultic practice continues in vv. 13-14 in a quatrain whose first and final lines form an inclusio marked by parallel syntax, rhyming Hebrew verb forms, and identical opening and closing verbs.[34]

1. (13)   On the mountain-tops they "perform sacrifices,"
                  and on the hills they "make offerings,"
2. (13)   Under oak and poplar
                  and terebinth—because its shade is good.
3. (13)   That is why their[35] daughters fornicate
                  and their daughters-in-law commit adultery;
4. (14)[36]   For they themselves "divide" with the prostitutes
                  and "perform sacrifices" with the hierodules.

The first two lines describe cultic activity in literal, but suggestive terms. The verbs, which resume the present tense (impf.) of the opening indictment, represent the primary terms for cultic action, *zbh* "to sacrifice" and *qtr* "to burn incense" or "present offerings,"[37] but both are given an unusual vocalization (*piel*) used elsewhere only of illicit cultic activity.[38] Introductory prepositional phrases place emphasis on the locus of the activity ("*on* the mountaintops" and "*on* the hills"), making location a key to the interpretation. This emphasis is underlined in the second line by a list of tree names introduced by a new preposition, without an additional verb. The preposition *tahat* "under" creates a complementary pair with the *'al* ("upon") of the preceding line, but also picks up the *tahat* of the *mittahat* ("from under") in v. 12: the people have *znh*-ed *from under* their God by "offering" *under* trees—because their shade is "good"![39]

The accented terms of location (*on* the heights and *under* shady trees) suggest what this "offering" really involves. As in the opening indictment, the message of sexual activity is carried by innuendo, without the use of explicitly sexual language; and as in v. 12, it is followed by an interpretive word employing the verb *zana*—only this time the usage is literal. Line 3 (v. 13b) describes the consequences of the activity condemned in lines 1 and 2: "That is why their (your) daughters fornicate and their (your) daughters-in-law commit adultery."[40] The structure of the argument is clear: what the men do has consequences in their daughters' behavior. But what kind of consequences? That is the central interpretive problem of the pericope.

It is commonly understood to mean that the women engage in some form of "cultic prostitution" and that this activity represents the female side of the male activity alluded to in 13a, and spelled out in 14a. Both context and syntax require a literal reading, but does this include a specialized cultic meaning? The following considerations point, I believe, to a non-cultic interpretation, at least as the "first reading."

1. The pericope as a whole envisions the worshiping community as a body of males, although in the author's mind they represent collective Israel ("my people," v. 12). The description of the daughters' behavior is not one of the series of charges against Yahweh's "people." It is, rather, an argument directed at the men themselves, aiming to bring home to them the consequences of their actions.

2. The function of the statement, as indicated by the initial *'al-ken* ("therefore," "for this reason"), is to draw a connection between two sets of circumstances that had not previously been linked (cf. 4:3). The revelatory force of the statement is in the correlation, not in the description of the activity itself, which must be clearly abhorrent. If the young women had been engaging in sexual activity at the sites of the men's "worship," the connection would be obvious and there would be no need for the *'al-ken*.

3. The intention of the *'al-ken* clause is best realized when the verbs are understood in their "plain sense," as describing the loose sexual conduct of those women for whom the men addressed bear responsibility. Fornication and adultery will be immediately recognized as the most serious of women's offenses; attributed to female dependents (daughters and daughters-in-law, not wives), these sexual improprieties also constitute an attack upon the men's honor.[41] The statement assumes a concern for the women's sexual morals; its message consists in linking their sexual activity to the men's cultic activity, a link that is dramatically substantiated in the climactic final statement (14a).

To summarize, the men are accused of cultic impropriety, the women of sexual impropriety. (The women's offense is obvious; the men's is "under cover.") It may be sexual activity that defiles the men's worship, but it is worship that is the central concern of the pericope, as the verbs show. The men's worst offense is to dishonor God by their perverted worship. The women's worst offense is to dishonor their fathers and fathers-in-law by their sexual conduct. The men dishonor their Lord (metaphorical use of *zana*, v. 12b); the women dishonor their lords (literal use of *zana*, v. 13b). This differential assessment of male and female behavior, as well as the overall male orientation of the pericope, illustrates the asymmetry of roles, activities, and values noted earlier as a characteristic of patriarchal societies. A further example is found in the concluding line.

Line 4 (v. 14a) of the reconstructed quatrain is linked to the preceding line (v. 13b) by repetition of the root *znh* (*tiznena* "fornicate," *hazzonot* "prostitutes"), which carries the decisive meaning in both lines, and by a focus on paired classes of women. It is tied to line 1 by parallel construction and repetition of the initial verb to form an inclusio. Line 4 resumes (with emphatic *hem* they "themselves") the 3mp subject of the first two lines, continuing the description of the men's activity and extending the series of prepositional phrases that define and condemn their action by reference to the circumstances in which it is performed. Here, however, for the first time, an explicitly sexual term (*zonot*) appears, revealing what lay behind the earlier veiled references; the "sacrifices" *on* the mountaintops and hills and *under* the trees were performed *with* (*'im*) prostitutes and hierodules. The final statement sharpens the charges by focusing on a single determining feature of the activity that correlates the men's behavior with that of the women in the preceding line.

The correlation achieved through the use of *znh* does not equate the two pairs of women, nor describe the same activity; rather it points to an underlying connection between the activities of the fathers and the daughters. Each line makes a single, and distinct, statement: line 3, the men's female dependents are promiscuous; line 4, the men perform their "worship" with promiscuous women.

It is usually argued that the pairing of *zonot* and *qedešot* means either that the *zonot* are "sacred prostitutes," at least here, or that the *qedešot* are (simply) prostitutes.[42] Neither argument fits the requirements of the passage. The classes must be distinct in order to be identified, and the *qedešot* must be understood as having an essentially cultic identity, as indicated by the etymology of the term and by the use of *zbḥ* ("sacrifice") to describe the activity performed with them. They represent a cultic role, but one associated in Israelite (prophetic) thought with "Canaanite" worship, not Yahweh worship. Thus the placement of the term *qedešot* in final position serves as the climactic revelation that these cult sites and cultic activities really belong to Baal, not Yahweh.[43]

The meaning of the paired terms, however, is given in this context by the initial *zonot*. Through this pairing and ordering the reader is meant to understand that *qedešot* are equivalent to prostitutes. But this directed reading is clearly polemical; it tells us what the prophet thought about the *qedešot*, but it does not give us any reliable information about the function or activities of these women, except that they must have been a recognized presence at the rural sanctuaries in Hosea's day. There may also be shock value in mentioning the *zonot* first. While *qedešot* belong in a cultic context, though not a Yahwistic cult, *zonot* do not. They belong in public squares and inns and along the highways (Josh. 2:1; Gen. 38:15; Jer. 3:2; Isa. 23:16; Prov. 7:10-12), not at sanctuaries. Naming them as the company with whom the men conduct their worship tells us that this is perverted worship; naming *qedešot* as the men's companions says that it is "Canaanite" Baal worship.

Zonot are defined by their sexual activity, *qedešot* by their cultic association. It is impossible to determine the nature of their cultic service from the biblical sources, which are too fragmentary and polemical. It is clear, however, from the limited OT references that the Israelite authors understood their role to include some form of sexual activity, which they identified with prostitution. Through juxtaposition with *zona* the term *qedeša* acquired the sense of "sacred prostitute." Neither the assumption of sexual activity, however, nor its equation with prostitution can be taken at face value. Since Israel appears to have recognized no legitimate role for women as cult functionaries during the period in which *qedešot* are attested,[44] it would be easy for Israelites to assume that the presence of women at a sanctuary involved sexual activity. It is possible then that the charge of "sacred prostitution" has no base in cultic sex, but is rather a false inference.[45] It is also possible to understand the charge as a polemical misrepresentation of a cultic role that did involve some form of sexual activity, but was not understood by the practitioners as prostitution; the identification of the hierodule's role with the prostitute's would represent a distorted, outsider's view of the institution. A final possibility is that the isolated biblical references to *qedešot* represent a perverted remnant of an earlier Israelite or Canaanite cult, perpetuated in a perverted Israelite cult.[46] That is suggested by the presence of *zonot.*

The text offers no justification for viewing the *zonot* as cultic functionaries. It does suggest that prostitutes found the rural sanctuaries an attractive place to do business, quite possibly by agreement with the priests. The verb *(prd* "divide, separate") offers little help in determining the role of the *zonot* at the sanctuary, since it has been conformed to the series of polemical *piels* and occurs nowhere else in this vocalization or in connection with *zonot.* Does it designate a cultic action as the other verbs of the series?[47] The usage appears to be deliberately veiled and avoids the common verbs of sexual encounter.

The *zonot* and *qedešot* of the rural sanctuaries must be viewed as a small, specialized class and therefore not descriptive of the general female population, whose younger generation is represented by the daughters and brides of v. 13b. They are not the daughters, or wives, of the men addressed by the oracle.[48] The argument of the concluding lines, which compares male to female activity, is not based on the identity of the actions or of the actors (strictly speaking, it is not a condemnation of the "double standard"). Rather it uses a case of transparent guilt in the secular sphere (*zana* of the daughters) to engage the male subjects and then exposes their involvement in similar activity in the sacred sphere (association with *zonot*), insisting that the men's behavior is equally reprehensible, *or more so,* since it defiles worship with sexual activity.[49] In the final analysis such "worship" amounts to a rejection of Yahweh for other love objects (metaphorical *znh*, v. 12b). The fact that Hosea does not use the verb *zana* to describe the men's activity in line 4, despite his attempt to compare male and female behavior, confirms the interpretation of its use in v. 12 as metaphorical.

To summarize, in the primary texts of Hosea the root *znh* has the same basic meaning exhibited elsewhere in historical-legal usage, namely "to engage in illicit/extramarital sexual activity, to fornicate"; and as a professional noun (*zona*), "a prostitute." The subject is always female[50] and the activity has, in itself, no cultic connotations. Alongside this basic meaning and corresponding to it in its primary images is a metaphorical usage created by Hosea to characterize and indict Israel's worship. In its original(?) form, Israel (represented as the land, mother of the inhabitants, but interchanging with the inhabitants themselves, always conceived as male) is depicted as a promiscuous wife who abandons her husband for lovers, behaving like a common prostitute in pursuit of hire. The activity represented by the metaphor is cultic activity, which the metaphor reveals to be in effect service of "the baals" rather than Yahweh. It exhibits the character of "nature worship" in its aims, location, and means, including activity of a sexual nature, which Hosea represents as "simply" fornication.

The metaphorical use of *znh* invokes two familiar and linguistically identified images of dishonor in Israelite culture, the common prostitute and the promiscuous daughter or wife. As a sexual metaphor, it points to the sexual nature of the activity it represents. Its female orientation does not single out women for condemnation; it is used rather as a rhetorical device to expose men's sin. By appealing to the common stereotypes and interests of a primarily male audience, Hosea turns their accusation against them. It is easy for patriarchal society to see the guilt of a "fallen woman"; Hosea says, "You (male Israel) are that woman!"

NOTES

1. This chapter presents preliminary and abbreviated arguments from a larger study in progress, titled provisionally "Harlot and Hierodule in Israelite Anthropology and Theology." In many cases the length and format of the present essay do not permit full argumentation or documentation of critical points, for which the reader is referred to the forthcoming work.

The only major study of the root is the unpublished Ph.D. dissertation of O. E. Collins, "The Stem *ZNH* and Prostitution in the Hebrew Bible" (Brandeis, 1977; University Microfilms International 77-13364), which, in my view, has serious flaws in literary-linguistic and sociological analysis. A superior, though less exhaustive, treatment is given by M. Hooks in chapter 3 of his dissertation, "Sacred Prostitution in Israel and the Ancient Near East" (Hebrew Union College, 1985), 65-151. The best summary treatment is that of S. Erlandsson, "*zanah*," *TDOT* 4 (1980): 99-104; cf. J. Kuhlewein, "*znh*, huren," *THAT* 1 (1978): 518-20. See also articles on prostitution or "sacred prostitution" and commentaries, especially F. Hauck and S. Schultz, "*pornē*," *TDNT* 6 (1968): 579-95; W. Kornfeld, "L'adultère dans l'Orient antique," *RB* 57 (1950): 92-109; and J. P. Asmussen, "Bemerkungen zur Sakralen Prostitution in Israel," *ST* 11 (1958): 167-92.

2. *Webster's Seventh New Collegiate Dictionary* (Springfield, Mass.: G. & C. Merriam, 1972).

3. The examples cited below are all of the *qal* (basic) stem. The *hiphil* (8x, all masc.) functions in most cases as a causative of the *qal;* on its use in Hosea see below.

4. Collins saw the problem of determining literal and figurative uses as one of the primary methodological problems in previous treatments of the root ("The Stem *ZNH*," 13-17).

5. See Hooks, "Sacred Prostitution," for a comprehensive review (survey of theories, 1-4) and critique of this assumption.

6. The functions of the women designated by these terms (which have limited geographical and chronological distribution) are still poorly understood. See J. Renger, "Untersuchungen zum Priestertum in der altbabylonischen Zeit," *ZA* 58 (1967): 114-87; R. Harris, "The NADĪTU Woman," in *Studies Presented to Leo Openheim* (Chicago: University of Chicago, 1964); and Hooks, "Sacred Prostitution," 10-23.

7. I use the Greek term, meaning "temple slave," as a convenient and arbitrary class term for all nonpriestly cultic personnel, since the languages in question lack a single designation.

8. Cf. Collins, "The Stem *ZNH*," 33-34; Hooks, "Sacred Prostitution," 10-45, 152-85.

9. The idea may also have arisen independently in classical sources. It has certainly been nourished by the sensationalist accounts of Herodotus (*Histories* I, 199) and Lucian (*De Dea Syria* §16) describing the strange religious and sexual customs of the Babylonians and Phoenicians. Neither, however, uses the expression "sacred prostitution" in his descriptions of practices which he attributes to the general female population, rather than to professional prostitutes or hierodules. See Hooks, "Sacred Prostitution," 32-36, 40-41.

10. So also Erlandsson, *"zanah,"* 100; followed by Hooks, "Sacred Prostitution," 70.

11. BDB also gives as a second basic meaning "be a harlot." In its classification of uses, however, it lists as 1. *"be or act as a harlot,"* offering the alternative "commit fornication" only for Num. 25:1, specified as a "man's act." Further categories are 2. "fig. *of improper intercourse with foreign nations,"* 3. *"of intercourse with other deities,* considered as harlotry, sts. involving actual prostitution," and 4. *"zwnh* of moral defection" (only Isa. 1:21). The *pual* and *hiphil* uses are all defined in terms of "fornication," further classified as "sexual" or "religious." Cf. HALAT, 263-64.

12. Hans Wehr, *A Dictionary of Modern Written Arabic*, ed. J. Milton Cowan (Ithaca, N.Y.: Cornell University, 1961). See further Collins, "The Stem *ZNH*," 4-12; Hooks, "Sacred Prostitution," 67-69.

13. *znh* is not used for incest or other prohibited relationships, such as homosexual relations or bestiality. It focuses on the absence of a marriage bond between otherwise acceptable partners.

14. Although Tamar is living in her father's house as a widow (Gen. 38:11), she is identified as Judah's daughter-in-law in the critical scene when she is accused of "playing the harlot" (v. 24). For a fuller discussion of this case, see my article, "The Harlot as Heroine: Narrative Art and Social Presupposition in Three Old Testament Texts," *Semeia* 46 (1989): 119-39.

15. On the legal and social status of the prostitute, see below and Bird, "The Harlot as Heroine"; cf. S. Niditch, "The Wronged Woman Righted: An Analysis of Genesis 38," *HTR* 72 (1979): 147.

16. Cf. Benjamin Kedar-Kopfstein, "Semantic Aspects of the Pattern *gotel,"* *Hebrew Annual Review* 1 (1977): 158, 164-65.

17. A major problem with Collins's study ("The Stem *ZNH*") is his understanding of the root in its "primary, literal sense" as referring to "actual prostitution" (13). As a result, he can only ask what *kind* of prostitution (secular or sacred) it designates and whether it is literal or figurative. Cf. Hooks, "Sacred Prostitution," 70. F. I. Anderson and D. N. Freedman (*Hosea*, AB 24 [Garden City, N.Y.: Doubleday, 1980], 160) appear to be alone in challenging the common English interpretations.

18. See Bird, "The Harlot as Heroine," 3-4; J. H. Gagnon, "Prostitution," *The International Encyclopedia of the Social Sciences*, vol. 12, ed. D. L. Sills (New York: Macmillan and Free Press, 1968), 592-98; P. H. Gebhard, "Prostitution," *The New Encyclopedia Britannica*, vol. 15, 15th ed. (Chicago: University of Chicago, 1980), 75-81; and V. and B. Bullough, *Women and Prostitution: A Social History* (Buffalo: Prometheus, 1987).

19. The prostitute has no male counterpart; male prostitution, which was homosexual, was a limited phenomenon and is poorly attested in our sources. There is no masculine noun corresponding to *zona*, which is paired with *keleb* "dog" in Deut. 23:19.

20. Collins emphasizes male concern for legitimacy of offspring as the primary motive in identifying activity by *znh* ("The Stem *ZNH*," 263).

21. Bird, "The Harlot as Heroine," 121-22, 127, 132-33.

22. For basic literary and historical analysis, see Anderson and Freedman, *Hosea*; J. L. Mays, *Hosea*, OTL (Philadelphia: Westminster, 1969); and H. W. Wolff, *Hosea. A Commentary on the Book of the Prophet Hosea*, Hermeneia (Philadelphia: Fortress, 1974).

23. Cf. JB "marry a whore, and get children with a whore"; NAB "a harlot wife and harlot's children." In contrast, Wolff argues that the term describes activity in the popular sex cult of the day and thus characterizes the woman as an "average, 'modern' Israelite woman" (14-15).

24. Cf. commentaries and G. Yee, *Composition and Tradition in the Book of Hosea: A Redactional Investigation*, SBLDS 102 (Atlanta: Scholars, 1987).

25. Heb. 2:7, 15. To avoid cumbersome double notation, only the RSV numbering is given for verse references in chapter 2.

26. Apparently a variant of *'etnan* (9:1; Deut. 23:19; Mic. 1:7; etc.), "a harlot's wages."

27. Wolff, *Hosea*, 34; cf. J. Huehnergard, "Biblical Notes on Some New Akkadian Texts from Emar (Syria)," *CBQ* 47 (1985): 433-34.

28. The emphasis is on cultic practice rather than on rival/foreign gods. Hosea never directly identifies the "lovers" with "the baals." The expression "other gods" (*'elohim 'aherim*) occurs only in 3:1, with *ponim 'el-* ("turning toward") as in Deut. 31:18, 20. I regard 3:1-5 as a redactional composition that does not reflect Hosea's own usage here. Cf. commentaries.

29. The clue to the condemnation is not in the names of the feasts, which represent a catalogue of Israel's traditional and mandated days of offering, but in the qualifying personal pronouns (*"her* pilgrim feast," etc.) and the cover term, *mesosah* "her rejoicing." The feasts commanded by Yahweh have become occasions for Israel's pursuit of her own pleasure or gain; and so Yahweh condemns them as "(feast) days of the baals" (v. 13).

30. For literary and textual analysis see commentaries and my forthcoming work. I take the people (*'ammi*, v. 11) to be the subject throughout and view *zenut* of v. 11a as secondary and belonging to v. 10.

31. Reading with MT, followed by RSV and Mays, *Hosea*, 72; cf. NJV; Wolff, *Hosea*, 72; and Anderson and Freedman, *Hosea*, 343, 364-65 (who read "my people" with the preceding verse). My translation is literal where necessary to bring out features of the Hebrew lost in a more idiomatic rendering.

32. The terms suggest the asherah pillars and standing stones (*maṣṣebot*) associated with open air sanctuaries in numerous texts (e.g., Deut. 16:21; Judg. 6:25); for idols, see Jer. 2:27; 10:8.

33. It might be argued that the metaphor of the promiscuous wife is lost altogether here, with the root becoming simply a figurative term for illicit cult and/or cultic sex. Or one might view this usage as drawing on a broader root-meaning, describing male as well as female involvement in extramarital sex. Attempts to "defeminize" the usage are made difficult, however, by *mit-taḥat* and by the pos-

sessive pronoun (*"their* God"; cf. Num. 5:19, 20, 29). The remaining occurrence of *zana min/me* in Hos. 9:1 (*ki zaneta me'al 'eloheka* "for you have fornicated from upon your God") clearly has a female model in mind although the verb is masculine, as here, addressing collective Israel. The accusation of fornication is followed immediately in 9:1 by the amplification, "you loved (a harlot's) hire (*'etnan*) upon (*'al*) all grain-threshing floors," recalling the figure of the prostitute and repeating other key terms (*'hb* "love" and *dagan* "grain") of chapter 2. We must conclude then that collective Israel is personified as female in each of these uses of *znh* and accused of "acting like a promiscuous woman/prostitute."

34. My reconstruction of the quatrain omits 14a as a later addition. The notion of punishment, even when negated, is out of place here, and the inclusion of this line obscures the symmetry and interconnections of the original oracle. The force of the argument is not substantially altered by the deletion. See commentaries.

35. MT (Hebrew) has 2mp suffixes ("your") on both nouns, which may be original, occasioned by a shift in the argument at this point to draw the consequences of the indictment for the listeners, addressed now directly (cf. Mays, *Hosea*, 73). The shift to 2nd person may also have been introduced when the secondary "no punishment" statement was added. Wolff (85) and Anderson and Freedman (369) see different groups addressed by lines 3 and 4. I have translated as 3rd person to enable English readers to connect the male subjects, whom I believe to be the same throughout, whether addressed directly or indirectly.

36. See n. 34.

37. The paired terms constitute a *merismus* intended to cover all forms and occasions of cultic activity. Cf. Wolff, *Hosea*, 86.

38. I have used quotation marks in translating all four of the *piel* verbs in the first and final lines as an attempt to duplicate the Hebrew use of a system of vocalization that suggests something else is intended by these terms than they usually convey. None of these verbs is normally used in this stem. Cf. Wolff, *Hosea*, 35. This polemical use of the *piel* is characteristic of Hosea, who provides the earliest examples of the usage and may well be its originator.

39. Cf. 14:7-8 (Heb. 8-9), where Yahweh is likened to an evergreen cypress (the largest of trees), and his protecting "shade" (RSV "shadow") is described by the same term used here (*sel*).

40. "Daughters" (*banot*) and "daughters-in-law" (*kallot*, lit. "brides," here = "son's brides") are paired for purposes of poetic parallelism. They are to be understood as a single class, viz. sexually mature, young, female dependents. Cf. Anderson and Freedman, *Hosea*, 369; Wolff, *Hosea*, 86-87.

41. Deut. 22:21; Lev. 21:9; cf. Gen. 34:31.

42. So M. Gruber ("Hebrew *qedešah* and her Canaanite and Akkadian Cognates, UF 18 [1986]: 133-48), who argues that the etymology points to a basic meaning of "set apart," in this case "for degradation," in other Hebrew uses and in Akkadian "for exaltation" (133, 148). Hooks ("Sacred Prostitution," 187) arrives at a similar conclusion, drawing on the notion of "taboo."

43. Cf. the placement of "days of the baals" in the final verse of 2:2-13 to reveal the identity of the previously mentioned "lovers" (vv. 5, 7, 10, 12) and feast days (v. 11).

44. See my essay, "The Place of Women in the Israelite Cultus," in *Ancient Israelite Religion: Essays in Honor of Frank M. Cross,* ed. P. D. Hanson, P. D. Miller, S. D. McBride (Philadelphia: Fortress, 1987), 405-8.

45. This is the burden of Hooks's argument, for Israel and for the entire ancient Near East ("Sacred Prostitution," 203-7).

46. What Hosea describes is an *Israelite* fertility cult, not a Canaanite cult. Survivals, and/or revivals, of older, pre-Yahwistic practices (among them the role of the *qedešot*) must be assumed, but it is impossible to learn from the biblical sources what role these may have played in the earlier cult or how the practices were understood by the practitioners.

47. The term is usually understood to mean something like "go aside" (so RSV; NJV; Wolff, *Hosea*, 72; Mays, *Hosea*, 762), with the idea of joining (sacred) prostitutes in groves adjacent to the sanctuaries. Anderson and Freedman (370) suggest, however, that it may refer to the dismembering of the sacrificial victim. Might it suggest a division of the priestly portion with the prostitute?

48. The professional women should probably be understood as recruited from the general Israelite population, but they are treated here as "other women." On the father's role in causing or permitting a daughter's promiscuity, whether casual or commercial, see Lev. 19:29 and commentary by Collins, "Sacred Prostitution," 103-5.

49. Cf. the argument employed in the judicial parables, 2 Sam. 12:1-7 and 14:2-20.

50. In addition to the texts treated, cf. 3:3 *tizni* (*qal* with feminine subject and literal meaning). Three instances of the *hiphil* occur in the book (4:10, 18; 5:3), all involving some textual problems. A provisional survey of these occurrences suggests that the *hiphil* is meant to represent the male activity in fornication, much as the male activity in giving birth to a child (*yld qal* with female subject) is normally represented by the *hiphil*, although in metaphorical usage the *qal* can have a male subject (e.g., Deut. 32:18, of God).

20

HENRI MOTTU

Jeremiah vs. Hananiah

Ideology and Truth in Old Testament Prophecy

The prophet enters a situation in which interpretation of events — and policies to change or influence the events — are being shaped. The prophet offers words and deeds (explicit cultural production) derived from a reading of the basic contradictions that the people face (implicit cultural formation). The prophecies compete with other words, deeds, and readings of the situation. The analyses and strategies of all the interpreters and persuaders are "ideology" insofar as they pretend to be universal and indisputable truth while being actually the point of view of a group or class. They become "truth" insofar as the conditioned character of the analyses and strategies can be overcome through changing the conditions by thoughtful action.

Hananiah and Jeremiah offer two different readings of the contradictions facing Judah in 594 B.C.E.

For Hananiah the primary contradiction is between the superpower Babylon and inferior Judah, while the secondary contradiction is between salvation prophecy that promises Judah early victory over Babylon (Hananiah's prophecy) and doom prophecy that promises a lengthy Judean defeat at the hands of Babylon (Jeremiah's prophecy). The two

---

Reprinted from *The Bible and Liberation: Political and Social Hermeneutics*, 1st ed., ed. N. K. Gottwald and A. C. Wire (Berkeley: Community for Religious Research and Education [Radical Religion], 1976), 58–67.

contradictions are smoothly aligned in Hananiah's mind, and there is no other contradiction to consider.

For Jeremiah, the undoubted political threat of Babylon to Judah is altogether overshadowed by the primary contradiction between the power- and wealth-seeking interests of the ruling class in Judah and the well-being and survival of the whole Judean people. The associated secondary contradiction lies between salvation prophecy (serving the ruling class) and doom prophecy (serving the common people). For Jeremiah the immediate resolution of the contradictions will be for Babylon to remove the oppressive Judean rulers from their positions over the Judean people, for the latter are not ultimately threatened by the Babylonians under whose "yoke" they will survive and be renewed.

ASSUMPTIONS

I begin these tentative "Marxian" reflections on Jeremiah 28 by explaining the two assumptions I make.

First, it seems to me that the problem the Old Testament and the New Testament faced long before us, the problem of pseudo- and authentic prophecy, could be reformulated today under the terms, analyzed by Marxist thought, of ideology and truth—or more precisely: *Logos* and *Praxis*. The question that I want to address to the text is this: What does it say to us as we face the problem par excellence that plagues our lives and thoughts: *how are we to differentiate an ideological from a true theoretical statement?* It seems to me that the old text of Jer. 28 was wrestling with this very question and that the text raised this question with the maximum consciousness available in his time. By this I do mean that we now have to "translate" the message or the text in our own language ("actualization"); that could be paternalistic. Rather, I mean we have to find again, in our own terms, the very question that the text was dealing with. My assumption is that the text was precisely dealing with Logos and Praxis. I call this process of interpretation "trans-interpretation."

As a matter of fact the text sounds very "modern," for it has to do with the question of authority: who has the authority to tell me what is true and what is false? Who is in a position to differentiate for me the deceitful Logos from the true Praxis? The Old Testament has an answer: only the true prophet is in such a position. But what constitutes the true prophet? Jer. 23, 26, and 28 are in fact wrestling with the conditions of true and false prophecy and provide us a sort of critique of what constitutes true or false Logos, Word of God or Word of Man. These texts, reflecting on Jeremiah's own praxis, grapple with the possibility and the actuality of such a differentiation. The modern problem, I believe, is not that of theism or atheism, of transcendence or immanence, of whether there is a God or not. Rather, what plagues us, Christians and atheists alike, is what makes a true statement true and a false statement false, and who in the last resort has the authority to teach us anything about it. This problem implies questions of source of authority, control, institutionalization, and politics. The *"diakrisis ton pneumaton"* of the New Testament necessarily involves the problem of the church or of the party.

My second assumption is that one cannot be satisfied today as an interpreter (and every theologian and philosopher is a decipherer of signs nowadays) with mere allusions to this problem or with basic unconscious and unexplained assumptions — as, for instance, when we identify from the outset with Jeremiah against his opponents, for that is precisely the beginning of a subtle hermeneutical lie. When for instance Van der Woude finishes a study of false prophecy with the remark: "The type of Zion-theology conceived of by the pseudo-prophets as an ideology does not in fact differ from any other ideology: its dogmatism, its objectivism, in particular its false hope for the future,"[1] one cannot avoid asking: on what basis does Van der Woude know that the theology of pseudo-prophetism was in fact an "ideology"? He simply assumes this and as an exegete has other things to do than to reflect on the matter. Nevertheless he does say such things in passing. As interpreters of the texts, however, we cannot avoid the problem and we must *try to clarify the process by which a given statement becomes false or true within the text itself as well as in our modern pre-understanding.* The same process of clarification is required from us concerning a myriad of other concepts or notions thrown out by exegetes and theologians as judgments in passing and sometimes even as cheap happy endings. In brief, our task is to decipher the hidden meaning of such unexplained assumptions; in other words, to make a critique of the dominant theological interpretation itself. We said earlier: *trans*-interpretation; we now say: *pre*-interpretation. It means: we want to provide critique of what *underlies* all these so-called "religious" or "Christian" interpretations.

THE PROBLEM

The problem has to be faced in its frightening and banal radicality without any attempt to transcend it too quickly or easily. And I must say, whereas the Old Testament itself has been quite honest in this regard, subsequent interpretations can be seen as an ongoing attempt to minimize and to domesticate it. For instance, the Old Testament never uses the equivalent of "pseudo" or "false" prophet. *Pseudoprophetes* comes from the Greek translation of the Old Testament and was taken up by some New Testament texts, but there is no comparable Old Testament expression. Behind this significant silence we may have the belief that only God himself is in a position to declare a prophet true or false. It is revealing that Jeremiah's opponents used a similar term. Shemaiah can describe Jeremiah as "a madman who sets up as a prophet" (Jer. 29:26), and the party of Azariah and Johanan can reply to Jeremiah on another occasion: "You are lying; the Lord our God has not sent you ... Baruch son of Neriah has incited you against us in order to put us in the power of the Chaldeans, so that they may kill us or deport us to Babylon" (Jer. 43:2-3). Here we encounter call of God against call of God, Word of God against Word of God, God against God. The abstract question as to whether there is a God — or as to what God, humanity, or the world is in reality—is here put in its sole concrete way: What makes the truth the truth and the lie the lie? Who is the true interpreter of the world in which we live? The problematic is not either God or Marx, either Lenin or Mao, either Barth or Bultmann, but rather: Where is the true God, the true Marx, the true Bultmann to be found and to be differentiated from the false?

The French Marxist Louis Althusser develops the notion of "epistemological break" precisely to answer the question: How can it be that our thinking, our Logos, is at the same time false by definition, since it is necessarily caught in its "practico-social function" as reflex (thus falsified) but still is, on the other hand, capable in some way of participation in the truth?[2] In fact, Althusser's epistemological break serves to describe both the fact that our Logos is a mere ideological reflex of socio-historical conditioning (our "lived relation" to the world) and the assumption that once the break has taken place, our discourse is then able to constitute itself as a theory of science. Among Christian exegetes, this process is presumably exhibited when they say: *Here* in Jeremiah, true prophecy! *There* in Hananiah, false prophecy! In their eyes Jeremiah is a so-called "canonical prophet," a dreadful designation that simply calls "scriptural" or "canonical" the text of the victors and rejects to abomination or forgetfulness the beaten text of the defeated.

When Jeremiah tries desperately to convince his people that "in very truth the Lord has sent me to you to say all this in your hearing" (26:15), he can only *assure* them that this is so. There is here no external legitimation, no public testimony; the legitimation comes solely from the truth itself, from internal legitimation and testimony. Only prophecy can decide about prophecy (see 1 Cor. 14:32). Only God can say which god is the true God; only the Spirit can judge other spirits. Yes, but like Pilate we are tempted to respond, "But *what is* truth?" (John 18:38).

Of course there are attempts in the Old Testament to give some formal as well as material criteria for differentiating true from false prophecy; but they are what Marxists call "rationalizations" or "reifications" of the problem to the degree that they replace the reality of lived-through history with objectifications and autonomous entities nowhere accessible to our actual consciousness. The formal criteria refer to Baal, morality, dreams, visions, fulfillment of prophecy, orthodoxy (as in Deut. 18:20-22); in this sense, Jer. 26 is mainly working on the level of the means of revelation and its critique. The material criteria refer to doom prophecy versus salvation and peace prophecy; free prophecy versus cult prophecy, etc. But, as Quell[3] and many others have shown, neither the external nor the internal criteria help very much, since they are all judgments after the fact. They do not help in the midst of the act of differentiating true and false prophecy. As André Néher says, not without irony, "There have been occasional attempts in biblical history ... to codify prophecy and to state a theory of false prophecy. But no one has ever been able to establish the code of true prophecy."[4] My assumption is that Jer. 28 is an eminent text, an eminent narrative, that contains a surplus of meaning concerning an underlying theory of false and true discourse capable of recovery with the help of Marxian tools. This is my wager.

IDEOLOGY

I begin with the comprehensive definition of ideology advanced by François Châtelet:

> ... an ideology is a cultural formation (implicit) or a cultural production (explicit) that expresses the point of view of a social class or caste; such a point of view concerns man's relations with nature, imagination, the others, and himself. Ideology presents itself as having a *universal* validity; but in reality it not only expresses a *particular* point of view, but also it tends to *mask* its particularity by proposing compensations and imaginary or fleeting solutions. By "ideological function" of a cultural production — a moral doctrine for instance — one has to understand the intellectual action that brings such a production, an action by which this particular conception is being presented as a universal conception.[5]

In Hananiah's statements and symbolic act (Jer. 28:1-4, 10-11) we have thus to differentiate three aspects:
1. The implicit cultural formation (what stands or lurks behind or beneath his discourse and act);
2. The explicit cultural production (what he explicitly says and does);
3. The ideological function of both (what the effects of his discourse and act are).

The *implicit cultural formation* that lies behind Hananiah's words and act may be summarized as follows:

1. There is the assumption that God protects his people and saves them from the Babylonian imperialism at any price (Zion-election tradition). Israel [i.e., the ruling class] is viewed as forever the chosen people of God, and its own actions or economic/political structures (e.g., the royal court) cannot change this enduring salvation.

2. There is the assumption that God acts in a repetitive way at any time and in any situation in the same way that he always has acted (God's truthfulness or fidelity is a given, a "thing" at our disposal). As God in Isaiah's time forced the Assyrians under Sennacherib in 701 miraculously to withdraw from the siege of Jerusalem, so now — in the same manner — the Babylonians under Nebuchadnezzar will be compelled by Yahweh to retreat and to let the first deportees of 597 (Jehoiachin and the ruling group with him) come back to Jerusalem safely and intact. What has happened in 701 will happen again in 594-593. We have to trust God's fidelity (to "trust" is Hananiah's key word, see Jer. 28:15).

Now what do we gain by calling this an "implicit cultural formation"? It is tempting to say: everybody knows that already and we have no need of this complicated conceptual apparatus. Answer: we gain two things. First, we are able to specify Hananiah's "unconscious motives" and his "concealed motivations" as a formation that *we* reconstruct and that *we* define as a theology, without immediately stigmatizing it as an "ideology," since this would be a statement after the event. J. Philip Hyatt asserts that "Jeremiah brought these concealed motivations into the open,"[6] but in truth it was not Jeremiah but *we* who try to bring into the open Hananiah's implicit cultural formation (I prefer the term "implicit" rather than the term "unconscious"). Jeremiah cannot be seen as taking the risk of reconstruction for us and apart from us. Second, when we speak of an implicit cultural formation we presuppose that such a construction—located "behind" or "beneath" any discourse or action that we undertake to decipher—lies behind Jeremiah's own statements as well. "May it be so!" he says, following Hananiah's Word of God (28:6). Consequently, it is not the mere existence of an implicit cultural formation as such, or for that matter its particular content, that can decide about truth and falsehood, reality and illusion. It is only the *function* of any formation that has become embodied in a specific production, the actual *use* made of them, that can decide about truth and falsehood, reality and illusion (see below on "Praxis").

The explicit cultural production takes the following form in the words and act of Hananiah:

Hananiah takes up the *universality* of Israelite prophetic speech: "Thus says Yahweh of hosts, the God of Israel: I have broken the yoke of the king of Babylon ... " (28:2). He explicitly takes up the Word of God as a universal Word, as *the* Word, whereas he in fact takes up *a* word, pronounced in a *particular* situation and responding to particular interests (cf. Isa. 9:4, "thou hast shattered the yoke that burdened them"). Such a process of making out of a particular statement a universal one, valid once and for all, is called by Jeremiah (23:30) a "stealing": the prophets "who steal my words from one another for their own use." And what Hananiah explicitly *does* is clear also: he acts symbolically, as is often the case in prophetism: he breaks the yoke and takes it off the neck of Jeremiah. Word against Word, symbolic act against symbolic act.

The ideological function of both cultural formation and cultural production may be analyzed in this way:

1. This discourse and this symbolic action have first the function of inter-jecting, so to speak, into the objective situation certain value-imbuing affirma-tions. These are value judgments or affirmations that deal with predictions of worth. Hananiah's discourse functions in reality as a predication of which leads the people to "trust" in Yahweh in terms of certain perceptions about good and evil, about friend and enemy, about what is near (and therefore of concern or value) and what is far (and therefore of little or no concern or value). The discourse functions in such a way that the people are led to see, to face, and to resist "the enemy"—namely, the Babylonian invader. Thus God is seen as the Friend, the Protector, the Near over against the "others" over there who intrude into our land, territory, and city. For Jeremiah, on the contrary, God is the Enemy: "am I a God only near at hand, and not far away?" (23:23). "Do I not fill heaven and earth?" (23:24). Nebuchadnezzar is bluntly designated by Jeremiah as "my [God's] servant" (27:6). God is beyond good and evil.

2. The ideological discourse functions secondly by leading the people to take into account only one aspect of the whole reality, one contradiction that is

elevated to the status of principal contradiction, whereas it is only a secondary contradiction [see below on "Contradiction"]. Hananiah sees only the contradiction between the Babylonian Empire and Judah (more precisely: between Babylon and the ruling class of Judah, esp. of Jerusalem) without taking any account of the fact that this contradiction is *overdetermined*[7] by the internal conflict between the people of Judah and its ruling class and by the conflict between God and Israel's fall into nationalism. Jeremiah, by contrast, understands the whole and rightly sees the necessity of history proceeding on its course under these painful circumstances—inevitably the "bars of wood" will be changed into "bars of iron" (28:13).

REIFICATION

As a beginning point I take the definition of reification by Peter Berger and Stanley Pullberg:

> By reification we mean the moment in the process of alienation in which the characteristic of thing-hood becomes the standard of objective reality. That is, nothing can be conceived of as real that does not have the character of a thing. This can also be put in different words: reification is objectification in an alienated mode ... Reification, on all levels to consciousness, converts the concrete into the abstract, then in turn concretizes the abstract. Also, reification converts quality into quantity.[8]

By means of the concept of reification, I shall attempt to reconstruct Hananiah's world—i.e., his subjective understanding of it or his "lived relation" to himself, to the people of Israel, to the world, and ultimately to God. The process of reification can be observed on four levels:

1. Process of Recurrence. To the degree that reification as a general phenomenon is "grounded in historically recurrent circumstances of human existence in society,"[9] one can say that Hananiah operates upon the belief that God's fidelity is simply a recurrent fact. "Recurrence" is a procedure of demonstration that consists in extending to all the terms of a series what is valid only for the first two terms. This is exactly what he does: he extends the events of 701 under Sennacherib to the events of 594/3 under Nebuchadnezzar without seeing those events in terms of the historical activity of Babylon and Judah. What is going on in Hananiah's mind is exactly "the autonomization of objectivity in unconnectedness with the human activity by which it has been produced."[10]

2. Process of Stealing. Reification occurs when certain people "steal" the praxis of others, which is the case when Hananiah "steals" (Isa. 9:4) from Isaiah and simply transfers a word said in a given situation into a quite different one. This process of "stealing" is a far-reaching one and covers many different situations, as illustrated by the German peasants who saw their praxis being "stolen" from their hands by the princes and by Luther,[11] or by the process in contemporary theology and church of "stealing" Marxian categories dislodged from their militant political context, or by the praxis and struggle of women today being "stolen" by males for their own advantages. So the text of Isaiah 9 becomes a "thing," even a commodity, at the disposal of anyone at any time. Jer. 23:30 speaks pointedly against this "reification" of the words of God.

3. Process of Fetishism. In his 1962 spring term lectures at Göttingen, Walther Zimmerli remarked that for Hananiah the "sacred" comes first and the people come only in second position. "Within two years I will bring back to this place all the vessels of the Lord's house . . ." (28:3), and the people come only after this: "I will also bring back to this place Jeconiah son of Jehoiakim, king of Judah, and all the exiles of Judah who went to Babylon" (28:4). "Reification in a capitalist society is a product of the fetishism of commodities, and it is spread through all social life by the institutions necessary to the market."[12] We can, I believe, transfer this to the situation of the text, even though the economy then was only a barter economy and not an industrial economy. Of principal importance are the vessels of the temple, and only secondarily the people of flesh and blood. The "world" of Hananiah is a world of sacred objects viewed as prior to people. The temple is the collective that concretizes the abstract, that incarnates dead vessels, frozen things. The fetishism of the temple is everywhere present among the "pseudo"-prophets (cf. Jer. 7:4 and Mic. 3:11). In addition, it is worthwhile to note that Hananiah is primarily concerned about the ruling class deported with the king.

4. Process of Reification in the Religious Realm. Marx has analyzed the process of reification (commodity, man as commodity, etc.) as a process paralleled by religious fetishism. It is clear that for Hananiah God is a product of what is seen as "given" in the representation. A fixed preconception stands opposed to what is actually present! God is a commodity or thing in the midst of other commodities and things, even if the most important and influential of them. So we meet a religious representation of reality concretized in the fetishism of the temple and the reification of the vessels, elevated above the people, combined in a thorough-going process of "thingification."

CONTRADICTION

We observed from the outset the decisive role played in the debate by the yoke as the medium for the two opposing symbolic acts: the wooden yoke that Jeremiah carries on his shoulders and the action of Hananiah in taking this yoke from the neck of his opponent, only to be replaced by Jeremiah with an iron yoke. We meet not only word against word but act against act, and this points up the fact that Judah lives under the pressure of history ("the yoke of Nebuchadnezzar," 28:11), under history's necessity. Thus the yoke in my view stands as a representation of the concept of necessity and, more precisely, for the basic contradiction that the people of Judah are living between the promise of their God and the actual inescapable reality posed by history. Judah is historically and theologically caught in the alternative: either to rebel against history's necessity and to restore Jerusalem and its temple or to let the events go their course. The latter alternative implies a radical new understanding of God's action in history and of the role of Jerusalem. Hananiah is a kind of zealot who united religious restorative thinking and political resistance. In my jargon: the symbolic gesture of Hananiah taking the yoke from Jeremiah's neck is the religious symbol of Judah's lived contradiction between rebellion and necessity.

Now let us try to make use of Mao Tse-tung's famous model of principal or dominant contradiction and nonprincipal or secondary contradiction; as well as the principal aspect of the contradiction and secondary aspect of the contradiction.[13]

1. Hananiah, like Jeremiah and all of the Judeans, sees the dominant contradiction as embodied in the unequal power relationship between Babylon and the royal court in Judah. This is first of all what lies objectively behind the entire situation. As far as the secondary contradiction is concerned, Hananiah envisions it as the antagonism between pseudo-prophetism as embodied in doom prophecy à la Jeremiah and authentic prophetism as incarnated in the Zion-election tradition à la Isaiah. He sees the situation exclusively in these terms, and there is no *reflection* on his part about the "aspects" of the two contradictions. For him the contradiction is really "pure and simple."

2. Jeremiah, by contrast, rightly points out the complexity of this twofold contradiction. The two contradictions imply aspects that are not reducible to the contradictions between Babylon and Judah and between doom prophecy and salvation prophecy. Jeremiah rightly sees that what Hananiah views as the dominant contradiction is in fact only the dominant *aspect* of the contradiction and that the secondary contradiction between doom prophecy (pseudo-prophecy in Hananiah's eyes) and salvation prophecy (authentic prophecy in his eyes) is only the secondary *aspect* of it.

What then is the actual dominant contradiction in the situation? It is, I think according to Jeremiah, *the overdetermination of the conflict Babylon-Judah by another conflict,* a conflict altogether ignored by Hananiah — namely, by *the conflict between the particular interests of the ruling class in Jerusalem and the objective interests of the people of Israel/Judah as a whole.* Note here the intriguing intervention on behalf of Jeremiah by "some elders of the land" (26:17) who probably represent the old North Israelite tradition of Amos and Micah (in fact, they quote Mic. 3:11-12). According to Jeremiah, the apparent principal contradiction of Babylon versus Judah is decisively overdetermined by the conflict between the people of the land and the people of Jerusalem who rule Judah. This internal conflict, because of its socioeconomic roots, is much more basic to the situation than the more easily observed interstate conflict between Babylon and Judah.

Consequently, as far as the secondary aspect of the contradiction is concerned, Jeremiah sees not only the religious aspect of the antagonism between pseudo- and authentic prophecy but also its concrete and practical social effects. Praxis against dogmatism. Hananiah's "world" remains a purely religious one. Jeremiah sees much better the socioeconomic aspects of this religious contradiction insofar as what is at stake in the last analysis is not the correct religion or doctrine but rather the *survival,* "the good" of people of flesh and blood (cf. Jer. 6:14, "They dress my people's wounds, but skin-deep only, with their saying

'All is well.' All well? Nothing is well!"). It is not only that sin brings forth doom, but also that at stake is the survival, the very life, of the people (cf. Jer. 27:12-13, 17, "serve the king of Babylon and his people and you shall save your lives"). For Jeremiah the secondary aspect of the contradiction is set into a social context in which the prophetic debate about truth and falsehood is merely a part. The secondary contradiction has an aspect that overdetermines it insofar as the question is not only a "theoretical" abstract one (truth/falsity) but a concrete one as well (survival). Thus, far better than his opponent, Jeremiah has seen the wholeness of the situation, a situation in which the religious secondary contradiction is never "pure and simple" but always overdetermined by the conflicts and power relationships among social groups with their respective interests (see the social components of Judah mentioned in Jer. 26).

What have we gained by this rather complicated analysis? I think we have gained two things:

1. First we have tried to recapture the complexity of the situation. We believe that the so-called "contradictions" pointed out by the exegetes to date are to some degree helpful but ultimately invalid. For it is simply not true to see the contradiction between true and false prophecy in the mere opposition between doom prophecy and salvation prophecy (e.g., Osswald[14]). In that case, what about Jonah and Nineveh? The contradiction between cult prophecy and "outsider" prophecy is somehow romantic and does not help very much. In that case, what about the fact that Jeremiah comes from a priestly family? The contradiction between group prophecy and solitary or individual prophecy is wrong too. In that case, what of the fact that Jeremiah was not "alone" (cf. the martyrdom of Uriah, Jer. 26:20-23, to say nothing of Jeremiah's "school" and disciples, such as Baruch). Finally, the contradiction between North Israelite land prophecy and Zion-election-temple prophecy (e.g. von Rad[15]) is somewhat more helpful, although this is not decisive either, since after all Hananiah and Jeremiah alike come from Benjamin and, moreover, Jeremiah is saved by the elders of the land only at the last minute without himself being located in their tradition.

Against these too facile "explanations," we have tried to differentiate dominant and secondary contradictions, viewed as mere external power relationships, from dominant and secondary *aspects* of these contradictions viewed as an *internal* overdetermination of the latter.

2. Secondly, I think we have shown that Marxism does not *reduce* the frightening question at stake to this or that *external* factor. On the contrary, the enigma remains intact while becoming analytically approachable and discernible in terms of the various forces at work and the various value predications which the disputants affirm. Naturally this judgment gives no blanket endorsement to all interpretations labeled "Marxist," since many of these have been crudely mechanistic or economist and quite as "undialectical" as the worst instances of biblical exegesis. We have emphasized here strands of Marxist analysis contributed by theoreticians such as Althusser and Antonio Gramsci.[16]

PRAXIS

Let us return to our main question: What is a true statement confronted with an illusory one? What differentiates Logos from Praxis? Since any kind of statement, whoever delivers it, is inescapably not only *dependent* on socio-historical conditioning but also necessarily *situated* in a web of power relationships, how can such a true statement simply *be?* There is no "human condition" as such, but only situation. All thought is situated and participates in the strategy of desire, of sociality, and of will for power. Where is the "line of demarcation" (Althusser) separating the true and the false and how can we simply "draw" it?

This is the problem of modernity: epistemology (What is knowing? How can I know any object?) is met from the angle of illusion (Kant and the "transcendental illusion"). It is at this point that Marx and Freud come together, Marx adding to Freud's analysis the power relationships and the relations of domination and dependence. As Ricoeur observes,

> ... in this respect, the fundamental contribution of Marx will not rest on his theory of class struggle, but on the discernment of the hidden relation which connects ideology to the phenomena of domination. This reading of ideology as symptomatic of the phenomenon of domination will be the durable contribution of Marxism beyond its political applications.[17]

Thus Hananiah not only lives in illusion (albeit a religious illusion) but also participates implicitly in the power relationships of his time. Without knowing it, he responds under the disguise of the prophetic Spirit to the wishful thinking of the royal court and of the temple fans. But still, how are we to draw the line of demarcation? How do we know that Jeremiah is right and who tells us that this is the case? From what source do we assume what we more or less consciously assume and identify with? There are, I think, three solutions that are available to us, and I will briefly discuss them: (1) History draws the line of demarcation with its sole necessity and certainty; (2) Philosophy of consciousness; the "true" and the "false" consciousness; (3) "Philosophy of the praxis" (Gramsci).

1. History as the Criterion. The sly "solution" of this line of interpretation rapidly proves itself to be a slovenly answer that no one can be satisfied with, but that has often been considered as the Marxist doctrine and as a secularization of the Christian predestination doctrine. This is in fact a dreadful escape, but a very cunning one that still lies in our minds as the way to read any text, including biblical texts. Even if success may prove the validity of our knowledge and practice, the difficulty is that such a realization always comes after the event. History, contrary to what Hegel has said, is not the ongoing self-recognition of the Spirit. History teaches us only one thing: that there are victors and victims, dominators and dominated, texts of victors that remain and texts of the defeated that have disappeared. In brief, such hermeneutics work under the delusive assumption of relations of domination and dependence.

It is sheer bad faith to give Jeremiah the pre-eminence over Hananiah simply because history has justified him a posteriori; here the sly moralism of many commentaries should be checked. This has often been the "moralistic theological" reading of Jer. 28: one saves Jeremiah from the ambiguity and opacity of history by using a posteriori the entire "Marxist" arsenal in order to disqualify

Hananiah. The "reflex" theory is then fully applied to Hananiah but *never to Jeremiah himself*, as if it would have been possible to differentiate them in the midst of the original action—which was precisely impossible. The proof from history is the false infinite of the theologian.

2. **Philosophy of Consciousness.** This is the exegetical solution of Edmond Jacob: "Thus what we customarily call 'false prophecy' would only be the temptation to which any prophet is constantly exposed."[18] This line of interpretation would focus on the "temptation" of Jeremiah as a prophet torn apart who exhibits the rise of personal subjectivity (who am I?); the temptation; the bad faith; etc. We would then have a *tragic* situation. Accordingly there is *no way* to draw our much-desired line of demarcation. We are in the dark of existence. Two duties, two spirits, two words equally valid and valuable in and of themselves; only existence can decide (decision!). But we thereby renounce any attempt to arrive at objectivity. The world is on the verge of disintegration within the choice of consciousness. Are we not back to idealism, whereby consciousness gives birth to the world?

3. **"Philosophy of the Praxis."** Against the assumption that every statement, whatever it may be and whoever announces it, is "ideological" and thus untrue, Marxism has always emphasized the breakthrough ("the working through") of the praxis. In Marxism the "epistemological break" only takes place under the auspices of the praxis (this is to be affirmed against Althusser). Praxis does not mean "to be where the action is," since it means in Marxism not only the practical response to a person's conditions of life (need, material conditions, work), but also "the comprehension of this practice" (Marx's Thesis 8 on Feuerbach). Ultimately praxis serves in Marxism the function of "authentic consciousness" in existentialism over against "false consciousness," insofar as praxis is the mediation necessary to solve the problem of human dependency on our conditioning and, at the same time, of human participation in the truth: "The coincidence of the changing of circumstances and of human activity can be conceived and rationally understood only as revolutionizing practice" (Marx's Thesis 3 on Feuerbach). Thus praxis in Marxism plays the role of paradox in existentialism. This is why Marxian tools are originally and fundamentally *open tools* of criticism, including self-criticism. *Praxis does not "solve" anything; it just poses the problem in its right terms and in its correct scope* and it does so in opposition to loose talk about history's automatic "judgment" and against a kind of existentialist irrationalism.

Jeremiah "works" the truth of his God, the hidden God. He is the man of the Praxis rather than of the Logos. Why? For four reasons:

1. There is in Jeremiah a tremendous *process of "working,"* of work that is not only external labor but of work turned upon interiority and then turning back to exteriority. Here we should refer to Hegel's analysis of the Slave/Master relation in *Phenomenology of Mind*, Chap. IV: the Master is idle, he encounters nature and raw material only through the mediation of the Slave who is in direct contact with the real world. Hence the Master cannot be ultimately "satisfied"; the Slave, on the contrary, "works through"—i.e., he forms and educates himself through his fighting for recognition and his struggle with

nature and other people. Hegel has a tremendous definition of "work": work, he says, is "repressed desire, an arrested passing phase" and therefore only work, not enjoyment, is able to "form-and-educate."[19] That is why only the slave is really able to make history. Marx of course will take up later these considerations of Hegel in his own concept of alienated labor.

One sees how readily we can apply such a scheme to the diametrically opposed attitudes of Hananiah and Jeremiah. Jeremiah is the Slave who confronts his God, disputes with him, works over the meaning of a God who remains fundamentally *hidden,* far away, and who therefore has to be searched. Nothing is taken for granted. *Tu es deus absconditus.* There is at work in Jeremiah a fight over meaning and against illusion, a process of purification (for him God's word is both hammer and fire, Jer. 23:29-30). Not in the givenness of culture and "tradition" is the intellectual locus of Jeremiah to be found, but in the process of formation-and-education, at once dramatic and prosaic. There is in his attitude something that we could call "critical reflection" which permeates his work and search. One recalls his "Amen. May it be so!" in response to Hananiah and his reflection following this sigh (28:6-9). This is not a "word," a powerful Logos said in the name of Yahweh; on the contrary, this is only a reflection, an objection addressed to Hananiah which says: this should give you pause for thought, this should be considered also! A human and even rational reservation is here subtly and ironically opposed to a so-called "Word of God."

2. Beyond this reflective capacity is the agony too, *the agonizing confrontation with the silence of God.* Previously we said that unlike Hananiah, for whom God is here and now given and revealed, for Jeremiah God is problematic, far away, not obviously given. Now we must even say that for him God is silent and absent. "And the prophet Jeremiah went his way" (28:11). It is interesting to note that Jeremiah always put himself on the side of the cheated and deceived, of his people's lostness and helplessness (e.g., 4:10). Praxis meant in our first point the critical "working through" of the truth, the reflection that takes *distance,* the difference; now praxis means also the deep *solidarity* of the prophet with his deceived people, with the lost and powerless.

3. We must also include here Jeremiah's concrete and theoretical fight against alienation and reification on every level. In addition to praxis as a critical reflection and as passion and agony, praxis means also *the concrete liberating struggle against alienation.* Note the critique of the idols, of Judah's infidelity and untruthfulness, of royal and ruling class deeds (e.g., 22:13-17, against Jehoiakim).

4. Finally, we must emphasize the openness of Jeremiah's praxis to newness and *innovation.* It is striking to notice Jeremiah's own attitude of openness toward new deeds that may be accomplished by God, new horizons opened by history. Zimmerli understands Jeremiah's going away and apparent escape and silence as a self-criticism (28:11): "The Word of God is not his own Word."[20] Of vss. 12-14, Zimmerli says: "To the prophet who has departed the scene obediently *to listen afresh,* the mission is given anew."[21] As far as the new horizons opened by history are concerned, I would say that Jeremiah is simply a far better interpreter of his time, and of the time to come, than Hananiah — a

better interpreter of Babylonian imperialism and, beyond that, of exile, purification, and possibility of renewal. (See the promise of a *new* covenant, Jer. 31:31-34.) "The Lord has not sent you" (28:15) can be translated: "You did not persevere in the discipline of listening," so that the discipline, cost of discipleship, means not only critical reflection but also discipline, hard work to *listen to new facts*, to the newly emergent.

To return to Châtelet's definition of ideology, one can say therefore that Jeremiah's implicit cultural formation (the hidden God as the Other/God coming under the auspices of history's inescapability and leading to the agony of Israel through exile, death, and loss of world toward the promise of new life) and his *explicit cultural production* (the transforming of the wooden yoke into "bars of iron," i.e., the relation of inexorable dependence on the Babylonian Empire) are just as much an "ideological" formation/production as Hananiah's own "ideological" formation/production. The only difference—which is decisive indeed—is *how* this formation/production is used and thus how it *functions* within the socio-historical conditions. Our assumption, our wager, is that Jeremiah's "ideology" functions as a praxis—as a breakthrough permitting the maximum *actual* consciousness of Israel's people to be transformed into the maximum *potential* consciousness, and as a "working through" of what has been made of them by history.

Praxis as critical reflection, as agony, as denunciation of alienation, and as innovating process makes possible a breakthrough toward newness, toward fresh fields of possibility, toward project. This is of course not to imply that Jeremiah's statement would suddenly and miraculously appear as a nonideological one (fairy's wand), but this is simply to say that praxis permits us to dispose of a relative criterion of differentiation and of a relative means of participating in the truth—despite, or better *because* of, our conditioning.

Against idealism, whereby consciousness itself seems to give birth to the world of things, the strength of Marxism has always consisted of its insistence that one succeeds in putting human thought *at a distance* from its conditioning—a conditioning that it never ceases to reflect—only to the degree that *human thought proves itself capable of transforming the world, of transforming the very conditioning that it reflects.* That is the deepest meaning of the philosophy of praxis, innovating praxis.

On the other hand, however, the great contribution of phenomenology is also that it reminds us that such a distance can only be achieved as thought proves itself capable of positing to itself, *of returning to itself the question of the foundation of what it affirms as true.* This is the phenomenological *epochè* or "suspension" of meaning (see again 28:6, "May it be so!"—suspension of judgment; Jeremiah simply does not know). Hegel asserted: "What is *familiar* is not *known*," which is exactly the epistemological presupposition of Jeremiah's whole attitude. This must be said against forms of materialism and naturalism whereby consciousness is seen as automatically engendered by the things, by the world, and by conditioning itself.

Praxis and Epochè: these are the two modern names for Jeremiah's words and deeds. How now to reconcile Marxism and phenomenology, Marx and

Kierkegaard, I do not know. This is the problem of my generation. In any case, throughout this whole discussion we have dealt with the central problem that I see as the modern problem par excellence: *where* does illusion cease and *where* does truth begin? What are the conditions for the actualization of such a process? What is a *critique* of theological Logos today in the light of Kant and of the three masters of suspicion: Marx, Nietzsche, and Freud?

We are brought to say that the stake of all importance, at the heart of ourselves, between the authentic and the inauthentic is the meaning that we give to the affirmation. What do we affirm? What is our source, our resource of affirmation?[22]

My wager, I repeat, is that this old text already knew and dealt before us and for us with this ultimate question. Logos *or* Praxis? *Nobody* can finally give us a sure answer to that—and this is good. Those who use Marxism to avoid this darkness with a lazy historicism or economism not only do not know Marxism but do not know themselves. What I have said only is that with praxis we may find the concept of our question, the origin of our agony; but we are still in search of a new source of affirmation.

NOTES

1. A. S. Van der Woude, "Micah in Dispute with the Pseudo-Prophets," *VT* 19 (1969): 260.
2. For the notion of "epistemological break" see Louis Althusser, *For Marx*, trans. B. R. Brewster (New York: Random House, Vintage Books, 1970), especially the introduction, pp. 21-39. For definitions of all the Marxist terms used in this article, see the glossary, pp. 249-57.
3. Gottfried Quell, *Wahre und falsche Propheten* (1952).
4. A . Néher, *L'Essence du prophétisme* (1955), p. 102.
5 . Quoted by J. P. Siméon, "Pensée et idéologie," *Esprit* 1 (1972): 31.
6. J. P. Hyatt, *Commentary on Jeremiah*, IB, p. 1016.
7. "Overdetermined" is Althusser's term, drawn from Freud, emphasizing that a contradiction or aspect of a contradiction may be "subordinated to" or even "deprioritized by" another contradiction or aspect of a contradiction. In other words, a contradiction is never "pure and simple." See *For Marx*, pp. 87-128, "Contradiction and Overdetermination."
8. P. Berger and S. Pullberg, "Reification and the Sociological Critique of Consciousness," *New Left Review* 35 (1966): 61, 68.
9. Ibid., p. 76.
10. Ibid., p. 59.
11. Jean-Paul Sartre, *Search for a Method*, trans. Hazel E. Barnes (New York: Knopf, 1963; Random House Vintage, 1968), p. 68.
12. B. Brewster, in discussion with Berger and Pullberg in *New Left Review* 35, p. 74.
· 13. Mao Tse-tung, "On Contradiction," *Selected Works*, 4 Vols. (New York: China Books, 1967, repr. of 1937 ed.), Vol. 1, pp. 311-47.
14. E. Osswald, *Falsche Prophetie im Alen Testament* (1962).

15. Gerhard von Rad, "Die falschen Propheten," *ZAW* 10 (1933): 109-20.

16. Antonio Gramsci, *Selections from the Prison Notebooks,* trans. Quinton Hoare and Godfrey Smith (New York: International Publishers, 1973), and Guiseppe Fiori, *Antonio Gramsci: Life of a Revolutionary* (New York: Dutton, 1971), with bibliography.

17. Paul Ricoeur, "The Critique of Religion," *USQR* 28 (1973): 206-7.

18. Edmund Jacob, "Quelques remarques sur le faux prophètes," *ThZ 13* (1957): 483.

19. A. Kojève, *Introduction to the Reading of Hegel,* ed. Allen Bloom, trans. James H. Nichols, Jr. (New York: Basic Books, 1969), p. 24.

20. W. Zimmerli, "Das Wort und die Träume," *Der Grundriss* (Schweiz. reform. Monatsschrift, 1939), p. 202.

21. Ibid.

22. Paul Ricoeur, "The Language of Faith," *USQR* 28 (1973): 224.

21

NORMAN K. GOTTWALD

Social Class and Ideology in Isaiah 40–55

An Eagletonian Reading

*This is a pioneering essay in ideological criticism, an effort to under-
stand the political functions of biblical texts. Recognizing that a text has
an integrity of its own, Marxist literary critic Terry Eagleton insists also
that a text is connected in a variety of ways with a specific situation in
the larger complex of social life. The function of criticism is to reconstruct the web of social forces at work in the production of a text. Isaiah
40-55 proclaims the imminent restoration of the Judean ruling class
exiled in Babylon to govern Judah under the sponsorship of the Persian
emperor Cyrus, whom it designates as the new* messiah. *The exiles view
themselves as the once and future privileged representatives of the cosmic-political order centered in Jerusalem/Zion. The "measurable
absences" of historical realities from the text may be as telling as what
is actually expressed. Most notably, these exiles, in their excitement over
their imminent restoration, assume that the indigenous Judeans who
were not deported (the vast majority) will simply acquiesce in their
leadership. Also, they apparently arrogate to themselves, as an aristocratic oligarchy, many of the former prerogatives of the Davidic mon-
arch. Because they had little sense of the injustices inherent in the
ancient tributary mode of production and in their own unchecked interests, in this text they "bequeathed to postexilic Judah and to Dispersion*

Reprinted from *Semeia*, vol. 59, 1992, pp. 43-57.

Jewry both their intended abounding self-confidence and their unintended, indeed totally unforeseen, dragon's teeth seeding divisiveness and disillusion."

Critical biblical scholarship has done much to clarify the genre and tradition-historical ingredients of Isaiah 40-55 and has been able to give it a plausible historical setting in the last decade or two of the Neo-Babylonian Empire. Because of the way these studies have carved out their subject matters, there has been little attention to the social and ideological dimensions of the work as a whole. How exactly is the category of history to become "social" and how is the category of theology/religious symbol to become "ideological," without simply producing tautologies? One way of trying to make good this lack is to work with Terry Eagleton's proposal for reading texts "obliquely" by observing how they actively determine themselves under the constraints of a distinctive conjuncture of general mode of material production (political economy), literary mode of production, general ideology, aesthetic ideology and authorial ideology—all of which produces a unique ideology of the text.

Eagleton makes two important points: (1) the text has an integrity of its own since it is no direct transcript of anything else and cannot simply be interchanged with anything outside itself ("for a text is made of words, not needs" [186]); and (2) the text exists in a specific space within the larger complex of social life with which it is connected in a variety of ways and, as a result, its very inviolate individuality as text is itself a form of social and ideological production whose full shape we cannot see unless we work to reconstruct the web of social forces at work in the production ("The function of criticism is to refuse the spontaneous presence of the work—to deny that 'naturalness' in order to make its real determinants appear" [101]).

I shall attempt to sketch the web of social forces at their conjuncture in Isaiah 40-55 along the lines of Eagleton's categories, in order to see if this way of looking at the text illuminates it significantly. Within so short a compass, I must presuppose a number of critically derived judgments about Isaiah 40-55 which I cannot take time to argue. Chief among these, I regard this section of Isaiah as a coherent whole addressed to Jewish deportees in Babylonia in the period 550-538 B.C.E. In my view, the Oppressed Servant figure is Israel, but Israel as mirrored and modeled in the author's own relationship to his audience. The work developed over time in active dialogue and open conflict between author and audience. The aim of the author was to enlist the audience in a program of return to Judah, and that goal was attained at about the time the text was completed.

GENERAL MODE OF PRODUCTION

The forces and relations of material production in the Babylonian Empire formed a tributary mode of production in which a strong centralized state dominated an agrarian economy, siphoning off the surplus of the productive populace by means of state taxation and privately controlled rent and debt. In conquered lands, the tributary system was two-tiered in that the native tributary system largely continued to operate, although often with new functionaries, beneath an overlay of tribute exacted by the Babylonian conquerors and a balance of trade that enriched the center at the expense of the periphery.

The audience of Isaiah 40-55 was inserted into this tributary mode of production as "neutralized" ex-officials and civil servants of the defunct State of Judah who had been in Babylonian detention for two or three generations. The biblical text, admittedly confused and elliptical on details (2 Kings 24:10-16, referring to the deportation in 597 B.C.E.), specifies some of these deportees as palace officials, military officers and artisans, but it is likely that priests, musicians and other categories of government servants were included. In Babylon, these detainees were a disempowered body of skilled professionals. To the best of our knowledge, they were kept intact (at least for some time) in self-sustaining agrarian communities. Since it was the habit of ancient Near Eastern empires to make use of the talents of those it deported, it is likely that as the decades of detention passed, numbers of the deportees were taken into the Babylonian governing apparatus according to the demand for their skills, or were permitted to engage in private business.

As former government personnel in Judah, the deportees had been at the heart of the native tributary mode of production and were thus fitted in attitude and skill to become variously integrated into the tributary mode of production of Babylonia without major strain on their social class identity. The primary contradiction for these Judahites was that the Babylonian tributary system was foreign in their eyes, governed by a sovereignty other than their own. The more that they integrated into the Babylonian tributary system, the more their religio-cultural distinctiveness was threatened and the less likely it appeared that a Judahite native tributary system could ever again be realized. They were on the way to being progressively "Babylonianized." This contradiction was possible because, unlike the policy of the Assyrians toward their Israelite captives after 722 B.C.E., the Neo-Babylonians appear to have kept the Judahite political prisoners in homogeneous communities which were granted some measure of self-government.

LITERARY MODE OF PRODUCTION

Under a tributary mode of production literature is not mass produced. It is written by hand and multiple copies are the exception rather than the rule. Most literature is produced to satisfy state administrative and ideological needs, including economic and religious texts. Production and preservation of these writings are secured by a scribal profession. Outside of these higher circles of power, communication is mostly oral. Even state documents intended to be shared with a considerable audience (political edicts, festival texts, etc.) are read aloud. Orality survives to a striking extent in writing that is politically or religiously declamatory.

What then is the literary mode of production in Isaiah 40-55? Vis-à-vis the Babylonian overlord, it was most assuredly not state-originated nor would it have been state-approved, since a central theme of the text is that Babylon is soon to be overthrown. But the text, whether heard or read, presupposes a high level of literate knowledge cultivated by the prior training of the deportees as Judahite public officials and servants of state. Although this professional literacy may have been attenuated by decades of political detention, the author employs so dizzying an array of genres and motifs that we must assume an appreciable mastery of the same in his audience. Isaiah 40-55 arises at a point of conflict between two state-formed identities, the one Judahite and powerless and the other Babylonian and all-powerful. However many of these Judahites had been incorporated into Babylonian government service, this particular writing with its insistent Judahite restoration mission could not be the expression of a new Babylonian identity. And it is highly probable that it was produced and consumed under clandestine and subversive conditions.

What kind of discourse is generated in Isaiah 40-55? It is certainly persuasive speech that draws upon an array of genres shaped by many older Judahite life-settings. In this, the writer capitalizes on earlier prophetic speech but does so with a maximum of cultic genres that saturate the political thrust of the document with powerful religious associations. The imagery is exceptionally rich, as are the concentrations of key words and tradition-historical motifs that relentlessly focus Judah's rich heritage on the crucial moment for the audience. The profuseness of verbiage is disproportionate to the argumentation, almost to the point of overkill, but the elegance of language and adroit interweaving of imagery, together with shifts in mood and pace, give the work a linguistic spaciousness. Why so much speech to make so few points? And why such intense and fevered, almost hysterical, speech?

Scholars have often pondered whether Isaiah 40-55 was at first oral or written. Even if we could know, and I doubt that we can, a solution would not be of much importance apart from the more crucial question: what was the relation of author and audience in the production of the book? In Eagleton's terms, how was it produced, distributed and consumed? The direct address throughout, the impassioned rhetoric, the incorporation of audience objections directly and indirectly—all these indicate a dialogical, even conflictual, matrix for Isaiah 40-55. We are hearing one voice in a community debate in which contrary voices reverberate: What are we Judahites to do about the deepening conflict between Babylonia and Persia? Where do our interests lie in these conflicts that we do not have much power to influence? What steps do we take to protect our community and assure its future? How realistic is it to expect a return to Judah after decades of statelessness? The controlling voice in Isaiah 40-55 couches this debate in heavily religious terms by drawing on an armory of traditions and by speaking in cultic theological language that has been provocatively "secularized" by its radical application to a present political crisis.

So it appears that the matrix for Isaiah 40-55 was gatherings of Judahites where all the facets of their life were deliberated and ritualized, where the lines between "town meeting" and "public worship" were not strictly drawn. This would be a context of spontaneous debate and ritualized celebration. Isaiah 40-55 draws these spheres of communal debate and worship together in a swirl of rhetoric. Some of it may have been orally delivered, other parts read from a written text, but, in any case, it was a spoken and heard argument in the community, an argument that was wrestled with under the urgency of gathering events in the community's environment. This internal communal debate of which Isaiah 40-55 was a part shows signs of having been spread over several years. Once deliverance came and the political tension was relaxed, the present Isaiah 40-55 may have been put together as a summary of those debates over many years, but with considerable loss in the urgency of the painful disputes in which they were a partisan voice. Clearly, the immediate "consumption" of these words before the fall of Babylon was more involving and disruptive than it became when read after the event.

GENERAL IDEOLOGY

Here we must take "general" on two levels: What was general to the Babylonian tributary mode of production and what was predominant within the community of deported Judahites? The Babylonian umbrella ideology was typical of ancient Near Eastern states: the existing order of the state and of society into classes was ordained by cosmic order and in turn helped to maintain cosmic order. Subject peoples such as the Judahites deserved their inferior position as a part of this cosmic-political hegemony. To be sure, the eccentric reign of Nabonidus, the last Babylonian ruler, was regarded by many Babylonians as a threat to political and social order, and it appears that this unrest contributed to the ease of the Persian victory over Babylonia, precisely because Cyrus was seen by some Babylonians as a more effective guarantor of the cosmic-political order.

The predominant ideology of the Judahite deportees in Babylon has to be reconstructed from what Isaiah 40-55 says or implies about them, taken together with other biblical data from sources such as Jeremiah, Ezekiel, and the Deuteronomistic History. My reading is that these deportees by and large held on to their own version of tributary ideology. They saw themselves as privileged representatives of the cosmic-political order once established in Jerusalem. They resisted strongly the judgments of prophets and the Deuteronomistic History which held that the State of Judah had forfeited its claims to be a legitimate state. They perceived a gross injustice in their present powerless condition. They kept their ideology of privilege alive but it was ingrown and could find no public expression. Thus, their religion existed in a kind of limbo, meaningful for sustaining honor in a dishonorable situation but without a hopeful future. Some of these Judahites, as they moved into Babylonian service, were ready to relinquish this nagging ideological contradiction by embracing Babylonian religion and culture, as implied by the satirical diatribes of Isaiah 40-55 against the alluring cults of Babylon.

AESTHETIC IDEOLOGY

An aesthetic ideology distinguishable from general ideology is not very visible in the ancient Near Eastern tributary systems. "The arts" seem not to be thought about as such, but always as immediate and "spontaneous" expressions of the right order of things. At any rate, the imagination as the realm of the aesthetic is harnessed to the ends of lending enchantment and persuasion to the order of state and society. And the imagination is so thoroughly controlled by religious images and motifs that for Babylonians and Judahites alike aesthetic expressions were at the same time largely religious expressions.

One important distinction can be made between the Babylonian and general Near Eastern "aesthetic ideology" and that of the Judahite and general Israelite "aesthetic ideology." Whereas the visual arts are important to the former, the latter focuses on words as the primary carriers of meaning. This preference for the "mobile" power of speech, oral and written, over the "immobile" icon is a reservoir of cultural and religious tradition that the author of Isaiah 40-55 skillfully draws upon to build an imaginary world of words that he finds nearer the true state of reality than the imaginary world of decorated palaces and temples with their murals and statues. We should not inflate this into an absolute opposition between Israelite word and pagan pictorial representation, as the biblical theology movement sometimes did. After all, the writer of Isaiah 40-55 wants to reestablish Judahite institutions in Jerusalem, including a temple. But he still feels the word to be of transcending power; Israel's God will help this author "to out-talk" the Babylonians.

AUTHORIAL IDEOLOGY

The author of Isaiah 40-55 is a cipher lacking direct autobiographical or biographical information. Since we have no other texts written by this author (even if we include all or part of Isaiah 56-66 as stemming from the same hand, we still get no direct data on the author), what we can say about authorial ideology distinct from the ideology of the text is limited. We may summarize that this author is a Judahite ex-official, a master of the cultic and historical traditions of preexilic Judah, a gifted rhetorician, a committed Yahwist with an expansive monotheistic outlook, a pronounced Persian sympathizer, and the vocal supporter of an anti-Babylonian political orientation and strategy for his community.

I would articulate the commanding authorial ideology as follows: the rise and fall of tributary sovereignties is in the hands of one divine being, the God of Israel who is also the unrecognized God of the world—not only unrecognized by other nations but by the Judahites as well. The former Judahite tributary system deservedly collapsed because of infidelity to its God, but it will be restored if the present Judahites commit themselves unreservedly to a readiness to return to their homeland when the opening to do so arrives in the near future. The overriding authorial ideology is sharply focused on the prospect of a Judahite restoration by the Persians and this seems to be based upon a close reading of events in the latter years of the Babylonian imperium. The extent to which this ideology was accompanied by political strategizing is uncertain, but that some specific measures of resistance and rebellion were encouraged by the author is highly probable when the text is read at the conjuncture of all the social forces described above.

One other facet of the author's ideology deserves to be commented on and that is his fascination with the role of suffering in bringing about political change. The Judahites have suffered a lengthy detention in Babylon, diminishing them in all aspects of their personal and communal existence. This has had a disciplinary intent, preparing the people to make the last necessary costly efforts to secure restoration. Some of this needed "surplus of suffering" is to bear the ignominy of being a people whose "god" appears to have failed, both in their minds and in the view of the Babylonians. The mandate of the author is to go on practicing their religion and moral code even if that brings discrimination and contempt on them. By now they have "paid for" their former wrongdoing, so that from now on the suffering they undergo will be voluntarily taken on in order to achieve restoration and to bring other peoples to a recognition of their worship as the only valid worship of the one true God. It is a grandiose and aristocratic ideology which puts these Judahites "on the inside track" with Yahweh, ruler and imminent rearranger of world affairs. But, this can only come about if they are willing to suffer present risk and loss in the interests of a future vindication.

It is at this juncture that the Oppressed Servant figure embodies imaginatively the costly project of staying faithful against the tide of the Babylonian hegemony and the subtle attraction of Judahites to adopt that kind of hegemonic thinking. This can only have been a compelling message if it was somehow encoded in the life of the author and in the lives of those who shared his outlook, however many or few they were (it is perhaps instructive that Isaiah 65:13-16, which continues the author's tradition in Palestine after the restoration, speaks in the plural of "servants of Yahweh"). This living witness risked suffering by persistently encouraging an attitude and line of action that split the Judahite community and invited Babylonian reprisals. For this reason the Oppressed Servant encodes personal experiences of the author and/or his associates in an active mission of persuasion and resistance, even of collaboration with pro-Persian forces. The author and his like-minded associates "hide" within the Servant figure just as the author "hides" behind the entire text and yet is everywhere present within it. The indirection of the Servant portraiture reflects personal experiences of betrayal by fellow-Judahites and of eventual vindication in their eyes, experiences which become in turn an exemplary pattern for others to follow, a veritable template of Israel itself as Yahweh's Servant.

THE IDEOLOGY OF THE TEXT

The literary text is the product of a specific overdetermined conjuncture of the elements or formations set out schematically above. It is not, how-

ever, a merely passive product. The text is so constituted by this conjuncture as to actively determine its own determinants—an activity which
is most apparent in its relations to ideology (Eagleton: 63).

When we take a stance within the text and analyze its relation to history by
way of its relation to ideology, what do we see? First of all, we see that it is an
enormous dramatic production, a bricolage of fantasy, portraying the deliverance of the Jewish exiles from Babylon and their restoration to Judah accompanied by a conversion of the nations to the worship of Yahweh. I take it that
the substance of Isaiah 40-55 is written before the deliverance, even though it
may have been assembled as it stands after that event. It describes what will
happen in ecstatic and ornate language. But it is by no means simple description
or prediction. It is persuasive speech inculcating a conviction of certainty about
the events to come and eliciting the agency of the audience to help make them
happen.

The forthcoming deliverance is enacted in the imagination of discourse
between author and audience, and the very discourse itself will assist in bringing
the events to pass because the word of Yahweh is effectual through this speaker
and in this audience. Or at least it ought to be! Yet the whole project is so
"iffy," depends upon so many variables, is so vulnerable to Judahite self-doubt
and irresolution, that author and audience don't know until the very last minute
if it will really happen. The dramatic production of the work is a creative act
to make the deliverance and restoration so palpable to the community's imagination that, believing it actual, the audience will join the author to make it
happen insofar as the deliverance depends upon them. Yahweh's "new thing"
is imaginatively enacted before the audience's eyes so that these blind and deaf
servants of Yahweh will see and hear, and thereby become "new beings" for
"the new day."

Such is "the pseudo-real" that Isaiah 40-55 conjures up. Is it capricious
fantasy or does it bear a coherent ideological formation that signifies history?

> History, then, certainly "enters" the text, ... but it enters it precisely as
> ideology, as a presence determined and distorted by its measurable
> absences. ... History, one might say, is the *ultimate* signifier of literature,
> as it is the ultimate signified. For what else in the end could be the source
> and object of any signifying practice but the real social formation which
> provides its material matrix? The problem is not that such a claim is false,
> but that it leaves everything exactly as it was. For the text presents itself
> to us less as historical than as a sportive flight from history, a reversal
> and resistance of history, a momentarily liberated zone in which the exi-
> gencies of the real seem to evaporate, an enclave of freedom enclosed
> within the realm of necessity. ... But it is precisely in this absence of the
> particular real that the text most significantly refers—refers, not to con-
> crete situations, but to an ideological formation (and hence, obliquely, to
> history) which "concrete conditions" have actually produced. The text
> gives us such ideology without its real history alongside it, as though it

were autonomous. . . . If it seems true that at the level of the text's "pseudo-real" — its imaginary figures and events — "anything can happen," this is by no means true of its ideological organization; and it is precisely because *that* is not true that the free-wheeling contingency of its pseudo-real is equally illusory. The pseudo-real of the literary text is the product of the ideologically saturated demands of its modes of representation (Eagleton: 72-74).

In the interests of gauging the ideological organization of Isaiah 40-55, I shall look into two noteworthy "measurable absences" of history from this text. Both of them have to do with the structure and leadership of the restored community of Judah which the text anticipates. Nothing explicit is said about the role of Judahites who are still living in Judah, and nothing explicit is said about the constitution of the new community. At most, we have scant hints about these crucial matters.

1. Judahites living in Judah. From the biblical texts we know that sizable numbers of Judahites remained in the land after the destruction of Judah in 586. They consisted of the poorer folk for the most part (2 Kings 25:12), but included Judahite armed units that had fled to the countryside as well as those officials willing to cooperate with the Babylonians by serving in the administrative apparatus of the Babylonian province whose capital was set up at Mizpah with Gedaliah as the governor (2 Kings 25:22-26, with an elaborated account in Jeremiah 40-43:7). Estimates of the size of the Babylonian deportation vary greatly, but, most generously, it would not have been more than 10 percent of the total populace. Even with attrition from subsequent deportations and flight, by the time of the restoration the population of Judah would have been vastly larger than the several thousand Judahite ex-officials who hoped to return. In short, they were not returning to an empty land. Oddly, it is only in their role as a faceless chorus welcoming the returnees that Isaiah 40-55 acknowledges these indigenous Judahites. What measure should we take of this absence?

One explanation is that the author is not concerned with the populace in Judah because he is so far removed from that land that he lacks knowledge of what is happening there. To be sure, we don't know how detailed his knowledge was, but we do know from Jeremiah and Ezekiel that communication between Judah and Babylon was thriving in the earlier exilic period and there is no reason to think that it stopped later on. Particularly because of their professional training and likely service in Babylonian administration, the Judahite ex-officials would have had every occasion to be informed about the general state of affairs in Judah as a Babylonian province, and in fact to know of it in a fairly detailed way from time to time. The omission of the undeported Judahites from the purview of Isaiah 40-55 must be accounted for in some other way.

The absence is most likely the result of disputed claims to leadership over the Judahite community. The deported Judahites were the officials who last ruled in Jerusalem when Judah was an autonomous state. They still wore the mantle of leadership as far as they were concerned. If Judah was to be rebuilt as a more autonomous political entity, they would be the ones to lead. In addition, the notion that exile had "purified" and uniquely qualified the deport-ees to lead a reconstituted Judahite polis was one of the ways they gave positive meaning to all that they had undergone in Babylonia. They had suffered much, and they apparently did not count the suffering of their fellows in Judah during the same period to have carried the same elevating disciplinary effect they had experienced. So Isaiah 40-55, sharing this sense of "exilic privilege" with its audience and savvy about Babylonian and Persian politics, does not seem to reflect any interest in what the Judahites at home will think about the return of the former Judahite elite. The assumption is either that they will welcome the returning deportees with open arms, or, whatever the attitude of the native Judahites, they will have to acquiesce in the leadership of the returning elite who will carry the stamp of Cyrus's approval. So it seems that either naiveté or "hard ball" politics, or an element of both, governs the author's disinterest in the people back home.

Judging from Isaiah 56-66, written after the return but in the style and tradition of chapters 40-55, the issue of the legitimacy of the returning lead-ership did become a major bone of contention during the decades following restoration. Because portions of Isaiah 56-66 question, even refuse to recognize, the legitimacy of the leadership in power, we may perhaps conjecture that the "innocence" of Isaiah 40-55 about the Judahites in Judah was the reflexive blindspot of an aristocratic ex-official who simply assumed that his confreres, having "learned their lesson" in exile, would be a noble and just body of leaders who would behave differently than had their forefathers who governed in Jeru-salem.

In Lamentations, on the other hand, we have a glimpse of the indigenous Judahite community that remained on the land and carried on its worship at the site of the destroyed temple. We read there of their disillusion with the Davidic dynasty and with the corrupt leadership of officials, priests and proph-ets. In 5:7 we probably find a dismissive reference to them, "Our fathers [= for-mer leaders?] sinned and are no more; and we bear their iniquities." It is hardly likely that these folk would gladly receive back the descendants of that dis-credited leadership "sight unseen" merely because they asserted a claim and had Persian authorization to back them. The one reference in Lamentations to the end of exile does not imply that the released exiles will initiate and lead the restoration of Judah (4:22).

In short, Isaiah 40-55 in its exuberance for return assumes a politically passive and culturally/religiously insignificant populace in Judah, waiting to be shaped by the very descendants of the officials who had led them to ruin in the first place. Thus, we must conclude that in the author's mind, and in the view of his audience as well, the imaginative figures of Jacob/Israel, Lady Zion and the Oppressed Servant of Isaiah 40-55 are supremely, even exclusively, those Judahites who were detained in Babylon.

2. The Constitution of the Restored Community. Apart from the overriding assumption that the returned exiles will form the leadership of restored Judah, there are I think only two oblique indicators of the anticipated governing shape of the restored community from which we may draw inferences about the way the ideology of this text signifies the concrete conditions of struggle over the political structuring of the restoration.

One indicator is the identification of Cyrus as Yahweh's "messiah" (45:1) and the other is the announcement of a covenant between Yahweh and the community addressed which is described as incorporating and continuing Yahweh's "dependable covenant loyalties to David" (55:3-5). What may we infer about the political framework of restoration otherwise absent from the author's program for the future?

The extraordinary designation of Cyrus as "messiah" is not simply a loosely awarded honorific title. It means that the political functions connected with the Davidic dynasty are to be transferred to the Persian head of state. This bold move rests upon the author's conviction that Cyrus will become a worshiper of Yahweh and give favored treatment to restored Judah as the center of worship and instruction for Yahwism in its new role as the religion of the empire. But the specifically "moral" and "religious" functions of the Davidic ruler as "witness" (*'ed*), "leader" (*nagid*) and "command-giver" (*meṣawweh*) to the nations will be assigned to the returning exiles. This transfer of aspects of Davidic authority to the community of exiles represents a certain "democratization" of royal rule, but it is hardly an egalitarian conception. It appears to operate within the controlling assumption that the purified exiles will be "more equal" than those who escaped exile. The announced covenant with the community of exiles implies an aristocratic oligarchy who, within the structure of the Persian political imperium, will have free hand to develop the internal life of restored Judah so as to make it an example and witness to the worshipers of Yahweh throughout the empire. As far as I can see, within this implied project there is no specification of separate priestly and lay roles.

My conclusion is that Isaiah 40-55 parcels out the functions of the former Davidic dynasty, some to Cyrus and some to the exiled community, thereby dissolving any need for a Judahite prince. This differs from other programmatic visions of the restored community deriving from exile. Ezekiel provided for a Judahite "prince" with sharply reduced powers so that social injustices could no longer corrupt the religious life of the people which henceforth would be fully under direct priestly control (45:7-12). The Deuteronomistic History, by closing with reference to favored treatment given Jehoiachin in exile in 561 B.C.E., also implies a continuation of the Davidic line as a possible kernel of hope for eventual restoration (2 Kings 25:27-30). The author of Isaiah 40-55 takes a step farther in discountenancing any Davidic rule, conferring instead a "Davidic" legitimacy on Persian overlordship and on supervision of Yahwism as the established religion of the empire by a cadre of purified exiles. In one stroke, the Davidic covenant, with its close intermesh of politics and religion, is preserved in principle—but without David's dynastic successors having a part to play.

That this apparent dismissal of the Davidic dynasty is never openly stated, but merely implied inadvertently, is probably due to internal communal disputes. Doubtless many of the exiles could only imagine a Judahite restoration that involved a renewal of the Davidic dynasty, at whose pleasure they had once served. It would have endangered the author's mission to unify the exiles in a pro-Persian stance had he stirred up "a hornet's nest" over the future of the Davidic dynasty. He could intuit that a Judahite restoration without a native prince would "sit better" with the Persians who could keep a closer political rein on the region if it were a Babylonian province rather than a vassal prince-dom. Possibly he shared the view of Ezekiel that a Davidic king might jeopardize the religious integrity of the community. In the last analysis, Isaiah 40-55 operates out of the reality of the exilic community as a more or less self-governing body which did not have a single head, much less a Davidic prince over it. By means of a collegial style of self-government, that community had managed to keep a Judahite and Yahwistic identity alive and thus constituted living proof that a viable Judahite entity could be reestablished and protected without a native dynasty. So our author chose the path of indirection in treating this topic, merely adumbrating that Davidic values and functions would not be lost when the Persian ruler and the purified exiles took power.

CONCLUSION

The measurable absences we have examined in the text of Isaiah 40-55, if I have discerned their ideological import aright, raise large questions about the "liberative" platform which has often been seen in this work. The exuberant universalist rhetoric has seemed to imply large humanizing goals. Taking the book of Isaiah as a whole, we are, I think, inclined to read into Isaiah 40-55 the same social ethical critique of Judahite political and religious power evident in major sections of chapters 1-12, 28-31 and 56-66. But our inquiry has shown that such a critique is at best presupposed or implied in chapters 40-55 and is, in any case, vitiated by the supreme confidence of the author that the exiled ex-officials in Babylonia are fully competent to lead a restored community with-out explicit provision of safeguards against the abuses and corruptions of the tributary mode of production that undermined the old Davidic rule in Jerusa-lem—and, moreover, with no felt need to enlist the undeported populace of Judah substantively in their project.

To be sure, it is not as though the author of Isaiah 40-55 rebuts the critique, or even quibbles with it; it is rather that he assumes it to have been vindicated and decisively transcended by the sufferings of exile. The fact that after the restoration some of those who shared his rhetoric and aspirations felt compelled to take up a severe critique of the new leadership (Isa. 56:9-57:13; 66:1-4) shows that the author's ideology of the exiles' virtue and competency to lead a reformed people was as precarious and excessive as his confidence that the inhabited world would convert to Yahweh.

The "hollow" that Isaiah 40-55 "has scooped out between itself and history" to use Eagleton's phrase, is the ideological formation of a professional political and religious elite possessing the means and confidence to be the bearers of historic change in the redivision of the political and religious map of the ancient Near East. As it turned out, this ideology and its bearers did contribute centrally to the restoration that slowly and arduously took root in Judah over the following century, although without the empire-wide effects that Isaiah 40-55 expected. They thereby bequeathed to postexilic Judah and to Dispersion Jewry both their intended abounding self-confidence and their unintended, indeed totally unforeseen, dragon's teeth seeding divisiveness and disillusion.

BIBLIOGRAPHY

Ackroyd, Peter R.
  1968   *Exile and Restoration: A Study of Hebrew Thought of the Sixth Century B.C.* Philadelphia: Westminster Press.

Amin, Samir
  1980   *Class and Nation: Historically and in the Present Crisis.* New York/London: Monthly Review Press.

Clines, David J. A.
  1976   *I, He, We, and They: A Literary Approach to Isaiah 53.* Sheffield: *JSOT Sup* 1.

De Gruchy, Steve and Guthey, Eric
  1986   "Deutero-Isaiah: Prophet to the Exiled Elite. Class Struggle in Isaiah 40-55." Paper submitted to a seminar on Deutero-Isaiah, Union Theological Seminary, New York, Fall Semester.

Eagleton, Terry
  1976   *Criticism and Ideology. A Study in Marxist Literary Theory.* London: Verso Editions.

Eissfeldt, Otto
  1962   "The Promises of Grace to David in Isaiah 55:1-5." Pp. 196-207 in *Israel's Prophetic Heritage. Essays in Honor of James Muilenburg.* Ed. B. W. Anderson and W. Harrelson. New York: Harper & Row.

Gadd, C. J.
  1958   "The Haran Inscriptions of Nabonidus." *Anatolian Studies* 8: 35-92.

Gitay, Yehoshua
  1980   "Deutero-Isaiah: Oral or Written?" *JBL* 99: 185-97.

Gottwald, Norman
  1985a   "Contemporary Studies of Social Class and Social Stratification and a Hypothesis about Social Class in Monarchic Israel." Paper presented to the Seminar on Sociology of the Monarchy, ASOR-SBL, Annual Meeting in Anaheim, CA.
  1985b   *The Hebrew Bible. A Socio-Literary Introduction.* Philadelphia: Fortress Press.
  1992   "Sociology of Ancient Israel." In *The Anchor Bible Dictionary* Vol. 6, pp. 79-89. Garden City, N.Y.: Doubleday.

Hollenberg, D. E.
  1969   "Nationalism and 'the Nations' in Isaiah 40-55." *VT* 19: 23-36.

Janssen, Enno
  1956   *Juda in der Exilszeit. Ein Beitrag zur Frage der Entstehung des Judentums.* Goettingen: Vandenhoeck & Ruprecht.

McLennan, Gregor
  1981   *Marxism and the Methodologies of History.* London: Verso Editions.

Miller, John W.
  1970   "Prophetic Conflict in Second Isaiah: The Servant Songs in the Light of Their Context." Pp. 77-85 in *Wort—Gebot—Glaube. Beitraege zur Theologie des Alten Testamens.* Ed. J. J. Stamm. Zurich: ATANT 59.
Oded, Bustenay
  1977   "Judah and the Exile" (Parts 6-7). Pp. 476-89 in *Israelite and Judaean History.* Ed. J. H. Hayes and J. M. Miller. Philadelphia: Westminster Press.
Smith, Daniel L.
  1989   *The Religion of the Landless. The Social Context of the Babylonian Exile.* Bloomington, IN: Meyer-Stone Books.
Smith, Morton
  1963   "II Isaiah and the Persians." *JAOS* 83: 415-21.
Smith, Sidney
  1924   *Babylonian Historical Texts Relating to the Capture and Downfall of Babylon.* London: Oxford University Press.
  1944   *Isaiah Chaps. XL-LV: Literary Criticism and History.* London: Oxford University Press.
Whybray, R. N.
  1978   *Thanksgiving for a Liberated Prophet: An Interpretation of Isaiah 53.* Sheffield: *JSOT Sup* 4.
Wilkie, J. M.
  1951   "Nabonidus and the Later Jewish Exiles." *JTS* 2: 34-44.

22

ROBERT B. COOTE AND MARY P. COOTE

Power, Politics, and the Making of the Bible

The Torah

It has long been recognized that the Hebrew Bible, and in particular the Torah or Pentateuch, was the product of several stages of collection, composition, reframing, and editing. Over several generations of investigation, scholars even reached consensus regarding the historical occasions of the various "strands" of the Pentateuch. As with the similar compositional layers in the prophetic books, however, it has seldom been asked what the political purpose of the various stages of composition may have been. In broad strokes the Cootes sketch how, at each stage in the making of the Torah, legends were recast, history rewritten, and legal traditions reformed to legitimate the newly dominant rulers. Thus the layers of the Pentateuch can be seen taking shape in the context of each successive major stage in the history of Israel and Judah. By gaining a sharper appreciation of the dominant ideology of the Torah as legitimation of the ruling regime, it should then be possible to discern the different "voices" or "layers" of material reused and reframed according to the interests of the rulers but nevertheless preserving frequent "subversive memories." Here also is a critical perspective for what has recently emerged as "canonical criticism," a recognition of the political interests dominant at each major stage in the process of "canonization."

Reprinted from Robert B. Coote and Mary P. Coote, *Power, Politics, and the Making of the Bible* (Minneapolis: Fortress Press, 1991), 3–5, 7, 23, 25–30, 40–42, 59–80, abridged.

Despite the variety of their contents, the Hebrew scriptures have one main subject—rulers of Jerusalem between 1000 and 150 B.C.E. and the people of Palestine under their rule. These people are variously called Israelites (Israelis are citizens of the modern state of Israel and played no role in the biblical period), Judeans, Jews, and, rarely, Hebrews, terms whose meaning will become clear. The Hebrew scriptures consist mainly of the scriptures of the temple cult of the god Yahweh in Jerusalem. The purpose of this cult was to legitimate rulers in Jerusalem, and this is what the scriptures are mostly about. Indeed, the writers of the scriptures became particularly active when rule changed hands and a new version of legitimacy had to be devised.

The initial purpose of the temple and its scriptures was to legitimate the ruling house of David (1000-520 B.C.E.) and after that the ruling priests established in David's name under Persian, Hellenistic, and Roman rule (520 B.C.E.-70 C.E.). For this reason, and not from a failure to realize that history means more than politics, the history of the biblical period pays particular attention to rule. Since the history of rule was mainly the history of men's rule, this history is mainly a history of men.

The three groups of the Hebrew scriptures in Jewish usage—Torah, Prophets, Writings—are of roughly equal length, but not of equal importance. The Torah was the most important. It contained the basic legal instruction and founding history of the nation Israel. (The concept of nation suggests a political consensus among the subjects ruled by Jerusalem; this rarely if ever existed, but the scribes who wrote the Bible worked for rulers who said it did.) The Torah legitimated the temple priesthood, the rulers of Jerusalem and its hinterland during the Persian, Hellenistic, and Roman periods—six hundred years. The Torah pictured the "nation" prior to its capture of Palestine, when Moses, who never set foot across the Jordan, delivered its laws. It described the priestly cult of a later period as though it originated in this early time. Surprisingly, it mentions neither Jerusalem nor the temple, both essential to its centuries-long importance.

The Bible's earliest history, which historians call "J," embedded in a third of the Torah, was written in David's court to present the history of David's nation as David saw it. It explained how Judah and Israel were supposedly united against the threat of Egypt, David's arch opponent. A generation later, when people in Israel, led by Jeroboam, overthrew the house of David, the rebel court retained David's history of Israel but made many additions to it. These additions are called "E." Another major addition, of priestly traditions called "P," was added by a class of Jerusalem priests exiled to Babylon after the destruction of Solomon's temple and then reinfranchised under Persian rule. The result was the Tetrateuch, or first four books of the Bible, consisting of three overlapping justifications of rulers' cults composed for three rulers or ruling groups at the beginning of their rule, when each seized power from another (David, Jeroboam, priests: J, E, P). Later Deuteronomy joined to make the Pentateuch (Greek for "fivefold unit"), or Torah.

Israel developed into a highland power on an expanding agricultural base as a result of three changes in the circumstances of empires competing in Palestine: the fall of the Hittite empire, the Philistine takeover of the Egyptian positions in Palestine, and the withdrawal of Egypt. A brief release from imperial pincers allowed the tribal confederation of Israel to expand its settlements from the northern lowlands and frontier to the central highlands and assert itself as a political power.

DAVID BEGINS THE BIBLE

With imperial competitors temporarily withdrawn, the two local powers took up the fight over the Palestinian bone. By the mid-eleventh century the Philistines, organized in a warlord confederacy of palace cities on the coast and lowlands, had consolidated their hold in the former Egyptian strongholds and were campaigning into the hills to seize trade routes, subdue tribal forces, and take over tribal lands and workers. Responding to this threat in the north and central highlands, the sheikhs of Israel tightened their traditional tribal form of rule, allowing the hierarchy to become more sharply defined. Before long encroaching Philistine urban rule was met by Israel's tribal monarchy.

Saul nearly succeeded in driving the Philistines and their allies from the highland watershed and upper Jordan Valley back to the coast. But the Philistines united to crush him, and Saul and three of his four sons perished in battle. What remained of Palestine not yet under Philistine control now fell into two parts. In the north, the surviving son of Saul, Ishbaal, whose name suggests a connection with the cults of Baal, took command of Israel, supported by Saul's cousin and commander Abner. Newly settled Judah in the south fell to David, a younger son in a large family from Bethlehem fathered by Jesse.

David had begun his ambitious rise in Saul's service and married Saul's daughter Michal. Looking to his own advancement, he was dismissed for insubordination. He relocated to the wilderness to the south and east of Judah and gathered an outlaw band of mercenary troops under his command. Apparently lacking support in his own family, except for some nephews, his sister's sons, whom he used and later discarded, and thus unhampered by kinship ties, David built his power by marrying into powerful and wealthy families. Although he temporarily lost Michal in his conflict with Saul, after Saul's defeat, from which he was conveniently absent, he acquired Saul's wife Ahinoam, who bore his first son. By then he had established marriage ties with the Calebites, the leading family of Hebron, by arranging the death of his own brother-in-law, a Calebite, and marrying the widow, his sister Abigail, thus becoming a wealthy landowner.

Aside from his marriages, David derived support mainly from Israel's enemy, the Philistines. In return for leading his gang for Philistine overlords in campaigns against desert tribes like the Amalakites, he received Ziklag south of Gath as a fief, a plentiful source of provisions and a base for handing out his own fiefs to his troops. Before long he became a quasi-tribal sheikh on the dryland border, with an urban base and control over extensive marginal and uncultivated lands and their flocks, as well as trade routes to the southwest and southeast. On his return to the hills with a large and eclectic troop that included Philistines and other European hired fighters, he captured Hebron and declared himself king of Judah. He then moved against Ishbaal to claim Saul's Israel. Linked to Saul's household by his alliance with the now-deceased Jonathan, Saul's son, and by reunion with Michal, David profited from the murders of Abner and Ishbaal to become king of Israel, though publicly he condemned the assassinations. Later he captured Jerusalem, a fortress town controlling an important route between coast and Jordan Valley, and moved his capital there, to the border between his united kingdoms. From this position he proceeded to overthrow rulers in all directions and create his own Asian empire. Thus, using Philistine forces, David, the one-time Philistine vassal, was able to fulfill for Israel the Philistine dream of controlling nearly all Palestine from the Red Sea to the northern Bika Valley in Lebanon. His next task was to co-opt the support of the tribes, to avert the hostility they were bound to feel toward one who had risen through the lowland network.

Except among his own gang, David was never popular, but he earned a measure of tolerance from his subjects thanks to his practical restraint in government and skillful public relations. (David's son Solomon, despite his reputation, was not nearly so clever.) David maintained royal rule over the tribal highlands by allowing tribal jurisdiction to take its traditional course in that area and by rewarding his supporters and palace staff with the yield of his external conquests rather than granting fiefs in Israelite territory. Lighter taxes were laid on the Israelite villagers than on conquered peoples. He achieved tenuous security on his borders through alliances, for example with the Phoenician coastal city Tyre, and by placing garrisons in strategic localities. He also settled Levites, a tribe of priests loyal to tribal ideals, with domicile and pasture rights but no permanent landholdings, in towns and villages on the frontier and lowlands and in Saul's former domain in Benjamin. He buttressed his throne with propaganda, promoting his success and the legitimacy of his rule in literature and ritual.

This one-man show could hardly last. Opposition to David's rule even at home came during his lifetime from defeated rivals in the families of Saul and Caleb, and from his own sons, most notoriously Abishalom (Absalom). His successor Solomon proved unable to retain the whole of David's realm and enforced such tyranny on the tribes that the next king lost all but Judah, where, however, the descendants of David (at least nominally) ruled for another four hundred years.

In David's realm, the traditional patterns of tribal jurisdiction prevailed in most aspects of highland life, while state jurisdiction on the Egyptian model, possibly learned from the Philistines, was superimposed where necessary to maintain royal authority, such as in requisitioning corvée labor (under the minister of labor, Adoram) to build the fortifications for Jerusalem. Parallel hierarchies, tribal and state, functioned in military and cult administration. Although the tribal militia was maintained under the command of David's nephew Joab, David's personal guard and troop of Europeans (Cerethites and Pelethites: Cretans and Aegeans), commanded by his crony Benaiah from the extreme south of Judah, formed the real heart of Israel's military force. In the cult, Abiathar of the house of Eli presided over the vestiges of the tribal cult of Shiloh and the tribal mobile battle palladium, the chest (ark) of Yahweh, and probably supervised the scattered Levite cults. Zadok, the reputed founder of the long-standing priestly line attached to the Davidic dynasty, ruled David's house cult in Jerusalem, which was probably conducted, at least at first, in a tent shrine in deference to tribal custom, as well as David's pilgrimage cult in the Sinai, on the border with Egypt. The state god to whom David's cult was devoted was Yahweh (translated LORD in many English versions), the Israelite manifestation of the warrior El as the chief god of the confederated tribes. (Yahweh was also referred to as El and, using an honorific plural, as Elohim, both usually translated God.) Benaiah and Zadok, the army and the cult, represented the twin bulwarks of David's throne and of Solomon's in the next generation.

Literature from David's court formed the germ of what became the Hebrew scriptures. It was not produced for popular consumption, literacy being limited to a few wealthy and the scribes in wealthy employ, but to appeal to the powerful few whose support David needed. Only a tiny fraction of David's subjects knew or cared what it said.

To legitimate his rule in broader terms, David, like any winner in historical conflict, needed a general history of his subjects that would show the inevitability of his success. This became the kernel of the later Torah. A large portion of Genesis and Exodus and some of Numbers, known as J (its writer is sometimes called the Yahwist), were composed as a history of early Israel from the creation of the world and its human inhabitants through the creation of Israel. Based in the literary tradition of Mesopotamia familiar to David's scribes, creation stories were appropriated to put Israel in a universal framework on a par with great powers like Egypt. The history was also designed to appeal for the loyalty of tribal sheikhs in the Negeb and Sinai, David's buttress against Egypt in the south, by suggesting that Israel's early chiefs, the patriarchs, were southern sheikhs like themselves rather than northern highland or presettlement sheikhs. Furthermore in the story Abram, introduced into Israel's tradition as its ancestor, must migrate from the east to facilitate a transition from Mesopotamian stories of early humanity to early Israelite history. Another new ancestor, Isaac, is pictured at peace with the Philistines: Egypt is the common enemy, contrary to what an Israelite might have continued to believe, given Egypt's earlier tie to Israel's chiefs and Egypt's support of Israel as the struggle against the Philistines developed.

David's scribe used tribal nomenclature and copied David's twelve-tribe structure of administration in order to foster the integration of tribes like Judah with Israel. History was reversed so that some historical latecomers to the highland conglomerate, members crucial to expansion of David's rule, like Simeon and Judah, were made older than Joseph and Benjamin, the representatives of heartland Israel. Manasseh and Ephraim, representing the territories settled first and the heartland of potential opposition to Davidic rule, were even placed in the following generation, mere sons of Joseph. All the tribal brothers, however, were reconciled to one another, in particular Judah and Joseph through the deference of Judah, in united opposition to the "national" enemy, Egypt. Egypt, on the brink of further adventurism in Palestine, was the principal enemy of David's Israel, now that his kingdom had been consolidated with the help of Philistines. So Egypt became the villain of the history, even though Israel in fact took form under Egyptian aegis.

Thus the formative event in David's history of Israel was escape from corvée labor for Egypt in the Delta, the main theme of the book of Exodus, not from the real threat to its heartland from the Philistines, with whom Israel had long contended, to say nothing of the threat from the likes of David himself. Moses, the putative forebear of David's supporters, the Levites, though in reality possibly a Palestinian in Egyptian administration, was linked with a traditional story of south Palestinian pastoral nomads and Hijazi Midianites and his authority made absolute, as by implication David's should be. Moses' name is given to the author of David's law, which was limited to the rules of David's cult, focused on an earthen altar and featuring the traditional harvest festivals of barley, wheat, and dry-season fruits. The conclusion of the history was that any attempt to subvert the sacral legitimation of David's rule and its blessings, endorsed by vassal kings, was an outrage against none other than the divine creator.

This history also includes reflections of pre-Davidic eleventh century compositions, shaped by their placement in the J document. Examples include Miriam's victory song in Exodus 15, Israel's blessing of his tribal sons in Genesis 49, and four blessings of Israel by a non-Israelite mantic named Balaam in Numbers 23-24. Similar to Miriam's song and possibly older, the song of Deborah in Judges 5, celebrating a tribal victory over urban forces out of Hazor in northern Palestine, indicates a pattern of women's victory song in Israelite tradition.

REVOLUTION IN ISRAEL

Solomon's son Rehoboam succeeded to the throne undisputed in Judah but needed confirmation from the local magnates in Israel that was not forthcoming. His attempt to intensify corvée labor in Israel for the royal court ("My father disciplined you with whips, but I will discipline you with barbed lashes") was rejected by a coalition of villagers, magnates, saints, and some factions dissatisfied with Solomon's tyranny and backed by Egypt. In a bona fide village revolt, rarely depicted in the Bible, time-worn Adoram, still administering corvée for David's grandson, was stoned to death and Rehoboam was forced to withdraw. Escaping from forced labor for Jerusalem, Israel in effect seceded from Judah and the rest of Solomon's kingdom and gained a temporary respite from tyranny.

The throne of Israel was restored by one Jeroboam, who had been Solomon's corvée administrator in Ephraim but, becoming disaffected with his royal master, had taken refuge in Egypt along with other rebels against Solomon's tyranny and gathered a band of supporters around him in exile, just as David had built his strength among the Philistines. Perhaps opportunely he was thus absent from Israel during the anti-Adoram putsch, just as David claimed to have missed the killing of Saul and Abner, but returned, a creature of the king of Egypt as much as of the people of Israel, to be offered the throne by the victorious forces. His installation as king was confirmed by the saint of Shiloh, Ahijah.

Jeroboam's power base was wide but shallow, requiring careful orchestrating. Once in power, he had to avoid antagonizing the tribal magnates, while proceeding to exercise the royal authority of his models David and Solomon. He recruited some support among the rebels against Solomon's rule by conceding authority to tribal magnates, restoring the village militia, protecting villagers' legal rights against magnates, and respecting tribal custom. But he himself undertook a royal building program, requiring corvée labor (in whose administration he happened to be expert), in Shechem and Penuel, then moved the capital to Tirzah, his Jerusalem, just northeast of Shechem.

Jeroboam's rise to power, as we have seen, paralleled David's in several ways. This meant that Jeroboam could read J, David's victory story of Israel's escape from corvée, perhaps available to him from a royal office in Shechem or Megiddo, as his own story, with Solomon and his successors in the role of pharaoh, and Jeroboam, belonging to the tribe of Joseph and with Egyptian court experience, taking the part of Joseph and Moses (David). Indeed, in J the house of David delivered a propaganda bonanza into the hands of Jeroboam. Here is the first, but by no means the only, use of the Bible story to defy the power that commissioned its writing.

So Jeroboam adopted the scripture of the royal house whose throne in Israel he had usurped; he also had it adapted to tell his own victory story. His revisions to the J document are known as E, standing for Elohim, the designation Jeroboam used for Yahweh in order to distance himself from Solomon's version of Yahweh.

The chief concern of E is to defend Israel's revolution in the person of Jeroboam and his judiciary, and to legitimate the succession to power by his son. By implication, it was to establish Jeroboam's right to revolt against the house of David. Jeroboam had been a fatherless child, and he probably had to leave one of his own sons as hostage in the court of pharaoh. At least one other son died young. Jeroboam was preoccupied with the safety of sons as heirs, and nearly every story in E takes this as its theme.

Moreover, many of the magnates who had just thrown off the yoke of one king were hardly eager to support another. They had an urgent question to put to Jeroboam of the tribe of Joseph: "Are you to be king over us?" In E, this is the question raised by the tribes when young Joseph told them he had dreamed that they were all out in the field binding sheaves and their sheaves bowed down to his. This question is answered in the rest of E's story of Joseph: the brothers devised evil against Joseph, but God devised that the same should turn out good in the end. The official history of Israel now showed that Jeroboam's rule was God's plan. In compensation, it also showed the cults of the magnates and their jurisdictions validated, and precedents from the customary law of the land defined in writing and thus ratified by the new Israelite ruler. Where J defined only cultic law, E's rulings began by defining the limits on debt slavery and went on to deal with the other categories typical of ancient Near Eastern law, thus raising royal jurisdiction to the level of that of the people's cults. Like all privileged, Jeroboam feared himself in other men, and hence projected this fear, in the guise of cultic and judicial respect, or the "fear of God," as public policy. This, too, is a major theme of E.

Although Jeroboam's kingdom was based in the north, in his scripture he made no effort to emphasize a specifically northern, or Israelite, tradition at the expense of the southern Judahite tradition fostered by David and Solomon. Indeed, E deals with personages associated with Israel and the north only as they relate to Jeroboam's own household and activities. This is the only reason for the emphasis on Joseph, patron of Shechem. Jacob, who stands for all Israel, figures in E only as a founder of shrines at Beersheba, Gilead, Mahanaim, Penuel, an oak south of Bethel, Rachel's tomb, and especially Bethel. With the exception of the first, these outline the probable eastern and southern bounds of the kingdom of Saul, when Israel was last independent of the house of David. Generally E avoids celebrating the tribal values promoted by J in support of David's royal rule to focus in the royal jurisdiction and cults of Jeroboam, the rebel against the royal house of David.

JOSIAH AND THE DEUTERONOMISTS

By the time [King] Manasseh died in 642, magnates of Judah had long since carved out domains at the expense of the house of David, which was forced to share the taxes of Judah more widely than it liked. The magnates could blame the burden of taxation on the empire, while neglecting to mention the empire's role in backing them. If the house of David were to slip its Assyrian shackle, however, the magnates' rapacity would be exposed as the house of David rescued its popular esteem. Josiah (640-609) accomplished precisely this, and in the process had a hand in writing a quarter of the Hebrew Bible, the broad revision of the temple scriptures often called Deuteronomistic because it follows the ideas and style of the book of Deuteronomy.

At Manasseh's death, factions of magnates, some linked to Assyria, some to Egypt, competed for control of the enervated palace, while Assyria's rulers were content to watch the controlled undermining of the house of David go on. Eventually Josiah, the eight-year-old son of Manasseh's heir Amon, was elevated to the throne.

A canny youth, tutored by advisers who clotted into a faction around him, Josiah resolved to follow Hezekiah's example and reassert the royal prerogatives, and so set himself free from the grip of regent and magnate, and his nation free from Assyria, whose meteoric decline gave his cabal their chance. Egypt's help was never far away. In the year of Josiah's accession, the pharaoh began a siege of Ashdod that, according to the Greek historian Herodotus, lasted the whole of Josiah's reign. For a decade prior to Ashurbanipal's death in 627, Egypt occupied the southern coast of Palestine. Though hardly admitted in Josiah's scriptures (see, however, Deut. 23:7), Egypt and Josiah's faction made common cause against Assyria, at least until late in Josiah's reign.

Josiah made no effort to bolster Judah to the south or east. In his southern marches, he supplied Greek mercenaries working for Egypt, probably the first time since Solomon that the house of David depended on Aegean guards. To the northeast Josiah could not hold the fertile hills of Gilead, and to the east Ammon and Moab were under attack by tribes whom Josiah had no mind to challenge. Departing from royal tradition and historical precedent, he set his kingdom's border at the Jordan River. This boundary, in the Bible confined mostly to Deuteronomistic texts, so influenced the modern popular concept of the territory of "Israel" that it was used to define the British mandate and Hashemite territory in Palestine in the 1920s and thus the Zionist state of Israel in 1948, whose fixed borders (including the Occupied West Bank) are like those of no kingdom or province in the biblical period and, like the borders of all industrialized states, fail to represent the extreme variability of preindustrial dominions. For Josiah, the focus of attack was to the north, into the productive lands of ancient Davidic tenure.

As Assyrian power waned in the provinces of Samarina and Magiddu and Gilead, Josiah began a series of military rampages that left resisters, whose tenure of land traced to Jeroboam or his successors or Assyria, dead, and joiners, if indigenous, with part of their lands confirmed—by their Davidic overlord. Thus much land fell to Josiah, who, wanting not just to demote the magnates of Judah but to make them join his movement, offered them liberated lands in Israel, to which the house of David had prior claim. Its claim was made clear in the greatest literary work of Josiah's court, the Deuteronomistic History, read aloud to preempted magnates invited to do battle for new land under Josiah's Joshua-like banner. Waverers in south and north found only weak support from Egypt, until late in his reign Josiah's success and Babylon's rise threw Egypt and Josiah into opposing camps.

Josiah devoted resources to conquest in a way Hezekiah could only dream about. As recounted in his own propaganda, Josiah's program began with the standard refurbishment of the dynastic temple. In 622, in the course of repair, a document containing a long-lost set of laws of Moses was reported discovered. A woman saint named Huldah was found to verify its authenticity. It was not divulged that the document, incorporating much archaic precedent, had been penned on Josiah's orders. Following the northern pattern of a single law for cult and countryside, Josiah promulgated this law based on E's model, the law of his refurbished cult, as the law for all Israel. The proclamation of a law of redress was likewise a standard act of new administration, as in the contemporary edicts of Draco and Solon in Athens. The heart of Josiah's law was its decree governing remission of debt: "At the end of every seven-year period, you shall write off all debt" (Deut. 15:1). This decree would have put a quick and certain end to poverty, toppling magnate creditors, if Josiah could and would have enforced it. With it and others like it, Josiah appealed over the heads—or under the heels—of the magnates of Judah to the villagers they oppressed. He offered villagers relief and restitution of their patrimonies, amounting to deliverance from their patrons, a pitch for popular support David himself could have admired.

The first and foremost of the discovered laws required that the cult of Yahweh, who was "one" (Deut. 6:4), be conducted at only one shrine (Deut. 12:1–14), the temple—where Yahweh would place his name, the basis of judicial oath. Following this radical decree, Josiah eliminated from the Davidic cult all foreign, especially Assyrian, elements and demolished local altars throughout Judah. The priests and saints of Judah's cults, clients and friends of Judah's magnates, were left in their localities, but deprived of their livelihood ate now at the pleasure, and from the supplies, of the king. Bethel, the northern shrine attributed to Jeroboam, the arch rebel against the house of David, likewise had to be destroyed. Josiah ordered the priests of Bethel slaughtered and their bones burned at the shrine to its permanent defilement and seized its treasures for the house of David. From there he ravaged the entire north, as far even as Gilead, wrecking every shrine and murdering every priest he could find. The jurisdictions of the north fell into utter disarray, to be reconstructed under Josiah's reform law. A new day had dawned—in blood.

In order to wrench the populace under his rule into the unprecedented channels required by the centralization of the cult in Jerusalem, Josiah decreed that the impending Passover and all pilgrimage feasts were to be held in Jerusalem, not at family and local shrines as always in the past. At the fall festival in Jerusalem that year, the new law, Josiah's law of Moses, was read out to the assembled nation, and a similar reading prescribed for every seventh year thereafter (in the interim it sufficed to know that the king would study it every day: Deut. 17:18–20). The law of centralization, and the carnage it justified, put the house of David once again at the hub of the amassing and allocation of wealth in Judah and Israel. Josiah's resolution and prowess had overwhelmed a host of opponents in the name of one God, one cult, one law, one ruling house, and one subject people.

On the seesaw of power, prior to Josiah the house of David had been held with its feet off the ground not only by the gentry but by the priests of the temple as well. Among these the Zadokite Aaronids established by Solomon ranked high. Hezekiah had enhanced their position by reducing the influence of priests outside Jerusalem or by loosing the lands of such priests altogether. By Josiah's time, although the Aaronids like the Davidids had compromised themselves by colluding with Assyria, they had also enlarged their powers in relation to the ruling house. While needing to centralize, Josiah did not exclude the rural Levites from his cult, but ordered that they be supported in Jerusalem as subordinate priests, a halfway attempt to create a counter to the Aaronids. For the next two hundred years, the descendants of these Levites lobbied the dominant priests and Yahweh to grant them position in the cult, with privileges appropriate to the custodians of the law of Moses, while the Aaronids continued to abase them and to raise one barrier after another against their menace.

Josiah's closest priestly supporters, who represented a Levite lineage and tradition connected with Shiloh and Moses in contrast to the Zadokites connected with Bethel and Aaron, spearheaded the attempt to exclude entrenched priests from the king's inner circle. These included Josiah's chief deputy Hilkiah, made a chief priest, Shaphan, Josiah's scribe, and Ahikam his son, Jeremiah, probably the same Hilkiah's son, Shallum, Jeremiah's uncle, keeper of the royal wardrobe, and Shallum's wife Huldah, who had verified that Josiah's law was Moses'. For years, though their fortunes rose and fell, members of this circle influenced affairs in Jerusalem and saw to it that Jeremiah's pronouncements over a long career, reaching to the fall of Jerusalem, were recorded in what developed into the longest document in the Bible. But Josiah died in embarrassing ignominy, and the group never regained the dominance they had in the heady days of 622.

Led by Shaphan, Josiah's scribes undertook a full-scale history of the house of David—whose longevity now appeared matched by its strength—in the light of Josiah's triumph. Hezekiah's retouched JE, with its unpopular anti-Egyptian stance and its total neglect of Jerusalem and the temple combined with veneration of Jeroboam's Bethel, was set aside unchanged. Starting with the history of royal legitimation already on file, based on the original documents justifying David's usurpation of Israelite lands and including accounts of Solomon's glory and the numerous scandalous deeds of northern kings, Josiah's scribes produced the Deuteronomistic History in some five scrolls, Deuteronomy and the Former Prophets. Other works incorporated included some version of the deeds of chiefs and gang leaders contained in Judges 3-16.

Within the existing work, the main additions consisted of protagonists' prayers and speeches, didactic explanations by the narrator, and repeated formulaic censures of Jeroboam. As usual in such revisions, a new beginning and ending produced a shift in the work's emphasis. The history's main theme became the law behind Josiah's resurgence, how it was produced, used by Joshua to conquer the land, then lost, then refound by Josiah. Drawing on much earlier tradition and record, the additions determined the basic meaning of the work: even more than David, Josiah was the fulfillment of Yahweh's plan for rule by the temple and the house of David.

The history began with two new episodes adapting the figures of Moses and Joshua to the pattern of saints in the existing work. The history commenced on the last day of Moses' life, as he reviewed for the nation the history of their trek from Sinai (leave aside Egypt), which like E Josiah's historian called Horeb, after adopting the organization of jurisdiction going back to E and espoused by Hezekiah (compare Deut. 1:9-18 with Exod. 18:13-26). At Horeb Yahweh had appeared so fearfully that all Israel begged him to say no more, except to Moses, who now must declare the laws that will make it possible for the nation to capture the land, or they will be lost with his death. This crisis typified the Deuteronomistic concept of the crucial last chance at many junctures in history, reflecting the stark choices offered by Josiah's radical reform. Once disclosed, the laws were written down, and Moses died.

In the second episode, Joshua, the Ephraimite hero, studied the laws like a future king and conquered the land of Israel. Already introduced into the work by Hezekiah if not before, he was recast as Josiah himself in disguise, Josiah by another name. Like Josiah, Joshua, leading the nation as one, attacked the heart of Benjamin, Galilee and the Judahite foothills. Like Josiah, Joshua allotted conquered land to his followers.

Under Joshua, Israel kept Josiah's law and captured land. When Joshua died, according to Josiah's history, they neglected the laws and started to lose land. Even the law seemed to have disappeared. According to the incorporated history of Israelite tribal ruffians, well-meaning leaders, called judges and saviors, accomplished sporadic victories but, ignorant of Josiah's law, led the people to suffer one reversal after another at the hands of their enemies. The stories of the judges, in the book of Judges, represented the exploits of local and tribal strongmen of just the sort on whom Josiah strove to impose his law.

Of his laws, the first was primary: as one people to worship the one God at one place, as yet unknown. It took a king, and none other than David, the ancestor of Josiah, to reveal, by conquest, that the place was Jerusalem. Furthermore, keeping Josiah's laws required a king and an energetic house of David. Anything less was not, as the magnates might claim, loyalty to Yahweh, who in Josiah's laws prescribes a law-reading king, but mayhem, in which "each did what was right in their own eyes" (Deut. 12:8; Judg. 17:6, 21:25).

With the narrative of Samuel and Saul, the Deuteronomist reached his main source which he left largely as it was. He composed a prayer for David on the occasion of Yahweh's promise to perpetuate his dynasty, one for Solomon at the dedication of the temple, and some other additions. Solomon's reign illustrated the glory of the house of David. His foreign alliances, relegated as a debacle to the end of his life, blemished his reign but did not alter its legal significance.

At Solomon's death Jeroboam founded the secessionist cult of Bethel, the most excoriable flouting of the law of centralization in the entire history. Josiah's historian cursorily cited the annals of the kings of Israel to prove that every one of them committed the same crime. Jehu's history of Omrid oppression showed the inevitable result. Even many Davidic kings of Judah violated the laws requiring purity of cult—no doubt because they were without the right laws. With Moses' law missing, its place was taken by the succession of saints representing Moses, as foreseen by Moses himself (Deut. 17:15-18).

The remedy to injustice—centralization in Jerusalem—had been declared but had to await fulfillment. At the instant Jeroboam had ascended to light the first sacrifice at Bethel, a nameless saint from Judah had stepped forward to proclaim, "O altar, altar, thus says Yahweh: A son shall be born to the house of David, named Josiah; he shall sacrifice upon you the priests who sacrifice on you" (1 Kgs. 13:1-2). It was only a matter of time, three hundred years. The fall of Samaria had verified Yahweh's judgment against Israel, but it had not put an end to the cult and jurisdiction of Bethel. The destruction of Bethel required an agent who could get rid of the Assyrians and their henchmen, and thus complete the ruin of those in Israel who persisted in violating the first law of Josiah.

The fall of Samaria, on which the Deuteronomist preached at length, and the deliverance of Jerusalem under Hezekiah brought the historian to the end of his base document. Hezekiah's pre-Josianic reform, from which Josiah had borrowed much, he passed over in almost total silence. The whole of Josiah's struggle to reconstitute the power of the house of David, the goal of the history, was compressed into a single year, tied to the discovery of the law in the temple—how it got there was not explained, the last reference to it probably being by David. In sum, the law of Moses emanated from the temple of the house of David in the reign of Josiah. Josiah lost no time carrying out its savage requirements. "Before Josiah," the historian concluded, "there was no king like him, who turned to Yahweh with all his heart, being, and strength, according to all the laws of Moses" (2 Kgs. 23:25, forming a frame with Deut. 6:5).

By transferring the judicial function of Bethel to Jerusalem and remarrying Moses and David, Josiah set the norm for the temple and its scriptures from then on. He did not, however, thereby create a constitutional monarchy. The law he promulgated was neither proposed nor imposed by the men who challenged his power. Quite the contrary, it set far more limits on his opponents than on Josiah. Their consolation was land in Israel. Josiah's revolution from above attracted support from the villages as well. The ameliorating norms of village custom made court law by Hezekiah were strengthened by Josiah, ingratiating him with his many subjects. This policy of making restitution to the poor, however, went against the tide of history as well as geography and could not endure as an administrative project or even as a standard for Jerusalemite law. As a prescript justifying jurisdiction in the eyes of the masses, later Jerusalemite rulers, royal as well as priestly, loved it.

By the end of his reign, Josiah was sliding increasingly into the camp of Nabopolassar of Babylon. In control of the pass at Megiddo, he let Egypt slip through to Assyria's aid in 616 and 610. In 609, however, when Necho, having just succeeded to the Egyptian throne, marched for Carchemish, Josiah seized the opportunity to make a clean break with Egypt. He mustered his forces, took the field against Egypt, and died in Necho's presence at Megiddo—cause not stated. The aegis of the house of David was shattered forever.

BABYLONIAN RULERS AND THE COURT IN EXILE

The contest between Egypt and Mesopotamia over Palestine went on, with Mesopotamia still holding the upper hand. Although the rule of Babylon was brief, only sixty-seven years, no period was more important for the formation of the scriptures. The radical realignment of power involved in the fall of Jerusalem and the destruction of the Davidic temple generated a burst of rewriting history and recording prophecy that brought the Torah and Former Prophets and most of the Latter Prophets into final form.

At Josiah's death, however, the more urgent threat came from Egypt. Judah's resurgent magnates once again elevated a younger son, Jehoahaz, to the throne, on the understanding that he would keep his hands off them and Egyptian hands off him. Three months later, the pharaoh Necho, whose dominion at that moment equalled Tuthmose III's, ordered Jehoahaz shipped to Egypt. He charged Judah one hundred talents of silver and one talent of gold and installed Josiah's eldest son, Eliakim, whom he renamed Jehoiakim, to collect it from the country's magnates. Necho's days in Palestine were also numbered. Following the battle at Carchemish in 605, Nebuchadrezzar's campaigns over the next twenty years established the rule of Babylon over Egypt's tributaries in Palestine.

When in 600 Jehoiakim withheld the tribute he was now paying to Babylon, Nebuchadrezzar besieged Jerusalem. The city fell in 598. Jehoiakim died shortly before the fall and was succeeded by his son Jehoiachin, who surrendered the city three months into his rule. Nebuchadrezzar plundered the palace and temple but left them standing and placed Zedekiah, another son of Josiah, on the throne. Jehoiachin and three thousand nobles, priests, court functionaries, and artisans were taken to Babylon to continue the house of David's royal government in exile. The people, of course, remained in the villages in Judah nominally ruled by Zedekiah.

Zedekiah paid the tribute until Egypt returned to campaign in Palestine in 591. He hosted an anti-Babylon congress in Jerusalem attended by delegates from Edom, Moab, Tyre, Sidon, and Ammon, but only Ammon stayed with him for the rebellion, which prompted the second siege of Jerusalem. The city fell again in 587. This time Nebuchadrezzar killed all Zedekiah's sons and deported Zedekiah, as well as another thousand of the ruling class, to Babylon, where Zedekiah died. The Babylonians plundered what was left in the palace and temple and went on to destroy the buildings. This event, unrecognized at the time, was to mark the end of Davidic temple rule in Palestine, a watershed in the history of the Bible matched in importance only by the destruction of the second temple in 70 C.E.

The Babylonian, and later the Persian, crown appointed governors to rule Palestine. The first, Gedaliah, was not a Davidid, but apparently once a member of Josiah's and Jehoiakim's courts. A cousin of the Davidid family, Ishmael, connived with the king of Ammon and his Egyptian backers against Gedaliah, assassinated him, and ended up hiding from Babylon in Egypt, where some in the Palestinian community looked to him as the rightful Davidid ruler in exile. The saint Jeremiah was also taken to Egypt, though he anxiously backed Jehoiachin, the Davidid in Babylon, rather than Ishmael. Ishmael may have been among the 745 Judahites taken to Babylon in 582 when during a lull in his thirteen-year fruitless siege of Tyre, Nebuchadrezzar invaded Ammon and Moab.

Along with the forced resettlement of the upper classes, other populations shifted during the Babylonian era. With Palestinian politics in disarray, Arab tribes moved into Transjordan in considerable numbers, just as Edomites, on friendly terms with Babylon, moved into the Negeb and southern Judah. From now on this area remained in the hands of Edomites, who became the Idumeans of later times. Many villages south of Jerusalem, where rural life was tied to the capital, declined. In most areas the villages were untouched, carrying on their agricultural routines and prospering through the sixth century. The coastal areas continued densely populated.

In Babylon the house of David was represented by Jehoiachin, the nominal king, who apparently enjoyed some income from royal estates in Judah. Although under house arrest, he and his five sons were not uncomfortable. About 560 his overlords allowed him to be restored to a position that a Judahite historian described as foremost among the subject kings resident in Babylon. The families of the deportees settled down, as Jeremiah had advised them after the catastrophe of 598, to build houses and establish households, plant lands, intermarry, and promote the welfare of Babylon. Their skills as artisans, scribes, and soldiers were well employed and well paid in their new homes in many Babylonian locales (thus in Nippur in the fifth century, Judeans are well attested in the financial records of the Murashu family). As they became assimilated to the dominant culture, they adopted Aramaic, the language of the northern tier of the Fertile Crescent that was replacing Assyrian and Babylonian as the language of the empire. People in the Davidid court assumed Babylonian manners and names: a son of Jehoiachin was called Shenazzar, from the Babylonian moon god Sin, later tactfully changed to Sheshbazzar, from the sun god Shamash, when the Persians ousted the moon god's devotee King Nabonidus; Jehoiachin's grandson, who was to be sent to govern in Jerusalem, was named Zerubbabel, the seed of Babylon. While many Judahites in exile kept their identity with the cult of Yahweh, others patronized the cults of Babylon.

In the court in exile, priestly scribes continued work on the cult's accumulated documents. They made a slight but significant revision of the Deuteronomistic History. Among the mostly minor changes, an addition to the beginning (Deuteronomy 4) changed the emphasis of Yahweh's covenant from enforcing obedience to Josiah's law to offering the gracious opportunity to repent. A new ending updated the history of the house of David to the restoration of Jehoiachin in Babylon in 563, placing the blame for the debacle mainly on Manasseh and his cults (2 Kgs. 21:10-15) but partly also on Hezekiah (2 Kgs. 20:16-18). Scholars sometimes refer to Josiah's history as Dtr 1 (for First Deuteronomist) and Jehoiachin's revision as Dtr 2. This completed the Former Prophets as they now appear in the Bible.

Nahopolassar's dynasty ruled Babylon in the shadow of Persian power rising in the northeast. The last of the regime, not of the same house, Nabonidus, resided at Taima in Arabia, leaving the capital and the state cult of Marduk in the hands of the crown prince, and in deference to his mother espoused worship of the moon god Sin. The priests of Marduk were annoyed by Nabonidus's religious policy and welcomed Cyrus of Persia to Babylon, as did an exilic scribe in the divan of Isaiah, as a deliverer. Cyrus took Babylon in 539, inaugurating the two hundred years of Persian rule in Mesopotamia that ended only with the conquests of the Greek Alexander the Great.

As the Persian armies advanced on Babylon, one brilliant scribe foresaw the change of administration — it was nothing more — in Babylon and declared Cyrus to be Yahweh's messiah. He urged his hearers to accept the announcement that Yahweh's plan for the overthrow of Babylon included returning them to Jerusalem. This scribe published his program by adding it to a slightly revised version of the divan of Isaiah, producing what appears now in Isaiah 2-55. He and his work in Isaiah 40-55 are known as Second Isaiah.

Resting on the successful prediction that Cyrus would take over Babylon, the burden of Second Isaiah was to persuade the second and third generation offspring of the deportees settled in Babylon to exile themselves from the capital of the world back to the provinces in Judah and Israel. This required a sustained effort of rhetoric unmatched in the Bible. The scribe chose to address the putative political nation, remnants of Jehoiachin's court, as the "servant of Yahweh," drawing on the imagery of the exodus from Egypt to evoke the notion of a new deliverance from Babylon, a deliverance few of his audience sought. The term implied that they should cry out as worshipers and suppliants to Yahweh to be saved, as the Babylonian priests cried to Marduk and were delivered. The term "servant" also suggested that like the "servants" who served as high officials in the Babylonian court, the people should be exalted to office in Yahweh's divine court, realized in a state that, chastened by the ordeal of exile, would broadcast and practice Yahweh's justice. This propaganda for restoring power in Jerusalem resonated with pre-exilic prophets' divans concerning the restoration of the temple.

Scripture writing in the Babylonian era was rounded off by the major literary product of the early Persian period (538-520), prior to the rebuilding of the temple. The Aaronid priestly families laid the conceptual groundwork for a revision of the royal history of Israel in their archives. Then, as with the support of the Persians they began to eclipse the house of David as rulers of Palestine, the priests carried out this revision, turning JE into their own legitimation document. The Deuteronomistic History was not suitable for revision, as it was in the hands of Levitical interests and spoke for Levitical prerogatives. The Aaronids took up the history of the nation prior to the reconquest of its land to elaborate on the cultic laws of Moses that went back to David's time, before Solomon's temple, by the addition of the rules for their own rites, often going back far into the monarchic period. The result was the priestly revision of JE called "P."

Changes were made throughout the JE history focusing on two issues: the complete reorganization of time and the calendar according to a novel concept developed under Babylonian influence, the seven-day unit of time (this is the origin of the week, one of few features of our secular culture that can be traced directly to the Bible), and the traditional priestly preoccupation with disposition of blood. Every cult requires an appropriate creation story. To represent these two issues, the Aaronids produced a new account of creation to buttress their restored cult, one devoted mainly to feeding Yahweh and themselves with meat at an elaborate tent shrine, akin to David's and ultimately El's tent. According to this account (Genesis 1), God made the world in six days and rested on the seventh. In the first three days God created light, the seas above and below, land and plants; in the second three days he created moving lights and moving water and land creatures. These move because they have blood. To keep moving they are appointed to eat plants.

At critical times in history subsequent to creation God made three eternal covenants of increasing exclusivity. By the first, made with the sons of Noah, that is, all humankind, people are allowed to eat animals as long as they do not eat blood (Genesis 9). The second, made with the sons of Abraham, that is, descendants of Israel, Edom, Ishmael, and other peoples to the south, prescribed the rite of circumcision that distinguished these people and limited the cult to men (Genesis 17). (Circumcision was in fact far more common than this.) The third, made only with the sons of Israel, ordained the keeping of the Sabbath, along with a set of other rules and taboos for the priestly cult dealing with the disposition of blood and the formulation of laws necessary for the purity of the land (Exodus 25 — Leviticus 26; cult in Exodus 35 — Leviticus 10; taboos in Leviticus 11 — 16; laws in Leviticus 17 — 25).

In order to counter the Levitical bias of the Deuteronomistic History, the Aaronid scribes made Aaron a hero equal to or greater than Moses and created their own version of what must be done to hold the land. Not yet restored to a rebuilt temple, the cult they envisioned was centered, like David's, in a tent, a tent of El revived with the tribal connotations but not the tribal politics of the archaic original. It was a cult of sacrifice, consisting of the slaughter, roasting and incineration, and consumption of meat. The taboos specified mainly what meats could be eaten, namely the flesh of animals that eat grass, not meat, and whose means of blood-based movement follow the pattern of the main herbivores of their class, that is, birds that have feathers and wings to fly, fish that swim with fins, animals like sheep that chew the cud and have cloven hoofs. Other rules governed cleansing rites to be observed after contact with menstrual blood, blood shed in sacrifice, and other bloodshed. The laws were filled out with detailed guidelines for legal and economic transactions. With the addition of a few further priestly touches, the Tetrateuch, the JEP document comprising the first four books of the Bible, and with the supplementation of Deuteronomy the Pentateuch (Torah), as we have them were completed. The authors of this revision were soon to be established under Persian hegemony as the rulers of Palestine in place of the house of David, with many of the Davidids' tenure privileges, as confirmed in JE, in their hands.

PERSIAN RULERS AND THE NEW TEMPLE

The Persian rulers inherited the Assyrian and Babylonian aspiration to extend an empire from central Asia to the Nile. They applied the familiar policy of asserting royal authority by buttressing royal cult to impose imperial control over conquered monarchies, just as they had done in Babylon itself in restoring the priesthood of Marduk. Cyrus's successor, Cambyses, who invaded Egypt in 525, was induced by collaborators to refurbish the dynasty's cult center in Saüs. Advised by the Egyptian priest Udjahorresnet, who received appointment as chief physician and chief scribe in the new regime, Cambyses expelled all aliens from the temple precinct, repurified the sanctuary, reinstated the "legitimate" priesthood, sacrifices, feasts, and festivals, while wiping out their rivals, and specified support to be donated by the Persian throne.

As the next ruler, Darius, struggled to confirm his succession, Udjahorresnet returned from service in the imperial court at Susa with a mission to undergird

Persia's tenuous control by codifying traditional Egyptian law under temple auspices. The code, drawn up in Aramaic and Egyptian, exemplified the Persian solicitude for local law and custom as pillars of imperial stability that resulted in the Persian word for law, *data*, being borrowed into not only Akkadian and Aramaic but also Hebrew and Armenian. Udjahorresnet inscribed his own apologia in the refurbished temple, concluding "O great gods who are in Saüs, remember all the useful things accomplished by Udjahorresnet."

Much the same procedure was followed in Jerusalem. The Persians' first move in the 530s was to restore the house of David, in the persons of Sheshbazzar and Zerubbabel, but as governors, not kings. However, the Davidids were, unlike Udjahorresnet in Egypt, a disappointment to their Persian overlords, and during the imperial clampdown after 520 disappeared, leaving Judean jurisdiction solely to the priesthood. The last notice of the house of David in government comes when Elnathan, the third Persian appointee as governor, attempted in vain to enhance his position by marrying a princess of the Davidic family.

When Cambyses died without an heir in 521, his successor Darius, from a different branch of the Achaemenid house, took two or three years to suppress the rebellions that broke out all around Persia's perimeter. During this lapse of imperial control, Haggai and Zechariah in Jerusalem announced that Zerubbabel and Joshua the high priest were to undertake jointly the rebuilding of the Davidic temple. By the time it was finished in 515, the house of David was out of the picture and the priesthood firmly in control, both the result of Darius's recovery. The temple was rebuilt in the name of the house of David, claiming Davidic legitimacy and preserving the Davidic scriptures, even though immediately the high priesthood superseded the monarchy as the main governing office in the Persian province of Judea (making P the concluding legitimating revision of the Torah). From now until the fall of this temple in 70 C.E. the high—high in contrast to chief, indicating additional authority—priest would be the judicial head of all Judeans.

Darius created the most powerful and integrated empire yet seen in the Near East, stretching from the Indus to the Danube, from Libya to Russia. According to Herodotus, it was divided into twenty satrapies, themselves subdivided into provinces and garrisoned by troops recruited from all over the empire. With road networks, coinage and banking systems, enlarged seaports and military fortresses, an efficient tax and toll collecting system, and a universal imperial Aramaic, the Persian regime created a common arena in which production thrived and many prospered. Like previous imperial rulers, the Persians enforced dependence by deporting and relocating portions of the population, both rulers and military garrisons (at a Judean garrison in the satrapy of Egypt, which may have predated Persian rule, numerous Aramaic documents have been discovered), with the added feature that they created quasi-ethnic enclaves for purposes of administration and tax collection. Settlement declined in the north of Palestine, but increased in Judah in the early Persian period as population moved into rural areas, some never settled before.

The Persians collected taxes on as much trade as they could and promoted the ideal, picked up by their clients in Jerusalem, of interdependence, that is, loyalty to Persia, as the only source of wealth. Their dominance in the eastern Mediterranean, however, soon met a challenge from the Greeks, whose stimulus of mercantile activity in the empire first benefited but later threatened Persia's tributary income. The Greeks, recovering from the collapse of Mycenean power, had by now spread widely in the eastern Mediterranean and established an enduring power base in the Levant. Many Persian subjects, notably the tribes of Arabs now moving into settled areas along the arc of the Syrian desert, from Sinai through the Negeb, Palestine, Transjordan, Syria, and the Middle Euphrates, managed to bypass the Persians and deal directly with the Aegean powers. An Arab chiefdom that extended into eastern Egypt through the "land of Goshen," where David's scribe had placed the Israelite tribes in J, had access to ports outside Persian Phoenicia. The exemption of Arabs from Persian commercial taxes and conscription suggests elasticity in imperial control. The Arabs paid only an annual "gift" of thirty tons of frankincense and served in the military for hire.

The Persian wars against Greece, highlighted by the Greek repulse of Darius at Marathon in 490 and defeat of Xerxes' invasion by the Athenian fleet at Salamis in 480 and culminating in the founding of the Athenian Empire, involved Palestine and Egypt as well. Archaeology shows that Palestine, particularly Judea, lay on the watershed between Persian and Greek spheres of influence during their half century of struggle for hegemony in the eastern Mediterranean. To the east, in the southern hills of Palestine and Transjordan, local Palestinian and Near Eastern culture prevailed. In the west, in Galilee and on the coast, wide trading contacts came under Greek, Cypriot, and Athenian influence. In Jerusalem the Aaronid priests put their family interests as large landholders ahead of temple interests and tied into the Athens-Arab trade network for personal gain.

Persia's response to the Greek threat was to put its local governors under tougher political supervision. Just after the Greeks helped Egypt recover their capital from the Persians in 459 and with it the Palestinian coast, the priest Ezra was appointed Persian high commissioner for Judean affairs and sent to Judea with an armed guard and a mass of silver and gold contributed by the throne and by wealthy Judeans in Babylon to refurbish the temple, that is, reassert Persian-style law and order in Jerusalem. Ezra's mandate included reorganizing the entire judicial system of Judea, reconfirming the temple-based Aaronid law of Moses as distinct, according to Persian policy, from the Persian civil law, and restoring the service of the temple, exempting all its priests and other officiants from Persian taxes. All this is explained in the book of Ezra, which contains the first signs of the use of Aramaic in place of Hebrew for writing scripture. (In Jerusalem the Aramaic script replaced the Hebrew script during the Persian period; the script known the world over as "Hebrew" is in fact descended from this Persian Aramaic script.)

The Treaty of Kallias between Persia, Egypt, and Athens in 448 allowed Persia to return to ordering unruly Judea. The court sent an expatriate Judean named Nehemiah, a high official close to the Persian crown, as governor (445-

432), with a picked military escort to reinforce Ezra's flagging mission, reestablish Jerusalem as a fortress, and impose Persian order from the temple out on the Judean people. Nehemiah inflicted stiff corvée duty on the populace to refortify Jerusalem in defiance of local warlords. This work force of villagers was kept in Jerusalem day and night and armed against proclaimed foreign subversion. To defuse their resentment, Nehemiah followed Josiah's policy of hearing their complaints against their patrons, the wealthy priests and magnates, against whom the temple was not protecting them. He republished the Levites' temple law, with its provisions for remission of debt, reversion of land to former owners, and outlawing of exorbitant interest rates, and required the magnates to ratify it. Nehemiah also reinstituted a pilgrimage feast, the feast of booths, and the 10 percent tax on produce to support the temple cult. In the interests of extending administrative control, he conducted a census.

Persia's governors in Judea were expected to see that the commercial bonds draining wealth away from Persia toward Greece were cut and that the Judean economy was reintegrated with the empire's tributary system. Ezra and Nehemiah therefore ruled against marriage alliances between Judahites and families of the coast and Athens-influenced interior. Nehemiah used the census to resettle one tenth of every village into Jerusalem, creating a new urban fortress population under his control and keeping the villages hostage to him. Local trade was strictly regulated: the rebuilt city walls were opened only at midday to admit non-Judean traders and the Sabbath ban on trade was enforced on everyone, Judean and non-Judean alike. Commerce, especially foreign trade, was denigrated as contrary to tributary interests; economic activity was relegated to despised and powerless social outcasts, thereby undermining merchants' power.

Additions made to Isaiah at this time reflect this policy. In keeping with the original divan, the poet envisioned the temple as the hub of a global stream of tribute, the "wealth of nations," flowing on, by implication, to the Persian capital. Adam Smith, champion of capitalist economic theory, later applied this phrase to the very commercial wealth that the Judean clients of imperial Persia decried. The Isaiah scribe also foresaw scattered Judeans streaming back to Jerusalem, not so much the exiles returning from deportation as the trading representatives recalled from travel in the Athenian Empire on business that was sapping temple and imperial wealth.

Representatives of these trading networks reaching beyond Persian Judea in all directions, such as Sanballat of Beth-horon near the coast, the governor of Samaria and Ashdod, Tobiah, strongman of Ammon, and Geshem the Arab, tried to counter the new regime by discrediting Nehemiah with his Persian masters. The book that bears his name is Nehemiah's defense before Yahweh and the Persian court against the charge of subversion and an epitome of the pro-Persian stance of the developing temple scriptures. At the conclusion of his public record placed in the Jerusalem temple, Nehemiah cried, like Udjahorresnet in Saüs, "Remember me, O my God, for good."

When the Persians gave up on the house of David in Palestine, the temple and its offices were left as the sole source of Judean jurisdiction. The priesthood, dominated by a surviving sector of Zadokite Aaronids, struck their own deal with the Persians. With no royal court to distribute land to its vassals, priests took over royal land attached to temple offices and became major land-holders and commercial operators. The supreme priestly family, the Aaronids, became surrogate royalty; to most of his subjects, the high priest chosen from that family was king in all but name.

The law at this stage was in two parts: the Aaronid law in the four scrolls of the main cult history JEP, and the law in the Deuteronomistic History, held at Josiah's behest by the Levites, but now, lacking protection from the house of David, under Aaronid control.

To avoid the implication of two laws and prevent Levite scribes from taking liberties with the main history, the Aaronids had the scribes join Deuteronomy to the Tetrateuch of JEP, thus forming the five-scroll Pentateuch, the canonical Torah. Its conclusion in Deuteronomy 34 made Moses the greatest of the saints, the first of several maneuvers to neutralize the saints as foci of discontent. Although this revision was not immediately accepted, by the time of Ezra and Nehemiah, the "laws of the temple" were understood as a composite. Thus when the Levites succeeded in recording Aaronid injustice in Isaiah (using explicit language but veiled referents), they claimed to be the true keepers of the law by virtue of their adherence to the law of the Sabbath, a principle based on the Aaronid section, P, not their own Deuteronomistic work.

Despite tension with Aaronids, the Levites continued to carry out their ancil-lary functions in the cult as cleaners, porters, cooks, and servants of priests. As liturgists and musicians they performed the elaborate service of choral song that David's prayer service had become. They assisted the priests in managing the temple treasury, the repository of Judea's public wealth, of private funds, tax-exempt donations to the temple, and of notarized contracts regarding inher-itance, land tenure, and debt. They kept custody of the temple scriptorium and library. As they had been Josiah's rural priests, they continued their profession of interpreting the law of the village, for the increasing number of villages that appeared during this period. Their prestige thus was based on their promotion of what gave Judah the little autonomy it had, the extension and application of ancestral laws and customs as widely as possible at the expense of imperial jurisdiction. Later the legal and scribal functions, as opposed to the menial ones, would be taken over by a class of scribes, and later still also by a group of free-lance teachers called pharisees.

Under Levite custody, the temple scriptorium set about producing the history of the temple and its cult that the new circumstances of rule without the Dav-idids required. The Aaronid cult history JEP, the Torah, still omitted to mention the temple; the Deuteronomistic History, now truncated of its first scroll, was preoccupied with the dead issue of Jerusalem's right against the usurpers of the north and included some scurrilous tales about the temple's founders, David and Solomon. Apparently drawing on archival material previous scribes had missed or ignored (the Greek translation was to be called the "Things Left Out"), the interpretive revision of the Deuteronomistic History that appears following Ezra and Nehemiah in Chronicles remedied these defects.

Chronicles linked the Torah to the temple by summarizing the Torah history in a series of extensive genealogies. The tent shrine of JEP was firmly equated with the temple: "the temple of Yahweh, the temple that was then a tent" (1 Chr. 9:23, assuming the phrase is not a gloss or conflation of two variant texts). Expurgated of unseemly incidents (for example, the circumstances of Solomon's birth), David's life story made clear that he had instructed Solomon in detail about the offices and services of the temple, in particular the role of the Levites. The secession of the northern kingdom was recast as a continuing rebellion against the enduring southern state, by overlooking all northern rulers except those loyal to the south. Hezekiah's refurbishment of the temple, always an absolute good, earned good press for his reform. And the history made extensive reference to the Levites, who had received but passing mention in Deuteronomy. Levite devotion and enthusiasm were credited with the nation's greatest triumphs; their songs of praise and deliverance were the new prophecy. Bolstered by fulfillment in the Persian restoration, they restressed the theme of exilic Deuteronomy: "If my people humble themselves, and pray and seek my favor [by maintaining the temple service], and turn from their wicked ways, then I will hear from heaven, and will forgive their sin and heal their land" (2 Chr. 7:14). The history concluded with the edict of Cyrus relaunching the Levites' temple, which confirmed that the Persian emperor, inspired by Yahweh, was the builder of the second Davidic temple.

23

NAOMI STEINBERG

The Deuteronomic Law Code
and the Politics of State Centralization

In analyzing issues such as the historical liberalization of marriage and inheritance laws ostensibly to the advantage of women, one must consider critically the motives of the "reformers" and the effects of the apparent liberalization. The two dominant social forms of life in ancient Israel were the patriarchal family and clan and the (equally patriarchal) monarchic state. Any "reform" or codification and publication of laws would have been undertaken by the monarchic state. The German sociologist Max Weber noted some time ago that the authority granted to the father of the family in Deuteronomy is far less than in the Covenant Code of Exodus 21–23. Recent cross-cultural studies indicate an explicit connection between laws regulating sexuality in particular and the centralization of political control. Accordingly, analysis of the laws in Deuteronomy 19–25 suggests that what appears as a granting of greater rights and autonomy to women in connection with the limiting of the powers of the paterfamilias *is likely only part of a broader legislation designed to strengthen central political power and judicial authority by weakening both the powers of the father-husband and local loyalties to extended family, clan or tribe.*

Reprinted from *The Bible and the Politics of Exegesis: Essays in Honor of Norman K. Gottwald*, ed. David Jobling, et al. (Cleveland: Pilgrim Press, 1991), 161–170.

Deuteronomy 19:1-25:19 appears on first glance to address a wide range of legal issues in ancient Israelite life. Upon closer reading, one discovers that the laws within this section of the Deuteronomic law code regularly concern one basic institution of Israelite society, the family. However, there has been no comprehensive interpretive sociological model that would enable a reader to understand these Deuteronomic legal provisions. This essay will assess these laws and propose the thesis that they gradually functioned to serve the interests of political centralization that began at the time of the inception of the monarchy.

I

Typically, scholars have explored the relationship of Israelite to other ancient Near Eastern laws. For example, Phillips[1] argues that, as a result of the seriousness of adultery in ancient Israel (it is an offense against God), it was treated not as a civil offense but as a crime.[2] Hence, punishment for a wife's behavior in such circumstances was not left to a husband's discretion but instead became a community concern and required the death penalty. Phillips views Deuteronomic thinking on both adultery and seduction as distinct from principles of ancient Near Eastern law, and an innovation in Israelite sexual ethics, because it construes women as legal adults responsible for their actions. For example, in comparison with biblical and cuneiform law, what is original about Deut 22:22, according to Phillips, is that in a case of adultery "both of them are to die."[3] Phillips contends that Deuteronomic legislation on adultery and seduction was designed to settle issues of paternity, and not, as is commonly argued, to protect a husband's or father's property, namely, his women. Concerning the emphasis on paternity, Phillips remarks, "This was of vital importance in a society which did not believe in life after death but rather that a man's personality went on in his children."[4] Phillips, and others who take this evolutionary approach, attempt to locate the biblical legal material on family life in the context of a developing moral consciousness that distinguished ancient Israel from her neighbors. They do this by highlighting one of the distinctive Deuteronomic humanitarian concerns, which Weinfeld and McBride have addressed,[5] namely, extending the scope of the law to include women. Phillips concludes that the death penalty for both the adulterous man and woman reflects the distinct ethical character of Israel's sacral criminal law and distinguishes it from the ancient Near Eastern legal tradition. For Phillips, the unique features of Deuteronomic legislation reflect Israel's particular theological foundation.[6]

In this essay, I will assess the singular qualities of the Deuteronomic legislation on family life by focusing on political concerns, not on moral evolution. I will analyze Deuteronomic laws on family life and sexuality as one arena in which political control is exercised. I am interested in refuting Phillips' argument for the putative uniqueness of Israelite family law in order to demonstrate that from a cross-cultural perspective these legal provisions can be interpreted as part of the politics of state centralization. State centralization altered judicial authority as exemplified in the Book of the Covenant, which is generally regarded as an earlier legal tradition. Using the perspectives of comparative legal studies, I will demonstrate that the change in ancient Israel's judicial administration was aimed at weakening local political boundaries in order to strengthen the authority of the central government under the united monarchy.

II

In order to understand the sociopolitical realities that lie behind the Deuteronomic legislation, we must appropriate the work of social historians who associate laws on marriage, family, and kinship patterns with attempts by politicians to exercise power. Such laws compel subjects to conform to institutionalized authority in a way that other laws (e.g., tax laws) do not. For example, a recent study by Goody[7] traces the connection between the growth of the church in medieval Europe and changing forms of domestic life to a "moment" parallel to the one I presume in ancient Israel for Deut 19:1-25:19. In particular:

> For the Church to grow and survive it had to accumulate property, which meant acquiring control over the way it was passed from one generation to the next. Since the distribution of property between generations is related to patterns of marriage and the legitimization of children, the Church had to gain authority over these so that it could influence the strategies of heirship.[8]

Goody's argument that early medieval Christianity benefited by passing legislation that, on the surface, appeared to provide independence for women parallels the sociopolitical dynamics behind the legislation in Deut 19:1-25:19. Changing laws, whether they be to discourage the remarriage of widows or to safeguard inheritance of paternal property by daughters, benefited church interests, because women were more likely than men to bequeath their property to the church. Further, legislation concerning marriage eligibility patterns (thereby altering notions of kinship) provided the church with an alternate source of revenue. If one violated prohibitions on marriage to near kin, one could be absolved of the sin by buying a dispensation from the local priest. Beyond providing revenue, legislation on sexual behavior succeeded in breaking down local autonomy and in establishing religious authority at the expense of lineage relationships. As a result, a woman gained a certain degree of freedom from the authority of her husband or her father as the church took control of family and marriage relationships, though whether women ultimately benefited from this "liberation" is open to question.

Goody provides evidence that suggests that political authority can be exercised through control of family life and sex roles; that is, general laws on sexuality may provide a centralized authority (either church or state) with a means of redirecting individual loyalty from one social institution to another, so that, in the case Goody presented, family allegiance was no longer in competition with the interests of church or state. For ancient Israel, legislation intended to accomplish that same goal may be identified in the Deuteronomic law code.

Only in the legislation of Deuteronomy 19-25 does one find laws where centralized authority is established at the expense of local political boundaries, thereby emphasizing the primary importance of the nuclear family unit. There are many examples of this concern. Besides the legislation concerning adultery considered by Phillips, Deuteronomy stipulates that foreign women who are taken captive in war will be protected from the capriciousness of their Israelite husbands (21:10-14). Moreover, the Deuteronomic law code legislates premarital sex. Deuteronomy 22:28-29 decrees that the man who rapes an unbetrothed woman must marry her.[9] Having done something dishonorable to her once, the new husband may not act in a similar fashion again; he can never attempt to divorce her. These laws establish rights for women in the interest of preserving nuclear family units whose existence depends on the protection of both spouses in the marriage.

The only legislation from ancient Israel on remarriage is found in Deuteronomy. Based on the many conditions specified in Deut 24:1-4, including the specification that a husband may not later remarry his wife, a husband must be serious about his decision to divorce. Another example of concern for the nuclear family unit, the law of Deut 24:5, mandates that the interests of the family be placed before those of the state, as when it exempts a bridegroom from military service for the first year following his marriage. This provision allows the alliance formed by the couple time to strengthen, such that their loyalties will now be to each other rather than to the families from which they originated. Maintenance of social order in ancient Israel, as represented in these laws, appears directly linked to the preservation of the nuclear social unit.

One law aimed at preservation of the nuclear family is worth examining in detail precisely because at first glance it appears to presume an extended family dwelling. This is Deut 25:5-10, the law of Levirate marriage. As stated here, the law appears to have two goals in mind: first, that the property of the dead man be kept within the family (presumably this is the reason that the responsibility the dead husband's brother is to show toward the widow falls only upon brothers who dwell together); second, that the name of the dead be perpetuated through the child born of a union between the widow and her brother-in-law.

The Deuteronomic formulation of this law allows for an element of choice. The brother of the dead man may elect not to fulfill his responsibilities to his dead brother and the widow. In that event, the widow is to make her brother-in-law's decision known to the local elders. She, rather than he, initiates this legal action. The law guarantees that the widow is not dependent upon her brother-in-law's unwillingness to acknowledge his obligations publicly. It protects the woman's interests through the sequence of events stipulated here. The denial of family responsibility by the living brother brings shame upon him, which must be witnessed before the local authorities. If the brother-in-law declines his Levirate duties, the woman informs the elders, who are instructed to quiz the man to determine the veracity of the widow's allegations. Having established that the brother-in-law will not fulfill his obligations toward his sister-in-law, the elders are directed to take legal actions to shame him publicly. The brother-in-law's sandal is pulled off by the widow; she then spits in his face, before renaming him, "The house of him whose sandal was pulled off" (v. 10).

Scholars have regularly understood this law to presume that the wife of the deceased man is legally the property of her husband's family.[10] Yet, the child born from the Levirate union not only allows for the continuance of the dead man's name, it also provides the widow with support in her old age.[11] The law maintains her right to a child, and protects her against her brother-in-law's refusal to redeem his brother's name, by placing authority for control of this family situation in the hands of individuals who administer the law from outside the setting of the nuclear family involved.

As noted above, a reader may get the initial impression that the Deuteronomic formulation of the Levirate law presumes an extended family unit. However, as Lemche notes, "if the custom has any meaning, it is that it points to the existence of nuclear and neolocal families, since it is the nuclear family that is threatened by extinction when the father of the house dies without having left sons behind him. Such a nuclear family simply ceases to be an autonomous unit."[12] Thus Deut 25:5-10 is another law that is concerned with preserving the nuclear unit.

Our survey of Deuteronomy 19-25 indicates that this legislation intends to preserve the nuclear family unit and guarantees that the nuclear family will endure by limiting the power of men and by creating rights for women. This protection is provided not because an individual is a woman; rather, this legal protection is mandated because the woman is defined by Israelite society as an integral member of the family unit. The law presumes that the nuclear family is more important than the individual.

III

Judicial practice in Deuteronomy purportedly safeguards justice for all people. For the nuclear unit, this norm is achieved through laws administered by Israelites outside the immediate family. Legal decisions connected to family problems are taken out of the hands of the individuals directly involved in the family relationship and placed in the hands of an impartial body, the elders, who are responsible for maintaining social stability.[13] If one compares Exod 22:16-17 with Deut 22:28-29, it is clear that what could have been resolved by the *paterfamilias* in Exodus is in Deuteronomy expressed in categorical terms. In fact, the father is not even mentioned in Deut 22:28-29. Such an arrangement for the administration of legal rights qualifies the power of adult males of the nuclear family and supposedly provides legal protection for women and children. The successful transition to a centralized state comes from both using and subverting existing judicial authority structures, in this case the elders.[14]

In comparing the Book of the Covenant to Deuteronomy, Weber remarks on the decline of authority granted to the father in the latter over against the former. He relates these changed social conditions to the rise of the monarchy.[15] The Deuteronomic law code effects a shift in social boundaries away from the kinship structure characteristic in the premonarchic period, in order to reduce local authority, which was seen as threatening to the nascent monarchy. As a result, the cohesiveness of the nuclear family is strengthened and the extended family is weakened; authority on both levels is, in the case of the laws of Deuteronomy, redirected to the control of the elders. The bureaucracy of the state promulgates law, which the local elders are responsible for enforcing over individual family units. The result is that what might formerly have been an ad hoc function exercised at the city gate by the elders becomes regularized through the regulation of behavior.[16] This is seen in the case of the law of the rebellious son (Deut 21:18-21) and the law guaranteeing the virginity of the bride (Deut 22:13-21). In effect, then, state centralization does not drastically renovate the organization of village life. In village life, the elders administer justice; with the imposition of monarchy, these individuals continue to regulate local business. In addition, they serve as liaisons to the central authority when necessary. One could argue that the rise of monarchy diminished the political functions of the elders while increasing their judicial role. Elders retain local power despite the monarchic overlay.[17]

A study by Y. A. Cohen that includes monarchic Israel in an attempt to comprehend the relationship between legal systems and the growth of political and economic organization builds on Weber's discussion of the legitimation of authority, and analyzes cross-cultural data from Murdock's "World Ethnographic Sample."[18] Cohen identifies an explicit connection between political control and laws of sexuality. He concludes that, concomitant with the centralization of political authority, a state ruler strives to manipulate allegiance to his government through the use of sexual controls; one mechanism for political control involves control of sexuality. Cohen maintains that the state places primary emphasis on the marital bond through legislation on adultery, incest, and celibacy. This is done in the interest of making the nuclear family – rather than the lineage, which can, but may not, have resided in the same town or village with other lineages – the primary unit in society.

Most relevant for our analysis of the laws in Deuteronomy 19-25 are Cohen's remarks on adultery:

> I interpret laws prescribing capital punishment for adultery as having four principal consequences: (1) the weakening of local corporate groups; (2) the strengthening of bonds that cannot serve as sources of rebellion; (3) the control of the polity through the encouragement of the conjugal pair's mobility; and (4) the maintenance of social distance between rulers and ruled. Common to the first three is the strengthening of the marital network's boundaries.[19]

Cohen concludes that an emerging and growing state is interested in redirecting individual loyalties in a way that will not conflict with allegiances to the political organization.[20] In a social system where lineage has previously been of primary importance, the local kinship relationship must be subverted, lest individuals unite in rebellion against the state. The possibility for such rebellion is seriously diminished when the strongest personal bond in society is based on the marital unit; the marital bond is strengthened at the expense of the kinship bond. In sum, Cohen interprets legislation regulating sexual behavior as a means of exercising political control in what he labels a "state organization."

For Cohen, state societies are those with centralized authority, stateless societies those with local autonomy, or what Cohen calls "horizontal organization." Chiefdoms are characterized by "multiple power centers; one of their central characteristics is a notable resistance to centralization of authority."[21] Thus, they are segmentary societies.

Cohen discerns a diachronic relation between state development and the sanctions imposed for the violation of adultery laws. Political organization in state societies moves along a continuum from early to late institutionalization of government. In the later stages of state organization, it is no longer necessary to enforce legislation guaranteeing the allegiance of the individual to the central leader. Local autonomy no longer threatens centralized authority.[22]

Potential obstacles to the imposition of state control over local autonomy through the use of control of sexual behavior may, according to Cohen, be overcome by couching the legislation in the language and ideology of local groups. In fact, it is not simply a matter of one group and its interests replacing another, but of a gradual shift that, over time, results in the disappearance of one type of control and its substitution by another.[23] Thus it would be incorrect to argue that, through laws of sexuality, the extended kin group is totally broken down and replaced by the nuclear family unit. The latter was present prior to the new legislation, and the larger kinship structures remain important (e.g., the "father's house"—a term recognized to refer to various social groupings).[24] Nonetheless, laws controlling sexual behavior reduce the emphasis on extended family units and replace it with a focus on the nuclear family.

IV

At this point it is appropriate to integrate Weber's discussion of the legitimation of authority with the work of Cohen and Goody, thereby linking analysis of sociopolitical organization with the regulation of family life. Most biblical scholars are familiar with informal theories of how a national leader might work to channel individual loyalty away from local authorities and toward the national level of government. At the time of the united monarchy, Solomon (961-922 BCE) recast tribal boundaries into fiscal districts in order to focus allegiance away from the tribal level and toward his own state organization (1 Kgs 4:7-19). This destruction of the old tribal boundaries was an attempt to prevent local rebellion through the erosion of kinship connections.[25]

Solomon's redistricting obviously violated tribal organization and raised the ire of many. Regardless of whether or not there is a connection between Solomon and the laws being discussed here, in both situations religion became a means to justify politics. In the case of Solomon, there is an appeal to the theology of Zion as the basis for royal prerogatives; in Deuteronomy the political motivation for the control of sexual behavior is made less offensive than it might otherwise be through the application of religious sanctions (e.g., in Deut 24:4 remarriage is an abomination to God). As a result, in Deuteronomy, laws on family life are understood as God's statement of proper social relationships within the Israelite community. Here one may identify the reciprocal influence of religion and politics.

Promulgation of the laws in Deuteronomy 19-25 may have met with little resistance from women because women appeared to benefit from these laws; power over them is taken out of the hands of their fathers and husbands, who become subordinate to the jurisdiction of the elders. The result of such a shift, ironically, is that women are actually controlled— along with men—in the interest of the politics of state centralization.[26] According to the newer legislation, women could be killed for lack of virginity (Deut 22:13-21) whereas men could not, just as in the issue of complicity of rape, women had to prove themselves in a way that men did not (22:23-27). Thus one may question whether Deuteronomic justice is truly egalitarian in intent, as some have claimed.[27] Women may have gained legal autonomy from their fathers and husbands through the legislation in Deuteronomy 19-25, but they were thrown on the defensive in ways that put them at a social disadvantage vis-à-vis men. These laws, which initially appear to relate to family status and roles, have less to do with gender as such, and more to do with political and social control of individual behavior of the entire "ruled" populace.

In light of comparative social histories, it seems reasonable to conclude that sanctions concerning sexual relations in Deuteronomy 19-25 should be seen as connected to a movement toward centralization, or tightening of control, on the national level. Although women appear less subject to the authority of the *paterfamilias* in the Deuteronomic legislation than in the Book of the Covenant, the former laws encourage nuclear family units and discourage extended family units. Rather, through these laws both men and women appear to be controlled by legal ordinances promulgated outside of the local group. All family issues are controlled to suit the sociopolitical aims of the form of government that replaced the old kinship-based social system.

There is one more point of contact between the comparative data and the biblical evidence. Cohen argues that adultery laws ultimately widen the social distance between the nation's rulers and their subjects. In other words, the laws of sexual behavior for commoners are not binding upon the royal court—despite what Deut 17:14-20 suggests. The ruler is separated from his subjects not only in the matter of sexual conduct, but in other social and political realms.[28] The pattern of family dynamics consistently revealed in the Deuteronomic law code exists in obvious contrast to the actions of the Davidic house.

V

Even though this essay is concerned primarily with examining the way in which comparative material can help us understand the relation of family law to state formation in ancient Israel, such perspectives may contribute to the discussion of the Deuteronomic legislation's date of composition. Although many scholars think that Jehoshaphat's reform (873-849 BCE) resulted in a shift in the administration of justice[29] such that professional judges (Deut 16:18) took over responsibilities formerly delegated to elders at the city gate, the analogy between the comparative data and the biblical texts suggests that we consider the inception of the monarchy as the beginning locus for the gradual promulgation of legislation emphasizing the nuclear family. In light of the present uncertainty on the issue of dating the Deuteronomic corpus and the range of dates already posited for this material, this suggestion should not overburden the discussion.

Using comparative social history, this study has argued that in the tenth century Deuteronomy 19-25 would have provided an important means for centralizing the political authority of the king by weakening local political boundaries and strengthening the nuclear family unit. This argument allows us to make sense of the fact that this legislation was promulgated at all: it was intended to reshape and maintain community organization. Laws need not be written down unless the collective disagrees with them and refuses to obey. Laws that are publicly formulated are those that society has failed to internalize. They require promulgation in order to be enforced.[30] In this regard, it is interesting to note that the statutes affecting family life in Deuteronomy 19-25 include sanctions for enforcement (the one noticeable exception is 24:5, which is more an abstraction than a legal decision). Thus it would appear that the Deuteronomic legislation was grounded in an actual sociopolitical reality. The analytical perspectives of comparative studies suggest that this reality began with the centralization of government under the monarchy.[31]

NOTES

1. A. Phillips, "Another Look at Adultery," *JSOT* 20 (1981) 3-25. Others who take this approach include M. Greenberg ("Some Postulates of Biblical Criminal Law," *The Jewish Expression* [ed. J. Goldin; New York: Bantam, 1970] 18-37) and S. M. Paul (*Studies in the Book of the Covenant in the Light of Cuneiform and Biblical Law* [VTSup 18; Leiden: Brill, 1970]).

2. In fact, this legislation receives even greater attention in the writings of C. M. Carmichael (e.g., *The Laws of Deuteronomy* [Ithaca: Cornell University Press, 1974]; *Law and Narrative in the Bible: The Evidence of the Deuteronomic Laws and the Decalogue* [Ithaca: Cornell University Press, 1985]). Cf. also his *Women, Law, and the Genesis Traditions* (Edinburgh: Edinburgh University Press, 1979). However, I have chosen not to address his prolific studies on the subject in this article because his attempts to harmonize law with narratives appear to be reductionistic. Carmichael's approach to the Hebrew Bible seems to reflect his apologetics toward ancient Israelite "patriarchy." Moreover, he asserts, "The premise is that the source of the problems taken up in the Deuteronomic legislation is not, as is most universally thought, matters that arose in the everyday life of the Israelites at various times and places, but matters that are found in the literary traditions available to the legislator in his time" (*Women, Law*, 4).

3. Phillips, "Another Look," 6.

4. Ibid., 7.

5. M. Weinfeld, *Deuteronomy and the Deuteronomic School* (Oxford: Oxford University Press, 1972) 284; S. D. McBride, "Deuteronomium," *Theologische Realenzyklopädie* 8 (1981) 534-35; "Polity of the Covenant People," *Int* 41 (1987) 242.

6. For a recent study arguing that the ethics of law in ancient Israel is no different from the ancient Near Eastern legal tradition, see R. Westbrook, *Studies in Biblical and Cuneiform Law* (Cahiers de la Revue Biblique 26; Paris: Gabalda, 1988).

7. J. Goody, *The Development of the Family and Marriage in Europe* (Cambridge: Cambridge University Press, 1983).

8. Ibid., 221.

9. This situation stands in contrast to Exod 22:16–17, which legislates that a father may choose to block the marriage of his daughter to the individual who raped her—with the result that the father would still receive the marriage present for his daughter. Thus, a father could reap monetary gain from the rape of his daughter. The law is such that it would in fact be in the father's economic interest to stop such a marriage. Either he could then marry his daughter to someone else and receive a second marriage gift, or he could keep her at home and have the benefit of her labor.

10. R. de Vaux, *Ancient Israel* (2 vols.; New York: McGraw-Hill, 1961) 1.40.

11. Cross-cultural studies of societies that emphasize patrilineal inheritance suggest that the strongest family bond is between a mother and her son. The mother works to further the interests of her offspring as heir to his father, resulting in the son's feelings of indebtedness toward his mother. See E. J. Michaelson and W. Goldschmidt, "Female Roles and Male Dominance Among Peasants," *Southwestern Journal of Anthropology* 27 (1971) 338–39. For further information on the plight of the widow in ancient Israelite society, consult P. S. Hiebert (" 'Whence Shall Help Come to Me?': The Biblical Widow," *Gender and Difference in Ancient Israel* [ed. P. L. Day; Minneapolis: Fortress, 1988] 125–41).

12. N. P. Lemche, *Early Israel* (VTSup 37; Leiden: Brill, 1985) 259.

13. F. S. Frick, *The City in Ancient Israel* (SBLDS 36; Missoula: Scholars Press, 1977) 126–27.

14. This is demonstrated by H. Niehr (*Rechtsprechung in Israel: Untersuchungen zur Geschichte der Gerichtsorganisation im Alten Testament* [Stuttgarter Bibelstudien 130; Stuttgart: Katholisches Bibelwerk, 1987]), who provides an extensive study of the interaction and transformation of judicial spheres from prestate to postexilic Israel. For a sociological study of the political/leadership role of elders in adapting to structural and historical changes in ancient Israel, see D. L. Smith, *The Religion of the Landless* (Bloomington, IN: Meyer-Stone Books, 1989) 94–99.

15. M. Weber, *Ancient Judaism* (Glencoe: Free Press, 1952) 61–70.

16. Lemche, *Early Israel*, 279.

17. There is extensive bibliography on this topic. Recent studies include Frick (*City in Israel*, 114–27), Lemche (*Early Israel*, 245–85), and Smith (*Religion of the Landless*, 94–99).

18. Y. A. Cohen, "Ends and Means in Political Control: State Organization and the Punishment of Adultery, Incest and the Violation of Celibacy," *American Anthropologist* 71 (1969) 658–87. See M. Weber, *The Protestant Ethic and the Spirit of Capitalism* (New York: Scribner's, 1930), and G. P. Murdock, "World Ethnographic Sample," *American Anthropologist* 59 (1957) 664–87. Although one may find fault with the ethnographic data in this sampling, it is the only such source available for comparative study.

19. Cohen, "Ends and Means," 665.

20. Cohen (ibid., 667–68) uses the example of Gen 2:22–25, which he believes

expresses the concerns of the Davidic monarchy to control marital relationships, to prove his point.

21. Ibid., 661.

22. This movement toward successful "vertical entrenchment" does not always follow the same course from state to state.

23. The same conclusion is reached by Goody, *Family and Marriage*.

24. Lemche, *Early Israel*, 269.

25. J. Bright, *A History of Israel* (3rd ed.; Philadelphia: Westminster, 1981) 221. However, recent works, such as Lemche's *Early Israel*, suggest that tribes were not as important as some have maintained.

26. This conclusion corresponds with Carol Meyers' argument concerning the diminution of women's social power with the advent of monarchy in Israel (*Discovering Eve* [Oxford: Oxford University Press, 1988] 189–96). This phenomenon is also evident in the contemporary world. Both Fascist and Communist regimes have promised women benefits that have not eventuated. For an account of women's perspectives on life in the Soviet Union that makes this same point, see the recent work by F. du Plessix Gray (*Soviet Women: Walking the Tightrope* [New York: Doubleday, 1989]).

27. For example, McBride, "Polity of the Covenant People," 242.

28. Cohen, "Ends and Means," 666–67.

29. Mentioned in 2 Chr 19:5. However, the historical accuracy of these details is questionable. See H. Donner, "The Separate States of Israel and Judah," in *Israelite and Judaean History* (ed. J. H. Hayes and J. M. Miller; Philadelphia: Westminster, 1977) 391–92.

30. L. Pospisil, *Anthropology of Law: A Comparative Theory* (New York: Harper & Row, 1971) 95.

31. I would like to thank David L. Petersen for his helpful comments on earlier versions of this essay.

24

GERALD T. SHEPPARD

"Enemies" and the Politics of Prayer
in the Book of Psalms

Modern readings of the Psalms have often been individualizing, even psychologizing, and/or narrowly formal and cultic. A combined social and literary approach, which asks more concretely what particular social situation has inscribed itself at the key stages in which the Psalms have taken their current literary form, opens up far more complex layers of meaning and sociopolitical functions of the psalms. Comparative materials available in anthropological studies suggest that the prayer represented in many of the biblical psalms, far from being a private individual exercise, was a form of public discourse, perhaps purposely spoken in the hearing of "enemies," hence a form of resistance against or protection from (further) harassment or exploitation. Exploring more precisely how prayer as a political *action may have functioned, Sheppard finds that it provided* public exposure *of the social conflict and* protection from further attack, *indictments or threats* against or commands and advice *to the "enemy." The question to ask about the psalms is not whether they are political, but what politics pertain to particular psalms uttered publicly in a concrete social situation.*

A persistent debate in the modern study of Psalms concerns how to interpret prayers that imprecate "enemies," "the wicked," "evildoers," and other antag-

Reprinted from *Bible and the Politics of Exegesis: Essays in Honor of Norman K. Gottwald*, ed. David Jobling, et al. (Cleveland: Pilgrim Press, 1991), 61–82, abridged.

onists. Key problems include the question of who are the enemies, why they remain unnamed within the prayers themselves, and what role such prayers actually played both in ancient society and, finally, in the later formation of scripture. This essay will first offer an analysis of the sociopolitical role of prayer in the biblical prehistory, and will then explore some theological implications that derive from the retentions and alterations of that same tradition history within the canonical context of Jewish and Christian scripture. One hermeneutical aspect of this essay is to show how even a canonical approach to theological interpretation still needs and benefits from the type of social-scientific analysis that Norman Gottwald has impressively pursued.

AN OVERVIEW OF THE DEBATE ABOUT ENEMIES IN THE PSALMS

One of the most common problems in the study of Psalms has been how to evaluate references to enemies and the accompanying graphic imprecations. The wish for violence against these enemies, whether God is summoned or the supplicant volunteers to retaliate, may seem harsh, childish, or "primitive." Commentators before the last century usually considered most of the enemies to be historical persons in the time of David. By the late nineteenth century the study of the cultic forms and functions of prayers, as well as the psychological-aesthetic nature of prayer itself, called for a radical change in the conception of enemies in the psalms. The "formulaic" quality of many statements about enemies proved that the poet often "assigned less value to the external events than to psychological impressions (*den seelischen Eindrücken*)."[1] Even if someone originally wrote a lament with quite specific enemies in mind, later usage of that psalm could blunt certain historically specific language in the psalm through slight modifications introduced by its ritualized recitation. Keel has sought to find an answer in a fresh assessment, found originally in Gunkel's work, of how prayer can be used to express in externalized, commonplace language deeply painful psychological or pious impressions associated with suffering. By describing many if not most references to enemies as evidence of pious, psychological projection derived from the psalmist's own unconscious self-criticism, Keel finally rationalizes these occurrences in a thoroughly modern way.[2]

Since the publication of his *The Tribes of Yahweh* in 1979, Norman Gottwald has sought to consider more fully the literary formation of scripture and what consequences the changes in literary presentation might entail for any sociopolitical interpretations. . . . The main question raised by the literary dimension is: "Exactly how does the social reality inscribe itself in language and in literary creations?"[3] Above all, in discussing Psalms, he singles out the problem of who constitutes concretely and politically the voice of the suffering one who prays in the psalms, and who are the enemies against whom such prayers are so often directed.

For Gottwald, the late historicizing titles that link certain psalms to events in the life of David as presented in 1 and 2 Samuel might mislead one into finding a warrant for "individualizing" or "psychologizing" the psalms. He argues that even in the postexilic usage, "David stood for the righteous leader of the community" and was, therefore, "not an object of purely past historical and personal speculation."[4] Further, the collecting of older psalms into written "books" obscured or obliterated any record of their originating socioeconomic settings. This loss of information pertinent to the prehistory of the prayers in the psalms has often led later interpreters to a false view of them as expressing concern for only private fears, illnesses, or the harm done by interpersonal shaming or witchcraft. Instead, Gottwald argues that in the psalms " 'rich' and 'wicked' are often spoken in the same breath" as a sign that the social dimension of the privileged has been retained even in the biblical psalms. Moreover, Gottwald proposes that "this wealth of language about socioeconomic conflict" should be "compared with and illuminated by speeches of the prophets and proverbs of the wise." Hence, the psalms and the prophets can be seen to express the same "world of socioeconomic oppression."[5]

On this same basis, Gottwald challenges the tendency of Christian scholars to treat the prophets as "ethical" champions over against the cultus and priests who are unfairly assumed to represent only "legalism" and social conformity. If language of the psalms and the prophets belongs to the same "world of socioeconomic oppression" with its opposition to "the *pauperization of the populace*," then the priests themselves must have been supportive of these prayers by oppressed people. Though priests required the sanction of the ruling elite, they still sought to be genuinely responsive to those whom the elite oppressed. Consequently, they were in "a difficult spot." Gottwald speculates that priests may have sought "to ameliorate the worst abuses by giving cultic support to the wronged even when the courts failed and by helping to build and disseminate a community climate for the defense of traditional rights." Finally, he conjectures that this tension in the social setting of the cult "may be one reason for the vagueness of language in the laments, because to have been more explicit might have brought further recriminations and penalties on the worshippers and priests alike." From the fact that thanksgiving songs, though fewer than lamentations, are also found in the psalms, Gottwald surmises that "sometimes the actions of oppressors were blocked and frustrated . . . [despite the ruling elite's] determination to smash the tribal landholding system."[6]

This treatment of Psalms is, in my view, one of the best examples of Gottwald's effort to hold literary description and social-scientific analysis together. He challenges literary approaches that underestimate the significance of specific social factors in textual production, or seeks, on a literary-canonical level, to describe how that knowledge about that social-scientific etymology still retains influence in the realism of the present biblical text within scripture. Although Gottwald explores in only a limited manner the frequent loss, alterations, or even reversals in the semantic transformation through tradition history leading to the biblical text, he still reminds us that the retentions of reference to a flesh and blood social world of justice and injustice in the ancient past can prove as illuminating of the biblical text as other appeals to the realism implicit solely in the later purely literary "shape" of a biblical book.

By identifying the enemies in the psalms frequently as the ruling elite or their sympathizers, Gottwald is able to explain plausibly why they would not be named and hence how the priests, who depend on support from the ruling elite, could often join with the populace in worshipful protest. Underlying Gottwald's observation is the assumption that the prayers are heard in public, and, therefore, those who pray take a political risk of response from the "enemies" who overhear, or hear about, these prayers. Though I would want to add several other dimensions to Gottwald's insight about the later association of the psalms with events in the life of David, including the messianic reorientation of royal psalms and other aspects of Psalms within the intertext of scripture, my concern in this essay will be restricted to the implications of references to enemies and, more specifically, those who are assumed to be antagonists within the immediate society of those who pray.

ENEMIES WHO OVERHEAR: SOME FURTHER SOCIAL-SCIENTIFIC CONSIDERATIONS

There have been some substantial anthropological studies of prayers and their reference to enemies in preindustrialized, peasant societies. These studies often highlight the recurring pattern of an individual's "blaming" of other persons within society. As in the psalms, prayers by persons in peasant societies rarely explain misfortune by appeal to either impersonal circumstances or poor planning. This evidence points to what sociologist F. G. Bailey calls one of the "limitations" of the "cognitive map" of peasant societies.[7] "Outsiders," even if they become "officials," are usually viewed as enemies or probable enemies. Likewise, peasants who become rich are commonly assumed to have "cheated" to do so. At a minimum, we are forewarned that the identification of enemies and the rationale for identifying them in ancient Israel's prayers may, at times, have little relation to "moral" outrage. Although social injustice may, indeed, provide a legitimate basis for accusation, xenophobia and the limits of one's cognitive map may also create a search for enemies alien to our modern notion of a just and proper indictment.

Furthermore, in peasant societies the "enemies" frequently include one's peers who become unfriendly, aloof, inhospitable, uncaring, or openly antagonistic. Likewise, the psalms are replete with comments about betrayal by friends, neighbors, and family. There is hope that God will protect the one praying from those "who speak peace with their neighbors, while mischief is in their hearts" (28:3). False witnesses are described as hypocrites who once relied upon the one praying when they themselves were sick (35:11-14). There is the fear that someone who amasses wealth easily becomes pompous and aloof to the needs of erstwhile friends (49:6-20, esp. v. 16). The psalms vividly describe wicked people in the immediate society who surreptitiously abuse widows, sojourners, and orphans because they think God will not take notice of their crimes (94:4-7). Psalm 86 presents a graphic picture of the poor who seek help from such "ruthless men" (v. 14). The enemies seem to be a common topic of prayer partly because social experience confirms that even in one's own neighborhood, "the wicked sprout like grass and all evildoers flourish" (92:7). So, if psalms often consider ruling authorities enemies, as Gottwald emphasizes, they just as often assume the enemy is a peer, a neighbor, or a member of the family.

We must also be careful not to assume that antagonism against ruling authorities in public prayer is uniquely characteristic of biblical psalms. Anthropologist I. M. Lewis reminds us that "ritual relates to the existing economic and social order in a way which is neither simple nor straightforward—nor, above all, is its thrust always in the same direction."[8] Though we normally think of cults as oriented toward supporting established authorities, Lewis observes that even official royal rituals "which primarily protect and hallow the existing power structure may, however, contain rebellious episodes."[9] Lewis observes the general rule that a single public liturgy can contain prayers both of support for the ruling elite and outrage over oppression and abuses of power by those in authority. For example, in the ancient Babylonian Akitu-festival, the king receives blessing and honor, but also ritually confesses his innocence, assuring the god, Marduk, that he "did not smite the cheek of the people under your [the god's] protection." The presiding cult functionary responds by slapping the king's face and pulling harshly on his ears. Tears by the king are a favorable sign to the public.[10]

For an explanation of such ritual behavior, Lewis draws on the studies of African tribal rituals by anthropologist Max Gluckman to show that "songs of hate and unedifying scenes of ritualized violence achieve their apotheosis in a glorious paean of praise celebrating the existing order despite its habitual inequalities and injustices."[11] Prayers of protest against authorities may, following Trotsky and Marxist theories, after the "early" Marx, often seem to serve primarily as a mode of ritualized catharsis and, in fact, to dissipate the will to take revolutionary action. However, Lewis acknowledges another, even if less common, occurrence, namely, that "such ritualized rebellions were frustratingly titillating and led eventually to a greater and more fundamental cataclysmic explosion."[12] Although the ritualized expressions of violence may usually dissipate and neutralize the desire actually to retaliate, to punish, or to take power from another person, the prayer does not preclude the possibility of action either on the part of the one who prays or, as I want to call more to our attention, on the part of those who overhear. These studies confirm that ritual prayers are spoken out loud or "sung" in public; therefore, people accused in the prayers are often present, able to overhear them or at least to hear about them from others who are present.

Furthermore, we may observe that, for the psalms, Gunkel presupposes too readily that the oral use of prayer requires an oral memory with no dependence on a written record, so that the oldest units of traditions must be short.[13] From the preservation of ancient Near Eastern prayers and on the basis of anthropological studies, we now know that the fact that a prayer occurs in written form in no way betrays a necessary transition away from orality. We can assume neither that written traditions always move in the direction of an increasingly learned style in contrast to more primitive oral types of literature, nor that written traditions by their very nature presume a tendency toward silent or privatized usage. Just as Augustine was shocked to find Ambrose reading a text in silence, so we are reminded that the Hebrew verb for reading, *qr'*, signifies principally "to call out," "read aloud," or "to recite." Recent studies have shown that up until the modern period virtually all "reading" of written texts would have been articulated out loud.[14]

For prayer, this same observation applies. Within the Bible, the account of Hannah's prayer in 1 Samuel 1 is the only full account of someone offering an individual lament in a holy city. In that narrative, Hannah came to "the house of the Lord" to ask for a child because she was barren. Eli sat by the doorpost at the time she made her vow, which was part of her prayer. She, then, "kept on praying" but "in her heart." At this point, Eli "watched her mouth," noticing that "only her lips moved, but her voice could not be heard" (vv. 12-13). For that reason alone, Eli accuses her of being drunk. Hannah asserts she is not drunk, but this extraordinary circumstance has occurred because "I have only been speaking all this time out of my great anguish and distress." Clearly, the tradition assumes that Eli's inability to overhear the prayer is exceptional rather than normal. As in the case of Job, prayers are not considered in general elsewhere in the Old Testament to be secretive, silent, or private exercises. The capacity of a prayer to be overheard is a characteristic rather than an incidental feature of it.

This social and political dimension of the prayer has begun to be recognized, but remains one of the most underestimated features in psalm study today. In Claus Westermann's often cited form-critical study of psalms, he puts emphasis on three parties involved: (1) the one praying, (2) God, and (3) the enemy. In this model, the enemy stands as a distant object of the prayer, someone unaware of the psalmist's defiant voice to God.[15] On this point, I am proposing the opposite circumstance, namely, that prayers are assumed to be overheard or, later, heard about by friends and enemies alike; and, furthermore, "enemies" mentioned in these prayers, as often as not, belong to the very same social setting in which one prays. The presence of overhearing "enemies" is integral to the prayer situation and influences the perceived function of prayer socially, rhetorically, religiously, and politically.

Just as Gunkel looked to the book of Job as a model of lamentation, we find there a confirming illustration of this position. Job is joined in mourning by "friends" (2:11). His opening lamentations are overheard and evaluated by them. Early on, as his friends become antagonistic, Job voices his disappointment in them: "My comrades are fickle, like a wadi" (6:15; cf. 6:21). The word *'oyeb*, "enemy," occurs in only three places in the book. Two of the occurrences belong to an argument in which Elihu appears to quote from Job's own words found in 13:24. In that instance, Job claims that God "counts me as his enemy" (cf. 33:10). Conversely, Job's accusations of God seem to treat God as his "enemy." The remaining reference to "enemy" belongs to Job's rebuttal of his friends, accompanied by the petition "Let my enemy be as the wicked, and let him that rises up against me be as the unrighteous" (27:7). In this context, "enemy" is clearly aimed at his friends who came originally to comfort him, but have stayed to torment him with accusations. The "friends" at the beginning of the book have become by its end Job's "enemies." This scenario also explains that an overheard lament traditionally may contain threats and instruction to the enemies, as here in Job. A similar case occurs in the so-called confessions of Jeremiah, where once again family and friends have either deserted him or become active antagonists (cf. Jer 9:4-5, 12:6). Likewise, even God has dealt unfairly with him, overpowering him in a manner that resembles sexual abuse (cf. Jer 20:7). These prayers are not portrayed as silent agonies, but complaints and indictments shared with an audience to which the enemies belong.

Applying this insight to the psalms, I find three principal ways in which the enemy is indirectly addressed in these prayers: (1) as someone whom the psalmist, through overheard prayer, implicitly exposes in public and from whom protection is now sought; (2) through indictments or threats against the enemy; and (3) by harsh commands, advice, or instruction given to the enemy, often in hope for the conversion of the enemy.

Public exposure and protection. Here we return to Delekat's question "When the ones praying and their enemies . . . are private persons, why do they turn to God for protection instead of the civil courts and how do they think of this protection?" My answer is that a prayer that is overheard does, in fact, offer some effective protection from an enemy. Alternatively, for example, a person might impugn an enemy through gossip and shunning, seek illicit revenge, name the enemy in a public curse, or bring a case against the enemy in the courts. Each of these strategies entails different political consequences and different real possibilities of protection. Although taking someone to court, for instance, might in certain cases be plausible and efficient, in many other circumstances courts might not consider some charges and could offer little valuable redress in others. Gottwald recognizes well that the authorities who control the courts might be exposed and threatened effectively in prayers. Furthermore, prayer, as the anthropological evidence confirms, may be less risky in its denunciation of the elite than would some other type of public discourse or court action. The hope by the elite for a cathartic effect may provide one reason for tolerance.

Prayer provides protection for the supplicant in various ways. For one, exposure of an enemy, even though not explicitly named, brings an end to abuse denied or endured in silence. Especially in a tight-knit peasant society these prayers about enemies undoubtedly invited those "in the know" to interpret the prayer in ways that could make obvious who the enemies were and what was the nature of their wrongdoing. The prayers could easily be "reused" to some effect by other parties. From the content of the psalms, we can see that the situation itself is presumed to be common knowledge already. So, in Psalm 41 an individual describes the "enemies" (vv. 3, 6-7, 12) who "come to visit me." Yet they are full of mischief and "go out . . . to tell it abroad," adding poignantly, "Even my bosom friend in whom I trusted, who ate of my bread, has lifted his heel against me" (v. 9). Elsewhere, the psalmist points to the irony of a time when he or she had comforted someone "as though it were a friend or my brother . . . like one mourning for his mother," but now the same person "fights against me" (Ps 35:14). Besides expressing frustration that there are no comforters and that the family no longer recognizes the one who prays, a fear is expressed in Psalm 69 that "I am the subject of gossip for those who sit in the gate." Elsewhere one observes, "Because of my foes I am the particular butt of my neighbors, a horror to my friends, those who see me on the street avoid me" (Ps 31:11-13; cf. the "empty folly" of the enemy in v. 6). Prayer is assumed to be only one moment in a larger web of intriguing words and actions in which the psalmist is fully involved. Indictments in prayer offer some protection for the psalmist because they expose actions taken by others and implicitly threaten further exposure and recognition of the same by everyone who overhears or hears from others present about the prayer.

Moreover, the words of prayer are distinguished from words used in gossip and can, consequently, be unusually blunt and graphic. In this regard, prayer becomes a significant alternative to gossip because, unlike gossip, it makes God the primary listener, maintains the intimacy of that discourse by not naming the enemy, and directly asks God, rather than neighbors, to respond in word and deed in behalf of the petitioner. As prophets are protected, despite their denunciations, by claiming that their words are God's rather than their own, the psalmist can argue that only God is directly addressed rather than the public. Just as the prophet when speaking prophetically cannot properly be charged with sedition, the psalmist when praying cannot properly be accused of gossip. In so doing, each finds protection while they publicly expose enemies, despite the need for those who overhear to interpret the ambiguous words in terms of specific parties.

Another protection sought by the psalmist through prayer is found in the actions that might be taken both by God and by those who overhear. The psalmist obviously hopes that prayer will evoke God's mercy and ensure that "the righteous will surround me" (Ps 142:7). The biblical psalms of lamentation and praise are filled with asides to those who overhear to join in prayer, to take up shouts, or even to repeat specific pious formulas.[16] In this way, prayer offers the prospect of protection both by God and by other persons who overhear and who join both in prayer and care for the one who suffers. Also, an assumption in the prayer is that those who overhear ought to be able to discern a fit between the words of the prayer and the discrete circumstances of the one praying in terms of specific persons and events. In the complaint of Psalm 38 about "enemies" (v. 19), the claim is made that "my friends and companions stand aloof from my plague, and my kinsmen stand afar off" (v. 11). This complaint presupposes that one's intimates should come near at the time of prayer and show themselves as publicly supportive. Prayers, therefore, become a unique political event that tests the loyalty of friends who must choose to stand either near or afar off. The prayer undermines the potential of secret treachery on the part of the enemy, because friends who are true sympathizers become alert to the perceived presence of an enemy.

Finally, there is some protection in the hope that the prayer itself might lead the enemy to repent and stop the wrongdoing. Although the address of prayer to God explains why the enemies do not need to be named, it also provides an opportunity for the enemies to save face, to alter their actions, or perhaps even to seek face to face reconciliation and reparation (see below, "Harsh commands, advice, and instruction to the enemy"). This circumstance stands in contrast to the real possibility of naming an enemy within prayer, as shown in the case of Neh 6:14. Furthermore, the commonplace ambiguity in the accusations of prayer hint at the possibility that the psalmist can resort to more explicit condemnation and other means of protection or remedy. Such prayers employ a less confrontative strategy than other possible verbal indictments on the part of the psalmist and, consequently, guarantee more protection for the one praying than some other type of discourse and action.

Indictments and threats. Frequently in the psalms we find appeals to God for judgment, and threats or hateful wishes directed against the enemies. God may be asked to slay the wicked (e.g., Ps 139:19), or a blessing is offered to whoever will do the same (e.g., Psalm 137). A hope for the destruction of the wicked and their families is common (e.g., Psalm 109). God's vengeance on the enemy provides an occasion to rejoice (e.g., Ps 58:9-10). These expressions seem less related to any specifically contemplated action on the part of the psalmist than to the vivid expression of anger and wish for protection or retaliation. Perhaps one underestimated implication of the overhearing of such prayers by the enemy is the degree to which the threat itself might be an effort indirectly to persuade the enemies to change their thoughts or course of action. So, in the prophets, Jonah hesitates to deliver a threat to the Ninevites because he suspects they might repent and begrudges any blessing God might grant them. This role of the prophetic threat is, of course, assumed in Jonah to be characteristic of prophecy in general. So, too, the consequences of the prophetic threat that Isaiah brings against Hezekiah in Isaiah 38 is, by God's response to the king's response in the form of a sincere prayer, delayed by fifteen years. Likewise, the indirect threat aimed at an enemy in prayer by its very public nature allows the possibility of the enemy's repentance, reconciliation, reparation, or the abatement of offensive actions.

More rarely, a prayer may contain an indictment reminiscent of a juridical charge. Psalm 55 complains bitterly of "the enemy" who causes "the oppression of the wicked" (v. 3). The supplicant is well into the prayer when a sudden and shocking revelation occurs:

> It is not an enemy who taunts me —
>   then I could bear it;
> it is not an adversary who deals insolently with me —
>   then I could hide from him.
> But it is you, my equal, my companion, my familiar friend.
>   (vv. 12-13)

This announcement of a friend who has become like an enemy is given plaintive depth by the further assertions: "We used to hold intimate conversations together, as we walked with the throng at the house of God" (v. 14). This past companion who worships at the same place is now accused of attacking his own friend, violating the covenant, and acting as one with words "smoother than butter, yet war was in his heart" (vv. 20-21). The social context suggests that the person indicted is present and overhears the prayer and should be convicted by its rhetoric.

The formula of accusation "But it is you" (*we'atta 'enoš*) occurs elsewhere in the prophets commonly as part of the accusation within juridical parables. For example, after Nathan tells David a parable and the king offers his judgment of the protagonist, the prophet responds, "You are the man!" (*'atta ha'iš;* 2 Sam 12:7). Similarly, in Isa 3:13-14 the prophet addresses the leaders in Judah, "It is you (*we'attem*) who devoured the vineyard!" This text has been displaced editorially from its original position with the rest of a juridical parable now found still preserved in Isa 5:1-7.[17] Psalm 55 shows at least the possibility of an accusation that surprises the friend who is unwittingly in attendance at the time of the prayer. This usage of prayer parallels exactly the use of a juridical parable by which someone is invited surreptitiously to make a judgment that, immediately, proves to be his or her own self-condemnation. Here a friend stands nearby and, therefore, supports and joins in the prayer of a lamenter. By staying close to the lamenter, the friend implicitly judges that the description of abuse is sufficient to deserve the severity of the prayer's complaint. Suddenly, the lamenter exposes the friend ("it is you") and capitalizes on the friend's unwitting self-condemnation. In this sophisticated manner, the friend is here exposed publicly as one who has, in fact, acted as an enemy.

Accordingly, the threats and wishes for opposition to the enemy in the prayer are heard as applicable to real situations rather than viewed as merely psychological projections. Besides specific indictments—for example, "You have caused friends and neighbors to shun me" (Ps 88:8, 18)—there are specific threats; for example, "May his memory be cut off from the earth" (109:13). The intensity of these accusations probably corresponds to the intensity of perceived pain, suffering, and need. If one takes seriously the degree of anguish that gives rise to these prayers, as well as the presence of the enemy so often within the community, then we must take seriously how violent ordinary life must have seemed for the ones who prayed these prayers. This violence points not only to the life-threatening power of the rich over the poor, but also to abuse within families, and between erstwhile friends and neighbors. The psalms suggest that contentment and harmony were fragile elements within the society for diverse reasons. Although threats expressed in silence toward an enemy may seem extreme to modern ears, they may become more understandable if they are overheard and pertain also to family violence, sexual abuse, and internecine conflicts that are common even today and increase when other economic injustices in society become more extreme. Although the expressed wishes for violent revenge are rhetorical, polemical, and sometimes exaggerated in tone, they should, nonetheless, be seen to reflect real feelings of hostility in response to an equally intense sense of pain and violation on the part of the petitioners.

Harsh commands, advice, and instruction to the enemy. In some of these psalms we find instructions to the enemy. Psalms often address the supportive members of the congregation in this same way. Prayers may contain admonitions, for example: "Love the Lord, all you his saints! ... Be strong and let your heart take courage" (31:23-24, cf. 32:6). Instructive descriptions may be offered, with blessings and condemnation of certain actions: "Blessed is the man who makes the Lord his trust" (40:4; cf. 62:8) and "Behold the wicked man conceives evil" (7:14-16; cf. 10:2-11; 14:1-6; 17:10-12). Didactic teaching, including the use of proverbs, occurs throughout the psalms and resonates even in introductory invocation: "I will instruct you and teach you the way you should go" (32:8-11; cf. 37:1-40; 49:1-20; 78:1-72). Other psalms indirectly address the enemy as well as any potential enemies among those who overhear. Prayers may contain statements in the second person, in the form of a command: "Depart from me" (6:8-10; cf. 35:19) or a repartee: "You would confound the plans of the poor, but God is his refuge" (14:6). The opening verses of Psalm 52 have exactly this same tone, with the rhetorical question "Why do you boast, O mighty man?" In Psalm 62 the enemies are addressed at the outset: "How long will you assail a person, will you batter your victim, all of you?" (v. 3). Then those tempted to join with the enemies are instructed: "Put no confidence in extortion and set no vain hopes on robbery" (v. 10). These statements fulfill some of the promise expressed in Ps 51:13: "I will teach transgressors your ways, that sinners may return to thee." Here is seen a side benefit of public prayer. The evildoer and the potential enemy may learn from the prayer and be admonished to alter his or her actions. Similarly, Ps 94:8-11 with its proverbs assumes the same role for prayer, that the wicked and foolish might gain insight through overhearing these well-said prayers. This is so, too, in Job; immediately after calling his friends enemies (27:7), Job volunteers to "teach you according to the hand of God" (v. 11) and offers a description of the wicked man who will not prevail (vv. 13-23) in a manner similar to that of the psalms.[18]

ENEMIES WHO OVERHEAR: A CANONICAL APPROACH

The preceding investigation has primarily been a social-scientific assessment of prayer in ancient Israel. In his *The Hebrew Bible,* Gottwald highlights some implications of the collecting of these psalms into a book, and of its role within a later canonical context of scripture. He argues that much of the biblical prehistory of these prayers is retained in this later scriptural presentation. My study will conclude with some further suggestions about how the originating sociopolitical situation is partially retained, but also how the scriptural presentation subverted, reoriented, or semantically transformed other moments in the same prebiblical traditions when they became a part of scripture.

1. When the ancient prayers were collected, they often gained secondarily an association with familiar biblical figures, and a few were given historicizing titles that play directly upon episodes in the life of David depicted in 1 and 2 Samuel. Consequently, most prayers in the book of Psalms are now presented in relation to a specific set of individuals (e.g., Moses, Solomon, David, Korah, Asaph). One effect of the historicizing titles is that *the reader* can sometimes know the identity of an unnamed enemy in David's use of a prayer both by the title and by appeal to the narratives in 1 and 2 Samuel (e.g., Absalom, Psalm 3; Cush, Psalm 7; Saul, Psalms 18 and 57; Abimelech, Psalm 34; Doeg the Edomite, Psalm 52; Philistines, Psalm 56). The titles permit readers of the

prayers in scripture to "overhear" them in a way similar to how they were once overheard in their biblical prehistory. Here, to a degree, the older living situation of prayer is retained and perpetuated in the later book of Psalms.

The psalms now contribute, within scripture, to the realistic depiction of David's activity of prayer, distinct from or in collusion with other rhetorical or physical responses of David to his enemies. Once again, prayer is seen as one option, or even as an alternative to other possibilities of discourse. As in Psalm 73, the one praying thought in response to the words of the enemy, "I will talk on in this way." But such use of words would have been "untrue," and, though prayer seemed "a wearisome task," the psalmist felt differently when he or she "went into the sanctuary" (vv. 15-17). So, the decision to use prayer rather than, or in conjunction with, some other forms of discourse is not self-evident, and entails a critical decision within faith. Admittedly, these depictions do not offer us "history" in the narrow modern sense, but as a part of scripture they can be heard as witness to God's revelation regarding the politics of prayer within history. From the standpoint of canonical context, we see that social-scientific knowledge of these ancient prayers can continue to illuminate those elements retained in the book of Psalms and refines the nature of the biblical witness to prayer itself.

2. Gottwald grants that the formation of the prayers in a book of scripture obscured or altered some elements of the originating prehistory. He warns against a tendency by some scholars to find in the association of psalms with named individuals a warrant for merely pietistic or individualistic interpretations of them. Our study may help us appreciate why complaints even about illness are often accompanied by accusations of enemies. In their own way, the psalmists assumed that "illness" is never just a "private" medical problem.[19] Today, we are even more aware of how illness can be related to stress, malnutrition, inhumane conditions of labor, lack of uncontaminated water, and so forth. Additionally, how society responds to the one who prays about an illness is another test of those who overhear.

Each of these features points again to a larger socioeconomic setting, so that illness, rather than being a private matter, belongs to the entire social fabric, in both the ancient period and in the present. As a contemporary example, whether Jewish and Christian believers will touch someone with AIDS, will stand near or afar, and how they will address the enemies who contribute through carelessness or prejudice to that suffering, are all questions that pertain to the testimony of the psalms regarding the theology and the politics of prayer.

Furthermore, because "David stood for the righteous leader of the community," Gottwald warns against either naive historical or psychological speculation. In this same direction, the presentation of David as speaking prophetically in the psalms shows a further semantic transformation of the older prayers (cf. 2 Sam 23:1-2; 1 Chr 25:1-3; 2 Chr 20:14, 24:19; Acts 2:29-30; Matt 22:43; Luke 12:36). As parts of the book of Psalms, the older prayers can now be read both as commentary on the Torah and as promises that find their fulfillment, for Christians, in how the sufferings of the oppressed participate in the redemptive sufferings of Jesus on the cross. This prophetic and messianic dimension in the context of scripture resists any reduction of the psalms to merely ancient examples of individual prayers.

3. Alongside Gottwald's proposal that the unnamed enemies were frequently members of the ruling elite, our study shows that the "enemies" could just as often be neighbors, friends, or members of the family. The prayers point, in my view, to a world of intimate enemies not so different from our own. Only in the recent period have churches begun to acknowledge the all too common occurrence of violence associated with addictions, incest, child abuse, date rape, sexism in the school and workplace, racism, and the abuse of wives by husbands. This admission might help us hear, for example, Psalm 55 as a resource in connection with the abuse of wives.[20] That these prayers were meant to be overheard invites any reader of scripture to ask not only "What prayers should I pray?" but also "What prayers might others pray about me?" The role of such prayers overheard would, furthermore, represent a form of discourse that does not perpetuate denial. Instead, it would show an awareness that accusations of an intimate enemy can take a variety of forms, in the determination to stop the violence and, at times, in the hope of some face-saving repentance and reparation. The complaint need not end in prayer, but at least the one praying is challenged to become fairly articulate to God about the injustice in order to name it and to instruct those who stand nearby, even when the enemy may be included in that group.

4. Gottwald, furthermore, suggests that we can "illuminate" the language of the psalms by linking it to the speeches of the prophets. In my view, this position finds its best support by appeal to the later canonical context of scripture. This context is constructed by dependence upon an intertextuality that requires interpretive links between different collections of biblical tradition, regardless of how anachronistic these links may be from a modern historical point of view. Such an intertextuality may blur social-scientific distinctions between different periods. One may question whether there is any constant and fixed "world of economic oppression" in the history of Israel, or if the social situation and referential import of the religious language of the postexilic psalter coincides originally and historically with the speeches of the preexilic prophets. For example, I would argue that many original possibilities once implicit in the term "enemies," including petty attitudes due to the limits of a peasant's "cognitive map," have been reoriented semantically when the earlier prayers are read as parts of the book of Psalms. In the interpretation of Psalms in the context of a later scripture, we find correlative information about enemies in the prophets (as Gottwald suggests) and in other parts of scripture as well. For one instance, the blunt antagonism against enemies in the psalms as scripture should be read within the larger intertext of admonitions to be kind to enemies in the Torah (Lev 19:17, 18; Exod 23:4-5) and in the Solomonic Wisdom books (Prov 24:17; 28:17). This larger context helps us understand, from a Christian perspective, how the teaching of Jesus about kindness to enemies finds its warrants in Jewish scripture and is not a "Christian" corrective to the "Old" Testament. Within Christian scripture, the Torah, Prophets, and Wisdom still warrant idiomatically how language about "enemies" in the book of Psalms belongs to the full human

witness of the text to God's revelation of the gospel and the role of prayer within it.

5. Finally, this investigation helps us realize that prayer is always "political," as is especially obvious if it is overheard and serves as one form of public discourse in comparison with others. We may argue that prayer even when spoken in private is a political activity. Prayer requires an economic use of times and places. Prayer seeks to articulate reality, attribute aspects of reality to God, summon God to act, and nurture courage to persevere or provoke changes in the conduct of the one who prays. The question is, strictly speaking, not whether a prayer is political, but what politics pertain to this or that particular prayer. Even in silent prayer, an assumption is usually present that something trans- formative is happening in the solitude of prayer. For all of these reasons, the choice between piety and politics, rights and ritual, is always a false one, from a socioeconomic as well as a theological perspective. This observation stands despite the common criticism of hypocrisy in prayer, when people pray accord- ing to one theo-political agenda but conduct their lives in a way that collaborates with or even promotes the very evils condemned in these prayers.

In sum, the core of this essay has been a social-scientific consideration of prebiblical prayers that later become parts of the biblical book of Psalms. In the final emphasis on the canonical context, my aim is to help define the arena in which theological interpretation of scripture takes place. Only a few features have been considered in terms of a canonical approach.[21] At a minimum, in a theology of prayer that uses scripture as its authoritative guide, the occurrence of "enemies" in the psalms reminds us of the political background integral to all language of prayer. These observations show how the intertextuality of the book of Psalms confirms the caution of Dietrich Bonhoeffer that such prayers do not depend merely on the imagination of the heart (including social and political analysis) but ultimately seek to be an expression informed by the Word of God.[22] There is, also, the perceptive reminder by Childs that the "right- eousness" underlying these prayers is not an "ideal" norm indicative of a "works righteousness."[23] Instead, "righteousness" and "justice" in the psalms both belong to the vocabulary of faith in the covenant that God freely established with Israel in association with acts of divine deliverance. For that reason, we are reminded that, as scripture, "these confessions functioned within Israel's worship as a declaration of loyalty to a prior claim."[24] In my view, it is this loyalty to a "prior claim" that requires of us a careful adjudication of modern social-scientific insight. Only by accepting that challenge can we in late modern- ity begin to understand profoundly how the book of Psalms as scripture still provides a normative witness to the politics of prayers for Jews and Christians alike.

A Christian response to these matters should, at the outset, acknowledge the independent value of Jewish scripture for Christian theology. Only with that full awareness may Christians seek, then, to hear properly the witness of Jewish scripture as "Old Testament" within the larger context of Christian scripture. In the latter case, Christians must look to the cross and its import for our understanding of the gospel. There are many great dangers if that effort loses its footing in the gospel, which is its true subject matter—if one finds, for example, a simple identification of "Jews" as the enemies of Jesus, or if the cross is seen as a warrant for masochism or other worldly acquiescence to injustice, or if the suffering of Jesus is viewed as a romantic, triumphalist apotheosis of pain. This important theological issue far exceeds the limits of this one essay. Its solution lies, in my view, in the direction of Bonhoeffer's challenge that Christians must learn from the New Testament witness how "the crucified Jesus teaches us to pray the imprecatory psalms."[25] This way of framing the question requires a careful consideration of both the continuity and the discontinuity that Christianity must maintain with its priceless legacy in Judaism and Jewish scripture.

NOTES

1. H. Gunkel and J. Begrich, *Einleiung in die Psalmen: Die Gattungen der religiosen Lyrik Israels* (Handbuch zum Alten Testament: Göttingen: Vandenhoeck & Ruprecht, 1933) 184. Cf. R. C. Culley, *Oral Formulaic Language in the Biblical Psalms* (Toronto: University of Toronto Press, 1967) 23-31.

2. O. Keel, *Feinde und Gottesleugner: Studien zum Image der Widersaeher in den Individualpsalmen* (Stuttgarter biblische Monographien 7; Stuttgart: Katholisches Biblewerk GmbH, 1969).

3. N. K. Gottwald, *The Hebrew Bible: A Socio-Literary Introduction* (Philadelphia: Fortress, 1985); see the section entitled "A Common Ground in New Literary and Social Scientific Criticism" (pp. 29-31).

4. Gottwald, *The Hebrew Bible*, 538.

5. Ibid., 539.

6. Ibid., 539-40.

7. F. G. Bailey, "The Peasant View of the Bad Life," *Peasants and Peasant Societies* (ed. T. Shanin; New York: Penguin, 1971) 314.

8. I. M. Lewis, *Social Anthropology in Perspective: The Relevance of Social Anthropology* (New York: Penguin, 1976) 140.

9. Ibid., 141.

10. H. W. F. Saggs, *The Greatness that Was Babylon* (New York: Mentor, 1962), 366.

11. Lewis, *Social Anthropology,* 142. Cf. M. Gluckman, *Order and Rebellion in Tribal Africa: Collected Essays* (London: Routledge & Kegan Paul, 1963).

12. Lewis, *Social Anthropology,* 144.

13. E.g., "Die Grundprobleme der israelitischen Literaturgeschichte," *Reden und Aufsätze* (Göttingen: Vandenhoeck & Ruprecht, 1913) 33-34. In the same essay, Gunkel describes the sad consequence of this progression to learned, written poetry and the canonization of scripture under the following characterization: "Zum Schluss dann die Tragödie der israelitischen Literatur: der Geist nimmt ab ... " (p. 36). For Gunkel, editors of scripture appear most frequently as clumsy and doctrinaire manipulators of the original, smaller, pristine unities of the oral *Gattungen.*

14. K. Grayson, "Murmuring in Mesopotamia" (forthcoming in a *Festschrift* for W. G. Lambert; London: School of Oriental and African Studies, 1992); J. Saenger, "Silent Reading: Its Import on Late Medieval Scripture and Society," *Viator* 13

(1982) 367-414. On the anecdote about Augustine and Ambrose, see Augustine's *Confessions,* Sect. VI, 3, lines 25-27.

15. C. Westermann, "Struktur und Geschichte der Klage im Alten Testament," *Forschung am Alten Testament (Theologische Bücherie* 24; Munich: Kaiser, 1964) 269-95.

16. The lament psalms frequently contain vows that promise to offer a thanksgiving psalm in the sanctuary and before the assembly of people there. So, Ps 35:18 promises that "I will praise you in the great congregation; in the mighty throng I will acclaim you" (v. 18, cf. 40:10; 22:22). Psalm 116:13-14 describes a ritual of lifting a cup at a banquet in the presence of friends. Psalms can expressly call upon the surrounding people to clap their hands, shout for joy, and join in the praise (e.g., 22:23; 33:1; 34:3-5; 47:1; 66:1-3, 8; 68:4), and sometimes prayers suggest the very words the listening congregation should say to God (e.g., 35:27; 66:3).

17. Cf. G. T. Sheppard, "The Anti-Assyrian Redaction and the Canonical Context of Isaiah 1-39," *JBL* 104 (1985) 204-11.

18. E. Gerstenberger properly detects in these psalms signs of a "dispute between opposing parties for individuals who are suffering" (*Psalms: Part 1. With an Introduction to Cultic Poetry* [FOTL 14; Grand Rapids: Eerdmans, 1988] 79). My proposal about the role of overhearing such prayers would, however, eliminate the need to speculate precariously, as Gerstenberger and other scholars have done, about the possibility of an open verbal accusation and response with an enemy as a formal part of worship activity. Speech addressed directly to the enemy certainly would invite a response, but prayer by its nature is addressed first to God and only secondarily to those who overhear. In the logic of prayer, God is always given the option to reply first!

19. This tendency is very common and might be grounds for criticizing, for example, Brevard Childs' discussion of psalms in the chapter "Life Under Threat" of his *Old Testament Theology in a Canonical Context* (Philadelphia: Fortress, 1986). Childs there explains the language of "death" by "the suffering community" solely in terms of the experience of one's own short life and of "illness" as a foretaste of each person's inevitable, natural death.

20. On a similar use of the psalms, see M. M. Fortune, "My God, My God, Why Have You Forsaken Me?" *Spinning a Sacred Yarn: Women Speak from the Pulpit* (ed. by the publisher; New York: Pilgrim, 1982) 65-71, and S. B. Thistlethwaithe, "Every Two Minutes—Battered Women and Feminist Interpretation," *Weaving the Visions: New Patterns in Feminist Spirituality* (ed. J. Plaskow and C. Christ; San Francisco: Harper & Row, 1989).

21. For more on this same subject, see my "Blessed Are Those Who Take Refuge in Him (Ps 2:11): Biblical Criticism and Deconstruction," *Religion and Intellectual Life* 5 (1988) 57-66, and "Psalms: How Do the Ordinary Words of Women and Men [to God] Become God's Word to Me?" *The Future of the Bible: How to Read a Book that Seems Intent on Reading You* (Toronto: The United Church Publishing House, 1990) 49-98.

22. D. Bonhoeffer, *Psalms: The Prayerbook of the Bible* (Minneapolis: Augsburg, 1970) 11-12.

23. Childs, *Old Testament Theology,* 231-32.

24. Ibid., 207-10.

25. Bonhoeffer, *Psalms,* 60.

PART III

SOCIOPOLITICAL READINGS
OF THE SECOND TESTAMENT

25

RICHARD A. HORSLEY

The Imperial Situation of Palestinian Jewish Society

By late second Temple and New Testament times, Palestinian Jews had been subject to one foreign empire after another for centuries. Imperial rule may have been indirect, but it nevertheless had a powerful impact on the lives of the people. The "imperial situation" under which the Jewish people lived meant that their high priestly rulers served in effect as the imperial representatives in ways that violated the interests of their own people. Groups of ostensible Jewish "leaders" were caught in the middle, functioning as mediators of imperial social control even as they fostered the observance of the native Jewish traditions in the Torah. The economic burdens imposed on the peasantry by the tribute to Caesar and the heavy taxation by the Herodian client kings contributed heavily to the disintegration of local village and family life. Under Hellenistic and Roman domination, the imperial situation in Jewish Palestine was highly conflictual and volatile, with repeated popular insurrections. The ministry of Jesus, the development of the Gospel traditions, and the emergence of rabbinic Judaism can hardly be understood without taking into account the pervasive impact of this imperial situation.

Reprinted from Richard A. Horsley, *Jesus and the Spiral of Violence: Popular Jewish Resistance in Roman Palestine* (San Francisco: Harper & Row, 1987), 3–19.

The Jews of Jesus' day were a subject people. Ever since the fall of Jerusalem to the Babylonian armies in 587 B.C.E., Jewish society had been subject to one imperial regime after another. The Babylonians destroyed the original Temple of Solomon, deported the ruling class to Babylon, and thus brought the Davidic dynasty to an end. When the Persians conquered Babylon in 538 B.C.E., they reversed the Babylonian imperial policy by allowing the Judean and other indigenous ruling classes to return to their native countries. Although the Persian empire thus appears relatively benign in our sources, most of which were produced by the governing elite, Judea remained a subject territory.

Alexander the Great and his Macedonian armies, who conquered all territory from Greece to Egypt and India in the 330s B.C.E., did not simply bring yet another foreign political rule but imposed a cultural imperialism as well. The little out-of-the-way territory of Judea, relatively isolated from the cosmopolitan currents of communication and trade, did not come immediately under the sway of the new Hellenistic cultural and political forms. Indeed, the Jewish aristocracy's attempt to implement a Hellenizing "reform" in 175 B.C.E. touched off the massive popular Maccabean revolt (after 168) that asserted the independence of Judean society once again.

Yet the tiny country ruled now semi-independently by the Maccabean or Hasmonean high priests was still part of a larger imperial system. As the Hellenistic empire of the Seleucids declined, the Romans exerted their influence and finally conquered the whole eastern Mediterranean, including Palestine, in 63 B.C.E. Thereafter, whether through the Herodian client kings or the collaborating Jewish priestly aristocracy, the Romans controlled affairs in Jewish society. Jesus was crucified by the Romans, and it was the Romans who placed the Pharisees (become rabbis) in control of Palestinian Jewish society after the Jewish revolt of 66-70. Thus, both Christianity and Rabbinic Judaism began under Roman imperial rule.

In the fields of biblical studies and Jewish history there has been a tendency to interpret biblical and other material on the assumption that we could deal with Jewish society by itself. There has also been the understandable tendency in biblical interpretation and study of religion to concentrate on the cultural dimension of history. Some have cautioned that Jewish phenomena of the second Temple period must be understood as part of a larger cosmopolitan whole—Hellenistic civilization in the eastern Mediterranean.[1] To the extent that such appeals have been heeded, however, adjustments have been made principally in the area of cultural history, particularly in examining the influence of "Hellenism."

Because Palestinian Jewish society was a constituent part of successive empires throughout the second Temple period, however, it was involved in something similar to what in modern times has been called a "colonial situation."[2] The particular structure of this "colonial" or "imperial situation" influences the orientation and actions of both "colonizer" and "colonized" and particularly the relations between them. It is important to recognize that relations between the dominant empire and the subject people are full of tension and conflict and cannot possibly be comprehended simply in terms of "culture contact" or "acculturation." If Jewish society had been occupied and exploited for only a short time, it would be less important to take the "imperial situation" into account. However, in a case such as ancient Judea, where the people had been ruled by one empire after another for a period of centuries, we must consider the antagonism and conflicts resulting from the prolonged forcible subjugation of a proud people by the dominant imperial regimes.

For example, such a society may have been almost continually in circumstances of crisis. To use only the most dramatic manifestations of the endemic tensions and conflicts between imperial domination and subjugated Judean society—that is, violent rebellion—late second Temple and New Testament times were framed by three of the major popular revolts in antiquity. In the Maccabean revolt, beginning in 168-167 B.C.E., the Judeans successfully rebelled against the Hellenistic empire of the Seleucid regime in Syria and against their own assimilationist, "Westernizing" aristocracy. Then twice within seventy years, in 66-70 and in 132-135 C.E., Palestinian Jews rose in prolonged popular rebellion against Roman domination and, in the revolt of 66-70, against their own priestly aristocracy as well. Between the Maccabean revolt and the anti-Roman revolts, moreover, there were several lesser Jewish popular rebellions against the imperial power or against their own semi-independent rulers or both: a rebellion against Alexander Jannai, popular resistance to the Roman conquest of Judea by Pompey in 63 B.C.E., prolonged popular rebellion and "civil war" during the great Roman "Civil War" in the 40s B.C.E., popular resistance to Herod's conquest of his realm as the client ruler for Rome in 38-37, and an outbreak of popular rebellion in every major district of Herod's kingdom at the latter's death in 4 B.C.E.

There was resistance and even rebellion in certain other subject societies in antiquity. The conflict and turmoil created in Palestinian Jewish society, however, was unusually intense and the "colonial situation" more volatile than elsewhere in Hellenistic-Roman antiquity. We must consider, finally, that these frequent armed rebellions were only the most violent manifestations. Underlying these highly visible rebellions were the continuing tensions and conflicts in which the more violent outbursts were rooted. It thus seems obvious that we should consider the principal aspects of the *imperial situation* in which the Judean people lived during the second Temple period.

DOMINATION BY FOREIGN EMPIRES

The relation between empire and subject people is one of power. Generally the imperial regime establishes domination initially by military force, often aided appreciably by technological superiority.[3] Domination is often maintained, however, by economic and cultural means. The relations between master and subject can thus be conveniently understood in terms of three interrelated but analytically separable dimensions: the economic, the political, and the cultural. Whereas some interpreters of modern colonialism have overemphasized the economic aspect, the tendency in biblical studies, with their focus on cultural-religious phenomena, has been to underemphasize or ignore the economic dimension. It is important to consider all dimensions and their interrelationship.

Pacification, domination, and development of a subject country is carried out in the interests of the imperial society. Modern colonizers sought trade and markets as well as materials. Economic exploitation by ancient empires, while including trade and materials, concentrated primarily on demanding tribute for the benefit of the dominant ruling groups. Development, in the form of cities, roads and aqueducts—all constructed with forced labor—was primarily in the interest of the imperial rulers and of their local upper-class allies. In order to extract its tribute from the primarily agricultural producers, the empire required a staff of tax collectors. The ostensibly "political" administration also basically served the purpose of economic exploitation. Even where cultural forms and psychological habits of dependency had been established, the country had to be held down—by occupying troops or by credible threat of military violence. Of course some areas were occupied not only for direct economic exploitation, but for their strategic importance in maintaining imperial control of other peoples or in protecting an uncertain frontier.

As we have noted, the Jews were subject to a succession of imperial regimes throughout the second Temple period, except for a brief interlude of about two generations when they were semi-independent under the Hasmonean high priests. If the legacy of the Babylonian conquest was the termination of the Judeans' existence as an independent people, along with the destruction of Jerusalem and of the original Temple, the legacy of the Persian empire was the reconstruction of Judea as a subject Temple-community under the imperially guaranteed authority of the high priesthood.

Alexander the Great's imperial successors, particularly the Ptolemies in Egypt and the Seleucids from Syria eastward, imposed Hellenistic political and cultural forms in addition to the usual exaction of tribute. The Ptolemies, who ruled Judea along with the rest of Palestine from 301 to 200, instituted an unusually efficient imperial bureaucracy that proved highly effective in the economic exploitation of Palestine as well as Egypt. The ubiquitous operation of the hated "tax" and "toll-collectors" (*telōnēs* in Greek) dates from Hellenistic times. For both the Ptolemies and the Seleucids (the latter took control of Palestine in 200), Judea was probably more important strategically as a link in their frontier defenses against each other than as a source of economic exploitation. Ptolemaic presence and, initially, Seleucid rule in Judea were primarily military and economic. In contrast to what was done in other areas, neither the Ptolemies nor the Seleucids imposed Hellenistic political forms directly on traditional Judean society. As the Seleucids' power became overextended, however, they became more desperate for funds and encouraged and then forcibly imposed the Hellenization of Judea through the Jerusalem ruling class. This Seleucid shift in imperial policy with regard to Judea proved fateful for subsequent Judean and Western religious history, for it led eventually to the successful Maccabean revolt.

The unusually predatory and oppressive treatment of the Jews by the Seleucid empire is vividly portrayed in the vision of four beasts recounted in Daniel 7. The first three beasts, representing the Babylonian, the Medean, and the

Persian empires, respectively, were fearsome enough. The bear, for example, "had three ribs in its mouth between its teeth; and it was told, 'Arise, devour much flesh.' " However, the fourth beast—the Hellenistic empire(s)—was "terrible and dreadful and exceedingly strong, and it had great iron teeth; it devoured and broke in pieces, and stamped the residue with its feet. It was different from all the beasts that were before it . . ." (Daniel 7:5, 7).

As the power of the Hellenistic empire declined, Rome easily dominated instead. Pompey "pacified" the eastern Mediterranean in 64-63 B.C.E. Augustus, the winner of the battle of Actium in 37 B.C.E., finally imposed the imperial *pax Romana,* which was to remain until its decline in late antiquity. As for the earlier empires, Judea probably held more of a strategic than an exploitative economic value for Rome. Tribute was nevertheless taken without fail; in Rome's eyes, nonpayment was tantamount to rebellion. Besides the tribute, Rome also collected numerous tolls. The "tax collectors" mentioned in the Gospels were probably the collectors of these tolls (and were apparently underling Jews working for the principal government tax agents). Under Roman rule, particularly under Rome's client King Herod, there was considerable "development" in the country, including Herod's rebuilding of the Temple and the construction of an aqueduct under the Roman governor Pontius Pilate. This "development," however, far from benefitting the ordinary people, was funded by the products taken from them in the form of taxes, tithes, and tribute. To hold the pacified people in check, the Romans depended on a relatively small occupying military force stationed primarily in Caesarea on the coast. But this force was backed by the well-known threat of overpowering retaliation in the event of serious trouble or resistance—as the Jews discovered on several occasions (in 63 and the 40s B.C.E., and especially in 66-70 and 131-135 C.E.).

The development of cultural and psychological mechanisms of domination and dependency (which supported imperial domination) included religious forms along with "civilization" through language and education. The modern Christian mission enterprise is not historically unprecedented. Ancient Near Eastern empires had long ago imposed their "gods" on subject people. The Old Testament is full of such stories. In modern colonial situations, "less sophisticated societies interpreting the impact of the West in their own categories, came to the conclusion that the superiority of the White man was so great that it must derive from quite supernatural sources. The White man clearly did not work. There must be some mystical secret."[4] In ancient Hellenistic and Roman empires, however, it was the *more* "sophisticated" (both the imperial courts and the aristocratic class in the subject cities and peoples) who interpreted the cosmically symbolized order and welfare brought to the world as due to the divine powers of the emperor.[5] The Romans appear to have been unusually cautious in dealing with Judea. Although they expected a daily sacrifice for the emperor in the Jewish Temple in Jerusalem, they generally respected the Jews' special sensitivity regarding "emperor worship." The points at which Roman officials were not sensitive, however, became occasions for some dramatic events.

SUBORDINATION AND CRISIS FOR THE SUBJECT SOCIETY

Control of a subject society has often been exercised through an already-existing indigenous ruling class or dominant aristocracy. The imperial regime compromised members of such a class by giving them a serious economic stake in the imperial system of domination. Often such nominally "indirect" systems of government "involved as much control over and manipulation of, the 'traditional' authorities ... as any system of 'direct' rule."[6] Indirect rule had another advantage. It provided a bridge of legitimation that enabled an empire to divide and rule. Popular resentment was deflected onto the local officials or aristocracy, while the imperial rulers remained more remote, less directly evident and involved.[7] Whether the system of government worked through imperial officials or indigenous aristocracy, the net effect on the subject society was the elimination of political participation by the people. All depended upon powerful control by the elite.[8] In these and other respects, the position and role of the Judean priestly aristocracy or of the Herodian client "kings" was typical of a colonial situation.

Whereas the Babylonians had deported the Judean ruling class, the Persians established a priestly government centered in the rebuilt Temple.[9] The two Jewish leaders who played the major role in the reconstitution of Judean society, Ezra and Nehemiah, held their authority and power as officers of the Persian emperor. This double role, however, was also true of the high priesthood once it was securely established. That is, the very representative of the Jewish people and their mediator with God was also the representative of the Persian imperial regime. From the Persian imperial viewpoint it made sense to sponsor both the restoration of "the House of the God who is in Jerusalem" and its attendant priesthood. The populace of Judea thus could focus their loyalty and worship on the God of Israel in Jerusalem—and of course bring their tithes and taxes in due season to the Temple, i.e., to the high-priestly officers, who in turn would render loyalty and tribute to the Persian court.

This same imperial arrangement of ruling through the priestly aristocracy remained in effect basically until the destruction of the second Temple, with the exception of the period of rule by Herodian client kings.[10] The Hellenistic empires, Ptolemies and Seleucids, both governed Judean society and apparently collected tribute through the Judean high priesthood. Indeed, the office of high priest itself became a virtual dynasty in the control of the same Zadokite family from the sixth to the second century. In 175 B.C.E., however, a strong Hellenizing faction of the aristocracy, with the cooperation of the Seleucid king Antiochus IV Epiphanes, carried out a successful coup and instituted a great *reform* that transformed Jerusalem into a Hellenistic *polis*. In Judea "indirect" imperial rule was effective only so long as the client aristocracy had credibility as representative of the people. When the usurping Hellenizing aristocracy attempted to transform the social-political order into the forms of the dominant Hellenistic civilization, the popular resentment was directed initially against them. Then when the emperor intervened directly and attempted to suppress the resistance, a widespread revolt erupted against Seleucid rule as well as against the apostate priestly aristocracy.

Following the successful Maccabean revolt, the Hasmonean high priests exerted some autonomy. Although their rule was conditional on Seleucid tolerance, they were able to play the Seleucids off against rapidly expanding Roman influence in the East. When the Romans finally took direct control of the eastern Mediterranean in 63 B.C.E., they also delegated rule of Judean society to the (Hasmonean) high-priestly regime. Following the devastating Roman and Judean civil wars in the 40s, in which rival Hasmoneans battled for control of the country, the Romans entrusted the rule of Jewish Palestine to the ambitious young opportunist Herod as client king. After conquering the country with the help of Roman troops, Herod set up an intensely repressive regime (37-4 B.C.E.). While posing as "king of the Jews," he instituted Roman-Hellenistic political and cultural forms, with mercenary troops manning his elaborate security apparatus. Because he maintained surveillance and tight control over the people, no serious opposition could effectively emerge. He also replaced the priestly aristocratic families who had held hereditary power since the Maccabean revolt, installing his own creatures in office. Thus, effective political participation of the people came to an end, even at the level of the aristocratically dominated high council, the Sanhedrin.

Upon the death of Herod the Great in 4 B.C.E., the Romans installed his sons in power: Antipas in Galilee, who ruled as tetrarch until 39 C.E., and Archelaus in Judea and Samaria. When the latter proved unsatisfactory as client king, Rome set up a system that combined "direct" and "indirect" rule. Ultimate authority was placed in the hands of a Roman governor, resident ordinarily at Caesarea. But domestic Jewish affairs were left to the priestly aristocracy again. From 6 to 66 C.E. four principal families dominated the society, with the office of high priest, in effect, alternating among them. Partially because of the awkward combination of Roman governor and Jewish priestly aristocracy, Roman control of Jewish Palestine was not as tight as it had been under Herod. But with all matters of importance in the hands of the high priests and the Roman governor, there was no legitimate channel for political participation by the people.

Such political decay in a "colonized" society was simply the most visible aspect of the extreme crisis in which prolonged imperial domination placed a subject people. Effects of imperial exploitation also began to break down the traditional socioeconomic infrastructure on which the society was based. Most fundamental and significant for its impact in other ways was the economic pressure brought on the peasantry for taxes and tribute. Rising indebtedness of the peasants led to loss of their land that was the base of their economic subsistence and of their place in the traditional social structure. Thus the traditional village-based social structure as well as the traditional economic structure began to break down. The peasantry in subject societies have especially experienced some degree of dispossession of land, destruction of the economic unity of the family, and disruption of traditional custom-regulated local socioeconomic relationships. Generally in the ancient world the native aristocracy (including newcomers) increased their landholdings as well as power in society, while formerly proud and independent peasant producers lost their self-respect along with their land and status as they became sharecroppers, day laborers, or simply vagabonds.[11] Imperial subordination thus creates or exacerbates the socioeconomic divisions within the subject society.

Under the Davidic monarchy, before Judean society was placed in the imperial situation, the prophets had bitterly protested the economic exploitation of the peasantry by the ruling class.

> The Lord enters into judgment with the elders and princes of his people:
> "The spoil of the poor is in your houses. What do you mean by crushing
> my people, by grinding the face of the poor?" (Isaiah 3:14-15)

The king, however, always had a concrete economic interest in protecting the productive base of his country and had the monarchy to help reinforce his moral or ideological motivation as protector of the "fatherless" and the "widow." Once the society was subject to a foreign empire, however, the Judean aristocracy, kept in power by, and responsible primarily to, their imperial overlords, had no corresponding interest and motive. Apparently they simply exploited the people for their own benefit, as well as for that of the empire—whether under the Persians, the Hellenistic regimes, or the Romans. Already by the time Nehemiah arrived to reorganize Judean affairs after 450 B.C.E., he found serious decay in basic socioeconomic relations: the wealthy and powerful were using indebtedness to weaken and subordinate the desperate peasants.

> There arose a great outcry of the people ... For there were those who
> said, "We have to pledge our sons and daughters to get grain, that we
> may eat and keep alive." There were also those who said, "We are mort-
> gaging our fields, our vineyards and our houses to get grain because of
> the famine." And there were those who said, "We have borrowed money
> for the king's tax upon our fields and our vineyards; ... some of our
> daughters have already been enslaved; ... (and) other men have our fields
> and our vineyards." (Nehemiah 5:1-5, RSV adapted)

Here is a classic picture of economic pressure on the peasantry for tithes and tribute, a pressure leading to increasing indebtedness that results in debt bondage and eventual loss of the family inheritance of land. But along with the economic decline of the peasantry went the decay of the traditional village-based social structure. Nehemiah's reform, the restoration of some sort of Mosaic covenantal law, must have done something to stem this decay; for the fourth-century B.C.E. Greek traveler Hecataeus found in Palestine a surprising situation (apparently unusual in his experience) in which ordinary people still had rights to their own land. A similar check to such socioeconomic decay may also have been one result of the Maccabean revolt. We can well imagine that the rebelling peasantry would have reclaimed their land lost or threatened with loss by indebtedness. Moreover, the expansionist policy and wars of the Hasmoneans would also have extended the territory open to the Jewish population.

With the Roman conquest, however, came a shrinking of available territory and a general shortage of land. Herod in particular intensified the economic exploitation of the people. In addition to supporting his elaborate regime and lavish court, he embarked on extensive building projects and made a name for himself in the Empire for his astounding munificence to the imperial family and to Hellenistic cultural causes such as athletic games, the whole funded by taxing his people. The intense economic pressure on the peasant producers continued under the Roman governors and Jewish high priests; the people struggled under a double burden of taxation: tithes and other dues paid to the Temple and priests as well as tribute and other taxes to Rome.[12] It is not difficult to imagine the resultant exacerbation of social-economic divisions within Palestinian Jewish society. The Galilee portrayed in the Gospels is a society of the very rich and the very poor.[13] Jesus' parables in particular give us illuminating insights into the socioeconomic conditions resulting from generations of intense economic pressure: heavily indebted peasants who cannot possibly avoid loss of their land or their freedom, tenant farmers and innumerable day laborers who have already forfeited their land or who must supplement their living by hiring themselves out. Over against the declining peasantry stands a class of wealthy absentee landowners who employ stewards to run their estates. Moreover, there is no love lost between the very wealthy and the desperately poor and threatened tenant farmers (see especially Matthew 18:23-33; 20:1-15; Luke 16:1-13; Mark 12:1-9). In fact, Luke's version of the parable of the pounds (Luke 19:11-27) is a miniature word-picture of the very imperial situation that had brought about a severe decline of socioeconomic conditions for the Jewish people and an intensification of the divisions within the society: A "nobleman" goes into a far country to receive "kingly power"; his servants (officials) meanwhile dramatically expand his capital, apparently by making usurious loans; but his people, having focused their resentment on him (not on the "far country"), are opposed to his ruling over them.

Simultaneous with and perhaps partly resulting from the perceived threat to the traditional social order and its sanctions, especially in situations of indirect rule, there was a tendency to "freeze" the social order, to inhibit change in the name of conformity with "immemorial custom."[14] This "freezing" of the social structure in the name of sacred tradition indicates how cultural domination aided political domination. The native aristocracy, legitimated in their position by tradition while themselves assimilating new cultural forms from the dominant imperial culture, perpetuated the traditional cultural forms as a way of keeping their people subordinated to the system as a whole. All the while, of course, the *culturally* productive groups were busy adjusting the tradition to the requirements of the "colonial situation" and of its impact on their society.

The very origins of second Temple Jewish society and religion can be understood in this light. Although Ezra, Nehemiah, and the high priests owed their power to their position as officers of the Persian empire, they and the "Priestly writers" of early postexilic times reconstructed and virtually *established* a religious tradition as a way of legitimating the "restored" Jewish sociopolitical order.

The priestly aristocracy's attempt at Hellenizing reform illustrates how, when they abandoned the sacred cultural traditions—even though they made no change in the actual social structure—they suddenly lost legitimacy in the eyes of the people. The Hasmoneans, who rode the Maccabean rebellion into power, far from claiming to be messianic kings (which would have been a departure from second Temple cultural tradition), immediately restored the traditional high-priestly regime with themselves as the new incumbents. However, the compromises and outright violations of tradition that they made in pretending to restore sacred customs (as well as in reestablishing socioeconomic stratification) did not sit well with some other priests and intellectuals among their former allies, the Hasidim (pious ones). The Dead Sea Scrolls provide vivid witness that to those who had hoped for a more egalitarian and revitalized social outcome of the revolt, the Hasmonean "Wicked Priests" simply reverted to the same old "frozen" stratified social order, while legitimating themselves by a putative restoration of traditions. Similarly, throughout the decades of more direct Roman rule in the first century C.E., the high priests appealed to sacred tradition to legitimate the preservation of the social structure as it stood, even though they themselves were not from the traditional Zadokite families.

POPULAR RESISTANCE AND RENEWAL

Colonized people, however, do not always cooperate. In a situation of tension, antagonism, and conflict with their traditional culture, with even their own sacred land visibly threatened, the subject people produce movements that attempt to adjust or to renew their traditional way of life. Indeed, the crises into which "colonized" societies are drawn often manifest themselves first "in the modification or disappearance of institutions and groups"[15] and even in the appearance of new groups and social patterns. As the old social structure comes under pressure, some social relationships persist even when the overall structures within which they previously functioned disintegrate, while new relationships may appear as a result of social conditions arising from imperial domination. Close attention to the specific conditions of this ordeal of subordination helps elucidate the processes of rejection or adaptation and the new patterns of behavior resulting from the destruction of the traditional social order. Attention to these "colonial" conditions and the processes of adaptation and renewal, moreover, can help elucidate the "pressure points" or "resistance points" of the subject people.[16]

Considering the structure of an imperial situation, we would expect that certain strata would be more likely to resist or to rebel or to attempt to renew the traditional way of life. Especially in a situation of indirect rule, the dominant aristocracy would have a substantial stake in maintaining the status quo. Even "middle strata" (those with some education or some regular contact with the imperial society and influenced by the imperial ideology) typically would make significant adjustments and find themselves a role in the colonial system. The resentment of such self-aware members of the subject society may well be rather intense; but they are in a position to have a more "realistic" sense of the actual imperial power relationship and therefore to hold to a more "conservative" stance. Villagers, however, who are more insulated from direct contact with the imperial system and its ideology are more likely to attempt to restore the old way of life or even to develop what might appear as "social revolutionary" notions.[17]

Large numbers of Jewish people reacted against the imperial situation or some particular manifestation of it, and various popular protests or renewal movements took shape among the people, under conditions resulting from the imperial situation, such as the decay of the traditional local socioeconomic structure. Even the literate priestly and/or scribal group or parties that we have usually looked upon as the most typical and important in Palestinian Jewish society in the late second Temple period were, in effect, all products of the imperial situation.

The Pharisees, the Sadducees, and the Qumran community were all responses to the crisis into which Jewish society had been drawn during its subjection to dominant empires. At some point in the postexilic period there emerged a type of "sage" or "scribe" not totally subordinate to, though still somewhat dependent on, the high priesthood, and highly dedicated to both individual and social practice of the Torah. In traditional societies the ruling class generally extracts its surplus and governs through "retainers" of various sorts, such as the military, tax collectors, and "bureaucrats," among whom skills of literacy and keeping of records, traditions, and laws are of special importance.[18] Judea may have been somewhat unusual insofar as it was governed by both the Temple, headed by the high priesthood, and the Torah. This made literacy and the role of scribes and interpreters-lawyers-teachers of the Torah especially important. Thus, while the scholars may have been supported by the high-priestly establishment, they would likely have developed some degree of independence and leverage over against the high priests. Moreover, as we might expect of professional scholars and teachers of the Torah, they would also have developed considerable personal loyalty or devotion to the traditions of which they were the guardians. Thus in an imperial situation in which the ruling class had become compromised by collaborating with the imperial regime, the scribes and scholar-teachers would not necessarily do likewise, but might be inclined to resist for personal as well as "professional" motives.

The most likely time when such scholar-teachers would have asserted greater independence from the high priesthood was during the Hellenizing reform, as the priestly aristocracy became more remote from the people who lived predominantly in the villages of Judea, while the "retainers" still functioned locally as teachers or sages knowledgeable in the now-threatened sacred traditions.[19] At the outbreak of the Maccabean revolt we find a group called the *maskilim* (Daniel 11:33). Perhaps the *maskilim* were simply one such association of "sages." The pre-Maccabean apocalyptic visions in Daniel 7-12 and the revelations in early sections of 1 Enoch must have originated from such circles of intellectuals.

According to one widely accepted hypothesis of the origins of the community at Qumran, a large group of Hasidim, hoping for just social-economic relations to emerge out of the Maccabean revolt, was disillusioned by the mundane climax brought about by the "Wicked Priest," i.e., the Hasmonean leadership of Jonathan and Simon. Persisting in their more apocalyptically informed expectations, they withdrew into the wilderness to "prepare the way of the Lord"; i.e., they carried out a new exodus and formed a new covenantal community in strict adherence to the Torah.[20]

Other groups of intellectual leaders devoted to the practice of the Torah, whom we have often referred to as Pharisees, may also have developed from the Hasidim or similar earlier groups. Instead of withdrawing to the wilderness when the Hasmoneans reverted to the old patterns of domination, the "Pharisees" attempted to influence or pressure the Hasmonean high priests to observe the Mosaic Law according to their own more progressive, popularly oriented interpretation. The "Sadducees" may have originated as the priestly aristocratic "party" of strict and conservative literal interpretation of the written Mosaic Law (written Law only) in opposition to the Pharisees. Against Alexander Jannai, the Pharisees led an open rebellion, and many Pharisees and others were killed or exiled as a result. Jannai's wife and successor, however, placed the Pharisees in positions of political influence. The Pharisees apparently opposed Herod in some sense and refused to sign his loyalty oath. Although they lost some political influence under Herod, they continued their active political involvement during the first century C.E., while forming brotherhoods devoted to rigorous study and practice of the Torah.

Most important to realize is that in response to the conditions created by the imperial situation of a widening gulf between the remote priestly aristocracy and the threatened peasantry, there emerged a small semi-independent *intellectual* but not economic middle stratum, however small, devoted to the preservation of the traditional way of life, oriented toward popular concerns, and eager to influence, even willing to offer resistance to, the ruling aristocracy. The development of changes in the character and social rule of the Pharisaic or similar groups, moreover, is directly related to the particular changes in the constellation of forces in the imperial situation of Jewish history during the second Temple period. The important final stage in this development, of course, was the emergence of the rabbis as the client rulers of Jewish society following the destruction of Jerusalem, including the Temple, and the termination of the priestly aristocracy in the great Revolt of 66-70.[21]

In sum, contrary to whatever inclinations some may have to find a stable and "traditional" social order and religious tradition, the imperial situation in which the Palestinian Jewish people were living entailed tension and conflict. Structural-functionalist social science has been especially influential in Anglo-American scholarship. Yet it is based on the assumption of a stable social system that undergoes certain tensions and adjustments while it is maintained basically intact. The colonial or imperial situation, however, requires by its very structure of dynamic tensions and conflictual relationships a more historically conscious and dialectical approach.

NOTES

1. M. Smith, "Palestinian Judaism in the First Century," in *Israel: Its Role in Civilization*, ed. M. Davis (New York: Harper & Row, 1956).

2. G. Balandier, "The 'Colonial Situation' Concept," in *The Sociology of Black Africa* (New York: Praeger, 1970), ch. 1, pp. 21–56; G. Balandier, "The Colonial Situation: A Theoretical Approach," in *Social Change: The Colonial Situation*, ed. I. Wallerstein (New York, London: Wiley & Sons, 1966), 34–61. P. Worsley, *The Third World* (London: Wiedenfeld & Nicolson, 1964), 21–49. The rest of this section consists of the application of Balandier's and Worsley's discussion to Palestinian Jewish history from the Babylonian to the Roman empires.

3. Worsley, *Third World*, 26.

4. Ibid., 30.

5. Ibid., 36.

6. Ibid., 38.

7. Ibid., 38.

8. Ibid., 42.

9. On Judea during the Persian period, see E. Bickerman, *From Ezra to the Last of the Maccabees* (New York: Schocken, 1962); N. K. Gottwald, *The Hebrew Bible: A Socioliterary Introduction* (Philadelphia: Fortress, 1984), 428-39; S. K. Eddy, *The King Is Dead* (Lincoln: University of Nebraska Press, 1961).

10. On Jewish Palestine under the Hellenistic and Roman empires, see V. Tcherikover, *Hellenistic Civilization and the Jews* (New York: Atheneum, 1970); M. Hengel, *Judaism and Hellenism* (Philadelphia: Fortress, 1974); and articles in two multivolume surveys: *WHJP*, vol. 6, and vol. 7; and *JPFC*.

11. Balandier, *Sociology*, 27–28.

12. J. Jeremias, *Jerusalem in the Time of Jesus* (Philadelphia: Fortress, 1969), 105; M. Stern, "The Province of Judaea," in *JPFC* vol. 1, 324–335.

13. A. N. Sherwin-White, *Roman Law and Roman Society in The New Testament* (Oxford: Oxford University Press, 1963), 139.

14. Worsley, *Third World*, 39.

15. Balandier, *Sociology*, 45.

16. Balandier, *Sociology*, 24–45.

17. Worsley, *Third World*, 29–30, 36.

18. See G. Lenski, *Power and Privilege* (New York: McGraw-Hill, 1966), 243–248.

19. See Tcherikover, *Hellenistic Civilization and the Jews*, 125–126, 196–198.

20. F. M. Cross, *The Ancient Library of Qumran* (Garden City: Doubleday, 1961), ch. 3; G. Vermes, *The Dead Sea Scrolls in English*, 2nd ed. (Harmondsworth: Penguin, 1975), ch. 3.

21. See J. Neusner; e.g., *From Politics to Piety* (Englewood Cliffs, NJ: Prentice Hall, 1973); and A. Saldarini, *Pharisees, Scribes, and Sadducees* (Wilmington, DE: Glazier, 1987).

26

RICHARD A. HORSLEY

The Kingdom of God and the Renewal of Israel

Scholarly interpretations of the "kingdom of God" proclaimed by Jesus have relegated it to the margins of history as a "cosmic catastrophe" and/or individualized and universalized it into the abstract spiritual "rule" of God. Concerned to make Jesus' teaching unique, as well as politically innocuous, they have also abstracted his ministry from its concrete social context. Jesus' discourse about the kingdom, however, is focused on people, not theology, and its principal metaphors envisage social extension, not individualistic spirituality.

In Jesus and the Spiral of Violence, *Horsley explored a concrete social reading of Jesus' teaching and practice in the historical context of peasant poverty, debt, and social disintegration driven by the exorbitant demands for tithes, taxes, and tribute by their high priestly, Herodian, and Roman rulers. The first step was a reexamination of what the "kingdom of God" may have meant for Jesus and his movement. Far from being eschatological or apolitical, the kingdom of God was the overarching symbol of a locally based popular movement attempting a renewal of the people of Israel. Seen most dramatically in the exorcisms, Jesus appears to have been generating a "social revolution" (to use modern political parlance), in the confidence that God was in the process of effecting the "political revolution" against the imperial forces of domination.*

Reprinted from Richard A. Horsley, *Jesus and the Spiral of Violence: Popular Jewish Resistance in Roman Palestine* (San Francisco: Harper & Row, 1987), 167-208, abridged.

THE KINGDOM OF GOD: SOCIAL AND CERTAIN

Jesus' preaching and action centered around the presence of the kingdom of God: "the kingdom of God has come upon you" (Luke 11:20), "the kingdom of God is in the midst of you" (Luke 17:21), or (in Mark's summary of the Gospel, 1:15) "the time is fulfilled, the kingdom of God is at hand." Before examining particular sayings of Jesus, it may be expedient to question some of our own assumptions and interpretative categories in order to mitigate somewhat our projections onto the historical material. The painstaking investigations of form-critics and, in particular, the important and influential studies of Norman Perrin on "the kingdom of God" and the "teachings" of Jesus generally provide a solid and indispensable foundation for any further investigation and interpretation.[1] Yet such "mainline" scholarship, precisely because it has worked faithfully out of the established religious scholarly tradition, tends to perpetuate certain concepts and assumptions that may obscure rather than elucidate some aspects of the synoptic gospel materials.

The Kingdom of God Is for People

The kingdom of God in Jesus' preaching is surely not to be understood as a "realm" existing in some place such as "heaven" ("kingdom of heaven" being Matthew's typically Palestinian Jewish circumlocution for "kingdom of God"). Understanding the kingdom of God as God's rule or ruling has been an important corrective to that misunderstanding. Yet "rule" may be far too vague, general, and neutral a concept to convey the active, partial, and engaged character of the kingdom of God in biblical literature. Thus, more precisely, the kingdom of God means the use of power, in "mighty deeds," to liberate, establish, or protect the people in difficult historical circumstances such as the exodus from bondage in Egypt (as in the ancient "Song of the Sea" in Exodus 15:1-18). Remembering the great historical actions of liberation, the prophets and apocalyptic visionaries symbolized God's imminent future liberating actions in terms analogous to those past events.[2]

Under the continuing influence of the older synthetic doctrinal understanding of apocalyptic eschatology in terms of "cosmic catastrophe," however, we tend to perpetuate certain interpretative concepts that are inappropriate to Jesus' sayings and to the comparative Jewish materials. "The kingdom of God" and related symbols do not refer to "the last," "final," "eschatological," and "all-transforming" "act" of God. Especially misleading in this context is the reified concept of the End or the *eschaton*. The apostle Paul had a "word of the [resurrected and exalted] Lord" that pictured the resurrection and parousia in "final" terms, seemingly discontinuous with the historical process, of the faithful being caught up to meet the Lord in the air (1 Thessalonians 4:15-17). But it is difficult to find any prophecies or other sayings of Jesus suggesting that the new saving action of God is "final" or "eschatological" in the sense of "the last." For example, if the original kernel of any of the sayings about "the son of man coming with the clouds of heaven" (or simply seated or standing in heaven; e.g., Mark 13:26; 14:62) stem from Jesus, then, like the image in Daniel 7:13 to which they refer, they are symbolizations of the vindication of the persecuted or suffering righteous.[3] God's action in the coming of the kingdom would be "final," not in the sense of "last" or "the end," but only in the sense of "finally!" or "at last!"

Similarly, it is difficult to think of Jesus' sayings that envisage an "all-transforming" action in God's ruling. "Heaven and earth will pass away, but my words will not pass away" (Mark 13:31) is a statement about "my words," not about "heaven and earth." The darkening of the sun and moon (Mark 13:24-25) is hyperbole elaborating on how astounding the events of ingathering and restoration of the people will be—and in any case is part of the "synoptic apocalypse" not usually thought to stem from Jesus himself. Jesus' sayings portray not an "all-transforming act" but a number of respects in which social relations (political-economic-religious) will be or are being transformed. Thus also Jesus' preaching of the kingdom of God does not refer to an "act" in the sense of one particular event. The kingdom of God clearly entails continuing action by God as well as response and participation by people. The liberating action or kingdom of God should also not be thought of as God's "intervention in history (and human experience)."[4] Jesus, like most of his contemporary Palestinian Jews and most of the biblical traditions, apparently, thought of God (and other divine or demonic forces) as integrally involved in history and human life.

Once we recognize that the kingdom of God in Jesus' preaching does not refer to a particular action or event, much less to the final act or the End, the whole convoluted debate about whether the kingdom as preached by Jesus was already present and "realized," or was still future but imminent, or somehow both present and future, appears to be a subordinate issue.[5] No longer diverted to that debate, we are free to explore the special liberating or saving activities involved in the "kingdom of God."

The divine activity of the kingdom of God is focused on the needs and desires of people.[6] In fact Jesus' preaching generally, and particularly his announcement of the kingdom of God, rarely calls attention explicitly to God, but concentrates on the implication of the presence of the kingdom for people's lives and on how people must respond.

The "kingdom" involves not a blissful rest in static beatitude, but social interaction such as feasting. Similarly, the saving activity of God does indeed bring wholeness to individual persons; but this does not stand in contrast to restoration of society.[7] Personal wholeness is integrally involved with the renewal of social life, apparently even with certain transformations in the patterns of political religious life.

It is important to keep in mind that "the kingdom of God" is a political metaphor and symbol. In Jesus' preaching and action the kingdom clearly includes the social-economic-political substance of human relations as willed by God. It is significant, as well as ironic, that we reach for the term "salvation" in order to express this substantive social aspect of the kingdom. Before it was spiritualized and etherealized in Christian discourse, "salvation" (*sōtēria*) meant the peace (especially law and order) and prosperity provided by the divine

(Hellenistic or Roman) emperor for his subjects, particularly those in the Hellenistic cities, the political-cultural elite. For Jesus and many of his Palestinian Jewish contemporaries, however, the blessings of individual and social-political life would be provided by God as king, in contrast to the emperor. "Kingdom of God" is Jesus' "comprehensive term for the blessings of salvation."[8] The socio-political dimensions are inseparable from the religious. Thus God's activity was political and Jesus' preaching of that activity was political — with obvious implications for the "imperial situation" then prevailing in Palestine.

The Certainty of Renewal, Vindication, and Judgment

First of all, Jesus presupposed as his cultural context what is usually called the Jewish "apocalyptic" lore and worldview. Like the Jerusalem scribes or Pharisees who accused him of being "possessed by Beelzebub" and of casting out demons "by the prince of demons" (Mark 3:22; Matthew 12:24; Luke 11:15), Jesus viewed individual and social life as caught up in the struggle for control between God and Satan. According to Matthew 26:53, at least, Jesus shared the long-standing biblical and widespread contemporary belief in the heavenly hosts by which God would defeat the oppressive historical and demonic enemies of the people at the appropriate time. Similarly, as Perrin has shown to be likely, he knew and used the "son of man" (as in Daniel 7) as a symbol of the vindication or restoration of the people.[9]

More significantly, Jesus shared the apparently widespread popular Palestinian Jewish perspective, attested in a variety of apocalyptic texts, that God was expected to effect the restoration of the people, which would include vindication of the suffering righteous and judgment of the unrighteous oppressors, domestic rulers, and alien imperial regime. Jesus symbolized the deliverance and renewal of the people by means of the banquet of the kingdom or feast of fulfillment, among other images. "I tell you, many will come from east and west and sit at table with Abraham, Isaac, and Jacob in the kingdom of heaven" (Matthew 8:11/Luke 13:28-29). The same image of the future banquet of the kingdom occurs again in the account of the "last supper," where Jesus declares: "Truly, I shall not drink again of the fruit of the vine until that day when I drink it new in the kingdom of God" (Mark 14:25 and parallels; cf. Luke 22:15-18).[10]

Symbolization of deliverance or fulfillment in terms of a great feast was a long-standing tradition from the prophets Isaiah and Jeremiah. In Isaiah 55:1-5 the image of a good and delightful feast parallels that of a renewed and "everlasting covenant" in the anticipated restoration of Israel. In Jeremiah 31:10-14, the future feast is linked with mourning turning into joy, as previously scattered Israel is gathered and redeemed from those who have overpowered it; the more fantastic imagery of the later text Isaiah 25:6-8 provides similar associations. From its frequent occurrence in the gospel tradition and from the form of the saying in Matthew 8:11, which was apparently originally a prophetic warning, it is clear that Jesus presupposed the banquet as a standard symbol of deliverance and was confident of, indeed more or less assumed, such imminent future fulfillment. In its content, Matthew 8:11 says nothing about outcasts, and it may be only from the current literary context in Matthew that we receive any sense of inclusion of Gentiles, and hence an implication of universalism from the phrase "come from east and west. . . . "[11] The saying appears rather to speak of the gathering of the people of Israel, as in Jeremiah 31 (see also Psalm 107:3, from which Luke may get the expansion "and from north and south"). The saying in connection with the last supper indicates that this image of the kingdom was also closely linked with the restoration of the people as a new-covenant society.

Another form in which Jesus expressed confidence in God's deliverance is the "Lord's Prayer," which is clearly a prayer for the kingdom, as the comprehensive principal petition indicates. A possibly more original version than either Matthew's 6:9-13 or Luke's 11:2-4 has been reconstructed by Jeremias:

> Father, hallowed be thy name. Thy kingdom come. Give us today the bread of tomorrow. Forgive us our debts as we herewith forgive our debtors. And lead us not into temptation.[12]

This is most likely a deliberate modification of the Kaddish, a prayer used regularly in Jewish synagogues in the time of Jesus.

> Magnified and sanctified be his great name in the world that he has created according to his will. May he establish his kingdom in your lifetime and in your days and in the lifetime of all the house of Israel, even speedily and at a near time.[13]

It is surely significant to recognize that the Kaddish was a prayer spoken by whole communities for the establishment of the kingdom. The same was surely true of the prayer for the kingdom that Jesus taught his followers, despite any implications that it might be a private or conventicle prayer in the current literary contexts in Matthew 6:5-8 and Luke. Noteworthy especially in the Lord's Prayer and in the saying about the banquet of the kingdom is Jesus' overall confidence that God is bringing the kingdom. Jesus speaks and acts in that confidence.

Although in many sayings Jesus often used highly distinctive images, he shared with other Palestinian Jews of his time an orientation toward the deliverance and renewal of the people, including vindication of the righteous and judgment against unrighteous rulers that God was already or imminently effecting. This conviction that God was acting in deliverance and judgment helps explain the confidence with which Jesus proclaimed and mediated the presence of the kingdom of God in highly distinctive ways.

THE PRESENCE OF THE KINGDOM

The thrust of Jesus' ministry, his practice and preaching, was to realize and to make others realize the presence of the kingdom of God. Not only is Jesus confident that God is acting imminently to liberate and renew the people and to vindicate those who join in that renewal, but Jesus manifests and mediates God's activity in his own actions and teachings. He declares in no uncertain terms that the kingdom of God has come upon and is among the people, available to be recognized, received, and entered.

Banqueting: Joys of the Kingdom Present

A strikingly distinctive activity of Jesus and his followers was their regular celebration with festive meals, almost certainly a celebration of the presence of the kingdom. Since the discovery of the Dead Sea Scrolls, the recognition that the Qumran community celebrated a similar "messianic banquet" has given us a greater appreciation of Jesus' anticipatory celebration of the kingdom of God. A surprising amount of the gospel tradition has to do with feeding, table fellowship, and related teachings, three or four kinds of material in particular leading to the conclusion that Jesus and his followers were indeed celebrating the presence of the kingdom.

Jesus had a reputation for "eating and drinking," one which led opponents to accuse him of associating with people who were indulgently enjoying life rather than observing the Torah. This behavior, moreover, was also a dramatic contrast to that of his supposed mentor, John the Baptist, who maintained an ascetic stance in the light of God's impending judgment. Thus the double criticism and accusation appearing in Q (Matthew 11:18-19 and Luke 7:33-34): "For John came neither eating nor drinking, and they say, 'He has a demon'; the Son of man came eating and drinking, and they say, 'Behold, a glutton and a drunkard, a friend of tax collectors and sinners!' "

Second, the central importance of festive table fellowship in the early church almost certainly was a continuation of Jesus' own "eating and drinking" with his followers.

Third, the core saying (generally thought to be genuine) in one of the controversy stories, Mark 2:19a, is in effect a brief parable "explaining" that the celebration by Jesus and his followers is the only appropriate response, given the present situation, i.e., the presence of the kingdom: "Can the wedding guests fast while the bridegroom is with them?" Also, although they are not reliable reports of particular events, the two great feeding stories (Mark 6:30-44 and 8:1-10) are nevertheless to be understood as portrayals of how God was finally feeding the people with miraculous abundance despite appearances of paucity.

The analogous "messianic banquet" celebrated at Qumran makes it clear that Jesus' festive "eating and drinking" was a present celebration of the banquet of the kingdom, the consummation of which he referred to in the saying about many coming from east and west to sit at table with Abraham, Isaac, and Jacob (Matthew 8:11 and parallels). Procedure for the banquet to be held by the Qumranites when the "messiahs" come is described at some length, 1QSa 2:17-21:

"[This shall be the ass]embly of the men of renown [called] to the meeting of the Council of the Community when [the Priest-] Messiah shall summon them ... [when] they shall gather for the common [table], to eat and [to drink] new wine, ... Let no man extend his hand over the first-fruits of bread and wine before the Priest; for [it is he] who shall bless the first-fruits of bread and wine, and shall be the first [to extend] his hand over the bread. Thereafter, the Messiah of Israel shall extend his hand over the bread, [and] all the Congregation of the Community [shall utter a] blessing. ... "

However, after thus stating explicitly that this is the order of procedure for the banquet when the messiahs come, the text continues: "It is according to this statute that they shall proceed at every me[al at which] at least ten men are gathered together" (similarly, 1QS 6:4-5). The Qumranites were thus celebrating their regular community meals as if the messiahs were already there, i.e., were celebrating in anticipation of the future consummation. Jesus' table fellowship would surely have been far less rigid and hierarchical than that of the priestly-led Qumran community's. Yet judging from this vivid analogy from another community that understood its own life and actions as already "preparing the way of the Lord," Jesus' festive "eating and drinking" must have been a celebration of the presence of deliverance in active anticipation of banqueting in the fully consummated kingdom of God.

Corresponding to the deliverance or renewal side of the feasting in the kingdom now present, of course, was the presence of judgment, i.e., the possibility of exclusion from the present kingdom if one did not respond. This can be seen in the parable of "the great supper" (Luke 14:16-24; Gospel of Thomas no. 64; cf. Matthew 22:1-10). The emphasis especially in the Gospel of Thomas no. 64 and in the story behind Luke 14:16-24 as well falls on the failure of those invited to come when summoned.[14] It is also relevant to note that two of the three groups in the Lucan version and perhaps all three in the Gospel of Thomas no. 64 are economically prosperous, in contrast surely to the vast majority of Galilean peasants. Thus the point of the parable must have been a warning about not responding to the presence of the kingdom, which the extended metaphor of a great banquet would surely have suggested for those familiar with one of the central prophetic symbols of God's future liberation and restoration of the people. Now that the summons to participate in the kingdom had been given, those otherwise preoccupied (such as with expanding their own property holdings) would find themselves excluded.

Healings and Forgiveness

Jesus' healings and exorcisms were not signs that the kingdom of God was soon to come, but indications that the kingdom was already present. They were direct manifestations of God's liberating and restorative activity in people's personal lives. In approaching the healings and exorcisms, however, we are in a complex and awkward situation with regard to the gospel stories. As form-critics have long since recognized, the healing and exorcism stories have typical forms, some of them even bearing striking resemblance to stories told about near-contemporary Hellenistic healer-philosophers such as Apollonius of Tyana. Virtually none of the stories in our Gospels provides reliable historical information about a particular incident in Jesus' ministry.[15] On the other hand, both within the gospel tradition and in later Jewish tradition, Jesus has an unshakable reputation as a healer and exorcist. Thus we are confident that Jesus performed a number of healings and did "cast out demons." Yet we must use the gospel healing and exorcism stories not as direct evidence for any particular incidents but rather as general and typical information that must be examined critically for any distinctive features.

Healings and other "miracles" by prophets who had been charged by God with rallying the people to resistance against domestic oppression and foreign influence, of course, were well known from the biblical traditions of Elijah and Elisha. Comparative material from other times and societies also indicates that it is not unusual at all for charismatic preachers or prophets to perform healings as part of their mobilization of people in acute states of distress. Moreover, it is worth noting, lest we simply accept a medically defined model of "disease," that many of the typical problems dealt with by such prophet-healers can most adequately be explained as partly or largely due to the extremely stressful situation of their people. Thus it could be argued that Jesus' healings dealt with problems typical of just such a situation: besides possession, we find stories about fever, lameness or paralysis, consumption, hemorrhage, deafness and dumbness, blindness, epilepsy, deformity, and dropsy. Thus, at the fundamental "psychosomatic" level, it seems highly likely that Jesus did function as the agent in a number of such cases of restoration to health.

It appears that God's forgiveness of sins announced or mediated by Jesus may have been connected with his healings. It comes as a surprise to many that the forgiveness of sins is not a more prominent element in the gospel tradition, particularly that there is very little by way of an interpretation of Jesus' death on the cross in terms of forgiveness of sins (Mark 10:45; Matthew 22:28; and Matthew's version of the Last Supper, 26:28 vs. Mark 1:4 and Luke 3:3, which understand John's baptism as having this function).

The forgiveness of sins, however, does appear to have been an important aspect of Jesus' practice. Besides the two passages in which Jesus explicitly pronounces God's forgiveness (Mark 2:1-12 and parallels; Luke 7:36-50, in which 7:48-50 is probably a Lucan composition on the basis of the other tradition in Mark), the petition in the Lord's Prayer (Luke 11:4 and Matthew 6:12) and the parable (Matthew 18:23-35) about passing on the forgiveness of debts are directly linked with, indeed presuppose, God's forgiveness of debts. The first half of the parable of the prodigal son and that about the Pharisee and the tax collector (Luke 18:9-14) also indicate that Jesus taught God's readiness to forgive, to "justify" a humble sinner. The connection of forgiveness of sins with healing is made primarily in the healing story behind Mark 2:1-12, which is compounded with a controversy in Mark 2:6-10.

Although this link may not have retained its importance in Matthew and Luke, which emphasize more the eucharistic celebration of Christ's death and Jesus' table fellowship with sinners, respectively, it is important for our examination of violence and injustice in an imperial situation because in Jewish society people's sickness and suffering were understood as caused by their sins. The Gospels themselves provide several indications that this understanding of sickness or misfortune and suffering were current assumptions in the context of Jesus' ministry (Mark 2:5 and parallels; John 9:2-3; Luke 13:2, where Jesus himself challenges the understanding only partially, in its extension to relative degree of sin and suffering). Now the understanding of suffering perhaps implicit in the old Deuteronomistic or predeuteronomistic view of life, i.e., as the result of one's (or one's parents') sins may have been adequate for traditional independent village or tribal life. In an imperial situation, however, in which one's suffering may be the direct or indirect result of conquest or other forms of institutionalized injustice and violence, such an understanding of the cause of suffering or sickness becomes problematic. This is the understanding of suffering disputed in some of the dialogue in the Book of Job (e.g., 4:7; 8:4, 20; 22:5), albeit without the benefit of a historical view of reality.[16] Despite efforts to counter such an understanding, such as the oracle concerning the new covenant by Jeremiah 31:27-34, especially 29-30, it persisted into the second Temple period, as is evidenced by a scribe such as Ben Sira (Sirach 38:9-11).

For the mass of ordinary people whom the system must keep in order, such an understanding of suffering or sickness can become "domesticating." In accordance with this understanding, they in effect blame themselves for their problems while they must simultaneously accept the necessity of an institutionalized system of atonement (sacrifices and offerings) in which God's forgiveness is conditional and is channeled through official mediators and regulators. Now if Jesus, when healing people's disorders, also dealt with the people's sense of sin in which (they and their officials believed) their sickness was rooted, then he would have been challenging one of the religious means by which the people were thus domesticated. By pointing to the forgiveness of God as directly available, Jesus was exposing the religious means by which the social restrictions on the people were maintained.[17] Thus, instead of the people continuing to blame themselves for their suffering, they were freed for a resumption of a productive, cooperative life in their communities.

Exorcisms and God's Defeat of Demonic Forces

The kingdom of God is manifested as present in the people's experience more dramatically and more explicitly in the exorcisms than in any other aspect of Jesus' practice and preaching. Judging from how prominent a feature exorcism is in the gospel tradition generally, Jesus must have encountered a number of people who were possessed by alien forces thought of as "demons" or "unclean spirits."

The significance of Jesus' exorcisms is articulated in two related passages, Mark 3:22-27 and the addition to that passage from Q in Luke 11:19-20 and Matthew 12:27-28.

And the scribes who came down from Jerusalem said, "He is possessed by Beelzebul, and by the prince of demons he casts out the demons."

And he called them to him, and said to them in parables, "How can Satan cast out Satan? If a kingdom is divided against itself, that kingdom cannot stand. And if a house is divided against itself, that house will not be able to stand. And if Satan has risen up against himself and is divided, he cannot stand, but is coming to an end. But no one can enter a strong man's house and plunder his goods, unless he first binds the strong man; then indeed, he may plunder his house." (Mark 3:22-27)

"And if I cast out demons by Beelzebul, by whom do your sons cast them out? Therefore they shall be your judges. But if it is by the finger[18] of God that I cast out demons, then the kingdom of God has come upon you." (Luke 11:19-20)

However this material may have been shaped or edited in the gospel tradition, the sayings in Mark 3:24-26 and 27, individually and collectively, presuppose the charge made against Jesus in Mark 3:22 or something very similar. The saying in Luke 11:20 presupposes both the same setting in the ministry of Jesus and, at least in its present form ("but if it is by the finger of God . . ."), the point or judgment based on the analogies in the preceding sayings (Mark 3:23-26; Matthew 12:25-26; Luke 11:17-18), i.e., "Since it is thus absurd that I would cast out demons by Satan, then it must be by the only other alternative." Although modern readers and interpreters have been uncomfortable dealing with demons, exorcisms, and the ancient apocalyptic dualism between God and Satan, these phenomena and these particular passages contain a number of implications that are extremely important for an adequate understanding of Jesus' practice and preaching.

The view of reality as involving a struggle between God and demonic forces must have prevailed among the ordinary people in Jewish society. It was certainly shared by Jesus and his opponents in the texts just cited. Moreover, besides the "scribes" of Mark 3:22 ("Pharisees" in Matthew 12:24), other literate strata in the late second Temple period shared this view, and the authors of the scrolls from Qumran articulated it in more systematic form, thus providing us with important comparative material.

In this view of reality, the struggle between God and demonic forces is taking place at three distinguishable but closely interrelated levels. Ostensibly, the struggle was one in the superhuman, divine-demonic world between God and Satan or, in Qumran literature, between the Prince of Light (or Angel of Truth) and the Angel of Darkness (or Belial or Satan; see especially 1QS 3:18—4:24; 1QM 1-2, 15-19). The apocalyptic dualism portrays rather a struggle between divine creative forces and demonic destructive forces for control of the historical process. The struggle between God and Satan, between the Prince of Light and Belial, explains, determines, and is thus concerned with what is happening on the second level, of the people and their historical situation. The Qumranites thought that the same decisive battle would involve the Kittim (i.e., the Romans, by the time of Jesus) as well as Belial Satan and the priests and people along with the heavenly hosts. At yet another, though obviously closely related level, the struggle between the two spiritual forces was taking place in the hearts of individual persons such that their personal behavior as well as their social-political group was determined by their relative portion of the two spirits, of truth and falsehood (1QS 4:2-12, 22-24). The views of Jesus and probably of the vast majority of Jewish society were not nearly as rigidly dualistic at the social-political and individual levels, yet they apparently thought of Satan as having a certain dominion socially-politically, and of the demons as controlling possessed persons.

This view of reality was both a revelation about and a mystification of the situation in which the people lived. Modern biblical interpreters thought of such apocalypticism as alienated from history. When we attend to the concrete imperial situation, however, it is clear that the violent struggle between God and demonic forces was simply a symbolization or reflection of the violent social-political-religious conflict in which the people were caught individually and collectively. Seeing their own conquest and subordination in the context of Satan's struggle against the divine purposes provided both reason for and significance to their otherwise inexplicable misfortune or fate. It would have been difficult to "explain" the degree and persistence of their subjugation and suffering without conceiving of superhuman forces involved. Belief that Satanic forces were the cause of their miserable situation enabled them not simply to further blame themselves. Believing that God was still ultimately in control of history and was locked in struggle against the superhuman oppressive forces enabled the people to live in their traditional way rather than to die, either by giving up or by assimilating to the dominant culture. Trust that God "had ordained an end for falsehood" and would finally win the struggle and liberate the people symbolized their own will to resist. It enabled them not simply to strike out blindly and go down fighting but to persist patiently and stubbornly in their traditional ways and commitments while probing patiently for appropriate forms of resistance.

The view of life as caught in the struggle between God and Satan, however, was also a mystification of the imperial situation. Believing that Satan and demonic forces were at work behind one's subjugation and suffering may have enabled the Jews individually and collectively not to strike out in frustration directly against the Romans, which would have been suicidal. But this belief may have also diverted attention from the concrete realities. Even possession by a demon (or a psychosomatic paralysis) may have been a self-preservative phenomenon insofar as it prevented (or replaced) an act of direct counterattack against Roman domination. But the cost was a partial self-destruction or self-diminution. Focusing on the struggle against demonic forces may have enabled the people to carry on a symbolic resistance, as was maintained collectively at Qumran (see the War Scroll) and individually by possessed persons, but this meant that resistance occurred in a way that proved very "functional" for the system. That is, aggressiveness stimulated among those subjugated by the violence of conquest and injustice was worked out in a way that did not disrupt the repressive *pax Romana*.

Besides having been functional simply by itself in channeling counteraggression into nondisruptive symbolic outlets, belief in Satan and demonic forces was useful to representatives of the established order in maintaining social control. A disruptive person could be accused of "having a demon." Or, more seriously, just as many a "wise woman" or folk healer was charged with effecting her cures by witchcraft in league with Satan in the great European witch hunts, so Jesus was accused of "casting out demons by the prince of demons."[19] Thus, besides the important ways in which the apocalyptic dualism was truly "revelatory" and preserved Jewish life and traditions, it was also undoubtedly mystified and helped maintain the very imperial situation it helped the people explain and deal with.

Jesus' interpretation of his exorcisms is revelatory and liberative at every level. He starts from the concrete experiences of people having been liberated from the hostile alien forces that had possessed them and from the accusations that he had effected them by the power of Satan. His analogies of the kingdom and home divided presuppose and refer to the struggle between God and Satan on the transhistorical spiritual level. Presupposing the integral relation or continuity of action between the two levels, he juxtaposes the concrete experiences of demons being driven out and the reality of God and Satan warring against each other for control. The analogies of Mark 3:24-26 call for the judgment that it would be absurd for Satan to be at war against himself (necessary if the accusation against Jesus were true). But the analogies also make the point that if Satan were divided against himself, then in any case his dominion "is coming to an end." The further analogy in Mark 3:26 makes the same point somewhat differently, juxtaposing the experience of exorcisms with the notion that a strong man must first be bound before his goods can be plundered. That is, if the demons are already being driven out, then Satan must already have been bound. It would be appropriate to consider in this connection also the brief saying of the "visionary" Jesus in Luke 10:18. The current setting is not only secondary but clearly editorial, but an exorcism context in the ministry of Jesus or the mission of his disciples could well have evoked or have been evoked by the saying "I saw Satan fall like lightning from heaven." If the visionary, in ecstasy, has seen Satan fall, then surely his power over people is coming to an end, and vice versa.

The saying in Luke 11:20 shifts the focus from the defeat of Satan to the victory of God, again starting from the concrete experience of people being freed from the hostile forces. "The finger of God" is an allusion to Exodus 8:19, in which God accomplishes a feat of magic (plague of lice) completely beyond the power of Pharaoh's magicians in effecting the liberation of the people from bondage. A rabbinic midrash (Ex R 10.7) says that the magicians recognized that the plagues "were the work of God and not the work of demons."[20] In the world of apocalyptic dualism there are only two alternatives, and Satan has been excluded. Thus, in a saying suggesting a new exodus is underway, "if it is by the finger of God that I cast out demons, then the kingdom of God has come upon you."

This saying also clearly focuses on the people, the societal-historical level, not the heavenly one. The "argument" of the saying goes from the experience of individuals having been freed of the demonic forces to the implications for the people and for the historical situation.[21] It has been suggested that another of the most important "kingdom" sayings, the one almost impossible to reconstruct in fully satisfactory form, "from the days of John the Baptist until now the kingdom of heaven has suffered violence, and men of violence take it by force" (Matthew 11:12 and Luke 16:16), should also be understood in terms of God's struggle against the powers of evil.[22] Although it is not explicit in the saying, the current social-political struggle of the people would probably have been understood in the context of the broader spiritual struggle between God and Satan. In any case, this is another key saying of Jesus indicating that the kingdom of God is present here and now in the experience of the people. Similarly, a third principal "kingdom" saying confirms this reading of "the kingdom of God has come upon you": "The kingdom of God is not coming with signs to be observed, nor will they say, 'Lo, here it is!' or 'There!' for behold, the kingdom of God is in the midst of you" (*entos hymōn* = "among you"; Luke 17:20-21). In all of these key sayings the kingdom is already present and active among the people.

Thus, strange as it may seem, Jesus' statements concerning the significance of his exorcisms have clear political implications. As was manifested precisely in the liberation of "possessed" individuals, Satan and the demonic force were being defeated. Insofar as all historical conflict would be comprehended in the perspective of the struggle against Satan, since Satan was now being defeated, the days of Roman domination were numbered, and broader societal liberation and renewal were now possible.

A last noteworthy point regarding Jesus' exorcisms — and one not made necessarily as evidence for the previous point, because Jewish scribes and rulers would not have known Jesus' interpretation of the significance of the exorcisms — pertains to the scribes' and Pharisees' and even Herod Antipas' reported concern about Jesus' healings and exorcisms. According to gospel traditions, it was the scribes and Pharisees who attempted to counter his activity with accusations of demon-possession and collusion with Satan. Then, in a most revealing bit of biographical tradition usually judged as early and "authentic," Antipas' concern to suppress Jesus appears to focus precisely on this healing and exorcising activity: "Get away from here, for Herod wants to kill you." To which he replied, "Go tell that fox, 'Behold, I cast out demons and perform cures today and tomorrow, and the third day I finish my course' " (Luke 13:31-32). Thus there are fairly solid traditions that the rulers and/or official representatives viewed Jesus' healing and exorcising activity as a threat to the established order. The liberation of persons from demonic alien forces, God's defeat of Satan, and the ending of the oppressive established social order were all happening simultaneously.

The Rule of God and the Society of God

In the gospel materials examined thus far, the distinctive ways in which Jesus portrayed and manifested the presence of the kingdom of God were all concerned with the welfare of people. In the earliest gospel traditions of the preaching of Jesus there is little or no concern directly with God. This may seem strange, perhaps because influential gospel passages such as the doxology added to the Lord's Prayer in Matthew loom so large in our consciousness. Yet it is striking, for example, in connection with the central proclamation of the kingdom of God, that Jesus rarely refers to God as king (e.g., only in passing, as it were, in Matthew 5:34). Instead, Jesus refers to God primarily as "Father." And although some sayings (relatively late ones? e.g., Mark 8:38) portray the "Father" in heavenly glory surrounded by the angels in royal splendor, the dominant tone is more the accessible (and very anthropomorphic!) figure who feeds the birds, clothes the flowers, and cares for his people, and whose mercy is to be imitated (Luke 12:22-31; 6:36). In the preaching and action of Jesus, including the "kingdom of God" sayings and references to God as Father, the focus is almost always on the people, and the concern is not abstract or even primarily religious, but is with the people's concrete circumstances, both somatic and psychic, both material and spiritual.

The shape of this concern for people can be further discerned and delineated through examining other kingdom sayings, particularly those speaking of being "in" or of "entering" the kingdom of God. In addition to the sayings already examined concerning "sitting at table" or "drinking the fruit of the vine in the kingdom of God" (Matthew 8:11; Mark 14:25; cf. Luke 14:15), the Q saying of Luke 7:28 and Matthew 11:11 and the saying in Matthew 5:19 speak of being located in, a member of, and participating in the activities of a community or society. Similarly, a number of sayings about "entering the kingdom of God" (Mark 9:47 and parallels; Mark 10:15 and parallels; Mark 10:23-25 and parallels; Matthew 5:20; 7:21; 23:13) and related sayings such as those about entering a gate (Matthew 7:13-14 and parallels), and "seeking" or "being fit for" the kingdom of God (Luke 9:62; 12:31) refer to a society or community of some sort.

Indeed, closer examination of these sayings indicates that Jesus had in mind some fairly definite and distinctive patterns of social relationship for the kingdom-society that is to be entered or as the requirements for entry. The disposition necessary for entry and continuing participation was childlike trust and humility: "whoever does not receive the kingdom of God like a child shall not enter it" (Mark 10:15 and parallels). Entry and enjoyment of the kingdom required rigorous observance of the will of God and/or of the teachings of Jesus: "Not everyone who says to me 'Lord, Lord,' shall enter the kingdom of heaven, but he who does the will of my Father" (Matthew 7:21); and "enter by the narrow gate, ... for the gate is narrow and the way hard, that leads to life" (Matthew 7:13-14; cf. further, Matthew 5:20; Mark 9:47 and parallels). The kingdom would also require egalitarian, nonexploitative, and nonauthoritarian social relations: "How hard it will be for those who have riches to enter the kingdom of God. ... It is easier for a camel to go through the eye of a needle than for a rich man to enter the kingdom of God" (Mark 10:23b, 25 and parallels); "Woe to you, scribes and Pharisees, hypocrites! because you shut the kingdom of heaven against men; for you neither enter yourselves, nor allow those who would enter to go in" (Matthew 23:13; cf. the parallel, Luke 11:52, without the "kingdom," 52a, but including the "entering," 52b). It is even evident that the kingdom as society has a historical location. Even though most of the "entering" passages speak in terms of an entry yet to be made, two sayings suggest that the kingdom began since (or with) John the Baptist: "I tell you, among those born of women none is greater than John; yet he who is least in the kingdom of God is greater than he" (Luke 7:28; Matthew 11:11); "the law and the prophets were until John; since then the good news of the kingdom of God is preached, and everyone enters it violently" (Luke 16:16; Matthew 11:12 has serious variations). These sayings, whatever their original form was precisely, suggest that the kingdom as society replaces that governed by the "law and the prophets," and yet is somehow the proper fulfillment of the law and prophets as well.

THE RENEWAL OF ISRAEL

If God was thus bringing the old order to an end and effecting a renewal in the individual and social life of the people in distinctive ways, then the social form of that renewal must have been a restoration of Israel.

Three themes or sets of material in the gospel tradition in particular indicate that Jesus was almost certainly working for the renewal of Israel: the location of his ministry in the villages and towns of Galilee (vs. the cities) and its restriction to "the house of Israel"; Jesus' continuity with John's call for repentance and the threats of judgment Jesus pronounced on whole villages or on "this generation"; and Jesus' constitution of the twelve disciples as symbolic of the renewal of the people of Israel.

The Twelve Disciples and the Twelve Tribes of Israel

One of the principal indications that Jesus intended the restoration of Israel was his appointment of the Twelve. Even apart from the key text of Matthew 19:28 and parallels, there appears to be solid evidence that the twelve disciples were symbolic of the restoration of the twelve tribes of Israel. The twelve tribes had become one of the principal images of the future restoration of the people. In one of the "servant songs" in Second Isaiah the restoration of the tribes is linked with the fulfillment of the promise to the ancestors; the servant is called "to raise up the tribes of Jacob" prefatory to becoming a light to the nations (Isaiah 49:6) . Ben Sira (Sirach 26:11) appeals to God to gather the tribes of Jacob and give them their inheritance, and anticipates that one of the appointed tasks of the returning Elijah will be "to restore the tribes of Jacob" (Sirach 48:10). Psalms of Solomon 17:28-31, 50 appeals for the reestablishment of the tribes on the land as well as their gathering together. Revelation 21:10-14 and Acts 26:7 indicate that the early Christian tradition had simply continued this standard symbolization of the fulfillment of the promise to the ancestors, the restoration of Israel according to the twelve tribes.

Most striking is the evidence from Qumran: that a contemporary community, acting in anticipation of the imminent fulfillment, structured its leadership in terms of twelve (symbolic) representatives of the twelve tribes: the Council of the Community consisting of twelve laymen along with the three priests (1QS 8:1-2); the twelve chief priests and twelve representative Levites, "one for each tribe" (1QM 2:2-3); the twelve chiefs of the twelve tribes, along with the "prince" and priestly leaders (1QM 5:1-3); and twelve loaves of bread offered by the heads of the tribes (11QTemple 18:14-16). Revelation 21:10-14 reveals the same symbolization of the twelve apostles as representative of the twelve tribes already well established in the communities of Jesus' followers. It seems highly credible, therefore, when New Testament scholarship claims (or simply assumes) that the twelve disciples, almost certainly appointed during Jesus' ministry, symbolized the imminent restoration of Israel in its twelve tribes.

Matthew 19:28 and Luke 22:28-30 then provide explicit evidence that Jesus was symbolizing the restoration of Israel in constituting the Twelve. Keeping in mind possible variations in the sequence of words and phrases, and antici- pating justification given below for the translation of certain terms, we can use a critically justified reconstruction of the saying as it may have stood in Q:

> You who have followed me, (in the restoration) when the son of man shall sit on his glorious throne, you yourselves will also sit on twelve thrones saving (effecting justice for) the twelve tribes of Israel.

Much of the previous interpretation of this passage illustrates how the (in)authenticity of a saying and its supposed meaning have been determined by the presuppositions of the modern interpreters and by their assumptions con- cerning the meaning of certain terms in the passage. Much modern New Tes- tament interpretation, whether by liberals, existentialists, and/or form-critics, presupposes that Jesus was primarily a teacher, that he addressed individuals, and that it is not necessary to bring concrete social (i.e., political-economic) context into consideration. Moreover, much of the interpretation of this passage has assumed that *krinein* meant "judging" (*richten*), or at most "ruling," that the passage referred to some sort of "last judgment," that "the Son of man" either referred to Jesus' return in judgment at the "end-time" or was an indi- cation of the inauthenticity of the whole passage, and/or that *palingenesis* in Matthew 19:28 meant "the new world" (RSV) somewhat in the Stoic sense of the regeneration of the world. None of these assumptions is valid. A change or shift in any one or more makes a considerable difference in how the passage is understood and in what context it would have made sense.

One of the principal points of our agenda is to take seriously the concrete social (i.e., political-economic as well as religious) context of Jesus' ministry and the movement he catalyzed. First of all, *palingenesis* need not be read in the Stoic sense of regeneration of the cosmos, as is usually assumed.[23] That was precisely the term used by Josephus when describing a historical renewal or restoration of the people in their land, and one, moreover, that he portrays also in terms of the twelve tribes (*Ant.* 11.66, 107). Even if the Aramaic equiv- alent of the term was not part of the original saying, but was added in Q or by Matthew, it provides a clear indication of how the passage as a whole was understood in the tradition: in terms of the future restoration or reconstitution of Israel in the land, i.e., as had happened previously in the return from the Babylonian exile.

Second, it is clear that the early church had indeed identified the exalted Jesus Christ with the "son of man" conceived as a figure coming in judgment, and hence that some of the "son of man" sayings should be viewed as stemming originally from that early church. Nevertheless, even as it is clear that in some sayings Jesus thinks of the "son of man" as a symbol or a figure different from himself, so it is highly likely that, especially Jesus himself, prior to exaltation as the risen Lord, could have used the symbol "son of man" in the original Danielic sense, perhaps even in direct allusion to the vision of Daniel 7. The saying of Jesus reported in his trial before the Sanhedrin in Mark 14:62 is clearly an allusion to the scene portrayed in Daniel 7. It is thus at least conceivable that the phrase "when the son of man shall sit on his glorious throne" in Jesus' saying in Matthew 19:28 should be read somewhat in the original Danielic sense as a symbol for "the people of the saints of the Most High" being granted rule and dominion themselves (Daniel 7:13-14, 27). That is, the meaning of "the son of man sitting on his glorious throne" would thus parallel, indeed be almost synonymous with, the *palingenesis*, the restoration of the people in their land.

The most determinative assumption has been that *krinein* means "judging" or "ruling." It is then supposed that the reference is to the Twelve judging Israel (e.g., for having rejected Jesus and his message), and that such judicial activity would contradict Jesus' concern for Israel in the light of the inbreaking of the kingdom.[24]

If we examine texts in which the "judging" terminology is used, it is clear that those who, filled with the Spirit of God, lead the people of Israel in reasserting their independence from conquerors or exploiters are "liberators" or "saviors," not "judges" (Judges 2:16; 3:10; 4:4, in context; even 11:27). Similarly, Yahweh does not "judge," but rather "liberates," "delivers," "saves," or "effects justice for" the orphan, widow, poor, or oppressed in passage after passage (see especially Psalms 9; 10:18; 35; 58; 72:4; 76:9; 82:1-4; 94; 103:6; 140:12; 146:7; note that the numbering of psalms is one lower in the Septuagint). Appealing to God's characteristic concern for and previous liberation of the poor and oppressed (e.g., Deuteronomy 10:18), the prophets castigate predatory rulers for their exploiting the "righteous" poor, etc. (e.g., Isaiah 1:17; 10:1-2). Expectations of God's future "judgment," or more properly "liberation" or "salvation," were almost certainly influenced by the portrayal of Yahweh's coming to deliver "the world with righteousness, and the people with his equity/truth" (Psalms 96:13; 98:9). For example, the "servant of Yahweh" who is to restore the twelve tribes of Israel in Isaiah 49:6 is expected to bring "justice" (not "judgment") to the people in Isaiah 42:1 (parallel surely to the "salvation" in 49:6). Thus the sense of the saying would have been that the Twelve would be sitting on the thrones "liberating/redeeming/establishing justice for" the twelve tribes of Israel.

This interpretation of Matthew 19:28 and parallels can be confirmed by comparison with two contemporaneous examples that also combine both the symbolic twelve tribes and a sense of fulfillment with the idea of the establishment of justice/salvation (i.e., more positively active and liberating than is connoted by "judgment"). Psalms of Solomon 17:28-32 expects that the anointed son of David will "gather together a holy people, whom he shall lead in righteousness," and . . . will "effect justice for" (or "deliver") the tribes of the people that have been sanctified by the Lord his God. This means, according to the following lines, that he will no longer allow any injustice in their midst, and that he will establish them according to their tribes in the land. What has been translated as "judging" was really a concrete liberating or justice-establishing aspect of the restoration of the people, the tribes of Israel, in their land. Secondly (and more striking in terms of the parallel to the twelve disciples), although the same term (*šapaṭ* or equivalent) may not be used, the representative "twelve men and three priests" who comprise "the Council of the Community" at Qumran are described as having a similar function (1QS 8:1-4), as they effect "righteousness, justice, loving-kindness, and humility, . . . preserve faith in the land, . . . and atone for sin by the practice of justice."[25]

Finally, according to this biblical way of understanding *krinein*, the liberating or justice-establishing activity of the Twelve in Matthew 19:28 and parallels stands in continuity with the "mission" they were given during Jesus' ministry, whereas it appeared as puzzlingly different when the Twelve were understood to be "judging" Israel (which was the principal grounds for denying the "authenticity" of Matthew 19:28!). According to the "mission discourse" in Mark and Q, the disciples are charged with healing, exorcism, preaching the presence of the kingdom, and spreading "peace" (i.e., *shalom* = salvation/ liberation) to those they visit and, in Q and Luke 10:10-11, pronouncing judgment against those towns that do not respond positively. The disciples are thus sent out to continue and expand Jesus' own mission of the liberation and renewal of the people. Some of the earliest gospel traditions (e.g., Matthew 11:5 and Luke 7:22) understand Jesus' activities as the fulfillment of the eagerly awaited deliverance prophesied by "Isaiah" (Isaiah 35:5; 61:1-2). Now, this is exactly what the future deliverance or *mišpaṭ* was expected to be: seeking the lost sheep of the house of Israel, binding up the crippled, and strengthening the weak; in sum, "feeding them in justice" (Ezekiel 34:16). The role of the Twelve thus continues and extends that of Jesus even as it fits within and acts out the very (temporal) structure of the historical fulfillment and renewal of Israel. Parallel to the way in which the kingdom of God is already present in the midst of the people, is available to be entered and yet is still to come "with power," the twelve disciples are already engaged with Jesus in saving activities (healings, exorcisms, preaching the kingdom's presence), and the same representative Twelve will continue their saving and justice-establishing activities in completing the renewal of the twelve tribes of Israel.[26]

When Jesus preached that the kingdom of God was at hand, he was not referring to a place or to some particular cataclysmic final eschatological act of God that would bring an end to history. The "kingdom of God" in Jesus' preaching refers to God's saving action, and the people who receive benefit from God's gracious action are expected to glorify God in gratitude. The focal concern of the kingdom of God in Jesus' preaching and practice, however, is the liberation and welfare of the people. Jesus' understanding of the "kingdom of God" is similar in its broader perspective to the confident hope expressed in then-contemporary Jewish apocalyptic literature. That is, he had utter confidence that God was restoring the life of the society, and that this would mean judgment for those who oppressed the people and vindication for those who faithfully adhered to God's will and responded to the kingdom. That is, God was imminently and presently effecting a historical transformation. In modern parlance that would be labeled a "revolution."

The principal thrust of Jesus' practice and preaching, however, was to manifest and mediate the presence of the kingdom of God. In the gospel traditions of Jesus' words and deeds, we can observe the kingdom present in the experience of the people in distinctive ways. Jesus and his followers celebrated the joys of the kingdom present in festive banqueting. In the healings and forgiveness of sins and in the exorcisms, individual persons experienced the liberation from disease and oppressive force and the new life effected by God's action. Jesus' interpretation of the exorcisms, moreover, points to the broader implications of God's present action among the people. That is, since the exorcisms are obviously being effected by God, it is clear that the rule of Satan has been broken. But that meant also that the oppressive established order maintained by the power of Satan (according to the apocalyptic dualistic view of reality that was shared by Jesus and his contemporaries) was also under judgment. The old order was in fact being replaced by a new social-political order, that is, the "kingdom of God," which Jesus was inviting the people to "enter."

NOTES

1. Esp. R. Bultmann, *History of the Synoptic Tradition* (Oxford: Blackwell, 1963); N. Perrin, *Rediscovering the Teachings of Jesus* (New York: Harper & Row, 1967); and *Jesus and the Language of the Kingdom* (Philadelphia: Fortress, 1976).

2. On this and the following paragraph, see Perrin, *Rediscovering the Teachings of Jesus*, 54-63.

3. As Perrin himself has argued, *Rediscovering*, 173-185.

4. Perrin, *Rediscovering*, 60.

5. See esp. W. G. Kümmel, *Promise and Fulfillment* (London: SCM, 1957).

6. Contra B. D. Chilton, *God in Strength: Jesus' Announcement of the Kingdom* (Freistadt, West Germany: Ploechl, 1979), 287.

7. Contra Perrin, *Rediscovering*, 67.

8. Perrin, *Rediscovering*, 59.

9. Perrin, *Rediscovering*, 173-185.

10. Bultmann, *History of the Synoptic Tradition*, 109.

11. Cf. Perrin, *Rediscovering*, 102-104.

12. J. Jeremias, *The Lord's Prayer* (Philadelphia: Fortress, 1973).

13. Perrin, *Jesus and the Language of the Kingdom*, 28-29, 47.

14. This is true once we recognize and peel away the Lucan interest in who turned out to be included, with "the poor and maimed and blind and lame" of vs. 21 repeating the list in 14:13 of the previous story.

15. Jeremias, *New Testament Theology* (London: SCM, 1971), 86-92, provides a

concise treatment of the situation. For a recent critical reconsideration of the oral transmission and shaping of the healing and exorcism stories, see W. Kelber, *The Oral and Written Gospel* (Philadelphia: Fortress, 1983), 46-55; cf., other recent literature in his notes.

16. See, e.g., Martin Buber, *The Prophetic Faith* (New York: Harper & Row, 1960), 188-197.

17. On how some healing stories thus expose the restrictions of the religious authorities, see further A. C. Wire, "The Structure of the Gospel Miracle Stories and Their Tellers," *Semeia* 11 (1978): 92-96; and on the purposeful challenge posed in the healings on the sabbath, see Elisabeth Schüssler Fiorenza, *In Memory of Her* (New York: Crossroad, 1983), 124-126.

18. Matthew must have changed "finger" to "spirit," since "spirit" is a favorite Lucan term (see esp. 4:18).

19. R. A. Horsley, "Who Were the Witches? The Social Roles of the Accused in the European Witch Hunts of the Sixteenth and Seventeenth Centuries," *Journal of Interdisciplinary History* 9 (1979): 689-715; and "Further Reflections on Witchcraft and European Folk Religion," *History of Religions* 19 (1979): 71-95.

20. See further Perrin, *Rediscovering*, 66.

21. Perrin, still working out of the modern individualistic orientation, argues just the opposite; *Rediscovering*, 67.

22. Perrin, *Jesus and the Language of the Kingdom*, 46.

23. W. D. Davies, *The Gospel and the Land* (Berkeley: University of California Press, 1974), 364-365.

24. E.g., M. Trautmann, *Zeichenhafte Handlungen Jesu* (Würzburg: Echter, 1980), 199; but far from a contradiction, judgment includes redemption as the alternative to its opposite punishment.

25. We should also note that the description of this function of the Council flows directly into the description of the Council as "a House of Holiness for Aaron, . . . precious cornerstone, . . . Most Holy Dwelling for Aaron, . . . an agreeable offering atoning for the Land. . . ." Jesus may have understood the new community he started in parallel terms as the new Temple.

26. It is worth noting also that the social-economic content of justice or deliverance to be looked for among the prophets in the [last?] judgment in Matthew 25:31-46 (probably a later tradition) is the same as that initiated by Jesus' ministry, continued in the disciples' mission, and to be established in their eschatological role of delivering and establishing justice for the twelve tribes of Israel.

27

CHED MYERS

The Ideology and Social Strategy
of Mark's Community

Preceding and continuing parallel to the development of social criticism of the Bible has been an increasingly sophisticated literary criticism, now branching into both "narrative" criticism and "reader-response" criticism. By and large the development of this literary criticism focused on Hebrew Bible narrative and the Christian Gospels has been separate from the use of social sciences and political hermeneutics in biblical studies. The newfound appreciation of narratives such as the Gospel of Mark as a complete story that has been plotted by an author with particular rhetorical techniques and with particular effects on the readers has made unavoidable the dramatic political conflicts portrayed in those biblical narratives. The obvious step is to bring critical social analysis and political hermeneutics together with a heightened appreciation of the features and effects of biblical narratives. Ched Myers has pioneered such a "political reading of Mark's Story of Jesus." Drawing heavily on a combination of Marxist and structuralist literary criticism and exercising a "hermeneutics of suspicion" on modern Western sociology as well as biblical texts, Myers illuminates how, in the course of the narrative, Mark both indicts the established political-economic-religious order and articulates a political-economic praxis constructive of a radical new kind of community.

Reprinted from Ched Myers, *Binding the Strong Man: A Political Reading of Mark's Story of Jesus* (Maryknoll, N.Y.: Orbis Books, 1988), 414–44, abridged.

THE HISTORICAL SITUATION OF THE PRODUCTION OF MARK

The purpose of this chapter is to summarize the socioliterary evidence that has been yielded by my reading of the gospel text, and to organize it into a brief portrait of Mark's community. I begin with a reconsideration of the historical "moment" in which Mark wrote, and then return to the hypothesis articulated at the outset of this commentary. There I postulated that the determinate social formation of Roman Palestine in Mark's era allows the possibility of a social group that was alienated from the dominant order, which advocated a radical alternative practice, and remained politically engaged yet nonaligned with the major sociopolitical groups. Before reconsidering this hypothesis, however, a word needs to be said about hermeneutical barriers to achieving an accurate and sympathetic portrait of Mark's community.

It has become a commonplace recently among biblical scholars to understand apocalyptic literature in terms of the conceptual frameworks established by the socioanthropological study of "millennial" communities.[1] There is much to be said for this approach; for example, K. Burridge's *New Heaven, New Earth* concludes that such movements closely resemble what we have seen in Mark:

> [They] involve the adoption of new assumptions, a new redemptive process, a new politico-economic framework, a new mode of measuring [humanity], a new integrity, a new community. . . . A prophet is he or she who organizes the new assumptions and articulates them; who is listened to and found acceptable; whose revelation is accorded authority.[2]

Burridge, however, also warned against the tendency of modern interpreters to caricature these new assumptions, ideals, and redemptive processes as social fantasy: "Whether or not they are bizarre is entirely subjective."[3]

Yet the prevailing attitude of historical sociology toward the social and ideological strategies of so-called sects, which dates back to Troeltsch's classic sociology of religion, continues to be pejorative. Similarly, in the biblical field, W. Beardslee wrote that scholars have been "able to clarify apocalyptic only by distancing themselves from its inner spirit."[4] But such objectification, at least according to the model of the hermeneutic circle advocated in this book, is itself the biggest barrier to a true political appreciation of the text.

There is a kind of circular logic to correlating sect-sociology and the study of biblical apocalyptic. For example, I have shown that late Jewish prophecy ("proto-apocalyptic") figures decisively in Mark. But listen to how Hebrew Bible scholar P. Hanson characterizes these traditions:

> The sociological setting of Daniel . . . like the communities behind Third Isaiah, the Isaiah Apocalypse, and Second Zechariah [is] a visionary minority living under oppression in a world seemingly fallen into the hands of enemies of Yahweh, convincing them that fulfillment of Yahweh's promises could no longer be anticipated within the existing order.

Clinging to their vision, the community of Daniel passively awaits Yahweh's intervention. . . . The dialectic [between vision and reality] has dissolved. . . . Connections with politico-historical realities have been lost:
neither the human community, nor any other human agent, takes part in
the conflict which would be won "by no human hand" (Dn 8:25); nor
does the kingdom given to the saints betray any connections with the
mundane; they are saved by being lifted out of this order into the cosmic
sphere of the vision.[5]

This illustrates the way in which apocalyptic symbolics are dismissed by a mainline liberal scholar as "pessimistic" and escapist. So caricatured, it is no wonder
that apocalyptic seems uninteresting to both Marxist and liberal reformist interpreters.

This bias is inevitably carried over into the study of Mark. So Kee, who
rightly defends the Danielic character of Mark, concludes: "In keeping with
the passivist tradition of the Hasidim, Mark portrays Jesus as refusing to take
any initiative against the political authority."[6] The same attitude characterizes
J. Wilde's more detailed study of Mark as a millennial community. Wilde
equates the Gospel's "nonaligned" discourse with a stance entailing socio-political ambivalence. Drawing upon the (notoriously slippery) method of "ideal
typologizing," Wilde argues that Mark articulates the "revolutionist" type as
defined in B. Wilson's influential sect-sociology:

[It] looks for the destruction and re-creation (transformation) of the basically alien social world by supernatural agency (not human) on a cosmic
level (not local or individual) very soon (not yet present); and therefore
sees men (by themselves) as basically powerless and weak in the face of
the oppression of the present world, but finds access to power and hope
solely in the salvation brought by divine agency in the approaching cataclysm.[7]

Admitting that this "pure" type occurs rarely because it is so absolutist, Wilde
nevertheless insists that it is the lens through which Markan radicalism should
be interpreted.

It is not hard to see in Wilde's sociological caricature the mirror image of
Hanson's theological one. Moreover, we can see in it an updated version of
Albert Schweitzer's old "thoroughgoing eschatology" thesis, which held that
because Jesus expected the literal and immediate end of the world, he abdicated
all political and historical responsibilities, offering at best an impractical
"interim ethic." In my view, such conceptual straitjackets are no closer to the
truth of apocalyptic symbolics than the crude literalizing of a Hal Lindsey or
the existentialist psychologizing of a Thomas Altizer.[8] Sectarian stereotypes fail
utterly to explain the militance of Mark's Jesus, his persistent political engagement with—and death at the hands of—the powers. They do not begin to do
justice to the activist ideology of discipleship that lies at the heart of the story.
Mark looks for the end of the old world and the inauguration of the new, but

it is discipleship—which he equates with a specific social practice and costly political engagement—that will inaugurate this transformation.

Mark could not have been ideologically further from groups such as the Essenes, who, as we *know* from historical records, pursued a social strategy of withdrawal in order to wait upon Yahweh's intervention. My reading has shown that Mark's Jesus is anything but "passive" toward political authority, his ideology anything but socially introverted. The problem with sect-sociology and the interpretation of apocalyptic literature is therefore hermeneutic: modern rationalists are unable to understand narrative symbolics in sociopolitical terms. Fortunately, there is a growing minority of scholars who has begun to interpret the documents of biblical apocalyptic, such as Daniel and Revelation, as political manifestoes of nonviolent movements of resistance to tyranny.[9] My commentary demonstrates that the same must be said of Mark.

In order to test my hypothesis about the Gospel as a document of "nonaligned radicalism" we must first return to the question of provenance. In chapter 2, I proposed that Mark was written in Galilee during the last years of the Jewish revolt. Let me address the question of time first. Brandon[10] and Kelber,[11] despite their entirely different approach and conclusions regarding Mark, agree on one thing: the literary novelty of Mark could be attributed only to the world-shattering destruction of the temple by the Romans in 70 C.E. Yet Kelber asks himself:

> But is the gospel nothing but a retrospective legitimization of a new Christian situation in the wake of the Roman victory? Does Mark merely sanction the facts after the Fall? [But] the gospel is not an exercise in confirming the obvious, but a creative reconsideration on the past so as to be of immediate service to the present of Mark.[12]

Kelber has put his finger on one of the central problems of a post-70 dating. Simply put: If the destruction of the temple state was a *fait accompli,* why did Mark need to launch his polemic against it?

The answer usually given, as Kelber notes, is that Mark was providing a theological justification of its demise. It is argued that Mark was using *ex eventu* (after the fact) prophecy in Jesus' prediction of the temple's destruction in 13:2 to "sanction" this world-shaking debacle. Now Mark is quite capable of making use of *ex eventu* prophecy, for it was a common apocalyptic literary device. But if this is the case with 13:2, why does Mark not use a more accurate description of events, as does Luke?[13] J. Collins's assessment of Daniel's use of *ex eventu* historical review is relevant here. He points out that the events recorded in Daniel 11:1-39 are verifiable based upon a history of the Hellenistic wars—that is, up until 11:40ff., at which point Daniel turns to the career of his own contemporary, Antiochus Epiphanes:

> We can tell at what point the book of Daniel was written, since beyond a certain point the "predictions" are no longer fulfilled. ... Antiochus, like Gog, is a king from the north, who will invade the land of Israel and

fall there. This is not how Antiochus met his death, so we know that this prophecy was composed before he actually died late in 164 B.C.E.[14]

In other words, *ex eventu* prophecy freely mixes historical reviews, contemporary commentary, and anticipation of imminent events. If we then apply the same logic to Mark, it follows that Jesus' "prediction" that the temple will be razed "stone by stone" must have been written before the destruction of the temple — by fire.

It is true that Mark wishes to assure Christians that a symbolic life can and must be reconstructed apart from the temple-based order. But it does not necessarily follow that he could only have advocated this after the temple was already destroyed. In fact his narrative indicates the opposite. The disciples' question in 13:1 suggests that the temple was very much a living and imposing edifice. This is further confirmed by Mark's symbolic discourse of "destruction," specifically the correlation between 11:23 and 5:13. The "legion" that "no one had the strength to bind" (5:3f.) is symbolically driven out of Palestine "into the sea" (5:9-13); similarly, after "exorcising" the commercial interests in the temple, Jesus promises that only through the power of faith can the "mountain" be overcome and ordered "into the sea" (11:23). The historical power represented by Roman legions and the temple mount was, in both cases, intact; that is precisely what makes the two "exorcisms" so remarkable as an anticipation of the "impossible," provoking amazement (5:15-20; 11:24).

Mark's criticism of the temple is not based upon "theological" considerations, but rather the exploitive political economy of the temple-based tributary system. This would hardly have been necessary once this system was overturned by the Romans. The same can be said of Mark's vigorous attacks upon the scribal and clerical aristocracy, which rapidly disappeared after 70 C.E.

Many of those who argue that Mark was theologically sanctioning the fall of the temple further assume that this is part of an overall pro-Roman apologia. This is not an implausible hypothesis; we know that some Jews did repudiate the popular revolt, and later justified the Roman victory. Moreover, we have an example of just such an ideological stance in the writings of Josephus. But the contrasts between Mark and Josephus are striking, all the more so given the fact that they had faced the same historical situation. Josephus, as a Jewish aristocrat, was vociferous in his criticism of the rebels, and sympathetic to the clerical elite. Although Mark does not agree with the rebels, he nevertheless refuses to criticize them directly, whereas he is strident in his attack upon the Jewish ruling classes. Similarly, Josephus, though openly pro-Roman, bemoans the temple's destruction; Mark celebrates the apocalyptic demise of both temple and legion.

If Mark wished to portray himself, like Josephus, as pro-Roman, he could scarcely have done a poorer job of it. His use of the anti-Hellenistic motifs of apocalyptic narrative, his veiled repudiation of imperial power (5:1ff.; 12:13ff.) and his parody of the procurator Pilate (15:2ff.) could hardly have curried Roman favor. We must conclude that Mark criticized the temple and the clerical aristocracy precisely because they were still operative. In other words, his struggle to overturn the dominant social order and its legitimating ideologies was a real battle in the war of myths not a rhetorical "exercise in confirming the obvious."

Another objection to a postwar dating of the Gospel arises from a consideration of Mark's discourse on suffering and martyrdom. At the most obvious level, it would have made no sense for Mark to anchor his discipleship ideology in the call to "take up the cross" if he agreed with Josephus's antirebel, pro-Roman stance. This image makes perfect sense, however, if his community was in fact subject to persecution on grounds of subversion. As B. van Iersel has demonstrated on purely literary grounds, "the significance of the book is most pregnant in an actual situation of persecution, when the reader or listener may be arrested at any moment."[15] Once the war was over, the crisis of temple-destruction may have continued to be a "theological" one, but it would not have been an existentially political one. During the war, on the other hand, a Christian community that refused to defect to the Romans but also refused to fight alongside the rebels would have been liable to persecution from both sides—which is precisely the situation the text reflects.

Virtually from the outset of Mark's portrait of the discipleship community, issues of polarization and solidarity find articulation. At the commissioning of the "confederacy," the shadow of the betrayer is present (3:19). In the catechism, the problem of apostasy is anticipated by the plot-theme of the disciples' "blindness." Indeed, the last days of Jesus are filled with undercover intrigue, and the community is riddled with self-doubt. But nowhere is the pressure of the historical moment more poignantly reflected than in Jesus' second sermon:

> Brother will deliver brother to death, and the father his child, and children will rise against parents and have them put to death; and you will be hated by all for my name's sake [13:12f.].

Not only must disciples stand political trial; they must also face the bitter prospect of betrayal from within the "family"—meaning both kin (for we know the war did divide relatives) and community. The seriousness of this prospect is reflected in the fact that the threat of eschatological judgment appears in Mark only in reference to such betrayal (9:42; 14:21).

That Mark builds his Gospel as a whole around an essentially tragic narrative—the disciples' failure—is explicable in terms of the historical reality of a community under persecution. Yet though "betrayal" is not lightly viewed, there is an equally strong counter-discourse of "pardon." Even as the solidarity of the community unravels in the story, Jesus assures his solidarity (14:22ff.). Mark asserts that even in the "fire" of persecution and apostasy, the "salt" of reconciliation must prevail (9:49f.). And this can happen only when the practice of forgiveness (11:25) is at the center of the community's life. And as the end of the story makes clear, even the most egregious "denial" of Jesus, the most blatant defection from the way, cannot bring the discipleship adventure to an end. Because Jesus "goes before" us (16:7), a new start can always be made on the discipleship adventure.

In sum, then, it was the crisis of the Jewish temple state engendered by the revolt against Rome, and the persecution of Mark's community for its "nonaligned" stance, that was the immediate context of the production of the Gospel.[16] We have both prewar and postwar texts from groups that responded differently to the same historical situation. Josephus, as noted, wrote a historical account that justified his defection and narrated the war from the victors' perspective. Later rabbinic writings obliquely reflect the strategy of many Pharisees, who responded to the defeat by reconceiving Jewish identity and practice in a way that maintained Jewish distinctiveness without a nationalist element. Qumran produced texts of monastic withdrawal, though its members, in the final hour, may have gone to fight in the defense of the temple. The rebels, for their part, left only the "texts" of coins minted during the period of liberated Judea — and the haunting witness of the ruins at Masada. And perhaps just as significant a testimony is the mute voice of those who were simply victims of the war, never its subjects.

Mark, a follower of Jesus, struggling and suffering through the apocalyptic moment of the late war years, responded with a story about a Nazarene and his followers. It legitimated neither defection, nor withdrawal, nor reform-minded moderation, nor Maccabean triumphalism, nor despairing acceptance of a world dominated by the powers. It called for resistance to the rule of the "strong man," and the creation of a new world: a practice of radical discipleship. This story heralded a way through the wilderness — and the war. But this way was the way of the cross: to the Romans a symbol of imperial hegemony, to Mark the sign of the kingdom come.

The place, like the time, of Mark's production, is something a socio-literary analysis can establish only plausibly, not conclusively. Kee's summary of the case against Roman provenance (still the majority thesis) confirms what I have found in reading the text:

> The preservation in Mark of cultural and linguistic features of the Eastern Mediterranean rural village culture — features which Luke, in writing for a Gentile audience, eliminates or alters — speaks against Rome. Marxsen, following the lines of reasoning developed by Lohmeyer and Lightfoot, proposes Galilee. The archaeological evidence from excavations there in recent years confirms the wide use of Greek in public inscriptions, including synagogues, so that for Mark to have written a Christian document there in the 60s as Marxsen suggests is not inconceivable. And the accurate reflection of practices having to do with agriculture, housing, employment, and land-ownership and taxation, that are characteristic of the whole of Syria-Palestine in the period do indeed speak for that larger area as the place of origin.[17]

The strong "narrative bias" in the Gospel toward Galilee, as Lightfoot and Marxsen argued, further confirms this area as the location for Mark's community. Because of alleged geographical ambiguities in the story, which he attributes to Mark's unfamiliarity, Kee opts for Syria over Galilee proper; I have argued that these ambiguities can be explained in socio-literary terms. I see no compelling reason not to place the production of the Gospel at the site of its own narrative center: Galilee. This is not historicism, but an argument from the ideology of the text.

If Galilee is the narrative center of gravity for the story as a whole, Capernaum is the narrative center of the Galilee narrative. Many of Mark's most detailed descriptions of social location are in or around Capernaum: the fisherman's workplace (1:16-20), a humble village dwelling (2:1-4), the agrarian parables (4:1ff.), storms on the Sea of Galilee (4:35ff.), and specific conflicts over social practice with the Pharisees (2:16ff.). To extend the logic still further, we have seen that the household is the narrative center in Capernaum (1:29; 2:1, 15; 3:20; 5:38; 9:33) as well as in other areas (7:17, 24; 9:28; 10:10; 14:3). Did Mark emphasize these aspects of life to color his realistic narrative because they were both familiar and important to the real life of his original audience? More specifically, were the households of the Markan community located in the vicinity of Capernaum? These details should not be abstracted from their narrative function in Mark's story, but they can yet serve as indicators of the social setting involved in the production of the Gospel. They do not *prove* that Mark's community was located in Galilee, much less Capernaum itself; but they certainly lend credence to my hypothesis that the Gospel was produced in a generally, if not specifically, Palestinian village setting.

THE GOSPEL AS SOCIOPOLITICAL CRITICISM

When discussing Mark's characterization of social structures, groups, and personalities, we must keep in mind that it was not his purpose to offer a dispassionate historical account of his world. He was involved in a fierce ideological struggle with his opponents in a world he assumed his audience knew; thus he employs shorthand, parody and caricature.

The Jewish ruling classes in the Gospel are represented by three groups: the Herodian nobility, the scribes, and the Jerusalem aristocracy (chief priests, elders, Sadducees). These groups are unequivocally opposed to Jesus throughout the story. The Herodians represent the old nobility of the half-Jewish house of Herod, whose political power, but not wealth or privilege, had largely dissipated under direct Roman administration of the colony. Jeremias notes three outstanding characteristics of the Jerusalem court during the rule of Herod the Great: the significant presence of Greeks and other aristocratic foreigners; its great affluence; and its strong security apparatus. The influential gentile contingent reflected the fact that though Herod's domain was Jewish, he looked to the Hellenistic world for his power, identity, and political style. Herod's state wealth was demonstrated in public building projects; his personal riches were manifested in palace opulence. The rabbinic writings tell of a widow in his court who complained when the scribes limited her daily expense account to 400 gold denarii![18] Finally, the king maintained a large personal police force, with a known and feared reputation for torture, used not only on dissidents but also on those within the court who fell into disfavor.[19]

In Mark's time the royal aristocracy was more concentrated in Galilee, south of Capernaum in the Hellenistic city of Tiberius on the Sea of Galilee. The mere mention of "Herodians" would have conjured up in the minds of Mark's readers all the abuses of this dynasty, singularly responsible for the Hellenization of Palestine and well known for its long record of brutal oppression. But it is the flashback account of the execution of John the Baptist by Herod Antipas that gives specific content to Mark's criticism of the Herodian class. That episode is a bitter parody of the whims of the royal aristocracy, whose marital-dynastic alliances are forged in defiance of Jewish Law, and whose political decisions are made at drunken parties. Yet Mark's vignette of Herod Antipas is far more plausible than Matthew's censorious parody (in Mt 2), which casts Herod (the Great) as the new murderous pharaoh of Exodus 1-2.

Both stories indicate class antagonism toward the house of Herod. But Mark's specifically reflects the popular outrage that lingered in the historical memory of Galileans regarding Antipas's martyrdom of the popular prophet John. His account of the party at the royal court with all the "leading men" of Galilee is highly realistic, including the custom of young Jewish maidens dancing for the nobility.[20] The scene reflects the practice of royal concubinage, and the fact that women were one of the prominent signs of wealth in the patriarchal oriental court.[21] We can infer from Mark's direct warning against the Herodians (8:15), and his portrait of their conspiratorial relationships with the Pharisees (3:6), that the royal house represented a continuing threat to Mark's radical community in Galilee (12:13f.).

The scribes are the archenemies of Jesus in the story and, as government investigators from Jerusalem (3:22; 7:1), they provide the link for the political machinations against Jesus. Mark thus accurately speaks of "scribal Pharisees" (2:16), their connection to the Sanhedrin (14:1; 15:1), and the tremendous social prestige they enjoyed (11:38-40). His criticism is twofold. He correctly perceives the scribes as the architects of the dominant ideology, whose respectability and authority must be refuted (see 9:12; 12:35). Therefore from the outset of the Gospel he pits Jesus' teaching directly against theirs (1:22; 2:6; 12:35). Mark also sharply attacks the way in which their social status becomes the pretext for economic exploitation and aggrandizement (12:38-40).

Finally, Mark repudiates the entire traditional Jerusalem power structure. The wealth and power of the leading patrician families derived primarily from landownership. The Romans acknowledged this power, and appointed them to positions of authority in the colonial structures. As for the Sadducees, Mark mentions them but once, and only in order to show how their conservative ideology legitimizes patriarchal rule (12:18-27). The fact that Mark is more concerned with scribal and Pharisaic social power is an accurate reflection of the situation of his time, in which the influence of the Sadducees was waning, and restricted largely to the Sanhedrin.

In considering the priestly aristocracy, Mark gives no indication of having the slightest interest in the disputes over the legitimacy of a non-Zadokite priesthood, a serious political conflict among the ruling classes, which dated from the period of the Hasmonean dynasty. To Mark priestly power was a function of economic class, not lineage, resulting from control over the temple cultus. This situation is directly reflected in Mark's report of their outrage over Jesus' attack upon the temple marketplace (11:27).

Mark's trial and execution narrative gives us a clear idea of his political estimation of the members of the Jerusalem hierarchy. On the one hand he portrays it as disdainful, yet fearful, of the discontentment of the masses (11:32; 14:2), whom they manipulate for their own ends (15:11). On the other hand he considers the Sanhedrin fully collaborative with Roman administration of Palestine. In the double trial they ape the imperial mechanisms of "justice," and even attempt to deny Jesus a proper burial after his execution. Their self-interest in maintaining the colonial arrangement predictably results in their rejection of any hint of popular kingship articulated in messianic terms (14:61; 15:32).

Mark summarizes his opposition to the ruling classes in his parable of the vineyard (12:2-9). In the classic prophetic tradition Jesus attacks the leaders of Israel. Although they should be servants (Lv 25:55), they make a pretense of "owning" the "vineyard." This is, in Mark's view, the *inevitable* result of economic and political power, which makes the ruling class "deaf and blind" to the message of the prophets, whom they murder—hence the "prophetic script." The subversive discourse of Jesus' parable, however, reverses the tables. The rulers are described as mere tenants who will be brutally punished for their insubordination by the true owner—for the landlord class, a taste of its own medicine! Mark roundly condemns this class (12:40), and in his mind there is no question of its compatibility with the new social order: "What will the owner of the vineyard do? He will come and destroy the tenants and give the vineyard to others" (12:9). These are the hardest, and most revolutionary, words in the Gospel.

Mark takes the same hard-line stance toward Roman imperialism. He relies upon two forms of more veiled discourse: the Jewish resistance tradition of apocalyptic and the literary device of parody. Though there are only six instances in which Mark alludes to the reality of foreign imperialism, each articulates his decidedly anti-Roman sociopolitical stance.

The first instance is his subversive expropriation of "gospel" as title for his story. This term suggests that this story will extol yet another Roman military victory in the provinces, and at the surface of the narrative this indeed appears to be the case. The Romans, through the agency of the collaborative native aristocracy, successfully capture and execute a subversive prophet and aspirant to popular kingship. Yet Jesus throughout the trial remains uncowed by the imperial power of Rome, causing the procurator to "wonder" (*thaumazein;* 15:5, 44). And in the discourse of Mark, the very moment of Roman triumph—the cross—is revealed by apocalyptic symbolics to be in fact the moment of Rome's defeat.

The true battle being narrated by the "gospel" is between Jesus the Human One and the domain of Satan, administrated by "strong men" such as Caesar. Just as Jesus first clashes with the Jewish ruling class through the symbolic action of the synagogue exorcism (1:21-27), so too he serves notice to the

Roman imperialists in the story of the Gerasene demoniac (5:1-20). Mark is nowhere politically bolder than in 5:9f., the only place where Jesus wrestles from a demon his "identity":

> Jesus asked him, "What is your name?" He replied, "My name is 'Legion,' for we are many." And he begged him earnestly not to expel them from the country [5:9f.].

Mark appears to acknowledge the reality that "no one had the strength to subdue" the demon of Roman military occupation (5:4). Yet he makes his revolutionary stance clear by symbolically reenacting the exodus story through a "herd" of pigs. With the divine command, the imperial forces are drowned in the sea. It is no accident that in the aftermath of this action the crowd, like Pilate, responds with "wonder" (*thaumazein;* 5:20).

To invoke the great exodus liberation story was, as it has been subsequently throughout Western history, to fan the flames of revolutionary hope.[22] Yet Mark realized that the problem was much deeper than throwing off the yoke of yet another colonizer. After all, biblical history itself attested to the fact that Israel had always been squeezed, courted, or threatened by the great empires that surrounded it. And the Maccabean revolt against the Seleucids had only resulted in recycling oppressive power into the hands of a native dynasty, one that in turn became an early victim of a newly ascendent imperial power, Rome. Thus the meaning of Jesus' struggle against the strong man is not reducible solely to his desire for the liberation of Palestine from colonial rule, though it certainly includes that. It is a struggle against the root "spirit" and politics of domination—which, Mark acknowledges matter of factly, is most clearly represented by the "great men" of the Hellenistic imperial sphere (10:42).

Mark believes that both parties of the colonial condominium are "possessed" by this spirit, and so assesses each in exactly the same terms. The discourse of "equation" is reflected at the outset in the parallelism between the two inaugural exorcisms, and again at the story's end in the double trial of Jesus. There Pilate is indicted along with the high priest for engineering the railroading of Jesus. The ruthless procurator, infamous for his defiance of Jewish political opinion, is parodied as "consulting" the Jewish crowd, yet nevertheless shrewd enough to release a convicted Sicarius terrorist instead of Jesus.

We can see the same discourse in Jesus' second campaign. On either side of the central political parable of 12:1-12 are conflict stories in which Jesus' opponents challenge him to reveal his ideological commitments, only to have their own duplicity revealed. They are unwilling to state their loyalty to the biblical vision of justice (represented by the prophet John, 11:27ff.) while implicitly advocating loyalty to Rome (represented by the coin, 12:13ff.). A political "trap" is set for Jesus in the tax question. It provided him with a good opportunity to unambiguously instruct his readers to collaborate with Rome, if he was so inclined. But in 12:17, as in 11:33, Jesus refuses to be caught. He appeals, as he does throughout the Gospel, to the sovereignty of Yahweh, who is true "lord of the house" (13:35) despite the counterclaims of Caesar.

But is Yahweh truly sovereign? This claim must stand the test of Caesar's ultimate claim over life, articulated not by the coin but the cross: Caesar's power of capital punishment, the threat that renders his subjects docile. And so, in his second call to discipleship, Jesus faces Caesar's "lordship" head on. Mark could not have chosen an image that indicated more unequivocally his opposition to the empire than the Roman executioner's stake. And Jesus *means* what he says about taking up this cross: Mark fully expects members of his community to "follow" Jesus in political trials not only before Jewish courts but Roman ones as well. "You will stand before governors (*hēgemonōn*) and kings" (13:9a), referring to procurator and Caesar.

By redefining the cross as the way to liberation rather than symbol of defeat and shame, Mark radically subverts the authority of the empire. The accepted meanings of "saving life" and "losing life," of being "convicted" and "acquitted," of what "belongs to Caesar" and what "belongs to God," are all turned upside down when the power of death, by which the powers rule, is broken. But to understand this takes "eyes to see" that the cross is the power of God, which alone can reanimate the exodus liberation story. It alone can drive the oppressive temple state and the repressive legions "into the sea."

Reform efforts among literate Jewish groups took two trajectories in Mark's era. The first strategy advocated withdrawal from the social mainstream in order to more rigorously attend to the demands of the symbolic order of debt and purity; it is represented by the Essene movement. The fact that Mark never addresses this movement directly may indicate he felt it less of an ideological competitor. His portrayal of John in the wilderness, and later his equation of the practice of John's followers with that of the Pharisees (2:18), may suggest that some of the Baptist's followers were drawn toward Qumran. It is noteworthy that Mark cites Isaiah 40:3, for this text appears to have been used by the Essene community to justify its monastic life in the desert. But the narrative movement of the Gospel, although it *begins* in the wilderness, does not *remain* there, proceeding inexorably from the periphery toward the center—that is, toward engagement.

Mark would not only have disagreed with the Essenes over their social strategy of elitism based upon intensification of the demands of the symbolic order, but their political eschatology as well, reflected in the so-called War Scroll, which narrates the final battle between the "Sons of Light and Sons of Darkness." Archeological evidence indicates that the community site at Qumran was abandoned late in the war years, and Qumranite writings have been found at Masada.[23] It appears therefore that once the siege of Jerusalem began, the Essenes joined the rebels in their defense of Jerusalem. This would strengthen my hypothesis that rebel recruiters operated abroad in Palestine in 69 C.E., and did in fact successfully draft many.

The other trajectory of reform and renewal pursued a strategy of extending the symbolic order to a greater number of persons. This was represented by the Pharisaic movement, a far more formidable competitor in Galilee. Mark's portrait strongly suggests protracted Pharisaic antagonism toward his community; Pharisees are always pictured on the offensive against Jesus. Conflicts erupt over issues of practice that were hallmarks of Pharisaic piety: strictly segregated table fellowship (2:16ff.), asceticism (2:18ff.), Sabbath observance (2:23ff.), and ritual purity with respect to meals (7:1ff.). In each case, Jesus eclipses the Pharisaic objection by raising a deeper issue concerning the place of the poor in the symbolic order. It is as if Mark is trying to convince those impressed by the Pharisaic social strategy practice that it is not the populist alternative it seems, but merely a cosmetic alternative to the oppressive clerical hierarchy.

At every point Mark's criticism of the Pharisees concerns social relationships. Mark does not stop with simply repudiating Pharisaic practices of ritual purity. By sandwiching the debate over *korban* into his consideration of kosher, Mark attacks the very heart of Pharisaic ideology: the halakah (7:6ff.). The halakah allegedly make the demands of the symbolic order more accessible for the common people. But Mark contends that this legislation is in fact quite elitist. It is this very commitment to the symbolic order (i.e., the temple treasury) that allows the "commands of God" regarding the weak *within* the community (in this case the elderly) to be ignored or overridden (7:9-13). The same issue is at stake in Mark's other reference to the halakah, the question of divorce legislation (10:2ff.). Again, the Pharisees are revealed to be wholly unconcerned with the weaker member (here the woman), not to mention the original scriptural vision of equality in marriage. Thus, Pharisaic *halakah* functions to guard the status quo, whether the political economy of the temple or patriarchy.

Mark's inclusive community, like Paul's, came under severe Pharisaic criticism, but his counterattack was just as vigorous. For Mark, Pharisaic concern for purity, allegedly in order to protect the social boundaries of Judaism, cannot possibly reflect a populist commitment if their own legislation is unconcerned with social equality *within* those boundaries. Segregation from gentiles, the poor, and the unclean did nothing to ensure that the "commands of God," which concern true justice for all, would be promoted. Mark concludes that the symbolic order and any group that supported it would never be able to fulfill Yahweh's vision of a humanity free of class and racial alienation. So does he reject the reform groups, withdrawn or engaged.

Jesus is portrayed as entering Jerusalem as a specifically nonmilitary, popular king (11:2-7); yet he is contrasted with [the rebel] Barabbas (15:7). We must also acknowledge, however, the distinct tone of solidarity that Mark weaves into his passion narrative. Jesus is first arrested (14:48) and then crucified (15:27) "as a social bandit." Mark appreciated the fact that the very conditions he protests against, the systematic oppression of the peasantry by both the Romans and the Jerusalem hierarchy, had led many of his Galilean compatriots to engage in social banditry. Some factions of the rebellion of 66-70 took the opportunity to settle class scores. Upon entering and gaining control of the city, certain rebels launched a series of attacks upon the houses of the royalists and high priests. The burning of the public archives building housing records of debt was certainly an action on behalf of those who had lost their land and become impoverished due to an inability to meet tax and tithe obligations. Noteworthy too were efforts to democratize the high priesthood and overturn the aristocracy's control of the temple during the civil war in 67-68. These actions against the institutions of autocracy suggest that there were many points of ideological affinity between Mark and the social bandits turned rebels.

Yet for all of this, and despite his unequivocal opposition to Roman colonialism, Mark did not advocate revolt. Why? According to the latter half of Jesus' second sermon, it had to do with his insistence that the real revolution must take place at a deeper level of both ends and means. Any attempt to restore a Davidic state meant a return to the politics of domination, and was thus counterrevolutionary (10:42f.). Mark therefore considered the prospect of the temple state's collapse a "sign" of liberation (13:28-31), whereas the rebels saw it as indicative of cataclysm and defeat, "the end" (13:7).

Mark then expropriates the great symbol of resistance to Rome, the cross. Jesus' call to a discipleship of the cross was directed not only to his disciples but to the "crowd" as well (8:34). Says Mark, our movement stands in resistance to Rome; after all, our leader was crucified (15:27). Our nonviolent resistance demands no less of us than does guerilla war—to reckon with death. But we ask something more: a heroism of the cross, not the sword. We cannot beat the strong man at his own game. We must attack his very foundations: we must render his presumed lordship over our lives impotent. You consider the cross a sign of defeat. We take it up "as a witness against them," a witness to the revolutionary power of nonviolent resistance (13:9b). Join us therefore in our struggle to put an end to the spiral of violence and oppression, that Yahweh's reign may truly dawn (9:1).

THE GOSPEL AS SOCIOECONOMIC CRITICISM

In the first part of the Gospel, Mark addresses the dominant ideological order as it manifested itself in the provinces. The three great dictums of the first campaign narrative—the two Human One sayings (2:10, 28) and the Deuteronomic ultimatum (3:4)—all make the same point: cultural systems must enhance and liberate human life, not marginalize it—or to put it in modern parlance, they must function "for people, not for profit." In the tradition of classical prophecy, Mark contends that the original intention of the symbolic order had been betrayed, and thus calls for justice and compassion over cultic obligation.

Mark's concern has to do, on the one hand, with the way in which the institutions of purity and debt have created socioeconomic stratification within the Jewish community and, on the other, the way in which they reinforce social segregation between Jew and gentile. Defying them, Jesus freely interacts with the sick/unclean and the foreigner, and instructs his disciples to do likewise. Included in Mark's criticisms are the dominant cultural codes of honor and status, which also function to promote social divisions. In the first construction section, Mark subverts cultural assumptions about propriety and what constitutes "first" and "least" in the hierarchy of status. For example, Jesus attends to the needs of an impure and destitute woman before the requests of a synagogue head, and concedes a debate to a gentile woman (5:21-43; 7:24-37). In the second construction cycle, Mark continues turning the social order upside down, this time through Jesus' teaching. Jesus gives priority to children and women over the rich and the "great"; a blind beggar is portrayed as a model of discipleship.

In the second campaign narrative, Jesus confronts the symbolic order at its heart, the temple. There he delivers yet another prophetic dictum concerning the purpose of the house of God (11:17). The decisive break with the debt code comes with his advocacy of a practice of communal forgiveness (11:25). When Jesus dies on the cross, not only are the powers pulled from their thrones (the sun darkens), but the symbolic order itself is overthrown (temple curtain is rent). The curtained Holy of Holies symbolizes the ideological justification for priestly elitism: in this order, Yahweh is exclusive (reclusive?), dwelling "apart from and above" the people, mediated by the priests. That which divides the people from Yahweh also divides them from each other: the priest also lives "apart and above." Thus the destruction of this curtain symbolizes the end of such an order. It is true that the symbolic order appears to prevail in the story, as Jesus' corpse (of the first order of impurity) is removed from the cross by a Sanhedrin representative so it will not profane the Sabbath. But the "absence" of that body from the tomb is the last word; the corpse does not need to be properly buried according to the demands of honor and purity, because the new order has now dawned. Moreover, that "body" becomes the center of the new order in the eucharistic feast— those who partake of it are "contaminated" with the subversive memory of Jesus.

The politics of the narrative reinforces Mark's contention that the messianic community must now live outside the bounds of the dominant order. From its genesis in the wilderness peripheries, the kingdom movement is put in spatial tension with the "center," whether that is conceived of as Judea/Jerusalem or the Hellenistic *polis*. Mark's Jesus travels throughout northern Palestine, which may well be an indication of the missionary scope of Mark's own community. Then the narrative slowly moves south toward the negative pole of Jerusalem for the final confrontation. But as soon as this mission is completed, Mark points immediately back to Galilee (16:7). This is the culmination to an ideology totally opposed to the dominant Jewish symbolic order, its institutions and its sites.

I stated above that Mark criticized the temple cult not as a theological rationalization of its demise but because it anchored an essentially oppressive political economy. To begin with, Mark portrays a world in which hunger and disenfranchisement among the masses is widespread—a situation that corresponds to the reality he knew in wartime Palestine. Mark is particularly preoccupied with eating and not-eating motifs. We might further consider the various expressions of economic deprivation, or "not enough," that we encounter throughout the story:

1. John's wilderness diet, 1:6
2. should we fast? 2:18ff.
3. disciples commandeer grain, 2:26
4. Jesus unable to eat due to press of crowd, 3:20, 6:31
5. Jesus' command to feed Jairus's daughter, 5:43

6. Jesus' command to go on mission without bread or money, 6:8
7. Syrophoenician woman's plea for crumbs, 7:24
8. Jesus hungers, 11:12
9. widow's impoverishment, 12:40, 44
10. famines, 13:8.

For Mark, the experience of economic marginality, land alienation, and social disruption was proof positive enough of the injustice of the temple-based tributary economy. He envisions the restoration of a system that will be committed to communal sufficiency.

Mark does more than criticize the economic disparity of class divisions within the Jewish community; he also recognizes the mechanisms by which those divisions are maintained. The Herodian class, for example, is portrayed as deeply complicit in the colonial system by which its wealth and power are maintained. It is the Herodians who, again in cooperation with the Pharisees, try to extract from Jesus a position on the imperial tribute (12:13-17). The Pharisees in turn are attacked where they are most vulnerable, from the peasant's perspective: their attempts to control the production and distribution of agricultural produce. Mark alludes, directly and indirectly, to each aspect of this control: their administration of purity regulations (2:16f.; 7:1ff.), which determined acceptable tithes, their jurisdiction over debt obligations (i.e., *korban*, 7:6ff.), and their enforcement of Sabbath law, which affected the peasant's ability to produce enough to survive (2:23ff.).

Patterns of landownership are reflected in Mark's frequent allusions to tenant farmers and absentee landlords. But it is the temple, as the central mechanism of this political economy, that is the focus of Mark's criticism. Jesus' attack upon the temple market, and the scriptural justifications that accompany this direct action, articulate a clear repudiation of this system. The poor are directly oppressed by cultic obligations they cannot meet, as illustrated in Jesus' lament over the impoverished widow in 12:41ff. Capital accumulates in the temple building and treasury, and landownership concentrates in the hands of those already privileged by the system—all of which is "robbery" of the poor. To claim that the temple is the domain of "thieves" (11:17) is the same as asserting that the rich are rich by "defrauding" the poor (10:18-21).

Throughout the Gospel there is a consistent narrative opposition between those representing the symbolic order on the one hand and the poor and marginal on the other:

1. priests (purity) vs. the leprous (1:41ff.)
2. scribes (debt) vs. the physically disabled (2:1ff.)
3. Pharisees (debt) vs. the dependent elderly (7:6ff.)
4. scribes (debt) vs. disenfranchised widows (12:40).

Although all the major social groups are indicted, it is the scribes, as ideological apologists for and economic beneficiaries of this exploitive political economy, who are singled out as the worst offenders. Mark's Jesus is unimpressed by their rhetorical affirmations of the prophetic insistence that "love of neighbor is more than burnt offerings and sacrifices" (12:34). The fact is that the system itself, which the scribes uphold, enforces the class stratification of Israel.

Mark, in other words, understands the nature of *structural* injustice, and for this reason refuses to consider strategies of reform. The disciples do not see this clearly, at least twice entertaining the idea that Jesus' concern for the poor might be satisfied by their making better use of their purchasing power in the market (see 6:37; 14:5). Their blindness is a result of a failure to see that the system cannot be redirected toward the purposes of justice. Instead, Jesus calls for its complete collapse (13:2), and in its place he advocates a genuine practice of equitable redistribution.

A NEW POLITICAL PRACTICE

Mark believed that the kingdom would not dawn by divine cataclysm, but rather would grow slowly, a small seed in hostile soil. Advocating a "revolution from below," the discourse of the Gospel includes both subversive and constructive elements. Mark does not simply criticize the present order; he offers instructions for the building of a new order, which will center around the community of discipleship. The Gospel functions to legitimate this community as a political "confederacy" (3:13-19), which represents a concrete alternative to the politics of domination.

How was this community organized? How was power exercised? The narrative undermines any absolute ideology of leadership: the leaders of the community are portrayed as failures. I would not characterize Mark's treatment of the male disciples as a "political polemic" against a Jerusalem-based Christian leadership, as does W. Kelber.[24] However, its sarcastic tone does suggest that pretensions to authoritarianism were not unknown in the experience of Mark's people. Jesus' taunt—"Oh, but this is not so among you!"— referring to the practices of domination so bitterly familiar from Roman colonialism, functions as a sharp warning against aspirations to power. And "discipleship" as a permanent state of following Jesus the true leader, in contrast to rabbinic schools in which the student became himself a master, further guarded against the reproduction of hierarchy in the community.

Still, Mark's alternative is not leaderlessness, but leadership accountable to the "least" in the community. What concretely did the "politics of servanthood" mean? Our reading has identified a radical break with the traditional Palestinian patriarchal structures of clan, kinship, and marriage. The new "family" is egalitarian, both in its marital and community forms, and the traditionally weakest members of the system, women and children, are given central place. Mark does not have a lot to say about marriage except where he considers the problem of divorce. The profile of women characters in the Gospel indicates that women were considered full persons outside their traditional roles as helpmeets. I have also argued that there is evidence that Mark's critique of patriarchy strongly implies that women are considered more suited to the vocation of servant-leadership than are men.

The unprecedented nature of such an ideology and practice in the context of Mediterranean antiquity cannot be overestimated:

At this period Jewish, Hellenistic, and Roman perceptions of family life are quite conservative. Strong family bonds were supported not only by social pressure but by a host of laws governing marriage, inheritance, and the relation of different members of the natural and extended family. The power of the head of the family (*patria potestas*) was a virtual law unto itself. A Christian community which evokes a saying of Jesus to claim that doing the will of God is more important than loyalty to the natural family and which actually counsels leaving the family to form a new family without the governing power of the father and which rejects those structures of interrelationship which govern normal family life would naturally evoke suspicion and persecution.[25]

Donahue goes on to note that many of the earliest attacks upon the Christians by Roman writers centered upon their socially aberrant community lifestyle.

Against Theissen's theory of "wandering charismatics," I believe Mark reflects a settled community in which the extended household model is maintained. The household, however, is now understood as the primary site not of reproducing dominant socio-cultural patterns, but resisting them; perhaps it is also the haven for underground activity. Under persecution, the community appears to be struggling with the question of internal discipline, but the Gospel clearly comes down on the side of leniency and understanding for those who have fallen to apostasy. The practice of reconciliation and forgiveness is crucial to the community's life. Importantly, Mark advocates an "open" community— that is, one whose boundaries are not rigidly defined. Not only must the door always be open to the poor and outcast, but non-Christians who do the works of justice and compassion must also be accepted.

On the whole, the Gospel concentrates more upon subversive than constructive politics, probably because the pressure from both Jewish and Roman authorities demanded clarity on these matters. Jesus is presented from the outset as a rival authority, challenging the hegemony of the powers who hold sway over the dominant political order. After being declared an "outlaw" (1:10f.) toward this order, Jesus proceeds to expropriate priestly authority over the purity apparatus (1:43), scribal authority over the debt system (2:10), and Pharisaic authority over Sabbath legislation (2:28). Later the conflict escalates as Jesus assaults the highest authority structure of his time: the temple. In each case he asserts that the original purpose of these institutions has been betrayed. Mark subsequently identifies Jesus as "Lord" not only of the "Sabbath," but of the "house" as well (13:35). As Malachi had warned (Mal 3:1ff.; cf. Mk 1:2), he has indeed come to judge the temple community according to the proper exercise of justice. All of this functions to justify the community's practice of resistance.

The ideology of resistance is clearly articulated in Jesus' "strong man" speech: the goal is to bring down the old order and liberate those captive to it. The practice of resistance consists of three elements, as we have seen: kingdom proclamation, healing and exorcism, and nonviolent confrontation. Jesus commissions and instructs his community in each aspect of this messianic vocation (3:13; 6:7).

The political strategy of the community, like so many modern revolutionary movements, begins with attempts to persuade the "base," or popular sectors, of the double imperative: the old order must be overturned and the new order welcomed. The community's proselytizing appears to consist of founding other cells of resistance, which become "safehouses" (6:7ff.). The mission is wholly contingent upon popular reception; thus the emphasis upon going without sustenance and the role of hospitality. It is anticipated that this preaching mission alone is enough to bring the disciples into conflict with the authorities, which is why it is juxtaposed to the story of John and Herod. Despite the danger, the "good news" of liberation must be spread abroad, not only to oppressed Jews but to "all peoples" (13:9f.).

The proclamation must be accompanied by concrete expressions of the new order. These are not thaumaturgical "signs and wonders" (8:11f.), but the works of justice and mercy: feeding the hungry (6:37), healing the sick (6:13), promoting fellowship with the socially outcast (2:16) and the gentile (7:1ff.), and above all, exorcism. Jesus' ministry of exorcism, portrayed as the most threatening aspect of his practice to the political authorities (3:22ff.), is a discourse by which Mark articulates his ideology of opposition to both Jewish and Roman politico-military hegemony. The new order means the end of scribal domination *and* liberation from the colonial boot of the imperial legions. But exorcism is not merely the symbolic declaration of intent: it takes on a decidedly concrete character when Jesus "casts out" the temple entrepreneurs. This episode links exorcism to the politics of symbolic direct action.

In both his first and second campaigns, Jesus employs the tactics of what we would today call "civil disobedience." The very first public action of his disciples is to break the law (2:23ff.)! Jesus then debates the true intention of the law in the ensuing "trial" (3:4). The same pattern of legal violation and defense occurs again in 7:1ff. The climax to Jesus' practice of symbolic direct action, however, is the parade from the Mount of Olives and the ensuing temple action. The procession, curse, and "cleansing" are, to be sure, painstakingly choreographed exercises in political theater; but we must not lose sight of the fact that they are also portrayed as specifically *disruptive*. Thus Mark legitimizes not only "classic" civil disobedience—in which the law is broken because it is unjust, as in the case of the Sabbath—but militant direct action as well.

The powerful practice of exorcism/direct action must not be exploited by the disciples in order to build their own power base (9:38ff.). Indeed, the power is linked to "faith," which means the ability not only to "name" the demons within and without, but to envision a new personhood and a new world free of the structures and patterns of domination (9:14ff.). Only by such faith can the "mountains" of the present order be overthrown (11:23f.). The disciples' struggle for faith-as-political-imagination is one of the central themes of the Gospel, narrated in counterpoint to Jesus' powerful practice. This indicates that Mark's community wrestled with self-doubt about the viability of its messianic vocation, and given the historical situation, it is not difficult to sympathize with its members. After all, their visible impact was small, and they were probably hard pressed by the rival claims of the Pharisees on the one hand and the rebels on the other. Yet Mark stuck by his belief that true subversive politics was to be found in neither reform nor rebellion.

In speaking of the political process, Mark offers his readers two key images: the "miracle" of a mustard seed and the "paradox" of the cross. The seed reminds us that a revolution from the bottom up is a slow process whereby the root causes of domination are exposed and transformed. It demands both patience and faith, for historical change will not be as evident as if the new order were imposed from the top. To believe in the "true" court of justice of the Human One is to believe that the smallest of seeds can grow into the tree in which all "the birds of the air" can nest. The cross reminds us that the powers cannot be overthrown by military means. But how was it that Mark (and all the early Christians) understood the cross to represent *victory* over, not defeat by, the powers?

I have shown how Mark weaves a sophisticated fabric of apocalyptic symbolics throughout the story. The combat myth in the wilderness is rearticulated in the parable of "binding the strong man and ransacking his house" (3:27). It is enacted in Jesus' direct action in the Jerusalem temple, and reaches its climax in Jesus' final confrontation with the authorities in his trial (14:62) and death. At this moment the apocalyptic signs of the "end of the world" occur (15:33-39): the Human One pulls the heavenly potentates down from their thrones (13:26f.). The "strong man," it turns out, is not identifiable *simply* with the scribal class or its political coalitions, or the temple, or even the "desolating sacrilege" of imperial Rome. Mark's apocalyptic discourse reveals the heart of the matter: Jesus is taking on the politics of domination itself.

W. Wink, in his study of "powers" discourse in the New Testament, has in my opinion correctly captured the meaning of this apocalyptic euphemism. His argument that we should interpret "the spiritual powers not as separate heavenly or ethereal entities but as *the inner aspect of material or tangible manifestations of power*" is worth citing at length:

> We encounter them primarily in reference to the material or "earthly" reality *of which they are the innermost essence*. . . . The expression "the Powers" should no longer be reserved for the special category of spiritual forces, but should rather be used generically for all manifestations of power, seen under the dual aspect of their physical or institutional concretion on the one hand, and their inner essence or spirituality on the other. Popular speech, often more accurate in unconscious matters than it is given credit for being, has quite properly referred to the whole range of phenomena as "The Powers That Be." . . . In all these cases, the simultaneity of heavenly and earthly events witnesses to the perception, mythically couched, that there is more to events than what appears. The physical actors and institutions are only the outer manifestation of a whole field of powers contending for influence.[26]

For Mark, then, the practice of domination is so deeply embedded in human history that no mere rebellion will do.

Genuine revolution demands a radical break with all the accepted canons of power politics, with every expression of violence, exploitation, and dehumanization:

> "For we are contending . . ." against the spirituality of institutions, against the ideologies and metaphors and legitimations that prop them up, against the greed and covetousness that give them life, against the individual egocentricities that the Powers so easily hook, against the idolatry that pits short-term gain against the long-term good of the whole.[27]

The means of the old order cannot bring about the ends of the new. Anything less than a politics of militant, nonviolent resistance is counterrevolutionary, a recycling of the old world. Mark's Jesus calls for a more radical (driving-to-the-roots) social transformation, a unity between means and ends. I have suggested at several points throughout this commentary that the cross is not only a reminder of the political "cost of discipleship," but can also be seen as a symbol of what Gandhi called *satyagraha*.

Mark's Gospel legitimates the transgression of established social and economic boundaries for the sake of the re-creation of human unity. The subjects of this practice of inclusivity are first the poor and outcast. This is articulated both generally, in terms of Jesus' ministry to the "crowd," and specifically, in terms of episodes involving the disabled (2:1ff.; 10:45ff.), the ritually unclean (1:45ff.; 5:25ff.), the socially marginalized (2:15ff.; 7:24ff.); and women and children (10:1ff.). This solidarity is perhaps best represented in the first episode of the passion narrative, in which Jesus is pictured residing at the house of a leper, and there teaches that one woman's act of compassion outweighs all the pretensions to faithfulness of his own disciples (14:3-9).

Because it is often raised in political readings of the Gospel, the question must be addressed: Does Mark's story portray Jesus as the author of a "mass movement"? This might be suggested not only by his clear "preferential option" for the poor of Palestine, but the evident class bias in the narrative. There are those who would see some of Jesus' "popular" actions, such as the wilderness feedings or the procession on Jerusalem, as indicative of mass organizing. But we must keep in mind that Mark's discipleship narrative articulates a definite strategy of minority *political vocation*. That is, Jesus creates a community that is expected to embrace the messianic way regardless of how the masses respond to the "objective conditions for revolution."

In what sense, then, do we understand Jesus' solidarity with the poor? Liberation theologians working in South Korea have illumined the question with a term drawn from their cultural and historical experience: *minjung*. Kim Yongbok defines *minjung*:

> Kingdoms, dynasties, and states rise and fall; but the minjung remain as a concrete reality in history, experiencing the comings and goings of political powers. ... Power has its basis in the minjung. But power as it expresses itself in political powers does not belong to the minjung. These powers seek to maintain themselves; and they rule the minjung.[28]

Kim calls them "protagonists in the historical drama," but distinguishes the politico-cultural definition of *minjung* from Marx's strictly socio-economic understanding of the proletariat:

> The former is a dynamic, changing concept. Woman belongs to minjung when she is politically dominated by man. An ethnic group is a minjung group when it is politically dominated by another group. A race is minjung when it is dominated by another powerful ruling race. When intellectuals are suppressed by the military power elite, they belong to minjung. Of course, the same applies to the workers and farmers.[29]

Ahn Byung-mu, sees *minjung* as analogous to Mark's "crowd." In Mark, argues Ahn, the *minjung* are outside the sphere of the dominant Jewish groups; they include the poor, the tax collector, the impure.[30] Mark clearly portrays Jesus as an advocate for the poor and outcast in his healing and symbolic direct action. Ahn refers to "passive" solidarity in the sense that Jesus does not objectify the Palestinian *minjung* in terms of its role in a revolutionary process "so that its name may be used to justify any kind of political dictatorship."[31]

Instead, Mark advances an ideology of "receptivity": the leper, the sinner, the woman, the child are all to be received unconditionally as subjects of the kingdom. Jesus teaches his disciples to live among them and look at life from their perspective. This receptivity is not based upon any inherent goodness on the part of the poor, but as a sign of Yahweh's unconditional acceptance of them as *minjung*. For Mark, the ideology of receptivity would appear to be rooted in the old Hebrew notion of reciprocity. The land belongs to Yahweh, and *all* who dwell upon it do so by grace, with equal status: "To me the people of Israel are servants, they are my servants whom I brought from the land of Egypt" (Lv 25:55).

In counterpoint to the portrait of economic deprivation that Mark paints of Palestine, he asserts the vision of abundance. The images of "enough" are:
1. eschatological harvest, 4:8
2. crowds satisfied in wilderness, 6:44
3. all food declared clean, 7:19
4. crowds satisfied in wilderness, 8:8
5. abundant leftovers, 8:19f.
6. communal abundance, 10:30.

These images imply a new practice over against the temple-based system of economic redistribution, which has failed. This is the practice of cooperative sharing, a return to the original Israelite vision of a community of production and consumption.

The old system will persist, of course, and the disciples on mission will be vulnerable to it (6:8); they are justified in commandeering food for sustenance (2:23ff.). Mark appears to reject asceticism (i.e., fasting) as a privilege of the affluent, offensive to those who genuinely hunger. But the central focus of Mark's ideology can be seen in Jesus' interaction with his disciples in the first feeding story. Note the dialectical play of Mark's discourse (6:36-38):

Disciples: "Send the crowds away into the villages so they can buy them-
selves something to eat."
Jesus: "You feed them."
Disciples: "Shall we go and buy two hundred denarii worth of bread and
give it to them to eat?"
Jesus: "How many loaves do you have? Go and see."

The disciples can imagine only market scarcity in the dominant economy.
Against this, Jesus keeps referring them to their own resources, challenging
them to forge an alternative economics. The "abundance" envisioned in Mark's
vision of the kingdom can be realized when the disciples learn to organize and
share available resources. This is the "miracle" narrated in the wilderness feedings; by it no one need "faint on the way" (8:3).

The community model of economic sharing is articulated in 10:29-31, there
standing in tension with the dominant order represented by the rich landowner
whose wealth "defrauds" the poor (10:19-22). The community re-creates the
redistributive system: private ownership of land and houses is abandoned in
favor of cooperative economics. This model is not intended to engender corporate affluence, but to provide surplus on behalf of the poor. The narrative
strongly suggests that Mark's community is in fact practicing some kind of
communal model (10:28), and experiencing social opposition because of it. It
was one thing for Qumran monks to practice a style of communal economics
in isolation in the wilderness; it was quite another to attempt it while residing
in the midst of a hostile economic system.

There may be, however, a more specific dimension to the "persecutions"
alluded to in 10:30. Did Jewish members of Mark's community refuse to cooperate with their tithing or other obligations to the temple-state? There is no
direct evidence of this, but certainly such a position could be extrapolated on
the basis of several episodes: the civil disobedience in the grain field (2:23ff.),
Jesus' attack on the temple (11:15ff.), his criticism of contributions to the treasury (12:41ff.), and his prediction of the temple's destruction (13:2). Moreover,
the tribute question suggests that some form of economic resistance was a live
issue for the community (12:13ff.). Mark's narrative bias against the city further
suggests that the community stood in solidarity with the plight of rural producers in the dominant system, and may have been promoting alternative models
of distribution that were considered subversive by authorities such as the Pharisees.

At the heart of Mark's political, social, and economic alternatives to the
dominant order lies a radical new symbolic system based upon the primacy of
human need (3:4). In place of the purity code Jesus exhorts moral imperatives
concerning exploitation (7:21f.). In place of the debt code he enjoins a community practice of forgiveness (11:25). Jesus' teaching functions to both ethicize
and democratize the traditional symbolic order, undermining the legitimacy of
those who mediate it—that is, priests, scribes, and Pharisees. Mark presses the
bold claim that the temple is not necessary in order for Yahweh to dwell among
the people. There is no sacred institutional site from which Yahweh must be

addressed in prayer: that site is faith (11:24). This point is made dramatically in the rending of the temple curtain at the moment of Jesus' death. The messianic "sacrifice" of Jesus has reconciled the people to Yahweh and each other, thus rendering void the priestly apparatus. Yahweh is no longer a recluse in the Holy of Holies, but present among the community.

Given the importance of table fellowship to Mark's social and economic experiment, it is not surprising that Jesus chooses this site as the new symbolic center of the community. In place of the temple is a simple meal, which represents participation in Jesus' "body" (14:22-25). Yet it is the meal, not the body, that is "holy," for the latter is absent at the end of the story. We are left, then, not with a ritual but the social event of table fellowship. This meal, which itself was an expropriation of the great liberation symbols of Passover, is meant to bring to mind the entire messianic program of justice and the cost of fidelity to it. But it is a meal for a community in flight, or more accurately, a community that follows its true center, Jesus, who cannot be institutionalized because he is always ahead of us on the road (16:7).

There is one more aspect to Mark's reconstruction of a symbolic life within the community: that is the primacy of the word. Jesus' teachings remain not only after he is gone, but stand at the center of history: "heaven and earth may pass away but my words shall not pass away" (13:31). And how is this word mediated? Through Mark's story, of course! The Gospel is an integral part of the symbolic center of the community, inseparable from Jesus himself. For the sake of Jesus and the Gospel, disciples give up the old order for the new (10:29) and pay the attendant price (8:35). And because the new story is linked to the old story, the community continues to read the Hebrew scriptures with "eyes to see" and "ears to hear."

To conclude, the literary *novum* called the Gospel of Mark was produced in response to a historical and ideological crisis engendered by the Jewish war. In this apocalyptic moment, a community struggled to maintain its nonviolent resistance to the Roman armies, the Jewish ruling class, and rebel recruiters, while sowing the seeds of a new revolutionary order through practice and proselytism. Mark's community does not fit in the strictures designed by sect-sociology, nor does it fit the caricatures of millennial groups. It must be taken seriously on its own terms, as a distinct socio-political strategy in a determinate formation, and indeed as an ideology of practice that begs to be heard in our own time.

NOTES

1. See the work of Howard C. Kee, *Community of the New Age: Studies in Mark's Gospel* (Philadelphia: Westminster Press, 1977), and John G. Gager, "Shall We Marry Our Enemies? Sociology and the N.T.," *Interpretation*, 36 (1982): 256-65.

2. Kenelm Burridge, *New Heaven and New Earth: A Study of Millenarian Activity* (New York: Schocken Books, 1969), pp. 13f.

3. Ibid., p. 8.

4. W. Beardslee, "N.T. Apocalyptic in Recent Interpretation," *Interpretation*, 25 (1971): 421.

5. Paul Hanson, "Old Testament Apocalyptic Reexamined," *Interpretation*, 25 (1971): 473, 476.

6. Kee, p. 146.

7. James A. Wilde, "A Social Description of the Community Reflected in the Gospel of Mark." Ph.D. dissertation, Drew University, 1974, pp. 61f.

8. Thomas Altizer, "The Dialectic of Ancient and Modern Apocalypticism," *JAAR* 39: (1971): 312ff.

9. John J. Collins, *The Apocalyptic Vision of the Book of Daniel* (Missoula: Scholar's Press, 1977); Adela Yarbro Collins, "The Political Perspective of the Revelation to John," *JBL* 26 (1977): 16-31.

10. S. G. F. Brandon, *Jesus and the Zealots* (New York: Scribner's, 1967).

11. Werner Kelber, *The Kingdom of Mark: A New Place and a New Time* (Philadelphia: Fortress Press, 1973).

12. Ibid., p. 131.

13. See B. Reicke, "Synoptic Prophecies on the Destruction of Jerusalem," in D. Aune, ed., *Studies in the NT and Early Christian Literature* (Leiden: Brill, 1972), pp. 121ff.

14. John J. Collins, *Daniel, 1–2 Maccabees* (Wilmington: Michael Glazier, 1981), pp. 105, 107.

15. B. van Iersel, "The Gospel According to Mark: Written for a Persecuted Community?" *Nederlands Theologisch Tijdschrift* 34 (1980): 15.

16. This is also the conclusion of Kee, *Community of the New Age*, pp. 100f.

17. Ibid., p. 102.

18. Joachim Jeremias, *Jerusalem in the Time of Jesus: An Investigation into Economic and Social Conditions during the New Testament Period* (Philadelphia: Fortress Press, 1969), p. 95.

19. See Josephus, *War*, I, xxiv, 708.

20. Jeremias, p. 362.

21. Ibid., p. 93.

22. Michael Walzer, *Exodus and Revolution* (New York: Basic Books, 1986).

23. Samuel Sandmel, *Judaism and Christian Beginnings* (New York: Oxford University Press, 1978), pp. 163ff.

24. Werner Kelber, *Mark's Story of Jesus* (Philadelphia: Fortress Press, 1979), pp. 88ff.

25. John R. Donahue, "The Theology and Setting of Discipleship in the Gospel of Mark." The 1983 Pere Marquette Theology Lecture (Milwaukee: Marquette University Press, 1983), p. 45f.

26. Walter Wink, *Naming the Powers: The Language of Power in the New Testament*, vol. 1 (Philadelphia: Fortress Press, 1984), pp. 104, 105, 107.

27. Ibid., p. 140.

28. Kim Yong-bock, "Messiah and Minjung: Discerning Messianic Politics over against Political Messianism," in *Minjung Theology: People as the Subjects of History* (Maryknoll, N.Y.: Orbis Books, 1981), p. 183.

29. Ibid., p. 185.

30. Ahn Byung-mu, "Jesus and the Minjung in the Gospel of Mark," in *Minjung Theology*, pp. 150f.

31. Kim Yong-bock, p. 185.

28

LUISE SCHOTTROFF

Women as Followers of Jesus in New Testament Times

An Exercise in Sociohistorical Exegesis of the Bible

Mary of Magdala was one of the women present with Jesus from the beginning of his public work, doubtless a single woman among the indigent beggar-wanderers, and not at all wealthy as Luke pictures the women accompanying Jesus. She was one of the disciples who proclaimed the imminence of the kingdom and who lived together as "the family of God." She was among the women who took the politically dangerous step of announcing the resurrection of Jesus, and became thereby, like Peter, a symbol of conquered fear. Mary exhibits the full partnership which the male and female followers of Jesus practiced. This equality of the sexes was born of a shared poverty and of the hope for the impending kingdom of God, for "the Jesus movement in Palestine was a self-help community of poor Jews."

Prisca, and her husband Aquila, were fellow missionaries with Paul, who as tentmakers were manual laborers who worked hard for meager wages, and were in this respect typical of the Pauline congregations. She is representative of a considerable number of women named or alluded to in the epistles and Acts as fully active in congregational affairs by organizing, speaking, prophesying, discussing, and praying in the public assemblies.

An address delivered at Union Theological Seminary, New York City, February 16, 1981.

Paul's attempt to restrict this lively ecclesial practice of women by encouraging signs of submission on the part of women toward men probably was his concession to pressure from a Roman public opinion that was suspicious of excessive public activities by women. From this concession of Paul, which he probably thought rather minor, there was a direct line to later New Testament texts that returned women to a passive position as silent churchgoers while channeling them into the role of nurturers of men and children.

ON FOLLOWING JESUS IN PALESTINE BEFORE A.D. 70

I begin with an example: Mary of Magdala was just as important for the emergence of the Jesus movement in Palestine as Peter—we just know much less about her. Less in the first instance because the Christian sources of the first century are only too ready to keep silent about the women in the Jesus movement. For example, Mark's Gospel reports only in connection with the Passion story that women were present right from the beginning of the Jesus movement in Galilee (Mark 15:40-41). Up to that point, Mark wrote only about the men who followed Jesus. A further reason why we know so little about Mary Magdalene is the theological and exegetical tradition. According to church tradition, we incorrectly associate her with "the woman who was a sinner," the prostitute whose many sins Jesus forgave in Luke 7:36-50. According to the exegetical tradition of historical criticism, we would at most say that she was an "important woman."[1]

Unusually, Mary of Magdala is written throughout with an indication of her origin (*hē Magdalēnē*) probably at first because one had to distinguish her from the other women called *Maria* (or *Mariam* = Heb. *miryam*). She was not however distinguished by the normal addition of the name of a male relative (for example *Maria hē Iakōbou*, Mark 16:1). If she had still been living in the setting of a Jewish family this would hardly have been explicable. She comes from Magdala by the Sea of Gennesaret, but her name shows that at the time of the Jesus movement she had given up or lost her homeplace and no longer lived in Magdala. For she could hardly have been called *hē Magdalēnē* by the people of Magdala. Other Jews within and outside the Galilean Jesus movement would have called her that.

So she was a single Jewish woman probably without settled abode, at any rate at the time of the Jesus movement. She wandered around Galilee with the group attached to Jesus and also took part in the journey to Jerusalem (Mark 15:40-41).[2] That a woman should lead an unsettled life could mean that like a wandering Cynic preacher, she had left home, family, and property. There is, as far as I know, only one reference in the classical sources to a female wandering Cynic philosopher: to Hipparchia, a beautiful young woman from a rich family, who journeyed as a Cynic philosopher in beggar's clothing, together with Krates, through Greece (Diog. L. VI, 96f). Luke imagined just this situation when thinking of the lifestyle of Jesus and his disciples: they leave their families, their wives, and all their property (see Luke 18:29; cf. 14:26).

However, for the women who follow Jesus this idea does not seem appropriate to Luke (8:1-3). Certainly Luke reports that women accompany Jesus and his disciples on the journey to the towns and villages of Galilee, but he imagines that, also on this journey, they have possessions with which they support Jesus and the twelve financially. The disciples take no money with them, not even a beggar's bag (Luke 9:3; cf. 10:4). They are poor beggar prophets. The wealthy women walk with them on this journey. (Are we to imagine that they carry large money-bags behind the disciples?) Luke illustrates here from his own context the traditional reports of the wanderings of Jesus and his disciples, among whom were also women. He does this for the men with the *idea* of the ascetic wandering philosophers, for the women with the *idea* of ladies from a well-to-do house who support religious groups with their own possessions. Such women are known, for example, as pillars of the Jewish congregations in Rome, or indeed, as we know from Luke's Acts of the Apostles, as pillars of Christian congregations in Philippi and in Thessalonica (Acts 16:14-15; 17:4, 12).

Luke did not notice the incongruence in his description of the Jesus movement in Galilee. For him it was important that right from the beginning in Galilee women were there too. For that reason he already mentions them very differently from Mark in the description of Jesus' way through Galilee. The women, among whom Mary Magdalene is mentioned first (24:10), have in this way, according to his categories, the quality of witnesses to all of Jesus' work (Acts 1:21f.), but not the status of apostles because, in Luke's opinion, twelve *men* were called (Luke 6:3; cf. Acts 1:21-22). Luke is interested from within the situation of his congregations to give emphasis to the women who followed Jesus. However he had no information about the historical reality of the women in Galilee at that time other than from Mark (15:40-41, 47; 16:1).

We return to the old pre-Marcan tradition which lies behind Mark 15:40—16:8. Mary of Magdala, like the other women who followed Jesus, shared his poor and vagrant life. We must not, like Luke, picture her life from the point of view of a relatively wealthy city-dweller far away from Palestine. We must work it out on one hand with help from the New Testament sources about the situation of the Palestinian Jesus movement, on the other hand from the extra-Christian historical sources from Josephus to archaeology. Mary Magdalene shared the life of the *ptōchoi*, "the poor," who formed the Jesus movement in Palestine.[3] She belonged to the apparently very broad class of the poor among the Jewish population at that time. These people were not poor because they had given up property on account of the kingdom of God. They were poor because the Herodian family and indirectly the Roman Caesars took more from the population than was bearable, and because the increasing cultivation in large estates stifled the small farmers economically without offering enough jobs for day-laborers.[4]

Without lapsing into historical speculation we can, despite the scanty sources about Mary Magdalene, deduce much about her from the situation of the Jesus movement and of the Jewish population. Like many other people she lived at subsistence level: she could not be sure whether she would have to go hungry tomorrow, if today she was able to buy some bread. She could try, like the men, to find casual work as day-laborers. Women have (not only) in Palestine done the hardest work in agriculture, in building, and certainly also in the fish-trade by Lake Gennesaret.[5]

From the beginning Mary Magdalene herself proclaimed the prophetic message of the coming of the kingdom of God. In Mark 15:41 it says that the women had already served Jesus in Galilee (*diēkonoun autō*). That cannot mean the *diakonia* of serving meals, because then the singular would not be intelligible: Jesus was not *alone* when journeying. Aside from that, it is hardly possible in the overall situation of poor homeless people to imagine a *diakonia* in the sense of a housewife's activity. The *diakonia Christou* is much more a proclamation that Jesus is the Messiah and that the kingdom of God is imminent (in the sense of the usage in 2 Cor. 11:23; 6:4f.).

The fact that Mary of Magdala and other women actively joined in the prophetic proclamation of the Jesus movement is shown also in their role after Jesus' death. We recognize from the largely pre-Marcan story of the so-called "empty tomb" that the execution of Jesus as a political troublemaker caused his followers to disappear. Perhaps it was similar to the way Mark describes it: they ran away terrified. It would have been at any rate extremely dangerous to be recognized as a member of this movement. The Jewish authorities were very quick, as is clear from Josephus, to flog potential troublemakers and to hand them over to the Roman procurator (see Josephus *B. J.* 6.300f.). Going to the grave on Easter Day, if we can imagine it from Mark 16:1-8, was a risky act of solidarity with a person who had been executed for political reasons. We ought not to understand Mark 16:1-8 as an historical account about Easter morning, but as a kerygmatic story about the beginning of the proclamation of the risen Jesus. In any case this text remains a document of courageous solidarity.

It is not in my opinion the intention of Mark 16:1-8 to show that the tomb was empty or that the empty tomb did not become known for such a long time because the women said nothing (as in W. Bousset or R. Bultmann). Mark 16:1-8 relates a vocational epiphany: the calling of Mary Magdalene and some other women to proclaim the resurrection of Jesus. Or put another way: from Mark 16:1-8 we can deduce the historical fact that it was only through the courage and activity of Mary Magdalene and some other women that the Jesus movement carried on after Jesus' death. Even Mark, who in the final verse situates the women in the group of the disciples who were overcome by fear, tells this whole story against the clear background that *this* frightened Peter and *this* shaking Mary Magdalene then became the carriers of the message. For the Marcan congregation, characterized by fear, Mary Magdalene—like Peter and other men and women who followed Jesus—is a symbol of conquered fear.

I should like at this point to make some remarks about method. I have already said so much about Mary Magdalene, about whom the sources apparently relate very little, that from shortage of space I must forego discussion of other possible aspects. If one asks about the real situation of the people who lie behind the New Testament tradition, one can say an astonishing amount about them. It is just for that reason that I chose initially one person to make the method clear. The New Testament tradition is not restricted, then, to the history of thoughts and religious ideas, but rather the thoughts become part of the history of the followers of Jesus, their suffering, their praxis, their experiences together, their hope.

The women who followed Jesus before and after his death played a full part in the proclamation of the prophetic message of Jesus. There are no traces in the old part of the Synoptic tradition of a discussion about the special role of women. There is no pleading for their subordination to men as in Paul and in later Christian texts, but also no expression of their equality with men "in Christ" as in Paul (Gal. 3:28). The story of Mary and Martha certainly reflects problems with the role of women, but is however part of Luke's own awareness. We see this awareness elsewhere in Luke. Luke 10:38-42 cannot be used to reconstruct the history of the Jesus movement in Palestine.

In the Jesus movement the women were clearly and without question partners of the men. I see the causes for this on two levels. First, the economic, social, and political situation, which is well summed-up in the Greek word *ptōchos,* led to increasing breakdown of the family and of the organized roles of women among the Jewish population. The men leave to look for work. The women have to work with small children in the fields from sunrise until sunset, or go with them to swell the crowds of beggars and sick in the villages. What was seen in the apocalyptic tradition as a terrible sign of the end of the world was now happening: "a man is set against his father and the daughter against her mother and the bride against her mother-in-law" (Matt. 10:35).

The break-up of families, which is mentioned in the Gospels, was also related to the fact that the message of Jesus could lead to division among families. We should, however, not see this division in isolation from the family break-up caused by economic relations. A woman like Mary Magdalene, and her Jewish sisters who have to struggle to survive, is a partner in need for the men in the same situation. The socially defined role of women is superfluous for her as much as for the female and male slaves who work on the large Roman estates described by the Roman writer on agriculture, Columella.

In my opinion it is not historically accurate if, as constantly happens, we describe the freedom of Jesus in contact with women in sharp contrast to the dark picture of Jewish rabbis, who despise women and do not talk with them in public. The background in which the Jesus movement should be seen is *not* the patriarchal opinion of Jewish rabbis. It is much more the living-situation of the whole Jewish people at this time. The background is hunger, family breakdown, exploitation of all, including women and children. In this background the Jesus movement shone out.

With that I come to the second reason for the equality between men and women in the Jesus movement: that is the *hope for the impending kingdom of God* and the collective life which resulted from that hope. They did not try to recreate the lost world of the patriarchal family, they founded a new family: the *familia dei.* They found the often accelerated break-up of existing families necessary (see for example Matt. 10:37). They did not try to define the special role of women, rather they understood the community of men and women as "one flesh" (Mark 10:8), as an indestructible community which they described in the enticing colors of a utopia: "from the beginning of creation God made them male and female. This is why a man must leave father and mother, and the two become one body. They are no longer two, therefore, but one body" (Mark 10:6f). Here speaks not a Jesus who anticipates church divorce laws, but a Jesus who shows us how wonderful it is to understand ourselves as God's creation. He shows that living with this understanding—as with living in the kingdom of God—turns sick beggars into people in a sense they could only dream about. This blissful experience of liberation, which speaks to us from many passages in the Synoptic Gospels, did not exist only in the *heads* of those involved. Above all in the healing miracles we can see that in the *familia dei* sick beggars become healthy people. We should not understand this as a metaphysical miracle to prove Jesus' divine qualities, but rather as a consequence, which we too can imagine, of the solidarity and love which was practiced in this movement of the poor.

Phrasing this as a fairly uninvolved historical report: the Jesus movement in Palestine was a self-help community of poor Jews. They tried in all ways to help each other, shared the little food that they had, and cared for each other's health. Those involved understood themselves as heirs of the religious tradition of Israel and their movement as the beginning of a bringing together of the entire people, as a restoration of the creation. Regarded politically, the execution of Jesus, and of many of his followers after his death, was from the point of view of the Romans thoroughly opportune. This movement could have become, at least in the long term, dangerous for Roman rule.

WOMEN IN THE PAULINE CONGREGATIONS

I begin again with an example.

Prisca, a Jewess with a Roman name, together with her husband Aquila, also a Jew with a Roman name, played just as important a role as Paul in the spreading of the gospel of the Messiah Jesus in the Roman Empire. Already in the old handwritten versions of the Acts of the Apostles there are changes in the text, which attempt to reduce the importance of Prisca, for example the Cantabrigiensis in Acts 18:2 (Paul *proselthen auto*, "went to see him [Aquila]," instead of *autois*, "went to see them [Aquila and Prisca]"), or in Acts 18:26 where in the same handwriting the word order is turned around: "Aquila and Prisca." The remarkable naming of the wife first, which is also to be found in Paul (Rom. 16:3), is, at least by such people as those who made such changes, understood as an expression of disproportionate importance for a woman.

We may infer that the married couple were full partners in the work for the gospel, if not that Prisca took on further tasks herself. It is anyway not a form of politeness when Paul and Luke name Prisca first. The work of this couple together ought not in any way to induce immediate associations for us ("Prisca probably wore the trousers in this marriage" or "Aquila preached while Prisca cooked"). Suitable associations would be much more Jesus' speech about the togetherness of man and woman in Mark 10:2-9: a married couple is trying here in extremely difficult circumstances to live in complete partnership. And Prisca and Aquila were not the only married couple. Philologus and Julia, whom Paul mentions in Rom. 16:15, perhaps Andronicus and Junia too (Rom. 16:7), can be regarded as couples who worked together for the gospel. Their partnership was not an expression of socially determined roles, but of a lifestyle according to the essence of the message; they tried to live as "one flesh." Prisca has however only found recent appreciation from Adolf von Harnack, who even wanted to assign to her the composition of the Letter to the Hebrews.[6]

Prisca and Aquila earned their living like Paul as *skēnopoioi* (Acts 18:3). This profession is not mentioned outside the New Testament. It is according to the letters of Paul a craft (1 Cor. 4:12) which if necessary can be done at night (1 Thess. 2:9). It is work which allows frequent change of residence, perhaps even requires it, for Prisca and Aquila like Paul frequently moved from one town to another. I relate *skēnopoios*, "tentmaker," to the production of tents out of leather or wool; it is thus either the work of sewing leather or of weaving material from wool. The *lanarius*, "worker in wool," who also made tents, earned according to Diocletian's wage-scales (C.E. 301) even less than an agricultural day-laborer. The greatest demand for tents must have been from the Roman army. It is certainly plausible that the production of army tents played a role in Rome, Corinth, Ephesus, and Tarsus.

But even if the substance of the occupation *skēnopoios* must remain hypothetical, the indications from Paul are enough to see that Aquila and Prisca are not "husband and wife employers,"[7] but manual laborers who work hard with raw material and who do not earn much. The wives of such manual laborers worked with them because the earnings of the husband were not sufficient. It is beyond doubt in this social situation that Paul worked with Aquila and Prisca together in Corinth (Acts 18:3); it is quite imaginable that the Western biblical tradition of the early church and of the Middle Ages had an interest in representing Aquila and Prisca as a well-off couple in whose business Paul was for a time employed, but who themselves did not have to work (see the history of the text, Acts 18:3: *ērgazeto*, "he worked"/*ērgazonto*, "they worked"). According to the Greek-speaking upper classes of the Roman Empire, Prisca, like Aquila and Paul, is a *penēs*, a person who lives from manual work. The *penētes* are not as poor as the *ptōchoi*—the destitute—but they have to lead a hard life full of risk.

Altogether, the social situation of Prisca, Aquila, and Paul is, in my opinion, representative of the Pauline congregations in general. There are certain social differences within the congregations (probably 1 Cor. 11:21 is indicative of this). There are also regional differences: the congregations around Corinth are better off than those in Macedonia (2 Cor. 8:1-5 in the context of 8:6-7). But the Corinthian congregation is also not rich; it argues that it does not want to become hard-pressed through the collections for the *ptōchoi* in Jerusalem.

I cannot deal fully with the sources about Prisca, but should still like to say something about her political and Christian life. She was driven from Rome by the edict of Claudius against the Jews (C.E. 49—see Acts 18:2), but she also had experience later of the firm measures of Roman authorities. Paul says in Rom. 16:3 that Prisca and Aquila had risked their necks to save his life. Risk to the life of Paul and others like him came about in confrontation with the Roman authorities (see above all 2 Cor. 11:23; 1 Cor. 15:32; Rom. 8:35). Even if we do not know the particular circumstances, the assertions of Paul in Rom. 16:3 show pointedly just what a dangerous life these congregations of Christians led, what an important role mutual solidarity played, and that the women were just as much endangered as the men in conflicts with the authorities.

Prisca's work for the spreading of the gospel that Jesus is the Messiah probably began in Rome; she went to the synagogue on the sabbath in Rome as in Corinth (Acts 18:4). Whether she was able to read from the Torah and attest that Jesus is the Messiah we do not know. But in the gatherings of the Christian assemblies in private houses the women did speak in public, pray, and prophesy (1 Cor. 11:5), and also took part in discussions such as those with Apollos in Ephesus, who only knew the baptism of John (Acts 18:26). The active role of women in public within the Pauline congregations can be deduced from their relevance for all congregations, shown especially in the greetings-list in Rom. 16:3-16. In that list one-third of the persons mentioned by name are women (nine out of twenty-six), and women like men are distinguished by their work for the congregations, without any ranking between women and men being apparent.

This clear praxis of the Pauline congregations is already opposed in Paul by a contrary theory. In 1 Cor. 11:2-16 Paul shows, with a rather overdeveloped display of theological arguments, that the woman should publicly express her submission to the man by covering her head when praying and prophesying.

I do not want to go into detail about this text, but of fundamental importance is the question how one could arrive at such a theory within the setting of a contrary praxis. The question is moreover of fundamental importance because from this opinion of Paul there is a direct line to those Christian texts which have had such a disastrous effect for women: texts which demand that the women should keep quiet in the congregation or declare that they become blessed through bearing children, etc.

Why did this development take place? I can only state my hypothesis here, without really being able to substantiate it. The Roman state had an obvious interest in fighting against freedoms which women claimed publicly. It had a tremendous interest in the constant repetition of the picture of the ideal woman: she is only the wife of the man (*univira*), she practices the *lanificium* — spins wool, works at home, and obeys her husband. If a woman speaks in public, says Valerius Maximus, that shows that the state is shaken by anarchy. Paul, and other Christians with him and after him, have clearly given in to this pressure from outside. Why did they do that? How often has it been that women have been the oppressed among the oppressed? It does not reduce Paul in my eyes that he was a human being like all others, that at a certain point he gave in to the pressure, which he probably did not find very important. It is *one* thing to make it clear why Paul behaved as he did in his historical situation. It is *another* how we deal with these expressions of opinion.

I should like to conclude by summarizing the methodological considerations concerning a sociohistorical exegesis. To do biblical exegesis means to see the connection between the realities of the lives of the people and the message of Christ they carried. I can, for example, only understand the message of the cross of Jesus when I grasp that those who preached that message were threatened by crucifixion, and that the symbol of the oppression of the Roman state became for them a sign of life. It is of critical importance theologically that the carriers of the gospel were the *ptōchoi* and the *penētes*.

The "reality of their lives" means their social reality in the widest sense: not only the spiritual and religious history, but also the political and social history. Or put in another way: Josephus is the most important New Testament commentator. It will not do that in New Testament studies the historical background remains a side-affair, and the social circumstances equally so.

To clarify further, biblical exegesis means that the social and political situation of the exegete is also part of the exegesis. As an exegete, it is necessary for me to consider my situation and to understand my exegesis in its own context. The phrase that man and woman should be one flesh can have quite a different sense depending on the context in which it is employed. It can also be a phrase which serves people's oppression.

Sociohistorical exegesis is an expression of *positive experience of the biblical tradition*, the experience that this tradition is capable of interpreting and changing my situation. From it we can understand that God is on the side of those who are made victims by the masters of this world.

NOTES

1. R. Pesch, *Das Markusevangelium II* (Freiburg, 1977), p. 505; M. Hengel, "Maria Magdalena und die Frauen als Zeugen," in *Abraham unser Vater, Festschrift O. Michel* (Leiden: Brill, 1963), pp. 243-56.

2. If Mark 15:40f has to be seen as the result of Mark's redaction-work, we can nevertheless draw the same conclusions from her name (Magdalene) and from her presence at the crucifixion of Jesus (Mark 15:47, 16:1).

3. Luise Schottroff and Walter Stegemann, *Jesus and the Hope of the Poor* (Maryknoll, N.Y.: Orbis, 1986).

4. See esp. S. Applebaum, "Economic Life in Palestine," in *The Jewish People in the First Century II* (Assen/Amsterdam, 1976), pp. 632-700.

5. L. Schottroff, "Frauen in der Nachfolge Jesu in neutestamentlicher Zeit," in W. Schottroff and W. Stegemann, ed., *Traditionen der Befreiung*, (Munich, 1980), Vol. 2, pp. 91-133.

6. Adolf von Harnack, *ZNW* 1 (1900): 16 ff.

7. K. Thraede, in G. Scharffenorth and K. Thraede, "Freunde in Christus werden . . ." (Gelnhausen: Burckhardthaus-Verlag, 1977), p. 97.

29

ELISABETH SCHÜSSLER FIORENZA

"You Are Not To Be Called Father"

Early Christian History in a Feminist Perspective

---

*The current discussion of the position of women in the early church,
reaching far beyond a narrow "woman's issue," goes to the heart of an
exegetical historical problem that exposes the contemporary societal and
ecclesial interests governing all interpretive models of early Christianity.
Already in later New Testament times, male-centered interpretation and
editing of earlier traditions both played down and covered over the
important roles of women at key points in Christian beginnings, because
their roles were seen either as unimportant or as threatening.*

*Patristic interpretation managed to present itself as the historically
prior "orthodox" view, while whatever the church fathers did not like,
such as equality of women in church leadership, was branded as
"heresy" which mutilated the ancient faith. In fact, supporters of the
ecclesial leadership of women could point to early support from
traditions which the church fathers defamed as late heresy.*

*The patriarchalizing and institutionalizing process in the early church
is not a mere fait accompli but an early move in a continuing "power
play" that requires a critical sociological and theological analysis to
recover biblical and theological ground for woman's full place in today's
church. The sexual equality of the Jesus movement and of the first
Christian missioners must be reaffirmed by an egalitarian interpretive*

Reprinted from *Cross Currents* 29/3 (1979): 301–23.

model that fully recognizes the conflict between equality and hierarchy within the early church — a battle that has been re-opened in our time.

For many Christians the reconstruction of early Christian history is not a problem. The impression remains widespread that Acts accurately reports what actually happened. Exegetes and historians of early Christianity, however, know all too well that this is not the case. But although most exegetes would agree that Jesus did not leave a blue-print for the organization of the church, their image of the actual development of early church history varies considerably. Questions regarding the historical importance of the Twelve, the relationship between charisma and office, the juxtaposition of Paulinism and early Catholicism, the issue of apostolic succession and heresy, and the practical-ecclesial implications of early Christian history are answered in different ways.[1] Moreover, exegetes today more readily acknowledge that a value-free interpretation of early Christian texts and an objectivist reconstruction of early Christian history are a scholarly fiction that fails to account for its own presuppositions and scientific models.

The question whether women had a leading position in the development of the early Church intensifies all these interpretative problems and at the same time formulates the debated issues in a new perspective.[2] Nevertheless, most scholars have been hesitant to perceive this problem as an exegetical-historical problem, but understand it as a "woman's issue."[3] Seen as a "woman's issue," the question belongs to conferences and papers about and for women, and is given no place on the program of an exegetical-scientific symposium or in a scholarly *Festschrift*. In this way most scholars continue to perceive this question only as a topical or thematic issue, not as an issue of heuristic value for the interpretation of early Christian texts and history.

One usually justifies this attitude by pointing out that such a topic is ideologically suspect and does not proceed from an historical-scientific interest since the topic is inspired by the women's movement, and therefore determined by ecclesial-societal modern interests. Such an argument, however, overlooks the fact that all scholarship on early Christian history is determined by contemporary questions and interests. Insofar as the Bible is not just a document of ancient history, but is Holy Scripture which claims authority and validity in the contemporary church, biblical-historical inquiries are always determined by ecclesial and societal interests and questions.

This dependency of historical-critical research on contemporary Christianity and society has, in my opinion, been correctly pointed out by J. Blank: "The interest in legitimization but also in the critique and reform of contemporary Christianity in all its forms and expressions is probably an essential and even the most fundamental motive for the study of the history of early Christianity."[4] The objection that the search for the role of women in the early Christian movement is greatly determined by societal and ecclesial political interests, and is therefore unscientific, applies to any reconstruction of early Christian history inspired by the quest for the identity and continuity of contemporary Christianity with the early church. An androcentric reconstruction of early Christian history, therefore, is not value-free and objective but, consciously or not, legitimizes the present hierarchical-male structures of the contemporary church.

All historical reconstruction is a selective, contemporary analysis of the past in the present; it is not limited to the extant sources but is also conditioned by the societal perspectives of the present. The understanding of the past is never just antiquarian but always related to the contemporary situation of the historiographer. The hermeneutic discussion has shown that historians, like other scholars, can never totally free themselves from their existential presuppositions, experiences, ideologies, and commitments.[5] The personal presuppositions and societal position of the historian and interpreter determine the selection and definition of what was important in the past, and what needs to be studied today. Although the hermeneutical discussion and the sociology of knowledge have driven home the insight that historiography is determined by the experiences and interests of those who write history, this scientific consensus seems to disappear when scientific historiography and theology are denounced as "male." The problem is not only that most scholars are men but that our very understanding of reality is androcentric.

It is not enough, however, to expose the existential presuppositions of male exegetes and scholars: we must analyze the interpretative models from which they reconstruct the history of early Christianity. While descriptive historical studies analyze the available information and texts of early Christianity and presuppose a certain understanding of early Christian history, a constructive historiography makes this understanding explicit by developing heuristic and interpretative models[6] which enable us to reconstruct a total view of early Christian development. Such interpretative models place diverse information into a coherent interpretative whole which enables us to see the intellectual contexts and practical patterns of action in a certain perspective. An interpretative model should, therefore, not only be judged by whether it adequately lists various traditions and information, but must also be scrutinized as to whether it provides a comprehensive vision of early Christian history, making its emancipatory life-praxis and theology available to the contemporary church and society.

ANDROCENTRIC INTERPRETATION AND REDACTION

The thematic approach to "women in the Bible" overlooks the fact that references to women are already filtered through androcentric interpretation and redaction. If study of this topic is to help us in the scientific reconstruction of early Christian history, we must understand and make explicit the androcentric perspective of scientific-historical models as well as of early Christian tradition and redaction.

The systemic androcentrism of Western culture is evident in the fact that nobody questions the fact that men have been historical subjects and agents in the church. The historical role of women and not that of men is problematic because maleness is the norm, while femaleness constitutes a deviation from this norm. Whenever we speak of "man" as the scientific and historical subject we mean the male.[7] For the Western understanding and linguistic expression of reality, male existence is the standard of human existence. "Humanity is male and man defines woman not in herself but relative to him. She is not regarded as autonomous being. He is the subject, the absolute; she is the other."[8] Therefore our societal and scientific structures define women as derivative and secondary to men. This androcentric definition of being human not only has determined the scholarly perception of men but also of women. In such an androcentric worldview woman must remain an historically marginal being. Therefore the androcentric scholarly paradigm has to thematize the role of women as a societal, historical, philosophical, and theological problem but cannot question its own androcentric scholarly horizon.[9]

Since the scientific reconstructions of early Christianity share in the androcentric paradigm of Western culture, they cannot integrate texts which speak positively about early Christian women into their overall interpretational framework. Because they generally presuppose that only men, and not women, developed missionary initiatives and central leadership in early Christianity,[10] texts that do not fit such an androcentric model are quickly interpreted in terms of an androcentric perspective. This happens in various ways. For example, most modern interpreters assume that Rom. 16:7 speaks about two leading men who had already become Christians before Paul and had great authority as apostles. However, there is no reason to understand Junia as a shortened form of the male name Junianus since Junia was a well-known female name. Even patristic exegesis understood it predominantly as the name of a woman.[11] Andronicus and Junia were an influential missionary team who were acknowledged as apostles.

Another example of androcentric interpretation is often found with reference to Rom. 16:1-3. In this passage Phoebe is called the *diakonos* and *prostatis* of the church at Cenchraea, the seaport of Corinth. Exegetes attempt to downplay the importance of both titles here because they are used with reference to a woman. Whenever Paul calls himself, Apollos, Timothy, or Tychicos *diakonos*, scholars translate the term as deacon, but because the expression refers here to a woman exegetes translate it as "servant, helper, or deaconess." While Kürzinger, for instance, translates the title in Phil. 1:1 as deacon, in the case of Phoebe he explains that "she works in the service of the community," and in a footnote he characterizes Phoebe as "one of the first pastoral assistants."[12] H. Lietzmann also understands the office of Phoebe in analogy to the later institute of the deaconesses which, in comparison to that of the deacons, had only a very limited function in the church. He characterizes Phoebe as an "apparently well-to-do and charitable lady, who because of her feminine virtues worked in the service of the poor and the sick and assisted in the baptism of women."[13] Origen had already labelled Phoebe as an assistant and servant of Paul. He concluded that women who do good works can be appointed as deaconesses.[14]

However, the text does not permit such a feminine stereotyping of Phoebe.

As we can see from 1 Cor. 3:5-9, Paul uses *diakonos* parallel to *synergos* and characterizes with these titles Apollos and himself as missionaries with equal standing who have contributed to the upbuilding of the community in different ways.[15] Since Phoebe is named *diakonos* of the church at Cenchreae, she receives this title because her service and office were influential in the community. That Phoebe could claim great authority within the early Christian missionary endeavor is underlined by the second title *prostatis/patrona*. In a similar way 1 Thess. 5:12 and Rom. 12:8 characterize leading persons as *pro-histamenoi*. Therefore, when Paul calls Phoebe a *patrona*, he characterizes her in analogy to those persons who had influential positions as representative protectors and leaders in the Hellenistic-religious associations.[16] G. Heinrici points out that in antiquity religious and private associations received legal protection and derived sociopolitical influence from the patronage of eminent and rich members.[17] Nevertheless, E. A. Judge insists on interpreting the patronage of women in the early church in an androcentric fashion:

> The status of women who patronized St. Paul would particularly repay attention. They are clearly persons of some independence and eminence in their own circles, used to entertaining and running their salons, if that is what Paul's meetings were, as they saw best.[18]

This misinterpretation reduces the influential role of women in the early Christian movement to that of housewives permitted to serve coffee after Paul's lectures!

Since exegetes of the New Testament take it for granted that the leadership of the early Christian communities was in the hands of men, they assume that those women mentioned in the Pauline letters were the helpmates and assistants of the apostles, especially of Paul. Such an androcentric interpretative model leaves no room for the alternative assumption that women were missionaries, apostles, or heads of communities independent of Paul and equal to him.[19] Since Paul's position was often precarious and in no way accepted by all the members of the communities, it is even possible that the women's influence was more established than that of Paul's. Texts such as Rom. 16:1-3 or 16:7 suggest that leading women in the early Christian missionary movement did not owe their position to Paul. It is more likely that Paul had no other choice but to cooperate with these women and to acknowledge their authority within the communities.

We must ask, therefore, whether it is appropriate to limit all leadership titles in the New Testament which are grammatically masculine to males alone. Predictably enough, androcentric exegesis interprets grammatically masculine terms in a twofold way, namely as generic and as masculine.[20] Grammatically masculine terms like saints, the elect, brothers, sons, which serve to characterize the members of the communities, are usually understood to refer to both men and women. Exegetes do not go so far as to understand Christian community in analogy to the Mithras-cult and to limit church membership or the New Testament admonitions and injunctions to men.[21] However, every time the New

Testament uses grammatically masculine titles such as prophet, teacher, deacon, missionary, co-worker, apostle, or bishop, which refer to leadership functions within the Christian community, exegetes assume that the reference is exclusively to men. They have no interpretative heuristic model that could do justice to the position and influence of women like Phoebe, Prisca,[22] or Junia or could adequately integrate them into its conception of early Christian leadership. Such an androcentric perspective is easily misused to legitimize the patriarchal practice of the contemporary church.[23]

One could reject such an analysis and maintain that the androcentric interpretation of early Christianity is conditioned and justified by our sources because they speak about women and their role in the early church only rarely and mostly in a polemic argument. The historical marginality of women is not created simply by contemporary exegesis, but by the fact that women were marginal in the fellowship of Jesus and in the early Christian male church from the very beginnings. Jesus was a man, the apostles were men, the early Christian prophets, teachers, and missionaries were men. All New Testament writings claim to be written by male authors and the theology of the first centuries is called the "theology of the Fathers." Women do not seem to be of any significance in the early church nor are they allowed any leadership or teaching functions. The Christian marginality of women has its roots in the patriarchal beginnings of the church and in the androcentrism of Christian revelation.

Such a theological conclusion presupposes, however, that the New Testament writings are objective factual reports of early Christian history and development. The rarity of women's mention in the sources adequately reflects the actual history of their activity in the early church. Such a presupposition, however, neglects the methodic insights of form, source, and redaction criticism which have pointed out that the early Christian writings are not at all objectivistic factual transcripts but pastorally engaged writings. The early Christian authors have selected, redacted, and reformulated their traditional sources and materials with reference to their theological intentions and practical objectives. None of the early Christian writings and traditions is free from any of these tendencies. All early Christian writings, even the Gospels and Acts, intend to speak to actual problems and situations of the early church and to illuminate them theologically. We therefore can assume that this methodic insight applies equally to the traditions and sources about women in early Christianity. Since the early Christian communities and authors live in a predominantly patriarchal world and participate in its mentality, it is likely that the scarcity of information about women is conditioned by the androcentric traditioning and redaction of the early Christian authors. This applies especially to the Gospels and Acts since these were written toward the end of the first century. Many of the traditions and information about the activity of women in early Christianity are probably irretrievable because the androcentric selection or redaction process saw these as either unimportant or as threatening.[24]

The contradictions in the sources indicate such an androcentric process of redaction, which qualifies information that could not be omitted. It is true that women were disciples of Jesus and witnesses of the resurrection, but none of them was a member of the twelve. Jesus healed women and spoke with them but no Gospel tells us a story about the call of a woman to discipleship. The images of the parables draw on the world and experience of women but the God-language of Jesus is totally masculine. The Gospels tell us that women discovered the empty tomb but the true resurrection witnesses seem to have been men.

Acts tells us about women, especially rich women who supported the early Christian missionary endeavor with their homes and wealth. However, the historical elaboration of Luke gives the impression that the leadership of the early Christian mission was totally in the hands of men. We find short references to widows and prophetesses, but Luke does not tell us any stories about their activity or function. Thus Luke's conception of history is harmonizing and does not acknowledge a "women's problem" in the early church.

Such a problem emerges, however, when one reads the Pauline letters. The meaning of the Pauline texts which speak directly about women is still unclear, although numerous attempts at interpretation have been made.[25] Exegetes are divided on the question of whether the influence of Paul was negative or positive with respect to the role of women in early Christianity. Paul presupposes in 1 Cor. 11:2-16 that women speak as prophets in the community worship but demands that in doing so they adapt to the prevailing custom. It is not clear, however, what the actual issue of discussion is between Paul and the Corinthians or how the individual arguments of Paul are to be evaluated and understood. The negative result of the injunction in 1 Cor. 14:33-36 is clear-cut, but exegetes are divided as to whether the famous *"mulier taceat in ecclesia"* (a woman is to keep quiet in church) is a later interpolation, since it seems to contradict 1 Cor. 11.

In Gal. 3:28 Paul proclaims that all distinctions between Jew and Greek, free and slave, male and female are obliterated, but he does not repeat in 1 Cor. 12:13 that maleness and femaleness no longer have any significance in the body of Christ. Therefore no exegetical consensus is achieved on whether Gal. 3:28, like 1 Cor. 12:13, applies to the Christian community, or to the eschatological future, or refers to the spiritual equality of all souls. The Pauline lists of greetings mention women as leading missionaries and respected heads of churches, but it is not univocal on how much they owe their leadership position to Pauline approval and support. It is true that Paul values women as co-workers and expresses his gratitude to them, but he probably had no other choice than to do so because women like Junia or Prisca already occupied leadership functions before him and were on his level in the early Christian missionary movement.

That the sources are unclear and divided about women's role in early Christianity is also evident when one compares the information supplied by different New Testament writings. The Pauline letters indicate that women have been apostles, missionaries, patrons, co-workers, prophets, and leaders of communities. Luke, on the other hand, mentions women prophets and the conversion of rich women but does not tell us any instance of a woman missionary or leader of a church. He seems to know of such functions of women, as his references to Prisca or Lydia indicate, but this knowledge does not influence his portrayal of early Christian history. Whereas all the Gospels know that Mary Magdalene was the first resurrection witness, the pre-Pauline tradition of 1 Cor. 15:3-5 does not mention a single woman among the resurrection witnesses. The Fourth Gospel and its tradition ascribe to a woman a leading role in the mission of Samaria, while Acts knows only of Phillip as the first missionary of this area. While Mark knows of the discipleship of women (*akolouthein*), Luke stresses that the women who followed Jesus supported him and his male disciples with their possessions.

Reference to the Lukan works,[26] the major source of our knowledge of early Christian history, demonstrates how much the androcentric interests of the New Testament authors determined their reception and depiction of early Christian life, history, and tradition. Since Luke is usually regarded as the most sympathetic to women of all New Testament writers,[27] such a hypothesis may sound strange. However, such an androcentric tendency becomes evident when one analyzes the Lukan Easter narratives. The discussions of Paul with his opponents indicate that the leadership function of the apostle was of eminent importance for the developing Christian church. However, according to Paul, the apostolate is not limited to the twelve but includes all those who had received an appearance of the resurrected Lord and whom the resurrected Lord had commissioned to work as Christian missionaries (1 Cor. 9:4). Luke not only limits the apostolate to the twelve but also modifies the criteria mentioned by Paul;[28] only those males who had accompanied Jesus in his ministry from Galilee to Jerusalem and had become witnesses of his death and resurrection (Acts 1:21f) were eligible to replace Judas as apostle. In terms of these criteria, Paul cannot be called apostle because he did not know the earthly Jesus, but some women would qualify. According to Mark,[29] women were witnesses of the public ministry of Jesus in Galilee and Jerusalem. They were the only ones who were eyewitnesses of his execution since the male disciples had fled, and women were the first to receive the resurrection news (Mark 15:40f, 47; 16:1-8). Whereas Mark does not tell us of an appearance of the resurrected Lord to anyone, Matthew and John report that Mary Magdalene, and not the male disciples, was the first to see the risen Lord.

Luke does not know of any appearance of the risen Jesus to women. His androcentric redaction attempts in a subtle way to disqualify the women as resurrection witnesses. He emphasizes that the twelve who heard about the empty tomb from the women did not believe them but judged their words as gossip (24:11). When the men checked out the message of the women, it proved to be true (24:24), but this did not provoke a faith response from the male disciples. Not until the appearance of the risen Lord before Simon (24:34) did the men believe in the resurrection of Jesus. However, this appearance before Peter is not narrated but proclaimed in a confessional formula. This formula corresponds to the tradition quoted by Paul in 1 Cor. 15: 3-5, which mentions Cephas and the eleven, but not Mary Magdalene and the women, as witnesses of the resurrection. That Luke is interested in excluding women from apostleship is also supported by his condition that only one of the male disciples is eligible to succeed Judas (Acts 1:21).

This Lukan stress on Peter as the primary Easter witness must be situated within the early Christian discussion of whether he or Mary Magdalene is the first resurrection witness. This discussion understands Peter to be in competition with Mary Magdalene insofar as he complains constantly that Christ has given so many revelations to a woman. The Gospel of Thomas reflects this competition between Peter and Mary Magdalene.[30] The gnostic writing *Pistis Sophia* and the apocryphal Gospel of Mary further develop this motif. In the Gospel of Mary,[31] it is asked, how can Peter be against Mary Magdalene because she is a woman if Christ has made her worthy of his revelations? The Apostolic Church Order evidences that this discussion presupposes an actual ecclesial situation. While the Gospel of Mary argues for the authority of Mary Magdalene on the ground that Christ loved her more than all the other disciples, the Apostolic Church Order argues for the exclusion of women from the priesthood by letting Mary Magdalene herself reason that the weak, namely the women, must be saved by the strong, namely the men.[32] This dispute about the resurrection witness of Mary Magdalene shows, however, that Mary, like Peter, had apostolic authority in some Christian communities even into the third and fourth centuries. It also makes clear that the androcentric interpretation of the egalitarian primitive Christian traditions serves a patriarchal ecclesial praxis.

PATRISTIC INTERPRETATION AND CODIFICATION

The necessity of such an androcentric interpretation of early Christian traditions provokes the question whether the early Christian traditions and sources canonized by the Fathers manufacture the historical marginality of women in the church. In other words, was early Christian life and community totally and from its very beginnings patriarchally defined or was the patriarchal marginality of women in the early Christian sources a by-product of the "patristic" selection and canonization process? Is it possible to unearth an emancipatory tradition in the beginnings of Christianity or is the question of the liberating impulses of Christian faith historically illegitimate and theologically inappropriate? This question becomes all the more pressing since scholars of antiquity point out that the "feminist question" was much debated and the legal position of women was quite good in the Greco-Roman world. In order to address this question one has to challenge the patristic interpretative model that understands early Christian history and community as the antagonistic struggle between orthodoxy and heresy.[33]

The classic understanding of heresy presupposes the temporal priority of orthodoxy. According to Origen all heretics were at first orthodox but then erred from the true faith.[34] According to this model of interpretation heresy is not only a free defection but also an intended mutilation of the true faith. The orthodox understanding of history knows that Jesus founded the church and gave his revelation to the apostles, who proclaimed his teaching to the whole world. By its witness the orthodox church preserves the continuity of revelation in Jesus Christ and establishes the personal continuity with Jesus and the just apostles by maintaining the apostolic succession.

Since this understanding of the Christian beginnings is shared by all groups of the early church, they all attempt to demonstrate that their own group and teaching are in apostolic continuity with Jesus and the first disciples. Montanism, gnostic groups of various persuasions, and the patristic church claim apostolic tradition and revelation in order to substantiate (and to legitimate) their own authenticity. Both parties, the opponents as well as the advocates of the ecclesial leadership of women, claim apostolic tradition and succession for such a leadership.[35] The advocates point to Mary Magdalene, Salome, or Martha as apostolic disciples. They stress the apostolic succession of prophetesses in the Old and New Testaments and call attention to the women of apostolic times mentioned in Rom. 16. They legitimate their egalitarian structures of community with reference to Gal. 3:28. Others preserve the Acts of Thecla as a canonical book.

The patriarchal opposition, on the other hand, appeals to the example of Jesus, who did not commission women to preach or admit them to the last supper.[36] They quote texts like Gen. 2-3, 1 Cor. 14, the deutero-Pauline household codes, and especially 1 Tim. 2:9-15. Whereas egalitarian groups trace their apostolic authority to Mary Magdalene and emphasize that women as well as men have received the revelations of the resurrected Christ, patristic authors pit the authority of Peter against that of Mary Magdalene. While groups that acknowledge the leadership of women search the Old Testament Scriptures and the Christian writings for passages that mention women, patristic authors attempt to explain away or play down the role of women whenever they are mentioned. Origen, for instance, concedes that women have been prophets, but stresses that they did not speak publicly and especially not in the worship assembly of the church.[37] Chrysostom confirms that in apostolic times women traveled as missionaries preaching the gospel but, he explains, they could do this only because in the beginnings of the church the "angelic condition" permitted it.[38] Whereas the Montanists legitimate the prophetic activity of women with reference to the Scriptures, the extant Church Orders justify the institution of deaconesses,[39] which granted women only very limited and subordinate ecclesial functions in relation to the prophetesses of the Old Testament and the primitive church.[40] While women who preached and baptized claimed the example of the apostle Thecla, Tertullian attempts to denounce the Acts of Thecla as a fraud.[41] This example indicates that the process of the canonization of the early Christian documents was affected by the polemics and struggle concerning the leadership of women in the church. The canon reflects a patriarchal selection process and has functioned to bar women from ecclesial leadership.

The acid polemics of the Fathers against the ecclesial leadership of women indicate that the question of women's ecclesial office was still debated in the second and third centuries. It also demonstrates that the progressive patriarchalization of church office did not happen without opposition, but had to overcome an early Christian theology and praxis that acknowledged the leadership claim of women.[42] We owe to these polemics the few surviving bits of historical, though prejudiced, information about women's leadership in various groups of the early Church. Unfortunately, early Christian historiography does not understand them as the outcome of bitter polemics but as historically adequate and theologically appropriate information.

The polemics of the patriarchal authors against women's ecclesial leadership and office ultimately resulted in the equation of women's leadership in the church with heresy. This progressive equation of women and heresy had as a consequence the theological defamation of Christian women. For example, the author of the Apocalypse prophesies against an early Christian prophetess whom he abuses with the name Jezebel.[43] This prophet apparently was the head of an early Christian prophetic school which had great influence and authority in the community of Thyatira. Since the author of the Apocalypse stresses that despite his warnings and denunciations the prophetess still was active within the community, her authority seems to have at least equaled that of John whom, in turn, she might have perceived as a false prophet. Her influence must have been lasting, since Thyatira, in the middle of the second century, became a center of the Montanist movement, where prophetesses had significant leadership and influence.

The attacks of Tertullian evidence how prominent women's leadership still was toward the end of the second century. Tertullian is outraged about the insolence of those women who dared "to teach, to participate in theological disputes, to exorcise, to promise healings, and to baptize." He argues that it is not permitted for women "to speak in the Church, to teach, to baptize, to sacrifice, to fulfill any other male function, or to claim any form of priestly functions."[44] He substantiates this exclusion of women from all ecclesial leadership roles with a theology that evidences a deep misogynist contempt and fear of women. He accuses woman not only of the temptation of man but also of that of the angels. According to him woman is the "devil's gateway" and the root of all sin. Finally, Jerome not only attributes to women the origin of sin but of all heresy.

> With the help of the prostitute Helena, Simon Magus founded his sect. Crowds of women accompanied Nicholas of Antiochia, the seducer, to all impurity. Marcion sent a woman before him in order to prepare the minds of men so that they might run into his nets. Apelles had his Philumena; an associate in the false teachings. Montanus, the mouthpiece of an impure spirit, used two wealthy women of noble origin, Prisca and Maximilla, in order to first bribe many communities and then to corrupt them. . . . Arious' intent to lead the world astray started by misguiding the sister of the emperor. The resources of Lucilla supported Donatus to corrupt so many wretched in Africa with his staining rebaptism. In Spain the blind woman Agape led a man like Elipidius to his grave. He was succeeded by Priscillian who was an enthusiastic defender of Zarathustra and a *Magus* before he became a bishop, and a woman by the name of Gall supported him in his endeavors and left behind a stepsister in order to continue a second heresy of lesser form.[45]

PATRIARCHALIZATION AND INSTITUTIONALIZATION

This process of ecclesial patriarchalization, which climaxed in the identification of women's leadership with heresy, was also operative in the selection and formulation of the canonical New Testament writings. This becomes explicit in the later writings of the New Testament, which in turn serve to reenforce and to legitimize the patriarchalizing tendencies in the patristic church.

Since the genuine Pauline letters know of leadership roles of women in the primitive church and since exegetes debate the meaning and authenticity of 1 Cor. 11:2-16[46] and 1 Cor. 14:33-36,[47] scholars discuss whether or not this process of patriarchalization was initiated, or at least supported, by Paul. However there is no question that the early Christian tendencies of patriarchalization claimed Paul for their cause and determined the history, theology, and praxis of the church in his name. Such an interpretation of Pauline theology is continued by modern historical-critical exegesis. Scholars presuppose the interpretative model of orthodoxy and heresy when they label the opponents of Paul as "gnostic" or "gnosticizing." The Christian women in the community of Corinth, who apparently occupied an equal position in the leadership and worship of the community, are, therefore, qualified as "heretic," whereas the theological admonitions and arguments of Paul are understood as "orthodox."[48]

The theological-historic claim of Gal. 3:28[49] is disqualified in a similar way when it is classified as a "gnostic" baptismal formula and denounced as enthusiastic spiritualization and illusion. Although the validity of this model for an historiography of early Christianity has been questioned, its patriarchal implications are not yet exposed. Even though exegetes disagree on Paul's own stance toward women, they acknowledge explicit tendencies of patriarchalization in the Deutero-Pauline and post-Pauline literature. The so-called household codes[50] of the Deutero-Pauline literature accept and legitimate the patriarchal family order. Ephesians especially gives a theological justification of the patriarchal relationship between husband and wife or slave and master, insofar as the author legitimizes it with reference to the hierarchically defined relationship between Christ and the Church.[51] First Peter, which belongs to the area of Pauline influence, identifies the missionary vocation of women with their subordination to their husbands, whom they can win over to Christianity without many words. The author admonishes women to imitate the example of obedience given by the women of the Old Testament. Sara becomes a prime example for the Christian woman because she acknowledged Abraham as her "lord." The husbands, in turn, are admonished to treat their wives with understanding since they are the "weaker sex." The expression "weaker vessel" implies the corporal, spiritual, intellectual, and social inferiority of woman. Peter concedes that women are also "heirs of the life," but theologically legitimates their secondary position. Indeed, the text not only justifies the submission of women, but also demands the submission of all Christians to the patriarchal political-societal order (2:13). Slaves are most especially enjoined to submit to the patriarchal domination; this is done with reference to the sufferings of Christ. The authors of 1 Peter, as well as Ephesians, do not shy away from developing a Christian theology that supports the patriarchal-hierarchical claims of the Greco-Roman state and society.[52]

1 Tim. 2:10-15 does not speak about the subordination of women to the patriarchal family order; but like 1 Cor. 14:33-36, it explicitly demands the

silence and subordination of women in the Christian community. The goal here, a patriarchalization of the ecclesial leadership functions, is evident in the injunction of the author that women should learn in total submission and the categorical prohibition of women teaching and having authority over men. This patriarchal injunction is theologically substantiated by the argument that man was created first and that woman sinned first.[53] This negative theological understanding of woman's functions is used to legitimize the exclusion of women from leadership and office in the church. Woman's vocation is not the call to discipleship or the missionary; it is her patriarchally defined role as wife and mother that accomplishes her salvation.

This demand of the Pastorals for the subordination of women is formulated in the context of a progressive patriarchalization of the church and its leadership functions. The Pastorals require that the structures and leadership of the Christian community should be patterned after the patriarchal family structure. This is seen in the criteria for the election of male leaders: they should be married to one woman and have demonstrated their patriarchal leadership qualities in their own household; they should know how to rule their children and to administer and order their household authoritatively.[54] In such a patriarchal church order, by definition, there is no room for women's leadership.

It is clear, however, that such a leadership structure developed in conflict with a more egalitarian church order which it worked to replace because it needed an ideological legitimization for the exclusion of women. Thus it becomes obvious that the misogynist expressions of patristic theology are not only rooted in a faulty anthropology of woman but are also provoked by ecclesiastical-patriarchal interests to theologically legitimate the exclusion of women from ecclesial leadership and office. Such an exegetical-historical delineation of the patriarchalization of the church does not prove the historical necessity and unavoidability of such a development; it does not call for theological justification but for a critical-theological analysis.[55]

Contemporary exegetes and theologians usually understand the process of ecclesial patriarchalization as the necessary development from charisma to office, from Paulinism to early Catholicism, from a millenarian radical ethos to a privileged Christian establishment, from the radical Jesus movement within Judaism to an integrative love-patriarchalism[56] within the Hellenistic urban communities, from the egalitarian charismatic structures of the beginning to the hierarchical order of the Constantinian church. Unlike the orthodoxy-heresy model, this interpretative framework does not justify the patriarchalization process of the early church on theological grounds, but argues with it in terms of sociological and political factors.

It implicitly maintains that, from a sociological-political point of view, the gradual patriarchalization of the early Christian movement was unavoidable. If the Christian communities were to grow, develop, and historically survive, they had to adapt and take over patriarchal institutional structures of their society. The institutionalization of the charismatic-egalitarian early Christian movement could not but lead to the patriarchalization of the ecclesial leadership functions—that is, to the exclusion of women from church office or to the reduction of their ecclesial functions to subordinate, feminine, marginal positions. The more the early Christian movement adapted to the prevailing societal institutions, thus becoming a genuine part of its patriarchal Greco-Roman society, the more Christian women had to be excluded from church leadership and office. They were reduced to powerless fringe groups or had to conform to the feminine stereotypes of the patriarchal culture. For example, the patristic office of widow and deaconess had to limit itself to the service of women, and finally disappeared from history. Moreover, these leadership functions could no longer be exercised by all women but only by those who had overcome their femaleness by remaining virgins.

This interpretative model of the early Christian development seems to describe accurately the consequences and casualties of the gradual patriarchalization of the Christian church. However, it does not reflect on its own theological androcentric presuppositions, insofar as it overlooks that the history of early Christianity is written from the perspective of the historical winners.[57] Christian history and theology reflect those segments of the church which have undergone this patriarchalization process and theologically legitimated it with the formulation of the canon. Insofar as the sociological-political model presents the elimination of women from ecclesial office and their marginalization in a patriarchal church as an historical necessity, it justifies the patriarchal institutionalization process as the only possible and historically viable form of institutional church structure. It overlooks, however, that the institutional structures of the patriarchal household and state were not the sole institutional options available to and realized by early Christians; collegial private associations, philosophical schools, guilds, and some of the mystery cults accepted women and slaves as equal members and initiates. These groups, like the early Christians, however, were always politically suspect because their egalitarian ethos challenged the patriarchal structures of their society. Since women such as Phoebe or Nympha were founders and leaders of house churches, the missionary house churches seem to have been patterned after such egalitarian private organizations and not after the patriarchal household.

The theological implications of the patriarchal sociological model for the reconstruction of early Christian history are obvious. Women can occupy only subordinate positions in the contemporary church since they could only do so in the early church. The patriarchal character of church office is given with the institutionalization of the church. Women who claim to be called to church office and leadership violate the essence of ecclesial tradition and institution. Therefore, the androcentric sociological model for the reconstruction of early Christian history prepares the grounds for the theological claim that patriarchal church structures are divinely revealed, and thus cannot be changed.

Both the androcentric theological model and the sociological model for the reconstruction of early Christian life and community presuppose that the process of the patriarchalization of the church was historically unavoidable. They claim that the early Christian theology and praxis, which acknowledged women as equal Christians and disciples, was either "heretical' or "charismatic," and hence theologically and historically nonviable. Neither model can conceive of a Christian church in which women were equal. Therefore, it is not enough to reinterpret the biblical texts that speak about women in early Christianity. What is necessary is to challenge the traditional interpretative models for the reconstruction of early Christianity and search for a new model which can integrate both egalitarian and "heretical" traditions into its own perspective. Since such an interpretative model presupposes and is based on the equality of *all* Christians, it could be called feminist. Insofar as such a perspective attempts to comprehend the equality of all Christians within the early Christian church, it has to employ sociological analysis.

AN EGALITARIAN INTERPRETATIVE MODEL: THE EARLY CHRISTIAN MOVEMENT AS A CONFLICT MOVEMENT

Such an egalitarian interpretative model is based on the insight that Christianity has not been patriarchally determined from its very inception, and has not been an integrated segment of the patriarchal Jewish or Greco-Roman society. If one asks which historical, as yet unrealized, emancipatory impulses in early Christianity, despite the patriarchalizing tendencies of tradition and church, are still accessible today, it is evident that the Jesus movement and the early Christian missionary movement have been "counter-cultural." These counter-cultural, egalitarian impulses have to become the defining elements of the interpretative model for the reconstruction of early Christian history.

Despite apparent patriarchal tendencies in the transmission and redaction of the Jesus traditions, the New Testament sources do not attribute to Jesus a single negative statement about women. This is remarkable because the Gospels were written at a time when the patriarchalization process of the Christian community was well underway. The stories about the healing of women especially indicate that tradition and redaction did not attempt to apologetically interpret Jesus' words and actions in a patriarchal way. Even New Testament texts which insist on the patriarchal submission of Christian women do not legitimize this injunction with reference to a word or action of Jesus but with reference to the Law and especially to Gen. 2-3.

The Jesus traditions are in no way patriarchally defined. The opposite is true.[58] They reflect that Jesus was criticized because he took women seriously, and that women were disciples and primary witnesses. Since discipleship and the community of the disciples dissolved and replaced traditional family bonds (Mark 3:35), the women disciples are no longer defined by the patriarchal order of marriage and family. It is not natural motherhood but Jesus' discipleship which is decisive. The commitment and fidelity of the women disciples is especially underlined in the Markan gospel. Women persevered with Jesus in his sufferings and execution. The women disciples were the primary witnesses of the empty tomb and the resurrection. The three women pericopes in Mark maintain that the women disciples were the primary witnesses for the three basic data of the kerygma: death, burial, and resurrection. These three women pericopes seem in narrative form to parallel the expression "Christ died . . . was buried . . . was raised" of 1 Cor. 15:3-5.[59] This tradition of the gospels concerning the women, especially Mary Magdalene, as primary witnesses and guarantors of the Christian gospel does justice to the critical criteria which historical-critical scholarship has defined for determining authentic Jesus traditions.[60] This tradition is found in two different areas, the Synoptic and the Johannine traditions. It cannot be derived from contemporary Judaism because women were not considered valid witnesses. It also does not owe its formulation to early Christian ecclesial interests, since later documents, as we have seen, attempt to play down the importance of the women disciples. Moreover, patristic and later church traditions speak of Mary Magdalene as "apostle to the apostles," although they attempt to diminish her importance, and in later ecclesial consciousness she becomes the "prostitute" and "sinner." Even modern interpreters attempt to explain away the significance of the women as primary witnesses and guarantors of Christian resurrection faith when they stress that, in distinction to Peter, the witness of Mary Magdalene was "unofficial."[61]

These traditions about the role of women in the discipleship of Jesus correspond to the character of the Jesus movement that has been worked out by the sociological interpretation of religion.[62] As a renewal movement the Jesus movement stands in conflict with its Jewish society and is "heretical" with respect to the Jewish religious community. The earliest Jesus traditions expect a reversal of all social conditions through the eschatological intervention of God; this is initially realized in the ministry of Jesus. Therefore, the Jesus movement can accept all those who, according to contemporary societal standards, are marginal people and who are, according to the Torah, "unclean"— the poor, the exploited, the public sinners, the publicans, the maimed and sick, and last but not least, the women. In distinction to other Jewish renewal movements, such as the Qumran community, the Jesus movement was not exclusive but inclusive; it made possible the solidarity of those who could not be accepted by other Jewish renewal groups because of religious laws and ideologies.[63]

Women could become disciples of Jesus, therefore, although they were socially marginal, religiously inferior, and cultically unclean persons. The sevenfold transmission[64] of the Synoptic traditions, which states that the first and the leaders should be last and slaves, shows that Jesus radically questioned social and religious hierarchical and patriarchal relationships. The fatherhood of God radically prohibits any ecclesial-patriarchal self-understanding. The lordship of Christ categorically rules out any relationship of dominance within the Christian community (Matt. 23:7-12). According to the gospel tradition Jesus radically rejected all relationships of dependence and domination.[65] This demand for inclusiveness and domination-free structures in the Jesus movement provides the theological basis for the acknowledgment of women as full disciples.

This ethos of the Jesus movement also finds expression in the early Christian missionary movement. All social distinctions of race, religion, class, and sex are abolished.[66] All Christians are equal members of the community. Gal. 3:28 is a pre-Pauline baptismal formula which Paul quotes in order to prove that in the Christian community all religious-social distinctions between Jews and Gentiles have lost their validity. This pre-Pauline baptismal confession clearly proclaims values that are in total opposition to those of the Greco-Roman culture of the time. The Christian missionary communities, like the Jesus movement, could not tolerate the religious-social structures of inequality that characterized the dominant Greco-Roman society. The new self-understanding of the Christians did away with all religious, class, social, and patriarchal relationships of dominance, and therefore made it possible not only for Gentiles and slaves but also for women to assume leadership functions within the urban missionary movement. In this movement women were not marginal figures but exercised leadership as missionaries, founders of Christian communities, apostles, prophets, and leaders of churches.

Contemporary exegetes, therefore, do not do justice to the text when they label this pre-Pauline baptismal formula as "gnostic."[67] As the Christian Jews remained racially Jews, so women remain sexually female although their patriarchally defined gender roles and dependency are annulled in the Christian community. Moreover, Gal. 3:28 does not claim, as later gnostic and patristic texts do, that "maleness" is the full expression of being human and Christian, and that women, therefore, have to become "male" in Christ. In addition Gal. 3:28 must not be misunderstood as purely spiritual or eschatological, since the text does not maintain Christian equality of Jews and Gentiles regarding their souls or with respect to the eschatological future. Finally, Gal. 3:28 should not be misinterpreted as purely charismatic but as applying to the structures and organization of the Christian community. Egalitarian structures were not unthinkable at the time. Such communal, organizational forms, which eliminated the societal differences between slaves and free as well as between male and female are found in the religious and secular associations of the time, although they were always suspected as capable of sedition if they did not conform to the social, patriarchal dominant order.[68] Like other cultic associations, especially Judaism and the cult of Isis, the Christians had to face the accusation that they upset the traditional patriarchal order of the household, and therefore, the order of the Roman state and society, by admitting women and slaves to equal membership. Therefore, the thesis of G. Theissen that the radicalism of the countercultural Jesus movement was assimilated by the earliest urban Hellenistic missionary communities into a "family style love patriarchalism," in which the societal distinctions survived although in a softer mitigated form, cannot be substantiated. The household code traditions of the Pauline school do not demonstrate such a love patriarchalism for the initial stages of the early Christian missionary movement in the Hellenistic urban centers.[69] They are better understood as an apologetic development of cultural adaption that was necessary because the early Christian missionary movement, like the Jesus movement in Palestine, was a countercultural conflict-movement that undermined the patriarchal structures of the Greco-Roman *politeia*. Only an egalitarian model for the reconstruction of early Christian history can do justice to both the egalitarian traditions of woman's leadership in the church as well as to the gradual process of adaptation and theological justification of the dominant patriarchal Greco-Roman culture and society.

In conclusion, I have attempted a critical analysis of the theological and sociological androcentric models which are presupposed in a historical and theological reconstruction of early Christian history and theology. I have proposed instead an egalitarian model, which can do justice to all the New Testament traditions and does not have to eliminate or to downplay the traditions of women's discipleship and leadership in the Jesus movement and the early Christian missionary movement. Like any historical interpretation, an egalitarian reconstruction and interpretation of early Christian history are not only analytical but also constructive. It is not only motivated by interest in the past but also attempts to set free the emancipatory and egalitarian impulses and traditions for the present, and especially for the future.[70] It seeks to engender an emancipatory praxis of church and theology that would set free the egalitarian impulses of the Jesus movement in Palestine and of the early Christian missionary movement not only for women and the Christian community but also for Western society and culture.

NOTES

1. A. Meyer, *Die moderne Forschung über die Geschichte des Urchristentums* (Leipzig and Tübingen: Mohr, 1898); D. Lührmann, "Erwägungen zur Geschichtedes Urchristentums," *EvTh* 32 (1972): 452-67; R. Schnackenburg, "Das Urchristentum," in J. Maier and J. Schreiner, *Literatur und Religion des Frühjudentums* (Würzburg: Echter, 1973), pp. 284-309; J. Blank, "Probleme einer Geschichte des Urchristentums," *Una Sancta* 30 (1975): 261-86; S. Schulz, *Die Mitte der Schrift: Der Frühkatholizismus im Neuen Testament* (Stuttgart: Kohlhammer, 1976); F. Hahn, "Das Problem des Frühkatholizismus," *EvTh* 38 (1978): 340-57; H. Paulsen, "Zur Wissenschaft vom Urchristentum und der alten Kirche—ein methodischer Versuch," *ZNW* 68 (1978): 200-230.

2. Since this article presupposes the studies about the history of early Christianity as well as the literature on women in antiquity and in early Christianity, it is impossible to quote the literature pertaining to the topic. Adequate discussion of divergent hypotheses and opinions must be reserved for a more extensive book-length treatment.

3. This is evident in the fact that the studies on women in the New Testament or women in early Christianity have not influenced the scholarly reconstruction of the Christian beginnings.

4. Blank, "Probleme," p. 262.

5. This is illustrated by the work of G. Heinz, *Das Problem der Kirchenentstehung in der deutschen protestantischen Theologie des 20 Jahrhunderts* (Mainz: Mathias Grünewald, 1974). Heinz highlights the theological presuppositions underlying the different reconstructions of early Christian beginnings. For the sociology of the biblical exegete, cf. also R. L. Rohrbaugh, *The Biblical Interpreter* (Philadelphia: Fortress Press, 1978).

6. For the concept of "model," cf. T. S. Kuhn, *The Structure of Scientific Revolutions* (Chicago: University of Chicago Press, 1970); I. G. Barbour, *Myths, Models, and Paradigms* (New York: Harper & Row, 1974); J. Blank, "Zum Problem ethischer Normen im Neuen Testament," *Concilium* 7 (1967): 356-62, uses model in a somewhat different way.

7. Cf. Vera Slupik, "Frau und Wissenschaft," in *Frauen in der Universität*, Journal No. 6 (Munich: Frauenoffensive, 1977), pp. 8-20; I. Kassner and S. Lorenz,

Trauer muss Aspasia tragen (Munich: Frauenoffensive, 1976); J. Janssen-Jurreit, *Sexismus/Über die Abtreibung der Frauenfrage* (Munich: Carl Hanser, 1976), pp. 11-93; H. Smith, "Feminism and the Methodology of Women's History," in B. A. Carroll, *Liberating Women's History: Theoretical and Critical Essays* (Urbana: University of Illinois Press, 1975), pp. 368-84.

8. Simone de Beauvoir, *The Second Sex* (New York: Knopf, 1953), p. 10; E. Janeway, *Man's World, Woman's Place* (New York: Dell, 1971), characterizes this as "social mythology."

9. Cf. my articles, "Für eine befreite und befreiende Theologie," *Concilium* 14 (1978): 287-94; and "Feminist Theology as a Critical Theology of Liberation," *ThSt* 36 (1975): 605-26; V. Saiving, "Androcentrism in Religious Studies," *JR* 56 (1976): 177-97; B. W. Harrison, "The New Consciousness of Women: A Socio-Political Resource," *Cross Currents* 24 (1975): 445-62.

10. Cf. my article on "Die Rolle der Frau in der urchristlichen Bewegung," *Concilium* 12 (1976): 3-9. For the relative emancipation of women in Hellenism, cf. G. Delling, *Paulus Stellung zu Frau und Ehe* (Stuttgart: Kohlhammer, 1931), pp. 2-56; C. Schneider, *Kulturgeschichte des Hellenismus* (Munich: Beck, 1967), Vol. 1, pp. 78-117; L. Swidler, "Greco-Roman Feminism and the Reception of the Gospel," in *Traditio-Krisis-Renovatio aus theologischer Sicht*, ed. Jaspert and Mohr (Marburgh: Elwert, 1976), pp. 39-52; W. A. Meeks, "The Image of the Androgyne," *History of Religions* 13 (1974): 167-80.

11. This is the reason why M. J. Lagrange, *Saint Paul, Epitre aux Romains* (Paris: 1916), p. 366, decided in favor of a woman's name although this textual reading was abandoned by Protestant exegetes.

12. *Das Neue Testament* (Aschaffendorf: Pattloch, 1956), p. 214.

13. H. Lietzmann, *Geschichte der alten Kirche* (Berlin: DeGruyter, 1961), Vol. 1, p. 149.

14. *Commenteria in Epistolam ad Romanos 10:26* (PG 14, 1281 B), 10:39 (PG 14, 1289A).

15. Cf. E. E. Ellis, "Paul and His Co-Workers," *NTS* 17 (1970/71): 439; M. A. Getty, "God's Fellow Worker and Apostleship," in *Women Priests*, ed. A. and L. Swidler (New York: Paulist Press, 1977), pp. 176-82.

16. This is stressed by Ramsey MacMullen, *Roman Social Relations, 50 B.C. to A.D. 284* (New Haven: Yale University Press, 1974), pp. 74-76, 124.

17. G. Heinrici, "Die Christengemeinde Korinths und die religiösen Genossenschaften der Griechcn," *ZWTh* 19 (1976): 465-526.

18. E. A. Judge, "St. Paul and Classical Society," *JBAC* 15 (1972): 28.

19. Cf. my article, "Word, Spirit and Power: Women in Early Christian Communities," *Women of Spirit: Female Leadership in the Jewish and Christian Traditions*, ed. Rosemary Ruether and E. McLaughlin (New York: Simon and Schuster, 1979), pp. 29-70.

20. For this distinction, cf. C. Miller and K. Swift, eds., *Words and Women: New Language in New Times* (New York: Doubleday, Anchor, 1977), especially pp. 64-74.

21. Small sectarian groups separate themselves from the world and distinguish between their members as insiders and the outsiders who are conceived as "the others." Not women but the non-Christians are the "others" in early Christianity. There is no evidence that church membership was restricted to males only, although the address of the Christians is usually masculine. Cf. my article "The Study of

Women in Early Christianity: Some Methodological Considerations," in *Critical History and Biblical Faith: New Testament Perspectives*, ed. J. T. Ryan (Villanova: Catholic Theology Society, 1979), pp. 30-58, and the contribution by W. A. Meeks, " 'Since Then You Would Need To Go Out of the World': Group Boundaries in Pauline Christianity," in the same volume, pp. 4-29.

22. Among the outstanding figures of early Christianity only Prisca is mentioned among the leaders in the Pauline churches by Hans Conzelmann, *Geschichte des Urchristentums* (Göttingen: Vandenhoeck and Ruprecht, 1971), in Appendix 1; Eng. *History of Primitive Christianity*, trans. John E. Steely (Nashville and New York: Abingdon, 1973).

23. This was already recognized and deplored by Elizabeth Cady Stanton, *The Woman's Bible*, new ed. (New York: Arno Press, 1974), in the last century. It is regrettable that the recent Vatican declaration against the ordination of women confirms this experience. For the international theological discussion of this document, cf. L. Swidler, "Roma Locuta, Causa Finita?" in *Women Priests*, pp. 3-18.

24. Many studies on women in the Bible do not perceive this process because they are often motivated by an apologetic defense of the biblical writers.

25. Cf. my article "Women in the Pre-Pauline and Pauline Churches," *USQR* 33 (1978): 153-66.

26. Cf. my plenary address "Women's Discipleship and Leadership in the Lukan Writings," at the CBA annual meeting in San Francisco in 1978.

27. Cf. e.g., C. F. Parvey, "The Theology and Leadership of Women in the New Testament," *Religion and Sexism*, ed. R. R. Ruether (New York: Simon and Schuster, 1974), pp. 137-46.

28. Cf. my articles "The Twelve" and "The Apostleship of Women in Early Christianity," in *Women Priests*, pp. 114-22 and 135-40 for the literature.

29. Since the Gospel of Mark portrays women positively, P. Achtemeier *(Mark* [Philadelphia: Fortress Press, 1975], p. 11) considers the possibility that the Gospel was authored by a woman. Although the tradition ascribes all New Testament writings to male authors, historical-critical scholarship has shown that we do not know the authors of most New Testament writings.

30. Logion 114, *PL* 99, 18-26. Cf. Edgar Hennecke, ed., *New Testament Apocrypha* (Philadelphia: Westminster, 1963), Vol. 1, p. 522.

31. Ibid., p. 343.

32. Cf. J. P. Arendzen, "An Entire Syriac Text of the Apostolic Church Order," *JThSt* 111 (1902): 71.

33. Cf. A. Hilgenfeld, *Die Ketzergeschichte des Urchristentums*, new ed. (Darmstadt: Wiss. Buchgesellschaft, 1963); W. Bauer, *Orthodoxy and Heresy in Earliest Christianity* (Philadelphia: Fortress Press, 1971); H. D. Betz, "Orthodoxy and Heresy in Primitive Christianity," *Int* 19 (1965): 299-311; J. Pelikan, *The Emergence of the Catholic Tradition* (Chicago: University of Chicago Press, 1971).

34. Origen, *Commentary to the Song of Songs* 3.2.2; similarly also 1 Clem. 42; Tertullian, *De Praescriptione* 20; Eusebius, *Ecclesiastical History* 4.22.2-3; cf. also John G. Gager, *Kingdom and Community: The Social World of Early Christianity* (Englewood, N.J.: Prentice-Hall, 1975), pp. 76-92.

35. For extensive references cf. my article, "Word, Spirit, and Power."

36. Cf. *Didascalia* 15 and *The Apostolic Church Order* III, 6.9; J. Kevin Coyle, "The Fathers on Women's Ordination," *Eglise et Theologie* 9 (1978): 51-101; C. Osiek, "The Ministry and Ordination of Women According to the Early Church

Fathers," in C. Stuhlmüller, ed., *Women and Priesthood* (Collegeville, Minn.: The Liturgical Press, 1978), pp. 59-68.

37. Origen, *Commentarium in I* ᵃᵐ/*Epistulam ad Corinthios 14:34-35*. Cf. C. Jenkins "Origen on 1 Corinthians, IV," *JThSt* 10 (1908/09): 41 f.

38. E. A. Clark, "Sexual Politics in the Writings of John Chrysostom," *AThR* 59 (1977): 3-20; D. F. Winslow, "Priesthood and Sexuality in the Post-Nicene Fathers." *St. Luke's Journal of Theology* 18 (1975): 214-27.

39. Cf. especially A. Kalsbach, *Die altkirchliche Einrichtung der Diakonissen bis zu ihrem Erlöschen* (Freiburg: Herder, 1926), and R. Gryson, *The Ministry of Women in the Early Church* (Collegeville, Minn.: Liturgical Press, 1976).

40. *The Apostolic Church Order* III, 6.1-29.

41. Tertullian, *De Baptismo* 17. For the *Acts of Thecla* cf. C. Schlau, *Die Akten des Paulus und der Thekla* (Leipzig: Hinrichs, 1877); W. M. Ramsay, *The Church in the Roman Empire before A. D. 170*, repr. of 1904 ed. (Kennebunkport, Maine: Longwood Press, 1977, and New York: Baker Books, 1979), pp. 375-428; and the very interesting dissertation of R. Kramer, *Ecstatics and Ascetics: Studies in the Function of Religious Activities of Women* (Ann Arbor: University Microfilms, 1976), pp. 142-49.

42. Cf. also F. Heiler, *Die Frau in den Religionen der Menschheit* (Berlin: De Gruyter, 1977), p. 114. He surmises, however, that in the heretical communities women in office were not disciplined enough.

43. The accusation of sexual licentiousness is a stereotypical accusation leveled by pagans against Christians and by Christians against each other. Cf. K. Thraede, "Frau," in *RAC* 8 (Stuttgart, 1973): 254-66; L. Zscharnack, *Der Dienst der Frau in den ersten Jahrhunderten der christlichen Kirche* (Göttingen: Vandenhoeck and Ruprecht, 1902), pp. 78ff.

44. *De Praescriptione* 41.5 and *De Baptismo* 17.4. Cf. also J. K. Coyle, "The Fathers on Women's Ordination," pp. 67ff.

45. Jerome 1.48.

46. Cf. W. Munro, "Patriarchy and Charismatic Community in Paul," in *Women and Religion, Proceedings of the American Academy of Religion, 1972-1973,* rev. ed., ed. Judith Plaskow and Joan A. Romero (Missoula: Scholars Press, 1974), pp. 189-98; W. O. Walker, "1 Cor. 11:2-6 and Paul's View Regarding Women," *JBL* 94 (1975): 94-110; J. Murphy-O'Conner, "The Non-Pauline Character of 1 Cor. 11:2-16," *JBL* 95 (1976): 615-21.

47. For the literature and discussion of this text cf. G. Fitzer, *Das Weib schweige in der Gemeinde* (Munich: Kaiser, 1963) and my article "Women in the Pre-Pauline and Pauline Churches."

48. Paul's reaction is often understood as inspired by his Jewish past. For the danger of anti-Judaism in such an exegetical feminist explanation cf. J. Plaskow, "Christian Feminism and Anti-Judaism," *Cross Currents* 28 (1978): 306-9.

49. Cf. W. Schmithals, *Die Gnosis in Korinth* (Göttingen: Vandenhoeck and Ruprecht, 1956), p. 227 n. 1; W. A. Meeks, "The Image of the Androgyne," pp. 180ff; R. Scroggs, "Paul and the Eschatological Woman Revisited," *JAAR* 42 (1974): 536.

50. Cf. J. E. Crouch, *The Origin and Intention of the Colossian Haustafel* (Göttingen: Vandenhoeck and Ruprecht, 1972); W. Leslie, *The Concept of Women in the Pauline Corpus* (Ann Arbor: University Microfilms, 1976), pp. 188-237.

51. Cf. J. P. Sampley, *And the Two Shall Become One Flesh* (Cambridge: Cam-

bridge University Press, 1971), and my article "Marriage and Discipleship," *The Bible Today* (April 1979): 2027-34.

52. Cf. the excellent analysis of D. Balch, *"Let Wives Be Submissive . . . ": The Origin and Apologetic Function of the Household Duty Code (Haustafel) in I Peter* (Ann Arbor: University Microfilms, 1974).

53. Cf. S. Roth Liebermann, *The Eve Motif in Ancient Near Eastern and Classical Greek Sources* (Ann Arbor: University Microfilms, 1975).

54. Cf. A. Sand, "Anfänge einer Koordinierung verschiedener Gemeinde-ordnungen nach den Pastoralbriefen," in *Kirche im Werden*, ed. J. Hainz (Paderborn: Schöningh, 1976), pp. 215-37, 220.

55. For a positive interpretation of this development, cf., for example, W. Schrage, "Zur Ethik der Neutestamentlichen Haustafeln," *NTS* 21 (1974): 1-22.

56. For this expression cf. E. Troeltsch, *Die Soziallehren der christlichen Kirchen und Gruppen* (Tübingen: Mohr, 1923), Vol. 1, pp. 67f, and especially G. Theissen, *Sociology of Early Palestinian Christianity* (Philadelphia: Fortress Press, 1978), and his various articles. However, in my opinion, Theissen too quickly ascribes the love-patriarchalism to the early Christian missionary movement in the Greco-Roman urban centers.

57. Cf. G. Gutiérrez, "Where Hunger Is, God Is Not," *The Witness* (April 1977), p. 6: "Human history has been written by a white hand, a male hand, from the dominating social class. The perspective of the defeated in history is different. Attempts have been made to wipe from their minds the memory of their struggles. This is to deprive them of a source of energy, of an historical will to rebellion."

58. Cf. also Evelyn and Frank Stagg, *Woman in the World of Jesus* (Philadelphia: Westminster, 1978), p. 102.

59. Cf. M. Hengel, "Maria Magdalena und die Frauen als Zeugen," *Abraham unser Vater*, ed. O. Betz and M. Hengel (Leiden: Brill, 1962), p. 246.

60. For a short discussion of these criteria cf. N. Perrin, *What Is Redaction Criticism?* (Philadelphia: Fortress Press, 1971).

61. Cf., e.g., R. E. Brown, "Roles of Women in the Fourth Gospel," *ThSt* 36 (1975): 692, n. 12.

62. Cf. in addition to the work of G. Theissen, J. Gager, R. Kraemer, and W. A. Meeks also the article by R. Scroggs, "The Earliest Christian Communities as Sectarian Movement," in *Christianity, Judaism and Other Greco-Roman Cults* (Leiden: Brill, 1975), Vol. 2, pp. 1-23; J. A. Wilde, "The Social World of Mark's Gospel," *SBLSP* (Missoula: Scholars Press, 1978), Vol. 2, pp. 47-70.

63. Cf. M. Völkl, "Freund der Zöllner und Sünder," *ZNW* 69 (1978): 1-10; L. Schottroff, "Das Magnifikat und die ältesten Traditionen über Jesus von Nazareth," *EvTh* 38 (1978), 298-312, and especially her excellent book, L. Schottroff and W. Stegemann, *Jesus and the Hope of the Poor* (Maryknoll: Orbis, 1986).

64. Mark 9:35; 10:41-45; Matt. 18:4; 20:25-28; 23:11; Luke 9:48; 22:24-27. According to Billerbeck, *Kommentar*, Vol. 4, p. 722, women had the same social standing as slaves did.

65. Cf. P. Hoffmann and V. Eid, *Jesus von Nazareth und seine christliche Moral* (Freiburg: Herder, 1975), pp. 199ff.

66. Cf., e.g., H. D. Betz, "Spirit, Freedom, and Law: Paul's Message to the Galatian Churches," *Svensk Exegetisk Årsbok* 39 (1974): 145-60.

67. It is often claimed that the text is "gnostic" because it does away with the creational differences between women and men. However, such a judgment, in my

opinion, does not sufficiently distinguish between biological sex and social gender roles. For such a distinction and its cross-cultural documentation, cf. Anne Oakley, *Sex, Gender, and Society* (New York: Harper & Row, 1973).

68. Cf. the documentation and elaboration of this point by D. Balch, *"Let Wives Be Submissive . . . ,* " pp. 115-33.

69. The interrelation between the organizational forms of private or religious associations and the house-churches needs to be clarified. Cf. A. J. Malherbe, *Social Aspects of Early Christianity* (Baton Rouge: Louisiana State University Press, 1977), p. 92.

70. Cf. H. M. Baumgartner, *Kontinuität und Geschichte: Zur Kritik and Metakritik der historischen Vernunft* (Frankfurt: Suhrkamp, 1972), p. 218.

30

CLARICE J. MARTIN

A Chamberlain's Journey and the Challenge of Interpretation for Liberation

Nothing reveals the Eurocentric orientation of New Testament studies more than the fact that many standard maps of NT times/early Christian history do not include Africa south of Egypt, e.g., Nubia or Ethiopia. Correspondingly, interpreters find abundant theological significance in the conversion of the Ethiopian in Acts 8, but fail to comment on the ethnographic and world-historical significance. But there is no ambiguity or unclarity in classical Greek and Latin sources, or in Luke's narrative. In the ancient Hellenistic-Roman world, an Ethiopian was clearly an African. And Ethiopia or Nubia/Meroë was thought of as situated at the edge of the known world. Thus, when Luke, at the very outset of his narrative, in Acts 1:8, has the risen Jesus announce the grand scheme of mission, that his apostles would be his witnesses "in Jerusalem, in all Judea and Samaria, and to the end of the earth," then has them scatter "throughout Judea and Samaria" in 8:1, and soon thereafter tells of the dramatic conversion of the Ethiopian, the implication is clear. The gospel and the movement had, in the person of the Ethiopian, reached "the end of the earth." Drawing on a wealth of sources from the ancient world, Martin here demonstrates how much broader were the biblical horizons and how much more inclusive was the biblical community than recognized by mainstream ethnocentric biblical studies.

Reprinted from *Semeia* 47 (1989): 105–35, abridged.

THE ETHIOPIAN'S CONVERSION: THEOLOGICAL TRAJECTORIES

The story of the Ethiopian's conversion has received scant attention in twentieth century biblical research. Traditional exegetical studies of Acts 8:26-40 have concentrated on several theological trajectories which echo recurrent Lucan motifs elsewhere in Luke-Acts.

First, the numerous allusions to the action of the Holy Spirit throughout the story (Acts 8:26, 29, 39)[1] recall the Lucan emphasis on the strategic role of the Holy Spirit in preaching and evangelism (Lk. 4:18; 24:44; Acts 1:8; 4:8-10; 7:55; 10:11-12; 13:4-10; 16:6-7).

Second, Philip's preaching to the Ethiopian highlights a second recurrent Lucan theme: the strategic role of the early Christians' witness to the significance of the events of Jesus' life, death, and resurrection (Lk. 1:1-4; 24:48; Acts 1:21-22; 4:33; 10:39-41; 22:14-15).

Third, the response of the Ethiopian to the conversion experience itself, "going home rejoicing," recalls the abundant expressions for "joy" in the Lucan writings (Lk. 1:44; 2:10; 15:4-7; 19:6, 37; 24:41; Acts 2:47; 8:8; 11:18; 16-33).

Chief among the theological motifs and interests in Acts 8:26-40 is a "prophecy-fulfillment" or "proof-from-prophecy" pattern which is acknowledged to be especially characteristic of the Lucan writings.[2] "Prophecy-fulfillment" here means the fulfillment of the Old Testament (promise, prophecy, etc.) in such a way as to establish historical continuity between Israel and the church (Talbert, 92). But in agreement with Talbert's thesis, the definition is broader than this, and includes the fulfillment of prophetic utterances or promises within the New Testament itself, as in prophetic statements uttered by the risen Christ regarding the evangelistic outreach of the church which are fulfilled (94).

For Luke, Isaiah 53:7ff. exemplifies such a prophecy-fulfillment function, and becomes the *locus classicus* for preaching Jesus in Acts 8:26-40. It is in response to the Ethiopian's inquisitive and unrelenting desire to know "about whom the prophet speaketh" that Philip the Evangelist, "beginning with this scripture" launches into his exposition of the "good news of Jesus."[3]

Luke's colorful depiction of Philip's exposition of Isaiah 53 indicates that already within the church there was an understanding of the Suffering Servant passages as fulfilled in Christ (Dodd, 132). Barnabas Lindars has suggested that Isaiah 53:7ff. was used with other Old Testament passages in the early preaching primarily for apologetic purposes, with Luke here drawing upon the stock of apologetic biblical material to illustrate how the mission of the Servant had been achieved in Jesus' death and resurrection. The particular value of Isaiah 53 for the early church is its revelation of a predetermined divine plan that the Messiah should suffer: "Jesus suffered because he is the Christ, and the Christ must suffer"(77).

Luke uses the Old Testament to confirm the fulfillment of God's promise in three additional ways. First, the conversion of the Ethiopian eunuch qua "eunuch" represents the fulfillment of Isaiah 56:3-7, which heralds a day when eunuchs will be accepted into the assembly of the Lord. Isaiah 56:3-7 contains a promise that the old regulation in Deut. 23:1 forbidding the entrance of eunuchs into the assembly of God will be abolished, and anticipates a time of "full class membership" for eunuchs—a move from communal isolation and marginality to communal inclusion and wholeness. For Luke, the conversion of the Ethiopian eunuch represents the realization of this vision. Williams argues that the Ethiopian eunuch's conversion qua "eunuch" is, in fact, the chief reason for its inclusion in the story, for Luke's main purpose is to show that "the Gospel was taken not only to the half-caste Samaritans but even to one who because he was a eunuch could never have belonged to the Old Israel" (118-19).

Second, the Ethiopian's conversion exhibits the fulfillment of the promise of an unconditional and prodigious acceptance of foreigners (*ho allogenēs*) into the community in accordance with Isaiah 56:3-7. The Ethiopian becomes a prototype of the "foreigner" who enjoys unconditional acceptance into the eschatological community. Finally, the conversion of the Ethiopian eunuch demonstrates the fulfillment of the prophecy in Psalm 68:31 that Ethiopia will "stretch out her hands to God."[4]

> Let bronze be brought from Egypt, let Ethiopia hasten
> to stretch out her hands to God.

Appropriately, in Acts 8:26-40, Luke portrays just such an eager reconnoiter in the figure of the Ethiopian treasurer.

THE ETHIOPIAN'S IDENTITY: ITS ETHNOGRAPHIC SIGNIFICANCE

Amidst the provocative mosaic of the theological motifs in Acts 8:26-40, however, the ethnic identity of the Ethiopian eunuch is virtually ignored. And when the ethnic identity of the Ethiopian is admitted explicitly as that of a recognizable black African from ancient Nubia, development of the significance of this data for the Lucan theological perspective is rarely attempted.

A survey of the literature reveals at least three approaches to the Ethiopian's ethnic identity. The first is "uncertainty": "*His ethnic origin is strictly undetermined*" (Gealy, 177-78, *italics mine*).

Dahl especially cautions the reader against concluding that the Ethiopian is black. Further, and most importantly—he concludes that the Ethiopian's nationality is of no consequence:

> What made his conversion to be remembered and told as a legend was neither his African provenance nor his black skin. (*It is quite possible that he was black, but that is never said. . . .*) In the Lucan composition his story has been placed between the evangelization among the Samaritans and the vocation of Paul, preparing for the mission to the Gentiles. Thus we get a picture of a progressive widening of the circle reached by the gospel; *but the question of nationality has no special importance* (Dahl, 1974:62-63, *italics mine*).

In a second and common approach to the Ethiopian's ethnic identity, his place of origin, Nubia, is admitted, but usually with only a cursory discussion of Nubia, and rarely with any explicit identification of Nubians (or "Ethiopians" as they were called in the Common Era) as black-skinned people (e.g., Dupont, 1953a; Haenchen; Foakes-Jackson; Marshall, 1983; Munck; Rackham).

A third approach more clearly describes the ethnic identity of an "Ethiopian" eunuch in the Lucan narrative. Writing as early as 1922, Theodor Zahn described him as "an Ethiopian" from a region bordering on the Egyptian Nile and inhabited by "more or less Negroid peoples" (311).

The glaring lack of concrete descriptive detail regarding the Ethiopian's identity in Acts 8:26-40 is surprising in view of the prodigious classical evidence. The word for Ethiopian, "Aethiops," a derivative of the Greek Aithiops, was the most common generic word denoting a Negroid type in Greco-Roman usage. A summary of Greek and Roman anthropological observations preserved in classical literature identifies Ethiopians as dark-skinned; in fact, as Snowden observes, "skin color was uppermost in the minds of the Greeks and Romans, whether they were describing Ethiopians in the land of their origin or their expatriated congeners in Egypt, Greece, or Italy" (1970:2). Snowden's graphic description of the significance of the Ethiopian's appearance in the Greco-Roman world is worth noting here:

> Blackness and the Ethiopian were . . . in many respects synonymous . . . The Ethiopian's blackness became proverbial, and gave rise to the expression, "to wash an Ethiopian white." . . . *Ethiopians were the yardstick by which antiquity measured colored peoples*. The skin of the Ethiopian was black, in fact, blacker, it was noted, than that of any other people. The Indians whom Alexander visited were said to be blacker than the rest of mankind with the exception of the Ethiopians (1970:2, 5, *italics mine*).

While the distinguishing mark of the Ethiopian was the color of his skin, several other characteristics were persistently applied to Ethiopians: "puffy" or "thick" lips, tightly curled or "wooly" hair, a flat or "broad" nose. In fact, as G.H. Beardsley observes, the extensive appearance of blacks in sixth-century Greek art was directly related to their memorable appearance — their characteristically "wooly" hair and "large everted lips" on vases and other art mediums "leaves no doubt that they served as models for the potter" (11-12).

In fact, one of the greatest witnesses of African migration northward to Egypt, Greece, and Italy is provided by classical art. From the sixth century onward artists have used the black as a model in almost every medium, and "as a favorite in many" (Snowden, 1970:23). Greek and Roman artists exhibited an incomparable and "continuous interest" in the Ethiopian. The popular depiction of the black in Greco-Roman art is corroborated by massive artistic evidence in stone, iron, marble, bronze, terra cotta and plaster. Negro images appeared on jewelry, tombs, shields, coins, pelikes, skypos, askos, lekythos, head-vases, busts, statues, and masks, and represented a wide range of occupational and other sociocultural involvements in Greece and Rome.[5]

Greco-Roman literary evidence for the Ethiopian as a recognizably black African is compelling. Most notable among the earliest numerous allusions to the Ethiopians' appearance is the Homeric description of Eurybates, the herald who attended Odysseus and accompanied him from Ithaca to Troy in the *Odyssey*.

> Furthermore, a herald attended him, a little older than he, and I will tell thee of him too, what manner of man he was. *He was round shouldered, dark of skin, and curly-haired,* and his name was Eurybates; and Odysseus honored him above his other comrades, because he was like-minded with himself[6] (*italics mine*).

The Greek adjective used to describe Eurybates, *melanochroos*, means "black" (Liddell and Scott, 1095). It was in reply to Penelope's request for a description of the comrades accompanying her husband that the disguised Odysseus mentioned Eurybates—and the mention of Eurybates was one of the sure tokens which Penelope recognized as proof of her husband (Snowden, 1979:102).

The Greek historian Herodotus, writing in the fifth century B.C., records numerous impressions of his visit to Africa, and frequently alludes to Ethiopians.[7] His description of the Ethiopians' hair betrays the perennial interest and familiarity with the appearance of Nubians in antiquity:

> ... but they of Libya have of all men *the wooliest hair*[8] (*italics mine*).

The Roman Seneca, writing in the Common Era, proposes that the African sun and heat are responsible for the Ethiopians' skin color:

> First of all, *the burnt color of the people* indicates that Ethiopia is very hot ...[9] (*italics mine*).

In a period when it was believed that the climate, flora, fauna, and topography influenced the appearance of the human inhabitants of a given region, Seneca's assertion would not be construed as unusual.

With our review of some of the massive classical evidence about the Ethiopian's ethnographic identity, the question which must be asked is: What is the significance *for Luke* of the inclusion of a story about a recognizably *black* African official? Since Luke's readers would not have suffered from nebulous illusions about the identity or appearance of Ethiopians, in what way would the inclusion of the story of the conversion of an Ethiopian eunuch *qua* "Ethiopian" eunuch coincide with Luke's general theological concerns (inclusive of the functions cited above under "Theological Trajectories")? We grant that the story may represent the first Gentile conversion in Hellenistic circles—a conversion effected by Philip—and perhaps a "rival" or parallel to the story of the first Gentile conversion effected by Peter (Haenchen, 315). But is it plausible that "the question of nationality has no special importance" for Luke (Dahl,

1974:62-63)? The subject deserves careful reexamination.

The story of a *black* African Gentile from what would be perceived as a "distant nation" to the south of the empire is consistent with the Lucan emphasis on "universalism," a recurrent motif in both Luke and Acts.[10] The declaration that the salvation accomplished in Christ is not ethnocentric, but is available to both Jew and Greek,[11] is already heard at the beginning of the Third Gospel (" 'All flesh' shall see the salvation of God," Lk. 3:6), and with the universal scope of the Christian kerygma given a most forceful and explicit expression at the end of the gospel ("Repentance and forgiveness of sins shall be preached to 'all nations' " Lk. 24:47).

Both Luke and Matthew preserve banquet scene traditions in which the invitation to the eschatological feast is issued to both the original invitees and subsequently, to those "outsiders" in the "thoroughfares and streets" (Mt. 22:9-10), and the "highways and hedges" (Lk. 14:23). We are elsewhere told that those who "sit at table" with Abraham, Isaac and Jacob will come from "east and west" (Mt. 7:8-12 par. Lk. 13:29), but Luke alone here adds "north and south" (cf. Lk. 13:29). Luke's explicit addition is interesting in view of the Ethiopian's provenance, for the Ethiopian's conversion enables the reader to envision proleptically just such an interloper from the "south" in attendance at the eschatological banquet.

Lucan universalism continues in Acts beginning with the proclamation of the mission to the "end of the earth" right at the outset (1:8). The sense of the eventual geographical expansiveness of the proclamation is evident in the Pentecost story (Acts 2), which has in view "Jews from every nation under heaven," including a specific list of nations represented.

The preaching to the Samaritans (Acts 8:4-8) marks yet another advance to the Gentiles, with the Cornelius story representing for Luke the decisive inauguration of the *Heiden Mission* (Acts 10:1-11:18). The Lucan theme of universal salvation and world mission unfolds throughout Acts as the Gospel advances northward from Palestine through Antioch (Acts 9:32-12:24), westward through Asia Minor (12:25-16:5), Europe (Acts 16:6-19:20), and finally to Rome (Acts 19:21-28:31), the "capital" of the Gentile world (Green, 112). Universalism in Luke-Acts underscores the certainty that the mission of Jesus and his church are "united in the plan of God for the salvation of all nations" (Navone, 187). The conversion of an "Ethiopian" eunuch provides a graphic illustration and symbol of the diverse persons who will constitute the Church of the Risen Christ.

In fact, the premise that the Ethiopian represents what Snowden calls "a symbol of the peoples out of whom the Church was destined to grow" (1979:198) has been admitted elsewhere in early Church tradition. Augustine proposes this symbolic function of "Ethiopia" in general in his comments on Psalm 68:31 ("Let bronze be brought from Egypt, let Ethiopia stretch out her hands to God") when he says:

Under the name of Egypt or of Ethiopia he hath signified the faith of all nations . . . he hath signified the nations of the whole world (Schaff, 298).

According to Jean Marie Courtès, the Augustinian interpretation is an example of "a strong bond . . . between the explication of the faith and the Ethiopian theme . . . intended to extend the promise and possibility of salvation to all of mankind [sic]" (30).

Athanasius also finds "Ethiopians" to be appropriate figures for representing the conversion of all nations. In his *Expositio in Psalmos*, he marvels of Psalm 68:31 that "by 'Kushites' God indicates the end of the earth . . . For how Kush ran to the preaching is possible to see from the believing Ethiopian . . . God shows that all the other nations also believe in Christ with their Kings."[12]

THE ETHIOPIAN'S PROVENANCE: ITS GEOGRAPHIC SIGNIFICANCE

By the first century of the Common Era the term "Ethiopia" was used especially of the kingdom of Meroë, the seat of government in Nubia. Located between the 5th and 6th cataracts, Meroë became the capital city of the region in about 540 B.C.E., when the royal family relocated there from Napata. Its strategic location near the Nile River proved advantageous for preserving the generally fertile, cultivable land used for crops and herds, and for facilitating travel for caravans traveling east and west.[13] Torgny Säve-Söderbergh's description of Nubia as the "Corridor of Africa" is no misnomer for this meeting place of cultures between the Mediterranean world and Africa (20).

The geographic significance of the Ethiopian's conversion is generally designated in missiological terms. Philip's missionary activity in Judea and Samaria (which includes the encounter with the Ethiopian) initiates mission to the world, effectively "breaking the bar between Israel and the people outside" (Munck, 8) and thus sets the stage for the great discussion between the Jerusalem church and the mission churches regarding the admission of Gentiles into the Church (Acts 15). The conversion of the Ethiopian is a "stepping-stone" between the conversion of the Samaritans and the Gentiles which illustrates the progress of the mission (Haenchen, 313, 316).

Mentioned less frequently is the significance of the Ethiopian's provenance for Acts 1:8, which many scholars consider to be the "keynote" or "programmatic" focus of the narrative of Acts. Here the Risen Christ declares to his followers:

> But you shall receive power when the Holy Spirit has come upon you, and you shall be my witnesses in Jerusalem and in all Judea and Samaria and to the end of the earth.

I suggest that Acts 1:8c, in particular, which forecasts mission "to the end of the earth" (*eschatou tēs gēs*),[14] finds a symbolic—though partial—fulfillment in Acts 8:26-40 when the converted Ethiopian returns home to "Ethiopia" (Nubia), for in ancient geography "Ethiopia" represented "the end of the earth" to the south in the Greco-Roman world. Proponents of the view that Acts 1:8c is fulfilled in Acts 8:26-40, though few, are explicit in identifying this correspondence. Luke included Acts 8:26-40 "to illustrate the fulfillment of the promise with which Acts begins of witnessing in Judea and Samaria and to the end of the earth" (Cadbury 1955:15), since "to Homer and to Isaiah the Ethiopians doubtless represented a geographical extreme," the Ethiopian "is certainly a representative of the ends of the earth" (1979:66).

> As a result of the expulsion of the "Hellenists" from Jerusalem, the gospel was passed on to Samaria and finally, *in the figure of the Ethiopian on his way home, reached the "end of the earth"* (Hengel, 80, *italics mine*).

The sole study of the correspondence between Acts 1:8c and 8:26-40 effectively challenges the popular thesis that mission to the "end of the earth" is fulfilled solely with Paul's arrival in Rome, the end point of the narrative of Acts (Acts 28:16) (Thornton, 35). With the Ethiopian returning home, the Gospel has "already reached the end of the earth, and this end is Ethiopia" (374). Previous arguments for the correspondence between Acts 1:8c and 8:26-40, however, lack specific documentation and elucidation. Ancient geographical literature in particular and classical literary documents in general provide formidable support for the identification of Ethiopia as the "end of the earth" to the south. Greek and Roman writers identified four major groups of peoples who lived toward the edges of the inhabited world: to the north were the "Scythians," to the south the "Ethiopians," to the east were "Indians," and to the west the "Celts" or "Iberians." It should be remembered that these geographical ideas were based primarily on literary and oral traditions rather than scientific investigations (Thornton, 374).

In primitive Homeric geography the earth was a circular plane surrounded on all sides by "Ocean," a continuous circumfluent stream flowing around the earth. Not a "sea" but a mighty river flowing around the earth in which the sun set and rose, Ocean was the parent of all waters, including rivers, seas and fountains (Bunbury, I:34,76). It was believed that Ethiopia bordered on the southern edge of the stream of Ocean, as attested by the *Iliad*. When we read that Iris is going to the land of the Ethiopians "near the Ocean" its significance is immediately apparent:

> I may not sit, for I must go back unto the streams of Oceanus, unto the land of the Ethiopians, where they are sacrificing hecatombs to the immortals, that I too may share in the sacred feast (Iliad, 23.205-207, Murray, 1960b).

Herodotus, writing in the fifth century B.C., traveled extensively, recording his experiences of the ethnic and geographic diversity of the world as he saw it, and as he heard it from traveler's tales and the experience of explorers. Herodotus described Ethiopia as the most distant country and peoples to the southwest.

> Where the south inclines westward, the part of the world stretching fartherest toward the sunset is Ethiopia; here is great plenty of gold, and

abundance of elephants . . . and the people are the tallest and fairest and longest-lived of all men. *These then are the Libyans* (Herodotus 3.114-15, Godley, *italics mine*).[15]

By the first century of the Common Era the perception of Ethiopia as an "end of the earth" was firmly entrenched. *The Geography of Strabo*, called one of the most important geographical works ever produced by any Greek or Roman writer (and representing the first attempt to condense all geographical knowledge attainable [Kish, 85; Bunbury, II: 209-293]), preserved this perception. Strabo assumed, like geographers before him, that the southern shore of Libya was surrounded by "Ocean," with the southernmost limit of the world extending "3000 stadia below Meroë" (Strabo 1.2.27-28; 2.2.2.). Strabo identified Ethiopia as the southernmost region of the world:

I maintain . . . that in accordance with the opinion of the ancient Greeks — just as they embraced the inhabitants of the known countries of the north under the single designation "Scythians" . . . and just as later, when the inhabitants of the west also were discovered, they were called Celts . . . I maintain, I say, that just so, in accordance with the opinion of the ancient Greeks, *all the countries in the south which lie on Oceanus were called Ethiopia* (Strabo 1.2.27, *italics mine*).

The Ethiopian's geographical provenance, like his ethnic identity, was of particular significance for Luke, and not parenthetical minutiae. It is extremely plausible that when the Lucan community read a story about an "Ethiopian" returning home southward to a region located on the edge of "Ocean," they would have considered that the Gospel had reached the "end of the earth" in that instance as a partial fulfillment of the prophetic and programmatic statement in Acts 1:8c. Thus, the Ethiopian's return home represents not only the extension of the Gospel beyond Israel to the Gentile world — it represents the symbolic (and partial) fulfillment of Acts 1:8c of mission "to the end of the earth." The Ethiopian's geographical provenance uniquely qualifies him to represent this fulfillment.

INTERPRETATION FOR LIBERATION AND "POLITICS OF OMISSION"

We have shown that while elements of the Ethiopian treasurer's "theological" significance in Acts 8:26-40 are readily acceded (e.g., the prophecy-fulfillment function), the significance of his geographical — and especially his ethnic — provenance receives far less attention and explicit analysis. At least three factors are proposed as contributing to this proclivity in the history of the interpretation of the pericope.

First, there is an "internal" phenomenon operative within the ideological framework of the New Testament itself which tends to circumscribe any detailed and expansive attention to Ethiopians. In his provocative study "Racial Ambiguities in the Biblical Narratives," Felder delineates the process by which the sociopolitical realities of the secular framework of the Christian authors in the New Testament led to a marginalization of the darker races. Specifically, the sociopolitical character of Rome as comprising a new and increasingly hegemonic center and symbol of the new center of God's redemptive activity (in contradistinction to Jerusalem) culminated in the perception of Rome as "ultimate destination of the Christian kerygma ... the new focus of the Christian missionary movement" (22). The confession of the Roman centurion in Mark's Gospel, for example, is situated as a major narrative climax in the story.[16] Luke's numerous allusions to "centurions" as positive, pious figures are also well known (Lk. 7:2ff; 23:47; Acts 10:1-11:18; 21:30-32; 22:25-28; 24:23ff; 27:42-44; 28:16). The significance of this increasing focus on Rome (certainly in the period post-70 C.E.) instead of Jerusalem is that "the darker races outside the Roman orbit are circumstantially marginalized by New Testament authors ... sociopolitical realities of the secular framework tend to dilute the New Testament vision of racial inclusiveness and universalism" (22). There is, in short, a decided ideological and geographical shift from the southeastern region of the Mediterranean world to the northwest region.

A second "external" phenomenon which contributes to a general lack of familiarity with "Ethiopians" and their provenance for twentieth-century students of the Bible is the failure of many Bible atlases to include the region south of Palestine and Egypt in its maps and illustrations. Of the useful atlases recommended by Joseph A. Fitzmyer in his excellent reference work, *An Introductory Bibliography for the Study of Scripture*, the majority do not include Meroë (or Nubia) in their maps of the world of the New Testament. An exception is the map "The Roman World at the Birth of Jesus" provided in George E. Wright and Floyd V. Filson's *The Westminster Historical Atlas to the Bible*.[17] Maps which purport to include regions reflective of the expanding evangelistic outreach of the church (such as a map entitled "The Background of the New Testament") should depict those regions to which New Testament narrative texts allude.

Finally, presumptions of the Ethiopian's ethnic identity as "marginally significant" or "inconsequential" for the Lucan theological perspective altogether may be traced to a larger and perennial problem in Western, post-Enlightenment culture wherein the signification and contributions of particular groups of persons have been historically marginalized or ignored. This ideological, psychosocial and cultural marginalization "omission" continues to foster a culturally or ethnically proscribed prism through which the biblical reader and interpreter envision and ascertain which data are "theologically significant" within a biblical text.

One illustration of this tendency to "marginalize" or treat as "inconsequential" the significance of, for example, racial minorities in ancient and modern literature may be seen in the treatment of the "black" or "black African" in antiquity in general. In this regard Snowden correctly calls into question the shocking dearth of documentary studies on Ethiopians in classical antiquity. Snowden observes that while Greeks and Romans were familiar with Ethiopians, modern scholarship has failed to relate archaeological and literary materials in a way which informs and enlarges our understanding of their status and involvements in Greco-Roman society:

> The Greeks and Romans knew a great deal about the physical features of the peoples whom they called Ethiopians. Their writers described the Ethiopian type in considerable detail. From the hands of their artists we have received an even more copious evidence which shows in a vivid manner the racial characteristics of many Ethiopian inhabitants of the Greco-Roman world. *Hence it is surprising that modern scholarship has virtually ignored Greek and Roman anthropological knowledge of the Ethiopian* (1970:1, *italics mine*).

Racial minorities and women in particular have challenged epistemological, analytical and interpretive constructs in modern academic discourse which render them invisible. In recent years, for example, female scholars in every academic discipline have been engaged in the assiduous—but inspiriting—task of recovering and reconstructing women's history. The general exclusion of women as both producers and subjects of knowledge (Spender, 1) and the consequential "mutedness" of women have perpetuated an "invisibility" of women and delegitimated women as subordinates and marginals.

A priori assumptions of the "inconsequential" nature of the Ethiopian's ethnic identity—whether conscious or unconscious, intentional or unintentional—are too often consonant with interpretive formulations which automatically assign a diminished valuation to the ethnographic significance of "blacks" or "black Africans" in general. In his impressive survey of the role of discursive factors in the codification of white supremacist ideals in the pre- and post-Enlightenment age, Cornel West argues that a combination of scientific investigation, Cartesian epistemology (wherein Descartes' emphasis on the primacy of the subject and the preeminence of "representation" became a controlling notion of modern discourse), and classical ideals "produced forms of rationality, scientificity, and objectivity which, though efficacious in the quest for truth and knowledge, prohibited the intelligibility and legitimacy of the idea of black equality in beauty, culture, and intellectual capacity. In fact, to think such an idea was to be deemed irrational, barbaric, or mad" (64). There is no dearth of literature on the subject of how these and other similarly negative ideological formulations have contributed to the invisibility, marginalization and omission of "black" persons in postmodern American literature and culture.[18]

In his important discussion of the role of "ideological suspicion" in the hermeneutical task in biblical interpretation and theology, Juan Luis Segundo observes that our way of experiencing reality leads us to "ideological suspicion" as we approach and interpret biblical texts. Four decisive factors are operative in this epistemic construct. First, one's way of experiencing reality prompts an "ideological suspicion"; second, an individual applies the "ideological suspicion" to the whole ideological superstructure (within the context of our discussion, biblical interpretation or hermeneutics receives particular focus); third, a new way of experiencing theological reality arises which leads to an "exegetical suspicion" that a prevailing interpretation of the Bible "*has not taken important pieces of data into account*"; and fourth, the interpretation of Scripture (the "fountainhead" of our faith) proceeds in new ways allowing the exegete to incorporate the new elements into his or her ideological superstructure (9).

Elisabeth Schüssler Fiorenza's extended analysis of the centrality of a "hermeneutics of suspicion" in feminist biblical interpretation provides a useful heuristic model for ascertaining ways in which a "hermeneutics of suspicion" can be utilized in assessing biblical interpretations wherein ethnographic data (which may illumine dimensions of a biblical writer's theological perspective) have, in fact, been minimized or ignored. A critical point of departure in the methodology of a "feminist hermeneutics of suspicion" is the admission that no interpretation or scholarship is "objective," "intellectually neutral," or "value free," for the exegete always brings his or her own presuppositions, assumptions, and subjectivity to the interpretive process (1984: 98, 118, 132, 137). Schüssler Fiorenza notes: "A feminist hermeneutics of suspicion questions underlying presuppositions, androcentric models, and inarticulated interests of contemporary biblical interpretation" (1984:16). It tests ways, for example, in which contemporary biblical interpretation promotes "linguistic sexism" which "creates the linguistic invisibility and marginality of women, characterizes them in stereotypical roles and images, and trivializes their contributions" (1984:17). Taking as its starting point the assumption that biblical texts are androcentric and serve patriarchal functions, feminist critical interpretation searches for the "lost traditions and visions of liberation" in androcentric biblical texts and interpretations in the same way that the woman in the parable sweeps the whole house in search of her lost coin:

> In order to unearth a "feminist coin" from the biblical tradition, it critically analyzes contemporary scholarly and popular interpretations, the tendencies of the biblical writers and traditioning processes themselves, and the theoretical models underlying contemporary biblical, historical and theological interpretations (1984:16).

The "search" which a feminist hermeneutic of suspicion engenders tests both the original biblical text and contemporary interpretations and translations of the text, thereby clarifying and exposing "hidden" presuppositions, assumptions and convictions operative in historical, critical methodology. Further, it incorporates both a cultural and theological critique (1983:21).

Segundo's and Schüssler Fiorenza's analyses of the role of a "hermeneutic of suspicion" in biblical interpretation are instructive in assessing the issues at stake in the minimalization or omission of the significance of the Ethiopian's ethnographic and geographic provenance in Acts 8:26-40.

Just as Gealy and Dahl's conclusions should trigger "hermeneutical suspicions" regarding the historical treatment of the Ethiopian's ethnic and geographic provenance in biblical research on Acts 8:26-40, so should they prompt a more critical stance toward interpretations of other pericopae which allude to "historically marginalized persons" — including women and "blacks" (Africans)—in the Hebrew Bible and the New Testament. Notions of what constitutes "significant" data continue to be applied selectively to historical sources and data in accordance with the theoretical models or perspectives which order an interpreter's information (Schüssler Fiorenza, 1984:99). When the ethnographic and geographic significance of the Ethiopian eunuch is relegated to the "back heap" of trivial minutiae and literary ornamentation, it is possible to miss the richness and breadth of theological data in biblical interpretation.

It is true that the Ethiopian eunuch was not a twentieth-century African-American male, but C. Eric Lincoln has correctly noted that, in African-American communities at least, the story of a black African convert to Christianity continues to comprise a culturally affirming and empowering tradition. African-Americans, whose experience of, in his words, a "white American Christianity" which has legitimized psychosocial and cultural marginalization in both church and society, are eager and "determined" to reclaim an ancient biblical heritage which helps African-Americans to "reestablish their connection with the faith at its inception" (Lincoln, 24). Lincoln argues that the explicit allusion to the Gospel promise extending to black Africa in Acts 8:26-40 should not be overlooked:

> But as if to underscore the divine intention that black Africa (which first touched the destiny of Israel when Abraham came out of Ur and settled in Egypt, and continued through all the centuries thereafter) should be a direct and unequivocal heir to that promise, after Pentecost, the divine imperative came to the evangelist Philip, directing him toward a rendezvous which made inevitable the inclusion of black Africans among the charter members of the faith ... an African nobleman ... received the good news from his lips, and accepted baptism at his hand (Acts 8:26-39), all of which symbolizes from the beginning the African involvement in the new faith that was to spread throughout the world (24).

If the ongoing process of interpreting biblical traditions is to be in any sense "interpretation for liberation"—that is, interpretation which effects full humanity, empowerment, and justice in church and society under God—interpreters must continue to discern critically ways in which a "politics of omission" may be operative in perpetuating the marginalization and "invisibility" of traditionally marginalized persons, groups, and ideologies in biblical narratives. It is only as we undertake such critical analysis that a potentially liberatory vision of biblical traditions can emerge and function as an empowering force in *all* contemporary communities of faith.

NOTES

1. The phrase "angel of the Lord" appears to be interchangeable with "Spirit of the Lord," denoting the "agency of the divine presence of God" (Bruce, 1984:141, 190). Williams calls both terms "synonyms" for God's acts of self-revelation (119). Haenchen notes that the only other story so distinguished by divine intervention determining the course of events in Acts "at every turn" is the Cornelius story

(315). For other examples of similar divine directives in Acts, cf. Acts 10:19; 13:2; 16:6f.

2. For discussions of this schema in the literature, cf. Lohse, Dupont (1953b), Tiede, Karris (1978), Schubert, Kurz (1976), and Dahl (1980).

3. The phrase "the good news of Jesus" is the rendering of *"euēggelisato"* in the Revised Standard Version of the New Oxford Annotated Bible, which is used throughout this essay unless otherwise indicated (May and Metzger).

4. Psalm 68:31 is but one of many Old Testament citations which refer to Ethiopia. Cf. Esther 1:1; Job 28:19; Isaiah 11:11; 18:1-2; 20:3-5; 37:9; Jer 13:23; 38:7-13; Ezek. 29:10; Amos 9:7; Nahum 3:9. Edward Ullendorf confirms that Ethiopia (Aihiopia) is rendered "Cush" by the LXX, and that it is generally used to refer to the entire Nile Valley south of Egypt including both Nubia and Abyssinia (5).

The Greek and Ethiopic texts of Psalm 68:31 are clear, but the Hebrew contains some textual problems, particularly the sense of *yadayw*. An alternative to the RSV translation cited above has been proposed by Mitchell Dahood and others. Dahood suggests that the sense of *yadayw*, "his hands," seems to connote "the product of his hands, his wares." The translation would then be: "Let Ethiopia bring her possessions to God." A. A. Anderson proposes that this translation would give a reasonable parallel to 68:31a. This sense is preserved by Roland Murphy: "Gifts are to be brought to Yahweh in Jerusalem from the 'nations' . . . This hymn urges 'kingdoms' to acknowledge Yahweh, enthroned in his sanctuary." See Dahood (151), Anderson (498), and Murphy (588).

5. Beardsley notes that the "Negro type" in classical art is so common that a complete list is difficult to amass (x). Her study, *The Negro in Greek and Roman Civilization*, contains illuminating and striking images dating from the fifth century B.C.: cf. Fig. 20, a bronze Ethiopian boy, possibly a musician, p. 98, Hellenistic period; Fig. 21, the conjoined heads in a tricephalic agate, with an Ethiopian woman who may be connected with the ruling family of Meroë, p. 109.

Also useful are the artistic depictions (often in color) found in Frank Snowden, Jr., "Iconographical Evidence on the Black Populations in Greco-Roman Antiquity," *The Image of the Black in Western Art. From the Pharaohs to the Fall of the Roman Empire* (Snowden, 1976b:133-245), and Jehan Desanges, "The Iconography of the Black in Ancient North Africa," *The Images of the Black in Western Art. From the Pharaohs to the Fall of the Roman Empire* (246-68). For other artistic renditions, cf. the work by Mary B. Comstock and Cornelius C. Vermule, *Sculpture in Stone: The Greek, Roman and Etruscan Collections of the Museum of Fine Arts*, Boston, which includes a striking figure entitled: "Negro Boy Seated," either a captive or genre study on an Alexandrian or Corinthian Street, 100 B.C.-100 A.D., Fig. 112; and David Finn and Caroline Houser, *Greek Monumental Bronze Sculpture*, who provide an illustrative depiction of the bronze "Negro Boy Jockey and Horse," ca. 2-3 century B.C., Pompeii.

6. Homer, *Odyssey* 19.244-248. A.T. Murray, trans. (1960a).

7. Herodotus 2.29-32; 3. 17-24; 4.183, 197.

8. Herodotus 7.70.

9. Seneca, *Naturales Questiones* IV A. 218. The *fons et origo* of this ancient anthropological formulation of ethnographic differences in humans was Hippocrates. See his *On Airs, Waters, Places* (Snowden, 1979:172).

10. Cf. John Navone, *Themes of St. Luke* (Navone); Jacob Jervell, "The Divided

People of God: The Restoration of Israel and the Salvation of the Gentiles" (Jervell); S.G. Wilson, *The Gentiles and the Gentile Mission in Luke-Acts* (Wilson); Robert F. O'Toole, *The Unity of Luke's Theology: An Analysis of Luke-Acts* (O'Toole, 1984).

11. Although Luke does preserve Israel's prerogative — salvation is to the Jew first, and also to the Greek (Acts 13:46).

12. I am indebted to Courtès for this citation in the Patristic literature (Courtès, 22). For Athanasius' translation, see Robert W. Thompson (108).

13. The history of ancient Nubia is divided into three major periods: the Napatan (751-542 B.C.) when Napata was the seal of government, the Meroitic (542 B.C.-339/350 A.D.), when Meroë became the seat of government, and the X-Group period (339/350-550 A.D.). For a helpful introductory survey of the history of ancient Nubia cf.: Margaret Shinnie, *Ancient African Kingdoms* (Shinnie); and works by William Y. Adams: *Nubia: Corridor to Africa* (Adams, 1977); "Post-Pharaonic Nubia in the Light of Archaeology, I," (Adams, 1964); and "Post-Pharaonic Nubia in the Light of Archaeology, II," (Adams, 1965).

14. There is widespread agreement among New Testament exegetes that Luke derived Acts 1:8c from Isaiah 49:6. For a thorough discussion of the use of the phrase in the LXX see W.C. Van Unnik.

15. Herodotus recognized a division of the world into three continents: Europe, Asia, and Libya (Africa). Egypt belonged to Asia, and Libya was surrounded by the sea on all sides except where it joined to Asia. "Arabia" was the most distant country to the southeast, Ethiopia the most distant to the southwest. Cf. Herodotus 3.107.

16. Mk. 15:39, 44, 45. Felder notes: "It is no coincidence that Mark, the earliest composer of the Passion Narrative, goes to such great lengths to show that the confession of the Roman centurion . . . brings his whole gospel to a climax" (22).

17. Plate XIII. Cf. L.H. Grollenberg (32); Pauline Lemaire and P. Donato Baldi, Map XII. But Yohanan Aharoni and Michael Avi-Yonah do include an illustration demarcating the region near Gaza where Philip would have encountered the Ethiopian. See Map 241. We are not engaging in historical reconstruction here, arguing that the story comes to us as objective history; nonetheless, we note that Nubia's significance in the Lucan theological framework in Acts 8:26-40 is such that students of the Bible should be familiar with the geographical designations mentioned in the pericope.

18. The literature of this subject is too massive to reproduce here, but see, for example, Wilmore and Cone; C.E. Lincoln; and for a helpful overview of the impact of racial formulations on American culture, see Winthrop Jordan.

BIBLIOGRAPHY

Adams, William Y.
  1964   "Post-Pharaonic Nubia in the Light of Archaeology, I." *JEA* 50:102-20.
  1965   "Post-Pharaonic Nubia in the Light of Archaeology, II." *JEA* 51:160-78.
  1977   *Nubia: Corridor to Africa*. Princeton University Press.
Aharoni, Yohanan and Michael Avi-Yonah.
  1968   *The Macmillan Bible Atlas*. New York: Macmillan.

Beardsley, G.H.
1929   *The Negro in Greek and Roman Civilization*. Baltimore: Johns Hopkins.

Bruce F. F.
1976   *The Book of Acts*. NICNT. Grand Rapids: Eerdmans.
1984   *The Acts of the Apostles: The Greek Text with Introduction and Commentary*. Grand Rapids: Eerdmans.

Bunbury, E.H.
1959   *History of Ancient Geography Among the Greeks and Romans from Earliest Ages Till the Fall of the Roman Empire*. 2 vols. New York: Dover Publications. First edition. New York: Century, 1932.

Cadbury, H.J.
1955   *The Book of Acts in History*. New York: Harper and Brothers.
1979   "The Hellenists." Pp. 59-74 in *The Beginnings of Christianity*, vol. 6. Ed. F.J. Foakes-Jackson and Kirsopp Lake. First edition. London: Macmillan, 1920-1933.

Courtès, Jean Marie.
1979   "The Theme of 'Ethiopia' and 'Ethiopians' in Patristic Literature." Pp. 9-32 in *The Images of the Black in Western Art: From the Early Christian Church to the Age of Discovery*. Vol. 2, Pt. 1. Ed. Ladislas Bugner. New York: William Morrow.

Dahl, Nils A.
1974   "Nations in the New Testament." Pp. 54-68 in *New Testament Christianity for Africa and the World: Essays in Honor of Harry Sawyer*. Ed. Mark E. Glaswell and Edward Fashole-Luke. London: SPCK.
1980   "The Story of Abraham in Luke-Acts." Pp. 139-158 in *Studies in Luke-Acts*. Ed. Leander Keck and J. Louis Martyn. Philadelphia: Fortress.

Dodd, C.H.
1952   *According to the Scriptures: The Substructure of New Testament Theology*. London: Nisbet.

Dupont, Jacques.
1953a   *Les Actes Des Apôtres*. Paris: Les Editions Du Cerf.
1953b   "L'utilization apologetique de l'ancien Testament dans les discours des Acts." *ETL* 29:289-327.

Felder, Cain.
1982   "Racial Ambiguities in the Biblical Narratives." Pp. 17-24 in *The Church and Racism*. Concilium 151. Ed. Gregory Baum and John Coleman. New York: Seabury.

Fitzmyer, Joseph A.
1981   *An Introductory Bibliography for the Study of Scripture*. Subsidia Biblica 3. Revised edition. Rome: Biblical Institute Press.

Foakes-Jackson, F.J.
1931   *The Acts of the Apostles*. New York: Harper and Brothers.

Gealy, F.D.
1962   "Ethiopian Eunuch." Pp. 177-178 in IDB, vol. 1.

Godley, A.D. trans.
1928   *Herodotus*. 4 vols. LCL.

Green, Michael.
1970   *Evangelism in the Early Church*. Grand Rapids: Eerdmans.

Grollenberg, L.H.
1960   *Atlas to the Bible. A Commentary.* Trans. and ed. Joyce M.H. Reid and H.H. Rowley. New York: Thomas Nelson.

Haenchen, Ernest.
1971   *The Acts of the Apostles: A Commentary.* Philadelphia: Westminster.

Hengel, Martin.
1979   *Acts and the History of Earliest Christianity.* Philadelphia: Fortress.

Jervell, Jacob.
1972   "The Divided People of God: The Restoration of Israel and the Salvation of the Gentiles." Pp. 41-74 in *Luke and the People of God: A New Look at Luke-Acts.* Minneapolis: Augsburg.

Jones, Horace Leonard, trans.
1932   *The Geography of Strabo.* LCL. 8 vols.

Jordan, Winthrop.
1968   *White Over Black: American Attitudes Toward the Negro, 1550-1812.* New York: W.W. Norton.

Karris, Robert J.
1978   *Invitation to Acts: A Commentary on the Acts of the Apostles with Complete Text from the Jerusalem Bible.* New York: Image Books.

Kish, George, ed.
1978   *A Sourcebook in Ancient Geography.* Cambridge: Harvard University Press.

Kurz, William B.
1976   "The Function of Christological Proof from Prophecy for Luke and Justin." Ph.D. Dissertation, Yale University.

Lemaire, Pauline and P. Donato Baldi.
1960   *Atlas Biblique. Histoire and géographie de la Bible.* Louvain: Editions Du Mont César.

Liddell, H.G., and R. Scott.
1961   *A Greek-English Lexicon: A New Edition Revised and Augmented Throughout.* Ed. Henry H.S. Jones with the assistance of Robert McKenzie. Oxford: At the Clarendon Press.

Lincoln, C. Eric.
1984   *Race, Religion, and the Continuing American Dilemma.* New York: Hill and Wang.

Lindars, Barnabas.
1961   *New Testament Apologetic: The Doctrinal Significance of the Old Testament Quotations.* Philadelphia: Westminster.

Lohse, E.
1954   "Lukas als Theologe der Heilsgeschichte." *EvT* 14:256-275.

Marshall, I.H.
1983   *The Acts of the Apostles.* TynNTC. Grand Rapids: Eerdmans.

Martin, Clarice J.
1985   "The Function of Acts 8:26-40 Within the Narrative Structure of the Book of Acts: The Significance of the Eunuch's Provenance for Acts 1:8c." Ph.D. Dissertation. Duke University.

May, H.G. and B.M. Metzger.
1977   *The Oxford Annotated Bible with the Apocrypha.* Revised Standard Version: Containing the Second Edition of the New Testament and an

Expanded Edition of the Apocrypha. New York/London: Oxford University.

Munck, Johannes.
1981 *The Acts of the Apostles*. AB. New York: Doubleday.

Murray, A.T., trans.
1960a *The Odyssey*. LCL. 2 vols.
1960b *The Iliad*. LCL. 2 vols.

Navone, John.
1978 *Themes of St. Luke*. Rome: Gregorian University Press.

O'Toole, Robert F.
1983 "Philip and the Ethiopian Eunuch (Acts VIII 25-40)." JSNT 17:25-34.
1984 *The Unity of Luke's Theology: An Analysis of Luke-Acts*. Good News Studies 9. Wilmington, DE: Michael Glazier.

Rackham, R.B.
1939 *The Acts of the Apostles: An Exposition*. London: Methuen.

Säve-Söderbergh, Torgny.
1987 *Temples and Tombs of Ancient Nubia*. New York: Thames and Hudson.

Schaff, Philip, ed.
1956 *Saint Augustine: Expositions on the Book of Psalms. A Select Library of the Nicene and Post-Nicene Fathers of the Christian Church*. Vol. 8. Grand Rapids: Eerdmans.

Schubert, Paul.
1957 "The Structure and Significance of Luke 24." Pp. 165-186 in *Neutestamentliche Studien für Rudolf Bultmann*. Ed. W. Eltester. Berlin: Töpelman.

Schüssler Fiorenza, Elisabeth.
1983 *In Memory of Her: A Feminist Reconstruction of Christian Origins*. New York: Crossroad.
1984 *Bread Not Stone: The Challenge of Feminist Biblical Interpretation*. Boston: Beacon.

Segundo, Juan Luis.
1976 *The Liberation of Theology*. Trans. John Drury. Maryknoll: Orbis.

Shinnie, Margaret.
1965 *Ancient African Kingdoms*. London: Edward Arnold.

Snowden, Frank M., Jr.
1970 *Blacks in Antiquity: Ethiopians in the Greco-Roman Experience*. Cambridge: Harvard University Press.
1976a "Ethiopians in the Greco-Roman World." Pp. 11-36 in *The African Diaspora: Interpretive Essays*. Ed. Martin L. Kilson and Robert I. Rottberg. Cambridge: Harvard University Press.
1976b "Iconographical Evidence on the Black Populations in Greco-Roman Antiquity." Pp. 133–245 in *The Image of the Black in Western Art. From the Pharaohs to the Fall of the Roman Empire*. Vol 1. Ed. Ladislas Bugner. New York: William Morrow.

Spender, Dale, ed.
1981 *Men's Studies Modified: The Impact of Feminism in the Academic Disciplines*. The Athene Series. New York: Pergamon.

Talbert, Charles H.
1984 "Promise and Fulfillment in Lucan Theology." Pp. 91-103, in *Luke-*

Acts: New Perspectives from the Society of Biblical Literature Seminar. Ed. C. H. Talbert. New York: Crossroad.

Thompson, Robert, trans.
1977 *Athanasius Syriaca: Expositio in Psalmos*. Corpus Scriptorum Christianorum Orientalium. Vol. 387. Louvain: Secretariat du Corpussco.

Thornton, T.C.G.
1977 "To the end of the earth: Acts 1:8." *ET* 89:374-75.

Tiede, D.L.
1980 *Prophecy and History in Luke-Acts*. Philadelphia: Fortress.

Ullendorf, Edward.
1968 *Ethiopia and the Bible*. London: Oxford University Press.

Van Unnik, W.C.
1973 "Der Ausdruck "ΕΩΣ ' ΕΣΧΑΤΟΥ ΤΗΣ ΓΗΣ' (Apostelgeschichte 1 8) Und Sein Alttestamentlicher Hintergrund." Pp. 386-401 in *Sparsa Collecta. The Collected Essays of W.C. Van Unnik*. Pt. I. Evangelia-Paulina-Acta. *NTSup* 29.

West, Cornel.
1982 *Prophesy Deliverance! An Afro-American Revolutionary Christianity*. Philadelphia: Westminster.

Williams, C.S.C.
1964 *A Commentary on the Acts of the Apostles*. London: Adam and Charles Black.

Wilmore, Gayraud S. and James Cone.
1979 *Black Theology: A Documentary History, 1966-1979*. Maryknoll, N.Y.: Orbis.

Wilson, S.G.
1973 *The Gentiles and the Gentile Mission in Luke-Acts*. SNTSM 23.

Wright, George E. and Floyd Vivian Filson, eds.
1956 *The Westminster Historical Atlas to the Bible*. Revised Edition. Philadelphia: Westminster.

Zahn, Theodor.
1922 *Die Apostelgeschichte des Lucas: Erste Hälfte kap 1-12*. Leipzig: A. Deichertsche Vorlagsbuchhandlung.

31

AMOS JONES, JR.

Paul's Message of Freedom

African Americans and women have long had serious reservations about Paul's letters because the apostle has for centuries been cited in support of slavery and the subordination of women, as Renita Weems points out in chapter 3. Indeed, the dominant stream of Eurocentric scholarly interpretation of Paul, heavily influenced by certain Protestant theological traditions, was at pains to emphasize that the apostle's mission and theology posed no challenge whatever to the dominant sociopolitical order of the Roman empire. Even the proclamation in Galatians 3:28 that now there was "neither slave nor free, . . . neither male nor female . . . in Christ," it was explained, meant only equality before God or in the nascent church, and no alteration in the concrete social status of the slave. While Paul's letters pose several severe problems for current liberationist concerns, the apolitical or conservative Paul may well be a product of traditional exegesis. In a sharp challenge to established Eurocentric exegesis of 1 Corinthians 7:20–24, Amos Jones argues that Paul was in fact proclaiming the freedom of slaves who joined the alternative society that was taking form as the intended result of his mission.

Freedom in America is not as free as it appears. Even those who seem to be free are ensnared by a peculiar kind of bondage. Bondage transcends

---

Reprinted from Amos Jones, Jr., *Paul's Message of Freedom: What Does It Mean to the Black Church?* (Valley Forge: Judson Press, 1984), 28–63, abridged.

national and continental boundaries. The blatant reality of this is demonstrated in South Africa, which employs the incarcerating system of apartheid; the Moslem world, which excludes women; India, which employs the caste system; Ireland and its religious oppression. Freedom is evasive; it is an illusion. There still stands before the children of bondage the pressing assignment to claim their freedom.

The exhortation for persons to claim their freedom is preponderant in the New Testament. Especially is it profoundly and provocatively set forth in the writings of the apostle Paul. Nestled within the corpus of his first letter to the Corinthians, as if it were an exploding bombshell, is the exhortation to the slave to claim freedom in Jesus Christ. First Corinthians 7:20-24 is the locus of this provocative and challenging passage, and it is the one with which we will shortly deal.

What was Paul's concern with freedom and slavery? And why was he so obsessed with the notion of freedom in Christ? Just a few years before Paul wrote First Corinthians, Caesar Augustus had instituted his Golden Age, the *pax romana*. For the mere investment of their allegiance to Caesar and the Roman state, every citizen and subject was guaranteed freedom. Each was guaranteed protection by the Roman army and the conveniences of the Roman state. So why was there a need for Paul to talk about freedom? Because the Roman guaranteed freedom was not as free as it appeared. In fact, there was a grave and insidious presence of human bondage in that society. Freedom à la the Roman Empire was, in a very real sense, bondage — bondage to the *kaiser kultus* (Caesar worship), social custom, racial and religious prejudice, and lust for luxury. Slavery was one of the sickening realities that stood in the midst of Caesar Augustus' Golden Age. It was a reality with which Paul had to deal. And deal with it he did.

CORINTH: A CITY OF ILLUSIVE FREEDOM

Corinth was a city in which the illusion of freedom was very present. The city was totally destroyed in 146 B.C. by the Roman general Mummius but was rebuilt by Julius Caesar in 44 B.C. as a Roman colony. Later, Emperor Augustus made it the capital of the great Roman province of Achaea. The geographical layout of Corinth made it one of the prominent trade centers of its time. It lay between the Aegean and the Adriatic Seas. Merchandise from distant lands came into its ports. The city also was a center of industry and banking. As a new and bustling city, it drew hundreds of thousands of tourists, and thousands settled there to remake it their home. Romans, Jews, and freedmen went there to live. Also hundreds of thousands of slaves were carried there aboard the many slave ships that landed in its ports. It is understandable that the problem of slavery was crucial in the Corinthian letter, for there was bondage of a very real sort in this thriving industrial port city.

MODERN MIXED REACTIONS ABOUT PAULINE FREEDOM

Bondage in its many varieties is the sickening reality that stands in the midst of the myth of freedom in America. Therefore, it would seem valuable for us to reexamine the early church's most articulate writer and his attitude toward bondage and the remedy of freedom in Christ as it is discussed in the First Letter of Paul to the Corinthians. Slavery in New Testament times could very well be a paradigm of the many and varied kinds of bondage faced by many in our society, especially blacks and other minorities.

However, one is ever conscious of the risks that are taken when the thesis is posited that Paul the apostle is an advocate for freedom. Women and minorities have had serious problems with Paul. Especially has this been true of blacks. Albert B. Cleage, Jr., insisted that Paul's deemphasis of the nation concept, which was promulgated and propagated by the black nation Israel and Jesus the black messiah, and Paul's emphasis of individualism provided the theological matrix for white preachers to justify the enslavement of the native sons and daughters of Africa.[1] James H. Cone thought Paul to be so vulnerable on the subject of slavery that he advocated that the apostle to the Gentiles be avoided at all costs; after all, he stated, Paul did acquiesce to slavery by instructing slaves to be obedient to their masters.[2]

What black theologians, black people, women, and others have failed to realize, it seems, is that we are dealing with a Paul who has been misrepresented, corrupted, perverted, and misused by the white church of the pre-Civil War era in America and, to a large degree, by the white church of today. The white church took from the deutero-Pauline writings (i.e., those letters not in the corpus: Ephesians, Colossians, and the Pastoral Epistles) the quasi-proslavery statement "Slaves, be obedient to your masters" (or its variant) and gave religious sanction and political legitimation to the peculiar institution of slavery in the name of Paul, although he neither wrote nor spoke those words. Whether knowingly or unknowingly, white preachers and the white church took those statements relating to slavery—albeit, taken completely out of the context in which they appear in these deutero-Pauline writings—and proceeded to pour holy water on the process of incarcerating the bodies and souls of black folk. They made it religiously right to dehumanize, ostracize, castrate, and kill those pitiable Ebony Children of Africa in order to feed their philosophy of racial superiority and sate their hunger for economic opulence.

So what we have today is a Paul who is trapped. On the one hand he is misrepresented, perverted, corrupted, and misused by the white church to perpetuate institutional racism. On the other hand black theologians castigate and disparage Paul for his seeming proslavery position. Women dismiss him for his seeming position of consigning the female to silence in the church. Whites have yet to admit their sin of willful misinterpretation. Blacks and women have yet to liberate the liberator. They have yet to wrestle with the man to find in him strong themes of liberation; they simply think of him as an unfortunate incident in the course of theological history, an opprobrious odium that hangs about the neck of the church. I think, however, that Paul offers something viable and dynamic in his understanding of Christian freedom, something powerful enough to destroy the idea and institution of slavery and every vestige of bondage. In their place he offers freedom in Christ in all of its dimensions.

In order to try to prove such a hypothesis, I will proceed by seriously considering the statement Paul makes regarding slavery and freedom, which is found in 1 Corinthians 7:20-24. It is my hope that from inquiring into the passage at hand I will be able to present a perspective on Paul yet to be seen by most black theologians, many women, and minorities or admitted by many white theologians as it relates to Paul on slavery and freedom—a perspective that would show Paul to be a rather militant opponent of slavery and an aggressive advocate of freedom.

There is a need to say a word about the general problem Paul faced in the Corinthian church, a church that he had established prior to writing this letter. The occasion for the First Letter of Paul to the Corinthians seems to be described in 1 Corinthians 1:10-11 (see also 1 Corinthians 11:18); there were dissensions and divisions. The problem, which seems to have been conveyed to Paul in several letters (cf. 1 Corinthians 1:11), may have been created by Gnostic elements within the Corinthian church. These were people who held that *gnōsis* (knowledge) was the highest of values and who claimed possession of the Spirit (*pneumatikoi*); from their belief that they possessed *gnōsis* and the Spirit, the Gnostics concluded that they were free to yield their bodies, albeit immorally, to anything they wished without reprisal. They engaged in intercourse with prostitutes (1 Corinthians 6:13-20), took part in sacrificing offerings to idols (1 Corinthians 8:1ff.; 10:23ff.), and even lived immorally with relatives (cf. 1 Corinthians 5:1ff.). Their possession of the Spirit led them to deny the future resurrection (1 Corinthians 15). The Jesus of history was to be cursed while a spiritual Christ was the only significant thing for them (cf. 1 Corinthians 12:1ff.); the cross was foolishness (1 Corinthians 1:18ff.). The Gnostics at Corinth demonstrated their spiritual prowess by speaking in tongues (1 Corinthians 14:1ff.), an act which proved their superiority over those who did not possess that kind of Spirit. In the final analysis, the problem at Corinth was that of runaway enthusiasm by Gnostic elements within the church; the problem was a misuse of and an abdication of Christian freedom.

It seems reasonable to conclude that 1 Corinthians 7:20-24 is a definite unit of material that is intimately connected with what goes before it and what comes after it. It serves the definite purpose of providing insight into the question of Paul's understanding of slavery and Christian freedom. If this be the case, we can proceed to answer this serious question. The result of our efforts should give us a more lucid picture of Paul's understanding of slavery in the context of Christian freedom. If positive data can be extracted from the material at hand, that data can be used to exonerate Paul from the charge of being pro-slavery; but more than this, we will use that positive data to relate to the present condition of black and oppressed peoples in America in an attempt to provide a viable theological alternative for liberation.

A HISTORY OF MISUNDERSTANDING AND MISINTERPRETATION

The problem with Paul and his writings started in the New Testament itself (cf. 2 Peter 3:15–16). The deutero-Pauline epistles of Ephesians and Colossians attempted to systematize Paul's theology (maybe the writers were Pauline students) but failed to grasp his understanding of slavery and freedom in 1 Corinthians 7:20-24. They understood Paul to be saying "Slaves, be obedient to those who are your earthly masters, with fear and trembling, in singleness of heart, as to Christ ..." (Ephesians 6:5; cf. Colossians 3:22). In the Pastoral Epistles' attempt to systematize Pauline theology and ecclesiology (the Pastorals were written sometime during the first half of the second century C.E.), there also was a failure to grasp what the apostle to the Gentiles was saying in 1 Corinthians 7:20-24. They, too, understood Paul to be saying "Let all who are under the yoke of slavery regard their masters as worthy of all honor, so that the name of God and the teaching may not be defamed ..." (1 Timothy 6:1-2; see also Titus 2:9-10). It is also important to note that the place of women in the church in the Pastoral Epistles is far removed from that of Paul's understanding (cf. 1 Timothy 2:9-12, where women are relegated to silence in the church, vis-à-vis 1 Corinthians 11:5a, where Paul makes a case for women prophets). The catholic epistle of First Peter reflects a similar failure to grasp Paul's understanding of slavery and Christian freedom (cf. 1 Peter 2:18ff.).

In the early history of Christian thought, the Apologists and Apostolic Fathers adopted a position on slavery that was far removed from the Pauline position and more akin to the deutero-Pauline, Pastoral, and catholic epistles schools. Clement of Alexandria, Ignatius, *The Didache*, and St. Augustine all religiously subscribed to the notion that slaves were divinely obligated to give obedience to their masters.[3] These ecclesiastical luminaries held that even if a slave held an office in the church of which his or her master was a part and the slave, while in the church, held authority over his or her master, once they were outside of the holy community, their relationship reverted back to that of master-slave. In such an arrangement, the slave was to be totally obedient to the master.

Although we run the risk of overgeneralizing and becoming utterly simplistic, it could be said that up to the time of the Reformation the church did not see the need to deal with, let alone grasp, Paul's understanding of slavery. Even when slavery was dealt with by the Reformers, the position of the deutero-Pauline epistles, the Pastorals, and the catholic epistles was amplified. John Calvin is a good example here.[4] The failure of the church to sort out Paul's genuine letters from those attributed to him caused the proslavery position of the deutero-Pauline epistles, the Pastorals, and the catholic epistles to become mixed with and attributed to be the same as the position of Paul, although Paul's position would be diametrically opposed to the subsequent positions. The result of this was the adoption of a formal position by the church that slavery enjoyed the sanction of Christianity and that becoming Christian did not alter the social status of the slave. A good example of this is the response that was given by the Anglican Bishop of London [in 1727] to the inquiry from American slaveholders as to the social status of the slave once he or she was baptized:

> To which it may be very truly reply'd, That Christianity, and the embracing of the Gospel, does not make the least Alteration in Civil Property, or in

any of the Duties which belong to Civil Relations; but in all these Respects, it continues persons just in the same State as it found them. The Freedom which Christianity gives, is a Freedom from the Bondage of Sin and Satan, and from the Dominion of Mens Lusts and Passions and inordinate Desires; but as to their *outward* Condition, whatever that was before, whether bond or free, their being baptized, and becoming Christians, makes no manner of Change in it.[5]

The deutero-Pauline position on slavery (namely that New Testament literature attributed to him, i.e., 2 Thessalonians, Ephesians, Colossians, and the Pastorals of 1 and 2 Timothy and Titus) became the biblical proof texts for white preachers and slaveholders in their interest of sanctioning slavery and holding black human flesh in perpetual thralldom.[6]

Modern biblical scholarship did little to grasp Paul's true understanding of slavery and Christian freedom and, therefore, get us back on track. For example, at the turn of the twentieth century, Albert Schweitzer could not see Paul's position on slavery in any other light than that of encouraging the slave to remain in servitude. In his interpretation of 1 Corinthians 7:20-24 (especially verse 21), Schweitzer asserts that "if ... a slave became a believer he should not, ... if he were afterwards offered freedom, accept it."[7]

There is still among more recent New Testament scholars the failure to grasp Paul's understanding of slavery in the light of Christian freedom. There is a strong penchant among many New Testament scholars today to adopt the more conservative (and maybe racist?) view of 1 Corinthians 7:20-24. For example, Günther Bornkamm, insists that

> ... the gospel [does not] call slaves and freemen to seek to change their existing social status, for "in Christ" the slave *has already become* a "freedman" of the Lord's, and the free man (in the social sense) a "slave of Christ's," both alike his property, body and soul (1 Cor. 7:17-24).[8]

It may not be fair to say that the history of failure to grasp Paul's understanding of slavery in light of Christian freedom on the part of the Christian church and its scholars is a racist proclivity (i.e., bent on keeping in subjection and even destroying a certain class or race of people), but it would be fair to say that there has not been a mad rush on the part of white theologians to the opinion that, for Paul, Jesus meant freedom for the slave in the church as well as in society. It has been because of this negatively skewed interpretation of Paul that the black church and black theologians have ignored the Apostle to the Gentiles and, in fact, have held him as an object of scorn. Therefore, the immediate task for black theology, and all theology, is to try to get at Paul's actual position on slavery. This will be our task in the pages to follow.

A CLOSE LOOK AT A CONTROVERSIAL PASSAGE

First Corinthians 7:20-24 is the locus of our concern. Paul's brief but powerful statement on slavery is introduced in verse 20: "Every one should remain in the state in which he was called." This verse harks back to verse 17. There Paul instructs each Corinthian to ". . . lead the life which the Lord has assigned to him, and in which God has called him." In elucidating the meaning of this for the Jewish and Gentile constituents of the Corinthian church, Paul says if the Jewish member of the congregation was already circumcised when he was called, he should not attempt to remove the marks of circumcision. Likewise, the Gentile member of the congregation who has never been circumcised should not seek to do so. It follows for Paul that neither circumcision nor uncircumcision counts for anything in the congregation of God's people; the only thing that counts is keeping God's commandments (cf. verse 19). The position Paul takes here is understandable, for it is altogether rational that a woman who is added to the church should not try to become a man, or a black man attempt to become a white man or a white man attempt to become a black man, and so on. Paul is correct; there is no need for one to change identity once he or she enters the church.

Paul takes a similar position on marriage (1 Corinthians 7:1-16, 25-40). He does not have any command from the Lord on the subject (1 Corinthians 7:25), but in his opinion, the person who is bound to a wife should not seek to get free; likewise, the person who is free of a wife should not seek to get married. There is no need to alter one's status as it relates to marriage because, in Paul's opinion, "the form of this world is passing away" (1 Corinthians 7:31).

If we were to extrapolate Paul's instructions to the circumcised and uncircumcised and the married and unmarried to what he says about slaves in verses 20 to 24, we would be forced to conclude that if people were slaves when they were called, they should not seek freedom afterwards. The same would apply to persons already free. But the question becomes, should the meaning of verses 17 to 19, as it relates to circumcision and uncircumcision, and the meaning of verse 27, as it relates to marriage, be applied to verses 20 to 24 and the question of slavery? Does Paul instruct persons who were slaves at their call to remain slaves after the call? This is the crucial question.

The answer to the question cannot be obtained by means of facile fundamentalism, i.e., literal interpretation without historical examination. We must raise some basic literary and historical questions and seek answers to those questions in order to answer the central question. We might begin by raising the question, What does Paul mean when he says, "Every one should remain in the state in which he was called" (v. 20)?

Hans Conzelmann sees the answer to the question as already given in verse 17. He thinks there is no need for one to change social status in order to obtain salvation. In the eschatological community, i.e., the church, social status and differences are obliterated.[9] Thus, in the eschatological community, the slave is equal with constituents and free (i.e., the internal self, the soul is already in heaven) while his or her external social condition remains the same. "Remaining in one's own particular status is, like remaining in the world, not a concession to the facts, but a logical consequence of genuine theology."[10] C. K. Barrett takes a similar position: "A man is not called (so far as this passage is concerned) to a new occupation; his old occupation is given new significance."[11]

One would concede that there is nothing a person can do before the fact of salvation that can enhance his or her possibility of attaining that blessed state of eschatological existence; thus, Conzelmann is right to say that salvation is *sola gratia*, by grace alone. But this seems not to be the answer to the question. Paul seems not to be dealing with the question of whether or not a slave must remain a slave or seek freedom in order to be saved; he is dealing with the question of slavery itself. Moreover, Barrett's suggestion that the slave's erstwhile occupation becomes glorified after the fact of salvation seems to be far from the point of verse 20 but certainly in conformity with racially biased interpretations of Paul and slavery.

The burden of Conzelmann's and Barrett's failure to grasp the intent of verse 20 rests on their emphasis of *en tautē menetō*, i.e., "in this let him abide." But to accuse Conzelmann and Barrett of blurred perception that results in unbearable conclusions elicits the obvious question of where the emphasis in verse 20 should be placed. Godet places emphasis in verse 20 on *tē klēsei*, "the call." "The word *klēsis*, call, vocation, . . . is applied here, as elsewhere, to the call to salvation."[12] Furthermore, "the idea of the call must be taken to embrace all the external circumstances which furnish the occasion and determine the manner of it."[13] Thus, the primal theological factor in verse 20 that opens up Paul's understanding of slavery is the "call." The call bears with it the determination of the slaves' external (social) circumstance as well as their internal (spiritual) circumstance. In virtually every case, Paul uses "call," as a technical term in the theological sense, viz., the call from God. Hence it seems justifiable to conclude that in verse 20 of the text, slaves are enjoined by Paul to remain in the calling received from God to which or in which they have been called.

I conclude that it is erroneous to translate *klēsis* as "state" (Revised Standard Version [RSV]), "station in life," "position," or "vocation" and permit that translation to stand.[14] If this were permitted, an obvious interpretation of verse 20 would be that Paul instructs slaves to remain in slavery even after they receive the call. However, the appearance of *tē klēsei* and *hē eklēthē* in verse 20 suggests that the verse should be translated thus: "each should remain in the state of the calling in which he was called" (see King James [KJV], Phillips, and Godet). If such a translation stands, the interpretation of verse 20 emerges as something different; it would take into account the change in religious and social status that comes as a result of the call and not assume the continuation of one's former social status though he or she has received the call. Therefore — contrary to those who, whether deliberately or inadvertently so, translate this verse to mean that slaves were to remain in their social condition of servitude even after they received the call — Paul seems to be instructing slaves to recognize the spiritual and social metamorphosis that comes about as a result of their call.

Our investigation of the importance of "call," in Paul's theology already opens up possibilities for seeing him in our text as an advocate of freedom and a liberator of slaves. But what was the specific state of existence to which slaves were called and in which they were to remain, according to Paul? The most prominent term that Paul uses to describe slaves' specific existence after the call and an existence in which they must remain is *ekklesia*, i.e., the church.

Ekklesia bore with it some very important meanings and possibly theological, social, and political ramifications for Paul.

THE DERIVATION AND MEANING OF *EKKLESIA*

Ekklesia had its origin in Greek culture and politics. There the term was descriptive of the assembly of citizens that was called together in the *polis* (city) to deal with political matters. The term also could mean a general gathering of people to deal with any matter that arose in the *polis*.[15] The Septuagint used *ekklesia* almost one hundred times as the translation of the Hebrew term *qahal* (congregation). The term described any gathering of people that had been assembled for any of many different reasons. Most significant among these gatherings in the Septuagint was the assembling of Israel before God to receive the Law (cf. Deuteronomy 4:10; 9:10; 10:4; and 18:16).[16] One could surmise that this gathering of Israel before God was significant politically as well as theologically. It was this Septuagint theological tradition, i.e., Israel as a people assembled before God or the people of God, that the early church (the Jerusalem church) and Hellenistic Christianity inherited.[17] Subsequently, by the time Paul adopted the term *ekklesia*, it had accumulated a rich tradition of meanings. On the one hand, its secular meaning was an assembly of citizens in the Greek *polis* that had gathered to deal with political matters; and on the other hand, its theological meaning was the assembly of Israel before God or, simply, the people of God.[18]

Just what was Paul's interpretation of the *ekklesia* into which slaves were called and in which they were to remain? What was his conceptualization of its locus in the world? What was his understanding of its worldly nexus? What, if any, were the political and social ramifications of its existence in the Corinthian society in which it found itself?

The *ekklesia* that has been baptized into Jesus Christ now has been raised to walk in the newness of eschatological freedom — such an existence has been described by Albert Schweitzer as the "already-not-yet" (cf. Romans 6:1-2). The locus of the *ekklesia* in the world is any place where people have been called together by God through Jesus Christ. At times, individual *ekklesiai* are referred to specifically by the geographical area in which they are located, e.g., "To the church of God which is at Corinth" (1 Corinthians 1:2; cf. 1 Thessalonians 1:1). Wherever located, individually or collectively, unity is maintained as the "body of Christ" (cf. Romans 12:4-5ff.). Also, members of the body of Christ are referred to as "brothers," *adelphoi,* who are members of the "brotherhood," *tou adelphou* (1 Corinthians 6:5-6).

The Separation of Ekklesia and the World

Bultmann suggests that in the *ekklesia* there was "a *consciousness of separateness and delimitation from the world.*"[19] He says further, "This separateness is first of all, of course, a self-exclusion from *non-Christian cults of every sort.* This is seldom mentioned in the text because it was taken for granted."[20]

Nowhere does Paul speak more about the separation of the *ekklesia* from the world than in his two letters to the Corinthians.

In the sixth chapter of the first letter, the Corinthians are caustically castigated for going before pagan courts with matters that should have been settled within the *ekklesia*. Paul chastens them because they dare go before an unrighteous judge in pagan courts rather than before the saints of the *ekklesia* to settle their disputes (1 Corinthians 6:1). In 1 Corinthians 10:20, Paul enjoins the Corinthians not to be partners with demons. Individual and collective members of the *ekklesia* are considered by Paul to be the *naos theou*, "temple of God," and are not to corrupt their bodies or spirits with vanity (e.g., chapters 5 and 6) or idolatry (e.g., chapters 8 and 10). The point of this complete separation from the world is made more poignantly in 2 Corinthians 6:14-18.[21]

Bultmann's observation that the *ekklesia* bore a "consciousness of separation and delimitation from the world" has opened up an even wider panorama of possibilities as it relates to liberation for Paul. The *ekklesia* was for Paul a self-contained entity: it was not to have religious intercourse with idolatry or idolatrous people; it was to have nothing to do with unbelievers; it was not to have social intercourse with the world; it was not to conform to the traditions of the world (Romans 12:2) for the form of this world was passing away (1 Corinthians 7:29-31); its citizenship was not in Corinth or the Roman Empire but "in the heavens" (Philippians 3:20); political institutions had no jurisdiction over it (i.e., the Roman Empire and the Corinthian municipal government), although there were times when its worldly engagements violated political conventions (for example, Paul's escape from the governor of Damascus in 2 Corinthians 11:32-33 had political overtones. It could be conjectured that his fight with the beasts at Ephesus was a battle with Roman soldiers, again reflecting political overtones. If Luke's account in Acts 17 bears any historical veracity, it details a most severe violation of political law by Paul. Acts 17:7 says of Paul and Silas, "they are all acting against the decrees of Caesar, saying that there is another king, Jesus"). Thus the *ekklesia*, the New Testament people of God, was called out of the world by God through Jesus Christ, called to be saints (1 Corinthians 1:2), sanctified, consecrated (set aside) to the worship of God and working God's purpose in the world (1 Corinthians 1:2 and Philippians 2:12-13).

The Ekklesia as an Underground Movement

In the final analysis, what we have in Paul's understanding of *ekklesia* is the concept of a religious secret society, an underground movement, that which was more popularly known in Roman culture as *collegia*. There were many *collegia* in the Roman Empire, although few of them had legal sanction from the Roman government.[22] As to their composition, *collegia* were something of a trade guild, a religious brotherhood, or a local association.[23] They were headed by a religious master.[24] Numbers of *collegia* began to increase as slaves and freedmen sought membership.[25] *Collegia* became the locus of ferment for freedom for slaves and freedmen; they often carried out the function of a mob or gang with military training, staging revolts and insurrections in an attempt to secure freedom for slaves and freedmen.[26] In 56 B.C., a provision was made for a law against membership in *collegia* in the *Lex lulia*.[27]

Such was the *ekklesia*. It was an underground movement. It was an illegal entity within the Roman Empire.[28] During the time of Nero (ca. 54-68 A.D.), Tacitus described Christians and Christianity as "the pernicious superstition" and "disease."[29] Eventually, the *ekklesia* came under attack and suffered flagrant persecution because of its theological tenets that amounted to serious aberrations from conventional Roman religion and posed a threat to the common political good of the Empire.[30]

It was into such an entity that slaves were called by God through Jesus Christ and it was in this calling where they were to remain, according to Paul. They were called in the *ekklesia* of freedom or *eleutheria* (see Galatians 3:28; 5:1, 13; 2 Corinthians 3:17; 1 Corinthians 9:1; 4:3-4; 2:15). For the slaves, there was no longer to be intercourse between the *ekklesia* into which they had been called and the world from which they had been called; more precisely, the slaves' membership in the *ekklesia* guaranteed their freedom from their erstwhile state of servitude and therefore delivered them from the requirement of returning to their master and slavery. (Such a conclusion raises serious questions regarding the interpretation of Philemon; Paul is charged by black theologians with flagrantly sending Onesimus back to his master. This question will be dealt with in more detail later.) If this is good reasoning, then we seem to have a clearer view and a more intelligible understanding of what verse 20 in the text meant for Paul. Our investigation seems to steer us away from an erroneous and racist interpretation of the verse, i.e., that of conventional white theology and the majority of New Testament translations of the verse that convey the notion that Paul is exhorting slaves to remain in their state of servitude even after they receive the call. Our investigation seems to disclose something altogether different. What is more, the foundation that we have laid as a result of our inquiry provides sounder footing on which a building of better understanding for what follows can be constructed. We have laid the foundation for showing Paul to be a theologian and preacher of liberation, in fact, the leader of an underground movement within an oppressive society, viz., the *ekklesia* within the Roman society and the Corinthian world. Now we must complete the structure.

PAUL'S RHETORICAL QUESTION TO SLAVES

"Were you a *slave* when called?" [*italics mine*] is the RSV's translation of *doulos eklēthēs* in verse 21. It is significant that the RSV translates *doulos* as "slave" because Edgar J. Goodspeed has noted, "slavery is so disagreeable a subject that it has been almost obliterated from the English New Testament."[31] An excellent example is the King James Version of the Bible, the version that dominated the English Bible-reading world and continues to be *the* Bible for many black people. The KJV never uses the word "slave" as the translation for *doulos*; its translation for *doulos* is "servant." In the KJV Paul's question in verse 21 reads, "Art thou called being a servant?" It is significant that the KJV, written at a time when slave traffic and bartering in cargoes of ebony flesh were beginning to flourish, mitigated the heinous force of such a sordid enterprise by rendering *doulos* "servant" instead of "slave." One is not sure whether this was done because the subject of slavery was so disagreeable, as Goodspeed suggests, or because it was a way of playing down its seriousness and importance. The fact is that by means of translation, the flagrance of slavery was played down by the KJV Bible. It is also interesting to note that only in a most recent supplementary edition of the *Interpreter's Dictionary of the Bible* does there appear an article on slavery during New Testament times, viz., Greek and Roman slavery that provided the blueprint for the form of slavery utilized by America to enslave black people.[32]

Now as for Paul's rhetorical question, "Were you a slave when called?" Barrett and Conzelmann fail to grasp the import and impact of it. Robertson and Plummer ignore it altogether.[33] The point seems to be that just as questions had been raised with Paul as to matters of conduct within the *ekklesia* (cf. 1 Corinthians 5:11; 7:1), there had been questions raised with him about slavery.[34] Of the question itself, we are not certain, for it is not stated. However, it is doubtlessly clear that there was grave concern within the sector of slaves who now had become members in the *ekklesia*. What was that concern? It could not have been concern for admittance into the congregation in the slaves' struggle for freedom, for the slaves to whom Paul was addressing himself were already called into the *ekklesia*. However (without presupposing the meaning of verses 22 to 24), possibly there was concern on the part of the slaves as to their security in the church. It is unlikely that the slaves would become homesick for the slavemaster and wish to return once the exciting wine of freedom in the *ekklesia* had been tasted; but how could the slaves keep the slavemaster from coming to them? How could they avoid being forcibly dragged back into that dehumanizing existence of servitude in Corinth? If these are some of the possible problems that lay behind Paul's rhetorical question, we can suppose that the slaves of Corinth were suffering serious anxiety and psychological trauma. It would be an unsettling thought to have to return to slavery: slavery in Greco-Roman culture was most flagrant.

Slavery's Degradation—What Paul Had to Address

Slavery, as it was practiced in the Roman Empire during Paul's era, was adequately defined some time before Caesar Augustus's Golden Age by Greek philosophers. Slaves were not to be a prominent part of the ideal state. Youths were to fear slavery more than death and were not to represent slaves or perform the offices of slaves.[35] Some three hundred and fifty years before Paul appeared in history, Aristotle posited the place of slaves in society as being part of the master's household, the master's possession, chattel property, his instrument of action. For Aristotle, society was neatly divided into two categories, the rulers and the ruled: "For that some should rule and others be ruled is a thing not only necessary, but expedient; from the hour of their birth, some are marked out for subjection, others for rule."[36]

From the philosophical theory of slavery, according to Aristotle's scheme, came its *praxis* in the republican era of the Roman Empire. The venality of slavery is reflected in the life of Cato the Elder. Cato, who had a penchant for luxury, as was the case of many Romans in his day, bought a large number of slaves for the sole purpose of profit.[37] For Cato, slaves were to be treated as animals and some were to be kept in chains.[38] It was his belief that slaves had to be either at work or asleep, at work in order to bring him profit, asleep to keep them docile.[39]

Slavery in the emerging Roman Empire became more vicious and venal. Quest for luxury led many Roman families to acquire and breed massive numbers of slaves. During the reign of Caesar Augustus, some slave owners had as many as four thousand slaves.[40] During the reign of Emperor Nero, the practice of Roman families accumulating slaves to insure luxurious living was probably at its highest level.[41] Although slaves facilitated luxury for Romans, they still were considered to be less than human. In the Roman Empire, slaves were designated as *res*, "a thing," *mancipium*, "chattel," and *res mortales*, "a mortal object to be bought or sold as property."[42] In Juvenal's *Satires* the Roman attitude toward slavery, that slaves were not human, is reflected:

> "Crucify that slave!" "But what has he done to deserve it? Who has witnessed against him? Who has informed on him? Listen—No delay's ever too long in the death of a human being." "A slave is a human being? You fool! All right, he's done nothing. This is my wish, my command; my desire is good enough reason."[43]

No reason was ever needed to kill a slave; a whim, a wish, this was all that was needed. He could be poisoned.[44] He could be crucified[45] or tortured.[46] Slaves were not permitted legally to marry,[47] and if they had families, the families could be torn apart at will[48] and members given away as presents.[49] It must have been a thoroughly traumatic experience for slaves to think of the possibility of having to return to this form of brutal life after having been called into the *ekklesia* of freedom.[50]

The freedman was probably no less anxious about his freedom. He certainly must have been aware that according to Roman law, he was obligated to show *obsequium* (respect), to perform *operae* (render service), and even give *munera* (gifts) to the erstwhile master.[51] Thus it was these kinds of prodigious problems that Paul was confronting when he addressed himself to the concerns of slaves and freedmen that had obviously been conveyed to him.

Paul's Answer to His Own Question

Paul's response to his rhetorical question follows in the remaining part of verse 21: *mē soi meletō*, "never mind" (RSV, Moffatt), "Don't let that worry you" (Phillips), "Care not for it" (Godet), or "Let not that trouble you" (Barrett). Is Paul being facetious? Was this response a reflection of his indifference to slavery?[52] Or was this response Paul's way of mitigating the slaves' anxiety and alleviating their fear of being reenslaved or of falling back into the power of their patron?

Certainly Paul was not being facetious; only a few times did he resort to comedy and sarcasm, e.g., the times he berated the *pneumatikoi*, "spiritual men" of the Corinthian congregation (cf. 1 Corinthians 4:6-13). It would seem correct to say that slavery was too serious for Paul to deal with it in lightness and levity. It was so awesome in its degradation of humanity that he could not ignore or be indifferent to it.[53]

The middle and ruling classes of the Roman Empire may have been indifferent to slavery, but not all were indifferent. The fact that flourishing *collegia* of slaves and freedmen were present in the Roman Empire, staging revolts for freedom and against the system of slavery, is indicative that the matter was not treated indifferently by all. The slave revolts of 61 C.E., during Nero's reign, and 100 C.E., during Trajan's reign, are reminders that there was disturbing discomfort with the system of slavery in those days. Most of all, the *ekklesia* did not treat slavery indifferently or ignore it. *Mē soi meletō* was not Paul's way of treating slavery indifferently; it was his way of comforting the slaves,[54] of relieving their anxiety and removing their trauma.

A Choice of Two Contrary Translations

This cannot rightly be understood aside from what follows in the verse. Paul continues: "But if indeed you are able to become free *mallon chrēsai*." The translation of this phrase is difficult.[55] But the difficulty of Paul's instructions to slaves at this point seems not to be dependent on unraveling the difficulty of grammatical construction.[56] Obviously, something must be added to *mallon chrēsai* "avail yourself of the opportunity," so that it might be understood what Paul is saying at this point. Conzelmann suggests the alternatives are (1) *tē douleia*, "slavery," and (2) *tē eleutheria*, "freedom." It seems logical that these are the only two alternatives. However, Conzelmann concludes that because the matter at hand is that of comfort for the slaves, *te douleia*, "slavery," is the only logical addition.[57] Barrett insists that *tē douleia*, "slavery," is the only logical alternative, in agreement with Conzelmann. He sees Paul's statement, "but even though you should be able to become free" (Barrett's translation), to be a reference to seeking emancipation according to Roman law. Thus, it is Barrett's conclusion that Paul is suggesting to slaves, who might be faced with the possibility of obtaining emancipation, to "put up rather with your present status"; more precisely, be content as a slave.[58]

But is *tē douleia*, "slavery," that which should be added to *mallon chrēsai*, as Conzelmann and Barrett suggest? One means of answering the question is to look at Conzelmann's and Barrett's conclusions in the light of what Paul would have to say about those conclusions. Conzelmann concludes that Paul would insist on slaves being content with servitude. Because of the function of eschatology in Paul's theology, according to Conzelmann, Paul would see civil freedom as a civil affair, an affair that was of no value in the church.[59]

The reasoning here is not logical; if civil freedom is a civil affair, as Conzelmann has said, what does Paul mean when he says, "For freedom Christ has set us free . . ." (Galatians 5:1)? Was not "freedom" an ecclesiastical and social (or civil) matter for Paul? Did not "Jesus" mean "freedom" in the social (or civil) as well as ecclesiastical sense (cf. 2 Corinthians 3:17)? Further, if civil affairs had no value in the church, why would Paul recommend *tē douleia*, "slavery," to those who were inquiring about their condition? If these slaves had tasted the eschatological freedom of the *ekklesia*, would Paul recommend that they continue in their social and civil servitude, making daily visits to their master and paying deference? If Paul were to suggest such, it would amount to double-talk in the most grandiose fashion. He had already said in verse 20 that all persons (slaves included) were to remain in the situation they were in when they were called by God, a calling that beckoned people to come out of the Corinthian world and into the *ekklesia*. It was without question that slaves were called out of the Corinthian world of sin into the *ekklesia* of righteousness; there was to be no passage back and forth between the latter and the former because the former no longer had jurisdiction over the latter.

In Romans 6, Paul addressed himself to the radical change or existence that comes about as a result of putting on Christ by baptism (cf. Galatians 3:27). Symbolically, the initiate who enters into the *ekklesia* dies with Christ in baptism (Romans 6:1-4) and rises to walk in a new life (cf. 6:4). The initiate's death is to sin; the initiate's resurrection is to righteousness.

In Romans 6:20-23, Paul says:

> When you were slaves of sin, you were free in regard to righteousness. But then what return did you get from the things of which you are now ashamed? The end of those things is death. But now that you have been set free from sin and have become slaves of God, the return you get is sanctification and its end, eternal life. For the wages of sin is death, but the free gift of God is eternal life in Christ Jesus our Lord.

If we interpreted this passage metaphorically, the following conclusion could be drawn: Earthly slavery for Paul was sin (Paul defined sin as anything that does not proceed from faith [cf. Romans 14:23b]. Certainly slavery did not proceed from faith). The result of slavery was death; slaves had no rights of their own; they were not their own; they belonged to their *dominus,* their master; they were dead to themselves. On the other hand, when slaves were baptized into the *ekklesia*, they were freed from sin (or slavery) and became slaves of God, sanctified or set aside for God's purpose, with the assurance of the eschatological reward of eternal life. The point of this is that *tē douleia*, "slavery," was not a continuing obligation for slaves once they had been called by God into the *ekklesia*. Thus the notion posited by Conzelmann that because of the function of eschatology in Paul's theology, slaves should choose "slavery" falls flat on its face.

Barrett's justification for choosing *tē douleia* as the alternative for *mallon chrēsai* is tenuous at best and confusing altogether. He never tells us why he thinks Paul would have the slave "put up rather with your present status." As he rushes to verse 22, we are told that the freedom that Christ gives the slave is freedom from "bondage to sin and death, and to the evil powers of this age."

There is no alteration in the slave's social status after the call.[60] In effect, slaves live in two worlds; on the one hand, they are a member of the *ekklesia*; on the other hand, they continue as slaves in the world. The slaves return to their master, in keeping with their obligation, to become totally subject to him as their *dominus*, lord, and master. They must participate in the family worship of images and celestial beings and hold the emperor to be divine. Then, when the church meeting is held, the slaves return to the congregation to worship Jesus the Savior of their souls, who only has fit them for heaven.

Ludicrous! Paul would have none of this fork-tongued religion. In the eschatological *ekklesia*, slaves now belong to God entirely (Romans 6:22); although "there are many 'gods' and many 'lords' " (1 Corinthians 8:5), for slaves in the eschatological *ekklesia*, "there is one God, the Father, from whom are all things and for whom we exist, and one Lord, Jesus Christ, through whom are all things and through whom we exist" (1 Corinthians 8:6). Barrett seems to fail to grasp in Paul's theology the inconsistency of being a part of the *ekklesia* while at the same time remaining in the world. Although for two different reasons, both Conzelmann and Barrett agree that, in Paul's theology, the slave could be both slave and Christian at the same time.

Of course, this has been the typical racist interpretation of Paul's understanding of the question of slavery and Christian freedom.[61] With what we have already seen in this discussion, the meaning of *klēsis*, the importance of the *ekklesia*, and the function of eschatology in Paul's theology, it seems reasonable to say that such conclusions about his understanding of slavery and Christian freedom are absurd.

It becomes obvious now that the meaning of verse 21 cannot be obtained on the basis of grammar or personal prejudices. C. F. D. Moule seems to be correct when he says it is not only a matter of grammar that causes clearer visions to come for the translation and interpretation of verse 21, it is also a matter of context.[62] Moule suggests that *mallon chrēsai* should be understood in the light of *tē eleutheria*, "freedom." Therefore, he suggests that the phrases should be translated to mean "but if you can gain your freedom, choose to use (the opportunity to do so)."[63]

If we were to take this statement in the context in which it stands, we would take it to mean that Paul is reminding the slaves of the freedom they have at their disposal as a result of the call they had received from God to become a part of the eschatological *ekklesia*; thus, they are to make use of that freedom.[64] The slaves had been called into the community of freedom; it is in this community that they were to remain (7:20).

An All-Encompassing Freedom

What is this freedom that is to be enjoyed by the slave in the church into which he or she has been called? The word Paul uses for "freedom," *eleutheria*, is the same as that which is used by Aristotle and Plato in their discussion of freedom in the Greek society or *polis*. For Aristotle and Plato, "freedom" meant "to be at one's own disposal, to be independent of others." However, such freedom was experienced only in the context of the state (*polis*) and was guaranteed only under the aegis of the law (*nomos*).[65] It is interesting that Paul makes use of the same term for freedom as Aristotle and Plato. However, contemporary theologians wish to allow the term for Paul to mean freedom only from sin, the Law, and death and not freedom in the social or political sense.[66] This seems to shield both the cryptic and candid political meaning of the term for Paul and his theology. Those slaves and others who became Christians at Corinth must have known this political meaning of freedom (*eleutheria*) when Paul used it.

It is even more interesting what Paul did with the term *eleutheria*. Although he used the same term as Aristotle and Plato when they spoke of political freedom in the state and under the law, his use of the term meant the freedom that was guaranteed to slaves and everyone united with the church and was given by Christ: "For freedom Christ has set us free . . ." (Galatians 5:1). It is freedom to which the slaves and everyone else were called (Galatians 5:13). The freedom that is promised to slaves was that which was promised to the citizen of the Greek city-state and to the citizen in the Roman Empire, but it was free from the encumbrance of political restraints of the city-state and the Roman Empire and the burden of Roman (and Jewish) law; it is freedom in Christ (the meaning of which we shall shortly discuss). Paul himself enjoyed this freedom (1 Corinthians 9:1). It was a freedom that exempted him from the judgment of any human court (1 Corinthians 4:3). Moreover, for the assembled congregation, freedom in Christ meant freedom anywhere and everywhere, for "where the Spirit of the Lord is, there is freedom" (2 Corinthians 3:17). So the Christian, whether former slave, man or woman, white or black, Jew or Gentile, was free wherever he or she went. So this is the freedom that is offered in the church, the *ekklesia*, the free community.

Verse 22 is explosive. It destroys any pseudo-interpretations that may have been drawn on what has been said before now. It is a commentary on verses 20 and 21: "For he who was called in the Lord as a slave is a freedman of the Lord. Likewise he who was free when called is a slave of Christ." Biblical translations of this verse generally concur with each other. (See KJV, *New English Bible*, Phillips, Moffatt, *The Jerusalem Bible, The Amplified New Testament*; see also, the nuance in the translations of *The Living Bible* and the *Good News Bible*.)

Conzelmann's interpretation of verse 22 is determined by his understanding of Pauline eschatology: the slave is free from sin.[67] In violation of all reason, Barrett argues that the slave's call into the *ekklesia* brings about no change in his or her social status but does bring about a change in spiritual status: "The slave who becomes a Christian, though he retains his social status, has been freed from bondage to sin and death, and to the evil powers of this age. . . ."[68] Godet's interpretation of this verse seems to be a transgression of what he already has said. Previously, Godet understood Paul's concern in verses 20 and 21 to be with the slave's external condition. But here he says, "The sentence of emancipation was pronounced by the Lord; by it He delivers this spiritual slave from the power and condemnation of sin; thenceforth this freedman belongs to Him as His servant."[69]

The reasoning here is inconsistent; the slave's deliverance is no longer linked with his external condition but with sin. We are not told what "sin" means. Thus, if we are dependent on the interpretations of Conzelmann, Barrett, and Godet for our understanding of what Paul is saying in verse 22, our conclusion would be that the slave's call into the *ekklesia* only assures freedom from the power of sin (whatever that means) and fits the soul for heaven. But is this really what Paul is saying? From the content of verse 22, the answer seems to be no.

The term *gar* seems to indicate that what follows is an elucidation on the point made in verse 21, i.e., make use of the freedom granted by the call into the *ekklesia*. Thus the slave who has been called in the Lord becomes the Lord's "freedman," *apeleutheros*. Walter Bauer[70] and Heinrich Schlier[71] spiritualize the meaning of *apeleutheros*, "freedman." They seem to see no connection, socially or politically, between the slave's former civil status and the new status in the *ekklesia*, viz., as the Lord's freedman. To be sure, Paul seems to be saying that a radical transition indeed has taken place, a transition that breaks the slave away from all social and political obligations. F. Lyall seems to be closer to the point of 1 Corinthians 7:22. He states:

> The point Paul is making is clearly the fundamental equality and worth of the individual believer. The slave Christian is a *freedman*, a full human being yet not detached from his patron. Christ has freed him and will perform the duties of a patron toward him, summed up shortly in caring for him. The freedman owes reciprocal duties to Christ, *obsequium, operae* and *munera* in their fullest extent. The free Christian is to consider that he is the slave of Christ, that he owns nothing and is subject to the direction of his owner, yet knowing that his owner will look after his welfare.[72]

If we can assume that Lyall's assessment of the meaning of 1 Corinthians 7:22 is plausible, we can conclude that upon the call, slaves are extricated from their social and political servile condition and immediately become the possessions of Jesus Christ. Unlike the former condition of the slaves (but similar to that of Roman freedmen), the former slaves owe respect, works, and gifts entirely to Jesus the Liberator.

The situation is similar as it relates to free persons (free Roman citizens) who are called by the Lord. The free persons become the slaves *in toto* of the Lord. Roman citizenship is given up (or the concern for that citizenship) in favor of the citizenship guaranteed to all members of the eschatological *ekklesia* (cf. Philippians 3:20). Pagan worship is renounced, e.g., worship of the emperor as divine (the *kaiser kultus*), and the multiplicity of gods in the Roman pantheon. The free persons are now totally slaves of Christ.

It seems that what is being said in verse 22 by Paul is that liberation is a matter of social importance (contrary to Conzelmann, Barrett, and possibly Godet) as well as spiritual significance. Nowhere is this interpretation of verse 22 seen more clearly than in Paul's position on the question of slavery in his letter to Philemon. It may appear suicidal to turn to Philemon for corroborative evidence for Paul's antislavery position in 1 Corinthians 7:20-24; many black theologians believe Paul was terribly wrong for sending Onesimus the slave back to his master, Philemon. But is this a legitimate criticism of the contents of Paul's letter to Philemon? A brief analysis should prove otherwise.

Philemon Concurs with Corinthians

From the information provided in the letter, Philemon seems to have been a member of the *ekklesia*; he is referred to by Paul as a "beloved fellow worker"; the *ekklesia* met in his house (Philemon, v. 2). Paul addresses Philemon as "my brother" (v. 7).[73] He declines the use of apostolic authority as a basis for his directive to Philemon (v. 8) but places his appeal in the context of love ("for love's sake," v. 9).[74] Thus the foundation is laid; the message to be heard by Philemon is that the community of believers, *hē ekklesia*, is comprised of *adelphoi*, "brothers," who relate to each other as equals (cf. 1 Corinthians 6:5, 8).

Paul uses the term for "brother" some one hundred and thirty times in his writings; his understanding of the term he learned from Judaism, viz., that Christians are "physical brothers" in the strict sense and "spiritual brothers" in the more general sense.[75] Regardless of the previous state of individuals, once they are converted by the Christ and added to the church, they are called to treat each other as brothers (and sisters) (cf. Acts 9:17).

The prevailing ethic within the Christian community of brothers is "love," *agapē* (cf. 2 Corinthians 5:14). It is a God-like, all-giving love that is to prevail in the church. This kind of love places one at the service of a brother or sister (cf. Galatians 5:13).[76] This is precisely what Paul is saying that Philemon is to do for Onesimus.

Now Paul assaults the central problem. His aim is to inform Philemon in no uncertain language that there is neither master nor slave in the *ekklesia*. Onesimus, who has become a convert to the faith as a result of Paul's preaching, is to be accepted now as a member of the brotherhood. Paul informs Philemon that he is sending Onesimus back to him "no longer as a slave but more than a slave, as a beloved brother, especially to me but how much more to you, both in the flesh and in the Lord" (v. 16). As a result of his call, Onesimus is now a brother with Philemon, both physically and spiritually. As one who has been called in the Lord, Onesimus no longer belongs to Philemon but belongs entirely to the Lord as his freedman.

In a most insightful essay on the social ethics in Paul's letter to Philemon, Theo Preiss says:

> If Paul had wished to reinstate Onesimus in a social order which must not be changed, if he had juxtaposed life in Christ to an order of creation, and love to civil justice, he would have written something like, my dear Philemon, in the Lord, you are brothers and one; in the life of the world you remain each in his place socially. Above all Paul would have respected the master's right of ownership over his slave. In actual fact Paul does no

such thing: fraternity, unity in Christ, seizes upon the relation of slave and master, shatters it and fulfills it upon quite another plane. Onesimus will be considered not merely as an equal, another member of the Church, he will be a member of Philemon's family, a full brother. Thus there remains no margin of paternalism, what we have is a total fraternity.[77]

Preiss seems to have captured the full force of Paul's intention. He understands Paul to be instructing Philemon to accept Onesimus on a fraternal level, as a Christian brother, both in the spiritual and physical (social) sense.

This discussion does at least three things: (1) it negates the erroneous conclusion by black theologians (because of the misrepresentation of Paul by white theologians) that the letter to Philemon represents Paul at his proslavery best; (2) it points up Paul's consistency in his concept of Christian freedom (e.g., the harmony between Philemon and Galatians 3:28); and (3) it negates the conclusion of conventional white New Testament scholarship that Paul's understanding of freedom for the slave was spiritual and internal, a matter of freedom from sin. It confirms the fact that the slave who was called in the Lord is liberated from civil and social servitude and becomes the Lord's freedman.

A FINAL WORD ABOUT RESISTANCE

Paul seems to presuppose possible misunderstanding of what he has already said as it relates to slaves and Christian freedom. He proceeds to drop his final bombshell that, on the one hand, clears the air for the inquiring slaves as to the security of their newfound freedom in the *ekklesia* and, on the other hand, provides a challenge for them to defend their freedom at all costs. Verse 23 reads: "You were bought with a price; do not become slaves of men."

The focus in this verse, as far as conventional theologians are concerned, is on *timēs ēgorasthēte*, "you were bought with a price." Barrett considers this to be a reference back to verse 21b where, he thinks, Paul instructs slaves to remain in their servitude. He thinks this phrase could be an echo of concern for Christian slaves who were seeking to sell themselves back into slavery.[78] The problem with this conclusion is that there is neither a direct nor indirect allusion from Paul regarding self-sale of freed slaves back into slavery. Further, self-sale of former slaves back into slavery seemed to be a rarity at best in the Roman Empire.[79] Conzelmann's comments on *timēs ēgorasthēte* are devoted to refuting Deissmann's theory that there is similarity between the position conveyed here by Paul and the pagan practice of slaves being liberated by being sold to the gods.[80] Godet's comments on verse 23 are confusing and his intention escapes me.[81]

Contrary to the interests of Barrett and to Conzelmann's and Godet's uncertainty, it would seem plausible to argue that 1 Corinthians 7:23a is a resonant reminder to the slaves that Jesus purchased their freedom on the cross. Not to remember this basic fact of liberation would cause a breach in the marching phalanx of Christian soldiers; it would empty the cross of its power (cf. 1 Corinthians 1:17). Paul's fear was that if former slave owners and men stealers were permitted to enter the *ekklesia* and seize their own or other former slaves, what would the world think of the power of Jesus' death on the cross to claim and sustain the freedom of slaves? Paul's concern seems to parallel that of Moses when he shouted in the wilderness to Yahweh, "Now if thou dost kill this people as one man, then the nations who have heard thy fame will say, 'Because the LORD was not able to bring this people into the land which he swore to give to them, therefore he has slain them in the wilderness' " (Numbers 14:15-16). If the slaves failed to remember that their liberation was claimed by the death and resurrection of Jesus and were returned, of their own volition or involuntarily, to slavery, the world would consider that death and resurrection to be of no effect. They would say of this Jesus, the Jew who was hanged on an ignoble gibbet, "He was able to bring the slaves out of the bondage of slavery but was not able to deliver them into the Promised Land of freedom." Paul was concerned that the cross not be emptied of its power, for the kingdom of God was to be known for its power (cf. 1 Corinthians 4:20).

Therefore, Paul's emphatic exhortation to the slave is "Do not become slaves of men." He does not say, "Do not become slaves of sin [*hamartia*]"; nor does he say, "Do not become slaves of another brother [*adelphos*]"; for these would be inconsistent with the principles of the *ekklesia*. He emphatically says, "Do not become slaves of men [*anthrōpōn*]" — any men; more precisely, "Do not allow slave masters, former slave masters, men stealers, or any man to make you a slave once you have gained your freedom in Jesus who now has become your Lord." Essentially, Paul is exhorting the slaves to claim their freedom in Jesus Christ. The emphatic tone of *mē ginesthe*, "do not become," bears the thought of resistance, resistance to any forceful attempt to reenslave a former slave. This seems not to be an illogical rationalization if we see Paul himself as an example *par excellence* for the slave.

Paul's life in Christ was one of incessant attempts to claim his freedom, of perpetual resistance and nonconformity against the norms and conventions of this world (cf. Romans 12:2). His mind-set was that of radical freedom; he was such a spiritual man that he could judge all things, but he was to be judged by no man (cf. 1 Corinthians 2:15). He counted it insignificant to be judged by any human court (or as Rudolf Bultmann put it, "dependent on the value judgments of men"[82]); it was the Lord who judged him (cf. 1 Corinthians 4:35). Paul was convinced he had the Spirit of God (1 Corinthians 7:40); therefore, he was free (cf. 1 Corinthians 9:1 and 2 Corinthians 3:17). It was this psychological mind-set, grounded in the theology of the cross and the call of God, that convinced Paul that no man had power over him, either physically or spiritually.[83]

For Paul the matter of psychological freedom that came as a result of Jesus' death on the cross and the call of God must inevitably be tested by physiological acts (*praxis*). Thus he takes great liberty, even to the point of boasting, to delineate his physical encounters for the cause of preaching the gospel (*euaggelion*) of freedom (cf. 2 Corinthians 11:23-33). Determined to defend the gospel of freedom from the oppression of the law, Paul physically opposed Cephas, face to face, when he came to Antioch (cf. Galatians 2:11). God only knows why Paul fought with the beasts (Roman soldiers?) at Ephesus; but we know that because Paul was assured of his eschatological reward in heaven, he dared to engage in physical fisticuffs with soldiers on earth (cf. 1 Corinthians 15:32). Because Paul was of Christ, he felt compelled to reflect his psychological mindset of freedom in the physiological act of resistance to any attempt to negate that freedom. Of such activity, Paul urges the Corinthians, and especially the erstwhile slave membership of the eschatological community, to "be imitators of me" (cf. 1 Corinthians 4:16; 11:1). Thus we conclude that, in verse 23, Paul is giving fighting orders to an army; he is instructing slaves to resist any attempt to make them once again slaves of men; he is urging them to claim the freedom for which Christ has set them free.

Verse 24 provides a powerful climax for all Paul has said. He winds up his argument for freedom by insisting "in whatever state each was called [the call being that which brought the slave into the *ekklesia*], there let him remain with God."

NOTES

1. See Albert B. Cleage, Jr., *The Black Messiah* (New York: Sheed and Ward, 1968), pp. 4, 110; also *Black Christian Nationalism: New Directions for the Black Church* (New York: William Morrow & Co., Inc., 1972), p. xxxviii.

2. James H. Cone, *A Black Theology of Liberation*, The C. Eric Lincoln Series in Black Religion (Philadelphia: J.B. Lippincott Co., 1970), p. 68.

3. See Clement of Alexandria, *Exhortation*, X, 107, 3; Ignatius, *To Polycarp*, 4; *The Didache*, IV, 10-12; and St. Augustine, *The City of God*, XIX, 15-16.

4. See John Calvin, *The First Epistle of Paul the Apostle to the Corinthians*, trans. John W. Fraser (Grand Rapids: Wm. B. Eerdmans Publishing Co., 1960), p. 154.

5. Quoted from the Anglican Bishop of London's letter of May 19, 1727, to "Masters and Mistresses." See Peter G. Mode, *Source Book and Bibliographical Guide for American History* (Menasha, Wis.: George Banta Publishing Co., 1921), p. 551.

6. Howard Thurman, *Jesus and the Disinherited* (Nashville: Abingdon Press, Apex Books, 1949), pp. 30-31.

7. Albert Schweitzer, *The Mysticism of Paul the Apostle*, trans. William Montgomery (New York: Seabury Press, 1968), p. 194.

8. Günther Bornkamm, *Paul*, trans. D. M. G. Stalker (New York: Harper & Row, Publishers, Inc., 1971), p. 175.

9. Conzelmann, *First Corinthians* (Philadelphia: Fortress Press, 1975), p. 126.

10. Ibid., p. 127.

11. Barrett, *A Commentary on the First Epistle to the Corinthians* (New York: Harper & Row, 1968), p. 170. A similar view appears in Karl Barth's statement on what Paul meant by saying that slaves should remain in the state they were called; see *Church Dogmatics*, ed. G. W. Bromiley and T. F. Torrance (Edinburgh: T. & T. Clark, 1961), vol. III. pt. 4, p. 605.

12. Frederic Godet, *Commentary on St. Paul's First Epistle to the Corinthians*, Clark's Foreign Theological Library, trans. A. Cusin (Edinburgh: T. & T. Clark, 1893), p. 356.

13. K. L. Schmidt, "Keleō," *Theological Dictionary of the New Testament*, ed. Gerhard Kittel and Gerhard Friedrich, trans. Geoffrey W. Bromiley, (Grand Rap-

ids: Wm. B. Eerdmans Publishing Co., 1965), vol. 3, pp. 491-492.

14. Walter Bauer, *A Greek-English Lexicon of the New Testament and Other Early Christian Literature*, ed. William F. Arndt and F. Wilbur Gingrich. 4th rev. and augmented ed. (Chicago: University of Chicago Press, 1957), pp. 436-437.

15. Bauer, *A Greek-English Lexicon*, p. 240; Acts 19:32; also Schmidt, "Keleō . . . ," *TDNT*, pp. 513ff.

16. See Paul S. Minear, "Idea of Church," *The Interpreter's Dictionary of the Bible*, vol. 1, pp. 607-617. See also J. G. Simpson and F. C. Grant, "Church," *Dictionary of the Bible*, ed. James Hastings, rev. Frederick G. Grant and H. H. Rowley (New York: Charles Scribner's Sons, 1963), pp. 160-162.

17. For this discussion, see Rudolf Bultmann, *Theology of the New Testament*, trans. Kendrick Grobel (New York: Charles Scribner's Sons, 1951, vol. 1), pp. 92-108.

18. If this succinct historical analysis of the term *ekklesia* and its possible meaning to Paul is substantial, the fact of *ekklesia* characterizing early believers for Paul as "the people of God" rather than a "church," as Western theology has interpreted it, would prove Albert Cleage and others wrong and negate the charge that Paul forsook the development of a "nation" or "people" and established churches. The term "church" primarily is the Western version of the more technical term *ekklesia*, cf. "church" (English), "kirche" (German), or "kerke" (Dutch). See *The Oxford Dictionary of the Christian Church*, ed. F. L. Cross, rev. F. L. Cross and E. A. Livingstone, 2nd ed. (London: Oxford University Press, 1974), pp. 286-287. These terms for church miss the intention Paul had for *ekklesia*.

19. Bultmann, *Theology*, p. 99.

20. Ibid., cf. p. 309.

21. In making the larger point of separation of the church from the world, Paul strings together several Old Testament passages, e.g. Leviticus 26:11; Isaiah 52:11; Ezekiel 37:27, 20:43; Jeremiah 51:45, 31:9; Zephaniah 3:20; 2 Samuel 7:8, 14; and Hosea 2:1. The significance of this seems to be that Paul adopted the Old Testament tradition of separation of the holy from the profane, cf. Leviticus 20:23, 24b, 26. Here, again, Albert Cleage's allegation that Paul failed to carry forward the concept of "nation" falls flatly on its face.

22. William W. Buckland, *A Textbook of Roman Law* (Cambridge: University Press, 1932), p. 177.

23. Andrew William Lintoldt, *Violence in Republican Rome* (Oxford: The Clarendon Press, 1968), p. 78.

24. Ibid., p. 82.

25. Ibid., p. 81. See also R. H. Barrow, *Slavery in the Roman Empire* (London: Methuen & Co., Ltd., 1928), p. 166.

26. Lintoldt, *Violence*, p. 78. See also A. R. Hands, *Charities and Social Aid in Greece and Rome* (Ithaca, N.Y.: Cornell University Press, 1968), p. 81.

27. Lintoldt, *Violence*, p. 123.

28. We are told by Suetonius that the Jews, probably meaning Christians, were expelled from Rome by Emperor Claudius (ca. 41-54 A.D.) because of disturbances due to the instigation of Chrestus (another form of Christus). See Suetonius, *The Lives of the Caesars*, V, xxv. See also Pliny's remarks about the resemblance of Christianity to a *collegium*, *The Letters of Pliny*, x, xcvi; cf. X. xxxiv.

29. See *The Annals of Tacitus*, XV, xliv.

30. Under Domitian, Christians suffered exile and martyrdom because of the

faith, cf. The Book of Revelation; so also under Trajan (ca. 112 A.D.). For a discussion of charges, trials, and punishment of Christians during these times, see Eusebius, *Ecclesiastical History*, IV, xv; V. i.

31. Edgar J. Goodspeed, *Key to Ephesians* (Chicago: University of Chicago Press, 1933), p. 7, note 4.

32. W. G. Rollins, "Slavery in the New Testament," *INDSup*, pp. 830-832.

33. A. Robertson and A. Plummer, *A Critical and Exegetical Commentary on the First Epistle of St. Paul to the Corinthians* (Edinburgh: T. & T. Clark, 1914), p. 147.

34. Inasmuch as Corinth was a port city, it stands to reason that it was a center for slave traffic and enjoyed a sizable slave population. It was obvious that the Corinthian congregation had former slaves within it (cf. 1 Corinthians 1:26, "Not many were powerful, not many were of noble birth . . . "). The faction referred to in 1 Corinthians 11:18-19 could very well have been the result of attempted discrimination against former slave members of the *ekklesia*. The reference to Stephanas's household, the first converts in Achaia, suggests that not only Stephanas's family became members of the *ekklesia* but his slaves did as well (see 1 Corinthians 16:15).

35. Plato, *The Republic*, trans. B. Jowett (New York: Alfred A. Knopf, Inc., n.d.), pp. 83, 96.

36. Aristotle, *Politics* I, v. 1254a. Aristotle (384-322 B.C.) argued that because slaves had little or no power of rationalization, they were slaves by nature (*Politics* I, v, 1254b). But more (or less) than this, slaves were things, not persons. Slaves became one of the instruments, or tools, by which the free man acquired wealth and comfort: " . . . in the arrangement of the family, a slave is a living possession, and property . . . " (*Politics* I, iv, 1253b). Essentially, slaves belonged to their master, body and soul; they had no rights that their master was obligated to respect.

37. Cato, *On Agriculture*, preface.

38. Ibid., LVI.

39. Plutarch, "Marcus Cato," *The Lives of the Noble Grecians and Romans*, trans. John Dryden, rev. Arthur Hugh Clough (New York: The Modern Library, 1864), p. 427.

40. For a discussion of slaves' importance to Roman luxury, see Michael Grant, *The World of Rome* (New York: The New American Library, Inc., A Mentor Book, 1960), pp. 121-148.

41. See J. P. Balsdon, *Life and Leisure in Ancient Rome* (New York: McGraw-Hill Book Co., 1969), p. 107. See also R. H. Barrow, *Slavery in the Roman Empire*, pp. 25ff., 43.

42. See J.A. Crook, "Law and Life of Rome," *Aspects of Greek and Roman Life*, ed. H.H. Scullard (London: Thames & Hudson, 1967), pp. 55-56; also W. W. Buckland, *The Roman Law of Slavery* (New York: AMS Press Inc., 1969), pp. 1, 3, 10.

43. Juvenal, *Satires*, VI, 11. 217-221.

44. See Tacitus, *Annals*, IV, 54.

45. See Tacitus, *History*, II, 72.

46. See Tacitus, *Annals*, II, 30. Another example of torture is cited in Balsdon, *Life and Leisure in Ancient Rome*, p. 52, when a household slave breaks some precious glassware and is thrown into a fish pond to feed man-eating lampreys.

47. Buckland, *Roman Law of Slavery*, p. 182.

48. Barrow, *Slavery in the Roman Empire*, p. 29.

49. See Suetonius, *Nero*, II. For other examples of atrocities inflicted upon slaves

in the Roman Empire during Paul's time, see the citations from Tacitus and Suetonius in Appendix I in Barrow, *Slavery in the Roman Empire*, pp. 237ff.

50. Could it be concluded from the use of *andrapodistais*, "men stealers, kid-
nappers, slave dealers," in 1 Timothy 1:10 that the early church was threatened
from without by intruders looking for runaway slaves or even from within by men
greedy enough for money to sell their brothers and sisters back into slavery? Either
possibility would have been traumatic for members of the *ekklesia* who were former
slaves.

51. There was a vast difference between a freeborn Roman citizen and a freedman. The freeborn Roman citizen gained citizenship by means of birth. The freedman, who was once a slave, gained citizenship by means of emancipation. In spite
of achieving citizenship via emancipation, the freedman was not equal to a freeborn
Roman citizen (see Barbara Levick, *Roman Colonies in Southern Asia Minor*
[Oxford: The Clarendon Press, 1967], p. 36).

A slave could gain freedom in at least three ways: 1) *Census*, placing his or her
name on the censor's list of citizens (under oath before a magistrate); however this
did not mean that he or she became a citizen of the Roman Empire; 2) *Vindicta*,
taking an oath before a magistrate to the effect that manumission would not mean
a change of citizenship; 3) *Testamenta*, being freed by means of a will upon the
death of master. Once a slave gained liberty, certain obligations to the master,
dominus (who still was to be regarded as sacred), were still expected: 1) *obsequium*
(respect); 2) *opera* (an oath at manumission agreeing to a certain number of days
of free labor for the former master); and 3) *bona*, the patron was assured of certain
property rights at the freedman's death. There was also the notion that freedmen
were to give *munera*, i.e., gifts to their patrons. For a discussion of the various
ramifications of freedmen's continuing obligations to their masters, see Buckland,
Roman Law of Slavery, pp. 185-231, and Levick, *Roman Colonies*, pp. 36-44.

52. S. Scott Bartchy argues that Paul was indifferent toward slavery (*Mallon
Chresai: First Century Slavery and the Interpretation of 1 Corinthians 7:21* [Missoula,
Mont.: University of Montana, 1973], pp. 103-104).

53. Bartchy insists that slavery was so accepted in Paul's day that no one gave a
thought to it. Ibid.

54. See Conzelmann, *First Corinthians*, p. 127, and Godet, *Commentary*, p. 357.

55. For example, Godet deals extensively with whether *ei kai* should be translated
"even if," "although," or "if therefore." He even suggests that *kai* might be sub-
stituted for *dē* to read *ei dē*, "but if." Godet, *Commentary*, pp. 358-359.

56. This is one point at which there is agreement with Bartchy. He argues convincingly that exegesis of 1 Corinthians 7:21 is not contingent on proper grammatical
analysis. Unfortunately, he concludes that the exegetical key to 1 Corinthians 7:21
is the understanding of slavery in the Roman Empire before, during, and after
Paul's time. He insists that attitudes, laws, and customs pertaining to slavery
affected Paul's attitude. This is in no way convincing. He does seem to be right to
conclude, however, that 1 Corinthians 7:21 is not understood best in the light of
grammatical excellence.

57. Conzelmann, *First Corinthians*, p. 127.

58. Barrett, *Commentary*, pp. 170-171.

59. Conzelmann, *First Corinthians*, p. 127. For a similar position, see Ernst Käse-
mann, *New Testament Questions of Today*, trans. W. J. Montague (Philadelphia:
Fortress Press, 1969), p. 208.

60. Barrett, *Commentary*, p. 171.

61. One can allude to several racist interpretations of Paul's attitude toward slavery based on 1 Corinthians 7:20-24. In every age, there have been strong representations of such racist interpretations. I am reminded of the instructions of 1727 A.D., which came from the Anglican Bishop of London, as they related to the Christian status of black slaves in America. Weiss, *Earliest Christianity*, 2, pp. 588ff., is another example from another era. Kenneth C. Russell is a representative of some segments of Roman Catholic thought on the subject of Paul and slavery, according to 1 Corinthians 7:20-24. Commenting on the passage he says, "Is he not suggesting that this individual who is a slave is so because God has permitted it and that this man, slave as he is, has been called in the total situation of his life to be a Christian? His secular condition cannot be separated from his divine call and, indeed, it is in the context of his worldly position that he must live out the divine summons to the Christian life." In a statement that sounds unreal coming from someone living in the latter half of the twentieth century, Russell says, "The Christian vocation must be translated into the ordinary acts of everyday life, and the slave cannot escape this obligation. Hard as it sounds, the only answer for the slave is that he will be a good Christian by being a good slave." See Kenneth C. Russell, *Slavery as Reality and Metaphor in the Pauline Letters* (Rome: Catholic Book Agency-Officium Libri Catholici, 1968), pp. 45-46.

62. C. F. D. Moule, *An Idiom-Book of New Testament Greek*. 2nd ed. (Cambridge: University Press, 1968), p. 21.

63. Ibid.

64. It is my conclusion that the freedom Paul talks about, which was acquired by the slave, was obtained as a result of the call. If this is true, I would be compelled to differ with Bartchy who suggests that the freedom in question was obtained as a result of the beneficence of a compassionate slave master. In his conclusion on the meaning of 1 Corinthians 7:21c, he says, "I conclude that Paul in 7:21c was speaking of any situation in which a Christian slave became a freedman. Thus his advice in 7:21d presupposes that the person addressed is a slave who has been set free by his owner." See Bartchy, *Mallon Chresai*, p. 208. Nowhere in the text at hand does Paul imply that the slave's freedom comes as a result of a gratuitous act of a master. According to Paul, freedom for the slave comes as a result of the liberating act of Jesus on the cross (cf. v. 23) and his call to the slave to enter into the *ekklesia*.

65. See Heinrich Schlier, "Eleutheros," *Theological Dictionary of the New Testament*, vol. 2, pp. 487-492.

66. Ibid., pp. 496-502.

67. Conzelmann, *First Corinthians*, p. 128. Conzelmann does not really tell us what freedom from sin meant for Paul as it related to slavery, whether it meant freedom from sin internally and morally or freedom from sin externally and socially or both. For what seems to be Conzelmann's position here, see the earlier discussion of verse 21 in this chapter.

68. Barrett, *Commentary*, p. 171.

69. Godet, *Commentary*, p. 363.

70. Bauer, *A Greek-English Lexicon*, p. 83.

71. Schlier, "Eleutheros," p. 501.

72. F. Lyall, "Roman Law in the Writing of Paul—The Slave and the Freedman,"

New Testament Studies, 17 (Oct. 1970), p. 79. For the complete discussion, see pp. 73-79.

73. *Adelphos*, "brother," denotes the mutual physical and spiritual relationship of all members of the *ekklesia*. See Hans Freiherr von Soden, "adelphos," *Theological Dictionary of the New Testament*, vol. 1, pp. 144-146.

74. Paul's concept of *agapē* is that it is the new and vital power which prevails in the *ekklesia* and holds it captive (2 Corinthians 5:14). See Ethelbert Stauffer, "agapaō," *Theological Dictionary of the New Testament*, vol. 1, pp. 49ff.

75. von Soden, "adelphos."

76. Stauffer, "agapaō."

77. Theo Preiss, *Life in Christ, Studies in Biblical Theology*, No. 13, trans. Harold Knight (Chicago: Alec R. Allenson, Inc., 1954), p. 40. For a refreshing commentary on Philemon, see Edward Lohse, *Colossians and Philemon, Hermeneia: A Critical and Historical Commentary on the Bible Series*, trans. Wm. R. Poehlmann and Robert J. Karrig, ed. Helmut Koester (Philadelphia: Fortress Press, 1971).

78. Barrett, *Commentary*, p. 171.

79. Barrow, *Slavery in the Roman Empire*, p. 12.

80. Conzelmann, *First Corinthians*, p. 128. For a description of the practice of slaves being liberated by being sold to the gods, see Adolf Deissmann, *Light from the Ancient East*, trans. Lionel R. M. Strachen, 2nd ed. (New York: Hodder and Staughton, 1911), p. 326.

81. Godet, *Commentary*.

82. See Rudolf Bultmann, *Primitive Christianity in Its Contemporary Setting*, trans. R. H. Fuller (Cleveland: World Publishing Company, 1956), p. 185.

83. Philo of Alexandria, a contemporary of Paul and a Jewish philosopher, seems to describe precisely Paul's psychological freedom. He argued that every good man is free. However, for Philo, freedom was not the work of Jesus' death on the cross, as Paul believed, but the result of a stoic kind of wisdom. See *Philo*, trans. F. H. Colson, The Loeb Classical Library (Cambridge, Mass.: Harvard University Press, 1941), vol. 9, pp. 2-102.

32

ELSA TAMEZ

The Scandalous Message of James

The Angle of Praxis

---

*Ferociously attacked by Martin Luther as "an epistle of straw," James
has repeatedly been downplayed, dismissed, or domesticated to fit a
religiosity uncomfortable with its sharp critique of the exploitation of the
poor by the wealthy and its uncompromising call for practice of
economic justice. Some churches avoid reading the letter and
established scholarship has clearly consigned it to secondary status. It
is surely not coincidental that it is a biblical scholar from Latin America,
Elsa Tamez, who insists that the letter be read more critically—just as
the indigenous peoples of Guatemala make more images of James than
of other, better-known saints (as she herself points out). Read more
carefully and seriously, James offers hope to the poor for an end to their
oppression, partly by proclaiming God's judgment against the
oppressors, and calls for a militant patience in resistance along with an
integrity in praxis, i.e., a consistency between belief, words, and actions
in the pursuit of justice.*

There is a surprising dearth of literature on James. This is probably due to
the privileged place given to abstract thought in our Western societies. The

---

Reprinted from Elsa Tamez, *The Scandalous Message of James* (New York: Crossroad, 1992),
5–6, 12–13, 52–69, abridged.

531

reasonableness of faith is valued more than the practice of faith; the latter is seen as separate from the former, or as a product of faith's reasonableness. That is, ethics, behavior, deeds, are considered of secondary importance by our logocentric societies. Thus a letter like that of James, which focuses its attention on the daily practice of Christian life, is easily marginated, while the "theological" letters of Paul are highly esteemed.

James's radical critique of the rich has contributed to this "crafty theft" of the letter. I know of churches where the letter is skipped over in the liturgies because there are many rich members in the congregation, and it is very uncomfortable to speak against them when they are sitting in the front seats. Certain parts of James, especially chapter 5, are very concrete and thus very difficult to "spiritualize."

Many of the ideas are to be found in the first chapter. Nearly the entire content of the letter appears there, so it strikes us as quite dense, difficult, and even incoherent. In chapters 2 through 4 we see an elaboration of the themes announced in the first chapter, and one or another new theme (for example, the call to conversion in 4:7-10). At the end of the letter we note that the main themes of the first chapter are taken up again: judgment against the rich, patience, prayer, suffering, consistency between words and deeds.

The framework is still not clear. We must focus more sharply, that is, read the letter again, several times. When we see the letter more clearly, we can look at it from three angles, distinct but complementary.

The Angle of Oppression-Suffering. There is a community of believers (*adelphoi mou*) that suffers. There is a group of rich people who oppress them and drag them before the tribunals. There are peasants who are exploited, Christian and non-Christian, by the rich farmers who accumulate wealth at the expense of the workers' salaries. There is a class of merchants who lead a carefree life, with no concern for the poor.

The Angle of Hope. This community of believers needs a word of hope, of encouragement, of reassurance concerning the end of the injustice. James gives it to them from the very beginning of his letter. We see hope in his greeting, his insistence on declaring the community happy, *makarios*, in his words about God's preference for the poor, God's judgment against the oppressors, the anticipated end of the oppression, and the coming of the Lord.

The Angle of Praxis. The content of the letter is concentrated in this angle. For James the denunciation of the present situation and the announcement of hope are not sufficient. Something more is needed: praxis. He asks of these Christians a praxis in which they show a militant patience, a consistency between words, belief, and deeds, a prayer with power, an effective wisdom and an unconditional, sincere love among the members of the community.

This is the picture that I see with the eyes of an "oppressed and believing" people. This is the focus I will give to the letter. In situations of oppression, James calls the communities to praxis, to make themselves felt in their environment by their testimony. James writes with a heavy pen here. We can see that he is truly concerned about the life of the Christian communities. He wants them to be signs of God's reign, focused on militant patience and integrity.

MILITANT PATIENCE

James insistently challenges his readers to "have patience." Traditionally the word "patience" has been understood as signifying a passive and submissive attitude. People are patient because nothing can be done about their situations. Such an interpretation has been prejudicial for the lives of Christians and their communities, for it encourages resignation, a lack of commitment to concrete realities, and a subjection to the governing authorities (Rom. 13:1). James is not referring in any way to this kind of patience. He calls for a militant, heroic patience, one that watches for the propitious moment. There are four Greek terms for patience: *anechomai, kartereō, makrothymia,* and *hypomonē.* These are strictly military terms and are used as metaphors referring to the battles of life.[1] The author of the epistle uses two of these four Greek terms to refer to patience: *hypomonē and makrothymia.* Although these can be used synonymously, they have significant differences. *Hypomonē* or the verb form *hypomenō* (used frequently in military situations), in 1:3-4, 12; 5:11, means to persevere, to resist, to be constant, unbreakable, immovable. Most scholars agree that there is an active meaning to the term.[2] James is very clear in this regard when he says in 1:3,4 that patience is accompanied by perfect works.[3] This is a militant patience that arises from the roots of oppression; it is an active, working patience. In 1:12 James speaks of those who resist the trial and overcome it, those who do not succumb to pain and oppression. Maccabees, which narrates the Jewish resistance to the Greeks, speaks of "the courage and the patience [*hypomonē*] of the mother of the heroes and their children" (4 Macc. 1:11). James 5:11 alludes to the patience (*hypomonē*) of Job. The more he experienced attacks, isolation, and suffering, the more he was strengthened, the greater his self-confidence.

At the end of his letter James employs the word *makrothymia* for patience, which appears in the context of the coming of the Lord and Judge (5:7-11). The attitude is that of awaiting, as it were, on alert. The farmers await with patience and joy the fruit that will come from the care of their plants. They can do nothing to make it come sooner, for everything takes time. So too the oppressed community of James knows that its difficult situation is going to change, that judgment has been pronounced in favor of those who suffer. It is important then that they do not despair but that they "continue to sow" and "cultivate the seedlings," which for James means that they should follow the law of freedom and live a life of integrity.[4]

INTEGRITY

For James, the core of praxis is integrity, that is, consistency in hearing, seeing, believing, speaking, and doing. This is a personal integrity and a communal integrity. For James the churches should be signs of God's reign, a model different from the values of the world. At a time when there are many poor, the landowners take advantage of the workers, the merchants plot to earn more money, and the Christians are marginated and dragged before the courts, the church out of concern for self-preservation runs the risk of imitating the values of that corrupt society. Therefore James exhorts them not to show favoritism toward the rich, not to seek the important places in the church (3:1), not to be envious, jealous, argumentative, not to be hypocrites speaking badly of one another.

For James and his community, Christians should be persons of integrity, sincere, transparent, consistent in everything they do. They should be sure of themselves, resolute, decisive. The author rejects shilly-shallying, for a community with indecisive members is doomed to failure. We see in the epistle great importance placed on unity among the members of the Christian community. This is a unity that helps strengthen them to confront a situation hostile not only to them as Christians but also to other poor people who have no one to defend them. It seems that for James unity arises from integrity, and God is the model of that true unity. The integrity of the Christians is demonstrated by their spiritual practice, which is pure and untainted before God the Father if it both practices justice and does not follow the values of this world (1:27). Let us look more closely at this core of praxis.

Integrity, Fruit of Painful Experience

From the beginning of the letter James introduces and focuses on the theme of integrity. After the greeting he makes explicit the process: joy, patience, tenacity, good and complete works, and the maturity that is the result, that is, to be complete and integral:

> My brothers, you will always have your trials but, when they come, try to treat them as a happy privilege; you understand that your faith is only put to the test to make you patient, but patience too is to have its practical results so that you will become fully-developed, complete, with nothing missing [1:2-4].

In his eagerness to encourage the Christian communities, James asks them to reflect on the positive side of the experience of oppression. He does not perceive the recompense for this unjust suffering at the end of time; rather it occurs now, in the heart of praxis, in the life of the communities; they experience wholeness and integrity within themselves. Paradoxically this is a humanizing process. In the very process of resisting dehumanizing forces, the communities and their members are humanized.

The experience of feeling perfect (*teleios*), which in James means complete, total, integral, should remind those who suffer that they are human beings, not things. In their experience of acute pain they should be able to integrate, within themselves, their flesh and their minds, their bodies and their souls. And because in this process the pain is almost palpable, the sensitivity of those who suffer to others who suffer is quite natural. Integralness, then, does not occur only in the body of one member of the community, but rather in the entire community, in which everyone becomes sensitive to the pain of the others within the community and outside of it. To feel what the other feels is truly a gift that should cause us to rejoice.

Integrity vs. Duplicity

James is against the two-faced person, or, as he puts it, the person living a double life.

> That sort of person, in two minds [*dipsychos*], wavering between going different ways [*akatastatos*], must not expect that the Lord will give him anything [1:81].

This text refers to those who pray with vacillation, with hesitancy. James says that they are like the waves of the sea moved this way and that by the wind. Such people are a problem for the community principally because no one can trust them, because they are both with the community and not with it. Moreover they have no will power, no decisiveness. With such members of the community the battle against oppression is lost. The word "wavering," "inconstant," *akatastatos*, intensifies the voluble quality of the ambiguous person. In praxis ambiguity, fickleness, and instability are highly destructive. "Clean your hands, you sinners, and clear your minds, you waverers" (*dipsychoi*) (4:8). This exhortation is addressed to those who tend to make friends with the world, or, in other words, to follow the values of the corrupt society described by James. Scholars agree that this passage refers to idolatry: the friend of the world is the friend of Mammon, the god of wealth,[5] and is therefore the enemy of God (4:4), for you cannot obey and worship two lords. Following this line of thought, 4:8 calls for integrity. These "adulterers," as James figuratively calls them, live a double life, are two-faced, are *dipsychoi*. Therefore he says that they must be purified, must clean their hearts and their hands. To clean one's hands means to cease doing evil,[6] to desist from corruption. James is probably alluding to certain members of the community who lived in a more or less comfortable situation and were driven by acquisitiveness, like the merchants in 4:13-17.

For James, then, you cannot live in ambiguity nor live two different lives. Either you believe that God generously answers prayers or God does not. Either you make friends with God or with the unjust world. Either you are in the community or you are out of it. A decisive option must be shown in praxis.

God, the Model of Integrity

James's understanding of God is closely linked to his concept of integrity. In James 1:5 God's attributes are contrasted with those of the divided (*dipsychos*) and fickle person:

> If there is any one of you who needs wisdom, he must ask God, who gives to all freely [*haplōs*] and ungrudgingly; it will be given to him.

The term to give "freely" is the translation of *haplōs*, "simply," "without second thoughts," a term opposed to *dipsychos*. The term can mean "give without reservation," "sincerely," to give of oneself generously and without hesitation.[7] For God gives disinterestedly to the needy who ask. James intentionally introduces both opposing words to indicate that we should act as God acts. This line of thought continues in 1:17:

> All that is good, everything that is perfect, which is given us from above, comes down from the Father of all light; with him there is no such thing as alteration, no shadow of a change.

As in 1:5 he again alludes to what comes from God. He employs an illustration from astronomy. God, the father of all lights, neither changes nor is changed by the shadow of rotation. Since God is the giver of good things, then, God never sends evil. God is faithful to God's own self and to God's children, born by God's own will with the Word of Truth (1:18). God, therefore, is a God of integrity; God is not two-faced or wavering, like the person in 1:8.[8]

But to know that God acts with integrity and then not to act like God is useless. This brings to mind 2:19-20: "You believe in the one God—that is creditable enough, but the demons have the same belief, and they tremble with fear. Do realize, you senseless man, that faith without good deeds is useless."

It has been said that in this text James refers to the classic formula for monotheism. Be that as it may, the close link between unity and integrity is clear. God is *one* not only because there are no other gods like God, but because God acts consistently with the divine purpose, which for James is the cause of the poor. The demons are frightened by this integrity of God, for God has been their steadfast enemy.[9] And since God does not change (1:17), the demons tremble.

Therefore, and here we come to the core of integrity, James challenges the communities to show their faith through works, for only in this way is the integrity of Christian life demonstrated. It is clear that James elaborates little theology in his letter and makes continuous reference to Christian practice. Nonetheless we must insist that his principal concern is not the general lifestyle of the communities, but rather as Donato Palomino says, "the theoretical-practical unity of biblical faith for discipleship, where he contrasts the character of the militants with the structures of the system,"[10] that is, with the economic, political, and religious system of his time.

Faith and Practice, the Core of Integrity

For James, the link between the experience of oppression and eschatological hope is the practice of faith. The Christian communities must avoid accommodation to this unjust world and not fall into the trap laid by its value system. Rather, the Christian communities should demonstrate the new values of justice, assisting the oppressed outcast from society. James links practice with the law of freedom, faith, and wisdom. These three, which could be considered in a theoretical way, are effective and alive only insofar as they are demonstrated in the practice of justice; otherwise they are false and dead. James challenges the community to hear the word and keep it, to contemplate the perfect law of freedom and practice it, to speak and act consistently, as befits those who are to be judged by the law of freedom. He is not referring here to rites but rather to the *mišpaṭim*, the Laws of the ethical tradition of Sinai. According to 2:8, the law consists in loving our neighbors as ourselves; the other commandments, then, must be understood in relation to this one.

With regard to the law of freedom, James exhorts his readers:

But you must do what the word tells you, and not just listen to it and deceive yourselves. To listen to the word and not obey is like looking at your own features in a mirror and then, after a quick look, going off and immediately forgetting what you looked like [1:22-24].

"Word," for James, means the perfect law of freedom (1:25). Those who only hear the Word, without practicing it, demonstrate a lack of integrity; they deceive themselves. If it is only heard, the Word loses its power, because it is only in fulfilling the Word that it takes on life and is verified as true. On the other hand, if those who hear it practice it steadfastly, says James, the practice itself will be a cause for joy, for it is a sign of consistency, integrity. Integrity as a cause for joy is referred to in 1:2-4.

In 2:12 James says, "Talk and behave like people who are going to be judged by the law of freedom." These words occur in chapter 2 where James also speaks against the lack of respect for the poor and the adulation of the rich. The law of freedom is a unity; you cannot fulfill one part of it and not another. If you do not commit adultery but do show favoritism against the poor, you have transgressed the royal law that "you must love your neighbor as yourself" (2:8-11). If the law of freedom is not fulfilled in its entirety, it is not fulfilled at all. Thus the author challenges his brothers and sisters to live with consistency and integrity in their words and deeds; if they have made a decision to obey the law of freedom they should act accordingly. If God chooses the poor to be rich in faith and heirs of God's reign, the brothers and sisters of faith should show a preference for the poor over the rich, rather than favoring the rich, as it seems that some were doing in the congregations.

After the description of discrimination, James continues in chapter 2 with his concern for integrity, situating faith and works together in a complementary unity. From a theological point of view, this is the most polemical part of the letter, for he seems to be contradicting Paul's view of justification by faith alone. In 2:24 James says: "You see now that it is by doing something good, and not only by believing, that a man is justified." This, together with the example of Abraham that he uses, leads us to believe that James knew well the expression "justification by faith." Some hold that it had become a slogan and that what Paul had meant was being distorted.[11] For some, justification by faith meant having faith without a commitment to others, without works. James, then, is trying to correct this idea by introducing works as an important element in justification.

We do not know exactly what James understands by faith, but he does make it very clear what he understands by works. Throughout his letter he refers to the good works continually spoken of in the Gospels as the liberating deeds of Jesus; they are deeds that effect justice. They are the social works that the prophets demand and that are spoken of in the Sinai tradition. Paul, on the other hand, assails works related to ritual, the sacrifices and other kinds of offerings and festivities. In his struggle against the Judaizers, Paul overturned the traditional thinking about the priority of these kinds of works to center on faith as the only way of salvation. At no time does he place the works of justice in opposition to justification. Rather he says they are the fruits of the spirit that are born of faith.

There is nevertheless a clear difference in the two approaches; this difference can perhaps be explained by the two different contexts. For James, faith cooperates with works, and through works faith achieves perfection (2:22). Works therefore justify together with faith (2:24). This may seem to be a heresy to Protestants, but this is what we read in James. The problem arises when we ignore the context of the passages. The intention of James, in the first instance, is not to speak about justification. He mentions this only in passing, probably because of misunderstandings of the Pauline phrase "justification by faith" (that is, if we hold that the author wrote later than Paul and knew Paul's teaching). From our angle of praxis we see that James wanted to emphasize the unity between faith and works as part of the necessary consistency in believing, hearing, saying, and doing. So he begins his reflection with a concrete example linking faith with the practice of justice:

> Take the case, my brothers, of someone who has never done a single good act but claims that he has faith. Will that faith save him? If one of the brothers or one of the sisters is in need of clothes and has not enough food to live on, and one of you says to them, "I wish you well; keep yourself warm and eat plenty," without giving them these bare necessities of life, then what good is that? Faith is like that: if good works do not go with it, it is quite dead [2:14-17].

As we can see, James holds to his concern for integrity and consistency between theory and practice. What is new in this section is the importance for justification that he gives to "doing." For many of us this is scandalous, and for that very reason we should study all the more James's contribution to the doctrine of justification by faith. Like James, we must recognize that faith without works is dead (2:26).

Finally, James also links wisdom with works. We have seen the Word (or the law of freedom) and faith given life by works. Some have said that wisdom here means the Spirit,[12] as can be seen by the fruits mentioned in 3:17. If this is the case, we can see in James a systematic relationship between the Word, faith, and the Spirit as elements that, together with praxis, make up true Christian life.

James links wisdom with integrity in both contexts where wisdom appears.

In the first (1:5), he says that those who lack wisdom should ask for it from God. He refers to those who have not achieved complete integrity, those who lack something. The verb "to lack" (*leipō*) makes the link. Wisdom, then, is important for integrity. All the following verses, as we have seen, speak in one way or another of consistency. James speaks of wisdom in 3:13-18 as well. Here he says that there are two kinds of wisdom, that from on high and the demoniacal. They produce different fruits. So those who think they have wisdom will have to show it by their works. These will reveal if their wisdom is true or false:

> If there are any wise or learned men among you, let them show it by their good lives, with humility and wisdom in their actions. But if at heart you have the bitterness of jealousy, or a self-seeking ambition, never make any claims for yourself or cover up the truth with lies—principles of this kind are not the wisdom that comes down from above: they are only earthly, animal and devilish [3:13-15].

This text is related with 3:1, where he speaks of the problem in the community when many want to be teachers.[13] Perhaps it is these who claim to have wisdom. James insists that they show their wisdom through their good works and then it will be known if their wisdom is from on high or not. If it is, their wisdom will be pure, peacemaking, kindly and considerate, compassionate, bearing good fruits, without hypocrisy (3:17). . . .

For James Christians should above all show a consistency in their faith and their deeds. Their faith is alive only if it is accompanied by good works. And good works for James have to do with justice.

NOTES

1. Colin Brown, *Dictionary of New Testament Theology* (Grand Rapids, Mich.: Zondervan, 1977), 2:764.

2. See James Adamson, *The Epistle of James* (Grand Rapids: Eerdmans, 1976); Peter Davids, *The Epistle of James* (Grand Rapids: Eerdmans, 1982); Martin Dibelius, *James*, revised by H. Greeven (Philadelphia: Fortress, 1976); Sophie Laws, *The Epistle of James* (New York: Harper & Row, 1980).

3. The term "perfect works" has been translated as "the patience that reaches perfection."

4. The term *makrothymia* has another meaning, even more common in the LXX and in other parts of the New Testament. In the Greek Old Testament it is used to refer to the patience of God. God is patient with human beings; God mercifully controls the divine anger to give human beings time to be converted and change their attitudes. In this case to have patience is to have mercy, to have clemency. In Rom. 2:4, the patience of God leads us to conversion—*metanoia*. In the parable of the unjust steward, Matt. 26, this meaning is clearly seen. The steward asked for patience from the Lord (*makrothymia*) for his debt and promised to pay back everything. In his mercy the master pardoned the debt, which the steward did not do with his peers, and so ended up in jail. This connotation does not easily fit into our text of James, for the author indicates the meaning we should use with his example of the laborer.

5. Adamson, *The Epistle of James* p. 170.

6. Davids, *The Epistle of James p. 167.*

7. *Kittel, Theological Dictionary of the New Testament,* vol. 1, pp. 386-387.

8. Sophie Laws, *A Commentary on the Epistle of James* (New York: Harper & Row, 1980), pp. 49-61, 126.

9. Ibid., p. 126.

10. In his unpublished dissertation, "Paradigmas bíblios para una pastoral obrera" (San José, Costa Rica: Seminario Bíblico Latinoamericano, 1984), p. 145.

11. Laws, *James*, p. 131.

12. See J. A. Kirk, "The Meaning of Wisdom in James: Examination of a Hypothesis," *New Testament Studies*, vol. 16, no. 1 (October 1969), pp. 24-38.

13. See Davids, *James*, p. 149; cf. Martin Dibelius, *James.* Hermeneia (Philadelphia: Fortress, 1976), p. 208.

Contributors

Phyllis A. Bird is Associate Professor of Old Testament Interpretation, Garrett-Evangelical Theological Seminary, Evanston, Illinois, and author of *The Bible as the Church's Book*.

Walter Brueggemann is William P. McPheeters Professor of Old Testament, Columbia Theological Seminary, Decatur, Georgia, and author of *The Prophetic Imagination* and *Interpretation and Obedience*.

Marvin L. Chaney is Nathaniel Gray Professor of Hebrew Exegesis and Old Testament, San Francisco Theological Seminary, San Anselmo, and the Graduate Theological Union, Berkeley, California, and contributor to *Palestine in Transition and the Books of the Bible I. The Old Testament/The Hebrew Bible*.

Mary P. Coote is Visiting Instructor in Biblical Greek at San Francisco Theological Seminary, San Anselmo, California.

Robert B. Coote is Professor of Old Testament at San Francisco Theological Seminary, San Anselmo, California, and the Graduate Theological Union, Berkeley, California, and author of *Amos Among the Prophets: Composition and Theology* and *In Defense of Revolution: The Elohist History*.

Kuno Füssel is Assistant Professor of Systematic Theology, University of Münster, Münster, Germany, and contributor to *So kennen wir die Bible nicht*.

Norman K. Gottwald is Wilbert Webster White Professor of Biblical Studies at New York Theological Seminary, New York City, and author of *The Hebrew Bible—A Socio-Literary Introduction* and *The Hebrew Bible in Its Social World and in Ours*.

Richard A. Horsley is Professor of Religious Studies at the University of Massachusetts, Boston, co-author of *Bandits, Prophets, and Messiahs: Popular Movements in the Time of Jesus* and author of *Sociology and the Jesus Movement*.

Amos Jones, Jr., holds a Ph.D. degree from Vanderbilt University and is pastor of the Zion Hill First African Church, Nashville, Tennessee.

Kwok Pui Lan is Assistant Professor of Theology at Episcopal Divinity School, Cambridge, Massachusetts, and formerly on the faculty of the Chinese University of Hong Kong.

David Lochhead is Professor of Systematic Theology at Vancouver School of Theology, British Columbia, and author of *The Dialogical Imperative: A Christian Reflection on Interfaith Encounter*.

Clarice J. Martin is Associate Professor of New Testament at Colgate Rochester Divinity School/Bexley Hall/Crozer Theological Seminary, Rochester, New York.

Arthur F. McGovern, a Jesuit priest, is Professor of Philosophy at the University of Detroit, co-author of *Ethical Dilemmas in the Modern Corporation*, and author of *Liberation Theology and Its Critics: Toward an Assessment*.

Carlos Mesters, a Dutch Carmelite priest, has worked for more than two decades with Christian base communities in Brazil, and is author of *Defenseless Flower: A New Reading of the Bible*.

541

José Míguez Bonino is Professor of Systematic Theology and Ethics at the Facultad Evangelica de Teología (ISEDET), Buenos Aires, Argentina, and author of *Doing Theology in a Revolutionary Situation* and *Toward a Christian Political Ethics*.

Itumeleng J. Mosala, Associate Professor of Religious Studies, University of Cape Town, South Africa, recently served a three-year term as Tutor and Research Scholar in African Studies at Wesley House, University of Cambridge, England, and is co-author of *The Unquestionable Right to Be Free and Hammering Swords into Ploughshares: Essays in Honour of Bishop Desmond Tutu*.

Henri Mottu, former director of an institute for adult theological education and pastoral training, is Professor of Homiletics and Dean of the Faculty of Theology, University of Geneva, Switzerland, and translator of Bonhoeffer's *Homiletics* into French.

Ched Myers is a peace activist and scholar, currently on the staff of the American Friends Service Committee in Los Angeles.

George V. Pixley is Professor of Bible, Seminario Teologico Bautista, Managua, Nicaragua, and author of *Exodus: A Liberation Perspective* and *Biblical Israel: A People's History*.

Luise Schottroff is Professor of New Testament, University of Kassel, Kassel, Germany, co-author of *Jesus and the Hope of the Poor*, and author of *Let the Oppressed Go Free: Feminist Perspectives in New Testament Studies*.

Elisabeth Schüssler Fiorenza is Krister Stendahl Professor of New Testament Studies, Harvard Divinity School, Cambridge, Massachusetts, and author of *In Memory of Her: A Feminist Theological Reconstruction of Christian Origins* and *Bread Not Stone: The Challenge of Feminist Biblical Interpretation*.

Juan Luis Segundo is Director of the Peter Faber Pastoral Center in Montevideo, Uruguay, and author of the four-volume *Jesus of Nazareth, Yesterday and Today* and *The Liberation of Dogma*.

Gerald T. Sheppard is Professor of Old Testament Literature and Exegesis, Emmanuel College of Victoria University and the Toronto School of Theology, University of Toronto, co-editor of *The Pilgrim Classic Commentary Series*, and author of *The Future of the Bible: Beyond Liberalism and Literalism*.

Naomi Steinberg is Assistant Professor of Hebrew Bible at DePaul University, Chicago, Illinois.

Elsa Tamez is Professor of Biblical Studies, Seminario Bíblico Latinoamericano, San José, Costa Rica, and author of *Bible of the Oppressed* and *Against Machismo*.

Renita J. Weems is Assistant Professor of Hebrew Bible, Vanderbilt University, Nashville, Tennessee, and author of *Just a Sister Away: A Womanist Vision of Women's Relationships in the Bible*.

Franklin J. Woo is Emeritus Director, China Program, Committee for East Asia and the Pacific, National Council of Churches.

Index of Scriptural References

Index of Names

Index of Subjects